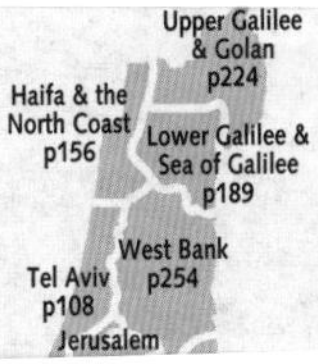

Upper Galilee
& Golan
p224
Haifa & the
North Coast   Lower Galilee &
p156   Sea of Galilee
p189
West Bank
Tel Aviv   p254
p108
Jerusalem

DATE DUE

IFORMATION TO
MOOTH TRIP

Safe T
Direct
Transp
Health
Langu
Index
Map Le

Michael Kohn, Dan Savery Raz, Jessica Lee, Jenny Walker

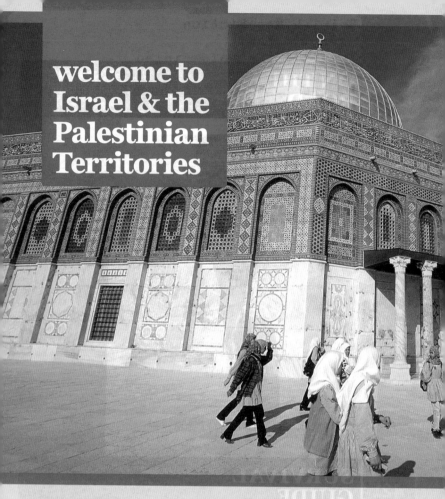

welcome to Israel & the Palestinian Territories

Holy Sites

The Holy Land, cradle of Judaism and Christianity and sacred to Muslims and Baha'is, offers visitors the opportunity to immerse themselves in the richness and variety of their own religious traditions – and to discover the beliefs, rituals and architecture of other faiths. Ancient Jewish sites, found throughout the country, include Jerusalem's Western Wall, which once surrounded the Second Temple, and Byzantine-era synagogues adorned with sumptuous mosaics. The Roman-era synagogues around the Sea of Galilee may have been used by Jews and Christians before they started thinking of themselves as belonging to separate religions. Both Christian pilgrims and tourists are welcome to visit sites associated with Jesus's birth (in Bethlehem), ministry (in Nazareth and around the Sea of Galilee) and crucifixion (in Jerusalem). For Sunni Muslims, only Mecca and Medina are holier than Jerusalem's Al-Haram ash-Sharif, known to Jews as the Temple Mount – perhaps the most contested real estate on earth.

Archaeology

Human beings have lived in Israel and the Palestinian Territories since long before recorded history, and thanks to the painstaking work of archaeologists, you can explore and ponder what they left behind. If the 10,000-year-old mud-brick

At the intersection of Asia, Europe and Africa – both geographically and culturally – Israel and the Palestinian Territories have been a meeting place of cultures, empires and religions since history began.

(left) The Dome of the Rock (p47) shines out in Jerusalem.
(below) The pomegranate is said to have as many seeds as there are Jewish commandments.

relics of Jericho don't impress you, you might find inspiration in Jerusalem's City of David, which dates from the time of Kings David and Solomon. Every conflict has two sides, so you could twin a visit to Masada, with its dramatic tale of resistance to the mighty legions of Rome, with a tour of the colonnaded thoroughfares and capacious theatres of Beit She'an, which still pulse with Roman opulence. Many of the country's most extraordinary finds – a silver amulet from the 6th century BCE inscribed with Judaism's Priestly Benediction, a 1st-century-BCE manuscript of the book of Isaiah (one of the Dead Sea Scrolls) – are on display in Jerusalem's Israel Museum.

Outdoor Activities

Few countries have so much geographic variety packed into such a small space. Distances are short so you can relax on a Mediterranean beach one day, spend the next floating in the mineral-rich waters of the Dead Sea or rafting down the Jordan River, and the day after that scuba diving in the Red Sea. Hikers can trek the length of the Golan Heights, follow spring-fed streams as they tumble towards the Jordan, explore verdant oases tucked away in the arid bluffs above the Dead Sea, and explore the multi-coloured sandstone formations of Makhtesh Ramon. Some trails are ideal for mountain biking.

› Israel & the Palestinian Territories ›

Top Experiences ›

Banias Nature Reserve
Gushing water and lush vegetation (p251)

Golan Heights
Wildflowers, canyons, volcanoes and snow (p244)

Sea of Galilee
Cerulean backdrop to Jesus's ministry (p212)

Nazareth
Holy sites and fusion cuisine (p191)

Jerusalem
Historic, holy, sublime – and contested (p38)

Dead Sea
Lowest, saltiest place on earth (p284)

Tsfat
Ancient centre of Jewish mysticism (p226)

Akko
Crusader ruins, Ottoman walled city (p181)

Caesarea
Ancient Roman theatre and port (p176)

Tel Aviv
Turquoise water and bronze bodies (p108)

Jaffa
Seafront promenade, galleries, flea market (p146)

Bethlehem
The original Nativity scene (p259)

MEDITERRANEAN SEA

LEBANON

SYRIA

Tyre

Rosh HaNikra

Nahariya

Montfort

Banias Nature Reserve

Kiryat Shmona

Quneitra

The Golan

Jordan River

Rosh Pina

Tsfat

Capernaum

Sea of Galilee

Akko

Peqi'in

Daliyat al-Karmel

The Galilee

Tiberias

Haifa

Atlit

Afula

Beit She'an

Nazareth

Megiddo

Caesarea

Jenin

Mt Ebal (940m)

Mt Gerizim (881m)

Nablus

Hadera

Netanya

West Bank

Ramallah

Abu Ghosh

JERUSALEM

Jericho

Qumran

Dead Sea

Herzliya

Tel Aviv

Jaffa

Rishon LeZion

Ramla

Rehovot

Bethlehem

Nebi Musa

Herodian

Hebron

Ashdod

Kiryat Gat

Beit Guvrin

Ashkelon

Gaza City

Gaza Strip

Irbid

Deraa

Mafraq

AMMAN

Jordan River

Dead Sea

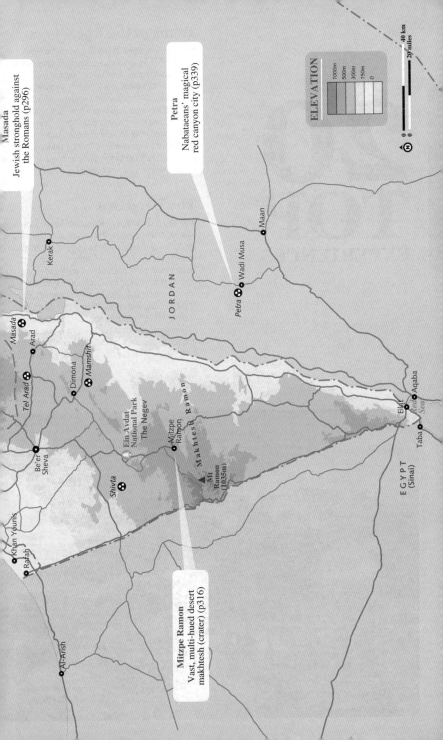

Masada
Jewish stronghold against
the Romans (p296)

Petra
Nabataeans' magical
red canyon city (p339)

Mitzpe Ramon
Vast, multi-hued desert
makhtesh (crater) (p316)

ELEVATION

1000m
500m
300m
150m
0

Khan Younis
Rafah
Al-Arish

Be'er
Sheva

Shivta

Dimona
Mamshit

Arad
Tel Arad
Masada

Kerak

Ein Avdat
National Park
The Negev

Mitzpe
Ramon

Makhtesh Ramon

Mt
Ramon
(1035m)

JORDAN

Petra
Wadi Musa
Maan

EGYPT
(Sinai)

Taba
Eilat
Aqaba

Red
Sea

N

0   20 miles
0   40 km

20 TOP EXPERIENCES

Dome of the Rock

1 The first sight of the Dome of the Rock (p47) – its gold cap shimmering above a mystical turquoise-hued octagonal base – never fails to take one's breath away. Perhaps that's what the architects had in mind more than 1300 years ago when they set to work on this impossibly gorgeous building. The best view is from the Mount of Olives but don't miss the chance to see it up close by taking an early morning walk up to the Temple Mount. Dome of the Rock, with Mount of Olives in the background

The Dead Sea

2 You pass a sign reading 'Sea Level' and then keep driving downhill, eventually catching glimpses of the Dead Sea's (p284) cobalt-blue waters, outlined by snow-white salt deposits, reddish-tan cliffs and tufts of dark-green vegetation. At the oasis of Ein Gedi you can hike through unique desert habitats to crystal-clear pools and tumbling waterfalls before climbing to the Judean Desert plateau above – or heading down to the seashore for a briny, invigorating dip. To the south around Mt Sodom, outdoor options include adventure cycling along dry riverbeds.

HANAN ISACHAR/LONELY PLANET IMAGES ©

Y. LEVY/ALAMY ©

Tel Aviv Beaches

3 Just over 100 years ago, Tel Aviv was little more than sand dunes. Now TLV is a sprawling cosmopolitan city bursting with bars, bistros and boutiques but the beach is still the epicentre of life. Here, sunbathers bronze their bodies, while the more athletic swim, surf and play intense games of *matkot* (beach racquetball). Each beach (p125) along the coast of Tel Aviv has its own personality – sporty, party, alternative, gay or religious – all against the deep-blue backdrop of the Mediterranean.

Golan Heights

4 From towering Nimrod Fortress, the 'Galilee Panhandle' (p244) spreads out before you like a topographical map, but turn around and the looming flanks of Mt Hermon, snow-capped well into spring, dwarf even this Crusader-era stronghold. Hikers can take on the alpine peaks of Mt Hermon, or follow the cliff-lined wadis of the Banias and Yehudiya Nature Reserves on their way to the Jordan River and the Sea of Galilee. The Golan's basalt soils are ideal for growing grapes, so the local boutique wines are some of Israel's finest. Nimrod Fortress, Mt Hermon

Western Wall

5 In Israel they say that every rock is holy in some way, but for Jews the holiest stones of all are those that make up the Western Wall (p49), the 2000-year-old western retaining wall of the Temple Mount. For centuries Jews have come here to pray and to mourn the destruction of the First and Second Temples. The wall's great stones have an almost magnetic power, drawing close the hands and foreheads of the faithful, who come here in search of a deep, direct connection with God.

5

BRIAN CRUICKSHANK/LONELY PLANET IMAGES ©

Church of the Holy Sepulchre

6 Israel is blessed with holy sites and there are few more holy than the site of Jesus's crucifixion and burial. The Church of the Holy Sepulchre (p55) is built on what Queen Helena believed to be that sacred place and it remains today a place of incredible spirituality. Join the constant parade of pilgrims as they shuffle solemnly through the darkened corridors viewing by candlelight the oldest traditions of the Christian faith.

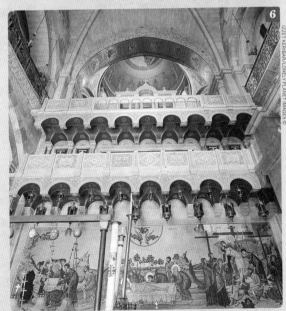

6

IZZET KERIBAR/LONELY PLANET IMAGES ©

Baha'i Gardens

7 One of the world's most progressive centres of spirituality, the Baha'i Gardens (p158) are an incredible fusion of ecology, spirituality, symbolism and design. Start at the top and make your way down the face of Mt Carmel breathing in the fragrances emanating from innumerable flowers in this one-of-a-kind sculpture. Or if you happen to be Baha'i, start at the bottom and make your way up the 19 terraces to fulfil a time-honoured spiritual pilgrimage.

Masada

8 The Romans had just destroyed Jerusalem when about a thousand Jewish Zealots took refuge on a remote mesa overlooking the Dead Sea. As you peer down from their towering redoubt, you can still see the eight encircling Roman camps (p296), connected by a siege wall, making it easy to imagine the dramatic, tragic events that unfolded here in early 73 CE. Eventually the Romans built a ramp and breached the walls, but all they found were a handful of survivors – everyone else had committed suicide rather than submit to slavery.

Tsfat (Safed)

9 The spirit of the 16th-century rabbis who turned Tsfat (p226) into the world's most important centre of Kabbalah (Jewish mysticism) can still be felt in the alleyways of the Synagogue Quarter, especially inside its ancient synagogues, and in the Artists' Quarter, where intimate galleries offer creative, joyous Judaica (Jewish ritual objects). A Kabbalistic vibe is also palpable in the hillside cemetery, where some of Judaism's greatest sages – the Ari, Yitzhak Luria, Yosef Caro – lie buried. Everything closes on Shabbat – supremely restful if you're in the mood. Jewish men studying Kabbalah

Old City, Bethlehem

10 For nearly two millennia Christian pilgrims have been making their way to the birthplace of Jesus and for just as long the people of Bethlehem have been feeding them in their restaurants and housing them in their inns. Bethlehem's Old City (p260) still retains the mystique of antiquity, almost unchanged through the generations. Get a feel for it by wandering up Star St, where you can haggle for keepsakes and savour the flavours of its myriad snack stalls. Star of Bethlehem in the Church of the Nativity, Bethlehem

Avdat

11 The harsh climate and lack of rainfall were no barriers to the ancient Nabataeans who built Avdat (p314) in the 3rd century BCE. Originally just a caravan stop from Petra to Gaza, Avdat's acropolis, bathhouse and catacombs were added later. Perched on top of a hill, the ruined city offers spectacular views of the surrounding desert through Roman arches and crumbled Byzantine church walls. Avdat's residents were also partial to a drop of wine and you can sample a modern merlot at the Carmey Avdat Winery across the highway.

JOHN ELK III/LONELY PLANET IMAGES ©

Petra

12 Hidden deep in the desert, Petra (p339) is undoubtedly the jewel in Jordan's royal crown. Voted one of the new Seven Wonders of the World, the ancient Nabataean capital is a global blockbuster and one of the world's great archaeological treasures. Famous for its swirling psychedelic rock, mysterious caves and glorious temple facades, the Red Rose City and its neighbouring town Wadi Musa are just a two-hour taxi ride from Eilat's Rabin border crossing. For a magical experience, don't miss the candlelit Petra by Night tour. The Monastery (Al-Deir)

Makhtesh Ramon

13 Standing on the edge of Makhtesh Ramon (p316) you can witness millions of years of evolution beneath your feet and barely imagine that this barren landscape was once a sea. Freezing cold at night, but baking during the day, the makhtesh, or crater as it's commonly known, is a place of extremes. The multicoloured rock formations of the Negev Highlands go on for as far as the eye can see and you can't help but wonder how such a small country can be home to such a vast secret.

Caesarea

14 Built on an exposed section of the eastern Mediterranean with heavy surf pounding it for half the year, Caesarea (p176) never really stood a chance. Within a few centuries of its creation the awesome port built by Herod was nothing more than a storm-battered stretch of dunes covering an ancient urban fabric. Archaeologists have since uncovered most of it and in doing so have patched together Caesarea's once-glorious history. Perch yourself on the edge of the sea and visualise the faded past. Crusader city ruins, Caesarea

DENNIS COX/ALAMY ©

Nazareth

15 The village where Jesus grew up has also grown up and is now a bustling Arab city. In the Old City, narrow alleyways are graced with churches commemorating the Annunciation and other New Testament events, and with Ottoman-era mansions. A new generation of restaurants has made Nazareth (p191) a star in Israel's gastronomic firmament. Alongside delicious old-time specialities, served with traditional Arab hospitality, you can sample East–West 'fusion' dishes – fresh local herbs with artichoke hearts, or wild Galilean pine nuts with chopped beef. Icon in Basilica of the Annunciation, Nazareth

ZVONIMIR ATLETIĆ/ALAMY ©

15

ICONOTEC/ALAMY ©

Akko

16 Time-warped Akko (p181) is Israel's hidden gem, a walled city by the sea where waves crash into time-worn towers and little fishing boats line up in the peaceful harbour. The town hasn't changed all that much since Marco Polo set foot here, with lots of underground passageways, a Knights Hall, towers and fortified walls. Akko used to be a place for a day trip from Haifa but with a growing number of hotels in all price ranges and an excellent selection of restaurants it's become a fine base for exploring northern Israel.
Harbour, Akko

Hunting for the Perfect Hummus

17 OK, hummus can be found all over the world today but in the Holy Land eating this chickpea dish is almost a religious experience. Popular with Israelis, Palestinians, Bedouins, Druze and just about everyone else in this neck of the woods, hummus here is hot, creamy and served with all kinds of herbs. Take a pilgrimage to Abu Ghosh or Old Jaffa to enjoy a plate of the beige stuff with tahina, fava beans, egg, onion, pita bread, felafel or all of the above.

Old Jaffa

18 While neighbouring Tel Aviv is only beginning its second century, Jaffa (p147) has some 4000 years behind it. Jaffa's history reads like a who's who of conquerors – the Greeks, Romans, Crusaders, Napoleon, Ottomans and British all used this Mediterranean port, once the gateway to the Middle East. Now a mix of Arab and Jewish neighbourhoods, Jaffa is a great place to smoke a nargileh pipe, haggle for antiques in the flea market or take a cycling trip along the redeveloped coastline.

Mount of Olives

19 The Mount of Olives (p71) is said to be where the dead have lined up for a first shot at redemption after the Apocalypse. Some 40,000 graves have been identified here dating back 3000 years. Some of Christendom's most important holy sites are also here, including the Garden of Gethsemane, the Tomb of Mary plus a half-dozen other churches and chapels built over sites associated with the life of Jesus. The nonreligious may simply want to enjoy the view – head up to the Seven Arches Hotel for a stunning panorama of the Old City.

Mahane Yehuda Market, Jerusalem

20 Ten years ago it was a grungy mishmash of fruit and vegetable stalls where grannies loaded up trollies with their daily groceries. Today it's one of the hippest spots in Jerusalem (p77), frequented by sophisticated urbanites dining at some of the city's most creative restaurants. Oh, there's still a fair bit of grunge in the fresh-food stalls but it's enlivened with colourful free-marketeers selling their goods and even a couple of beer bars where you can watch the action roll past. Halva for sale in Mahane Yehuda Market

19

20

need to know

Currency

» Israel and the Palestinian Territories – Israeli new shekel (NIS or ILS); Jordan & the West Bank – Jordanian dinar (JD or JOD); Egypt & Gaza – Egyptian pound (E£ or EGP)

Language

» Israel – Hebrew & Arabic (official), English; Palestinian Territories, Jordan and Egypt – Arabic (official), English

When to Go

- Desert, dry climate
- Dry climate
- Warm to hot summers, mild winters

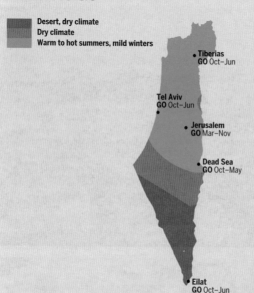

Tiberias GO Oct–Jun

Tel Aviv GO Oct–Jun

Jerusalem GO Mar–Nov

Dead Sea GO Oct–May

Eilat GO Oct–Jun

High Season (Jul–Aug)

» Warm in Jerusalem, muggy in Tel Aviv, infernal in Eilat, Tiberias, Dead Sea

» Hotels prices spike and rooms are scarce

» Jewish holidays of Passover, Rosh HaShana and Sukkot are also high season

Shoulder (Oct–Nov, Mar–Jun)

» Sometimes rainy but more often warm and sunny

» Spring wildflowers make March and April ideal for hiking

» Local tourist demand spikes during the week-long Jewish holidays of Passover and Sukkot

Low Season (Dec–Feb)

» Chilly or downright cold in the north, especially at higher elevations

» Popular time to head to the warmth of Eilat and the Dead Sea

Your Daily Budget

Budget less than 300NIS

» Dorm bed: 100NIS

» Meals of felafel or hummus, and supermarket picnics

» Travel by bus, train or sherut (shared taxi)

» Swim at free public beaches

Midrange 500NIS–600NIS

» Double room at midrange hotel (per person): 220NIS

» Meals at midrange restaurants

» Intercity travel by small rental car

Top end over 800NIS

» Luxury double room or B&B (per person): from 300NIS

» Meals at the finest restaurants

» Travel by mid-sized rental car or with guide

Money

» ATMs widely available in Israel, less so in Palestinian Territories, absent from Israel's land borders. Credit cards almost universally accepted in Israel.

Visas

» Israel and Jordan grant on-arrival visas to most nationalities, so does Egypt for visitors to Sinai's Red Sea coast

Mobile Phones

» All but the remotest areas have excellent 900/1800 MHz mobile phone coverage. Local pre-paid SIM cards available.

Transport

» Getting around by public transport is possible but complicated and slow. Outside cities, renting a car gives unmatched flexibility and convenience.

Websites

» **Israel Nature & Parks Authority** (www.parks.org.il) Nature reserves and archaeological sites.

» **Israel Ministry of Tourism** (www.goisrael. com) Background, events and a virtual tour.

» **ILH-Israel Hostels** (www.hostels-israel. com) Independent hostels.

» **This Week in Palestine** (www.this weekinpalestine.com) Cultural goings-on.

» **Lonely Planet** (www.lonelyplanet. com) Destination information, hotel bookings, traveller forum and more.

Exchange Rates

		NIS	JD	E£
Australia	A$1	3.96	0.76	6.39
Canada	C$1	3.79	0.71	6.10
Euro	€1	4.95	0.93	7.98
Israel	NIS1	1.00	0.19	1.62
Japan	¥100	4.49	0.85	7.23
NZ	NZ$1	3.10	0.59	4.98
UK	UK£1	5.95	1.12	9.58
USA	US$1	3.70	0.71	6.00

For current exchange rates see www.xe.com.

Important Numbers

Police/Ambulance/Fire	☑100/101/102
Israel country code	☑972
Palestinian Territories country code	☑972 or 970
Jordan country code	☑962
Egypt country code	☑20

Arriving in Israel

» **Ben-Gurion airport** Taxi – 242NIS/126NIS to Jerusalem/Tel Aviv Sherut (shared taxi) – 58NIS to Jerusalem Train – 15NIS to Tel Aviv

» **Jordan River/ Sheikh Hussein Crossing (Jordan)** Taxi – 50NIS to Beit She'an

» **Allenby/King Hussein Bridge (Jordan)** Taxi – 160NIS to Jerusalem

» **Yitzhak Rabin/ Wadi Araba Crossing (Jordan)** Taxi – 35NIS to Eilat

» **Taba Crossing (Sinai)** Bus – 7.50NIS to Eilat

News in English

The English edition of **Haaretz** (www.haaretz.com), Israel's left-of-centre newspaper of record, is sold at news stands bundled with the **International Herald Tribune** (the global edition of the *New York Times*). The right-of-centre **Jerusalem Post** (www.jpost. com) is also widely available. The biweekly **Jerusalem Report** (www.jpost.com/Jerusa lemReport) covers current affairs.

On the radio, **IBA World** (Reshet Reka; www.iba.org.il/world) has 15-minute English news bulletins daily at 6.30am, 12.30pm and 8.30pm (Jerusalem: 100.3 MHz and 101.3 MHz; Tel Aviv: 101.2 MHz; Galilee: 105.1 MHz and 104.8 MHz; Negev: 107.3 MHz). The BBC World Service, broadcast from Cyprus, can be picked up on 1323 kHz AM/MW.

Israel TV's **Channel 1** broadcasts nine minutes of English news at 4.50pm from Sunday to Thursday. Cable and satellite packages, including those in hotels, almost always include BBC, CNN, Sky, Fox and other TV news channels.

if you like...

Beaches

Hedonists preen and bronze along the Mediterranean, while at the Dead Sea they float and apply mud packs. At the Red Sea the most colourful creatures are under the water. The Sea of Galilee offers old-fashioned family fun.

Metzitzim Beach A family-friendly half-bay just south of the lively Tel Aviv port (p126)

Coral Beach Nature Reserve Eilat's best beach is a utopia for snorkellers (p324)

Ein Bokek Broad, clean and sandy – the Dead Sea's best free beach (p298)

Sea of Galilee Some are free, others come with fees and amenities, all are refreshing on a scorching summer's day (p209)

Dahab Sinai's premier beach resort for independent travellers (p359)

Herzliyya Pituach Fine Mediterranean sand between the marina and some of Israel's most expensive villas (p151)

Akhziv About as far north as you can go along Israel's Mediterranean coast (p188)

Hiking

Israel's hills and valleys burst into flower after the winter rains, making spring the ideal season to hit the hiking trails. Marked routes (p427) range from easy strolls for the whole family to multi-day treks requiring topographical maps (p431).

Ein Gedi Two spring-fed canyon oases are home to a profusion of plant and animal life (p289)

Makhtesh Ramon Hike through this vast desert crater, famous for its multicoloured sandstone (p316)

Banias Cool, burbling spring water tumbles down waterfalls and nourishes Edenic vegetation (p251)

Wadi Yehudiya Canyons, waterfalls and pools on the western edge of the Golan (p247)

Jesus Trail Links Nazareth with the Sea of Galilee (p190)

Ein Avdat A hidden spring-fed oasis deep in the Negev Desert (p312)

Golan Trail Runs the entire length of the Golan Heights (see p253)

Wine Tasting

Grown here since biblical times, grapes thrive in Israel's varied microclimates, producing wines of surprising richness and subtlety that have recently been winning international awards. Some top wineries (p237) produce over a million bottles a year, others just a few barrels.

Golan Heights High altitudes, cool climate, well-drained volcanic soils and top-rate savoir faire (p245 and p251)

Dalton Plateau High in the Upper Galilee, 'Israel's Tuscany' produces some of the country's most highly regarded vintages (p237)

Negev Highlands Hot daytime temperatures, cool nights, sandy soils, the latest drip-irrigation technology – and inspiration from the ancient Nabataeans (p307)

Zichron Ya'acov A winemaking centre since the late 1800s, this town, overlooking the northern coastal plain, has a typically Mediterranean climate (p175)

EDDIE GERALD/ALAMY ©

» Fermentation tanks at the Golan Heights Winery (p245), Katzrin

Ancient Synagogues

The focus of Jewish ritual shifted from temple sacrifices to synagogues after the Romans destroyed Jerusalem in 70 CE. Impressive ancient synagogues, some adorned with ornate stone carvings or gorgeous mosaics, can be visited all over the country.

Beit Alpha Famed for its extraordinary mosaics depicting a zodiac circle, a menorah, a shofar and a Torah ark (p205)

Tiberias Features beautiful mosaics, including a zodiac and two seven-branched menorahs (p206)

Korazim Decorated with exceptionally fine basalt carvings, many depicting floral and geometric designs (p215)

Tzipori Byzantine-era synagogue with an extraordinary mosaic floor (p201)

Bar'am Solidly built of finely hewn limestone during the late Talmudic period (p238)

Katzrin A Talmud-era synagogue made of local basalt (p246)

Gamla One of the world's oldest synagogues, believed to date from the 1st century BCE (p248)

New Testament Sites

The historical Jesus was born in Bethlehem, grew up in Nazareth, preached in Galilee and was crucified in Jerusalem. Many sites associated with his life and ministry, identified by both tradition and archaeology, have become places of Christian pilgrimage.

Church of the Holy Sepulchre The traditional site of Jesus's crucifixion, death and resurrection is Christendom's holiest site (p55)

Church of the Nativity Believed to be the site of Jesus's birth since at least the 4th century (p260)

Basilica of the Annunciation Where many Christians believe the Annunciation took place (p193)

Capernaum Jesus's home base during most of his Galilean ministry (p214)

Qasr al-Yahud Reputed place of Jesus's baptism by John, reopened in 2011 (p276)

Mt Tabor Traditional hilltop site of Jesus's Transfiguration (p201)

Mount of Temptation Where Jesus is said to have been tested by the Devil (p275)

Outdoor Adventures

Israel's cliffs, canyons, deserts, rivers and seas offer ample options for adventurous travellers in the mood to burn some calories, confront their fears or just pump some adrenalin.

River rafting The Jordan offers everything from a sedate family float to wild white-water rapids (p245)

Scuba diving Explore the spectacular Red Sea from underneath the waves in Eilat (p325) or at Sinai's Dahab (p361)

Mountain biking Cycle the desert at Wadi Sodom (p300)

Parachuting Jump tandem above the Dead Sea and Masada (p297)

Cliff rappelling You'll need ropes and reliable friends to follow Wadi Daraja down to the Dead Sea (p295)

Skiing Hit the pistes at Israel's only ski resort (p253)

month by month

Top Events

1 **Passover**, April

2 **Easter**, April

3 **Ramadan**, July

4 **Hanukkah**, December

5 **Christmas**, December

Jewish holidays follow the lunisolar Hebrew calendar and fall somewhere within a four-week window relative to the Gregorian (Western) calendar. The Islamic calendar is lunar so each year festivals arrive 11 or 12 days earlier than the Gregorian dates. Jewish and Islamic holidays begin at sundown and last until sundown of the following calendar day; the dates given below include the eve of the holiday. Eastern Orthodox churches use a combination of the Julian calendar and, for Easter, the Paschal cycle. To check the dates of religious holidays, go to www.bbc.co.uk/religion/tools/calendar.

January

The coolest and wettest month of the year. Chilly in Jerusalem and the north; sometimes sunny along the coast; usually sunny at the Dead Sea and in Eilat. Occasional snow in Jerusalem and Tsfat. Low-season room prices.

☆ New Year's Day
An official holiday in the Palestinian Territories, a regular work day in Israel (1 January).

☆ Christmas (Orthodox)
Commemorates the birth of Jesus in Bethlehem (celebrated by Eastern Orthodox churches on 6 and 7 January and by Armenians in the Holy Land on 18 and 19 January).

☆ Tu Bishvat
(New Year of the Trees) Jews plant trees, and eat nuts and fresh and dried fruits (26 January 2013, 16 January 2014, 4 February 2015).

☆ Prophet's Birthday
(Mawlid al-Nabi) Celebrations mark the birthday of the Prophet Mohammed (23–24 January 2013, 12–13 January 2014, 2–3 January 2015).

March

Thanks to the winter rains, hillsides and valleys are green and wildflowers are in bloom – a great time for hiking. Often rainy in the north. Low season room prices.

☆ Purim
Celebrates the foiling of a plot to wipe out the Jews of ancient Persia. Children and adults put on costumes for an evening of revelry (23–24 February 2013, 15–16 March 2014, 4–5 March 2015; celebrated one day later in walled cities, including Jerusalem).

☆ Land Day
(Yom al-Ard in Arabic, Yom HaAdama in Hebrew) A Palestinian day of protest against Israel's expropriation of Palestinian land (30 March).

April

Hillsides and valleys are alive with spring wildflowers – this is the best month for hiking. Accommodation prices spike during Sukkot and, near Christian sites, around Easter.

☆ Passover
(Pesach) Weeklong celebration of the liberation of the Israelites from slavery in Egypt. Jewish families hold a *seder* (ritual dinner) on the first night (in the Diaspora, on the first two nights). The sale of *chametz*

(bread and other leavened products) is forbidden in Jewish areas (supermarkets hide such items behind plastic sheeting). Shabbat-like closures on the first and seventh days. Lots of Israelis go on holiday so accommodation is scarce and room prices skyrocket (25 March–1 April 2013, 14–21 April 2014, 3–10 April 2015).

★ Mimouna
North African Jews celebrate the end of Passover with sweets, picnics and barbecues (2 April 2013, 22 April 2014, 11 April 2015).

★ Good Friday
Commemorates Jesus's crucifixion in Jerusalem. Falls on the Friday before Easter Sunday (for Protestants and Catholics, 29 March 2013, 18 April 2014 and 3 April 2015).

★ Great Friday
Commemorates Jesus's crucifixion in Jerusalem (for Eastern Orthodox churches, on 3 May 2013, 18 April 2014 and 10 April 2015).

★ Easter (Western)
Commemorates the resurrection of Jesus on the third day after the crucifixion; marks the end of Lent (40 days of penance and fasting). Catholic pilgrims throng Jerusalem's Via Dolorosa and the Church of the Holy Sepulchre, and many Protestants gather at the Garden Tomb (for Catholics and Protestants, on 31 March 2013, 20 April 2014 and 5 April 2015).

★ Easter (Orthodox)
Commemorates the resurrection of Jesus (for Eastern Orthodox and Armenians, on 5 May 2013, 20 April 2014 and 12 April 2015).

★ Holocaust Memorial Day
(Yom HaSho'ah) Solemn remembrance of the six million Jews, including 1.5 million children, who died in the Holocaust. Places of entertainment are closed. At 10am sirens sound and Israelis stand silently at attention wherever they happen to be (7–8 April 2013, 27–28 April 2014, 15–16 April 2015).

★ Yom HaZikaron
(Memorial Day) Commemorates soldiers who fell defending Israel and the victims of terrorism. Places of entertainment are closed. At 8pm and 11am sirens sound and Israelis stand silently at attention wherever they happen to be. Falls on the day before Israel Independence Day (14–15 April 2013, 4–5 May 2014, 22–23 April 2015).

★ Israel Independence Day
(Yom Ha'Atzma'ut) Celebrates Israel's declaration of independence in 1948. Marked with official ceremonies, public celebrations with live music, picnics and hikes (16 April 2013, 6 May 2014, 23 April 2015).

★ Palestinian Prisoners Day
Palestinians remember their countrymen imprisoned in Israeli jails (17 April).

★ Armenian Genocide Remembrance Day
Commemorates the genocide of Armenians by the Ottoman Turks during WWI (24 April).

May

Sunny but not too hot, with nice long days. School's in session in Israel, Europe and North America so few families are travelling. The last rains often fall in early May.

★ International Labour Day
An official holiday in both Israel and the Palestinian Territories (1 May).

★ Naqba Day
Palestinian commemoration of the *naqba* (catastrophe) of refugees' displacement in 1948 (15 May).

★ Shavuot
(Pentecost) Jews celebrate the giving of the Torah at Mt Sinai. Dairy products are eaten and all-night study sessions held. Shabbat-like closure of shops and public transport. Popular time for domestic tourism so accommodation is scarce and room prices are high (14–15 May 2013, 3–4 June 2014, 23–24 May 2015).

★ Lag BaOmer
A break in the Jewish semi-mourning period between Passover and Shavu'ot. Celebrated with picnics, hikes, weddings and bonfires (27–28 April 2013, 17–18 May 2014, 6–7 May 2015).

Leilat al-Mi'raj

(Al-Israa' wal-Mi'raj) Commemorates Mohammed's 'Night Journey' from Mecca to Jerusalem and from there to heaven (4–5 June 2013, 24–25 May 2014, 14–15 May 2015).

June

Long days and sunny, warm weather. The coast is not as hot and humid as in July and August. Almost never rains. High-season room prices in some places.

Israel Festival

(www.israel-festival. org.il) Four weeks of music, theatre and dance performances, some of them free, in and around Jerusalem (see p87).

Israeli Opera Festival

(www.opera-masada.com) Brings dazzling opera productions to Masada (early June).

Naksa Day

Palestinian commemoration of the *naksa* (setback) of the 1967 Six Day War (5 June).

Gay Pride Parade

Tel Aviv is bedecked with rainbow flags for Israel's biggest and most colourful gay and lesbian extravaganza.

July

Sweltering along the coast but pleasantly dry in Jerusalem. Sizzling hot at the Sea of Galilee, the Dead Sea and Eilat.

Accommodation is pricey, especially in northern B&Bs and in cities popular with French tourists.

Ramadan

Holy month of dawn-to-dusk fasting by Muslims. Celebratory break-fast meals are held after dark. Offices may have shorter hours, and restaurants may close during daylight (9 July–8 August 2013, 28 June–28 July 2014, 18 June–17 July 2015).

Eid al-Fitr

(Festival of Fast-Breaking) The end of Ramadan is marked by celebrations with family and friends (7–8 August 2013, 27–28 July 2014, 16–17 July 2015).

Tish'a B'Av

(Ninth of Av) Jews commemorate the destruction of the Temples in Jerusalem. Restaurants and places of entertainment are closed (15–16 July 2013, 2–3 August 2014, 25–26 July 2015).

August

The hottest month of the year. Sweltering along the coast but pleasantly dry in Jerusalem; infernal at the Sea of Galilee, the Dead Sea and Eilat. Accommodation expensive, especially in northern B&Bs and cities popular with French tourists.

Tsfat Klezmer Festival

Eastern European Jewish soul music high in the Galilee (see p233).

Red Sea Jazz Festival

(www.redseajazzeilat.com) Eilat sizzles with the coolest jazz (last week of August; see p328).

September

Israeli schools are in session so fewer families are travelling, though room prices skyrocket at Rosh HaShanah and during Sukkot. Flights are often full around Rosh HaShanah and Yom Kippur.

Rosh HaShanah

(Jewish New Year) Shabbat-like closures last two days. Some Israelis go on holiday so accommodation is scarce and room prices rise (16–18 September 2012, 4–6 September 2013, 24–26 September 2014).

Yom Kippur

(Jewish Day of Atonement) Solemn day of reflection and fasting – and cycling on the empty roads. In Jewish areas, all businesses shut and transportation (including by private car) completely ceases; Israel's airports and land borders close (25–26 September 2012, 13–14 September 2013, 3–4 October 2014).

October

The start of the rainy season, though most days are dry and sunny. Accommodation prices skyrocket during the Sukkot holiday. Sites and activities that are only open in the warm season often close right after Sukkot.

✦ Sukkot

(Feast of the Tabernacles) Weeklong holiday that recollects the Israelites' 40 years of wandering in the desert. Jewish families build *sukkot* (foliage-roofed booths) in which they dine and sometimes sleep. The first and seventh day are Shabbat-like public holidays. Popular vacation time for Israelis so accommodation is scarce and room prices skyrocket (30 September–7 October 2012, 18–25 September 2013, 8–15 October 2014).

✦ Simhat Torah

Concludes and begins Jews' annual cycle of reading the Torah. Singing and dancing in synagogues (7–8 October 2012, 25–26 September 2013, 15–16 October 2014).

✦ Eid al-Adha

(Festival of the Sacrifice) Muslims commemorate the willingness of Ibrahim (Abraham) to sacrifice his son Ishmael. Marks the end of the hajj (annual pilgrimage to Mecca). Sheep are sacrificed (25–26 October 2012, 14–15 October 2013, 3–4 October 2014).

✦ Oktoberfest

(www.taybehbeer.com) Pints, Palestinians and lederhosen at this beer festival in the pretty Palestinian village of Taybeh (see p274).

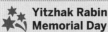

November

Sometimes rainy and chilly but frequently sunny. Often pleasantly warm along the coast, at the Dead Sea and in Eilat. Days are short. Low-season prices.

✦ Yitzhak Rabin Memorial Day

Honours Prime Minister Yitzhak Rabin, assassinated on 4 November 1995. A rally is held at Tel Aviv's Rabin Square.

✦ Islamic New Year

(Hijri New Year) Marks the beginning of the Islamic year. Gifts and cards are exchanged (14–15 November 2012, 3–4 November 2013, 24–25 October 2014).

December

Sometimes rainy and chilly but not infrequently sunny and even warm. Low-season room prices except in Christian areas around Christmas. Days are short.

✦ Hanukkah

(Festival of Lights) Jews celebrate the rededication of the Temple after the Maccabean revolt. Families light candles over eight nights using a nine-branched candelabra; waistlines bulge due to jelly doughnuts (8–15 December 2012, 27 November–5 December 2013, 16–24 December 2014).

✦ Christmas (Western)

Commemorates the birth of Jesus in Bethlehem. Midnight Catholic Mass is celebrated in the Church of the Nativity in Bethlehem. Christmas is a public holiday in the West Bank but not in Israel or Gaza (celebrated by Catholics and Protestants on 24–25 December).

✦ Holiday of the Holy Days

(HaChag shel HaChagim) Haifa's Wadi Nisnas neighbourhood celebrates Hanukkah, Christmas and Ramadan with art and music (weekends in December; see p165).

itineraries

Whether you've got one week or four, these itineraries provide a starting point for the trip of a lifetime. Want more inspiration? Head online to lonelyplanet. com/thorntree to chat with other travellers.

Two Weeks
Best of Israel

> Spend your first four days in and around **Jerusalem**, including a couple of days wandering the alleys of the **Old City**, walking from the Western Wall up to Al-Haram ash-Sharif/Temple Mount, and following the **Via Dolorosa** to the **Church of the Holy Sepulchre**. Break out your swim suit and hiking shoes for a full-day excursion down to the **Dead Sea** and up the storied stronghold of **Masada**. Then head to the Mediterranean coast for three days around **Tel Aviv** and **Jaffa**, dividing your time strolling, cycling, lounging on the beach, fine dining and watching the world go by. Next, head up the coast for a peek at Roman-era **Caesarea** before pushing on to **Haifa**. Check out the views from atop **Mt Carmel** and the **Baha'i Gardens** before a day trip to the walled city of **Akko** and the grottoes of **Rosh HaNikra**. After a day in **Nazareth**, concluded with a tongue-tingling 'fusion' dinner, head to **Tiberias** for a day exploring the shores of the **Sea of Galilee**. On the drive back to Jerusalem, stop at the Roman ruins of **Beit She'an**.

Four Weeks
Israeli Odyssey

After four or five days in and around **Jerusalem**, including a couple of days exploring the **Old City** and a half-day visit to the **Israel Museum**, take a day trip down to the wondrous caves at **Beit Guvrin**, stopping at a winery on the way. Next, stir it up in **Tel Aviv** for a few days, strolling along the beachfront promenade to historic **Jaffa**, biking along the **Yarkon River** to the **Tel Aviv Port**, and working on your Mediterranean tan. On your way north to **Haifa**, stop at the Roman ruins of **Caesarea** and the quaint town of **Zichron Ya'acov**, famed for its vintage winery. After touring Haifa's sublime **Baha'i Gardens**, visit **Mt Carmel** and the Druze village of **Daliyat al-Karmel**. The next day, continue north to **Akko**, with its enchanting mixture of Crusader ruins and Ottoman relics. Then go as far north as politics permit, to the subterranean grottoes of **Rosh Ha-Nikra**, before heading inland for a couple of days in **Nazareth**, exploring Christian sites and dining on traditional Arab delicacies and East–West fusion dishes. Based in **Tiberias** for a couple of days, relax around the **Sea of Galilee**, combining ancient synagogues and Christian sites with quiet beaches and, perhaps, white-water rafting on the **Jordan River**. Loop east to the **Golan Heights**, visiting the hilltop ruins of **Gamla**, the Golan Archaeological Museum in **Katzrin** and towering **Nimrod Fortress**; sleep in a B&B. Circle west via the lush vegetation of **Banias Nature Reserve** to the wetlands of the **Hula Valley**, beloved by migrating birds; the quaint, cobbled streets of **Rosh Pina**; and **Tsfat (Safed)**, suffused with the spirituality of the Kabbalah (Jewish mysticism). Finally, head south through the Jordan Valley, strolling the colonnaded Roman thoroughfares of **Beit She'an** and visiting the Palestinian city of **Jericho**, whose ruins go back to the very beginning of civilisation. After a starlit night on the shores of the **Dead Sea**, rise early to catch the sunrise from high atop **Masada**. Continue south into the **Negev Desert** for a day or two around **Mitzpe Ramon**, including a hike into **Makhtesh Ramon**. Next stop, for a spot of sea, sun and snorkelling, is **Eilat**. Finally, cross into Jordan to visit the awe-inspiring 'red city' of **Petra**; plan on at least two days if you're keen to do some hiking in the area.

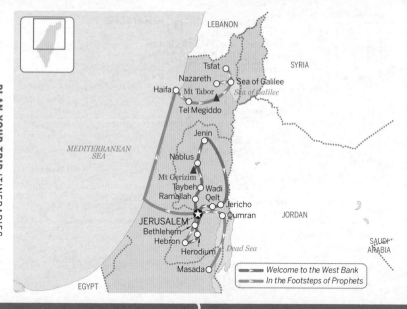

LEBANON

SYRIA

Tsfat

Nazareth

Sea of Galilee

Haifa

Mt Tabor

Sea of Galilee

Tel Megiddo

MEDITERRANEAN SEA

Jenin

Nablus

Mt Gerizim

Taybeh

Wadi Qelt

Ramallah

Jericho

JERUSALEM

Qumran

JORDAN

Bethlehem

Hebron

Herodium

Dead Sea

SAUDI ARABIA

Masada

EGYPT

➤➤➤ *Welcome to the West Bank*

➤➤➤ *In the Footsteps of Prophets*

Two Weeks
Footsteps of Prophets

➤ Even travellers who aren't religious will be intrigued by the vibes that make the Holy Land holy to so many. **Jerusalem** is, of course, the country's crown jewel, and you could spend days visiting sites sacred to Judaism, Christianity and Islam – and, in some cases, to all three. Take a day trip below sea level to **Qumran**, where the Essenes hid the Dead Sea Scrolls, and **Masada**, where Jewish Zealots defied the Roman legions. Then head south of Jerusalem to friendly **Bethlehem**, birthplace of Jesus, and the troubled city of **Hebron**, burial place of Abraham, Isaac and Jacob and their wives (except for Rachel, who's back in Bethlehem). In the north, the formal beauty of the **Baha'i Gardens** in **Haifa** inspires people of all faiths. Doomsdayers might want to visit **Tel Megiddo**, better known as Armageddon, mentioned in the New Testament as the venue of the last great battle on earth. To the northeast, there are inspirational views from atop **Mt Tabor** and in **Nazareth**, boyhood stomping ground of Jesus. Continue northeast to the **Sea of Galilee**, where Jesus spent much of his ministry and the Jerusalem Talmud was redacted, and to spiritual **Tsfat (Safed)**, renowned centre of Kabbalah (Jewish mysticism).

One Week
Welcome to the West Bank

➤ From the Arab bus station in **East Jerusalem**, hop on a bus to **Ramallah**, where you can drop in on the **Muqata'a**, last resting place of Yasser Arafat. Spend the afternoon sipping coffee, scooping hummus and clacking backgammon tiles, then get ready for a night on the town. The next day, drop by the only brewery in the Palestinian Territories, **Taybeh**, returning to Ramallah to catch a concert or theatre performance at one of the city's many arts venues. Next, head north – through olive orchards and terraced hills – to **Nablus** for a day of shopping in the enchanting market, scrubbing up at an ancient hammam, visiting the Samaritans atop **Mt Gerizim**, and feasting on *kunafeh* (a warm, syrupy cheese-based pastry). Then travel north to the Christian sites near **Jenin** and that city's renowned **Freedom Theatre** before looping east and south to **Jericho** for some extraordinary hiking in **Wadi Qelt**. Then slip southwestward to beautiful **Bethlehem**, with its winding lanes and ancient churches. Finally, stop off at Roman-era **Herodium** before heading down to the West Bank's troubled gem: the extraordinary city of **Hebron**, passionately sacred to both Jews and Muslims.

Crossing Borders

Peace Borders

The borders between Israel and the two countries with which it has signed peace treaties, Egypt and Jordan, are open to both tourists and locals.

West Bank Crossings

For details on getting through Israel Defence Forces (IDF) roadblocks between the West Bank and Israel, see p265 and p190.

Colourful Frontiers

Israel's UN-certified border with Lebanon is known as the Blue Line; the Israeli–Syrian ceasefire line of 1974 is known as the Purple Line; and the pre-1967 border between Israel and the West Bank is known as the Green Line.

Border History

In the secret Sykes-Picot Agreement of 1916, Britain and France determined the future borders of Palestine, Syria, Lebanon, Transjordan (Jordan) and Iraq.

Planning Your Crossing

Visas, Security & Entry Stamps

» For details on **visas** to Israel, Jordan and Egypt, see p433.

» For tips on getting through **Israeli border control**, see p30.

» If you don't want an **Israeli stamp** in your passport (see p30), mention this as soon as you hand it over to border control.

Land Crossings: Your Options

» **Israel–Jordan:** Jordan River/Sheikh Hussein crossing, south of the Sea of Galilee; Yitzhak Rabin/Wadi Araba crossing, just north of Eilat/Aqaba

» **West Bank–Jordan:** Allenby/King Hussein Bridge, just east of Jericho (controlled by Israel)

» **Israel–Egypt**: Eilat/Taba crossing, on the Red Sea just south of Eilat

» **Gaza–Egypt:** Rafah

Fees for land border crossings are as follows:

	ARRIVAL	DEPARTURE
Israel	None	103NIS (176NIS at Allenby/King Hussein Bridge)
Egypt	E£30	E£2
Jordan	JD5	JD8

Border Closings

Israel's borders (and airports) are closed on Yom Kippur. Crossings with Jordan are also closed on Al-Hijra/Muslim New Year), and with Egypt on the Muslim holiday of Eid al-Adha.

Northern Frontiers

Israel's borders with Syria and Lebanon are shut tight. Unless you're a UN peacekeeper, the only way to get to the other side is through Jordan, but if you've already been in Israel this can be tricky (see p30).

To/From Jordan

Although the crossings to Jordan from Israel and the Palestinian Territories are a bit quirky – this is especially true of the Allenby/King Hussein Bridge crossing – tourists shouldn't have too much trouble getting across.

Jordan River/Sheikh Hussein Crossing

Situated in the Jordan Valley 8km east of Beit She'an, 30km south of the Sea of Galilee, 135km northeast of Tel Aviv and 90km northeast of Amman, this **crossing** (☑04-609 3400; www.iaa.gov.il; ⊙6.30am-9pm Sun-Thu, 8am-8pm Fri & Sat, closed Yom Kippur & Al-Hijra/Muslim New Year) is generally far less busy than Allenby/King Hussein Bridge.

The Israeli side lacks an ATM but currency exchange services are available whenever the terminal is open.

For travellers heading to Jordan, getting through Israeli border formalities usually takes about a half-hour. You then have to take a bus (4.50NIS, twice an hour) to cross to the Jordanian side of the river, a distance of about 500m.

Getting There & Away

The Israeli side is connected with Beit She'an (17 minutes, three daily Sunday to Thursday, two on Friday) by Kavim bus 16. **Taxis** (☑04-658 5834) can take you to Beit She'an (50NIS) and destinations around Israel.

On the Jordanian side, frequent service taxis travel to/from Irbid's West bus station (JD1, 45 minutes), and to Amman. **Nazarene Tours** (☑04-601 0458; Paulus VI St, Nazareth) links Nazareth with Amman (75NIS, five hours), via the Jordan River/Sheikh Hussein crossing, on Sunday, Tuesday, Thursday and Saturday. Departures are from the company's Nazareth office (near the

Bank of Jerusalem and the Nazareth Hotel) at 8.30am; and from Amman's **Maraya Hotel** (www.marayahotel.com; University St) at 2pm. Reserve by phone at least two days ahead.

Yitzhak Rabin/Wadi Araba Crossing

Located just 3km northeast of Eilat, this **crossing** (☑08-630 0530/555; www.iaa.gov.il; ⊙6.30am-8pm Sun-Thu, 8am-8pm Fri & Sat) is handy for trips to Aqaba, Petra and Wadi Rum. Most hotels and hostels in Eilat offer day trips to Petra; prices vary.

Getting There & Away

A taxi from Eilat costs 35NIS. If you're coming by bus from Be'er Sheva, the Dead Sea or Jerusalem, ask the driver to let you out at the border turn-off.

Once you are in Jordan, you take a cab to Aqaba (JD8), from where you can catch a minibus for the 120km ride to Petra (JD5, 2½ hours); the latter leave when full between 6.30am and 8.30am, with an occasional afternoon service. Alternatively, bargain for a taxi all the way from the border to Petra (around JD50, two hours).

Allenby/King Hussein Bridge

Situated 46km east of Jerusalem, 8km east of Jericho and 60km west of Amman, this busy **crossing** (www.iaa.gov.il; ⊙8am-early afternoon Sun-Thu, 8am-about noon Fri & Sat, closed Yom Kippur & Eid al-Adha, hours subject to change) links the West Bank with Jordan. It is the only point at which West Bank Palestinians can enter Jordan so traffic can be heavy, especially between 11am and 3pm. Though it's in the West Bank, it's under Israeli jurisdiction. Israeli citizens (including dual citizens) are not allowed to use this crossing.

This was once merely a bridge from Jordan's East Bank to its West Bank, and as the Jordanians see it, when you travel to the West Bank and Israel you're still not crossing a proper international frontier. As a result, you won't need a new visa if you cross back into Jordan through Allenby/King Hussein Bridge within the period of validity of your Jordanian visa – just show your stamped exit slip. On the Israel side have the border officers stamp your Jordanian slip rather than your passport.

If you are going into Jordan for the first time you'll need to arrange a Jordanian visa in advance – visas are *not* available at the crossing. You can get one at the Jordanian embassy in Tel Aviv (see p429).

Try to get to the border as early in the day as possible – times when tourists can cross may be limited and delays are common.

The bus across the frontier costs 5NIS from Israel; from Jordan, the fee is JD4, plus JD1.500 per piece of luggage.

Bring plenty of cash (Jordanian dinars are the most useful) and make sure you have small change. Both sides have exchange bureaux but don't count on them being open. There are no ATMs.

This crossing can be frustratingly long-winded, especially if you're travelling into the West Bank and/or Israel. Chaotic queues, intrusive security, luggage X-rays (expect to be separated from your bags) and impatient officials are the norm, and expect lots of questions from Israeli security personnel if your passport has stamps from places like Syria or Lebanon or you're headed to less touristed parts of the West Bank.

Getting There & Away

From opposite Jerusalem's Damascus Gate, shared taxis run by **Abdo** (②02-628 3281) leave for the border twice per hour until around 11am; the price is 40NIS per person. After 11am it offers private taxis (150NIS to 180NIS), with hotel pick-up as an option.

Egged buses 961, 948 and 966 from West Jerusalem's central bus station to Beit She'an (and points north) stop on Rte 90 at the turn-off to Allenby Bridge (12NIS, about hourly, 45 minutes). Walking the last few kilometres to the crossing is forbidden so you'll have to take a taxi, which can cost as much as 50NIS. From Amman, you can take a *servees* (shared taxi) or minibus (JD8, 45 minutes). **JETT** (②962-6-566 4146; www.jett.com.jo) runs a daily bus from Abdali (JD7.250, departure at 7am).

To/From Egypt
Taba Crossing

This **crossing** (②08-637 2104, 08-636 0999; www.iaa.gov.il; ⊙24hr), on the Red Sea near Eilat, is currently the only border post between Israel and Egypt that's open to tourists. There's an exchange bureau on the Egyptian side. At the time of research, it was not possible to take a car across.

You can get a 14-day Sinai-only entry permit at the border, allowing you to visit Red Sea resorts stretching from Taba to Sharm el-Sheikh, plus St Katherine's. If you're planning on going further into Egypt, you'll need to arrange an Egyptian visa in advance, eg

at the Egyptian consulate in Eilat or the embassy in Tel Aviv (see p433 and p429).

Getting There & Away

For details on getting to Eilat from places around Israel, see p332. Local bus lines 15 and 16 link Eilat's central bus station with the Taba crossing (7.50NIS, 30 minutes, hourly 9am to 2.30 or 3pm daily), or you can take a taxi (about 30NIS).

For details on onward travel on the Egyptian side, see p356. Tight security sometimes results in delays at the border and frequent passport checks on buses within Sinai.

Mazada Tours (②in Tel Aviv 03-544 4454, in Jerusalem 02-623 5777; www.mazada.co.il; 141 Ibn Gabirol St, Tel Aviv or 6 Yanai St, Jerusalem) runs overnight buses from Tel Aviv and Jerusalem to Cairo (one way/return US$146/165, 12 hours) via Taba, and vice versa.

Rafah Crossing

As a result of the Arab Spring, this crossing between Gaza and Sinai was unsealed by Egyptian authorities in May 2011. It is now officially open between 10am and 6pm Saturday to Thursday (excluding public holidays) but is often closed for days at a time, eg when the Egyptian border officials can't handle the traffic flow or for security reasons. Foreign nationals wishing to cross must first seek special permission from the Egyptian Ministry of Foreign Affairs' **Palestinian Affairs Division** (②in Cairo 02-2574 9682, call noon-3pm).

If you enter Gaza through Rafah, you cannot continue on to Israel – you must also exit through Rafah. Be prepared to wait for an extended period (possibly weeks) for the crossing to open, or while you wait for approval from Egyptian authorities to let you back into Egypt.

Jordan–Egypt Ferry

If you are travelling between Petra and Sinai, you can avoid passing through Israel by taking one of the two Aqaba–Nuweiba ferries. The 'fast-ferry' service (economy/first class US$75/95, two hours) leaves Nuweiba at 3.30pm Sunday to Friday, though we have received numerous complaints about this service leaving late. Be at the port two hours ahead of time to guarantee a ticket.

There's also a 'slow-ferry' service (economy/first class US$65/70, five hours), leaving Nuweiba at 2pm daily. While the fast ferry isn't always fast – or even on time – we can't

BANNED: ISRAELI PASSPORT STAMPS

Arab and Muslim countries have widely varying policies on admitting travellers whose passports show evidence of their having visited Israel. Jordan and Egypt, with which Israel has peace treaties, have no problem at all, and the same goes for Turkey (which has direct flights to Israel), Tunisia, Morocco and many of the Gulf emirates (but *not* Saudi Arabia). These places, as well as a variety of other Arab and Muslim-majority countries, even allow in Israeli passport holders, at least under certain circumstances. However, with parts of the Arab world in a state of ongoing revolution and Islamic parties in the ascendancy, policies could change.

If there's any chance you'll be heading to Arab or Muslim lands during the life of your passport, your best bet is to make sure that it shows no indication that you've been to Israel. Fortunately, Israeli passport inspectors are usually amenable to issuing your entry stamp on a separate piece of paper. When you hand over your passport, just say 'no stamp, please' (make sure they've heard you!) and keep the insert until you depart.

Unfortunately, Egyptian and Jordanian officials are not so obliging about their own stamps, even though having a chop from one of those countries' land crossings to Israel or the West Bank may be no less 'incriminating' than having an Israeli one. This is especially true of Syria, Lebanon and Iran, which have been known to put travellers on the next plane out if they find even the slightest evidence of travel to Israel. Saudi Arabia is also known to be very strict – except when, for some reason, it isn't. Malaysia and Indonesia restrict (but don't entirely ban) the entry of Israeli passport holders but Israeli stamps are not a problem.

Some countries, including the United States, allow their citizens to carry more than one passport.

stress how much more comfortable it is than the slow ferry.

Tickets can be paid in either US dollars or Egyptian pounds, and you must also pay your Egyptian departure tax (US$10 or E£50) when you buy them. Tickets must be purchased on the day of departure only at the **ferry ticket office** (☏352 0427; ☺9am-3pm), in a small building near the port.

Israeli Border Control

Entrance procedures for Israel are a source of annoyance for some and a breeze for others. Rigorous at the best of times, you can expect a barrage of questions about your recent travels, your occupation, any acquaintances in Israel and possibly your religious or family background.

If you are meeting friends or family in Israel, have their phone number, full name and address handy (a letter in Hebrew from them, confirming you're staying with them, works wonders). A printout of your hotel reservations may also help.

If border officials suspect that you're coming to take part in pro-Palestinian political activities, or even visit the West Bank for reasons other than Christian pilgrimage, they may ask a lot of questions. Having a Muslim name and passport stamps from places like Syria, Lebanon or Iran may also result in some pointed questions. The one sure way to get grilled is to sound evasive or to contradict yourself – the security screeners are trained to try to trip you up.

One more tip: when immigration asks how long you plan to stay in the country, if you say 'two weeks' that may be what they write on your entry card. For the maximum time allowed, you should specifically ask for three months.

Travel with Children

Top Activities for Kids

Underwater Red Sea Observatory
Scuba-quality reef views without even getting wet; also has a petting pool.

Play Areas in Malls
Many shopping malls have a *mee-schakiya* (play area) for babies and toddlers – a great place to meet local kids (and on occasion their colds), especially on rainy days.

Water Hikes
Israelis love hiking along – and through – spring-fed streams, especially during the hot, dry days of summer (try the Ein Gedi, Banias, Yehudiya and Majrase Nature Reserves).

Desert Cycling
Mountain biking through the desert along a dry wadi bed – great for tweens and teens.

Israel Museum
The Art & Youth Education Wing has some superb art programs for children.

Mini Israel
Midway between Jerusalem and Tel Aviv, this park shrinks 350 of Israel's best-known attractions down to scale-model size.

Travel with children in Israel and the Palestinian Territories is a breeze: the food's good, the distances are short, there are child-friendly activities at every turn and the locals absolutely love children. For general tips, see Lonely Planet's *Travel with Children*.

Israel for Kids

Israel is extremely family-oriented, so children are welcome pretty much everywhere. When parents go on holiday – to a B&B on the Golan, say, or hiking near the Dead Sea – so do the little ones. At every turn, your children will encounter local children out-and-about with their parents, especially during school holidays (July, August and Jewish holidays) and on Saturday.

Children's Highlights

Among Israel's biggest drawcards for children are the beaches, which are usually clean, well equipped with cafes and even playgrounds, and great for a paddle, a sandcastle or a swim. Make sure you slather on the sunblock, especially in summer, and stay out of the midday sun. (The Dead Sea, because of its altitude, poses the least risk of sunburn but kids have to be extra careful to keep the water out of their eyes.)

Most of Israel's nature reserves are fantastic for kids, and older children will enjoy the hikes – some gentle, some more challenging – on offer throughout the country. As parks' wheelchair access has improved in recent years, so has the ease of getting around with a stroller (pram). The cities, too, have lots of amusements for children young and old,

CHILDREN'S DISCOUNTS

At nature reserves, archaeological sites and museums, children generally get in free through age four, and receive significant discounts from age five through 17 or 18. Young children qualify for moderate discounts on buses and trains. Places whose main clients are children, such as amusement parks, tend to charge full price starting at age three.

and there's always a toy shop, ice-cream parlour or other diverting activity for when a bribe's the only thing that will work.

For a run-down of kid-friendly activities in Tel Aviv, see p128. Eilat also has a wide variety of things kids will love.

Child-friendly highlights in the north include:

» Watching migrating cranes at **Agamon HaHula**

» Fruit picking at **Bustan HaGolan**

» The chocolate-making workshop at the **Chocolate House** in Ein Zivan

» **Ya'ar HaYe'elim** deer park

» Bottling your own grape juice at **Tabor Winery**

Planning

Disposable nappies (diapers), wet wipes, powdered milk, baby bottles and dummies (pacifiers) are available in supermarkets and pharmacies, but prices are higher than in most Western countries. If your baby is picky, it pays to bring familiar powdered milk from home. Jars of baby food are also available, though in fewer flavours than in the UK or USA; organic baby food is slowly making an appearance. Medicines for children are easily obtained; almost all pharmacists speak English and are happy to assist.

A lightweight, collapsible (umbrella-style) stroller is convenient for travelling, but it's also a good idea to bring a wearable kid-carrier for the narrow cobblestone alleys and staircases in places like Jerusalem's Old City, Akko, Safed and Bethlehem.

Sleeping

With the exception of a few B&Bs (*tzimmerim*) that fancy themselves as 'adult-oriented', children are welcome to stay almost everywhere. In the vast majority of hotels, guesthouses and B&Bs, babies and toddlers can sleep in their parents' room for free (cots are provided); older children (often from age three) incur an extra charge. Most rooms in HI hostels and SPNI fields have at least four beds, making them ideal for families.

Eating

Virtually all restaurants welcome children, with both the servers and other diners taking the disruptions of kiddie mealtime in stride. Almost all have high chairs, and some also offer special kids' portions for child-sized prices. Most eateries, except the most upscale, are open all day long so meal times can be flexible. Israeli breakfasts are famously copious and usually include at least a couple of breakfast cereals.

Many children take an instant liking to felafel, hummus, *sabich* and shwarma but as these fast foods (including their sauces and salads) are more likely than most to play host to microbes unknown back home, you might want to go easy, or eat only at sit-down places.

Travelling by Car

» Babies up to one year old or who weigh less than 9kg must sit in a back-facing child seat (also recommended for children up to two years old). A portable baby seat is known in Hebrew as a *salkal*.

» A child seat (*kiseh b'tichut*) is required for toddlers aged two and three; it can face the direction of travel.

» Children aged three to eight must sit on a booster seat.

» Child seats must not be placed in the front seat if the car has a passenger-side airbag.

» Car seats are theoretically required for travel in a taxi but unless you bring your own you'll have to hold the child on your lap.

The Palestinian Territories for Kids

Children receive a warm welcome in the West Bank and will often be whisked away to meet local children or be treated to cakes and cookies. But travelling in the area has its own special challenges. Pushing a stroller (pram) around chaotic West Bank towns like Ramallah, Nablus and Bethlehem can be laborious, and then there's the matter of getting through checkpoints. If you're travelling from Jerusalem to Ramallah, you might want to give the prison-style turnstiles at Qalandia a miss, preferring instead a guided tour with a car and driver. In any case, remember to bring their passport as well as yours.

regions at a glance

Jerusalem

History ✓✓✓
Sacred Sites ✓✓✓
Culture ✓✓✓

History
Visit the City of David, established more than 3000 years ago, and the Citadel (Tower of David), a castlelike structure full of exhibits on Jerusalem's history.

Sacred Sites
Seek solace at the Western Wall, the Church of the Holy Sepulchre or the Dome of the Rock. Jerusalem's many religious sites could keep you busy for weeks.

Culture
Jerusalem is a cauldron of culture, a fascinating blend of peoples that include ultra-Orthodox Jews, Palestinians, religious pilgrims and others. Tour the neighbourhoods, attend a religious service or see a cultural performance. Ground zero of the Holy Land, this is where millions come each year to walk in the footsteps of prophets, connect with their religion or simply marvel at the overlapping and interconnecting cultures that have made a home here.

p38

Tel Aviv

Food ✓✓✓
Shopping ✓✓✓
Museums ✓✓

Food
Yes, Tel Aviv has fantastic beaches but it's really a city dominated by food. From felafel stalls, hummus joints and ice-cream parlours to European-style cafes, sushi bars and chef restaurants, you won't go hungry here.

Shopping
Tel Aviv, with its old-fashioned street markets and modern shopping malls, has the best shopping in Israel. Shop 'til you drop at boutique designer stores at the HaTachana complex, Sheinkin and Dizengoff Sts.

Museums
It may not have the history of Jerusalem but Tel Aviv is Israel's capital of cool. Check out the Tel Aviv Museum of Art, Holon Design Museum and smaller specialised museums such as Bialik House.

p108

Haifa & the North Coast

History ✓✓
Sacred Sites ✓✓
Scenery ✓✓

History
Caesarea was one of the great ports of antiquity while Megiddo was one of the worlds' oldest civilisations. Akko is brimming with history and was a stop for Marco Polo before his sojourn to Asia.

Sacred Sites
The Baha'i Gardens are a spiritual highlight of northern Israel, an incredible swath of green venerated by the world's Baha'i community. Also worth visiting is Elijah's Cave in Haifa, sacred to Jews, Christians and Muslims.

Scenery
Rosh HaNikra is a jagged corner of coastline punched with grottoes that make for some stunning natural scenery. But for excellent coastline views, perch yourself on Haifa's mountaintop promenade.

p156

Lower Galilee & Sea of Galilee

Christianity ✓✓✓
Archaeology ✓✓✓
Dining ✓✓

Christianity
Mary is said to have experienced the Annunciation in Nazareth, later Jesus's childhood home. It is believed that the Transfiguration took place at Mt Tabor, and Jesus spent much of his ministry around the Sea of Galilee at Tabgha, Capernaum, Bethsaida and Kursi.

Archaeology
Top excavations include the Roman and Byzantine city of Beit She'an, ancient synagogues at Hamat Tverya, Korazim, Capernaum and Tzipori, and the Belvoir Crusader castle.

Dining
Nazareth is known for its East/West fusion cuisine; in Kfar Kisch you can dine the French way or sample delicious cheeses; in Kfar Kama you can try Israel's only Circassian restaurant.

p189

Upper Galilee & Golan

Hiking ✓✓✓
Bird Life ✓✓✓
Wineries ✓✓

Hiking
Trails for all fitness levels abound, from the alpine summit of Mt Hermon (elevation 2000m) to the banks of the Jordan River (elevation -200m), and through the cliff-lined canyons of the Banias and Yehudiya Nature Reserves.

Bird Life
Half-a-billion birds migrate through the Hula Valley – you can spot local and migrating species in the wetlands of the Hula Nature Reserve and Agamon HaHula, especially in spring and autumn.

Wineries
Many of Israel's finest wineries, some of them boutique, can be visited – and wines sampled – at Katzrin, Ein Zivan and Odem on the Golan and on the Dalton Plateau northwest of Tsfat.

p224

West Bank

Bazaars ✓✓
Food ✓✓
Religion ✓✓✓

Bazaars
West Bank cities revolve around their lively bazaars. Shop for fresh fruits, taste sweets and haggle over handicrafts in the colourful markets of Hebron, Nablus and Bethlehem.

Food
Don't pass up any invitation for a home-cooked meal in the West Bank, where the dinner table overflows with spicy, tangy Middle Eastern delicacies. The best restaurants are in Ramallah.

Religion
For Jews and Muslims the Cave of Machpelah is an important pilgrimage site. Christian sites include the Church of Nativity and the Mount of Temptation. No spiritual journey to the West Bank is complete with a trip to Mt Gerizim.

p254

Dead Sea

Beaches ✓✓✓
Archaeology ✓✓✓
Hiking ✓✓✓

Beaches
Float on your back while reading the newspaper – a cliché but eminently doable in the hypersaline waters of the Dead Sea, which will relax your nerves and soothe your skin.

Archaeology
The Romans had already destroyed Jerusalem but high atop Masada, a thousand Jewish Zealots resisted the besieging might of Legion X, in the end preferring death to slavery.

Hiking
Year-round springs feed the dramatic desert oases of Ein Gedi and Ein Bokek, where hikers encounter cool streams, luxuriant vegetation, Edenic waterfalls and rare wildlife such as the majestic Nubian ibex.

p284

The Negev

Hiking ✓✓✓
Diving ✓✓
Archaeology ✓✓✓

The Gaza Strip

Inaccessible ✓✓✓
Beaches ✓
Religion ✓

Petra

Ruins ✓✓✓
Hiking ✓✓✓
Scenery ✓✓✓

Sinai

History ✓
Resorts ✓✓✓
Wilderness ✓✓✓

Hiking

The Negev desert is filled with life. Hike through the wilderness of Makhtesh Ramon, Sde Boker or Ein Avdat and you'll likely spot an ibex, camel or bird of prey.

Diving

If you want to explore a coral reef and see schools of tropical fish, then come to the Red Sea. Great for diving and snorkelling, just dip your head underwater and enjoy the show.

Archaeology

Home to biblical ruins like Tel Be'er Sheva and Tel Arad, plus the ancient Nabataean cities of Avdat, Shivta and Mamshit, the desert is an historical treasure trove.

p303

Inaccessible

Gaza is definitely not a tourism destination. Almost impossible to enter unless you are an aid worker or diplomat, this thin strip of land remains a danger zone.

Beaches

If you can get in, the one thing Gaza does have to offer is a long sandy coastline. Expect to see luxury hotels, restaurants and sprawling refugee camps.

Religion

Despite its troubles, Gaza is home to the historical Great Mosque, a Greek Orthodox Church and the tomb of the Prophet Mohammed's great-grandfather, Hashim.

p333

Ruins

There are not enough superlatives to describe the ancient city of Petra. Make sure you allow enough time to reach the Treasury in early morning, picnic at a High Place by noon, watch the sunset at the Monastery and walk the siq by candlelight at night.

Hiking

Petra has some great, accessible hikes. Engaging a local Bedouin guide will help bring the recent history of Petra to life.

Scenery

Outrageously colourful sandstone, wind-eroded escarpments and oleander-trimmed wadis make the rose-pink landscape of Petra a worthy consort of the ancient architecture. Don't forget your camera!

p339

History

Moses allegedly laid down the law here at Mt Sinai, a popular hike for religious and secular travellers alike. At St Katherine's Monastery, see rare early Byzantine icons.

Resorts

The laid-back beach camp was perfected on the coast between Taba and Nuweiba and in backpacker-built Dahab. At the other end of the scale, Sharm el-Sheikh offers a glitzy holiday scene, beautiful reefs and good eats.

Wilderness

If it's desert you're after, the interior of the Sinai is the place for starlit treks with Bedouin guides. You can spot flocks of flamingos in the Zerenike Protectorate or explore the coral wonderland of Ras Mohammed National Park.

p353

> Every listing is recommended by our authors, and their favourite places are listed first.

> Look out for these icons:

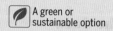 Our author's top recommendation

 A green or sustainable option

FREE No payment required

See the Index for a full list of destinations covered in this book.

On the Road

Jerusalem ירושלים القدس

02 / POP 780,200

Best Places to Eat

» Amigo Emil (p93)

» Mahane Yehuda Market (p77)

» Hamarakia (p93)

» Little Jerusalem (p94)

Best Places to Stay

» Harmony (p88)

» Abraham Hostel (p87)

» Lutheran Guest House (p89)

» St Andrew's Guesthouse (p88)

Why Go?

Jerusalem has been seducing travellers, pilgrims and curiosity seekers since time immemorial. Holy to Jews, Christians and Muslims, the city is overflowing with sites of intense religious importance, not the least of which are the Dome of the Rock, the Western Wall and the Church of the Holy Sepulchre. Even for the nonreligious, it's hard not to be moved by the emotions and history that come alive in the narrow alleys of the Old City.

Jerusalem feels like a loosely connected patchwork of 20 or so distinct villages, each inhabited by a unique subset of the population. A cross-town journey could pass through Muslim East Jerusalem to ultra-Orthodox Mea She'arim and onto the progressive German Colony. Take a wander through each area to contemplate the historical significance of the city and to better understand its passionate citizenry: Muslims, Jews and Christians warily co-habiting in order to keep a toehold on the most spiritual city on Earth.

When to Go
Jerusalem

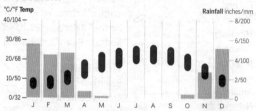

Apr Temperatures are pleasant and flowers are blooming, but prepare for crowds around the Easter holiday.

May Jerusalem hosts the Israel Festival, a good time for arts and culture events.

Sep–early Nov The best time weather-wise, with blue skies, pleasant temperatures and fewer tourists.

Getting Around

The Jerusalem Light Rail (JLR) passes in front of Central Bus Station. You can hop on the JLR for a ride down Jaffa Rd to Zion Sq and East Jerusalem. For Jaffa Gate, take the JLR to City Hall and walk downhill for five minutes. For Mamilla and the German Colony, take bus 18 from Central Bus Station.

A taxi to/from the airport costs 250NIS on weekdays or 300NIS on Shabbat. Nesher service taxis provide a door-to-door airport shuttle service charging 60NIS per head. The public bus costs 35.80NIS per head but requires a bus change; see p103 for details.

ORIENTATION

Navigation in Jerusalem is complicated by the rolling topography, winding roads and one-way streets, not to mention the labyrinth of alleys in the Old City. In the New City, the main artery is Jaffa Rd, which is now only open to the new Jerusalem Light Rail (JLR).

In West Jerusalem, the main areas of shopping and commerce are located on and near Ben Yehuda and Hillel Sts. In East Jerusalem the main road is Salah ad-Din St.

Most visitors enter the Old City at Jaffa Gate (which has a tourist information office) and work their way downhill. It's easy to get lost, but just walk one or two minutes in any direction and you eventually reach a familiar landmark or street.

Egged 99 Circular Line, which makes a loop around the city while providing commentary in English, is a good way to orient yourself upon arrival.

Climate & Holidays

» Summer temperatures here are milder – with daytime averages of between 20°C and 25°C – than in other parts of the country, making this a good time to visit. However, tourist numbers rise, so book ahead to make sure you get a room.

» In winter (mid-October to mid-March), daylight hours are reduced (it gets dark as early as 4.30pm) and, with daytime temperatures down to between 8°C and 10°C, you'll need to come equipped with warm clothes and rain gear.

» During major holidays such as Passover (April) and Jewish New Year (September), visitor numbers spike and hotel prices increase.

MEDIA

The *Jerusalem Post* (www.jpost.com) and *Ha'aretz* (www.haaretz.com) newspapers are both in English and are great for local news and events.

Top Views

» Citadel (Tower of David)
» Mount of Olives
» Haas Promenade
» Rooftop cafe, Hashimi Hotel
» Church of the Ascension tower

Internet Resources

» Jerusalem Municipality website (www.jerusalem.muni.il)
» Jerusalem Shots (www.jerusalemshots.com)
» Il Museums (www.ilmuseums.com)

Handy Tips

» Some sights, including the Western Wall Tunnels tour, Chain of Generations Centre and the Herzl Museum, require reservations.

» Visit the Muslim and Christian Quarters on Shabbat (Friday afternoon and Saturday), when other parts of the city close down.

» Egged buses and the light rail don't run on Shabbat but the Arab buses from East Jerusalem do, allowing you to reach the West Bank cities and the Mount of Olives.

» Most places of interest are religious in nature, so modest dress – pants for men and long skirts for women – is respectful.

Jerusalem Highlights

① Walk along the sacred **Via Dolorosa** (p58), long considered the final path of Jesus on his way to Calvary

② Gaze at the architectural magnificence of the **Dome of the Rock** (p47), Jerusalem's most recognisable symbol

③ Explore the narrow alleys of **Mahane Yehuda Market** (p77), jam-packed with some of the most delicious fruits and vegetables in the Middle East

④ Feel the spiritual power of the **Western Wall** (p49), Judaism's holiest place

⑤ Go underground in the **City of David** (p69), the tunnel-laced original settlement of Jerusalem

⑥ Get acquainted with Israel's history, ancient and modern, at the exceptional **Israel Museum** (p81)

⑦ Visit the **Church of the Holy Sepulchre** (p55), Christendom's holiest site and a unique piece of architecture built over a period of centuries

⑧ Clamber up the **Mount of Olives** (p71), the biblical site associated with Jesus and the End of Days

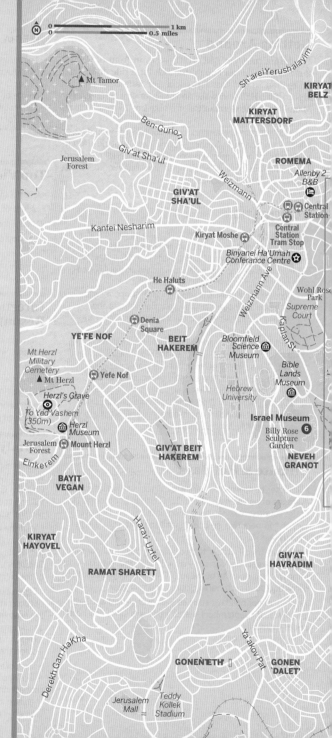

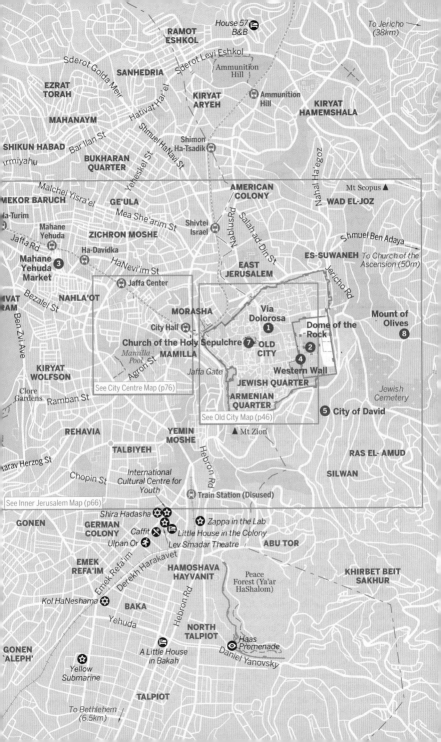

History
FIRST TEMPLE

The first settlement on the site of Jerusalem was on the Ophel Ridge, immediately to the southeast of the present-day Jewish Quarter. This was a small Jebusite (pre-Israelite tribe) city, mentioned in Egyptian texts of the 20th century BCE. It was conquered in 997 BCE by the Israelites under King David, who brought the Ark of the Covenant to Jerusalem and made the city his capital.

Under King Solomon (David's son), the boundaries of the city were extended north to enclose the spur of land that is now Al-Haram ash-Sharif/Temple Mount. The construction of the First Temple began in 950 BCE.

Some 17 years after Solomon's death, the 10 northern tribes of Israel split off to form the separate Kingdom of Israel and Jerusalem became the capital of the Kingdom of Judah. In 586 BCE Jerusalem fell to Nebuchadnezzar, king of Babylon, and both the city and the First Temple were destroyed; the people of Jerusalem were exiled to Babylonia. Three generations later, the king of Persia, Cyrus, allowed them to return.

SECOND TEMPLE

The Second Temple was constructed around 520 BCE, and around 445 BCE the city walls were rebuilt under the leadership of Nehemiah, governor of Judah.

The next notable stage in the history of Jerusalem came with Alexander the Great's conquest of the city in 331 BCE. On his death in 323, the Seleucids eventually took over until the Maccabean Revolt 30 years later. This launched the Hasmonean dynasty, which resanctified the Temple in 164 BCE after it had been desecrated by the Seleucids.

ROMANS

Under the leadership of General Pompey, Jerusalem was conquered by the Romans around 63 BCE. Some 25 years later they installed Herod the Great to rule what would become the Roman province of Judaea (Iudaea). A tyrant's tyrant, Herod (often known as 'the Great') had his wife and children, as well as rabbis who opposed his rule, put to death. But he is also known for his ambitious construction and infrastructure projects, including expansion of the Temple Mount to its present form.

Upon the death of Herod, the Romans resumed direct control, installing a procurator to administer the city. Pontius Pilate, who is best known for ordering the crucifixion of Jesus around 30 CE, was the fifth procurator.

The Great Jewish Revolt against the Romans began in 66 CE, but after four years of conflict, the Roman general (and later emperor) Titus triumphed. Rome's Arch of Titus, with its famous frieze of Roman soldiers carrying off the contents of the Temple, was built to celebrate his victory.

With the Second Temple destroyed and Jerusalem burnt, many Jews became slaves and more fled into exile. Jerusalem continued to serve as the capital of the Roman province of Judea, but Emperor Hadrian decided to destroy it completely in 132 CE due to the threat of renewed Jewish national aspirations. This provoked the Jews' unsuccessful and bloody Bar Kochba Revolt (132–35 CE), led by Simon Bar Kochba. After the uprising was crushed, Jerusalem was renamed Aelia Capitolina and Judaea given the name Syria Palaestina. The Romans rebuilt Jerusalem, but Jews were banned from the city.

BYZANTINES & MUSLIMS

In 313 CE – with the granting of the Edict of Milan, requiring tolerance of all previously persecuted religions – Christianity was legalised by Emperor Constantine, founder of the Eastern Roman Empire (later known as the Byzantine Empire) and his mother visited the Holy Land searching for Christian holy places. This sparked off the building of basilicas and churches, and the city quickly grew to the size it had been under Herod the Great.

The Byzantine Empire was defeated by the Persians, who conquered Jerusalem in 614. Their rule lasted just 15 years before the Byzantines succeeded in retaking the city. That victory, however, was short-lived, for within another 10 years an Arab army, led by Caliph Omar under the banner of Islam, swept through Palestine. In 688 the Dome of the Rock was constructed on the site of the destroyed Temple. Under the early Islamic leaders, Jerusalem was a protected centre of pilgrimage for Jews and Christians as well as Muslims, but this came to an end in the 10th century. Under the mercurial Fatimid Caliph al-Hakim, non-Muslims were persecuted and churches and synagogues destroyed, actions that eventually helped provoke the Crusades.

FROM CRUSADERS TO MAMLUKS TO OTTOMANS

The Crusaders took Jerusalem in 1099 from the Fatimids, who had only just regained control from the Seljuks. After ruling for almost 90 years, the Christians' Latin Kingdom was defeated in 1187 by Saladin (Salah ad-Din), whose efficient administration allowed Muslims and Jews to resettle in the city. From the 13th to the 16th centuries, the Mamluks constructed a number of outstanding buildings dedicated to religious study.

Although a Muslim academic centre, Jerusalem became a relative backwater. In 1517 the Ottoman Turks defeated the Mamluks, adding Palestine to their large empire. Yet although they too are remembered for their lack of efficiency in local administration, their initial impact on the city is still much admired today. The impressive Old City walls that you see now were built in the mid-1500s by Sultan Süleyman, aka Süleyman the Magnificent. But after his reign, Jerusalem's rulers allowed the city, like the rest of the country, to decline. Buildings and streets were not maintained, and corruption among the authorities was rife.

In the wake of the Turkish sultan's 1856 Edict of Toleration for all religions, Jews – by this time a majority of the city's population of about 25,000 – were allowed to establish Jerusalem's first neighbourhoods beyond the city walls. Some of the first projects, begun in the 1860s, were inspired and financed by an Italian-born English Jew, Sir Moses Montefiore. As Jewish immigration rapidly increased, scattered neighbourhoods developed into what is now the New City.

BRITISH RULE & DIVISION

British forces under the command of General Allenby captured Jerusalem from the Turks in late 1917, turning the city into the administrative capital of the British-mandated territory of Palestine. In these times of fervent Arab and Jewish nationalism, the city became a hotbed of political tensions, and the city was the stage for terrorism and, occasionally, open warfare, both between Jews and Arabs and among rival Arab factions (eg between supporters of the Nashashibi and Husseini families).

Under the United Nation's 1947 Partition Plan, Jerusalem was to be internationalised, separate from the two states – one Jewish, the other Arab – the resolution called for. Accepted in principle by the Jews but rejected by the Arabs, the Partition Plan was outpaced by events as the 1948 Arab–Israeli War engulfed the city and the country. However, it still serves as the basis for the US State Department's opposition to moving the US embassy to Jerusalem.

During the 1948 Arab–Israeli War, the Old City and East Jerusalem, along with the West Bank, were captured by Jordan, while the Jews held onto most of the New City. Patches of no-man's-land separated them, and the new State of Israel declared its part of Jerusalem as its capital.

For 19 years Jerusalem – like Berlin – was a divided city. Mandelbaum Gate served as the only official crossing point between East and West Jerusalem for the few who were permitted to move between them. In the Six Day War of 1967, Israel captured the Old City from Jordan, reunifying the city and beginning a massive program of restoration, refurbishment, landscaping and construction.

CONTROVERSIAL CAPITAL

Controversy continues to surround the status of Jerusalem, and as a result most countries maintain their embassies in Tel Aviv.

Both Israelis and Palestinians see Jerusalem as their capital. At present, the Palestinian Authority is based in nearby Ramallah but it hopes one day to move to East Jerusalem. Israel is determined to never let that happen and since the suicide bombings of the Second Intifada has been constructing a security fence (see p268) that effectively seals the city off from the West Bank.

Various peace plans suggested by Israeli and Palestinian doves propose that the city be partitioned, with Jewish neighbourhoods in Israel and Arab neighbourhoods in Palestine. There is little agreement on exactly how to handle the Old City, especially Al-Haram ash-Sharif/Temple Mount, Judaism's holiest site and Islam's holiest site after Mecca and Medina.

Dangers & Annoyances

Demonstrations and marches by both Jews and Arabs are pretty common in Jerusalem and while they are usually peaceful, it's still a good idea to remain vigilant in case things get rowdy, such as outside Damascus Gate. The Mount of Olives has not always been the friendliest area to walk in and some female travellers strolling there alone have been hassled. If possible, visit the area in pairs. Ultra-Orthodox Jewish Haredi groups sometimes stone buses, burn trash bins and confront the police in Mea She'arim, which even on quiet days can turn hostile when tourists (especially immodestly dressed ones) saunter in. For more general tips on staying safe in Israel and the Palestinian Territories see p422.

JERUSALEM IN...

Four Days

Visitors to Jerusalem usually schedule at least a week to see the main sights of the city, so if you are pressed for time you'll need to be selective.

Spend your first day visiting the highlights of the Old City, including the **Temple Mount**, the **Western Wall**, the **Church of the Holy Sepulchre** and the **Citadel (Tower of David)**.

On day two, utilise **Egged 99 Circular Line** to explore the major sights in West Jerusalem, including **Yad Vashem**, **Mt Herzl** and the **Israel Museum**. Bus 99 will also give you a peek into East Jerusalem and Mt Scopus. Make some time for **Mahane Yehuda Market** before an evening around the shops and cafes of Ben Yehuda and Rivlin Sts.

With a third day, see the sights of the **Kidron Valley**, including the City of David, before moving onto the **Mount of Olives**. Here you should make time for the **Church of the Pater Noster** and the **Tomb of the Virgin Mary**. Finally, visit East Jerusalem and the **Garden Tomb**.

Use day four to tick off more sights in the Old City, including **Mt Zion**, the **Jerusalem Archaeological Park & Davidson Centre**, the museums and synagogues around the **Jewish Quarter** and the **Western Wall Tunnels** tour, for which you need a prebooking.

A Week

On day five hire a bike and explore some of Jerusalem's neighbourhoods, such as the **German Colony**, **Mea She'arim**, **Nahla'ot** or **Ein Kerem**.

Save day six for any sights you've left behind, notably the **Via Dolorosa**, **Hurva Synagogue** or the **Rockefeller Museum**.

Even God needed to rest on the seventh day; you should do the same. Take a look at Jerusalem, Shabbat & You, p87, for ideas (even if it's not Shabbat).

During your stay also make sure you take advantage of some of Jerusalem's unique cultural activities. A highlight is to visit the **Western Wall** on Friday evening to watch the masses welcome Shabbat. Dances at the **International Cultural Centre for Youth** also make for a one-of-a-kind Jerusalem experience. And if you get a chance, don't miss an opportunity to join a local family for a Shabbat dinner.

⊙ Sights

Jerusalem's major sights can be broken down geographically, with the highest concentration in the Old City. The Kidron Valley (which contains the City of David) and Mt Zion are both within walking distance of the Old City, but touring the area involves lots of walking, much of it uphill.

West Jerusalem contains a number of sights, including the Israel Museum, Mt Herzl, Yad Vashem and Ein Kerem, but these are spread out and are best reached by bus or taxi.

Sights around East Jerusalem can be reached on foot once you are in the area. But getting over here from other parts of the city usually requires a taxi or a trip on the new Jerusalem Light Rail (JLR).

OLD CITY

In the late afternoon, as sunlight turns the ancient stone buildings golden, the Old City is a feast for the senses: church bells clang in the distance, the smell of spices wafts out of the bazaars, and there's a distinct tension in the air. Within its mighty walls you can sleep in 700-year-old edifices, haggle over everything from souvenir T-shirts to ancient artefacts, and taste the delectable food of the Levant.

But far from being merely ancient and spectacular, the Old City is above all a holy place, containing sites sacred to Judaism, Christianity and Islam. The Western Wall, the Dome of the Rock and the Church of the Holy Sepulchre are hardly more than a stone's throw from each other.

Most visitors enter through Jaffa Gate, from where the rest of the Old City is downhill. Roads circle the Old City, so you could take a taxi to any of the gates, including Damascus Gate for the Muslim Quarter and Dung Gate for the Western Wall and the Temple Mount.

**Al-Haram ash-Sharif/
Temple Mount** ANCIENT SITE
(Map p46; www.noblesanctuary.com, www.tem
plemount.org; admission free; ☺7.30-11am &
1.30-2.30pm Sat-Thu Apr-Sep, 7.30-10am & 12.30-
1.30pm Sat-Thu Oct-Mar) A walk up to the
Temple Mount is a time-honoured privilege
sanctified by the thousands of pilgrims who
have trod before you. An open plaza of cypress trees and ancient paving stones, much
of the architecture that exists today dates
back to the first Muslim conquest, around
1400 years ago, including the unmistakable Dome of the Rock. But the history of
the mount goes back much further, with the
first Jewish temple having been built here a
thousand years before Jesus. There are few
patches of ground as holy, or as disputed, as
this one.

The Temple Mount, known to Muslims
as Al-Haram ash-Sharif (Noble Sanctuary)
and Jews as Har HaBayit (Temple Mount),
started with a large slab of rock protruding
from the ridge Mt Moriah. According to Jewish lore, this rock was identified as the foundation stone of the world. The Talmud states
that it was here that God gathered the earth
that was used to form Adam; and that biblical figures such as Adam, Cain, Abel and
Noah all performed ritual sacrifices here.
The most well-known account appears in
Genesis (22:1-19): as a test of faith, Abraham
was instructed by God to sacrifice his son
Isaac Genesis but in the 11th hour an angel
appeared and a ram was sacrificed instead.

It was atop Mt Moriah that Solomon built
the First Temple, probably pretty much where
the Dome of the Rock now stands (because of
religious sensitivities, archaeological excavations are out of the question). It took seven-
and-a-half years to complete, but for reasons
unknown it stood unused for 13 years. When
it was finally consecrated, Solomon placed
the Ark of the Covenant inside and celebrated with a seven-day feast. After weathering
a number of raids, the temple was destroyed
in 586 BCE by Nebuchadnezzar II of Babylon. The Second Temple was erected in 515
BCE, and King Herod later upgraded the site
by building a wall around the mount and filling it with rubble, levelling off the enormous
plaza we can see today. The biggest of the
stones holding up the Temple Mount (eg in
the Western Wall) weigh over 500 tonnes.

Jews coming to the Temple Mount ap-
proached from the south. Pilgrims were
required to enter a *mikveh* (Jewish ritual

bath) for purification purposes before ascending the steep steps. Inscriptions on
stones warned that any gentile entering the
mount would do so on pain of death. Only
the high priest could enter the inner sanctum of the temple; he did so once a year on
Yom Kippur.

Any civic improvements made by Herod
were for naught, however, as the Second Temple was destroyed by the Romans in 70 CE.

Despite the destruction they had wrought,
the Romans, too, felt a spiritual affinity for the
Temple Mount and erected a temple to Zeus
that was later turned into a Christian church.

Fast forward to the mid-7th century in
Mecca, where the Prophet Mohammed is
believed to have announced to his fellow
Meccans that in a single night he had travelled to the 'farthest mosque' and led other
prophets in prayers. Although Mohammed
did not mention Jerusalem by name, the
farthest mosque was interpreted to be Al-
Haram ash-Sharif, thus making Jerusalem a
holy place for Muslims. The Temple Mount
is considered Islam's third-holiest place after
Mecca and Medina.

Immediately following the 1967 Six Day
War, Israeli commander Moshe Dayan handed control of the Temple Mount to Jerusalem's Muslim leaders. Their control of the
mount has never gone down well with Jewish extremists and there have been a number
of protests and incidents of violence, including failed plots to blow up Muslim holy sites
in the early 1980s. According to many Orthodox Jewish authorities, Jews are forbidden from visiting the Temple Mount because
they may inadvertently tread on the sacred
ground on which the Temple once stood.

For the uninvolved visitor, the Temple
Mount provides a relaxing contrast to the
noise and congestion of the surrounding
alleyways. It's a flat paved area the size of
a couple of adjacent football fields, fringed
with some attractive Mamluk buildings
and with the Dome of the Rock positioned
roughly in its centre. Below the surface of
the pavement 19th-century explorers discovered more than 30 cisterns, some of them 15
to 20m deep and up to 50m long. Because
of religious prohibitions modern archaeologists are not allowed into the cisterns;
today they rely largely on drawings and descriptions made by Sir Charles Wilson, who
mapped the cisterns in 1861.

There are nine gates connecting the enclosure to the surrounding narrow streets, but

JERUSALEM SIGHTS

Old City

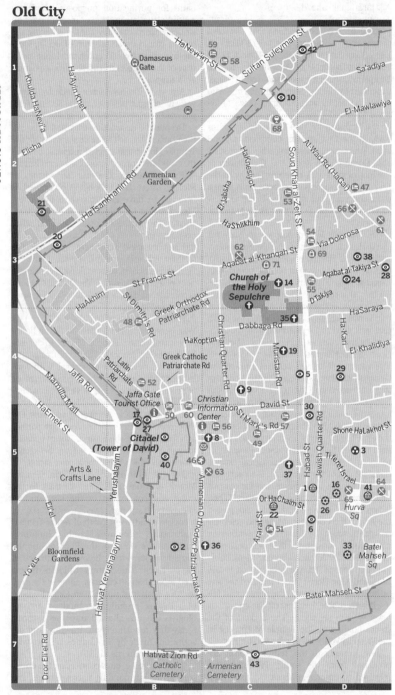

Damascus Gate

HaNevi'im St

59

58

Sultan Suleyman St

42

Sa'adiya

10

El-Mawlawiya

68

Al-Wad Rd (HaGai)

47

Souq Khan al-Zeit St

HaKnesiyot

53

66

61

HaShlikhim

Via Dolorosa

54

69

Armenian Garden

HaTsankhanim Rd

Khulda HaNevi'a

Ha'Ayin Khet

Elisha

21

20

HaAkhim

St Francis St

St Dimitri's Rd

Greek Orthodox Patriarchate Rd

El-Jabsha

62

Aqabat al-Khanqah St

71

38

Aqabat al-Takiya St

24

28

Church of the Holy Sepulchre

14

55

D Takiya

HaSaraya

Ha-Kari

El-Khalidiya

48

35

Dabbaga Rd

HaKoptim

Greek Catholic Patriarchate Rd

Christian Quarter Rd

19

Muristan Rd

5

29

Latin Patriarchate Rd

Jaffa Rd

Mamilla Mall

HaEmek St

52

Jaffa Gate Tourist Office

Christian Information Center

9

17

27

50

60

56

David St

30

Shone HaLakhot St

3

Citadel (Tower of David)

8

49

St Mark's Rd

57

37

1

16

41

64

40

46

63

Habad St

Jewish Quarter Rd

Tiferet Israel

65

Hurva Sq

Arts & Crafts Lane

El-rei

Yo'ets

Bloomfield Gardens

Yerushalayim

Hativat Yerushalayim

2

36

Armenian Orthodox Patriarchate Rd

Ararat St

Or HaChaim St

22

51

26

6

33

Batei Mahseh Sq

Batei Mahseh St

Dror Eli'el Rd

7

Hativat Zion Rd

Catholic Cemetery

43

Armenian Cemetery

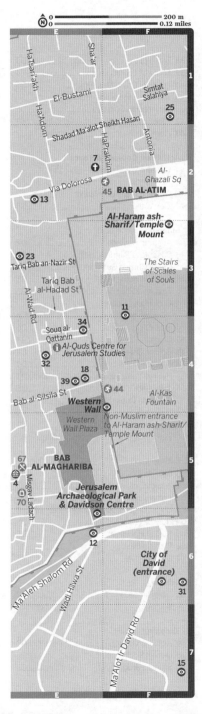

although you can leave the compound by most of them, non-Muslims are allowed to enter only at the Bab al-Maghariba/Sha'ar HaMugrabim (Gate of the Moors), reached from the Western Wall plaza. Line up early for security checks and bear in mind that the site closes on Muslim holidays. Modest dress is required.

See Map p50 for further sites within Al-Haram ash-Sharif/Temple Mount.

Al-Aqsa Mosque

(Map p50) The name Al-Aqsa means 'farthest mosque' and is in reference to the journey Mohammed is believed to have made on his way to heaven to receive instructions from Allah. While the Dome of the Rock serves more as a shrine than a mosque, Al-Aqsa is a functioning house of worship, accommodating up to 5000 praying supplicants at a time.

Al-Aqsa stands on what is believed to have been a marketplace on the edge of the Temple Mount. This might be where Jesus turned over the tables and drove out the moneychangers with a makeshift whip (Matthew 21:13).

The building in place now is believed by some to be a conversion of a 6th-century Byzantine church, although Muslims maintain that Al-Aqsa was built from scratch in the early 8th century by the son of Abd al-Malik, patron of the Dome. Clarification of the issue is complicated because nothing much remains from the original structure, which was twice destroyed by earthquakes, in 746 and 774 (another big earthquake damaged the structure again, in 1033). The Crusaders thought Al-Aqsa was Solomon's Temple and made their own additions.

The present-day mosque is a compendium of restorations, with columns donated, strangely enough, by Benito Mussolini, and the elaborately painted ceilings courtesy of Egypt's King Farouk. The intricately carved mihrab (prayer niche indicating the direction of Mecca), however, dates from the time of Saladin, as did an equally magnificent carved wood pulpit that was lost in a 1969 fire started by a deranged Australian Christian.

Dome of the Rock

(Map p50) The jewel in the Temple Mount crown is the gold-plated Dome of the Rock (Qubbet al-Sakhra in Arabic), the enduring symbol of the city and undoubtedly one of the most photographed buildings on earth. As its name suggests, the dome covers a slab of stone sacred to both the Muslim and Jewish faiths. According to Jewish tradition, it

Old City

◎ Top Sights
Al-Haram ash-Sharif/Temple
  Mount F3
Church of the Holy Sepulchre C3
Citadel (Tower of David).....................B5
City of David (entrance).......................F6
Jerusalem Archaeological Park &
  Davidson Centre................................E6
Western Wall...F4

◎ Sights
1 Alone on the Walls Museum D5
2 Armenian Compound...........................B6
3 Broad Wall...D5
4 Burnt House..E5
5 Butchers' Market..................................D4
6 Cardo Maximus D6
  Chain of Generations Centre.......(see 44)
7 Chapel of the Flagellation E2
8 Christ Church.......................................C5
9 Church of St John the Baptist..............C4
10 Damascus Gate C1
11 Dome of the Rock..................................F3
12 Dung Gate E6
13 Ecce Homo Convent of the
  Sisters of Zion...................................E2
14 Ethiopian Monastery C3
15 Hezekiah's Tunnel F7
16 Hurva Synagogue D5
17 Jaffa Gate...B5
18 Khan al-Sultan E4
19 Lutheran Church of the
  Redeemer...C4
20 New Gate...A3
21 Notre Dame de France Hospice...........A2
22 Old Yishuv Court Museum....................C6
23 Ottoman Sabil.......................................E3
24 Palace of the Lady Tunshuq D3
25 Pool of Bethesda F1
26 Ramban Synagogue..............................D6
27 Ramparts Walk Entrance......................B5
28 Ribat Bayram Jawish.............................D3
29 Rooftop Promenade..............................D4
30 Rooftop Promenade..............................D5
31 Royal Quarter (Area G) F6
32 Sabil Suleyman.....................................E4
33 Sephardic Synagogues.........................D6
34 Souq al-Qattanin...................................E4
35 St Alexander's Church C4
36 St James' (Jacques') Cathedral...........C6
37 St Mark's Chapel C5

38 Tomb of the Lady Tunshuq D3
39 Tomb of Turkan Khatun E4
40 Tower of David Museum........................B5
41 Wohl Archaeological Museum
  (Herodian Quarter) D5
42 Zedekiah's Cave D1
43 Zion Gate C7

◎ Activities, Courses & Tours
44 Western Wall Tunnels
  Entrance...F4
45 Western Wall Tunnels Exit....................F2
46 Zion Walking Tours B5

◎ Sleeping
47 Austrian Hospice...................................D2
48 Casa Nova Pilgrims' Hospice B4
  Christ Church Guesthouse............ (see 8)
49 Citadel Youth Hostel C5
50 East New Imperial Hotel B5
  Ecce Homo Convent
  Guesthouse...................................(see 13)
51 El Malak...C6
52 Gloria..B4
53 Golden Gate Inn....................................C2
54 Hashimi Hotel..D3
55 Hebron Youth Hostel D3
56 Jaffa Gate Hostel..................................C5
57 Lutheran Guest House...........................C5
58 New Palm Hotel.....................................C1
59 Palm Hostel C1
60 Petra Hostel..B5

◎ Eating
61 Abu Shukri D3
62 Amigo Emil...C3
63 Armenian Tavern...................................C5
  Christ Church Guesthouse Cafe... (see 8)
64 Holy Bagel...D5
65 Keshet HaHurva D5
66 Pizzeria Basti..D2
67 Quarter Café E5

◎ Drinking
68 Cafe Rimon Himo C2
  Versavee ....(see 50)

◎ Shopping
69 Aweidah Gallery.....................................D3
70 Moriah Bookshop E5
71 Studio Varouj...C3

was here that Abraham prepared to sacrifice his son and from which, according to Islamic tradition, the Prophet Mohammed ascended to heaven. The building was constructed between 688 and 691 CE under the patronage of the Umayyad caliph Abd al-Malik. His motives were shrewd as well as pious – the caliph was concerned that the imposing Christian Church of the Holy Sepulchre was seducing Arab minds.

In asserting the supremacy of Islam, Abd al-Malik had his Byzantine architects take as their model the rotunda of the Holy Sepulchre. But not for the Muslims the dark, gloomy interiors or austere stone facades of the Christian structures; instead, their mosque was covered, both inside and out, with a bright confection of mosaics and scrolled verses from the Quran, while the crowning dome was covered in solid gold that shone as a beacon for Islam.

A plaque was laid inside honouring Abd al-Malik and giving the date of construction. Two hundred years later the Abbasid caliph Al-Mamun altered it to claim credit for himself, neglecting to amend the original date.

During the reign of Süleyman the Magnificent, what remained of the original interior mosaics was removed and replaced, while the external mosaics were renewed by Armenian artisans in the early 1900s and again in 1963. The original gold dome also disappeared long ago, melted down to pay off some caliph's debts. The dome is now covered with 1.3mm of gold donated by the late King Hussein of Jordan. The 80kg of gold cost the king US$8.2 million – he sold one of his homes in London to pay for it.

Essentially, however, what you see today is the building as conceived by Abd al-Malik. Inside, lying centrally under the 20m-high dome and ringed by a wooden fence, is the rock from which it is said Mohammed began his *miraj* (ascension to heaven). According to the Quran, the stone also wanted to join him in heaven and began to rise from the earth; Mohammed pushed the stone down with his foot, leaving a footprint on the rock (supposedly still visible in one corner). Jewish tradition also has it that this marks the centre of the world. Steps below the rock lead to a cave known as the 'Well of Souls', where the dead are said to meet twice a month to pray.

Unfortunately most travellers will only be able to admire the exterior of the building as the interior is only accessible to Muslims.

Small Wall

(HaKotel HaKatan; Map p50; Iron Gate St) The Small Wall is a continuation of the Western Wall located between the Bab al-Hadad and Bab al-Nazir gates. It's worth visiting this section briefly after you exit the Temple Mount.

Western Wall   RELIGIOUS

(HaKotel; Map p50) The builders of the Western Wall could never have fathomed that one day their massive creation would become the most important religious shrine for the Jewish people. Indeed, when it was built some 2000 years ago it was merely a retaining wall supporting the outer portion of the Temple Mount, upon which stood the Second Temple. But following the destruction of the Temple in 70 CE, Jews were sent into exile and the precise location of the Temple was lost. Upon their return they purposely avoided the Temple Mount, fearing that they might step on the Holy of Holies, the ancient inner sanctum of the Temple barred to all except the high priest. Instead they began praying at an exposed outer wall; according to rabbinical texts, the *Shechina* (divine presence) never deserted the wall, and it's regarded as the most holy of all Jewish sites.

The Wall became a place of pilgrimage during the Ottoman period and Jews would come to mourn and lament the destruction of the Temple – that's why the site is also known as the Wailing Wall, a name that Jews tend to avoid. At this time, houses were pressed right up to the Wall, leaving just a narrow alley for prayer.

In 1948 the Jews lost access to the Wall when the Old City was taken by the Jordanians and the population of the Jewish Quarter was expelled. Nineteen years later, when Israeli paratroopers stormed in during the Six Day War, they fought their way directly to the Wall and their first action on securing the Old City was to bulldoze the neighbouring Arab houses to create the plaza that exists today.

The area immediately in front of the Wall now operates as a great open-air synagogue. It's divided into two areas: a small southern section for women and a larger northern section for men. Here, black-garbed Hasidic men rock backwards and forwards on their heels, bobbing their heads in prayer, occasionally breaking off to press themselves against the Wall and kiss the stones. To celebrate the arrival of Shabbat there is always a large crowd at sunset on Friday. The Wall is

Al-Haram ash-Sharif/ Temple Mount

A TOUR OF THE TEMPLE MOUNT

The Temple Mount encompasses multiple sites that span an area the size of one or two city blocks. A visit requires a little planning and may need to be accomplished over a couple of days.

Ascend the rickety wooden ramp at the Western Wall plaza to reach the Temple Mount at the Bab al-Maghariba (Gate of the Moors). Passing through the gate, continue ahead to view the understated facade of the **Al-Aqsa Mosque 1** and the sumptuous detail of the **Dome of the Rock 2**. Take a slow turn around the Dome to admire its surrounding structures, including the curious **Dome of the Chain 3** and the elegant **Sabil of Qaitbay 4**. Don't miss the stunning view of the Mount of Olives seen through the stone arches known as the **Scales of Souls 5**.

Exit the Temple Mount at the **Bab al-Qattanin (Gate of Cotton Merchants) 6**; and return to the Western Wall plaza where you can spend some time at the **Western Wall 7** and visit the **Jerusalem Archaeological Park & Davidson Centre 8**.

Scales of Souls
Muslims believe that scales will be hung from the column-supported arches to weigh the souls of the dead.

Bab al-Qattanin (Gate of Cotton Merchants)
This is the most imposing of the Haram's gates. Make a point of departing through here into the Mamluk-era arcaded market of the Cotton Merchants (Souq al-Qattanin).

Sabil of Qaitbay
This three-tiered, 13m-high structure is one of the finest pieces of architecture on the Temple Mount. It was built by Egyptians in 1482 as a charitable act to please Allah and features the only carved-stone dome outside Cairo.

Dome of the Rock

The crown jewel of Israel's architectural heritage, the Dome famously contains the enormous foundation stone that Jews believe is the centre of the earth and Muslims say is the spot where Mohammed made his ascent.

Dome of the Chain

Some believe this structure was built as a model for the Dome of the Rock. Legend has it that Solomon hung a chain from the dome and those who swore falsely while holding it were struck by lightning.

Al-Aqsa Mosque

One of the world's oldest mosques, Al-Aqsa (the Furthest Mosque) is 75m long and has a capacity for more than 5000 worshippers. The Crusaders called it Solomon's Temple and used it as a royal palace and stable for their horses.

Solomon's Throne

Bab Hitta

A Dirty Problem

The large pile of dirt and debris on the east side of the Mount was left here after the excavation of an underground vault in 1990.

2

3

Summer Pulpit

4

5

Al-Kas Fountain

Dome of Learning

Musala Marwani Mosque (Solomon's Stables)

Mamluk Arcade

Bab al-Maghariba

1

7

Western Wall Plaza

8

Coming Clean

Al-Kas Fountain, located between Al-Aqsa Mosque and the Dome of the Rock, is used for ritual washing before prayers.

Western Wall

Today it's the holiest place on earth for Jews and an important cultural nexus on Shabbat, when Jews from around the city come to sing, dance and pray by the Wall.

Jerusalem Archaeological Park & Davidson Centre

This is the place to see Robinson's Arch, the steps that led up to the Temple Mount and ancient *mikveh* (Jewish ritual bath) where pilgrims washed prior to entering the holy temple.

DON'T MISS

WESTERN WALL TUNNELS

For a different perspective on the Western Wall, join a tour of the Western Wall Tunnels (Map p46; ☎02-627 1333; www.thekotel.org; adult/child 30/15NIS; ⊗7am-6pm Sun-Thu, to 12.30pm Fri), a 488m passage that follows the northern continuation of the wall. Dug out by archaeologists, the tunnels burrow down to the original street level (nicknamed Market St by tour guides because it was believed to have been a shopping area). The foundation stones here are enormous – one is a 517-tonne monster the size of a small bus. You can only visit the tunnels on a guided tour, which takes about 75 minutes and must be booked in advance. Try to book at least a week ahead of time – these tours are very popular and fill up fast!

also a popular site for bar mitzvahs, held on Shabbat or on Monday and Thursday mornings. This is a great time to visit as the area is alive with families singing and dancing as they approach the wall.

Notice the different styles of stonework comprising the Wall. The huge lower layers are made up of 'Herodian stones', identifiable by their carved edges, while the strata above that, which are chiselled slightly differently, date from the time of the construction of Al-Aqsa Mosque. Also visible at close quarters are the wads of paper stuffed into the cracks in between the stones. Some Jews believe that prayers and petitions inserted into the Wall have a better-than-average chance of being answered (it's also possible to email your prayers for insertion into the Wall).

On the men's side of the Wall a narrow passage runs under Wilson's Arch, which was once used by priests to enter the Temple. Look down the two illuminated shafts to get an idea of the Wall's original height. Women are not permitted into this area.

The Wall is open to members of all faiths 24 hours a day, 365 days a year. Modest dress is recommended and head covering is required for men (paper kippas are available if you don't have one). Be discreet when taking photos and don't take any photos at all during Shabbat. Up-to-the-minute live shots can be viewed at www.aish.com/wallcam.

Chain of Generations Centre EXHIBITION
(Map p46; ☎02-627 1333; www.thekotel.org; adult/senior/student 25/12.50/15NIS; ⊗7am-6pm Sun-Thu, to 12.30pm Fri) This new exhibit uses multimedia to describe the origin of the Jewish people, dating back to Abraham 6000 years ago. Darkened galleries contain glass sculptures etched with the names of ancient ancestors of the Jewish people, while an audio guide describes the trials and tribulations of their existence. Some 77 tonnes of glass were used to build the exhibit. It finishes with a short film that tells the story of Moshe Amirav, one of the first paratroopers to reach the Western Wall during the Arab–Israeli War of 1967. It can be a moving experience for visitors interested in learning about the history of the Jewish people.

Jerusalem Archaeological Park & Davidson Centre HISTORIC SITE
(Map p46; www.archpark.org.il; adult/concession 30/16NIS; ⊗8am-5pm Sun-Thu, to 2pm Fri) On the southern side of the Western Wall, the Jerusalem Archaeological Park & Davidson Centre offers a peek into the history of the Temple Mount and its surrounding areas, displaying the remains of streets, columns, walls and plazas exposed by modern archaeologists. Byzantine and Arab structures are among the ruins, as well as finds from the Herodian period.

As you enter you'll notice on your left the remains of an arch protruding from Herod's wall. This is Robinson's Arch (named after a 19th-century American explorer), which was once part of a bridge that connected the Temple Mount and the main commercial area. The paving stones on the Herodian-era street below the arch are crushed, damage caused when the massive stone from the bridge came crashing down, presumably when Roman soldiers destroyed the bridge in the process of levelling the Second Temple. Also on this street is a metal fence with steps leading below; this is the entry to a drainage tunnel that leads 500m downhill to the Pool of Siloam (p70).

Towards the back of the complex, you'll find a long, wide staircase that was once the main entry for pilgrims headed to the Temple Mount. Near the bottom of the steps you can spot ancient ritual baths that Jewish pilgrims used to purify themselves before they walked to the temple complex.

The Davidson Visitor's Centre, in an underground vault near the entrance, has a multimedia presentation and virtual tour of the Temple Mount as it looked 2000 years ago.

Citadel (Tower of David) HISTORIC SITE

(Map p46) The Jaffa Gate area is dominated by the Citadel, which includes Roman-era Herod's Tower and the Tower of David (actually a minaret). It's occupied by the highly worthwhile Tower of David Museum (Map p46; www.towerofdavid.org.il; adult/child 30/15NIS; ◉10am-5pm Mon-Thu & Sat, to 2pm Fri May-Sep, 10am-4pm Mon-Thu & Sat, to 1pm Fri Oct-Apr), which tells the entire history of Jerusalem in a concise and easily digestible format. Revolving art exhibits in the halls and gardens add an especially pleasant angle. There are also good views of the city from the highest ramparts.

One of the highlights is a detailed large-scale model of Jerusalem, made in the late 19th century and discovered almost 100 years later, forgotten in a Geneva warehouse. It's displayed in an underground chamber reached from the central courtyard garden. For sight-impaired visitors, there is also a series of relief aluminium models of the city at several stages of its history.

The Citadel started life as the 1st-century palace of Herod the Great. A megalomaniacal builder, Herod furnished his palace with three enormous towers, the largest of which was reputedly modelled on the Pharos of Alexandria, one of the Seven Wonders of the Ancient World. The chiselled-block remains of one of the lesser towers still serve as the base of the Citadel's main keep. Following Herod's death the palace was used by the Roman procurators as their Jerusalem residence until it was largely destroyed by Jewish rebels in 66 CE. The Byzantines, who came along some 250 years later, mistook the mound of ruins for Mt Zion and presumed that this was David's palace – hence the name Tower of David. They constructed a new fortress on the site.

As Jerusalem changed hands, so did possession of the Citadel, passing to the Muslim armies and then to the Crusaders, who added the moat. It took on much of its present form in 1310 under the Mamluk Sultan Malik an-Nasir, with Süleyman the Magnificent making further additions between 1531 and 1538. Süleyman is responsible for the gate by which the Citadel is now entered, and it was on the steps here that General Allenby accepted the surrender of the city on 9 December 1917, ending 400 years of rule by the Ottoman Turks.

The Night Spectacular (adult/student 55/45NIS) is a 45-minute sound-and-light show played on the walls of the Citadel. In summer it's played daily and in winter it runs four times a week; start times vary depending on what time the sun sets.

Rooftop Promenade VIEWPOINT

(Map p46) For some great views of the Old City, climb the metal stairway on the corner of Habad St and St Mark's Rd or the steep stone stairs in the southwestern corner of the Khan al-Sultan, both of which lead onto the rooftops around the David St and Al-Wad markets. Come up during the day for a peek through the ventilation ducts at the bustle below, but also make a night-time visit to appreciate the Old City's moonlit silhouette.

WALLS & GATES

The walls as they exist today are the legacy of Süleyman the Magnificent, who oversaw their construction between 1537 and 1542. The northern wall, including Damascus Gate, was built first and then extended south, at which point it was delayed by a dispute over whether or not Mt Zion and the Franciscans' monastery should stand inside or outside the wall. To save time and expense the builders decided against looping the wall around the monastery, leaving the Franciscans out in the cold. Popular legend has it that when news reached Süleyman of the miserly cost-cutting exercise, he was furious and had the architects beheaded.

There were seven gates in Süleyman's walls, and an eighth was added in the late 19th century. All but Golden Gate on the southern side of Al-Haram ash-Sharif/Temple Mount are accessible and, time permitting, you should try to make a point of entering or leaving the Old City by each of them.

The following begins with Damascus Gate and continues clockwise around the wall.

Damascus Gate GATE

(Map p46) The scene in front of Damascus Gate, known in Hebrew as Sha'ar Shchem (Nablus Gate), is a microcosm of the Palestinian world – vendors heave goods in and out of the Old City, families picnic on the steps and Israeli soldiers tap their truncheons. You'll also spot elderly Palestinian women from the villages trying to sell herbs and produce; most of them wear intricately embroidered dresses that are a part of their dowry and identity.

The gate itself dates in its present form from the time of Süleyman the Magnificent, although there had been a gate here long before the arrival of the Turks. This was the main entrance to the city as early as the time of Agrippa, who ruled in the 1st century BCE.

The gate was considerably enlarged during the reign of the Roman emperor Hadrian.

A long-disappeared column erected by Hadrian once stood in the square, which is why the gate is also known in Arabic as Bab al-Amud (Gate of the Column).

Herod's Gate   GATE
(Map p66) It was just 100m east of this gate that the Crusaders breached the city walls on 15 July 1099. The name was derived from a mistaken belief held by 16th- and 17th-century pilgrims that a nearby building was at one time the palace of Herod Antipas. In Hebrew the gate is called Sha'ar HaPrahim and in Arabic, Bab al-Zahra; both names mean Flower Gate.

St Stephen's Gate (Lions Gate)   GATE
(Map p66) This is the gate that gives access to the Mount of Olives and Gethsemane. It is also where, from their positions on that biblically famed hillside, Israeli paratroopers fought their way in on 7 June 1967 to capture the Old City from the Jordanians.

Although Süleyman called it Bab al-Ghor (Jordan Gate), the name never stuck and it became known as St Stephen's Gate after the first Christian martyr, who was stoned to death at a spot nearby. The Hebrew name, Sha'ar Ha'Arayot (Lions Gate), is a reference to the two pairs of heraldic lions carved on either side of the archway.

Golden Gate   GATE
(Map p66) Uncertainty surrounds this sealed entrance to Al-Haram ash-Sharif/Temple Mount. The Jewish Mishnah mentions the Temple's eastern gate and there are Herodian elements in the present structure. Some believe it to be where the Messiah will enter the city (Ezekiel 44:1-3). The gate was probably sealed by the Muslims in the 7th century to deny access to Al-Haram ash-Sharif/Temple Mount to non-Muslims. A popular alternative theory is that the Muslims sealed it, and established a cemetery just outside, to prevent the Jewish Messiah from entering the Haram. Golden Gate is known as Sha'ar HaRahamim (Gate of Mercy) in Hebrew and either Bab al-Rahma or Bab al-Dahriyya (Eternal Gate) in Arabic.

Dung Gate   GATE
(Map p46) In Hebrew it's Sha'ar HaAshpot (Refuse Gate). The popular theory as to how this unflattering appellation came about is that at one time the area around the gate was the local rubbish dump. Its Arabic name is Bab al-Maghariba (Gate of the Moors), because North African immigrants lived nearby in the 16th century.

Presently the smallest of the city's gates, at one time it was even more diminutive. The Jordanians widened it during their tenure in the city in order to allow cars through. You can still make out traces of the original, narrower Ottoman arch.

Zion Gate   GATE
(Map p46) This gate had to be punched through to give access to the Franciscan monastery left outside the walls by Süleyman's architects. During the 1948 Arab–Israeli War, Israeli soldiers holding Mt Zion also tried to burst through here in a desperate attempt to relieve the besieged Jewish Quarter. First they tried to dynamite the wall at a spot 100m east of the gate (it still bears the scar), and when that failed they launched an all-out assault, which ended disastrously. A memorial plaque to the fallen is inset within the gate, while the bullet-eaten facade gives some indication of how ferocious the fighting must have been. Note the *mezuzah* (box containing extracts from the Torah) on the doorpost; it was fashioned from bullet casings collected after the fighting.

To the Jews, the gate is Sha'ar Tziyon (Zion Gate), while in Arabic it's Bab Haret al-Yahud (Gate of the Jewish Quarter).

Jaffa Gate   GATE
(Map p46) The actual gate here is the small block through which the dog-legged pedestrian tunnel passes (the dog-leg was to slow down any charging enemy forces – you'll find the same arrangement at Damascus and Zion Gates); the breach in the wall through which the road now passes was made in 1898 in order to permit the German Kaiser Wilhelm II and his party to ride with full pomp into the city.

Just inside the gate, on the left as you enter, are two graves said to be those of Süleyman's architects, beheaded for leaving the Mt Zion monastery outside the walls. A few steps past the gate on the left is the Jaffa Gate Tourist Office (as well as a tour operator that calls itself 'Jerusalem Tourist Information Center' in order to lure you inside).

The Arabic name for the gate is Bab al-Khalil (Gate of the Friend), which refers to the holy city of Hebron (Al-Khalil in Arabic). In Hebrew it is Sha'ar Yafo (Jaffa Gate) because this was the start of the old road – Jaffa Rd – to the port city of Jaffa.

New Gate
GATE

(Map p46) Opened in 1887 by Sultan Abdul Hamid to allow direct access from the newly built pilgrim hospices to the holy sites of the Old City's Christian Quarter, New Gate is the most modern of all the gates. In Hebrew it's HaSha'ar HeChadash, and in Arabic, Al-Bab al-Jadid; both names mean New Gate.

Ramparts Walk
CITY WALLS

(Map p46; ☑02-627 7550; adult/child 16/8NIS; ◯9am-4pm Oct-Mar, to 5pm Apr-Sep) The Ramparts Walk is a 1km jaunt along the top of the city wall – from Jaffa Gate north to Lion's Gate, via New, Damascus and Herod's Gates; and Jaffa Gate south to Dung Gate, via Zion Gate. It isn't possible to do a complete circuit of the wall because the Al-Haram ash-Sharif/Temple Mount stretch is closed for security reasons. Tickets are sold at the 'Jerusalem Tourist Information Center' (near Jaffa Gate), which in fact is a private company and not the official tourist information centre. Note that the north side of the wall is closed on Fridays because of Muslim prayers. The south side is open seven days a week. Most walkers only go as far as Damascus Gate, the section that provides the best views.

CHRISTIAN QUARTER

Jerusalem's Christian Quarter is an attractive blend of clean streets, souvenir stalls, hospices and religious institutions belonging to 20 different Christian denominations. At its centre stands the Holy Sepulchre, and everyone, tourists and pilgrims alike, tends to be drawn towards it.

As you enter from Jaffa Gate, the first two streets to the left – Latin Patriarchate Rd and Greek Catholic Patriarchate Rd – indicate the tone of the neighbourhood, named as they are after the offices there. The roads lead to St Francis St and in this quiet area around New Gate the local Christian hierarchy resides in comfort.

Heading straight across Omar ibn al-Khattab Sq from Jaffa Gate you'll find a narrow passage that leads down David St, a brash tourist bazaar dedicated to filling up travellers' suitcases with glow-in-the-dark crucifixes and 'Don't Worry Be Jewish' T-shirts. Everything is overpriced and it's expected that you'll bargain.

Towards the bottom end, David St switches over to food – a row of cavernous vaults on the left with fruit and vegetable stalls inside dates from the Second Crusade. David St ends by crashing into a trio of narrow streets that, if followed to the left, converge into Souq Khan al-Zeit St, one of the main thoroughfares of the Muslim Quarter; while to the right they become the Cardo Maximus and lead into the Jewish Quarter. The first of the narrow alleys leading to the Muslim Quarter is Souq al-Lahamin, the **Butchers' Market** (Map p46).

For more details on the Christian Quarter see the Via Dolorosa walking tour, p58.

Church of the Holy Sepulchre
CHURCH

(Map p46; ◯4.30am-8pm) While the Dome of the Rock glistens and the Western Wall wails, the holiest Christian site in the Old City, the Church of the Holy Sepulchre, passes quietly through the centuries in sombre reflection of the last hours of Jesus. The church, somewhat huddled in the Christian Quarter between otherwise insignificant edifices, is considered by Christians to be the biblical Calvary (Latin for skull), or Golgotha, where it is said Jesus was nailed to the cross, died and rose from the dead. For the past 16 centuries Christian pilgrims have arrived at this spot from every corner of the globe, and while it may not look as regal as even the most average medieval church in Europe, their tears, laments and prayers have done much to sanctify it.

The decision to place the church here was made by Helena, the mother of Emperor Constantine, 300 years after the Crucifixion. While on pilgrimage in the Holy City, she took note of Hadrian's pagan temple to Venus and Jupiter (built in 135 CE), and believed it had been placed here to thwart early Christians who had worshipped at the site.

Excavations at the site revealed the grave of Joseph of Arimathea, as well as three crosses, leading Helena to declare the site as Calvary. Work on Constantine's church commenced in 326 CE and it was dedicated nine years later. If you are a little confused as to why Jesus is said to have been crucified in the middle of the city, bear in mind that 2000 years ago this was an empty plot of land outside the former city walls. Shrines and churches were built on the site from the 4th century, occasionally destroyed by invading armies and rebuilt.

When his armies took the city in 638 CE, Caliph Omar was invited to pray in the church but he refused, generously noting that if he did his fellow Muslims would have turned it into a mosque. Instead, in 1009

Church of the Holy Sepulchre

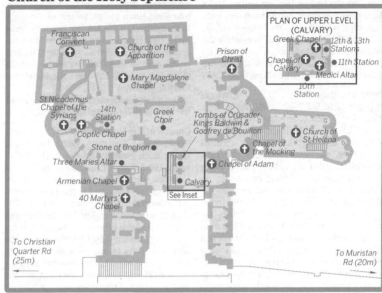

PLAN OF UPPER LEVEL (CALVARY)

Greek Chapel — 12th & 13th Stations
Chapel of Calvary — 11th Station
Medici Altar
10th Station

Franciscan Convent
Church of the Apparition
Prison of Christ
Mary Magdalene Chapel
St Nicodemus Chapel of the Syrians
14th Station
Greek Choir
Tombs of Crusader Kings Baldwin & Godfrey de Bouillon
Church of St Helena
Coptic Chapel
Chapel of the Mocking
Stone of Unction
Three Maries Altar
Chapel of Adam
Armenian Chapel
Calvary
See Inset
40 Martyrs' Chapel

To Christian Quarter Rd (25m)

To Muristan Rd (20m)

the church was destroyed by the mad Caliph Hakim – which no doubt wouldn't have happened if Omar had prayed there all those years before.

Unable to afford the major repairs necessary, the Jerusalem community had to wait until 1042 when the Byzantine Imperial Treasury provided a subsidy. It wasn't enough to pay for a complete reconstruction of the original church, so a large part of the building was abandoned, but an upper gallery was introduced into the rotunda and an apse added to its eastern side as a sort of compensation. This was the church that the Crusaders entered on 15 July 1099 as the new rulers of the city. They made significant alterations and so the church as it exists today is more or less a Crusader structure of Byzantine origins.

A fire in 1808 and an earthquake in 1927 caused extensive damage; however, due to serial disagreements between the different Christian factions who share ownership, it took until 1959 for a major repair program to be agreed upon. Due to the rivalries, the keys to the church have been in the possession of a local Muslim family since the days of Saladin and it's still their job to unlock the doors each morning and secure them again at night.

Visitors to the Church of the Holy Sepulchre should dress modestly – the guards are very strict and refuse entry to those with bare legs, shoulders or backs. The main entrance is in the courtyard to the south and can be reached from two points: via Christian Quarter Rd or Dabbaga Rd, running from Souq Khan al-Zeit St past Muristan Rd. Another two possible entry points are via the roof (see the Ethiopian Monastery, p57).

There are a number of holy relics and spots within the church, including the final five of the 14 Stations of the Cross. (For the first nine Stations, see the Via Dolorosa walking tour, p58).

Before entering the church, stand at the back of the courtyard and look above the portico and you'll spot a small ladder just below a window. This ladder, known as the immovable ladder, has been here in almost the exact same spot since sometime in the early 19th century because of the Status Quo agreement (see p407). Pictures of the church from the early 1900s prove that the ladder has long been part of the scene.

As you enter the church, head up the steep stairway immediately to your right. The chapel at the top is divided into two naves. The right one belongs to the Franciscans, the left to the Greek Orthodox. At the entrance to the Franciscan Chapel is the **10th Station of the Cross**, where Jesus is said to have been stripped of his clothes.

The **11th Station**, also in the chapel, is where it is said Jesus was nailed to the cross. Look to the right and you'll see a mosaic of Isaac being bound by Abraham; this story from the Hebrew Bible is shown as being linked to Jesus's crucifixion.

The **12th Station**, in the Greek Orthodox Chapel, is said to be the site of Jesus's crucifixion. The earthquake that struck when Jesus died is believed to have created the crack you can see in the rock.

The **13th Station**, where the body of Jesus is said to have been taken down and handed to Mary, is located between the 11th and 12th Stations.

As you walk to the 14th Station, you'll pass the Stone of Unction, where the body of Jesus was cleansed. Pilgrims pour oil on it and rub it with a handkerchief as a way to take home some of the holiness of the place. On the wall behind the station, you'll see a beautiful mosaic donated in 1964 to mark the visit by Pope Paul VI.

The **14th Station** is the Holy Sepulchre, the tomb of Jesus. Walk down the narrow stairs beyond the Greek Orthodox Chapel to the ground floor and you will see that the Holy Sepulchre is to be found in the centre of the rotunda, which would be on your left if you were entering from outside. The actual tomb is inside the Sepulchre. Candles lit by pilgrims who make a donation dominate the small tomb, with the raised marble slab covering the rock on which it is believed Jesus's body was laid.

Around the back of the Holy Sepulchre is the tiny **Coptic Chapel**, where pilgrims kiss the wall of the tomb, encouraged by a priest who expects a donation.

As you wind your way through the church you'll eventually reach the **Church of St Helena**. Legend has it that it was here that Helena dug into the ground and discovered the three crosses. The True Cross was identified after a sick man touched the crosses and was healed by one of them. The cross was put on display, but when pilgrims bent over to kiss it many took a bite out of the wood, which they took home as a memento. Eventually there was nothing left.

Coming back towards the entrance, look on your left for the **Chapel of Adam**, which contains the Rock of Adam. This sits below the 12th and 13th Stations. It is said Jesus's blood ran down the cross onto the Rock of Adam, thus cleansing Adam of his sins.

Christ Church CHURCH

(Map p46; Omar ibn al-Khattab Sq) Located just across from the Citadel in the Jaffa Gate area, Christ Church was the Holy Land's first Protestant church, consecrated in 1849. It was built by the London Society for Promoting Christianity Among the Jews (known today as CMJ, the Church's Ministry Among the Jews). The society's founders were inspired by the belief that the Jews would be restored to what was then Turkish Palestine, and that many would acknowledge Jesus Christ as the Messiah before He returned.

In order to present Christianity as something not totally alien to Judaism, Christ Church was built in the Protestant style with several similarities to a synagogue. Jewish symbols, such as Hebrew script and the Star of David, figure prominently at the altar and in the stained-glass windows.

Later the compound became the first British Consulate in Palestine. It now serves as a Christian hospice and a cafe. There is also a museum featuring old documents and models of the city. Among the more interesting relics are a Syriac New Testament from 1664 and, amazingly, a guidebook to Jerusalem printed in 1595. Below the museum is an ancient cistern that is still in the process of excavation.

St Alexander's Church CHURCH

(Map p46; 9am-1pm & 3-5pm Mon-Thu) On a corner just east of the Holy Sepulchre stands St Alexander's Russian Orthodox Church. The attraction for visitors is a much-altered triumphal arch that once stood in Hadrian's forum, built here in 135 CE. Through the arch and to the left at the top of the steps you can see a section of the pavement that was once part of the platform of Hadrian's temple to Aphrodite. Ring the bell to enter.

Ethiopian Monastery CHURCH

(Map p46; daylight hrs) Located on the northwestern corner of the Holy Sepulchre complex, the Ethiopian Monastery houses a few monks who live among the ruins of a medieval cloister erected by the Crusaders where Constantine's basilica had been previously. The cupola in the middle of the roof section admits light to St Helena's crypt below. Once inside you may find monks and nuns praying or prostrating. Around the walls are paintings of Ethiopian saints, the Holy Family and the Queen of Sheba during her visit to Jerusalem. It was during this visit that the Queen

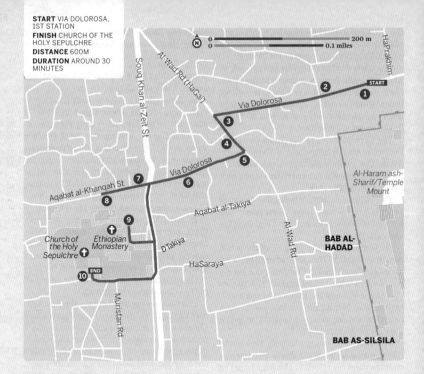

START VIA DOLOROSA, 1ST STATION
FINISH CHURCH OF THE HOLY SEPULCHRE
DISTANCE 600M
DURATION AROUND 30 MINUTES

Walking Tour
Via Dolorosa

❯ The ultimate Jerusalem walking tour is, of course, the Via Dolorosa (Way of the Sorrows), the route that Jesus is believed to have taken as he carried his cross to Calvary. The walk is easily done on your own, but for a somewhat more unique experience join the Franciscan Fathers on Friday as they lead a cross-bearing procession along the route. The walk is held at 3pm October to March and 4pm April to September.

The history of the Via Dolorosa goes back to the days of the Byzantine pilgrims, who trod the path from Gethsemane to Calvary on Holy Thursday, although at the time there were no devotional stops en route.

By the 8th century, pilgrims were performing ritual stops to mark the Stations of the Cross; the route had also changed considerably and now went from Gethsemane around the outside of the city walls to Caiaphas' house on Mt Zion, then to the Praetorium of Pilate at St Sophia near the Temple, and eventually to the Holy Sepulchre.

In the Middle Ages, with Latin Christianity divided into two camps, the Via Dolorosa was split and each of the two factions claimed routes primarily visiting chapels belonging to either one or the other faction. In the 14th century, the Franciscans devised a walk of devotion that included some of the present-day stations but had as its starting point the Holy Sepulchre. This became the standard route for nearly two centuries, but it was eventually modified by the desire of European pilgrims to follow the order of events of the gospels, finishing at the believed site of the Crucifixion rather than beginning there.

If historians had their way, the route would probably begin outside the Citadel, as this was the residence of Pilate when he lived in Jerusalem. Various Bible references to the trial of Jesus taking place on a platform (Matthew 27:19) and in the open (Luke 23:4, John 18:28) support this theory, as the palace is known to have had such a structure. Hence, it's believed that a more probable route for Jesus to have taken would be east along

David St, north through the Butchers' Market of today and then west to Golgotha.

To begin the route known today, head deep into the Muslim Quarter, in the direction of St Stephen's (Lions) Gate. Before embarking on the walking tour, you might want to visit **St Anne's Church** (p60) and the **Ecce Homo Convent of the Sisters of Zion** (p61), both located close to the first station.

The **❶ 1st Station** is actually inside the working Islamic Al-Omariyeh school, whose entrance is the brown door at the top of the ramp on the southern side of the Via Dolorosa, east of the Ecce Homo Arch. Entry is not always permitted so don't be surprised if you are asked to leave (entry is sometimes allowed after school hours, from 3pm to 5pm). The college offers nothing of official Christian value to see nowadays, but the location does offer a spectacular view of Al-Haram ash-Sharif/Temple Mount through the barred windows on the upper level.

The **❷ 2nd Station**, located across the street from the school in the Franciscan Church of the Condemnation, is where it is believed Jesus received the cross. The **Chapel of the Flagellation** (Map p46; admission free; ⊙8am-noon & 2-6pm Mon-Sat Apr-Sep, 8am-5pm Mon-Sat Oct-Mar) to the right is where he is said to have been flogged. Built in 1929, the design on the domed ceiling incorporates the crown of thorns and the windows of the chapel around the altar show the mob who witnessed the event.

Continue down a short hill until you reach Al-Wad Rd, a bustling street corner where cultures mingle in the form of Israeli police warily eying passers-by, Palestinian children kicking soccer balls, shop merchants moving carts and Christian pilgrims navigating through the crowds.

Turn left on Al-Wad and walk just a few steps to the **❸ 3rd Station**, where it is believed Jesus fell for the first time. The station is marked by a small Polish chapel, adjacent to the entrance of the Armenian Catholic Patriarchate Hospice.

Beyond the hospice, next to the Armenian Church (the wonderfully named Our Lady of the Spasm), the **❹ 4th Station** marks the spot where Jesus is said to have faced his mother in the crowd of onlookers.

As Al-Wad Rd continues south towards the Western Wall, the Via Dolorosa breaks off to climb to the west; right on the corner is the **❺ 5th Station**, where it is said that the Romans ordered Simon the Cyrene to help Jesus carry the cross. The station is marked by signs around a door.

Further along the street, the **❻ 6th Station** is marked by a brown wooden door on the left. This is where Veronica is believed to have wiped Jesus's face with a cloth. The Greek Orthodox Patriarchate in the Christian Quarter displays what is claimed to be the cloth, which shows the imprint of a face.

A bit further along you'll enter bustling Souq Khan al-Zeit St, a major marketplace of restaurants, hostels, sweets stalls and jewellery shops. The **❼ 7th Station**, where it is believed Jesus fell for the second time, is a small chapel marked by signs on the wall of the souq. In the 1st century, this was the edge of the city and a gate led out to the countryside, a fact that supports the claim that the Church of the Holy Sepulchre is the genuine location of Jesus's crucifixion, burial and resurrection.

The **❽ 8th Station** can be easy to miss. To find it, cut straight across Souq Khan al-Zeit St from the Via Dolorosa and ascend Aqabat al-Khanqah. Opposite an internet cafe on the left is the stone and Latin cross marking where it is said Jesus told some women to cry for themselves and their children, not for him.

Return the way you came, back to the Souq Khan al-Zeit, and turn right (south, away from Damascus Gate). Head up the stairway on your right and follow the path around to the Coptic church. The remains of a column in its door mark the **❾ 9th Station**, where it is believed Jesus fell for the third time.

Retrace your steps to the main street and head for the **❿ Church of the Holy Sepulchre**; the remaining five stations of the Via Dolorosa are inside. For information on the final five stations, see p55.

of Sheba, together with King Solomon, produced heirs to both royal houses, one of whom (according to Ethiopian legend) brought the Ark of the Covenant to Ethiopia.

To find the monastery, follow the route to the 9th Station of the Cross: up the steps off Souq Khan al-Zeit St, at the point where the street to the Church of the Holy Sepulchre turns to the right, there is a small grey door directly ahead that opens onto a roof of that church. The cluster of huts here has been the Ethiopian Monastery since the Copts forced them out of their former building in one of the many disputes between Jerusalem's various Christian groups.

Access to the Church of the Holy Sepulchre is also possible via two nearby points. One is through the Ethiopian Chapel and the other way is to go left out of the Ethiopian monastery and through the Copts' entrance.

Lutheran Church of the Redeemer CHURCH
(Map p46; ⊘9am-1pm & 1.30-5pm Mon-Sat) Dominating the Old City skyline with its tall white tower, the Lutheran Church of the Redeemer was built in 1898 on the site of the 11th-century church of St Mary-la-Latine. The closed northern entrance porch is medieval, decorated with the signs of the zodiac and the symbols of the months. The tower is popular for its excellent views over the Old City.

Church of St John the Baptist CHURCH
(Map p46) The oldest church in Jerusalem, the Church of St John the Baptist is rather hidden by the Christian Quarter homes that surround it. Coming down David St from Jaffa Gate, make the second left turn and then look for the church on the left; the signposted entrance leads you into the courtyard of a more recent Greek Orthodox monastery, where a monk will usually be present to open the church for you. Originally built in the mid-5th century, it was restored after the Persians destroyed it in 614. In the 11th century the merchants of Amalfi built a new church, which became the cradle of the Knights Hospitallers, using the walls of the earlier building. The present facade with the two small bell towers is a more recent addition, along with a few other alterations made to ensure the building's stability.

MUSLIM QUARTER
Strolling does not come easy in the Muslim Quarter – visiting the sights here is more a matter of dodging, weaving and ducking. You'll need agility as heavily laden carts trundle past, children zip by with reckless abandon and merchants bundle you into their shops. Challenging as it may seem, the hustle and bustle of the Muslim Quarter is relieved by the fragrance of the spice shops, the sight of colourful headgear bobbing amid the crowd and the joy of a hot tea taken on the roof of a guesthouse, with the Dome of the Rock dominating every view.

The Muslim Quarter runs from the melee at permanently congested Damascus Gate east and south towards Al-Haram ash-Sharif/ Temple Mount. About 100m in, the street forks; there is a busy felafel stall wedged between the two prongs. Bearing to the left is Al-Wad Rd, lined with vast showrooms of brass items such as coffee pots and trays, in among sweet shops, vegetable stalls and an egg stall. This route leads directly to the Western Wall, along the way crossing the Via Dolorosa.

Bearing to the right at the fork is Souq Khan al-Zeit St, which is even busier than Al-Wad Rd. Its name means 'Market of the Guesthouse of the Olive Oil' – in addition to its namesakes you'll find shops selling fruit, vegetables, sweets, hardware, spices and nuts.

For an interesting perspective on this part of town, try to visit around midday on Friday. Position yourself around the bottom of Aqabat al-Takiya St and watch the streams of Muslim faithful flood through the alleys towards the Temple Mount on their way to prayers. The alleys will be heaving with freshly baked goods, including some delicious *manaish* (Palestinian pizza) to feed the hungry mosque-goers. Some of the best pizza (costing 4NIS to 6NIS) comes from the little stall near the Ottoman Sabil (Map p46).

St Anne's Church CHURCH
(Map p66; admission 7NIS; ⊘8am-noon & 2-6pm Mon-Sat Apr-Sep, 8am-noon & 2-5pm Mon-Sat Oct-Mar) Surrounded by trees and rubble from bygone eras, St Anne's Church looks like a lost archaeological site in the midst of the Old City. Traditional belief holds that this was once the home of Joachim and Anne, the parents of the Virgin Mary, while next to the church are the impressive ruins surrounding the biblical Pool of Bethesda (Map p46).

Aside from its biblical ties, St Anne's Church is also the finest example of Crusader architecture in Jerusalem. It was built in 1140, at the same time as a small adjacent chapel with a stairway leading down to the pool where Jesus is supposed to have healed a sick man (John 5:1-18). The building is unusually asymmetrical – columns, windows and even steps all vary in size and dimension.

MAMLUK ARCHITECTURE

One of the best features of the Muslim Quarter is its wealth of buildings constructed during the golden age of Islamic architecture. A short scuttle through the Muslim Quarter brings you past some of the best examples.

This area was developed during the era of the Mamluks (1250–1517), a military dynasty of former slaves ruling out of Egypt. They drove the Crusaders out of Palestine and Syria, and followed up with an equally impressive campaign of construction, consolidating Islam's presence in the Levant with masses of mosques, madrassas (theological schools), hostels, monasteries and mausoleums. Their buildings are typically characterised by the banding of dark and light stone (a technique known as *ablaq*) and by the elaborate carvings and patterning around windows and in the recessed portals.

All of these features are exhibited in the Palace of the Lady Tunshuq (Map p46), built in 1388 and found halfway down Aqabat al-Takiya – 150m east of the Hebron Youth Hostel. The facade is badly eroded; however, the uppermost of the three large doorways still has some beautiful inlaid marble work, while a recessed window is decorated with another Mamluk trademark, the stone 'stalactites' known as muqarnas. The palace complex now serves as workshops and an orphanage. Opposite the palace is the 1398 Tomb of the Lady Tunshuq (Map p46).

Continue downhill to the junction with Al-Wad Rd, passing on your right, just before the corner, the last notable piece of Mamluk architecture built in Jerusalem, the 1540 Ribat Bayram Jawish (Map p46), a one-time pilgrims' hospice. Compare this with the buildings on Tariq Bab an-Nazir St, straight across Al-Wad, which are Jerusalem's earliest Mamluk structures, built in the 1260s before the common use of *ablaq*. This street is named after the gate at the end, which leads through into Al-Haram ash-Sharif/Temple Mount, but non-Muslims may not enter here.

Some 100m south on Al-Wad Rd is Tariq Bab al-Hadad St; it looks uninviting but wander down, through the archway, and enter a street entirely composed of majestic Mamluk structures. Three of the four facades belong to madrassas, dating variously from 1358 to 1440, while the single-storey building is a *ribat* (hospice), dating from 1293.

Back on Al-Wad Rd, continuing south, the road passes the Souq al-Qattanin (p62) and then, on the left, a *sabil* (public fountain) dating from Ottoman times, Sabil Suleyman (Map p46). The road terminates in a police checkpoint at the mouth of the tunnel down to the Western Wall plaza. However, the stairs to the left lead up to the busy Bab al-Silsila St and the Bab al-Silsila Gate (which leads to the Temple Mount). Just before the gate is the tiny kiosk-like 1352 Tomb of Turkan Khatun (Map p46), with a facade adorned with uncommonly asymmetrical carved geometric designs.

Look out also for the restored Khan al-Sultan (Map p46), which is a 14th-century caravanserai (travellers' inn and stables) at the top end of Bab al-Silsila St. A discreet entrance just up from the large 'Gali' sign leads into a courtyard surrounded by workshops, and from a staircase tucked in the left-hand corner as you enter you can climb up to the Old City rooftops.

When Jerusalem fell to the armies of Saladin, St Anne's became a Muslim theological school – an inscription that can still be seen above the church's entrance testifies to this. Successive rulers allowed the church to fall into decay, so by the 18th century it was roof-deep in refuse. In 1856 the Ottoman Turks presented the church to France in gratitude for its support in the Crimean War against Russia, and it was reclaimed from the garbage heap.

In addition to the architectural beauty of the church, inside it the acoustics are excellent, prompting not a few Christian pilgrims to break out into song (soprano and tenor voices sound particularly good here). You can sing too, but house regulations require that you pare your playlist down to religious songs only.

Ecce Homo Convent of the Sisters of Zion
RELIGIOUS

(Map p46; www.eccehomoconvent.org; 41 Via Dolorosa; adult/child 9/6NIS; ⊙8.30am-noon & 2-5pm Mon-Sat) This convent is named for the Ecce Homo arch that crosses the Via Dolorosa outside. The arch (part of which has been enveloped by the wall of the convent) was at one time thought to be the gate of Herod's Antonia Fortress and therefore believed to be the spot that Pontius Pilate took Jesus out and proclaimed 'Ecce Homo' (Behold, the man!). Researchers now dispute this as the arch is now considered to be a 2nd-century-CE triumphal arch built by the Roman emperor Hadrian.

Inside the convent, down in the basement, is a cistern with a barrel-vault roof, a likely creation of Hadrian. You can also find here the *lithostratos* (stone pavement) etched with the games played by Roman guards, including the 'Kings Game', the goal of which was to execute a mock king.

Souq al-Qattanin   MARKET

(Market of the Cotton Merchants; Map p46) The Souq al-Qattanin was originally a Crusader market, improved by the Mamluks in the mid-14th century. Almost 100m long, it has 50 shops on the ground floor, with residential quarters above. The market also included two hammams (public baths). One is located in the Al-Quds University Jerusalem Studies Centre, located halfway down the souq. The hammam has been converted into a gallery with occasional shows and performances.

JEWISH QUARTER

Unlike its more bustling neighbours to the north, the Jewish Quarter is decidedly residential, with scrubbed stone, proper rubbish collection and the occasional children's playground. This is due largely to the fact that the area was heavily shelled by Jordan's Arab Legion during the 1948 fighting and later demolished by the Jordanians, so most of the quarter had to be rebuilt from scratch after 1967.

While few historic monuments above ground are in evidence, there are a number of interesting archaeological finds below street level, some of which date back to the time of the First Temple (around 1000 to 586 BCE). The finds are on display in a couple of exhibits, the Burnt House and the Wohl Archaeological Museum. The website www.rova-yehudi.org.il is an excellent resource, providing overviews of several attractions in this quarter.

The Jewish Quarter is the only part of the Old City that is fully equipped to accommodate wheelchair users. A designated route for wheelchair users begins at the car park south of Hurva Sq. Call ☎02-628 3415 for details.

You can also reach the Jewish Quarter by Egged bus 38 or 38A, which continues to the Western Wall, goes back to Mt Zion, then Cinematheque, Keren HaYesod St and Mamilla Mall.

Cardo Maximus   STREET

(Map p46) Cutting a broad north–south swath, the Cardo Maximus is the reconstructed main street of Roman and Byzantine Jerusalem. At one time it would have run the whole breadth of the city, up to what's now Damascus Gate, but in its present form it starts just south of David St, the tourist souq, serving as the main entry into the Jewish Quarter from the Muslim and Christian areas.

As depicted on the 6th-century Madaba Map of the Old City, a copy of which is displayed here (the original mosaic is in Jordan), the Cardo would have been a wide colonnaded avenue flanked by roofed arcades. Part of it to the south has been restored to something like its original appearance, while the rest has been reconstructed as an arcade of expensive gift shops and galleries of Judaica. There are wells to allow visitors to see down to the levels beneath the street, where there are strata of a wall from the days of the First Temple and the Second Temple.

Close to the large menorah (seven-branched candelabrum) near the southern end of the Cardo, the Alone on the Walls Museum (Map p46; adult/senior/student 12/6/10NIS; ◎9am-5pm Sun-Thu, to 1pm Fri) documents the May 1948 campaign for control over the city. The small but interesting exhibit includes a 15-minute documentary and a photo gallery. You can buy a combined ticket for this museum, the Burnt House and the Wohl Archaeological Museum (any combination of two of these or all three is possible).

Broad Wall   RUIN

(Map p46) Just east of the Cardo and north of Hurva Sq, looking like a derelict lot between blank-faced apartment blocks, is a stretch of crumbling Jerusalem stone known as the Broad Wall. This is actually an exposed portion of the remains of a fortified stone wall dating from the First Temple period, from the time of King Hezekiah (c 701 BCE).

Old Yishuv Court Museum   MUSEUM

(Map p46; 6 Or HaChaim St; adult/child 18/8NIS; ◎10am-5pm Sun-Thu, to 1pm Fri) This small museum tells the story of daily life in the Jewish Quarter during the latter years of Ottoman rule in Jerusalem. Housed in the remains of two synagogues, it contains period artefacts, clothing and personal effects of the families who lived nearby. The last room contains some interesting propaganda posters from the British Mandate period.

Hurva Square & Hurva Synagogue
SYNAGOGUE

Hurva Sq is an uncommon patch of open space in the middle of the Jewish Quarter. It's flanked by cafes and shops and is a fine place to rest your legs after some serious Old City exploration.

The recently reconstructed **Hurva Synagogue** (Map p46; ☎02-626 5900; adult/student 25/15NIS; ☉8am-6pm Sun-Thu, 9am-1pm Fri) stands on the western side of the square. The land on which the synagogue stands was originally purchased by a group of Jewish immigrants from Poland following their arrival in the Holy Land in the 1700s. Money to build the synagogue was loaned to them by local Arabs but the loan came with an interest rate of around 40%; when Jews fell behind on their payments the Arabs burned down the building in 1720. A new name, Hurva (the ruin), was bequeathed on what was left.

Lithuanian Jews built a new synagogue here in 1864 and fitted it with 12.8m-high arched windows and a 24.9m-tall domed ceiling. The ark (cabinet used to hold the Torah scrolls) was shipped here from the city of Kherson in Ukraine.

During the 1948 war Jewish soldiers used the synagogue as a bunker; after a pitched battle the Arab Legion of Jordan captured the synagogue and later blew it up with 200kg of dynamite. After a lengthy reconstruction job the building reopened in 2009.

Visits are conducted by tour only. The guides bring you into the basement and show the remains of a Second Temple–era *mikveh* that was found during reconstruction. The tour also includes a visit to the roof for excellent views of the Jewish Quarter.

Ramban Synagogue
SYNAGOGUE

(Map p46; admission free;) Adjoining the Hurva Synagogue, Ramban Synagogue – its name an acronym for Rabbi Moshe Ben Nahman, also known as Nahmanides – was established in the year 1400 in a stable bought from an Arab landlord. Problems were later caused by the construction of a neighbouring mosque (the minaret of which still

stands); the upshot was that in 1588 the Jews were banned from worship and the synagogue was converted into a workshop. It was reinstated as a house of worship only in 1967, some 380 years later.

Sephardic Synagogues
SYNAGOGUE

(Map p46; admission free; ☉9.30am-4pm Sun-Thu, to noon Fri) South of Hurva Sq, on HaTupim St, are four Sephardic synagogues, two of which date back as far as the 16th century. In accordance with a law of the time stating that synagogues could not be taller than neighbouring buildings, this grouping was sunk deep into the ground – a measure that certainly saved the buildings from destruction during the bombardment of the quarter in 1948. Instead, the synagogues were looted by the Jordanians and then used as sheep pens. They have been restored using the remains of Italian synagogues damaged during WWII and are back in use for morning and evening services.

If you only have time for one, visit the 400-year-old **Ben Zakai Synagogue**, which is named after a rabbi who escaped Roman persecution at the time of the Second Temple. Inside, a window high above the floor contains a *shofar* (ram's horn) and a flask of olive oil. The purpose of the *shofar* is to announce the coming of the Messiah and the oil is there to anoint him upon his arrival in the synagogue. Legend has it that a tunnel was once built from the synagogue all the way to the Temple Mount so that the Messiah could easily walk there without the hindrance of street traffic.

The other three synagogues can also be visited. The **Istanbuli Synagogue**, the largest of the four, came into use in 1764 as a house of worship for Jews from Turkey, Kurdistan and North Africa. Nearby **Eliahu Ha'navi Synagogue** is the oldest of the bunch, founded during the 16th century. Finally, there is little **Emstai Synagogue**, wedged in between the others. Emstai was originally nothing more than a courtyard next to the Ben Zakai Synagogue. A roof was built over the courtyard in the mid-18th century, thus creating the 'middle' synagogue.

Burnt House
MUSEUM

(Map p46; ☎02-626 5921; Tiferet Israel St; adult/senior/student 25/12.50/20NIS; ☉9am-5pm Sun-Thu, to 1pm Fri) One of the more interesting sights of the Jewish Quarter is the Burnt House, located below the Quarter Café. The house, buried under rubble for centuries and only recently excavated, dates back to the Roman period, as evidenced by the many Roman coins found here. It was destroyed in 70 CE when the Romans put the city to the torch (hence the name of the house). Aside from the coins, a spear was found here, as well as the skeletal remains of a woman and a stone weight with the name 'Kathros' on it (Kathros was a priestly family living in the city at this time). Piecing together history, the museum has created a well-made multimedia presentation shown in a number of languages, including English. Movies begin every 40 minutes, so be prepared to wait around for a bit until the next show (or call ahead for times).

Wohl Archaeological Museum
(Herodian Quarter)   ARCHAEOLOGICAL SITE
(Map p46; 1 HaKara'im St; adult/senior/student 18/9/13NIS; ⊙9am-5pm Sun-Thu, to 1pm Fri) Down a narrow alleyway east of Hurva Sq, the impressive Wohl Archaeological Museum features a 1st-century home and several Herodian archaeological sites, plus interpretive displays. The museum details the lavish lifestyle enjoyed in the Jewish neighbourhood of Herod's city. Exhibits include frescos, stucco reliefs, mosaic floors, ornaments, furniture and household objects.

ARMENIAN QUARTER
Somewhat shuttered behind high walls and enormous wooden doors, the Armenian Quarter of Jerusalem plods along unnoticed, as it has for centuries. If the very presence of an Armenian Quarter strikes you as a bit odd, consider that Armenia was the first nation to officially embrace Christianity, when its king converted in 303 CE. Armenians established themselves in Jerusalem sometime in the following century. The Kingdom of Armenia disappeared at the end of the 4th century and Jerusalem was adopted as its spiritual capital. They have had an uninterrupted presence here ever since.

The core of the quarter is actually one big monastic compound. The Armenian presence in Jerusalem was traditionally purely religious, but a large secular element arrived early last century to work on retiling the Dome of the Rock and to escape Ottoman Turkish persecution. That persecution culminated in 1915, when more than 1.5 million Armenians were killed in an act of genocide.

The community today numbers about 1500 and is still very insular, having its own schools, library, seminary and residential quarters discreetly tucked away behind stone parapets. The gates to this city within a city are closed early each evening.

The compound contains a museum but it has been 'closed for renovations' the last three times we visited. When asked when it would reopen the caretaker replied simply, 'When God wills it'.

Armenian Compound   RELIGIOUS
(Map p46) Fewer than 100 Armenians now live in what used to be a large pilgrims' hospice. The Armenian Compound became a residential area after 1915 when refugees from the Turkish massacres in Anatolia settled here. Such empty, wide courtyards are a rare sight in the Old City. It is usually open to visitors during daylight hours, but it can close without notice, so it's best to call ahead (☏02-628 4549) or ask at the entrance to St James' Cathedral to make an appointment for a visit.

St James' (Jacques') Cathedral   CHURCH
(Map p46; Armenian Orthodox Patriarchate Rd; admission free; ⊙6-7.30am & 3-3.30pm Mon-Fri, 2.30-3pm Sat & Sun) The glowing lamps that hang from the ceiling and the richly patterned carpets strewn across the floors give St James' Cathedral a palpable aura of mystery lacking in many other Christian sites of Jerusalem.

It was the Georgians in the 11th century who first constructed a church here in honour of St James, on the site where he was beheaded and became the first martyred disciple. The Armenians, in favour with the ruling Crusaders, took possession of the church in the 12th century and the two parties shared restoration duties. The tiles date from much later – the 18th century – and were imported from Turkey.

The cathedral is only open for services; the most impressive are held on Sunday when nine hooded priests take part. There is quite a bit of toing and froing around the altar area from the numerous helpers and there is impressive choral chanting from a 45-person choir – all in Armenian.

St Mark's Chapel   CHURCH
(Map p46; admission free; ⊙7am-noon & 2-5pm Mon-Sat) The venerable St Mark's Chapel is the home of the Syrian Orthodox community in Jerusalem, whose members number about 200. (There are only about three million worldwide, of whom two million are in Malabar in central India.) The Syrian Orthodox believe the chapel, on Ararat St,

occupies the site of the home of St Mark's mother, Mary, where Peter went after he was released from prison by an angel (Acts 12:12). The Virgin Mary is claimed to have been baptised here, and according to their tradition this, not the Cenacle on Mt Zion, is where the Last Supper was eaten. One thing to look out for is the painting on leather of the *Virgin and Child*, attributed to St Luke. The nuns here take real pride in their chapel and will probably act as an escort; with a little luck one of them may sing to you the Lord's Prayer in Aramaic.

MT ZION

An eclectic mix of histories, Mt Zion contains sites holy to Christianity, Islam and Judaism. The Last Supper is said to have occurred here, as well as the eternal sleep of the Virgin Mary. It is also the site of David's tomb.

Although once encompassing the entire ridge of the upper Old City (including the Citadel), Mt Zion is now defined as the stern hill south of the Old City beyond Zion Gate. The name change came in the 4th century, based on new interpretations of religious texts.

Grave of Oskar Schindler CEMETERY
(Map p66; ⊗8am-5pm Mon-Thu, to 1pm Fri) Among the ancient sites on Mt Zion is one relatively new site, the grave of Oskar Schindler, the Austrian industrialist who saved more than 1200 Jews from the gas chambers (and whose story was captured by filmmaker Steven Spielberg in the Oscar-winning film *Schindler's List*). From Zion Gate in the Old City walk directly ahead, downhill, bearing left at the fork to go past the Chamber of the Holocaust, round the bend and head across the road to the entrance of the Christian cemetery. Once inside the cemetery head down to the third (lowest) level. Schindler's grave is not well marked but you can look for the cenotaph covered in stones.

FREE **King David's Tomb** RELIGIOUS
(Map p66; ⊗8am-6pm Sun-Thu, to 2pm Fri) A Crusader structure erected two millennia after his death, King David's Tomb provides little spectacle. What's more, the authenticity of the site is highly disputable – the likelihood is that David is buried under the hill of the original Mt Zion, east of the City of David. However, this is one of the most revered of the Jewish holy places, and from 1948 to 1967, when the Western Wall was off limits

to Jews in Jordanian-held territory, the tomb was a stand-in centre of pilgrimage. It still serves as a prayer hall. The sombre room is divided into sides for men and women, both leading to the stone cenotaph draped in velvet. Behind is a small alcove that researchers believe is a synagogue dating back to the 5th century CE. To get to the tomb head south from Zion Gate, bear right at the fork and then left. Modest dress is required.

FREE **Room of the Last Supper (Cenacle)** RELIGIOUS
(Map p66; ⊗8.30am-5.30pm) The Last Supper is one of the most familiar icons of Christianity, captured in artwork most famously by Leonardo da Vinci. Venerated as the room where Jesus and his disciples had their final meal together, the Room of the Last Supper is considered to be the fourth-most holy place in the Christian world.

Also known as the Coenaculum (Latin for dining hall) or Cenacle (derived from *cena*, Latin for supper), the room is believed to be the place where the disciples received the Holy Spirit on the Pentecost and started speaking in 'foreign tongues' (Acts 2). The event culminated with the baptism of 3000 followers of Jesus, marking the birth of Christianity.

The original building was the site of the first Christian church, but was destroyed twice before being rebuilt in its current form by the Crusaders. To the right of the entrance there is a pair of faded Crusader coats of arms (blackened from rubbings). Look up to see a lamb (a Christian symbol) on the ceiling (the chandelier is attached to it). In the Middle Ages the Franciscans acquired the building, but were later expelled by the Turks. Under the Turks the room became a mosque, and Christians were barred from entering, just as Jews were kept from King David's Tomb, located in the room below. The southern wall still bears the niche hollowed by the Muslims as a mihrab when they converted the chapel into a mosque; the minbar (pulpit used for mosque sermons) contains a column with a pelican on it, also a Christian symbol. During the Mandate period, the British forbade prayer here because of the sensitivities between the various religions and sects.

The room is reached via a stairway from the courtyard of King David's Tomb. The entry is not well marked, so you may need to ask a passing tour group.

Inner Jerusalem

Church & Monastery of the Dormition CHURCH

(Map p66; ⊙8am-noon & 2-6pm) The beautiful Church & Monastery of the Dormition is one of the area's most popular landmarks and is the traditional site where the Virgin Mary is believed to have died, or fell into 'eternal sleep'; its Latin name is Dormitio Sanctae Mariae (Sleep of Holy Mary). The current church and monastery, owned by the German Benedictine order, was consecrated in 1906.

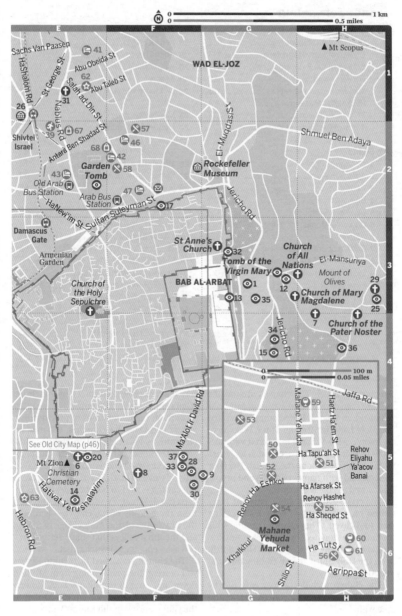

It suffered damage during the battles for the city in 1948 and 1967. During the latter, Israeli soldiers occupied its tower overlooking Jordanian army positions on the Old City ramparts below. The soldiers nicknamed the tower 'bobby' because its tower resembles the helmet worn by London policemen.

The church's interior is a bright contrast to many of its older, duller peers nearby. A golden mosaic of Mary with the baby Jesus is set in the upper part of the apse; below are the

Inner Jerusalem

Prophets of Israel. The chapels around the hall are each dedicated to a saint or saints: St Willibald, an English Benedictine who visited the Holy Land in 724; the Three Wise Men; St Joseph, whose chapel is covered with medallions that feature kings of Judah as Jesus's forefathers; and St John the Baptist. The floor is decorated with names of saints and prophets, as well as zodiac symbols.

The crypt features a stone effigy of Mary asleep on her deathbed with Jesus calling her to heaven. The chapels around this statue were donated by various countries. In the apse is the Chapel of the Holy Spirit, with the Holy Spirit shown coming down to the Apostles.

The church includes a cosy cafe run by German volunteers, with coffees, snacks and free wi-fi.

Church of St Peter of Gallicantu CHURCH
(Map p66; admission free; ⊙8-11.45am & 2-5pm) Almost hidden by the trees and the slope of the hill, the Church of St Peter of Gallicantu is the traditional site of the denial of Jesus by his disciple Peter (Mark 14:66-72) – 'be-fore the cock crow thou shalt deny me thrice' (Gallicantu means 'cock crow').

Built on the foundations of previous Byzantine and Crusader churches, the modern structure is also believed to stand on the site of the house of the high priest Caiaphas, where Jesus was believed to have been taken after his arrest (Mark 14:53). A cave beneath the church is said to be where Jesus was incarcerated. Whatever your beliefs, the view from the balcony of the church – across to the City of David, the Arab village of Silwan and the three valleys that shape Jerusalem – is reason enough to justify a visit.

The church is reached by turning east as you descend the road leading from Mt Zion down and around to Sultan's Pool. Roman steps lead down from the church garden to the Gihon Spring in the Kidron Valley.

KIDRON VALLEY
Historically the oldest section of Jerusalem, the Kidron Valley has archaeological remnants that date back more than 4000 years. This is the site of the legendary City of David, which was actually a city long before David slung any stones. There are also a number of

69

JERUSALEM SIGHTS

graves and tombs in the area, particularly in the Valley of Jehoshaphat. Steep topography has isolated the valley from the rest of the city (the best access is via Dung Gate or St Stephen's (Lions) Gate in the Old City), but it's definitely worth trekking down here for a morning of exploration.

Valley of Jehoshaphat　　　RELIGIOUS
The word Jehoshaphat (Yehoshafat) in Hebrew means 'God shall judge', and this narrow furrow of land located between the Temple Mount and the Mount of Olives is where it is said that the events of Judgment Day will take place. The Book of Joel describes how all nations will be gathered here and the 'heathens' (non-believers) will be judged.

At the southern end of the Valley of Jehoshaphat is a series of tombs. The northernmost is the **Tomb of Jehoshaphat** (Map p66), a 1st-century burial cave notable for the impressive frieze above its entrance. Just in front of the Tomb of Jehoshaphat is **Absalom's Pillar** (Map p66), the legendary tomb of David's son (II Samuel 18:17). Just beyond Absalom's Pillar is the **Grotto of St James** (Map p66), where St James is believed to have

hidden when Jesus was arrested nearby. Next to the grotto, carved out of the rock, is the **Tomb of Zechariah** (Map p66), where Jewish tradition believes the prophet Zechariah is buried (II Chronicles 24:25).

Despite their names, the tombs most likely belong to wealthy noblemen of the Second Temple period. The Grotto of St James is believed to be the burial place of the Bnei Hezirs, a family of Jewish priests.

City of David　　　ARCHAEOLOGICAL SITE
(Map p46; www.cityofdavid.org.il; adult/student 27/14NIS, guided tour 60NIS, movie 13NIS; ⏰8am-5pm Sun-Thu, 8am-2pm Fri) The oldest part of Jerusalem, the City of David was the Canaanite settlement captured by King David some 3000 years ago. The excavations are the result of work, still ongoing, started in 1850. There is much to see here, and quite a bit of walking is involved, so set aside a good part of your morning.

From Dung Gate, head east (downhill) and take the road to the right (on the side of the road is a metal fence which you can peer through to see an archaeological dig in progress); the City of David entrance is then on the left. At the visitors centre you can watch a 3D movie about the city. The site is spread out and contains numerous paths, so signing up for the guided tour (10am or 2pm, Friday 10am only) is recommended. If you intend to walk through the water-filled Hezekiah's Tunnel you can change into swimming trunks in the bathrooms and leave your gear in a locker (10NIS).

Once you get down to the bottom of the hill you can walk back up or take the shuttle bus (5NIS) to the top.

Royal Quarter (Area G)

(Map p46) Area G, also called the Royal Quarter, was first constructed in the 10th century BCE, most likely as a fortification wall for a palace on the ridge. During the First Temple period an aristocrat's home (Achiel's House) was built against the wall, but was destroyed along with the temple in 586 BCE. Judean and Babylonian arrowheads found at the site are vivid reminders of the bloody battle waged here. Archaeologists have also located 51 royal seals (in ancient Hebrew script) here, including one belonging to Gemaryahu Ben Shafan, the scribe of the prophet Jeremiah, who is mentioned in the book of Jeremiah 36:10. The seals were all located in one chamber, indicating that the room served as an office in the days of old.

Warren's Shaft

(Map p66) The long, sloping Warren's Shaft was named after Sir Charles Warren, the British engineer who rediscovered it in 1867. The tunnel, which runs underneath the City of David to the Spring of Gihon, allowed the Jebusites to obtain water without exposing themselves to danger in times of siege. It's just inside their city's defence wall and is possibly the tunnel that David's soldiers used to enter and capture the city, as mentioned in II Samuel 5. Modern archaeologists, however, tend to doubt this theory, suggesting the invaders used a different tunnel. From Warren's Shaft, you can proceed down to Hezekiah's Tunnel at the bottom of the hill.

Hezekiah's Tunnel

(Map p46) The highlight of a visit to the City of David complex is Hezekiah's Tunnel, a 500m-long underground passage of waist-deep water that ends at the Pool of Siloam, where it is said that a blind man was healed after Jesus told him to wash in it. The purpose of the tunnel was to channel water flowing from the Gihon Spring, a temperamental source of water that acts like a siphon, pouring out a large quantity of water for some 30 minutes before drying up for several hours.

Gihon, appropriately, means 'gushing', and the spring is the main reason the Jebusites settled in the valley rather than taking to the adjacent high ground. There is believed to be enough water to support a population of about 2500 people. The tunnel was constructed in about 700 BCE by King Hezekiah to bring the water of the Gihon into the city and store it in the Pool of Siloam, to prevent invaders, in particular the Assyrians, from locating the city's water supply and cutting it off (II Chronicles 32:3).

Although the tunnel is narrow and low in parts, you can wade through it; the water is normally about 0.5m to 1m deep. Due to the siphon effect it does occasionally rise, but only by about 15cm to 20cm.

About 20m into the tunnel, the cavern turns sharply to the left, where a chest-high wall blocks another channel that leads to Warren's Shaft. Towards the tunnel's end the roof rises. This is because the tunnellers worked from either end and one team slightly misjudged the other's level. They had to lower the floor so that the water would flow. A Hebrew inscription was found in the tunnel (a copy can be seen in the Israel Museum): carved by Hezekiah's engineers, it tells of the tunnel's construction.

The walk through Hezekiah's Tunnel takes about 20 minutes; wear shorts, suitable footwear, and bring a torch (flashlight). There are no lights in the tunnel but it's impossible to get lost. You can buy a keychain light from the ticket office for 4NIS. If you don't want to get wet there is a second tunnel without water, which takes about 15 minutes to walk through. To find the entrance to the dry tunnel, go left just before the opening to Hezekiah's Tunnel.

Pool of Siloam

(Map p66) As you exit from Hezekiah's Tunnel there is a small pool with round stones. Many visitors mistakenly believe this to be the Shiloach Pool – it's not. This is the Byzantine Pool of Siloam, which was built in the 5th century to commemorate the Christian tradition of the healing of the blind man (John 9). The Byzantines built the pool because they could not find the Shiloach Pool, which was buried under a thick layer of debris and garbage.

Shiloach Pool

(Map p66) From the Pool of Siloam, head up the stairs and out to an open area with

TOURING THE MOUNT OF OLIVES

Tackling the Mount of Olives on foot can be hard work, especially on a hot summer day. You can make things a little easier by starting at the top of the hill and working your way down. Take Arab bus 75 from the East Jerusalem bus station and get off at the Church of Ascension (you'll spot the sign outside the gate that reads: 'Augusta Victoria Hospital'); arrive early, because this church closes at 1pm. From the church you can walk down the main road for 10 minutes to the Russian Chapel of the Ascension, the Mosque of the Ascension, the Church of the Pater Noster, the Tomb of the Prophets, and then downhill to the remaining sites at the bottom of the Mount of Olives. From the Tomb of the Virgin Mary (your final stop on this walking tour), it's a short hike uphill to St Stephen's (Lions) Gate and the Old City.

crumbling steps that lead down to a small pond. This is the Shiloach Pool. Discovered during excavations in 2005, the pool was built during the Second Temple period and was used for purification rituals. Archaeologists and historians have theorised that this is the pool where Jesus healed a blind man.

Eastern Stepped Street

(Map p66) From the Shiloach Pool head up the flight of wooden steps to the Eastern Stepped Street, an ancient flight of stone steps. A drainage ditch is located under the steps and it was here that archaeologists found Roman-era coins and pottery, leading historians to believe that the ditch served as a hideout for Jews while the city was being sacked in 70 CE.

Temple Road Ascent

(Map p66) This recently discovered 650m-long tunnel is another drainage ditch that channelled water out of the Temple Mount area. The bottom of the tunnel is near the Shiloach Pool; from here it's possible to walk uphill back to the Old City. There are two exits, one near Dung Gate and the second inside the Jerusalem Archaeological Park & Davidson Centre (p52).

If you take the tunnel to the Archaeological Park you'll need to have a ticket for that site purchased in advance. The tunnel itself is largely barren, although during its excavation archaeologists found vessels containing food dating back 2000 years (most likely hidden here during the Roman siege). Note that the ceiling is low and the walls are narrow in spots, so if you are unusually tall or wide maybe give this one a miss.

MOUNT OF OLIVES

Offering visitors a big slice of biblical history, along with some of the most spectacular views over Jerusalem, is the Mount of Olives.

According to the Book of Zechariah, this is where God will start to redeem the dead when the Messiah returns on Judgment Day. In order to get a good place in the line, Jews have always preferred to be buried here, and to date some 150,000 people have been laid to rest on these slopes. Aside from being the world's oldest continually used cemetery, there are many churches commemorating the events that are believed to have led to Jesus's arrest and his ascension to heaven.

As a cemetery, the Mount of Olives fell on hard times during Jordanian occupation. Graves were desecrated and headstones were used as paving stones. The Seven Arches Hotel was built at this time, a move that stirred huge controversy because it was built over part of the cemetery.

Today the Mount of Olives is a quiet slope of churches, pilgrims and tour groups. Most of the churches and gardens are open in the morning, closing for at least two hours towards noon and reopening again mid-afternoon. The Mount of Olives also happens to be one of the best spots to catch a panoramic view of the Old City. Head up to the promenade near the Seven Arches Hotel for the best views; try to visit in the early morning, when you'll get the best light.

Church of the Ascension   CHURCH

(off Map p40.; admission 5NIS; ☺8am-1pm Mon-Sat) In 1898 the Ottomans granted Germany eight hectares of land on the Mount of Olives during Kaiser Wilhelm II's visit to the Holy Land. The Kaiser set the land aside for a church and hospice, naming it after his wife Augusta Victoria. Completed in 1910, the church featured outstanding mosaics and frescos, and a 60m-high bell tower to afford unobstructed views of Jerusalem and the Judean Desert. The Turkish army occupied it during WWI and later the British converted it into a military hospital – it's still a hospital today. A Bible signed by Augusta Victoria can be seen near the entrance to the church. The lively Café Auguste (⊘10am-4pm, to 9pm Wed; ☎), run by German volunteers, is located outside the church. Arab bus 75 stops outside.

Mosque of the Ascension
(Chapel of the Ascension) RELIGIOUS
(Map p66; admission 5NIS) Another holy site honoured by multiple faiths (this time Muslims and Christians), the Bible tells that this is the site from where Jesus ascended to heaven (Luke 24:50-51).

A church was first built here in 390, destroyed and rebuilt a couple of times before Saladin captured it in 1197 and converted it into a mosque.

The building is a circular tower located inside an odd little octagonal Crusader-built structure. Hooks on the walls were used to string up tents used during the Feast of Ascension. Hours are irregular but someone is usually around most mornings to open it up.

The stone floor bears an imprint said to be the footstep of Jesus. Perhaps the reason for its unconvincing appearance today is that pilgrims in the Byzantine period were permitted to take bits of it away. Note that only the right footprint is visible today as the left footprint was taken to Al-Aqsa Mosque during the Middle Ages. Unusually, the caretakers say that the structure is both a Muslim mosque and a Christian chapel.

There is no explanation of the site in any language, so the return on your 5NIS entry fee is marginal at best.

Russian Chapel of the Ascension CHURCH
(Map p66; ⊘9am-1pm Tue & Thu) Marked by a needle-point steeple – the tallest structure on the Mount of Olives – the Russian Chapel of the Ascension is built over the spot from which the Russian Orthodox Church claims Jesus made his ascent to heaven. It was constructed in the late 19th century and during WWI housed a battalion of Turkish soldiers. Today it's a working convent with nearly 40 nuns. It's hard to find, so look for a narrow alleyway leading off from the main street, in among the shops and cafes. Note that it's only open two days a week.

Church of the Pater Noster CHURCH
(Map p66; admission 7NIS; ⊘8.30am-noon & 2.30-5pm) Beside the cave in which Jesus is believed to have spoken to his disciples, Queen Helena, mother of Emperor Constantine, constructed the Church of the Pater Noster. The church, also known as the Church of the Eleona – a bastardisation of the Greek word *elaionas* (olive grove) – was destroyed by the Persians in 614. The site later became known as the place where Jesus is believed to have taught the Lord's Prayer, a belief that inspired the Crusaders to construct an oratory among the ruins in 1106 and a church in 1152. These both fell into disrepair by the mid-14th century.

Princess de la Tour d'Auvergne, an Italian woman married into a French noble family, purchased the property in 1886, excavated the site and built the neighbouring Carmelite convent. Her tomb is located in the entrance to the current church, which was modelled on the Camposanto in Pisa. The most interesting things here are the attractive tiled panels on which are inscribed the Lord's Prayer in over 160 languages.

The cave itself is located between the church and the garden, reached via a short flight of steps.

Tombs of the Prophets RELIGIOUS
(Map p66; admission free; ⊘9am-3pm Mon-Thu) Slightly to the north of the Church of the Pater Noster and below the viewing promenade (near the Seven Arches Hotel) are the Tombs of the Prophets, a set of ancient tombs in which are buried the three prophets Haggai, Zachariah and Malachi, who lived in the 5th century BCE. To find it, take the staircase downhill, just next to a TV satellite dish. The tomb is on private property and the caretaker can usually give a short tour by donation.

Church of Dominus Flevit CHURCH
(Map p66; admission free; ⊘8.30am-5pm) Built in the 1950s, the Church of Dominus Flevit is one of the latest additions to the Mount of Olives' collection of sites. The original church on this site was built by medieval pilgrims who claimed to have found the rock on the Mount of Olives where Jesus had wept for Jerusalem (Luke 19:41) – hence, Dominus Flevit, meaning 'the Lord wept'.

When the present-day tear-shaped church was being built, excavations unearthed a 5th-century monastery, the mosaic floor of which is on display.

Church of Mary Magdalene CHURCH
(Map p66; admission free; ⊘10am-noon Tue, Thu & Sat) The seven golden onion domes of the Russian Church of Mary Magdalene are still one of Jerusalem's most attractive and surprising

landmarks. Built in 1888 by Alexander III in memory of his mother, the church is now a convent and has one of the city's best choirs. A section of the Garden of Gethsemane is claimed to be within the church's grounds.

Church of All Nations
CHURCH

(Map p66; admission free; ⊘8.30-11.30am & 2.30-4pm) Glistening golden mosaics mark the facade of the classically styled Church of All Nations, designed by prolific architect Antonio Barluzzi and dedicated in 1924. The mosaic depicts Jesus assuming the suffering of the world, hence the church's alternative name – the Basilica of the Agony.

Despite the name, not *all* nations are represented, but you can see the seals of the 12 countries that financed the project, located in the ceiling of the church. The church is the successor to two earlier churches; the first was erected in the 4th century but destroyed by an earthquake in the 740s, and the second was an oratory built over the ruins by the Crusaders but abandoned in 1345 for reasons unknown.

Garden of Gethsemane
GARDENS

(Map p66; ⊘8am-noon & 2-6pm) Around the church is the popularly accepted site of the Garden of Gethsemane, the garden where Jesus is believed to have been arrested (Mark 14:32-50). The garden has some of the world's oldest olive trees (in Hebrew *gat shmanim* means 'oil press'), three of which have been scientifically dated as being over 2000 years old, making them witnesses to whatever biblical events may have occurred here. The entrance is not from the main road but from the narrow, steeply inclined alleyway that you'll find leading up beside the church.

Tomb of the Virgin Mary
RELIGIOUS

(Map p66; admission free; ⊘6am-noon & 2.30-5pm) One of the holiest sites in Christianity, the Tomb of the Virgin Mary is a dim and somewhat forlorn place, hung with ancient brass lamps and infused with a millennium of must.

On her death, sometime in the middle of the 1st century, Mary was supposedly interred here by the disciples. A monument was first constructed in the 5th century but was repeatedly destroyed. The current structure dates back to the Crusader period of the 12th century, built on Byzantine foundations. It is now owned by the Greek Orthodox Church, while the Armenians, Syrians and Copts have shares in the altar.

On the main road beside the stairs down to the tomb, the small cupola supported by columns is a memorial to Mujir ad-Din, a 15th-century Muslim judge and historian.

EAST JERUSALEM
Predominantly Arab, East Jerusalem occupies the land that before 1967 belonged to Jordan. The old border between Israel and Jordan was Cheyl HaHandasa Rd (the JLR runs along this road). East of Cheyl HaHandasa Rd, the major roads running north and south are Nablus Rd and Salah ad-Din St. During your rambles make sure to visit the American Colony Hotel (p91), one of the top hotels in Jerusalem and a historic attraction. Legend has it that when the Ottomans finally surrendered the city to British rule, the Turkish governor of Jerusalem snatched a sheet from one of the beds (it was a hospital at the time) and used it as a flag to surrender. The 'flag' is now in the Imperial War Museum in London.

FREE Rockefeller Museum
MUSEUM

(Map p66; Sultan Suleyman St; ⊘10am-3pm Sun-Mon & Wed-Thu, to 2pm Fri) Archaeology buffs who do not get their fill at the Israel Museum should also visit East Jerusalem's Rockefeller Museum. The historic, octagonal-shaped building was set up with a gift of US$2 million donated by the Rockefeller family in 1927, and in its heyday was the leading museum of antiquities in the region. Highlights include the carved beams from Al-Aqsa Mosque, the stone ornamentation recovered from Hisham's Palace (see p276), and the famed 'Lachish Letters' that describe the last days of the Kingdom of Judah (6th century BCE). Take note of the abbreviated opening hours.

FREE Garden Tomb
GARDENS

(Map p66; ✆02-627-2745; www.gardentomb.org; ⊘9am-noon & 2-5.30pm Mon-Sat) The slightly incongruous walled patch of green in the middle of East Jerusalem is the Garden Tomb, a site considered as an alternative to the Church of the Holy Sepulchre for the crucifixion and resurrection of Jesus. While enjoying little support for its claims, it is appreciated by many for its tranquillity and charm. As one Catholic priest is reported to have said, 'If the Garden Tomb is not the true site of the Lord's death and resurrection it should have been'.

Biblical significance was first attached to this location by General Charles Gordon (of Khartoum fame) in 1883. Gordon refused to believe that the Church of the Holy

Sepulchre could occupy the site of Golgotha, and on identifying a skull-shaped hill just north of Damascus Gate he began excavations. The suitably ancient tombs he discovered under the mound further strengthened his conviction that this was the true site of the crucifixion and burial of Jesus.

Archaeologists have since scotched the theory by dating the tombs as being from the 5th century BCE. Several cynics suggest that the continued championing of the Garden Tomb has more to do with the fact that it's the only holy site in Jerusalem that the Protestants, its owners, have any stake in.

To get there from Sultan Suleyman St head north along Nablus Rd and turn right at Schick St. The site is wheelchair accessible. Free guided tours are available in several languages but reservations are required for any language other than English.

Museum on the Seam   MUSEUM
(Map p66; www.mots.org.il; 4 Hel Handasa Rd; adult/concession 25/20NIS; ⊘10am-5pm Sun-Thu, to 2pm Fri; ⊕Shivtei Israel) Conflict, prejudice and racism (and occasional coexistence) are on display at the Museum on the Seam, a sociopolitical/contemporary-art museum that speaks to issues both global and local.

Globally recognised modern artists have displayed their work here, presenting ideas of human rights and universal conflicts translated into the language of art. Exhibitions are theme based, including recent displays such as 'The Right to Protest' (freedom of speech), 'Nature Nation' (provoking political and natural borders) and 'West End' (clash of civilisations).

The name of the museum comes from its location, set smack dab between East and West Jerusalem. The building itself is known to most locals as the Turjeman Post, and served as a forward military position for the Israeli army from 1948 to 1967. Still today the facade bears the scars of war.

Do not mistake it for a museum about the Israeli–Palestinian conflict; the issues here are broad and the Middle East conflict is just one small piece of the larger puzzle. Some of the content in the museum may not be suitable for small children.

St George's Cathedral   CHURCH
(Map p66; admission free; ⊘variable) Named after the patron saint of England, who is traditionally believed to have been martyred in Palestine early in the 4th century, St George's Cathedral belongs to the Anglican Episcopal Diocese of Jerusalem and the Middle East.

The church was consecrated in 1910. During WWI the Turks closed the church and used the bishop's house as their army headquarters. After the British took Jerusalem in 1917, the truce was signed here in the bishop's study. The cathedral has two congregations, Arabic- and English-speaking, and the complex includes a popular guesthouse (see p91).

The church compound is a piece of the British Mandate frozen in time, featuring many symbols of the British presence in Jerusalem, including a font given by Queen Victoria, memorials to British servicemen, a royal coat of arms, an English oak screen and the tower built in memory of King Edward VII.

Zedekiah's Cave   HISTORIC SITE
(Map p46; admission 16NIS; ⊘9am-5pm Sun-Thu; ⊕Damascus Gate) A good bit of the stone that makes Jerusalem so famous was excavated from what is today known as Zedekiah's Cave, a rock quarry and holy site located a short walk east of Damascus Gate, along the Old City wall.

For centuries the cave has been the source of many legends, folk tales and biblical lore. The most prominent legend recalls how Zedekiah (Tzidkiyahu), the last King of Judah, used the cave to escape from the Chaldean troops dispatched by King Nebuchadnezzar of Babylon. But when Zedekiah emerged from the cave (in Jericho), the soldiers were there to capture him. He was blinded on the spot.

The cave is also known as Solomon's Quarries because legend has it that King Solomon built his temple from stones excavated from here. The Freemasons attach particular importance to the cave because they believe King Solomon to be the first Freemason.

The mouth of the cave is natural but slaves excavated the rest, some five city blocks' worth of stone. In some of the rooms you can see nearly finished blocks that the stonecutters abandoned for one reason or another. It's particularly nice to visit on a hot summer day as the cave remains cool year-round.

CITY CENTRE
The city centre, or the New City as it's sometimes called, is the area northwest of the Old City. Its central axis is Jaffa Rd, running from Tzahal Sq to the Mahane Yehuda Market area. To the south of Jaffa Rd is the

main shopping and dining area of the city. The main pedestrian road, Ben Yehuda St, is filled with souvenir shops, moneychangers and buskers. At the bottom of Ben Yehuda, Zion Sq is a handy landmark and meeting point. Despite its status as Jerusalem's downtown, the area is pleasantly devoid of traffic and busy thoroughfares, making it easy to get around on foot or bicycle.

Notre Dame de France Hospice   HISTORIC BUILDING

(Map p46; www.notredamecenter.org; 3 Paratroopers Rd; ☺2-6pm; ⓂCity Hall) Built as a hostelry for French pilgrims, Notre Dame takes the form of a vast, imposing fortress that even manages to dominate the Old City walls. It's thus unsurprising that between 1948 and 1967, when Jerusalem was divided, the south wing of the Notre Dame was used as an Israel Defence Forces (IDF) bunker and frontier post. As a result the building suffered heavy battle damage, but it underwent major renovation in the 1970s and now Notre Dame operates as a busy hotel and restaurant. It also has a cafe and an arts centre promoting traditional local Christian art.

Russian Compound   CHURCH

(Map p76) Between Jaffa Rd and HaNevi'im St and dominated by the green domes of the Church of the Holy Trinity, the Russian Compound was acquired by the Russian Orthodox Church in 1860. In addition to the cathedral, facilities were constructed here for the many pilgrims from Russia who visited the Holy Land until WWI. The cathedral occupies the site where the Assyrians camped in about 700 BCE, and in 70 CE Roman legions assembled here during the Great Jewish Revolt. In front of the cathedral, the 12m-high Herod's Pillar is believed to have been intended for the Second Temple; however, it cracked during chiselling and was abandoned here.

In the last years of the British Mandate, the Russian Compound and nearby streets were turned into a fortified administrative zone nicknamed 'Bevingrad' by Palestinian Jews after the reviled British foreign secretary Ernest Bevin. Today it is home to Jerusalem's central police station and law courts.

Mea She'arim   NEIGHBOURHOOD

Walk northeast from Zion Sq and you'll soon enter a neighbourhood with squat, stone-fronted buildings, balconies adorned with drying laundry, bearded figures in black, and long-skirted mums pushing shopping carts trailed by a gaggle of smartly dressed children. If you have the sense that you've stumbled upon an Eastern European *shtetl* (ghetto) of the 1880s then you are probably standing somewhere near Kikar Shabbat, the main intersection of Mea She'arim, Jerusalem's oldest ultra-Orthodox Jewish (Haredi) neighbourhood.

A throwback to older times, Mea She'arim was developed by ultra-Orthodox Eastern European immigrants who modelled their Jerusalem home on the ones they remembered back in Poland, Germany and Hungary. Despite their transition to the Holy Land, residents have maintained the customs, habits and dress of 18th-century Eastern Europe. Fashions are conservative, including black fedoras for men and floor-scraping dresses for women; even in the height of the Middle Eastern summer it's still customary to wear thick padded coats and fur hats.

In a few of the most traditional families, women shave their heads and wear wigs covered by a beret. Yiddish is the preferred language on the street as the ultra-Orthodox believe Hebrew to be a language only fit for religious purposes. Days are often spent in prayer and business is a secondary pursuit – religious study is frequently financed by fellow ultra-Orthodox communities abroad.

Families are typically large and this fact has made Mea She'arim one of the fastest-growing neighbourhoods in Jerusalem, as well as contributing to the increasingly religious nature of the city.

In the most traditional families, married women shave their heads and cover their bald scalp with a scarf, in the name of modesty. For some religious zealots, though, this is not enough, and in 2011 extremist groups tried to segregate areas of Mea She'arim's sidewalks – men on one side, women on the other. The campaign, opposed by many mainstream ultra-Orthodox Jews, was declared unconstitutional by Israel's Supreme Court.

As this is a religious neighbourhood, visitors are expected to dress and act in a conservative manner – rules stating as much are posted on banners that hang from buildings. It is requested that visitors not take pictures of the residents (snapping photos of street scenes or buildings is possible, but be discreet) or speak to children. Do not walk arm in arm or even hand in hand with anyone; kissing is definitely taboo. Disobeying local customs will lead to verbal objections or

City Centre

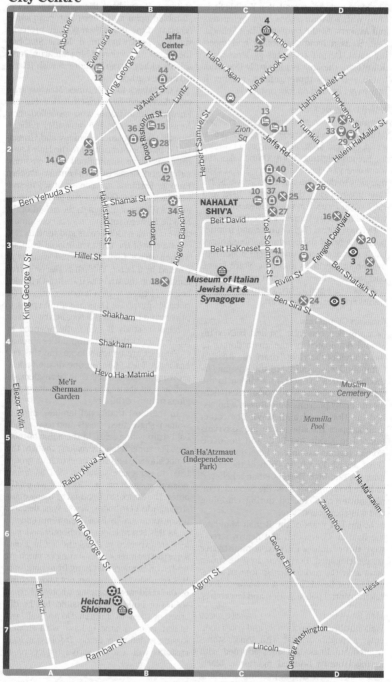

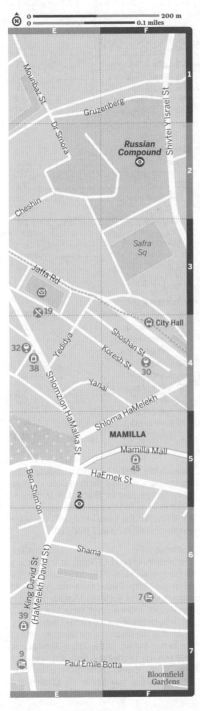

even stone throwing. If a confrontation with the police seems to be brewing, steer clear.

Friday is perhaps the liveliest day to visit as you'll see families heading to and from market in their preparations for Shabbat. Neighbourhood bakeries are open all night on Thursday, baking *challah* (traditional braided soft bread eaten on Shabbat). On Friday nights the streets are awash with people taking a break from their sparkling Shabbat dinners. Another interesting time to visit is during the days leading up to Passover, when you can find local residents kashering (making kosher for Passover) their pots in giant boiling vats.

Mea She'arim is a few minutes' walk from both Damascus Gate and the Jaffa Rd/King George V St junction.

Ethiopia Street   STREET

Tucked away on narrow, leafy Ethiopia St is the impressive bronze-domed **Ethiopian Church** (Map p66; admission free; ⊙9am-1pm & 2-6pm). Built between 1896 and 1904, the church's entrance gate features the carved Lion of Judah, an emblem believed to have been presented by Solomon to the Queen of Sheba, Ethiopia's queen, when she visited Jerusalem. The gate also has inscriptions in Ge'ez, an ancient language of Ethiopia. Visitors are asked to leave their shoes at the door before entering.

Opposite the church is the **Ben Yehuda house** (Map p66), where the great linguist Eliezer Ben Yehuda lived and did much of his work to revive the Hebrew language. A plaque marking the house has been stolen repeatedly by ultra-Orthodox Jews who strongly disapprove of the language's every-day use.

On your left as you leave Ethiopia St and descend HaNevi'im St towards the Old City is the **Ethiopian consulate** (Map p66), with its mosaic-decorated facade.

Mahane Yehuda Market   MARKET

(Map p66; ⊙8am-sunset Sun-Thu, 9am-2pm Fri; 🚊Mahane Yehuda) All walks of Jerusalem life converge at the bustling Mahane Yehuda Market, a fascinating spectacle for the first-time visitor and a bargain food fair for city residents. The marketplace is crammed with fresh fruit, oils, nuts, vegetables and just about anything else grown or picked from the Israeli soil. Spices abound and the smell of cinna-mon, pesto, paprika and black pepper fills the air. There is also plenty of imported coffee and teas, not to mention fresh fish hauled up from

City Centre

the Mediterranean. The names of the alleyways within the market relate to the products available; eg HaEgoz means 'the nut'. Creative types and gourmets have discovered the area in recent years, opening up trendy restaurants, bars and art shops.

One of the most interesting personalities in the market is **Uzi Eli** (cnr Agos & Tuut), an organic drink seller who will give you a spritz of citron treatment on your face whether you want it or not. His treatments are based on Yemenite traditional medicine and methods developed by the 12th-century Spanish-born philosopher and physician Maimonides (the Rambam).

The market is at its most-bustling best on Thursday and Friday during the pre-Shabbat scramble. As the market closes down on Friday a couple of Hassidic blokes walk

through the market blowing trumpets at the stall owners, warning them to close shop, go home and prepare for Shabbat. In the last 30 minutes or so you can get a big bag of bread for 1INIS. See the boxed text, p77, for some recommended cafes and food stalls.

Nahla'ot   NEIGHBOURHOOD
The neighbourhood of Nahla'ot is a warren of narrow alleys in West Jerusalem, founded in the 1860s. There are a number of old synagogues and yeshivas (Jewish religious seminaries) hidden down these lanes, many set in large stone-walled compounds.

Among the dozens of synagogues, one of the better known is the **Ades Synagogue** (Map p66; cnr Be'ersheva & Shilo Sts), built by Jews from Aleppo (Haleb), Syria in 1901. The synagogue was named for Ovadia and Yosef Ades, the Syrian-Jewish brothers who financed the project. It quickly became a centre for Syrian *hazzanut* (Jewish liturgical singing) and saw the training of many a Jerusalem cantor. Inside, you'll find a classically Middle Eastern–styled interior with a walnut ark that was carried here from Aleppo by donkey cart. Today it maintains the rare tradition of *bakashot*, a set cycle of Kabbalistic poetry sung in the early hours of Shabbat during the winter months. The synagogue has two morning services and a combined afternoon/evening service, which visitors can attend.

The most interesting street is HaGilboa, where you'll find small gardens and a number of historic homes; each contains a plaque that describes the family that built the home. One street over, on HaCarmel, look for the attractive synagogue Hased ve-Rahamim (Map p66), with its unmistakable silver doors.

A community of students and artists have moved into the neighbourhood – see what they are up to at Barbur (Map p66; www.barbur. org; 6 Shirizili St; admission free; ⊙4-8pm Mon-Thu, 11am-2pm Fri), a small contemporary art gallery and community centre. Movie screenings, lectures, book readings and workshops often take place here, so check its website for a listing of events.

Time Elevator
THEATRE

(Map p76; ☎02-624 8381; www.time-elevator -jerusalem.co.il; Beit Agron, 37 Hillel St; adult/student 54/46NIS; ⊙10am-5pm Sun-Thu, to 2pm Fri, noon-6pm Sat; ⊜Jaffa Center) If you prefer to have your history delivered to you in a Disney-type format, check out the Time Elevator, a cross between a museum, a theatre and a carnival ride. Once inside the theatre, spectators are jolted around in their seats along with the on-screen action as Chaim Topol (one-time star of *Fiddler on the Roof*) leads them through Jerusalem's equally moving history. It's especially recommended if you have children with you (but only children over the age of five are allowed). Reservations are required.

FREE Ticho House (Beit Ticho)
MUSEUM

(Map p76; www.imj.org.il; 9 HaRav Kook St; ⊙10am-5pm Sun, Mon, Wed & Thu, to 10pm Tue, to 2pm Fri; ⊜Jaffa Center) Dr Abraham Ticho, an Austrian-born ophthalmologist, purchased this 19th-century stone mansion in 1924. Dr Ticho established an eye clinic here, saving hundreds of Palestinian Arabs from blindness. Following Dr Ticho's death, his wife, Anna, donated the building as an art centre and museum, for which it is still used today.

Among the exhibits are Dr Ticho's study and some documents and letters of interest, in particular those dealing with his work for the Arabs, as well as his collection of Hanukkah (Festival of Lights) lamps. Anna was also an artist and some of her work is on display.

However, the appeal of the museum is secondary to the popularity of its charming ground-floor cafe, Little Jerusalem, the tables from which spill out onto a terrace overlooking a large, tranquil garden. For details, see p94.

Museum of Italian Jewish Art & Synagogue
MUSEUM

(Map p76; 27 Hillel St; adult/child 20/15NIS; ⊙10am-5pm Sun, Tue & Wed, noon-9pm Thu, 10am-1pm Fri; ⊜Jaffa Center) This museum contains a rich collection of tapestries, Torah arks and other Judaica brought here from Italy in the 1950s. The entire interior of the building, in fact, originally comes from an 18th-century synagogue in Conegliano Veneto (near Venice) that was transported across the Mediterranean and rebuilt here. It now serves the needs of Italian Jews in Jerusalem and is the only synagogue outside Italy where the ancient Italian liturgy is performed.

Heichal Shlomo
RELIGIOUS

(Map p76; 58 King George V St) The seat of the Chief Rabbinate of Israel is Heichal Shlomo, a vast complex designed in the 1950s and styled along the lines of Solomon's Temple – Heichal Shlomo literally means 'Solomon's Mansion'. Check out the semicircular balcony, intended for the use of the Chief Rabbi as he addressed, pope-like, throngs of believers. The Wolfson Museum (Map p76; adult/child 15/10NIS; ⊙9am-3pm Sun-Thu), housed inside the massive building, features presentations of religious and traditional Jewish life.

Great Synagogue
SYNAGOGUE

(Map p76) Next door to Heichal Shlomo, and forming part of the same complex, is the Great Synagogue. The building has been condemned by many as an extravagant and tasteless waste of money, but attendance at a Shabbat service here is, nevertheless, popular.

KING DAVID STREET (HAMELEKH DAVID STREET)
The most coveted piece of real estate outside the Old City lies along King David St (Map p76), on a hillside west of Jaffa Gate that is dominated by the venerable King David

Hotel. The area includes parks, gardens, some of the best hotels in the city and, in Mamilla, rows of new luxury apartments – many owned by Jews who live overseas for most of the year – that look out on the walls of the Old City. Important landmarks include the Reform Movement's Hebrew Union College (Map p76; www.beitshmuel.co.il), part of which was designed by Moshe Safdie (1986) and, facing the King David Hotel, the 1933 YMCA (Map p66) – for a cheap thrill, take the elevator (5NIS) to the top of the 46m bell tower.

Yemin Moshe & the Montefiore Windmill   NEIGHBOURHOOD

The small Yemin Moshe neighbourhood can be identified immediately by the Montefiore windmill (Map p66; ☺ museum 9am-4pm Sun-Thu, to 1pm Fri), one of the first structures to be built outside the secure confines of the Old City.

The neighbourhood was part of a scheme developed by English Jewish philanthropist Sir Moses Montefiore, who visited the Holy Land seven times in the mid-19th century. Hoping to aid the Jews living in Jerusalem, and seeking to ease overcrowding within the city walls, Montefiore built a block of 24 apartments, a development known as Mishkenot Sha'ananim (Tranquil Dwellings). The windmill was built in 1857 to provide the basis for a flour industry. The scheme failed and the windmill now serves as an exotic landmark and a museum dedicated to Montefiore.

St Andrew's Church   CHURCH

(Map p66; 1 David Remez St; ☺ museum 9am-4pm Sun-Thu, to 1pm Fri) Also known as the Scottish Church, St Andrew's Church was built in 1927 to commemorate the capture of the city and the Holy Land by the British in WWI. Based on the design of one Clifford Holliday, the buildings are an intriguing mix of Western and Arabic influences; take note of the exquisite Armenian tiles outside the entrance to the guesthouse and church (these were designed in a workshop on the Via Dolorosa). The floor features an inscription to the memory of Robert the Bruce, who requested that his heart be buried in Jerusalem when he died. Sir James Douglas made an attempt at fulfilling Bruce's wish but en route he was killed in Spain, fighting the Moors. The heart was recovered and returned to Scotland, where it's now buried at Melrose.

GERMAN COLONY

(Map p40) Lounging in a cafe, sipping lattes and reading the morning Ha'aretz newspaper seems to be the main daily activity for residents of Jerusalem's German Colony. Built in the late 19th century by members of a German Protestant sect called the Templers (not be confused with the Crusader-era Knights Templar), the German colony remains a pleasant, tree-lined neighbourhood of Arab villas and European homes. It has always carried an air of affluence and continues to attract a mix of moneyed foreign investors and students socializing in aromatic coffee shops. Evenings are a pleasant time to stroll here and experience some of the best restaurants in the city.

REHAVIA & TALBIYEH

With Talbiyeh built by wealthy Christian Arabs and Rehavia by Jewish intellectuals in the early 20th century, these are among the city's more fashionable neighbourhoods. The official residences of the prime minister and president are here. The upper (northeastern) section of Gaza (Aza) Rd – the old route to Gaza – and Ramban St are particularly homey, and their cafes and restaurants get lots of student traffic.

Talbiyeh, also known as Kommemiyut, has some wonderfully self-indulgent architecture; take a look at Beit Jalad (Map p66; 17 Alkalay St), built by an Arab contractor with a fondness for the imagery of The Thousand and One Nights.

These neighbourhoods lie south of Bezalel St and west of King George V and Keren HaYesod Sts.

LA Mayer Museum for Islamic Art   MUSEUM

(Map p66; ☎ 02-566 1291; www.islamicart.co.il; 2 HaPalmach St; adult/child 40/20NIS; ☺ 10am-3pm Sun, Mon, Wed & Thu, to 7pm Tue, to 2pm Fri & Sat) At the southern fringe of Rehavia, close to the President's Residence, the LA Mayer Museum for Islamic Art showcases art from Islamic cultures stretching from Spain to India. The museum and research centre, completed in 1974, was founded as a way to bridge the cultural divide between Jews and their Arab neighbours. Exhibits include jewellery, carpets, brassware, glasswork and paintings – and, for something completely different, a world-renowned collection of historic clocks and watches, including many of the timepieces stolen in 1983 in Israel's most spectacular heist and recovered

JERUSALEM SYNDROME

Each year tens of thousands of tourists descend on Jerusalem to walk in the footsteps of the prophets, and a handful come away from the journey thinking they *are* the prophets. This medically recognised ailment, called Jerusalem Syndrome, occurs when visitors become overwhelmed by the metaphysical significance of the Holy City and come to the conclusion that they are biblical characters or that the Apocalypse is near.

The ailment was first documented in the 1930s by Jerusalem psychiatrist Dr Heinz Herman, who identified, for example, an English Christian woman who was certain that Christ's Second Coming was imminent and regularly climbed Mt Scopus to welcome Him back to earth with a cup of tea.

In more recent times, there were reports of a Canadian Jew who, claiming to be Samson, decided to prove himself by smashing through the wall of his room to escape. Or there was the elderly American Christian woman who believed she was the Virgin Mary and went to Bethlehem to look for the baby Jesus.

In the most serious case so far, in 1969 an Australian Christian fanatic set fire to Al-Aqsa Mosque, causing considerable damage. He believed that he was on a mission from God to clear the Temple Mount of non-Christian buildings to prepare for the Messiah's Second Coming.

Doctors estimate that Jerusalem Syndrome affects between 50 and 200 people per year, and although many have a recorded history of mental aberration, about a quarter of recorded cases have no previous psychiatric record. You can occasionally see these people standing on Ben Yehuda St, dressed in colourful garb or wearing togas, and holding placards that describe soon-to-be-occurring events of an apocalyptic nature.

Most sufferers are taken to the state psychiatric ward, Kfar Shaul, on the outskirts of West Jerusalem. Patients are monitored and then sent home. Doctors explain that the syndrome generally lasts a week and when the patient resumes his or her old self, they become extremely embarrassed and prefer not to speak of the incident. Doctors at Kfar Shaul have found it virtually pointless to try to persuade the deluded that they are not who they claim to be.

in France in 2008. There are guided tours in English upon request (call ahead).

TALPIOT

Haas Promenade   VIEWPOINT

(Map p40) The main reason to venture down to Talpiot is to walk along the Haas Promenade, a garden-fringed walkway that offers spectacular views over the Old City. To the east, atop the forested Hill of Evil Council, stand the UN's Jerusalem headquarters, until 1948 the seat of the British high commissioner of Palestine. To get here take bus 8 from King George V St and get off at the Kiryat Moriah stop.

GIVAT RAM & MUSEUM ROW

The political seat of the Israeli government, along with its accompanying government buildings, is located in the rather forlorn area of Givat Ram, south of Central Bus Station. There is no great plaza and roads run haphazardly around the area, seemingly in circles. It's home to the Knesset (the seat of the Israeli parliament), the Prime Minister's Office, the foreign ministry, the Bank of Is-

rael and several museums. You can get here from Central Bus Station on bus 9.

Israel Museum   MUSEUM

(Map p40; www.imj.org.il; adult/child 48/24NIS; ⊙10am-5pm Sun, Mon, Wed, Thu, 4-9pm Tue, 10am-2pm Fri, 10am-5pm Sat) Consider the Israel Museum to be a road map for your travels throughout the country. By visiting early in your stay you'll get a good grounding on the 5000 years of history that you are about to explore. Don't forget to pick up a complimentary audio guide from the visitors centre. Note that in August, Tuesday opening hours are 10am to 9pm.

Heading out the back of the visitors centre, take your first right to the Shrine of the Book, where some of the Dead Sea Scrolls (see p295) are on rotating display. The distinctive pot-lid-shaped roof is meant to symbolise the pots in which the Dead Sea Scrolls were kept. The scrolls, totalling 800 in all, were found in 1947 and date back to the time of the Bar Kochba Revolt (CE 132–35). They deal with both secular and religious issues and were thought to have been written by an ascetic group of Jews called the Essenes, who inhabited the area for about 300 years. The most important of the Dead Sea Scrolls is the Great Isaiah Scroll, the largest and best preserved. It is the only biblical scroll that has survived in its entirety, and takes centre place in the room. The 54 columns of the scroll contain all 66 chapters of Isaiah without an apparent division between what modern scholars regard as First and Second Isaiah. It predates the previously oldest biblical document ever found by about 1000 years. Note that some scrolls (including the Isaiah scroll) may be rotated out for reasons of preservation.

Just past the Shrine of the Book is a huge 1:50 scale model of Jerusalem as it was towards the end of the Second Temple era. A paved promenade leads from the Shrine of the Book to a Sculpture Garden with works by Moore, Rodin and Picasso.

Inside the main building, the Judaica wing includes three complete synagogues brought from various locations and reconstructed. Of the three, the Vittorio Veneto Synagogue is the most impressive. It dates from 1700 and was transported from Vittorio Veneto in Italy in 1965. The second part of this exhibition focuses on Jewish ethnography. Foremost among the exhibits are a Jewish bride's outfit from San'a in Yemen, which dates back to the turn of the 19th and 20th centuries, a Druze woman's apparel from Galilee dating back to the late 19th century, and richly embroidered Palestinian costumes from Bethlehem of the 1930s. Look out also for costumes from Jewish communities in Ethiopia and Kurdistan.

In the Archaeology Wing look out for the 'House of David' Victory Stele (audio guide No 233), a fragmentary inscription from the First Temple period discovered at Tel Dan (p243). It is the only contemporary, extra-biblical reference to the Davidic dynasty to have come to light so far. The Roman period is well represented by Jewish sarcophagi, ossuaries and some impressive statues, including a bronze bust of Hadrian from the 2nd century CE. Found at Beit She'an, it is considered one of the finest portraits of Hadrian ever discovered. Also in this section is a nail pierced through a human anklebone, dated to the 1st century BCE: a victim of Roman crucifixion. The

item is a replica, as according to Jewish law, Kohanim (the descendants of the Temple priests) cannot enter buildings that contain human remains.

The highlight of the Arts Wing is the great section on Impressionist and post-Impressionist art, containing work by Renoir, Pissarro, Gauguin and Van Gogh. One of the most arresting displays is a complete French Salon from the 18th century (viewed from two entrances leading off from the post-Impressionist art gallery). Israeli art is well represented in the Israeli Art pavilion, with striking paintings by Reuven Rubin and Yosef Zaritsky, and less conventional work by Igael Tumarkin (see his odd exhibit made of wood, textiles, iron, a stretcher and paint, entitled *Mita Meshunah – Unnatural Death*).

Bible Lands Museum   MUSEUM
(Map p40; www.blmj.org; 25 Granot St, Givat Ram; adult/student/senior 40/20/30NIS; ⊘9.30am-5.30pm Sun-Tue & Thu, 9.30am-9.30pm Wed summer, 1.30-9.30pm Wed winter, 9.30am-2pm Fri, 10am-3pm Sat) This museum chronologically presents the material culture and history of both the Holy Land and neighbouring civilisations with a wealth of well-displayed artefacts and background information.

The museum was founded by Dr Elie Borowski, a Polish-born academic who fought the Nazis in Germany and later moved to Switzerland, where he became known as one of the leading dealers of art from the antiquities. In his fascination for biblical times, Dr Borowski had it in mind to establish an institute where people of different faiths could join together and return to the morals and ethics laid out by the Bible. This museum is the result of his work.

Exhibits date from 6000 BCE to 600 CE and include some 2000 artefacts ranging from mosaics, objets d'art, seals and bronzes to household items from all over Asia, Europe and Africa. The unusual organisation of artefacts can be a little confusing, so take the free guided tour, daily at 10.30am.

FREE **Knesset**   LANDMARK
(Map p66; ☎02-675 3333; www.knesset.gov.il; Ruppin Blvd) Israel's 120 lawmakers convene at the Knesset, a building whose bland, colonnaded exterior hardly personifies the rousing atmosphere found inside its hallowed halls.

Belonging to the multistorey-car-park school of architecture, the building was inaugurated in 1966 – previously the parliament had met in an unobtrusive building on King George V St. The Knesset is a lot more attractive inside than out and it has a foyer decorated with three tapestries and a mosaic by Marc Chagall.

The building is open to the public on Sunday and Thursday from 8.30am to 2.30pm, when free guided tours are given. Call ahead to sign up for a tour in English and don't forget to bring your passport – and leave sharp objects at home. You can also see the Knesset in session on Monday or Tuesday from 4pm to 7pm, and Sunday and Thursday from 11am to 7pm. The proceedings are conducted mainly in Hebrew and occasionally in Arabic.

Next to the bus stops opposite the Knesset is a giant bronze menorah, a gift from the British Labour Party in 1956. It's decorated with panels representing important figures and events in Jewish history.

Monastery of the Cross　MONASTERY
(Map p66; Rehavia Valley; admission 10NIS; ⊘9am-4pm Mon-Fri) The fortress-like Monastery of the Cross was founded in the early 4th century CE by King Bagrat of Georgia. According to tradition, this was the site of the tree from which Jesus's cross was made. Persians laid waste to the building in 614 and Muslims destroyed the replacement in 1009. Construction began again in 1038, although various additions have been made since then, including a Spanish-style rococo tower in the mid-19th century. The Greek Orthodox Church purchased the complex in 1685.

The interior of the church contains some interesting 17th-century frescos, a bit of 6th-century mosaic floor in the chapel and a small museum. In the frescos, note the small, white-bearded fellow in the red robe at the feet of the two church fathers; this is Shota Rustaveli, the famed Georgian poet who came to this monastery in the 12th century and lived here until his death.

The monastery can be reached by walking through Rehavia along Ramban St, crossing Hanasi Ben Zvi and following the path down the Valley of the Cross (Emeq HaMatzleva). From the city centre take bus 17 (from either Gaza Rd or Shivtei Yisra'el) and get off at Derekh Rupin. Then follow the path down.

HAR HAZIKARON
On the far western fringe of the city, between rows of housing blocks and the Jerusalem forest, quietly sits Har Hazikaron (Mount of Remembrance). This high ground of wooded slopes and spectacular views includes Mt Herzl, a military cemetery and Yad Vashem, Israel's main memorial to victims of the Holocaust. The area is close to Ein Kerem, so for the sake of convenience, try visiting both areas in one trip.

Herzl Museum　MUSEUM
(Map p40; ☑02-643 3266; www.herzl.org.il; adult/child 25/20NIS; ⊘9am-3.30pm Sun-Thu, to 12.30pm Fri; ⊠Mt Herzl) The history of the Zionist dream is detailed in the Herzl Museum, a multimedia journey into the life of Theodor Herzl. The tour is by appointment only.

Herzl's story, as covered by the museum, began in fin de siècle Paris, where the secular, Budapest-born journalist was working as a correspondent for a Vienna newspaper. After witnessing violent outbreaks of anti-Semitism in the wake of the 1894 Dreyfus treason trial, he dedicated himself to the creation of a Jewish state where Jews would not be subject to such hatred. Three years of campaigning culminated in the first World Zionist Congress, held in Basel, Switzerland in 1897. He continued campaigning over the next seven years, until his death in 1904.

Herzl's grave (Map p40), a simple black marker with his name etched upon it, is on a small knoll west of the museum. Nearby are the graves of several Israeli prime ministers and presidents, including Golda Meir, Yitzhak Rabin and Menachem Begin. A short walk north leads to the military cemetery, or you can continue west down a dirt path that leads to Yad Vashem.

FREE **Yad Vashem**　MEMORIAL
(off Map p40; www.yadvashem.org; ⊘9am-5pm Sun-Thu, to 2pm Fri; ⊠Mt Herzl) In 1953 the Knesset set forth a plan to memorialise the six million Jews who died at the hands of the Nazis, and honour those who tried to save them. The result was Yad Vashem, a vast, landscaped complex with a visitors centre, a museum and a dozen memorials scattered over 18 hectares of the Mount of Remembrance.

The centrepiece of Yad Vashem (the name was taken from Isaiah 56:5 and means 'A Memorial and a Name') is a prism-like history museum. Architect Moshe Safdie explains that the triangular design represents the bottom half of a Star of David, because the population of Jews worldwide was almost cut in half as a result of the Holocaust. Towards the end of the structure is the Hall of Names, the physical repository for the Pages of Testimony – forms filled out by friends and family of Holocaust victims; three million have so far been collected. The hole dug out of the floor honours those victims whose names will never be known because they, and their entire families, all their friends and everyone who had known them was killed, leaving no one to testify – or say the Kaddish (Jewish memorial prayer).

Closer to the visitors centre is the Children's Memorial, also designed by Safdie, and dedicated to the 1.5 million Jewish children who died in the Holocaust. Dug into the bedrock, the sombre underground memorial contains a solitary flame reflected infinitely by hundreds of mirrors. Recorded voices read the names of children who perished.

The Avenue of the Righteous winds along the ridge of the mountain and is lined with trees dedicated to the Gentiles who risked their own lives to save Jews from the Nazis and local collaborators; among them are Oskar Schindler and King Christian X of Demark. In the Hall of Remembrance, an eternal flame burns near a crypt containing ashes of victims brought from the extermination camps. The floor is inscribed with the names of 22 of the most infamous extermination and concentration camps. At the southern edge of the complex is the Cattle Car memorial, one of the original train cars used to transport Jews from the ghettos to the death camps. Nearby is the Valley of the Communities, a moving, one-hectare monument carved out of the valley floor. Columns of stone are inscribed with the names of 5000 Jewish communities wiped out by the Nazis.

It takes about three hours to get around Yad Vashem. Egged 99 (as part of its city-wide tour) stops here. The JLR has a stop near Mt Herzl, a 10-minute walk from Yad Vashem (there is also a free shuttle that comes up to the junction but it only runs once every 30 minutes, so you are better off walking).

EIN KEREM

Hidden in a valley on Jerusalem's western outskirts is a pretty village of Arab-built stone houses surrounded by Lebanese cedars and native pine trees. The small community is home to several important churches related to John the Baptist, and the Chagall

---

JERUSALEM FOR CHILDREN

Spare your kids the agony of visiting another treasure of antiquity and let them loose in the excellent Biblical Zoo (Map p104; www.jerusalemzoo.org.il; Zoo Rd; adult/child 47/37NIS; ⊗9am-6pm Sun-Thu, 9am-4.30pm Fri, 10am-6pm Sat), a 25-hectare park in the southwest of the city. The zoo contains animals mentioned in the Bible that have become extinct in Israel, including lions, bears and crocodiles. Another section displays endangered animals from other parts of the world. The best way to reach the zoo is to take the light rail to Mt Herzl, where you can pick up bus 33 to the zoo.

Kids also love the Bloomfield Science Museum (Map p40; www.mada.org.il; Hebrew University, Ruppin Blvd; admission 34NIS, under 5yr free; ⊗9am-6pm Sun-Thu, 9am-4.30pm Fri, 10am-6pm Sat), a hands-on experience with loads of activities and introductory science exhibits. It's a 25- to 30-minute walk from the city centre or take bus 9 from Central Bus Station. It's 10 minutes on foot from the Israel Museum.

Other possible diversions include Jerusalem's Train Theatre (Map p66; ☏02-561 8514; www.traintheater.co.il; Liberty Bell Park; admission 15-60NIS), which puts on occasional puppet performances and the Time Elevator (p79).

The City of David (p69) is good for older kids as they can make like Indiana Jones and wade through a spooky water-filled tunnel. In the Old City, there is a good playground for small children a few steps north of Hurva Sq (tucked into a courtyard, behind the Broad Wall).

If choosing a restaurant tends to provoke a family schism, try Spaghettim (Map p76; 35 Hillel St; dishes 40-55NIS), a centrally located and reasonably priced Italian place with yummy pastas and pizzas that will please all ages.

Windows at Hadassah Medical Centre are not too far away. It's busiest on weekends, when locals descend on the place for brunch.

The history of the town was rather ordinary until the middle of the 6th century, when Christian pilgrims identified it as the likely home of Elizabeth, mother of John the Baptist. Inevitably, shrines and churches were built over holy sites. The 1948 Arab–Israeli War caused the local Arab residents to flee the town; their homes were later taken over by immigrants from Morocco and Romania. A growing student population has breathed new life into the community.

To reach the village, take bus 27 from Central Bus Station or bus 28 from Mt Herzl.

Church of St John
CHURCH

(admission free; ⊘9am-noon & 2.30-5pm Sun-Fri) The blue-and-white interior of the Franciscan-owned Church of St John is reminiscent of European churches – not surprising, as it was funded and built by the Spanish monarchy in 1674. The paintings are by Spanish artists and there is a royal coat of arms above the entrance.

Towards the front of the church is the grotto where it is believed John came into the world (Luke 1:5-25, 57-80); a small marble circle under the altar marks the spot.

The church is located on the street to the right of the main road.

Church of the Visitation
CHURCH

(admission free; ⊘8-11.45am & 2.30-6pm) The Church of the Visitation is built over what is said to have been the home of Zacharias and Elizabeth, across the valley from the Church of St John and uphill from Mary's Spring. The name of the church is in remembrance of Mary's visit to Elizabeth (Luke 1: 39-49). The prayer that Mary is said to have uttered ('My soul exalts the Lord'; Luke 1: 46-56) is inscribed on the walls of the church in 41 languages. Brilliant paintings adorn the walls of the upper church; in the apse, Mary stands in the desert flanked by her devotees and below angels who prepare to crown her with wreaths. From the main intersection in Ein Kerem, walk along the narrow road that heads south and the church appears on the left after about 10 minutes of walking.

Chagall Windows
SYNAGOGUE

(Map p104; ☑02-641 6333; admission 10NIS; ⊘8am-1.15pm & 2-3.30pm Sun-Thu) The Hadassah-Ein Kerem Medical Centre (not to be confused with the Hadassah-Mt Scopus Medical Centre across town) is the Middle East's largest hospital. It's known internationally for its synagogue featuring stained-glass windows by Jewish artist Marc Chagall. Each of the 12 colourful abstract panels depicts one of the tribes of Israel, based on Genesis 49 and Deuteronomy 33.

Guided tours are conducted in English, but you'll need to call ahead to confirm times. Take bus 19 or 27 and get off at the last stop. You can also walk up here from Ein Kerem.

⭐ Courses

Ulpan Or
HEBREW LANGUAGE

(Map p40; ☑02-561 1132; www.ulpanor.com; 43a Emek Rafa'im Rd) Short- and long-term Hebrew language classes are available. One-week (US$1149) or two-week (US$2299) intensive language courses are available. The one-on-one course is pricey but includes practical experience in the field.

Gerard Behar Centre
HEBREW LANGUAGE

(Map p66; ☑02-624 0034; 11 Bezalel St) Morning and evening Hebrew-language classes with ongoing enrolment. Five days a week costs 920NIS per month, three days a week 613NIS.

Hebrew Union College
HEBREW LANGUAGE

(Map p76; ☑02-620 3303; hsaggie@hotmail.com; 13 King David St; ⏚City Hall) Three-month courses (1800NIS) meet twice a week in the evenings. A popular option for long-term tourists.

Palestinian Arabic Institute
ARABIC LANGUAGE

(☑052-227 3874; palestinianarabic@gmail.com) One-month intensive Arabic lessons that meet four days a week. Call or email for current class locations.

YMCA East Jerusalem
ARABIC LANGUAGE

(Map p66; ☑02-628 5210, 054-920-3932; 29 Nablus Rd) Offers three-month Arabic-language courses for 1200NIS. Classes meet twice weekly in the evenings. Contact Malda.

☞ Tours

There are a number of excellent national tour operators that offer day trips in Jerusalem; see p440 for details. The following list is for tours that operate primarily in Jerusalem.

Egged 99 Circular Line
BUS TOUR

(☑02-530 4704; non-stop tour adult/child 60/48NIS, hop-on hop-off tour 80/68NIS) A good introduction to the city is the Egged 99 Circular Line. This open-air coach service cruises past 35 of Jerusalem's major sites, providing

RELIGIOUS SERVICES IN JERUSALEM

Experience a slice of holiness in Jerusalem by attending a Shabbat service, Sunday-morning church service, or Friday prayers.

Shabbat services are typically held on Fridays shortly after candle lighting (36 minutes before sunset) and on Saturday morning from about 9.30am. Dress modestly. Among Jerusalem's more interesting and innovative synagogues:

Kol HaNeshama (Map p40; ☎02-6724878; www.kolhaneshama.org.il; 1 Asher St, Baka) Reform congregation.

Shira Hadasha (Map p40; www.shirahadasha.org.il; 12 Emek Refa'im St) Liberal Orthodox congregation.

Kehilat Har-El (Map p66; ☎02-625 3841, 054-474 2314; www.kharel.org.il; 16 Shmuel HaNagid St) Israel's oldest Reform congregation.

For details on church services, see the Christian information centre website (www.cicts.org) and click the link 'Liturgy in the Holy Land' (the tabs on the left allow you to choose between the denominations). The following are English-language services:

Narkis Street Congregation (Map p66; www.narkis.org; 4 Narkis St, City Centre) Baptist community.

Lutheran Church of the Redeemer (Map p46; ☎02-627 6111; Old City) English-language services are held Sundays at 9am.

Muslims can join Friday prayers in **Al-Aqsa Mosque** (p47) on Al-Haram ash-Sharif.

commentary in eight languages along the way. Stops include Yad Vashem and the Israel Museum. The first bus leaves Central Bus Station at 9am. You can catch it at Jaffa Gate, the King David Hotel or other stops. The Egged website (www.egged.co.il/eng, click the tourism link) lists the stops and times.

Zion Walking Tours   WALKING TOUR
(Map p46; ☎02-627 7588, 050-530 5552; Omar Ibn al-Khattab Sq) Operates a three-hour Old City walking tour (120NIS per person) at 10am and 2pm from Sunday to Thursday (there must be at least four participants). It hits the major historic spots.

Sandemans New Jerusalem Tours
                                        WALKING TOUR
(Map p66; ☎052-346 4479; www.newjerusalemtours.com; 67 Hanevi'im St) Has free daily tours of the Old City (though tips are appreciated). Meet at Jaffa Gate Sunday to Thursday at 9am, 11am or 2.30pm. On Friday and Saturday the tour is at 9am and 11am only. The free tour is a great introduction to the city; try to do this on your first day in town to get better acquainted with the place. More in-depth paying tours (60NIS to 85NIS) go around the Old City and other parts of Jerusalem.

EcoBike   CYCLING TOUR
(☎054-426 2187; www.ecobike.co.il) If you prefer to tour the city by bicycle, contact EcoBike,

which offers a Saturday ride past Jerusalem's neighbourhoods and landmarks. The guides give excellent commentary throughout the journey and the price includes the hire fee. Since the tour is on Shabbat, the streets are pleasantly car-free. EcoBike also does night rides, a great time for riding through the Old City. You can also do a lower-cost self-guided tour (they give you a detailed map and printout of sights to see). Check the website for rates.

Jerusalem Reality Tours   SOCIOPOLITICAL TOUR
(☎052-363 4370; www.jerusalemrealitytours.com) Good for tours of East Jerusalem, the Separation Wall, Silwan, the Old City and other places of sociopolitical interest. Walking tours cost 120NIS for adults and 80NIS for students. Knowledgeable local guides discuss the political and historical issues of the areas, visit local families and have lunch with a family. Trips are usually by appointment, so call ahead for details.

✬ Festivals & Events

Some festivals and events to keep an eye out for if you're in town at the right time (see p20 for more information).

Jerusalem International Book Fair   BOOKS
(February) For dates and venue see www.jerusalembookfair.com.

Jerusalem Day   HOLIDAY

(May or June) Not so much a festival but a holiday of celebration as Israelis mark the reunification of the city.

Israel Festival   CULTURAL EVENTS

(June) A 16-day event that offers a raft of concerts, dances and theatre performances around the city.

Jerusalem Film Festival   FILM

(July) One of the largest film festivals in the Middle East. Check out www.jff.org.il for details.

Jerusalem Wine Festival   WINE

(early August) Held at the Israel Museum, this festival allows you to sample wines from around the country and meet Israeli winemakers.

🛏 Sleeping

Most budget accommodation is located in the Old City or in the city centre along Jaffa Rd. There are some great midrange options, including atmospheric Christian hospices in the Old City and boutique hotels in the city centre. High-end category picks are found in Mamilla and East Jerusalem.

While the Old City hotels offer much in the way of rustic atmosphere and access to Jerusalem's historic places of interest, the area is crowded and filled with steps and narrow streets, inconvenient if you have a car or lots of luggage.

CITY CENTRE

TOP CHOICE **Abraham Hostel**   HOSTEL **$**

(Map p66; ☎02-650 2200; www.abraham-hostel -jerusalem.com; 67 Hanevi'im St; dm 70-100NIS, s 240NIS, d 270-360NIS, tr 400NIS; ✿@🛜; 🚇Ha-Davidka) A mecca for budget travellers looking for centrally located accommodation, Abraham has 77 clean, functional rooms, all with private bathroom and shower. The ever-busy lounge/bar has an attached kitchen for communal cooking (the hostel organises Shabbat dinners for up to 40 people here). Tours can be arranged and the well-organised, helpful staff put on special events such as Hebrew and Arabic language lessons and open mic music nights. The entrance is on HaNevi'im St near the bus stop.

JERUSALEM, SHABBAT & YOU

An hour before sunset you can hear the drone of a horn bellowing over the Jerusalem hills. This signifies the start of Shabbat and with it comes a pronounced spiritual vibe that permeates the streets. All across the city you can see Jerusalemites dressed in their Shabbat best, drawn to the Western Wall or carrying backpacks full of food as they head to the home of a friend or relative for the customary Friday-night dinner.

Put on the best clothes you've got and follow the crowds down to the Western Wall to marvel at the singing, dancing and prayer that ignite this magical place. Alternatively, visit a synagogue for Friday-night services.

Try to make arrangements beforehand to join a Shabbat dinner with a local family. If you can't manage that you'll need to scope out a restaurant ahead of time as kosher places (except hotel restaurants) will be closed. Later in the evening, much to the chagrin of Orthodox Jews, the downtown bars will be open for business.

While the city centre and the Jewish Quarter of the Old City are closed on Saturday, this is just another day for Jerusalem's Arab population, and most of the sights are open in the rest of the Old City, Mt Zion, the Mount of Olives and East Jerusalem.

You can join a free three-hour **walking tour** (☎02-531 4600), sponsored by the municipality, departing from **Safra Sq** (Map p76); the route changes weekly. To find the schedule online go to www.jerusalem.muni.il and click on the link that says 'FREE Weekend Walking Tours'. Another option is to join EcoBike (p104) for its Saturday ride around town.

While the Egged buses and the light rail system (but not taxis) are taking a sabbatical, the Arab bus network and service taxis are still operating from the Damascus Gate area, and Shabbat is as good a time as any to visit a West Bank city such as Jericho or Bethlehem. Ein Gedi, Masada and the Dead Sea are other popular day-trip options – all-inclusive tours are offered by tour operators and hostels in Jerusalem (see p285). These depart at either 3am or 7am Saturday morning, depending on availability.

JERUSALEM B&BS

Jerusalem is filled with atmospheric B&Bs. Some are individual apartments while others are attached to the home of a local family. Check the website www.bnb.co.il for details.

TOP CHOICE Harmony
BOUTIQUE HOTEL **$$$**

(Map p76; ✆02-621 9999; www.atlas.co.il; 6 Yoel Solomon St; s/d US$219/238; ❄@⛱; ☐Jaffa Center) This popular new place has a great location on Yoel Solomon St. It has 50 rooms built in a stylish atmosphere with a welcoming lobby and a lounge with billiards, chess, books and a computer. A happy hour between 5pm and 7pm includes free snacks and drinks in the lounge. This place gets exceptional reader feedback.

Jerusalem Hostel & Guest House
HOSTEL **$**

(Map p76; ✆02-623 6102; www.jerusalem-hostel. com; 44 Jaffa Rd, Zion Sq; dm 80NIS, s 200-260NIS, d 250-280NIS, tr 360NIS; ❄@⛱; ☐Jaffa Center) With a prime location overlooking Zion Sq, this is a fine option for budget travellers looking for a place in the city centre. Rooms are clean and there is a healthy traveller vibe here, with lots of info tacked on the walls and plenty of other guests willing to lend free advice. In summer it offers basic accommodation on the roof for 80NIS; you get a mattress and linen, and share facilities. In addition to the main backpacker wing the hostel has a new section in a separate building with private rooms (single/double 310/340NIS) and a quieter atmosphere – a good option for those early to bed.

Zion Hotel
HOTEL **$$**

(Map p76; ✆02-623 2367; 10 Dorot Rishonim St; s/d/tr 310/360/490NIS; ☐Jaffa Center) Run by a chatterbox granny, this place has an ideal location over the bars and restaurants of the city centre. Inside, the double rooms are simply furnished and have basic bathrooms. While everything functions reasonably well, it's a little neglected.

City Center Suites
APARTMENT **$$**

(Map p76; ✆02-650 9494; www.citycentervacation. com; 2 HaHistadrut St; r 400-500NIS; ⛱; ☐Jaffa Center) These well-appointed, fully equipped studio and two-room apartments are perfect for travellers who want a central location and a little room to spread out. Amenities include TV, free use of the washer and dryer,

and a kitchenette with fridge. Discounts are available if you book for at least three nights.

Hotel Palatin
HOTEL **$$**

(Map p76; ✆02-623 1141; www.palatinhotel.com; 4 Agrippas St; s 350-450NIS; d 380-480NIS; ⛱; ☐Jaffa Center) Located near the hub of Jerusalem's shopping and cafe district, the 29-room Hotel Palatin has smallish but comfortable rooms. There are two types of rooms: cheaper non-renovated rooms with old furniture, and newly renovated rooms that cost 100NIS extra and have a fresh, boutique-hotel feel. A substantial Israeli breakfast is included.

Lev Jerusalem
HOTEL **$$$**

(Map p76; ✆02-530 0333; www.levyerushalayim. com; 18 King George V St; s/d US$135/168; ❄@⛱; ☐Jaffa Center) Located in the heart of the city centre, this all-suite hotel is a good family option, with spacious rooms that have kitchenettes and a bedroom/living room set-up. Rooms are large and comfortable, just a little bland. For an added fee you can get a room with a kitchenette.

Hotel Kaplan
HOTEL **$**

(Map p76; ✆02-625 4591; natrade@netvision.net. il; 1 HaHavatzelet St; s/d/tr US$45/65/75; ❄@; ☐Jaffa Center) Rooms are basic and the furniture is a little ragged, but you do get a private bathroom and views of Jaffa Rd. No breakfast, but guests can cook in the small kitchen.

MAMILLA & YEMIN MOSHE

Beit Shmuel Hostel
GUESTHOUSE **$$**

(Map p76; ✆02-620 3456; www.beitshmuel.com; 6 Shamm'a St; s/d/tr/q US$100/120/150/180; @⛱) Part hotel, part community centre and part social hall, Beit Shmuel can get pretty busy. Standard rooms are no-frills affairs that feel like college dorms (ask for one facing the Old City). Rooms in the newer wing have bland, Swedish-style layouts, with plain white decor and hard surfaces (these cost about US$40 more than the standard rooms).

TOP CHOICE St Andrew's Guesthouse
GUESTHOUSE **$$**

(Map p66; ✆02-673 1711; www.scotsguesthouse. com; 1 David Remez St; s/d/tr US$120/160/180; @⛱) Set on a hill overlooking the Old City, with leafy gardens and an imposing stone facade, St Andrew's feels like a bit of Scotland transported to the Middle East. Rooms are plainly furnished with desk, phone, heater and fan. Some rooms include balconies and those that don't still have access to a large sun deck. It's a great place for atmosphere and views, but does require a little extra walking to reach sights and facilities.

YMCA Three Arches Hotel HOTEL $$$
(Map p66; ☑02-569 2692; www.ymca3arch.co.il; 26 King David St; s/d/tr US$150/164/242; @🛜🏊) As a centre for learning, sport and culture, this YMCA is an important local landmark and a great place to spend a few nights. The hotel's 56 rooms are simply furnished; you're paying more for the atmosphere than the quality of rooms. The Y has an excellent restaurant and use of gym and pool is included in the price.

King David Hotel HOTEL $$$
(Map p66; ☑02-620 8888; www.danhotels.com; 23 King David St; r US$470-600, ste $960; 🌐@🛜🏊) The King David is a blast from the past, a 1930s-era hotel that is both grandiose and charming. The extraordinary lobby is furnished with velvet couches, gold drapery and marble-top tables. Meals are taken in a grand ballroom down the hall, or out on the back patio, which overlooks a lawn and pool. The rooms are modern but some of the standard rooms are awfully small. Ask for a deluxe room, which is generally larger and has better views.

Eldan Hotel BUSINESS HOTEL $$$
(Map p76; ☑02-567 9777; www.eldan.co.il; 24 King David St; s/d US$120/190; 🌐@) Although lacking in style, this spotless business hotel offers convenience and comfort in the midst of a posh neighbourhood. All 75 rooms have a TV, safe and minibar.

OLD CITY

TOP CHOICE Austrian Hospice GUESTHOUSE $$
(Map p46; ☑02-626 5800; www.austrianhospice.com; 37 Via Dolorosa; dm/s/d/tr €22/62/104/135; @🛜) This castle-like guesthouse was opened in 1863 as a pilgrims' hospice and later became the Austrian consulate in Palestine. There is a garden in front and the cloistered exterior is a popular hang-out for guests chatting over rounds of beer. Rooms are simply furnished but comfortable. The hospice is on the corner of Al-Wad and Via Dolorosa. Ring the bell to get inside (reception is open 7am to 11pm). Non-guests can still come to enjoy the atmosphere and the wonderful cafe (open 10am to 10pm), which serves Austrian cakes, soups, pastries and sausages.

TOP CHOICE Lutheran Guest House GUESTHOUSE $$
(Map p46; ☑02-626 6888; www.luth-guesthouse-jerusalem.com; St Mark's Rd; s/d/tr €53/82/105; ❄) Beyond the heavy steel door of this guesthouse is a bright, welcoming lobby where cheerful staff will check you in. Upstairs is a gorgeous reading room where you can pull a book off the shelf and enjoy views of the Church of the Holy Sepulchre. The modern double rooms are simply furnished but comfortable. A breakfast buffet includes meats, cheeses, fruits, vegetables and yoghurt. To get here from Jaffa Gate walk down David St, then take the first right up a narrow staircase; the guesthouse is about 100m down on the left.

TOP CHOICE Christ Church Guesthouse GUESTHOUSE $$
(Map p46; ☑02-627 7727; www.cmj-israel.org; Omar Ibn al-Khattab Sq, Jaffa Gate; s/d/ste 295/465/525NIS; 🛜) This wonderfully maintained Christian hospice gets high marks for its period atmosphere, prime location and welcoming staff. Simply furnished rooms have stone floors and domed ceilings. There is no TV in the rooms but you can relax in the cafe or watch a DVD in the lounge. There is a mix of foreign and local staff comprising Christians, Jews and Muslims, all hired as a way to promote cultural unity.

East New Imperial Hotel HISTORIC HOTEL $$
(Map p46; ☑02-628 2261; www.newimperial.com; Jaffa Gate; s/d/tr US$70/100/120; @🛜) The distinguished owner of this hotel, Abu El Walid Dajani, provides a warm welcome and can spin some nice stories about the hotel's history. Notably, Kaiser Willhelm II was but one of its many VIP guests. Recent improvements have given the rooms a clean, fresh look, but without ruining the historic atmosphere of the place. On the downside, the plumbing is a bit erratic, so you cannot count on hot water all the time. It's located just inside Jaffa Gate, and is thus accessible by taxi.

Hashimi Hotel GUESTHOUSE $$
(Map p46; ☑02-628 4410, 052 257 2121; www.alhashimihotel-jerusalem.com; 73 Souq Khan al-Zeit St; dm/s/d/tr/q 125/290/360/450/520NIS; 🌐@🛜) Rising out of the chaos that is the Muslim Quarter, the Hashimi is famed for its spectacular views from the rooftop cafe. Inside, there's a mishmash of family suites, dorms, doubles and lounge areas, all painted in bright colours and surrounding a sunlit atrium. Rooms are clean, if unspectacular,

and there's a nice cafe (breakfast is included in the price). Strict Islamic house rules prevent unmarried couples from sleeping in the same room.

Ecce Homo Convent Guesthouse
GUESTHOUSE $

(Map p46; ☎02-627 7292; www.eccehomo convent.org; 41 Via Dolorosa; dm/s/d/tr/q US$26/52/84/108/144) If staying a few nights in a convent sounds intriguing, book yourself a room at this 150-year-old pilgrim guesthouse, with its front door on the Via Dolorosa. The stone walls and dim corridors evoke the feeling of a time gone by and the ever-present brown-robed Franciscan monks only add to the effect. Rooms are simply furnished and there is a comfortable reading lounge. Door are locked at 11pm.

Casa Nova Pilgrims' Hospice
GUESTHOUSE $

(Map p46; ☎02-628 2791, 627 1441; 10 Casa Nova St; s/d US$60/80) Among the many Christian hospices in the Old City, this one is most geared towards the Christian pilgrim. It's a bare-bones place with simple furnishings, big doors, cavernous hallways and an 11pm curfew. To get there from Jaffa Gate, take the second left onto Greek Catholic Patriarchate Rd and follow it until it becomes Casa Nova St; the hospice is on the left as you enter a narrow alley. Reception is open from 7am to 11pm.

Gloria
HOTEL $$

(Map p46; ☎02-628 2431; www.gloria-hotel.com; 33 Latin Patriarchate Rd; s/d/tr US$120/150/180; ❄☎) A hidden gem of a hotel in the Old City, the 100-room Gloria offers clean and well-maintained single, double and triple rooms. Only a couple have decent views, and you'll probably need to book in advance to secure one of these. It's about 100m uphill from Jaffa Gate.

Jaffa Gate Hostel
GUESTHOUSE $

(Map p46; ☎02-627 6402, 054 495 7145; jaffa_gate_hostel@yahoo.com; Jaffa Gate; dm/s/d/tr 85/220/250/300NIS; ❄@☎) This reasonably priced hostel has a handy location close to Jaffa Gate and good views from the roof. The rooms are a bit small and rough around the edges but most do have a private bathroom. Note that Muslim house rules prevent alcohol on the premises. Breakfast is not included.

Hebron Youth Hostel
GUESTHOUSE $

(Map p46; ☎02-628 1101; ashraftabasco@hotmail.com; 8 Aqabat al-Takiya St; dm 60-70NIS, d 250NIS, without bathroom 200NIS; @☎) One of the longest-running hostels in the Old City, Hebron is a character-filled place with stone walls, arches and Arab decor. The narrow staircase leads up to a small reception area, a billiards room and cosy guest quarters. The rooftop additions are not as nice but do offer a little more sunlight. On the downside, the share dorm bathroom gets busy in mornings.

Petra Hostel
HISTORIC HOTEL $

(Map p46; ☎02-628 6618; www.newpetrahostel.com; Omar Ibn al-Khattab Sq; dm 70NIS, s/d 180/250NIS, without bathroom 160/200NIS; @) Built in the 1820s, this is the oldest hotel in Jerusalem. Some of its illustrious former patrons include Mark Twain and Herman Melville. The antiquated charm is still in effect and it retains a busy traveller vibe with bright and somewhat musty rooms; in summer you can even sleep on a mattress on the roof (50NIS). The helpful night manager, Gabriel, can answer most of your questions. The price includes breakfast.

Citadel Youth Hostel
HOSTEL $

(Map p46; ☎02-628 5253, 054 580 5085; citadel-hostel@mail.com; 20 St Mark's Rd; dm 65NIS, d 180-210NIS, without bathroom 140-180NIS; @☎) This quirky hostel has ancient walls of stone, a twisting staircase and great views from the roof. Scattered across the building are a hodgepodge of oddly configured rooms; lower rooms are part of the original home while the upper levels are modern add-ons that are poorly insulated and get hot in summer and cold in winter. It has nice decor and a friendly owner but the kitchen facilities and showers are a tad basic.

El Malak
GUESTHOUSE $

(Map p46; ☎02-628 5382, 054 567 8044; 18 El-Malak & 27 Ararat; dm/s/d 75/100/200NIS) One of the more unusual places in the Old City, El Malak is basically a series of rooms set inside a renovated basement under the home of an Armenian granny named Claire Ghawi. While a bit dark, it manages to stay quite cool when other guesthouses are baking. Otherwise, there are two better rooms available in the house upstairs (these range between 250NIS and 350NIS). The place is difficult to find; from the steps at the end of the Cardo, walk south on Habad Rd, turn right after 30m, go up the alley and then turn left. Look for No 18.

Golden Gate Inn
GUESTHOUSE $

(Map p46; ☑02-628 4317; www.goldengate4.com; 10 Souq Khan al-Zeit St; dm/s/d 50/150/200NIS; ✳🛜) The Golden Gate has the makings of a great guesthouse. Set inside an atmospheric old home, it has clean and spacious rooms with attached bathroom, cable TV and aircon. The communal kitchen is spacious and well maintained. Despite these niceties, the vibe here is muted and lacks the communal travellers' air of places nearby. Breakfast is included. Alcohol is forbidden on the premises.

EAST JERUSALEM

Jerusalem Hotel
HOTEL $$$

(Map p66; ☑02-628 3282; www.jrshotel.com; 4 Antara Ben Shadad St; s/d US$140/190; ✳@🛜; 🚇Shivtei Israel) With stone-clad walls, antique furnishings and personal service, this place is a combination heritage and boutique hotel. The thick walls keep the building cool even in the height of summer (but there is also air-con). An excellent buffet breakfast is served in the vine-trestled garden patio. You can also book a tour from here to the West Bank with Abu Hassan Alternative Tours (see p440).

St George's Cathedral Pilgrim Guesthouse
GUESTHOUSE $$

(Map p66; ☑02-628 3302; stgeorges.gh@j-diocese.org; 20 Nablus Rd; s/d/tr US$110/150/190; ✳@🛜) Located on the property of a 110-year-old Anglican church, this tranquil guesthouse has simply furnished guest quarters with twin beds, cable TV and wi-fi. The lovely garden of rose bushes and citrus trees sets the place apart. The distinguished reading room is a nice place to relax with a thick novel.

American Colony Hotel
HISTORIC HOTEL $$$

(Map p66; ☑02-627 9777; www.amcol.co.il; 23 Nablus Rd, Sheikh Jarah; s/d/ste from US$235/315/900; ✳@🛜🏊) This historic hotel, built in 1902, was a popular lodging for wealthy westerners in the early 20th century and still today is a destination of choice for many VIPs and international correspondents. Winston Churchill, Jimmy Carter, Mikhail Gorbachev and John Steinbeck are but a few of the illustrious names that have checked in here. Pricier junior suites have domed ceilings, arched windows, cushions, alcoves and wrought-iron-frame beds. Rooms in the newer block lack traditional decor, but are no less luxurious.

Capitol Hotel
HOTEL $

(Map p66; ☑02-628 2561; www.jrscapitol.com; 17 Salah ad-Din St; s/d US$75/99; 🛜; 🚇Damascus Gate) This small hotel was built when Jordan controlled East Jerusalem. Not much has changed since then and the hotel still retains an air of the 1960s. Slight renovations have kept it in decent shape and there is a comfortable lounge where you can use the free wi-fi.

Rivoli Hotel
HOTEL $

(Map p66; ☑02-628 4871; 3 Salah ad-Din St; s/d US$70/85; 🛜; 🚇Damascus Gate) A no-frills place just a few steps away from Herod's Gate. Rooms are simple if a little bland but there is a small lounge and the price includes breakfast.

National Hotel
HOTEL $$$

(Map p66; ☑02-627 8880; Al Zahra St; www.nationalhotel-jerusalem.com; s/d/tr US$145/185/225; 🛜) The recently renovated National Hotel is an island of tranquillity in bustling East Jerusalem. Rooms are small but clean and well appointed, and the top-floor restaurant has a nice view of the Mount of Olives.

Palm Hostel
HOSTEL $

(Map p46; ☑02-627 3189; newpalmhostel@yahoo.com; 6 HaNevi'im St; dm 50-70NIS, s/d 170/200NIS; @🛜; 🚇Damascus Gate) A fixture in East Jerusalem, the Palm is reached through a narrow fruit and vegetable stand in a busy marketplace near Damascus Gate. At the top of the stairs turn left for the hostel, a shabby collection of dorms and basic private rooms. Although cleanliness is not a major priority and the staff can be a little glum, the low prices still draw a few hardy backpackers.

New Palm Hotel
HOTEL $

(Map p46; ☑02-627 3189; newpalmhostel@yahoo.com; 4 HaNevi'im St; s/d 200/230NIS; @🛜; 🚇Damascus Gate) This hotel is attached to the Palm Hostel. A separate staircase reaches it and the wing is a bit nicer than the hostel but the staff are essentially the same. Rooms in the back don't have windows but are quieter than those overlooking the street.

GERMAN COLONY & REHAVIA

Little House in Rehavia
HOTEL $$

(Map p66; ☑02-563 3344; www.jerusalem-hotel.co.il; 20 Ibn Ezra St, Rehavia; s/tw/q US$119/149/229; @🛜) Quaint set-up in Rehavia with singles, doubles and some family units. A glatt kosher dining hall (ie where food is prepared under very strict kosher rules) serves simple meals and there is a relaxing garden in the back. It's located in one of Jerusalem's prettiest neighbourhoods, a 1.5km walk to the Old City.

Little House in the Colony
HOTEL $$

(Map p40; ☑02-566 2424; www.jerusalem-hotel. co.il; 4a Lloyd George St, German Colony; s/tw/q US$119/149/229; @�﹫☞) The newest branch of the Little House chain is a renovated Templer building located on a quiet lane in the German Colony. Rooms are charmingly antiquated but comfortable.

SOUTH JERUSALEM

A Little House in Bakah
HOTEL $$

(Map p40; ☑02-673 7944; www.jerusalem-hotel. co.il; 80 Hebron Rd & 1 Yehuda Rd; s US$79-99, d US$99-129; ✳@☞) A friendly boutique hotel with spacious rooms, an excellent cafe, high ceilings and a retro spin back to the 1920s, this is a good pick in the mid-price range. The main drawback is the city-fringe location. It's located 2.5km south of the Old City; take bus 7 from Central Bus Station.

RAMAT ESHKOL

House 57 B&B
B&B $$

(Map p40; ☑02-581 9944; www.house57.co.il; 57 Sinai Desert Rd; s/d 250/350NIS; ✳☞; ⬚Ammunition Hill) House 57 offers a variety of rooms accessed through a private entrance that includes a small kitchen area (used by all guests). There is one studio with its own kitchenette. A filling breakfast is included.

ROMEMA & MEKOR BARUCH

TOP CHOICE Allenby 2 B&B
B&B $

(Map p40; ☑052 257 8493, 02-534 4113; www.bnb. co.il/allenby; Allenby Sq 2, Romema; s US$25-55, d US$35-70; ✳@☞; ⬚Central Station) One of the most popular B&Bs in Jerusalem, Allenby 2 combines a warm atmosphere with excellent service. With nine rooms, it's one of the larger B&Bs in the city. There are a couple of studios that have separate entrances (plus studios in nearby buildings). Enthusiastic owner Danny Flax is a mine of information and a keen cyclist who can offer great advice on offbeat trips. There is no reception, so advanced bookings are essential.

✖ Eating

Jerusalem is home to an array of restaurants in all categories – from your basic hole-in-the-wall shwarma joints all the way up to sushi bars and haute cuisine taken in the leafy gardens of a historic home. Befitting Jerusalem's religious nature, a significant percentage of restaurants are kosher; when almost everything in Jerusalem's Jewish neighbourhoods shuts down for Shabbat, head to East Jerusalem or out of town to Abu Ghosh (p105).

OLD CITY

Most Old City restaurants stick to kebabs, shwarma and other Middle Eastern fare. But what they lack in diversity is often made up for by quaint atmosphere and great views. Finding a meal after dark can be challenging as the Old City shuts down when the crowds go home.

Abu Shukri
HUMMUS $

(Map p46; 63 Al-Wad Rd; hummus platters 20NIS; ☺8am-4pm; ☑) Our constant search to find the best hummus in Jerusalem landed us at this place, as recommended by many a local. The standard platter includes a bowl of fresh hummus, sliced tomato, pita bread and a couple of felafel balls. Add 10NIS for a cup of freshly squeezed OJ. It's located near the Fifth Station of the Cross.

Christ Church
Guesthouse Cafe
EUROPEAN $$

(Map p46; ☑02-627 7727; Omar Ibn al-Khattab Sq, Jaffa Gate; breakfasts/lunches/dinners 40/50/65NIS; ☺breakfast 7.30-8.30am, lunch noon-2pm, dinner 6.30-8pm) The cafe inside the Christ Church Guesthouse offers an English-style buffet lunch with a main dish and various sides for 50NIS. Breakfast and dinner are also available but for dinner you'll need to make a reservation by 1pm that day.

Pizzeria Basti
PIZZERIA, KEBAB $

(Map p46; 70 Via Dolorosa; dishes 25-35NIS; ☺7.30am-9pm) The display of ancient photos on the walls adds significant charm to this Old City eatery. The menu offers a choice of 20 kinds of pizza, plus steaks, kebabs and burgers. It's located opposite the Third Station of the Cross.

Keshet HaHurva
ISRAELI $

(Map p46; 2 Tiferet Israel St; meals 30-60NIS; ☺8am-midnight) Owners Nissim and Veronica can be found each morning serving up hot breakfasts to hungry tourists and locals alike. Pastas and salads appear later in the day. It's Mehadrin kosher.

Armenian Tavern
ARMENIAN $$

(Map p46; 79 Armenian Orthodox Patriarchate Rd; meat dishes 55-70NIS; ☺11am-10.30pm Tue-Sun) Walk down the steps into this basement restaurant and relax in an old-world atmosphere, with Armenian pottery hung on stone walls, and a gently splashing fountain. The strongly flavoured meat dishes are excellent, including *khaghoghi derev,* a spiced minced-meat mixture bundled in vine leaves. Other specialities include Armenian pizza and *soojuk* (spicy sausages).

TOP CHOICE Amigo Emil   MIDDLE EASTERN $$
(Map p46; Aqabat al-Khanqah St; dishes from 55NIS; 10.30am-9.30pm Mon-Sat) A 400-year-old building and former workshop, Amigo Emil has been chiselled down to the bare stone foundations and decorated with pictures of old Jerusalem. There are some nice appetisers, including a mezze of hummus, *muttabal* (purée of aubergine mixed with tahina, yoghurt and olive oil) and Arabic salad. The house speciality is *musakhan,* a chicken casserole spiced with sumac stuffed into Bedouin bread (40NIS). The friendly owner Costandi may sit down with you for a drink or two and can explain the history of the building.

Holy Bagel   BAKERY $
(Map p46; Tiferet Israel St; 8am-9pm Sun-Thu, to 2pm Fri) Sells fresh bagels and cream cheese for around 17NIS.

Quarter Café   EUROPEAN, ISRAELI $
(Map p46; Tiferet Israel St; snacks 22-25NIS, meals 40-60NIS; 9am-6pm Sun-Thu, to 3pm Fri) Coffee, cakes and light meals, with views of the Western Wall.

CITY CENTRE
The City Centre is jam-packed with restaurants and cafes. There are a half-dozen places on Yoel Solomon St that cater to the tourist market, but scattered around the area are lots of places frequented by locals.

Pinati   HUMMUS $
(Map p76; 13 King George V St; hummus 17NIS; 9am-7pm Sun-Thu, to 4pm Fri; Jaffa Center) The old photos of loyal customers that cover the walls are a testament to the longevity of this popular hummus joint. Even today it's something of a magnet for customers young and old, and almost impossible to get inside during the lunchtime rush.

HaShomen Shwarma   KEBAB $$
(Map p76; 2 Shlomzion HaMalka; pitas/plates 30/45NIS; 11am-2am, closed Shabbat; City Hall) At most shwarma joints the meat on the spit looks like it has been spinning since last Tuesday. Not so at HaShomen Shwarma,

where the constant stream of customers ensures that the meat gets used quickly and is therefore very fresh. It's reputedly the best shwarma in West Jerusalem.

TOP CHOICE Hamarakia   SOUP $
(Map p76; 4 Koresh St; soups 28NIS; 6pm-1am, closed Shabbat; City Hall) Old drums, typewriters, records and a beat-up piano line the walls of this purposely ramshackle restaurant. The name of the place (Soup Pot) pretty much sums up the menu – you have your choice of about five different soups. *Shakshuka* (eggs poached in a skillet of tangy stewed tomatoes; 25NIS) is also available. It's a very social atmosphere, with just a few tables, so you may end up eating with new friends. Live music (jazz jams and acoustic grunge) is sometimes played here.

Kadosh   CAFE $$
(Map p76; 6 Shlomzion HaMalka St; 7am-12.30am, closed Shabbat; City Hall) There are a lot of great cafes in Jerusalem and Kadosh is one of the best. The ambience is 'French bistro' and the waitstaff and regular customers are all very engaging. Meals are made from scratch, so you can be sure that the sandwiches, lasagne, quiche and baked goods are tasty and fresh. Ask about the specials; the salmon bruschetta (35NIS), stuffed mushrooms (39NIS) and ravioli aubergine with goat's cheese (49NIS) are all excellent.

T'mol Shilshom   CAFE $$
(Map p76; 5 Yoel Solomon St; salads 45-56NIS, mains 56-83NIS; 8.30am-midnight Sun-Thu; Jaffa Center) This funky cafe has books galore lining the shelves, creating a hip vibe that attracts a literary-minded crowd. Soups and sandwiches dominate the menu; it's pricier than its competitors, but there's free wi-fi and a great atmosphere (concerts and book readings are sometimes held here). It's a little tricky to find: go through the arch on Yoel Solomon St, turn left and walk to the end of the courtyard, then look for the black-and-white sign, next to Lion's Den bar.

Village Green   VEGETARIAN $
(Map p76; 33 Jaffa Rd; 9am-10pm Sun-Thu, to 3pm Fri; Jaffa Center) A vegetarian's delight, this kosher restaurant offers home-made dishes produced from the freshest ingredients. It's cafeteria style, with various offerings of vegetable soups, quiches, veggie burgers, pizza, blintzes, savoury pies and lasagne, all served with home-baked bread.

Meals are sold by weight (8.50NIS per 100g). If you still have room for dessert, try one of the freshly baked pies.

TOP CHOICE Focaccio Bar
MEDITERRANEAN $$

(Map p76; 4 Rabbi Akiva St; dishes 30-50NIS; ⊙10am-1am; ⊉; ▣Jaffa Center) The combination of good food at reasonable prices has made this one of the most popular restaurants in town. The speciality of course is focaccia, baked fresh in the *taboun* (clay oven) and eaten on a sunny patio. A variety of toppings is available and portions are large and reasonably priced; try the Bulgarian cheese and olive spread (35NIS). The menu also includes a nice 350g entrecôte steak, deep-fried calamari and fried mushroom dishes.

Barud
MIDDLE EASTERN $$$

(Map p76; 31 Jaffa Rd, Feingold Courtyard; dishes 65-85NIS; ⊙12.30pm-1am Mon-Sat; ▣Jaffa Center) Come to Barud for cosy atmosphere and dazzling (non-kosher) Sephardic cooking. Meatballs with eggplant is a speciality, as well as *pastalikos* (a pastry with pine nuts, minced meat and onion; 59NIS). Owner Daniella Lerer is also very proud of her fruit-based moonshine, which is surprisingly good. Live jazz is played once or twice a week. To find it, first locate Gent Bar at the bottom of Rivlin St. The steps left of Gent Bar lead into Feingold Courtyard and Barud is at the end of the alley.

Little Jerusalem
MEDITERRANEAN $$

(Map p76; ⊉02-624 4186; Ticho House Museum, 9 HaRav Kook St; meals 52-80NIS; ⊙10am-11pm Sun-Thu, 9am-3pm Fri, 7pm-midnight Sat; ▣Jaffa Center) The peaceful patio overlooking a grove of pine trees is the perfect place to enjoy a quiet dinner or late Israeli breakfast. The kitchen mixes Western and Mediterranean menus, with a nice selection of seafood and meat dishes. On Tuesday at 8.30pm the restaurant hosts a wine, cheese and dinner evening (95NIS) with live jazz music. Live classical music is played on Wednesday at 8pm (for an additional fee), while Jewish traditional music is played on Saturday evening. Advance bookings are essential.

Zuni
EUROPEAN $$$

(Map p76; 15 Yoel Solomon St; ⊙24hr; ☎; ▣Jaffa Center) Zuni offers a range of excellent-quality Western dishes, such as baked eggplant with garlic aoli (42NIS) and seafood risotto (89NIS), in a dimly lit, sophisticated setting. Everything is made from scratch,

including the delicious breads and desserts. It's open all night and tends to mop up some of the late-night revellers from nearby Rivlin St, keeping the place hopping until 4am.

Darna
MOROCCAN $$$

(Map p76; ⊉02-624 5406; 3 Horkanos St; dishes 90-130NIS; ⊙noon-3.30pm & 6-10pm Sun-Thu, 6-10pm Sat; ▣Jaffa Center) Darna offers traditional Moroccan ambience and delectable treats, such as *pastilla fassia* (43NIS), a flaky pastry stuffed with Cornish hen, almonds and cinnamon. If you've come with a friend, try as a main course the *mechoui* (310NIS), a marinated lamb shoulder roasted in an oven. Reservations are required.

Mahane Yehuda
FRENCH, ITALIAN $$$

(Map p66; ⊉02-533 3442; 10 Beit Ya'akov St; starters 47-62NIS, dishes 98-166NIS; ⊙12.30-4pm & 6.30-11pm; ▣Mahane Yehuda) A trio of local chefs – Uri, Yossi and Asaf – have collaborated on this popular new place, a kitchen that creates food from ingredients solely from nearby Mahane Yehuda Market. Even the restaurant is designed to look like a market stall. Influences come from Bedouin traditional meals, Arab cuisine and grandma's recipes. The menu changes daily and through the seasons but you can count on some type of fish, steak or pasta dish. Reservations are essential.

KING DAVID STREET

The high-rent district around King David St is home to a handful of posh restaurants; some of the nicest are strung along the flashy new Mamilla Mall.

Arca
WESTERN $$

(Map p66; 26 King David St; mains 55-110NIS; ⊙7am-10.30pm) Located in the historic YMCA, this non-kosher kitchen serves up excellent steaks, fish, pastas and salads. Don't miss the eggplant with tahina starter. Early risers can indulge in a 48NIS breakfast buffet. Meals are served in a leafy courtyard amid fountains and flowers, a great spot to relax in the heat of summer. It's a good place to dine during Shabbat when most other restaurants are closed.

GERMAN COLONY

Jerusalem's 'restaurant row' is in the German Colony along Emek Refa'im St. It's fun to just head down here and stroll the street until something catches your fancy.

Caffit
EUROPEAN $$

(Map p40; 35 Emek Refa'im St; mains 48-88NIS; ⊙7am-1am) This fun, lively place has a varied Western-style menu that includes salads,

MAHANE YEHUDA MARKET

Boasting an abundance of fresh fruit, vegetables and fish, teas, coffees and a huge variety of other foodstuffs, the Mahane Yehuda Market (Map p66; ☺8am-sunset Sun-Thu, 9am-2pm Fri; ⓜMahane Yehuda) is crammed with excellent cafes and food stalls. The restaurant scene is surprisingly hip and diverse, with places specialising in Georgian, Italian and Indian cuisine, fish and chips, organic food, and classic Israeli meals. The following are open normal market hours unless otherwise noted, and all appear on the Inner Jerusalem map, p66:

Azura (Souq HaYorekrom; ☺8am-4pm, closed Shabbat; ✐) The competition for great hummus restaurants is very stiff in Jerusalem, but this one manages to hold its own. Diehard fans say it's the best hummus Jerusalem has to offer. Try a bowlful yourself. It also serves a nice kuba (dough stuffed with ground beef and pine nuts) soup (30NIS to 35NIS).

Hagas Ehad (Rehov Eliyahu Ya'acov Banai 11; ✐) Izikial, the owner of this tiny cafe, slings the healthiest food in Jerusalem. Options include tofu burgers (28NIS), stuffed vegetables (35NIS), a sizzling hot shakshuka (a rich egg-and-tomato breakfast dish served in a frying pan) and some delicious herbal teas and juices (try the unique hibiscus juice). The cafe also serves special meals for coeliac sufferers (people who cannot eat wheat).

Itchikidana (Rehov HaEshkol 4; ✐) This colourful Indian vegetarian cafe specialises in thali (set meal with dhal, rice and vegetables; 39NIS to 64NIS) and masala dosa (22NIS). It opens at 9am for chai (tea) but food is not served till noon. The folks who run the place are very friendly and will help explain the finer points of the menu if you're not familiar with Indian food.

Mizrahi Coffeeshop (Rehov Hashet) Serves the best coffee in the market, but also offers sandwiches (22NIS to 38NIS), pastries (16NIS to 38NIS) and tasty breakfasts (38NIS to 54NIS). Grab a seat on the mini porch and watch the crowds sweep past.

Pasta Basta (Ha Tut; ☺noon-midnight, closed Shabbat) Pasta lovers should make a beeline to this nook, where you choose the type of pasta, the sauce and the other ingredients then let the chef do his magic. If that sounds complicated, there are staff recommendations such as 'Revitals Dish', which includes beetroot, goat's cheese and pesto. A dish costs around 40NIS.

See p77 for more details about the market.

---

burgers and pastas, plus some tasty specialities, such as salmon with halloumi and mushrooms. If you're flying solo, grab a seat at the bar and hang out with the friendly bartender, Tilan.

EAST JERUSALEM

The restaurant scene in East Jerusalem is slowly maturing, with a handful of upmarket restaurants in the Sheikh Jarah neighbourhood and an improving crop of midrange places on and around Salah ad-Din St. In addition to the following places, you can eat light meals at the Educational Bookshop cafe (see p98).

Zad   CAFE $
(Map p66; 9 Salah ad-Din St; ☺7.30am-10pm; ☎) Zad means 'food and drink' in old Arabic and this place has plenty of it, with sandwiches, pastas, salads and Syrian shwarma, set to an Arabic soundtrack. Owner Mohammed welcomes all comers but it's especially popular with East Jerusalem–based expats and Palestinian students.

Jerusalem Hotel   MEDITERRANEAN $$
(Map p66; ☎02-628 3282; 4 Antara ben Shadad St; mains 50-100NIS; ☺7.30-10.30am & noon-11pm; ✐; ⓜShivtei Israel) The Jerusalem Hotel has an attached restaurant in an open courtyard, pleasantly set under grape trestles and cooled by fans (the courtyard is covered in winter). The grill menu features yalla yalla chicken (65NIS), a house special of chicken stuffed with mushrooms and vegetables. Some good vegetarian options are available too. Arabic music and dancing is organised here on Monday and Fridays (call to make a reservation).

Askadinya   ITALIAN $$
(Map p40; 11 Shim'on Ha Tsadik St; pastas 55-65NIS; ☺noon-midnight; ⓜShim'on Ha-Tsadik) Injecting a cosmopolitan air into East Jerusalem, Askadinya is an upmarket Italian restaurant located inside an elegant 120-year-old home.

The house speciality is the Askadinya platter (63NIS), an appetiser for two with seafood, roca cheese and vegetables. You can wash your meal down with a wine from South Africa, Spain or Italy.

Philadelphia
MEDITERRANEAN $$
(Map p66; Al Zahra St; meals 40-90NIS; ⊘noon-midnight) This old standby has spent decades doling out some of Jerusalem's best Mediterranean cuisine. Friendly owner Zoher can put out a phenomenal spread of salads (mezze) followed by tasty mains such as grilled sea bass, *musakhan* chicken or roast lamb leg. In the summer months, grab a seat in the lovely garden.

 Drinking

Jerusalem's city centre is well set up for pub crawling, with a number of bars clustered in close proximity, especially on Rivlin and Yoel Solomon Sts. They tend to be crowded with American teenagers on study breaks, but there are a few local places among them. East Jerusalem bars tend to be inside hotels, while the Old City is almost as dry as the Negev.

OLD CITY

Cafe Rimon Himo
CAFE
(Map p46; Damascus Gate; ⊘7am-10pm; Damascus Gate) We spent some quality time on the porch of Cafe Rimon, soaking in the frenetic atmosphere around Damascus Gate. It's one of the best places in town for people-watching. You can get fresh juice (€3.50), nargileh (€5), or try the famed Taybeh beer (€4.50) from the West Bank.

Versavee
BAR
(Map p46; Jaffa Gate; ⊘9am-midnight;) The four brothers who run this place – Gabi, Jamil, Joe and Jack – went all out to make it a classy little setting. It has a long drinks menu, and meals, including pastas, shwarma and grilled chicken, are also available (the kitchen is open from 9am to 9pm). Versavee is located in the same courtyard as the East New Imperial Hotel.

CITY CENTRE

Bolinat
BAR, CAFE
(Map p76; 6 Dorot Rishonim St; ⊘24hr; Jaffa Center) In the late afternoon the patio in front of Bolinat is jam-packed with young Jerusalemites sunning themselves and downing pints of beer. Basic meals such as sandwiches and salads are also available. Since it's always open, it gets busy on Shabbat and late on weekend nights.

HaCasetta
BAR
(Map p76; Horkanos St; ⊘8pm-5am Sat-Thu, 2pm-6am Fri; Jaffa Center) If you're walking down Horkanos and spot a metal door covered with old cassette tapes you've arrived at HaCasetta (The Cassette), a pint-sized bar with just two tiny rooms but a lot of character. The hipster crowd drinks into the night, serenaded by '80s punk or sometimes live local grunge bands. At the back of the bar is a narrow passage that leads to another bar called HaTaklit (The Record).

TOP CHOICE Uganda
BAR
(Map p76; 4 Aristobulos St; ⊘noon-3am; Jaffa Center) Uganda is an alternative bar named after the alternative territory offered by the British to Herzl. Taybeh (made in Palestine) beer is served and East Jerusalem hummus is usually available. Comfy chairs, a relaxed vibe and good music go down well with locals and visitors alike. DJs and parties are often organised, so ask about upcoming events.

Sira
BAR
(Map p76; 1 Ben Shatakh St; ⊘5pm-late; City Hall) This tiny bar is smoky, dark, crowded and loud; the beer flows pretty fast and well into the night. If you are over the age of 23 you might feel old here. It has a mini dance floor and a semi-private room in the back. It also goes by its old name, D1, if you are asking around for it.

Fifth of May
BAR
(Map p66; 56 Ha'etz Ha'em; ⊘almost 24hr; Mahane Yehuda) Barely big enough to squeeze in 12 Apostles, this micro bar is a convivial place run by a group of young friends who have designated 5 May as their own personal holiday. The sign above the entrance confusingly says: 'Danesi Coffee'.

TOP CHOICE Casino de Paris
BAR
(Map p66; Georgian Market; ⊘noon-3am; Mahane Yehuda) During the British Mandate this building used to be an Officers Club for British soldiers. Known as the Casino de Paris, it housed a bar downstairs and a brothel on the 2nd floor. It reopened in 2011 as a tapas bar, serving up tasty Spanish snacks and 25 types of Israeli boutique beers such as Negev, Shapira and Malka. Come around midnight and see the place in full swing.

GAY & LESBIAN JERUSALEM

Owing to Jerusalem's religious nature, the city's gay, lesbian, bisexual and transgender scene is much more subdued compared with Tel Aviv's. Public displays of affection, especially between same-sex couples, will be unwelcome in Jewish Orthodox areas and East Jerusalem. One place to flaunt it is Mikveh (Map p76; 02-623 3366; mikvehbar@gmail.com; 4 Shoshan St; 9pm-late Mon-Sat; City Hall), a small bar on a quiet alley south of Safra Sq. It has drag shows on Mondays from 11pm and parties on Thursday and Friday. It's a good mixture of people with various religions, ethnicities and backgrounds coming together. According to one patron we met, 'it's not necessarily a sane place'. During the day, T'mol Shilshom (p93) is a gay-friendly meeting place. Zuni (p94) is a gay hang-out and is open 24 hours.

In late June, the Jerusalem Pride march clogs downtown streets.

If you want more information on the GLBT community, visit the Jerusalem Open House (Map p76; 02-625 0502; www.joh.org.il; 2 HaSoreg St; City Hall). New visitors are invited to come Sunday to Thursday from 10am to 5pm to learn about community events. It organises a variety of events, many of which are English-speaker friendly.

Rivlin Street BAR
(Map p76; Rivlin St; Jaffa Center) Half a dozen bars are located on this tiny alley, each offering drink specials to lure in the punters. The crowd here is mostly Israeli soldiers and American high-school and college kids.

EAST JERUSALEM

Cellar Bar WINE BAR
(Map p66; 23 Nablus Rd; noon-1am) Tucked inside the historic American Colony Hotel (p91), this vaulted basement bar is an intimate nook dating back to the late 19th century. It's popular with journalists taking a break from covering one war or another.

☆ Entertainment

Nightclubs

Yellow Submarine CLUB
(Map p40; 02-570 4646; www.yellowsubmarine.org.il; 13 HaRechavim St, Talpiot; 11pm-late Thu & Fri) Usually a venue for live music, the Yellow Submarine also hosts DJs and dance parties. It's best to call first to see what's on, as you may need to order tickets in advance.

Wallenberg CLUB
(Map p66; 6 Raul Wallenberg St; 9pm-late Thu-Sat; Ha-Davidka) This centrally located nightclub, popular with the 30s crowd, plays techno, Israeli and house music. Admission is free Thursday and Saturday but costs 20NIS on Fridays.

Dancing

International Cultural Centre for Youth CULTURAL CENTRE
(ICCY; Map p40; 02-566 4144; 12 Emek Refa'im St) The ICCY building hosts folk dancing on Tuesdays (25NIS) from 10.30am to 12.30pm. It's not a performance; it's locals coming to dance, and you can join in (an instructor is available at the beginning of the session). Thursday night is an all-ages dance party. Participants form conga lines, the hora and any other possible dance formation. There are dances most nights of the week but you might want to call ahead to find out what's on.

Cinemas

Cinematheque CINEMA
(Map p66; 02-606 0800; www.jer-cin.org.il; 11 Hebron Rd) The Jerusalem Cinematheque, a bastion and favoured hang-out of secular, left-leaning Jerusalemites, features quality foreign films and classics. This is also the home of the respected Jerusalem Film Festival (www.jff.org.il).

Lev Smadar Theatre CINEMA
(Map p40; 02-566 0954; www.lev.co.il; 4 Lloyd George St; admission 38NIS) A quaint neighbourhood art-house movie theatre showing independent and foreign films. It has an attached cafe and you can bring food into the theatre.

Theatre & Classical Music

Jerusalem has a rich tradition of theatre and music. You can check what's on in the Friday edition of the *Jerusalem Post* or the monthly tourist bulletin published by the Ministry of Tourism. You can book advance tickets through Bimot (Map p76; 02-622 2333; 8 Shamai St; Jaffa Center).

Classical performances are sometimes held at the YMCA (Map p66; 02-569 2692; 26 King David St) and at Beit Shmuel (Map p76;

02-620 3427; www.beitshmuel.com; 6 Shamm'a St), part of the Hebrew Union College (Saturday morning).

Jerusalem Centre for the Performing Arts
CONCERT VENUE, THEATRE

(Map p66; 02-560 5755; www.jerusalem-theatre. co.il; 20 David Marcus St) The Jerusalem Centre for the Performing Arts includes a concert hall, theatres and a cafe. Its Sherover Theatre (admission 200NIS) has simultaneous English-language translation headsets available for certain performances. Comedy, music, children's theatre and dance performances are held here; it's also home to the Jerusalem Symphony Orchestra. Free concerts are held on Monday at 5pm from October to June.

Al-Masrah Centre for Palestine Culture & Art and Al-Kasaba Theatre
THEATRE

(Map p66; 02-628 0957; www.pnt-pal.org; Al-Masrah Centre, Abu Obeida St) Off Salah ad-Din St in East Jerusalem, these venues stage plays, musicals, operettas and folk dancing in Arabic, often with an English synopsis.

Khan Theatre
THEATRE

(Map p66; 02-671 8281; www.khan.co.il; 2 David Remez St; adult/student 150/120NIS) Sometimes stages English-language performances.

Binyanei Ha'Umah Conference Centre
CONCERT VENUE

(Map p40; 02-622 2481; www.iccjer.co.il; Central Station) The Jerusalem venue of the Israel Philharmonic Orchestra (www.ipo.co.il).

Live Music

Dublin
LIVE MUSIC

(Map p76; 4 Shamai St; 5pm-3am; Jaffa Center) This Irish pub has live English and Hebrew music on Monday and Irish on Tuesday. It's best to call ahead to reserve a table on these nights.

Zappa in the Lab
LIVE MUSIC

(Map p40; 02-622 2333; www.zappa-club.co.il, in Hebrew; 28 Hebron Rd; admission 80-160NIS) Crafted out of a disused railway warehouse, this innovative live-music venue stages local talent for a sophisticated crowd. Doors open at 8.30pm and shows start at 10pm. Dinner is available from the kosher kitchen before the show. It's open most days of the week but you need to check the website or call for upcoming events.

Sport

Beitar Jerusalem
FOOTBALL

(www.bjerusalem.co.il, in Hebrew) The 20,000-seat Teddy Kollek Stadium (Map p40) is home to Beitar Jerusalem and Ha'poel Jerusalem football clubs. Beitar is known for having the most dedicated (and nationalistic) fans in the country, prone to burning things down when a match does not go their way (or even when it does). Ha'poel matches are rather more laid-back. You can buy tickets on the day of the game. The stadium is close to the Jerusalem Mall; take bus 6 from Central Bus Station.

Shopping

Jerusalem is a great place for niche shoppers looking for quality Judaica, Middle Eastern and Jewish art, ceramics, jewellery and antiques. West Jerusalem is generally the best place to shop for these items, while the Old City shops sell low-end souvenirs by the overpriced boatload. Food products are best bought in Mahane Yehuda Market (p77 and p77), while standard items like electronics, camping gear, books and clothing can be purchased in the city centre or shopping malls spread around town.

Agfa Photo Shwartz
PHOTOGRAPHY

(Map p76; 11 Mordechai Ben Hillel St, Allenby; Jaffa Center) Sells photo equipment; as a free service it will charge the battery for your digital camera if you've lost the charger.

Lametayel
OUTDOOR EQUIPMENT

(Map p76; 5 Yoel Solomon St; Jaffa Center) Sells quality camping supplies, outdoor gear, maps and travel guidebooks.

Bookshops

TOP CHOICE Eucational Bookshop
BOOKS

(Map p66; www.educationalbookshop.com; 19 Salah ad-Din St; 8am-8pm) East Jerusalem's best bookshop has an impressive range of books and DVDs pertaining to the Arab–Israeli conflict, as well as a good selection of magazines and Palestinian music CDs. It also boasts a reading balcony, cafe and function room. Journalists, aid workers, activists and other politically aware people make this place a regular stop on their East Jerusalem wanderings.

Moriah Bookshop
BOOKS

(Map p46; 40 Misgav Ladach St) Moriah has the largest selection of books in the city on Judaism; it's also endowed with souvenirs, CDs and books on current events of the Jewish state.

Sefer VeSefel
BOOKS

(Map p76; 2 Ya'vets St; ⒢Jaffa Center) This Jerusalem institution houses floor-to-ceiling new and secondhand fiction and non-fiction titles. It's upstairs in an alley linking Jaffa Rd with Mordechai Ben Hillel St.

Steimatzky
BOOKS

(Map p76; Mamilla Mall) Chain bookshop with several branches around town. The largest is the new three-storey outlet in Mamilla Mall, which includes a cafe.

T'mol Shilshom
BOOKS

(Map p76; www.tmol-shilshom.co.il; 5 Yoel Solomon St; ⒢Jaffa Center) Bohemian cafe and secondhand-book shop; this place often hosts poetry readings or lectures by authors and journalists. Check its website for upcoming events.

Crafts & Souvenirs

A crafts fair is held every Friday on Schatz St, near the Bezalel Art School. It's a good place to pick up high-quality artwork directly from the artists who produce them.

David St in the Old City is a great place to shop for T-shirts, nargileh, chess boards, handicrafts and all manner of tat. Bargain hard for everything.

In the city centre, there are plenty of souvenir shops on Ben Yehuda St.

Studio Varouj
SOUVENIRS

(Map p46; 36 Aqabat al-Khanqah St; ⊘8.30am-5pm Mon-Sat) This photo shop sells black-and-white prints of old Jerusalem for 50NIS. The multilingual Armenian gent who runs the place is quite a character.

Arman Darian
CERAMICS

(Map p76; www.darianart.com; 12 Shlomzion Ha-Malka St; ⒢City Hall) Perhaps the most well-known ceramicist in Israel, Arman has installed his Armenian ceramic designs in many public buildings, including one floor of the Empire State Building.

Armenian Ceramics
CERAMICS

(Map p66; www.armenianceramics.com; 14 Nablus Rd) This studio and shop has been in business since 1922. Tiles are hand-painted and you can have items designed to your taste. It's opposite the US consulate in East Jerusalem.

Altogether 8
CERAMICS

(Map p76; 11 Yoel Solomon St; ⒢Jaffa Center) A co-operative of ceramicists who come from all over Israel.

Kippa Man
KIPPOT

(Map p76; 5 Ben Yehuda St; ⒢Jaffa Center) If you are looking for a good kippa (yarmulke; skullcap) or want one specially made, try Avi the Kippa Man.

Judaica, Fine Art & Antiques

Jerusalem is the best place in the country to shop for Judaica (Tsfat also has a fine selection). In the Old City, browse the shops in the Cardo, which has some reliable outlets. There is an Arts & Crafts Lane (Hutzot Hayotzer in Hebrew) just outside and downhill from Jaffa Gate. The products here are mainly Judaica and of excellent quality. It's open daily except Shabbat. Some of the best Judaica and fine-art shops are right along Yoel Solomon St in the city centre. If you are a serious shopper, avoid the Judaica shops on David St in the Old City as the products here do not necessarily conform to Jewish law (despite what the salespeople will tell you) and are generally of inferior quality.

Aweidah Gallery
ANTIQUES

(Map p46; www.aweidah-gallery.com; 4 Via Dolorosa) Looks like a museum but is actually a gallery that sells artefacts dating back hundreds, if not thousands, of years. You get a certificate that allows you to take it out of the country. (While artefacts certainly *look* genuine only a real expert could spot a fake, so buy with caution before handing over your credit card.) There are also several other antique galleries down this street.

Arta Gallery
JUDAICA

(Map p76; 22 King David St) Specialises in contemporary Judaica, with an eye-pleasing array of *mezuzahs,* menorahs and *birkat bait* (house blessings).

Daniel Azoulay
JUDAICA

(Map p76; 5 Yoel Solomon St; ⒢Jaffa Center) Creates hand-painted porcelain and beautiful *ketubas* (Jewish wedding contracts).

Greenvurcel
JUDAICA

(Map p76; www.greenvurcel.co.il; 27 Yoel Solomon St; ⒢Jaffa Center) Deals with beautiful silver Judaica, including candlesticks, Seder (Passover) plates and menorahs.

Shopping Malls & Streets

Mamilla Mall
MALL

(Map p46) This gorgeous outdoor shopping street has international shopping outlets, several excellent cafes, a beautiful Steimatzky bookshop, art galleries and shops

HANAN ISACHAR/LONELY PLANET IMAGES ©

1. Monastery of the Dormition (p66)
The Church & Monastery of the Dormition is
where the Virgin Mary is believed to have died.

2. Dome of the Rock (p47)
The enduring symbol of the city and one of the
most photographed buildings on earth.

3. Church of the Holy Sepulchre (p55)
At the holiest Christian site in the Old City,
pilgrims reflect on the last hours of Jesus.

4. Western Wall (p49)
A mere retaining wall when it was built, now the
most important Jewish shrine.

specialising in modern Judaica. It's located between Jaffa Gate and the David Citadel Hotel, so you can use it as a thoroughfare to transit between the Old City and West Jerusalem.

Ben Yehuda Street STREET
(Map p76) Jerusalem's tourist-friendly pedestrian boulevard, crammed with souvenir shops and cafes.

❶ Information

Emergency
Fire (☏102)

First aid (☏101)

Police (☏100, 539 1360; 107 Jaffa Rd; ⊗8am-4pm Sun-Thu) This police station has a lost-property office.

Tourist police (☏100) Old City (Armenian Orthodox Patriarchate Rd); Russian Compound (Central Police Station) The Old City station is near the Citadel (Tower of David). These are the best police stations for tourists to use.

Internet Access
If you're hanging around Central Bus Station, internet terminals (10NIS per 30 minutes) are located on the 4th floor. Most hotel and cafes have free wi-fi.

Internet Café (31 Jaffa Rd; per hr 14NIS; ⊗9am-5.30am; 🚇Jaffa Center) Located near Zion Sq.

Mike's Centre (☏02-628 2486; www.mikes centre.com; 9th Station, 172 Souq Khan al-Zeit St; per hr 10NIS; ⊗9am-11pm) In the Old City, this all-in-one tourist stop has internet, international phones and laundry services. Mike also runs tours to the Dead Sea, the Galilee, Jordan and Egypt.

Laundry
In the Old City, try Mike's Centre, which washes 2.5kg of laundry for 30NIS.

Laundry Place (12 Shamai St; ⊗9am-8pm Sun-Thu, 8.30am-3pm Fri; 🚇Jaffa Center) Washing and drying costs 52NIS.

Rotem Laundry (202 Jaffa Rd; ⊗6am-midnight; 🚇Ha-Turim) Self-service facility. Wash and dry is 50NIS and a bag of detergent 3NIS.

Media
The *Jerusalem Post* (www.jpost.com) is an excellent source of local news and events listings. On Friday, the *Post* includes an extensive 'What's On' weekend supplement.

Medical Services
Hadassah Medical Centre (☏02-677 7111; www.hadassah.org.il) Above Ein Kerem.

Orthodox Society (☏02-627 1958; Greek Orthodox Patriarchate Rd; ⊗9am-2pm Mon-Fri) In the Old City's Christian Quarter, the Orthodox Society operates a low-cost medical and dental clinic that welcomes travellers.

Superpharm (☏02-636 6000; 9 Mamilla Mall; ⊗8.30am-11pm) Pharmacy located between Jaffa Gate and the city centre.

Terem (☏1-599-520-520; www.terem.com; 80 Yirmiyahu St, Romema; ⊗24hr; 🚇Central Station) Efficient walk-in medical clinic that handles everything from minor ailments to emergencies. A consultation with a doctor costs 400NIS. It's a five-minute walk from Central Bus Station.

Money
The best deals for changing money are at the private, commission-free exchange offices in the New City (around Zion Sq), East Jerusalem (Salah ad-Din St) and in the Old City (Jaffa Gate). Some moneychangers, especially around Ben Yehuda St, will also change travellers cheques. Note that they close early on Friday and remain closed all day Saturday.

Banks with ATMs, such as Mizrahi and Leumi, are found on every block in the city centre.

American Express (☏02-623 8000; 18 Shlomzion HaMalka St; 🚇City Hall) Cashes travellers cheques (3% commission) but cannot replace lost cheques.

Post
DHL (☏1-700-707 345; www.dhl.com)

FedEx (☏1-700-700 339; www.fedex.com)

Post office Main post office (Map p76; ☏02-624 4745; main section, 23 Jaffa Rd; ⊗7am-7pm Sun-Thu, to noon Fri); city centre (Map p66; cnr Bezalel & Shilo Sts); East Jerusalem (Map p66; cnr Salah ad-Din & Sultan Suleyman Sts); Old City (Map p46; Omar ibn al-Khattab Sq) The main post office in the city centre is the place to pick up poste restante; letters can be addressed to: Poste Restante, CPO, Jaffa 23, Jerusalem.

Tourist Information
Al-Quds Centre for Jerusalem Studies (Map p46; ☏02-628 7517; www.jerusalem-studies. alquds.edu; Souq al-Qattanin) Located deep in the Arab Quarter of the Old City, this micro-university has a gallery, sponsors cultural events and runs tours around the city. It welcomes tourists so stop by and see if any events are planned during your stay.

Christian Information Centre (Map p46; ☏02-627 2692; www.cicts.org; Omar ibn al-Khattab Sq; ⊗8.30am-5.30pm Mon-Fri, to 12.30pm Sat) Opposite the entrance to the Citadel; provides information on the city's Christian sites. Also gives out handy maps that detail walking tours around the Old City.

Jaffa Gate Tourist Office (Map p46; ☏02-627 1422; www.tourism.gov.il; Jaffa Gate; ⊗8.30am-5pm Sat-Thu, to 1.30pm Fri) This is the main tourist office for Jerusalem. You can pick up free maps and reams of literature on sites around town. Don't confuse it with the 'Jerusalem Tourist Information Center', a private tourist company next door which sports an 'information icon' above the door, often fooling visitors into thinking it's an official tourist office.

Travel Agencies

ISSTA HaNevi'im St (☑02-621 3600; 31 HaNevi'im St); Herbert Samuel St (☑02-621 1188; 4 Herbert Samuel St; ⬛Jaffa Center) Israel's student travel agency. Organises inexpensive flight tickets. The second branch is near Zion Sq.

Websites

www.gojerusalem.com Useful website with everything from car rental and bus schedules to hotel reviews and festival dates.

www.jerusalem.com Excellent overview of the city, its attractions and events. Virtual tours of important sites and even an application that allows you to leave prayers at holy places!

www.jerusalem.muni.il Run by the municipality, this website has thorough and up-to-date pages on events and festivals. It also has a list of art exhibits and cultural institutes.

ℹ️ Getting There & Away

Air

Jerusalem's Atarot Airport has been closed since 2001.

The **El Al office** (☑03-977 1111; 4th fl, Gan Technology Malha) is located in a building opposite the Malha Mall.

Bus

From **Central Bus Station** (Map p40; www.bus.co.il; Jaffa Rd; ⬛Central Station), you can get to all major cities and towns in Israel. Buses travel to Tel Aviv (bus 405, 20NIS, one hour, every 15 minutes), Haifa (bus 940 or 960, 40NIS, two hours, every 15 minutes), Tiberias (bus 962, 40NIS, 2½ hours, hourly), Be'er Sheva (bus 446 or 470, 32.50NIS, 90 minutes, twice hourly), and Eilat (bus 444, 70NIS, 4½ hours, four daily).

For details on making a day trip to the Dead Sea, see p288.

To get to parts of East Jerusalem such as Abu Dis (7NIS) and Mount of Olives (5NIS), use the **Arab bus station** (Map p66) in East Jerusalem, located on Sultan Suleyman St.

If you are headed into northern areas of the West Bank such as Ramallah (7NIS), use the **old Arab bus station** (Map p66) on Nablus Rd, opposite the Garden Tomb.

For Bethlehem, take bus 21 (7NIS) from the **Damascus Gate bus station** (Map p46). For Hebron, change in Bethlehem. For Nablus, change in Ramallah.

For Jericho, take a bus to Abu Dis from the Arab bus station and change for a *servees* (shared taxi) to Jericho. Alternatively, take a bus to Ramallah and change there.

Car

Most Jerusalem-based rental-car agencies forbid you to take their cars into the Palestinian Territories (Rte 1 to the Dead Sea is generally not a problem); check the agency's policy.

Avis (☑02-624 9001; 22 King David St)

Budget (☑02-624 8991; 23 King David St)

Eldan (☑02-625-2151; 24 King David St)

Green Peace (☑02-585 9756; www.greenpeace.co.il; Shu'fat, East Jerusalem) Will deliver the car to you wherever you are in Jerusalem; does permit cars to be taken into the Palestinian Territories.

Hertz (☑02-623 1351; 19 King David St)

Sherut (Shared Taxi)

Sheruts (shared taxis, *servees* in Arabic) are much faster than buses, depart more frequently and cost only a few shekels more; on Shabbat they're the only public transport to destinations in Israel. Service taxis for Tel Aviv (23NIS per person on weekdays, 33NIS on Friday and Saturday) depart from the corner of HaRav Kook St and Jaffa Rd, near Zion Sq (Map p76).

Train

Jerusalem's **railway station** (Jerusalem Malcha; ☑02-577 4000; www.rail.co.il) is located in the southwest of the city, near the Jerusalem Mall. Trains to Tel Aviv's Savidor Center/Merkaz station (adult/child 22/17.50NIS, 1¾ hours) depart every hour or two between 5.43am and 9.43pm Sunday to Thursday. The last train on Friday is at 3pm. A combo train/bus ticket saves a few shekels. The station is reached on bus 6 from Central Bus Station. Ring ☑*5770 (note the star) for more details.

ℹ️ Getting Around

To/From the Airport

Ben-Gurion airport is 51km west of Jerusalem, just off Rte 1 to Tel Aviv. Bus 947 departs from Central Bus Station for Ben-Gurion airport (23NIS, 40 minutes, twice hourly) from 6.30am to 8.30pm Sunday to Thursday, 6am to 4.30pm Friday, and 8.20pm to 10pm Saturday. Get off at the Airport City Commercial Complex, a transit point, from where you have to switch to bus 5 (6.40NIS) to reach Terminal 3. From the airport, take bus 5 (6.40NIS) to the transit point, where you catch bus 947 to Jerusalem.

Alternatively, **Nesher service taxis** (☑02-625 7227, 1 599 500 205) pick up booked passengers from their accommodation 24 hours a day (60NIS). The service also travels from the airport to Jerusalem – don't believe unscrupulous taxi drivers who tell you it's no longer running. Book a seat 24 hours in advance (or 48 hours in advance if you are departing on a weekend).

Bicycle

The hills of Jerusalem make biking tough going, but if you want a bike try **Nitzan Bike Shop** (02-623 5976; 137 Jaffa Rd; Mahane Yehuda), which rents out bikes for a pricey 100NIS per day.

If you are serious about cycling and want a good quality, well-maintained bike, contact **EcoBike** (077-450 1650; www.ecobike.com), which rents out top-of-the line hybrids for US$25 a day or US$125 per week. The bikes are available to pick up at Abraham Hostel (p87).

Bus

Jerusalem is laced with a good network of city bus routes (6.40NIS per ride). If you need to transfer to another line the ticket is good for 90 minutes. A pass for 10 rides costs 55NIS, while a one-month pass is 216NIS. For the latest route information, call *2800.

Bus 1 Central Bus Station via Malchei Yisra'el St, Mea She'arim St, HaNevi'im St, Damascus Gate, Western Wall

Bus 2 Central Bus Station, Bar Ilan St, Shivtei Y'Israel St, Damascus Gate, Western Wall

Bus 4a Mt Scopus, Yehezkel St, King George V St, Keren HaYesod, Emek Refa'im, Jerusalem Malha Train Station

Bus 7/7a Central Bus Station, King George V St, Ramat Rachel

Bus 9/9a Central Bus Station, Knesset, Givat Ram (Hebrew University)

Bus 17/17a Ein Kerem, Israel Museum, Aza Rd, King George V St, Central Bus Station

Bus 18/18a German Colony, Malha Railway Station, Mt Herzl, Central Bus Station, Jaffa Rd

Bus 20 Yad Vashem & Mt Herzl, Central Bus Station, Jaffa Rd, Jaffa Gate

Bus 23 Mt Herzl, Central Bus Station, Saladin St, Mt Scopus

Bus 24a Israel Museum, Givat Ram (Hebrew University), Malha Mall

Bus 26/26a Mt Scopus, Central Bus Station, Yad Vashem & Mt Herzl, Biblical Zoo

Bus 38a Jewish Quarter, Western Wall, King George V St, HaNevi'im St, Shlomzion HaMalka St, Jaffa Gate

Light Rail

Inaugurated in 2011, **Jerusalem Light Rail** (JLR; *2800; www.citypass.co.il, in Hebrew) consists of a single line that runs from Mt Herzl in the west of the city to Cheyl HaAvir in Pisgat Ze'ev, in the city's far northeast. It has 23 stops along a 13.9km route and passes a handful of landmarks including Central Bus Station, Mahane Yehuda Market, Zion Sq and Damascus Gate. It runs from 5.30am to midnight daily except on Shabbat. Tickets cost 6.40NIS. A JLR

Around Jerusalem

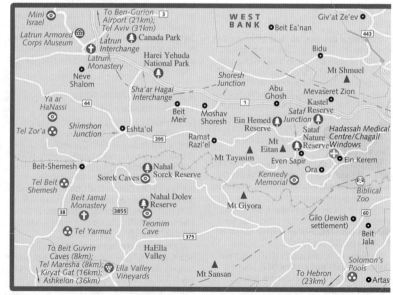

ticket is good on any Egged bus for 90 minutes from the time of purchase.

Taxi

Plan on spending 20NIS to 25NIS for trips anywhere within the central area of town. Always ask to use the meter. To order a taxi, call **Hapalmach taxi** (📞02-679 2333).

AROUND JERUSALEM

There are a number of sites near Jerusalem that you can visit on a half-day or full-day trip. With a day off, most travellers head for the Dead Sea or Bethlehem, but there are also lesser-known sights worth your time. The highlights include the Sorek stalagmite cave and the bell caves at Beit Guvrin.

Abu Ghosh ابو غوش אבו גוש
📞 02 / POP 5500

Shaded by trees and lorded over by a grand old church, the picturesque Arab town of Abu Ghosh, 13km west of Jerusalem off the main highway to Tel Aviv, makes for a pleasant half-day trip from Jerusalem. It's known in the Bible as Kiryat Ya'arim (Town of Forests), where the Ark of the Covenant was said to have been located for 20 years

until David moved it to Jerusalem (I Chronicles 13:5-8). Nowadays it's equally known as a contender for the hummus capital of Israel.

There are two interesting churches here. The first, **Our Lady of the Ark of the Covenant** (Notre Dame de l'Arche; admission free; ⊙8-11.30am & 3.30-6pm), was built in 1924 and is a local landmark, with its statue of Mary carrying the baby Jesus. It belongs to the French Sisters of St Joseph of the Apparition, and they believe that it stands on the site of Abinadab's house, where the Ark was kept (I Samuel 7:1). The church is built on the same site as a larger Byzantine church, and you can see its mosaic floor inside and out. The church is located at the top of the hill overlooking the village and facing Jerusalem.

The **Crusader Church and Monastery** (admission free; ⊙8.30-11am & 2.30-5.30pm) is one of the country's best-preserved and most attractive Crusader remains. It was built about 1142 and destroyed in 1187. It is believed that the monastery stands on the remains of a Roman castle. A stone from it is displayed in the church and bears an inscription of the 10th Legion, a renowned Roman unit stationed in Jerusalem in the 1st century. The complex is next door to the mosque, so look for the minaret in the valley.

✗ Eating

Abu Ghosh is known throughout Israel as having some of the best hummus restaurants in the country. Locals make day trips here just to try the hummus and it can get very crowded on weekends and holidays.

Abu Shukhri HUMMUS $
(hummus bowls 10NIS; ⊙8am-9pm; 🖋) This is one of the oldest places in town, a family-run business that prides itself on quality food (it has won several awards). Hummus, felafel and drink costs 30NIS. To get here, walk past the mosque and take the first left. It's the third building on the right.

Caravan MIDDLE EASTERN $$
(meals 50-90NIS; ⊙10am-10pm) A step up from the hummus joints, Caravan offers a choice of tasty meats or kebabs stuffed in vine leaves. Desserts are also good and you can't beat the views across the valley towards Jerusalem. It's located halfway between the two churches.

Sorek Caves

مغارة سوريق   מערות שורק

One of Israel's most spectacular natural wonders, the Sorek Caves (☎02-991 1117; adult/child 25/13NIS; ⏱8am-5pm Sat-Thu, to 3pm Fri) were only found by accident in 1967 when a local quarry crew blasted away some rock to reveal this underground cavern. Also known as Avshalom (Absalom's) caves, they contain stalactites, stalagmites and rock pillars in every form and shape. Tours are held throughout the day (except Friday). Because of the fragile nature of the caves, photography is only allowed one day per week (Friday). The caves are located some 20km west of Jerusalem along the road from Ein Kerem. There is no bus to the caves.

HaElla Valley

وادي السنط   עמק האלה

HaElla Valley's place in history was secured long ago as the battlefield where it is believed David slew the Philistine giant Goliath. Past the Rte 38 and Rte 383 junction (HaElla Junction) the highway crosses a dry stream, possibly where David picked up the 'five smooth stones' as described in I Samuel 17. Then out in the field, according to the Bible, 'David left the line of battle and ran to meet the Philistine. Putting his hand in his bag, he took out a stone and slung it and struck the Philistine on the forehead.'

There is really nothing to mark the spot, but you can stop your car, wander into the field and let your imagination conjure up the battle.

Beit Guvrin & Tel Maresha

تل مريشا   بيت جبران
בית גוברין ותל מראשה

The Beit Guvrin Caves & Tel Maresha (☎08-681 1020; adult/student 27/14NIS; ⏱8am-4pm) is an archaeological site, natural wonder and feat of human ingenuity all rolled into one. Around this national park are some 4000 hollows and chambers that create a Swiss-cheese landscape. Some of the caves are natural, the result of water eroding the soft limestone surface. Others, however, are thought to be the result of quarrying by the Phoenicians, builders of Ashkelon's port between the 7th and 4th centuries BCE. During the Byzantine period the caves were used by monks and hermits and some of the walls are still discernibly marked with crosses. St John the Baptist is said to have been one of the pious graffitists.

Tel Maresha's excavations have uncovered remains from a 3rd-century synagogue and various Greek and Crusader artefacts, all of which are now on display at Jerusalem's Rockefeller Museum. Some Byzantine mosaics also found here are now in the Israel Museum in Jerusalem. Among the finds that

---

THE GOAT'S CHEESE GURU

Long and windy is the road to the goat farm on Mt Eitan. Fortunately, every mile or so we spotted a tiny sign emblazoned with a goat, indicating we had not yet lost our way.

At last we arrived at the farm and with a shout of 'Shai!' our host poked his head from the tiny abode on the hillside. Shai Seltzer, Israel's most famous maker of goat's cheese, emerged wearing a white frock and thick white beard, an arrangement that made him appear like Charlton Heston when he played Moses in The Ten Commandments.

Shai shooed us into a little cave that housed a bar. A young woman behind the bar explained the menu and we decided on the deluxe cheese platter: a 110NIS gourmet bonanza that included four types of goat's cheese, bread, yoghurt and sun-dried tomatoes. It seemed like a lot to pay for a plate of cheese, but when the meal came out we were convinced it was worth every shekel.

We tried to interview Shai about his cheesemaking techniques but he disappeared back into his home to resume his work. Only his goats, crowded into a pen near the cave, seemed to take any interest in us.

You may have better luck. Visit Shai's cave bar or, better yet, take one of his cheese-making workshops. The bar is most active on Friday and Saturday (on other days it's best to call ahead to make sure Shai will be around).

The road to Shai's home begins at the car park at the entrance to Sataf Nature Reserve. You can get more info at www.goat-cheese.co.il or by calling ☎054-440 3762.

DIG THIS TEL

For amateur archaeologists, Israel is simply one big playground. What aspiring Indiana Joneses find most intriguing are the numerous 'tels' scattered about the country. A tel is a mound of earth created when successive civilisations built on top of an earlier city: sometime after one city was destroyed, another people came along, built on the ruins and lived there until someone else came and put them out of business. The process repeats itself a few times until – voila! – the ruins form a low hill.

Because of its soft earth and wealth of history, Tel Maresha is chock-full of bits and pieces from history. Every summer, amateur archaeologists descend on the place and carefully scoop up the earth, often uncovering shards of pottery, coins, oil lamps and other items discarded by our civilisation's ancient ancestors.

Tourists are often brought along as a source of cheap labour. If this sounds appealing, contact Archaeological Seminars (☎02-586-2011; www.archesem.com), which charges around US$25 per person for a three-hour dig and seminar.

haven't been transported elsewhere are the ruins of the 12th-century Crusader Church of St Anna (or Sandhanna).

The easiest caves to explore are those west of Tel Maresha – you can see tracks leading from the road. Some of the caves have elaborate staircases with banisters leading down below ground level. The rows of hundreds of small niches suggest that they were created for raising small domesticated doves to be used in the worship of Aphrodite by the Sidonian colony between the 3rd and 1st centuries BCE.

The park is fairly large and the sights are spread out. The only practical way to visit is by private car. To get there, take Rte 38 south until it hits Rte 35. Take Rte 35 west for 2km until you see the entrance to the park. If you don't have a car, take the 8am bus from Kiryat Gat to Kibbutz Bet Guvrin and ask the driver to let you out at the national park. A bus returns to Kiryat Gat from here at 5pm.

Latrun اللطرون לטרון

Halfway between Tel Aviv and Jerusalem, the area of Latrun is a worth a stop for its Trappist monastery and a couple of offbeat sites.

The Latrun Monastery, founded in 1890 by the French Trappist Order of monks, is now widely renowned for its wine, and its lovely location, architecture and gardens. The winemaking started around 1899. The

monks reclaimed and cultivated the land and planted olive groves, grain and vegetables as well as vineyards. In WWI the monks were expelled by the Turks as enemy aliens, but they were able to return, and in 1926 the present monastery was constructed. There is an on-site shop (☺8.30-11.30am & 2.30-4.30pm Mon-Sat) selling the wine, spirits and olive oil produced here.

Aficionados of military history will want to visit the Latrun Armored Corps Museum (adult/child 30/20NIS; ☺8.30am-4.30pm Sat-Thu, to 12.30pm Fri), one of the largest tank museums in the world. The main building was originally built by the British in the 1930s as a fortress to safeguard the road to Jerusalem. It now holds a museum of history from ancient times to modern, and a theatre screening an introductory video. Surrounding the museum are 160 types of armoured vehicles, including Israel's mighty Merkava tank.

If you want to feel like Gulliver in the land of Lilliput, visit Mini Israel (☎1-700-559 569; www.minisrael.co.il; adult/2-5yr/5-18yr 79/24/59NIS, audio guide 15NIS), which shrinks 350 of Israel's famed attractions down to scale-model size. A 3D movie that covers Israel's major sights is available for an additional 10NIS. The attraction is a good break if you have kids. Check the website for opening hours, as they shift during the year.

Tel Aviv تل ابيب תל אביב

♪03 / POP 404,400

Best Places to Eat

» Ali Caravan (p150)
» Raphael (p133)
» Adora (p133)
» Benedict (p136)
» Goocha (p133)

Best Places to Stay

» Center Hotel (p129)
» Beit Immanuel (p150)
» Hotel Montefiore (p130)
» Old Jaffa Hostel (p150)
» Art Plus Hotel (p128)

Why Go?

While the State of Israel hits the headlines, the state of Tel Aviv sits back with a cappuccino. Lovingly nicknamed the Bubble, Tel Aviv (TLV) is a city of outdoor cafes, leafy boulevards and long sandy beaches. A favourite with Europeans looking for some year-round sun, Tel Aviv is fast becoming a bubble of boutiques, bistros and brasseries. All over the city old Bauhaus buildings are getting a well-needed facelift and skyscrapers aspire to build a kind of Manhattan in the Middle East. Yet the real Tel Aviv is found in humble hummus joints, wine bars hidden down alleyways, fresh-fruit-shake stalls, quiet memorial gardens and chaotic marketplaces.

With its plethora of pick-up bars, nightclubs and all-night parties, Tel Aviv has been labelled 'Sin City'. But appearances can be deceptive. The diversity of its people, music, museums, art galleries and graffiti all testify that Tel Aviv has soul.

When to Go
Tel Aviv

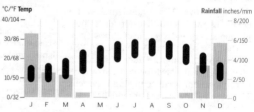

Mar–May Tel Aviv blooms in springtime with bright bougainvillea flowers.

Jun–mid-Sep Party at the Gay Pride Parade (June) and cool down at the beach or pool.

Dec–early Mar Cold with sporadic rain; the city is still blessed with winter sun.

Lie of the Land

Tel Aviv is very easy to get around, as its bustling central area focuses on five parallel north–south streets that follow 6km of seafront. Nearest the sand is Herbert Samuel Esplanade, while the hotel-lined HaYarkon St lies a block inland. East of HaYarkon St is Ben Yehuda St, home to backpackers and souvenir shops, and the fourth parallel street is the trendy Dizengoff St, which marks the geographic centre of the city. Further east again, Ibn Gabirol St forms the eastern boundary of the city centre. The Neve Tzedek and Florentine districts mark the southernmost reaches of the city centre before Jaffa, while Park HaYarkon and the Old Port (Namal) mark the northernmost.

BICYCLE BOOM

Being a compact city, there is no better way to see Tel Aviv-Jaffa than on two wheels. The Big Orange (Tel Aviv's answer to the Big Apple) now has over 100km of dedicated bike paths running along many of the major thoroughfares. There's a bunch in Park HaYarkon, and one follows the coastline from a bit north of Sde Dov airport south, via Jaffa, to the suburb of Bat Yam. A free map of the bike-path network can be picked up at tourist information offices. For more information see p145.

In 2011, the municipality introduced **Tel-O-Fun** (✆6070; www.tel-o-fun.co.il), a citywide bike-rental scheme similar to Paris' Vélib'. You pick up and drop off the green bicycles in over 75 docking stations; the first half hour of use is free. Subscriptions cost 14NIS (daily) and 60NIS (weekly); pay with your credit card at any Tel-O-Fun station.

Tel Aviv's Best Beaches

» Hilton Beach (p126) is the city's unofficial gay beach and is popular with dog owners. Although crowded on weekends, during the week it is calmer and can be a great spot for sunset swimming or surfing.

» Gordon Beach (p126) in the centre is close to most of the major seafront hotels and has beach volleyball courts, a small outdoor gym and plenty of butch bronze bodies playing serious games of *matkot* (beach tennis).

» Alma Beach (p126), nearer Jaffa, is where the cool kids from Florentine come to chill, smoke a nargileh pipe and drink a beer.

THE NAME GAME

Tel Aviv streets are generally named after people and this eclectic mix includes names from Britain (Allenby), Eastern Europe (Jabotinsky) and Moorish Spain (Ibn Gabirol).

Fast Facts

» Area: 51.4 sq km
» Synagogues: 544
» Bauhaus buildings: over 4000
» Age of Jaffa: over 4000

Boutique Beer

» The Dancing Camel (p139) brews its own pale ales and stouts.
» Norma Jeane (p139) offers a range of international beers on tap.
» Porter & Sons (p139) sells boutique European and Israeli beers.

Resources

» Tourism office: www.visit-tlv.com
» Municipality: www.tel-aviv.gov.il/english
» Tel Aviv guide: www.telavivguide.net
» Tel Aviv city: www.telavivcity.com

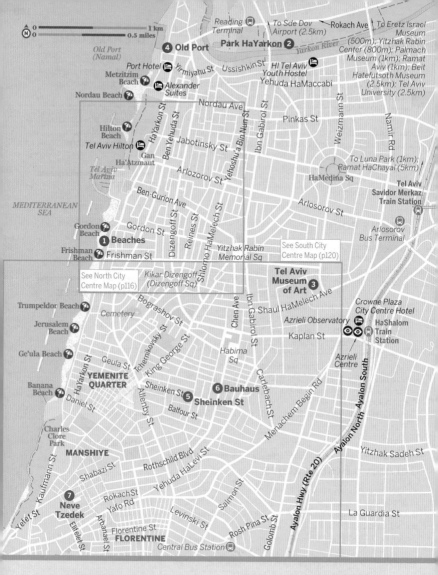

Tel Aviv Highlights

1 Swim in the warm Mediterranean or sink your toes into the sand at one of the city's boisterous **beaches** (p125)

2 Join the joggers, cyclists and frisbee-throwers at **Park HaYarkon** (p124), TLV's very own Central Park

3 Visit the ultramodern **Tel Aviv Museum of Art** (p118),

home to contemporary art, design and photography

4 Enjoy a fine farmers market in the daytime and go clubbing at night in the renovated hangars of the **Old Port** (p115)

5 Slip on a pair of super-sized sunglasses and shop a

frenetic Friday away on ultra-hip **Sheinken St** (p114)

6 Tour through the 'White City', a Unesco World Heritage Site thanks to its 4000 **Bauhaus** (p124) buildings

7 Take a lazy stroll through **Neve Tzedek** (p119), the city's oldest European-style neighbourhood

History
OUT OF JAFFA

While the history of Jerusalem makes for a grand epic spanning millennia, the making of Tel Aviv is a modern short story whose main themes are ambition, vision and drive, coupled with some rather eccentric town-planning choices.

Tel Aviv was created by small groups of Jews who decided to leave the cramped, unsanitary and sometimes unfriendly confines of the long-established, predominantly Muslim and Christian Arab town of Jaffa. Initially they settled in two small communities, Neve Tzedek (1886) and Neve Shalom (1890), nestled among the sand dunes just north of Jaffa. In 1906 they were joined by 60 families led by Meir Dizengoff, an ambitious businessman and politician born in modern-day Moldova, who planned to create a major new Jewish town. The families purchased 12 acres of empty sand dunes, divided it into 60 lots, and held a lottery – using seashells – to divvy up the land around what is now the intersection of Herzl St and Rothschild Blvd.

Taking as a model the English 'garden city' (a self-contained, structured community surrounded by greenbelt land – only two were ever actually built in England), several town planners were invited to submit schemes for the new town, with Dizengoff sitting at the head of the town planning committee. The plan adopted was that of Professor Boris Schatz, founder of the Bezalel Art School in Jerusalem, and centred on what is now Herzl St. The new town was officially inaugurated in 1909. The name Tel Aviv (Hill of Spring) comes from the title of the Hebrew translation of Theodor Herzl's novel *Altneuland* (it's also mentioned in Ezekiel 3:15).

ECLECTIC BEGINNINGS

The building of Tel Aviv ground to a halt when the Ottoman administration expelled the Jewish population from the Tel Aviv area in 1917. But after WWI the British Mandate in Palestine made it possible for the city to resume its exponential growth. Arab riots in Jaffa in 1921 sent many Jews fleeing to Tel Aviv, swelling the population to around 34,000 by 1925. In the mid-1930s, more anti-Zionist rioting in Jaffa caused the city's entire Jewish population to flee north; many refugees settled in shacks along the seashore. The boycott of Jewish passengers and

cargo by the Jaffa's Arab port workers led Tel Aviv to build its very own port.

Tel Aviv grew quickly to accommodate the newcomers, but development veered, on occasion, erratically away from the simple, logical, garden-city planning. Allenby St, designated the new main thoroughfare, was intended to run north–south, parallel to the seafront, but was diverted in order to reach a coffeehouse built on stilts over the beach. Likewise, the Neve Sha'anan district in the south was laid out in the shape of the seven-branched Jewish menorah simply because of the symbolism. Meanwhile, the immigrants kept on coming. The 1930s saw waves of arrivals from overseas, many fleeing Nazi Germany, and by 1939 Tel Aviv's population had reached 160,000, one-third of the country's total Jewish population.

As war clouds gathered in Europe, Jewish architects who had fled Nazi Germany set about turning Tel Aviv into a Bauhaus-inflected 'White City'. With the outbreak of WWII in 1939, Tel Aviv played host to Allied troops while simultaneously serving as a centre of Zionist resistance against Britain's anti-immigration policies. The city was bombed by Mussolini's air force in 1940.

In late 1947 and into 1948, as the British prepared to pull out of Palestine, tensions rose on the Jaffa border, with Arab snipers firing at Jews from the minaret of the Hassan Bek Mosque. The Haganah and Irgun (Jewish underground forces) responded by laying siege to Jaffa and by spring 1948 much of its Arab population fled, leaving the old port city in the hands of the newly declared State of Israel.

TRIALS & TRIBULATIONS

In April 1949 Tel Aviv and Jaffa were joined together to create a single municipality.

The decades after Israeli independence saw Tel Aviv expanding in every direction, turning neighbouring towns such as Ramat Gan and Holon into bustling suburbs. Early restrictions on the height of buildings had to be amended when authorities realised the only place to go was up – and that if Tel Aviv didn't get the skyscrapers neighbouring Ramat Gan would.

During the First Gulf War (1991), greater Tel Aviv was hit by about three dozen Iraqi Scud missiles, damaging thousands of apartments. And in the mid-1990s the city centre was hit by a wave of Palestinian suicide bomb attacks. In 1995, Prime Minister Yitzhak Rabin was assassinated by a right-wing Orthodox Jew during a peace rally at what is now Rabin Sq. Life in the city looked bleak – at least for a while.

BOUNCING BACK

Tel Avivians, however, are survivors. Despite the implosion of the late-1990s dot-com bubble and more than a dozen suicide bombings during the second Palestinian intifada – targeting civilians on buses, in cafes and at night-clubs, they left Tel Aviv's beach-based tourism industry in tatters – the early 21st century saw a rejuvenated economy largely based on high-tech wealth. Young Israelis started to move back to TLV and older neighbourhoods such as Neve Tzedek and Jaffa's Ajami underwent gentrification. Ever-taller buildings sprouted, with high-profile residential projects such as Phillipe Starck's prestigious Yoo Towers creeping up into the skyline.

Over the past decade, Tel Aviv has reinvented itself as an international-level dining destination, with a wealth of top-end brasseries and restaurants, a vibrant nightlife, a busy gay scene and shopping opportunities galore. In 2003 it gleefully accepted Unesco World Heritage status for its (sometimes dilapidated) Bauhaus buildings, and in 2009 the city celebrated its 100th birthday with 100km of bike paths and a series of extravagant street parties and events. The city's rejuvenation continued during the second decade of the 21st century – ravishing new projects include an expansive boardwalk linking Tel Baruch Beach (north of the Yarkon River) with Jaffa and Bat Yam; and the Old Railway Station in Neve Tzedek, now a boutique tourist centre.

Though infrastructural obstacles remain (lack of parking, stray cats, litter and poor public transport), Tel Aviv's reinvention has seen New York journalist David Kauffman describe it as the Mediterranean 'capital of cool'. According to Mercer, in 2011 Tel Aviv ranked as the most expensive city in the Middle East (and 24th in the world).

Although since 2008 Tel Aviv has missed the worst of the economic crisis that engulfed North America and much of Europe, the sky-high prices of food, education and housing led to a 'Summer of Discontent' in 2011, with thousands taking to the streets calling for social justice.

Dangers & Annoyances

Despite the spectre of suicide attacks (the most recent of which occurred in 2006), Tel Aviv is a remarkably safe city, and even lone women will rarely feel intimidated walking its central streets at night. The area around the old central bus station, Neve Sha'anan, has a reputation as a haunt for prostitutes and drug dealers, but it's also the home turf of many foreign workers and African refugees, remaining lively – thanks to legions of Indians, Filipinos, Thais, Romanians, Eritreans and Sudanese – well into the wee hours.

As when visiting almost any city, it pays to keep your valuables locked up in your hotel room safe or deposited with the hostel receptionist. When hitting the sands, never leave your bag, wallet, camera or mp3 player unattended (you can usually find a congenial neighbour to keep an eye on your belongings while you're taking a dip).

For general tips on personal safety see p422.

Sights

Aside from beaches, Tel Aviv sports a number of interesting museums and a selection of neighbourhoods well worth a wander. Most sights of interest are within walking distance of the city centre. You'll need a short hop by bus or taxi to venture out to the attractions of outlying Ramat Aviv, home to Tel Aviv University and its excellent museums. Jaffa, to the south, is linked to Tel Aviv by one long boardwalk, which makes a wonderful stroll (unless during midday in August).

CENTRAL CITY CENTRE

If you're looking for the hub of Tel Aviv's action, head direct to the busy intersection between Allenby, King George and Sheinken Sts. Here, where six shopping streets collide, is a great place to begin your Tel Aviv explorations, with a trip through the covered Carmel Market, a shopping spree on chic Sheinken St or a browse of the craft market on Nahalat Binyamin St.

Alternatively, head into the quieter Yemenite Quarter, where an older world awaits, or historic Bialik St, home to a few unique museums.

Carmel Market   MARKET
(Map p120) The Carmel Market (Shuk HaCarmel) is, in many ways, the frenetic heartbeat of Tel Aviv. The total opposite of air-conditioned shopping malls, it's an old passageway marketplace, squeezed between the Yemenite Quarter and Nahalat Binyamin St.

Here, passionate, mainly Sephardi men and women shout (and sometimes sing)

TEL AVIV IN...

Two Days

Kick off day one with a stroll along the seafront to familiarise yourself with the city and perhaps have a quick dip in the sea. Stop for lunch and boutique buys on fashionable Sheinken St before exploring the more earthy wares of the **Carmel Market** and the scents and sights of the ramshackle **Yemenite Quarter**. In the evening, stroll around arty **Neve Tzedek** and end the night with a dance performance at the **Suzanne Dellal Centre**. The next day head down to swanky Rothschild Blvd to visit **Independence Hall** and the redesigned **Haganah Museum**, then spend the afternoon in **Jaffa** bartering in the **flea market**, before stopping off for dinner at one of Jaffa's great **restaurants**.

Four Days

An extra couple of days will give you time to rent a bicycle and ride through **Park Ha-Yarkon** to Ramat Aviv, where you can pop in to see **Beit Hatefutsoth** at Tel Aviv University. You could also go out of town to spend a peaceful afternoon on a beach in **Herzliyya** or **Netanya**. When you get back to Tel Aviv, go for dinner at one of our recommendations and rev up for a nightclub in **Florentine** or at the **Old Port**.

while selling everything from fresh flowers to piles of paprika. This bubbling cauldron of commerce offers the cheapest and freshest food around. So leave your manners at the entrance and push on past the fake fashion stalls to the aromatic, enticing stalls of fruit and veg, nuts, hot breads, fresh fish, olives and spices beyond.

The best prices are to be had as the market closes, especially around 3pm or 4pm Friday, when everyone wants to sell up before Shabbat. Look out, meanwhile, for a handful of restaurant choices tucked quietly away beyond the bustle.

Nahalat Binyamin Street ARTS & CRAFTS

Formerly the run-down territory of the textile and haberdashery trade, Nahalat Binyamin St has been transformed into a busy pedestrianised precinct that hosts a popular open-air craft market (⊙10am-5pm Tue & Fri) complete with buskers and jovial atmosphere. Divert your eyes upwards, too, where vestiges of elegant architecture are in various states of repair and renovation, including No 16 (Rosenberg House), No 8 (Degel House) and No 13 (Levy House).

Yemenite Quarter NEIGHBOURHOOD

Tel Aviv may be the city that never sleeps, but the Yemenite Quarter is one parcel of land smack in the centre that seems to have slumbered though the better part of the 20th century. A tightly packed and crumbling quarter of narrow lanes, ramshackle houses and smoky kitchens, the neighbourhood is just a couple of blocks away from the hustle and bustle of Allenby St, but a world away from its frantic pace. Stroll here at lunchtime to see old men playing backgammon, and stop in for lunch at one of its hole-in-the-wall hummus restaurants.

Bialik House MUSEUM

(Map p120; ☏03-525 5961; 14 Bialik St; adult/child 20NIS/free; ⊙10am-3pm Mon, Wed, Thu & Fri, to 8pm Tue, 11am-2pm Sat) A short street lined with attractive buildings, Bialik St is a repository of Tel Avivian history. The highlight is the former home of Chaim Nachman Bialik, Israel's national poet, which contains memorabilia connected with his life and work. It was reopened in 2008 after being restored to its former glory.

Part of the Bialik complex, Beit Ha'ir (Map p120; ☏03-724 0311; 27 Bialik St) is the old Town Hall, set in a handsome renovated white mansion at the end of the street. It showcases art exhibitions and relics from Tel Aviv's past, plus a reconstruction of the original office of the first mayor, Meir Dizengoff.

Reuven Rubin House GALLERY

(Map p120; ☏03-525 5961; www.rubinmuseum.org.il; 14 Bialik St; adult/child 20NIS/free; ⊙10am-3pm Mon, Wed, Thu & Fri, to 8pm Tue, 11am-2pm Sat) Not far from Bialik House is the former residence of Reuven Rubin, an artist whose long career spanned from the WWI era to the 1970s. He was referred to as the 'Gauguin of Palestine', and his vibrant paintings and private photographs are an account of Jewish immigration and the early years of Israel.

THE REVIVAL OF HEBREW

Many Israelis feel that one of the greatest cultural achievements of the Zionist movement was the resurrection of the Hebrew language, which had not been used for everyday living for a couple of thousand years.

After the Jews were dispersed into the Diaspora following the destruction of the Second Temple – even before then, Judean Jews were already conducting most of their day-to-day affairs in Aramaic – they adapted to local cultures and picked up the local lingo wherever they settled, combining it with Hebrew to create uniquely Jewish languages such as Yiddish (based on medieval German) and Ladino (Judeo-Español; based on medieval Spanish). Classical Hebrew was preserved in sacred texts and synagogue prayers, but on the street it was about as useful as Latin would be these days in Paris' Latin Quarter.

The turning point came when early Zionists began publishing secular literature in Hebrew in the mid-1800s and, in the latter decades of the 19th century, settling in Palestine. Among them was Eliezer Ben Yehuda, born in Lithuania in 1858. Like most Jewish children of his era, he was introduced to Biblical Hebrew as part of his religious upbringing. When he arrived in Palestine in 1881, he was determined to turn Hebrew, the archaic language of study and prayer, into a secular tool of everyday communication, thus enabling Jews from all over the world to communicate with each other. (Herzl never spelled out what language he thought would be spoken in the Jewish State, but it appears that he assumed it would be German.)

When Ben Yehuda began living a Hebrew-speaking life, he found himself at a loss when trying to describe modern inventions such as trains and incandescent light bulbs. He began updating the language while simultaneously spreading it, as a spoken language, among his peers. His oldest son was the first all-Hebrew-speaking child in modern history.

Ben Yehuda's persistence and proselytising – and generations of Hebrew-language *ulpans* (language schools) for new immigrants – paid off, and today there are some nine million Hebrew speakers worldwide, including quite a few Palestinian Arabs. (By contrast, on the eve of WWII there were 11 million to 13 million speakers of Yiddish, while today there are fewer than two million.) People working to preserve shrinking minority languages such as Irish and Corsican often look to Hebrew – the only case of a 'retired' language having been completely resurrected – for inspiration and methods of propagation.

As in ancient times, when all sorts of Greek, Aramaic, Persian and Egyptian words crept into Hebrew, latter-day globalisation has resulted in an influx of words and concepts from languages such as English, German, French, Russian and Arabic. A classic case of word adoption is the @ symbol, which Israelis call a *shtrudel* because it looks like the Austrian pastry. However, although Hebrew has far fewer words than languages such as English, there are seemingly endless ways of saying 'What's up? How's it going?'

On the streets of Tel Aviv – which once proudly billed itself as 'the 1st Hebrew city' – you may hear some 'Hebrish', as Israelis tend to drop English (including obscenities) into the middle of Hebrew sentences. Much Israeli slang comes from Arabic – for instance, you'll often hear the words *sababa* (cool, OK) and *achla* ('excellent' or 'sweet'). A classic Arabic-English-Hebrew hybrid phrase, used when hip young people are saying goodbye to each other, is 'Tov, yallah, bye' (OK, let's go, bye).

Sheinken Street STREET

Feeling beautiful? Join others who feel the same on trendy Sheinken St. The hub of Tel Aviv's gay community, this narrow street – soon to become a pedestrian mall – is packed with boutiques selling designer sunglasses, Brazilian bikinis and cool clothes for adults and children alike. Arrive early on a Friday morning, pick a prime pavement-side perch at one of the street's many comfortable cafes, and settle in for a coffee and some supreme people-watching.

FREE **Jabotinsky Institute** MUSEUM
(Map p120; ☎03-528 7320; 38 King George St; ☺8am-4pm Sun-Thu) Also on King George St, you'll find the Jabotinsky Institute, a histori-

cal research organisation with a museum on the 1st floor presenting the history and activities of the Etzel (Irgun), a pre-state underground militia founded by Ze'ev Jabotinsky. Several departments show his political, literary and journalistic activities, and also document the creation of the Jewish Legion (five battalions of Jewish volunteers who served in the British army during WWI).

Almonit Alley STREET

(Map p120) It's easy to miss Almonit Alley (literally, Anonymous Alley), a tiny side street on the eastern side of King George St, originally named after Getzel Shapira, an American Jew who financed civic projects in Tel Aviv in the 1920s. Shapira built this neighbourhood and erected a statue of a lion on the adjacent Plonit Alley for his wife Sonia. Later, Mayor Dizengoff, irritated that anyone with money could have a street named after them, ordered the street names changed and a clerk gave the alley its current name. Almonit nowadays sports a couple of nice cafes and some grand old buildings in need of restoration.

Gan Meir Park PARK

(Map p120) To escape the city pace, head to Gan Meir Park, on the western side of King George St, where dog walkers release their four-legged friends in a specially designated dog run, and parents do the same to their two-legged charges at the playground. There's a good stretch of grass, too, for some lunchtime lounging.

NORTH CITY CENTRE

Old Port (Namal) PORT

(Map p110; www.namal.co.il) Originally opened in 1936 to give then-newly-established Tel Aviv sea-trafficking independence from Jaffa, the port soon went into decline with the construction of a better, deeper harbour at Ashdod. In the early 2000s the Tel Aviv municipality finally overhauled the area, creating a wide wooden boardwalk and transforming the derelict warehouses into a commercial centre.

By day it's buzzing with families wandering around its waterfront shops, restaurants and cafes, while planes swoop in low overhead to land at nearby Sde Dov airport. After dark and on weekends, hordes of young clubbers descend on the strip of bars and nightclubs. The Old Port also has a permanent indoor market housed inside Hangar 12.

Tel Aviv Marina HARBOUR

(Map p116) Between Gordon and Hilton beaches, the Tel Aviv Marina is a small harbour filled with a mixture of luxury yachts and old fishing boats. Join the joggers or strollers along the boardwalk, go for a swim in the restored Gordon Swimming Pool or put down anchor in one of the seafront cafes.

FREE **Ben-Gurion Museum** MUSEUM

(Map p116; ✆03-522 1010; 17 Ben-Gurion Ave; ⊙8am-3pm Sun & Tue-Thu, to 5pm Mon, to 1pm Fri) Built in 1930, this modest house was the Tel Aviv home of David Ben-Gurion, Israel's first prime minister. Maintained more or less as it was left on Ben-Gurion's death, the small rooms are simply furnished and contain part of the revered politician's library of some 20,000 books, as well as photographs of him meeting other 20th-century figures such as Nixon and Einstein.

Gan Ha'Atzmaut Park PARK

(Map p116) Overlooking the Mediterranean, Gan Ha'Atzmaut (Independence Park) was reopened in late 2009 and is next to the Hilton Hotel. It has a small outdoor gym, children's playground, a few weird sculptures and plenty of grass for a picnic.

Dizengoff Street STREET

(Map p120) Named after the city's first mayor, in office almost continually from 1911 to 1936, Dizengoff St is a long high street, where you'll find restaurants, pubs and fashion shops. It becomes increasingly lined with expensive designer clothing boutiques, mellow neighbourhood cafes and dozens of glitzy wedding-gown shops the further north you go.

Dizengoff Square SQUARE

(Map p116) Kikar Dizengoff – a 1970s landmark or eyesore, depending on your view – is the geographic heart of the city and a popular meeting point. It is located on a raised platform over the street, a block north of the Dizengoff Center shopping mall.

The Fire and Water Fountain in the centre of the square, designed by Ya'acov Agam, a leading Israeli artist known for his (obvious) predilection towards rainbow colour schemes, makes for an outlandish but appropriate symbol of the city. At the time of writing it was being renovated.

There are plans to return Dizengoff Sq, named after Meir's wife Tzina, to street level.

North City Centre

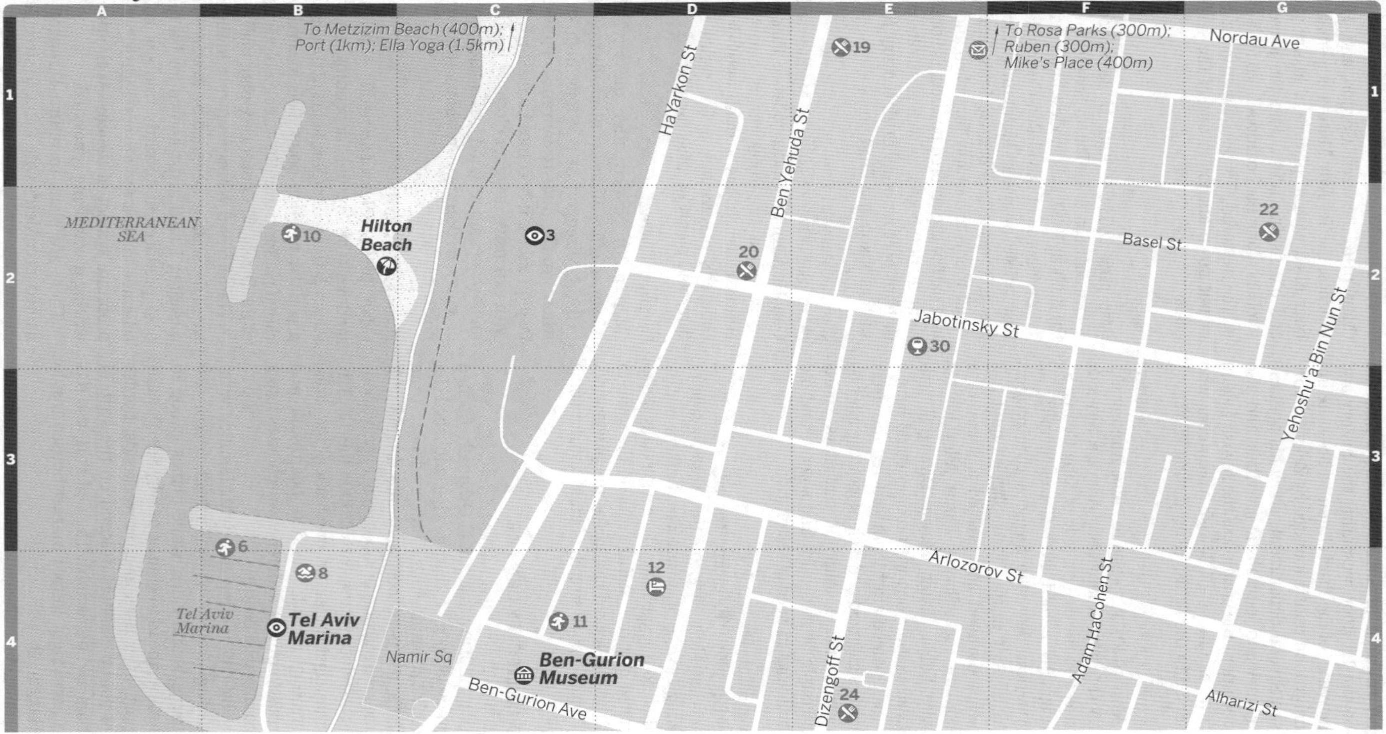

N

0   0.2 miles

0   400 m

MEDITERRANEAN
SEA

To Metzizim Beach (400m);
Port (1km); Ella Yoga (1.5km)

Hilton
Beach

Tel Aviv
Marina

Tel Aviv
Marina

Namir Sq

Hayarkon St

Ben Yehuda St

Jabotinsky St

Nordau Ave

Basel St

Yehoshu'a Bin Nun St

Adam HaCohen St

Arlozorov St

Dizengoff St

Alharizi St

Ben-Gurion Ave

Ben-Gurion
Museum

To Rosa Parks (300m);
Ruben (300m);
Mike's Place (400m)

10

7

3

8

6

11

12

20

19

30

24

22

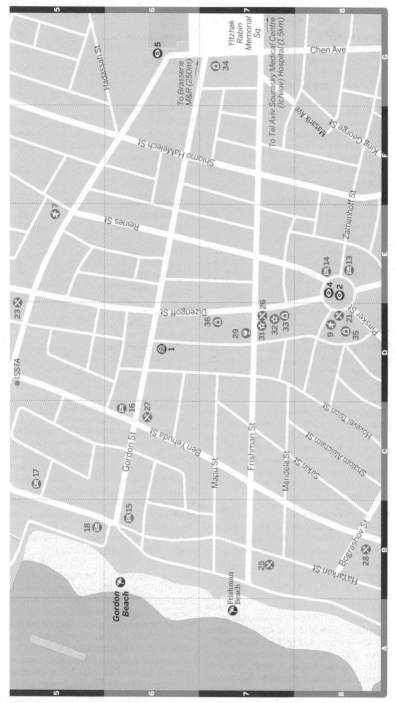

TEL AVIV

North City Centre

FREE Dan Contemporary   GALLERY
(Map p116; ☑03-524 3968; www.dancontempo
rary.com; 36 Gordon St; ⊙11am-6.30pm Mon-Thu,
to 2pm Fri) Providing a blank white canvas
for the finest Israeli art and photography,
the Dan is compact, contemporary and cool.
Check the website for details of the latest
exhibition.

EAST CITY CENTRE

Tel Aviv quietens down as you head east,
an area of the city basically bordered, to the
west, by Rabin Sq, which plays host to the
city's major celebrations, music concerts and
protests. South of here is the redeveloped
Habima Sq, home to the Habima Theatre.

Tel Aviv Museum of Art   MUSEUM
(Map p120; ☑03-607 7020; www.tamuseum.com; 27
Shaul HaMelech Ave; adult/child 42/34NIS; ⊙10am-
4pm Mon-Wed & Sat, to 10pm Tue & Thu, to 2pm Fri)
The recently opened, ultramodern 'envelope'
building by Harvard architect Preston Scott
Cohen adds another reason to visit the Tel
Aviv Museum of Art. The museum is home

to a superb permanent collection of Impressionist and post-Impressionist works, as
well as some fine 20th-century avant-garde
pieces. Works by Picasso, Matisse, Gauguin,
Degas and Pollock feature prominently, as
do Jewish post-Impressionists Chagall and
Soutine. The jewel of the collection has to be
Van Gogh's *The Shepherdess* (1889). The museum often screens films and holds special
exhibitions by Israeli artists, so check online.
To get to the museum take bus 9 from Ben
Yehuda St or 70 from Rothschild Blvd. Otherwise, walk from Kikar Dizengoff.

FREE Helena Rubenstein Pavilion   GALLERY
(Map p120; ☑03-528 7196; www.tamuseum.com; 6
Tarsat Blvd; ⊙10am-4pm Mon, Wed & Sat, to 10pm
Tue & Thu, to 2pm Fri) Named for the woman
behind the cosmetics empire, the Helena Rubenstein Pavilion of Contemporary Art is part
of the Tel Aviv Museum of Art and is used for
temporary exhibits by guest artists, both Israeli and foreign. Call ahead before going, as
the place is closed when exhibitions are in

transition. The Pavilion is just off HaBima Sq and can be reached by bus 5 or 26.

Rabin Square   SQUARE
(Map p116) The biggest public square in the city, this huge expanse of paving stones was repaved and upgraded in 2011. It now has an ecological pond filled with lotus flowers and koi, a fountain that's lit up at night, and some cool cafes around the perimeter. On the northern edge towers City Hall, which looks like a 1960s communist-style block (though not when it's lit up with laser beams).

Rabin Sq used to be called Malchei Israel (Kings of Israel) Sq but was renamed after the assassination of Prime Minister Yitzhak Rabin in 1995. On Ibn Gabirol St next to City Hall, a small memorial marks the spot where he was shot.

SOUTH CITY CENTRE
The southern fringe of the city centre is Tel Aviv's hippest area, loaded with exquisite restaurants, boutiques and wine bars. It's also the most historic part of the city, where, in Neve Tzedek the first buildings were laid down a century ago, while on Rothschild Blvd, the State of Israel was declared in 1948.

Neve Tzedek   NEIGHBOURHOOD
Stepping out of downtown Tel Aviv and into the narrow streets of Neve Tzedek (meaning 'Oasis of Justice'), the decibel level immediately drops a few notches. This was Tel Aviv's first Jewish neighbourhood, founded in 1887, and is well worth a wander. Its old European-style houses are now the most expensive real estate in town. The district's cute boutiques, cafes, wine bars and restaurants are centred on Shabazi St (named after a 17th-century Yemenite poet); meanwhile, the controversial modern Neve Tzedek tower looms large overhead, a chic apartment high-rise which went ahead despite locals' fears for the character of the neighbourhood.

Independence Hall   HISTORIC SITE
(Map p120; ✆03-517 3942; 16 Rothschild Blvd; adult/child 20/16NIS; ☺9am-2pm Sun-Fri) This slightly neglected hall was where on 14 May 1948, Ben-Gurion declared the establishment of the State of Israel. Previous to that the building had been the home of Meir Dizengoff, one of the founding fathers of Tel Aviv. Entry includes a short introductory film and a tour of the room where Israel's Declaration of Independence was signed.

FREE Haganah Museum   MUSEUM
(Map p120; ✆03-560 8624; 23 Rothschild Blvd; ☺9am-4pm Sun-Thu) The Haganah Museum chronicles the formation and activities of the Haganah, the military organisation that was the forerunner of today's Israel Defence Forces (IDF), originally a guerrilla force working against the British Mandate. The museum is housed in the former home of Eliahu Golomb, the founder of the Haganah.

Rothschild Boulevard   STREET
This pleasant, palm-tree-lined upscale boulevard was named after the famed Jewish family of financiers. Lining the boulevard on both sides today is a string of sleek

---

STREET WISE

Walk around south and central Tel Aviv and you may begin to notice strange things happening around you. Walls appear to talk, move and even tell stories. In recent years, derelict and disused buildings have become a backdrop for the city's astonishing street art.

The antithesis of billboard advertising, street art aims to reclaim public spaces, creating colourful and often thought-provoking images, free for all to see, that is, before the municipality covers them up. From tagging names and simple slogans, Tel Aviv street artists have branched out into complex compositions displaying various styles and techniques (aerosol, acrylic, pasting and stencils).

The backstreets of Florentine provide the best place to catch a glimpse of this underground graffiti world and the best-known name is undoubtedly Know Hope, Israel's very own Banksy. Know Hope has created sad and uplifting images featuring his 'everyman' character, with his trademark long arms and open heart. Now an international artist in his own right, Know Hope has published two books and even exhibited at the Helena Rubinstein Pavilion.

Other artists such as Broken Fingaz, Dede, Foma, Klone and Zero Cents have followed Know Hope's success into the gallery. But the real home of this daring and sometimes disturbing art is on the street.

South City Centre

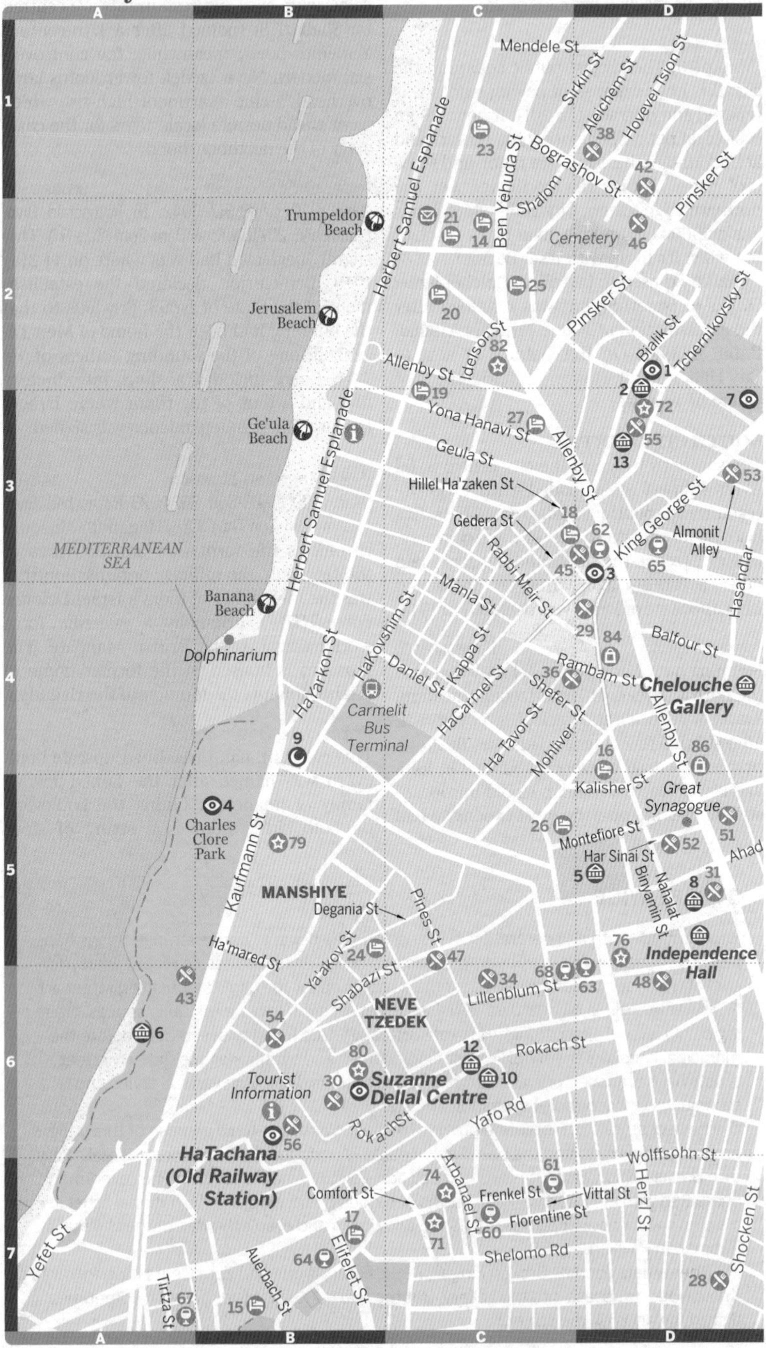

Mendele St
Sirkin St
Alechem St
Hovevei Tsion St
Mendele St
Bograshov St
Shalom
Ben Yehuda St
Pinsker St
Herbert Samuel Esplanade

Trumpeldor Beach

Jerusalem Beach

Ge'ula Beach

MEDITERRANEAN SEA

Banana Beach

Dolphinarium

Herbert Samuel Esplanade

Allenby St
Yona Hanavi St
Geula St
Idelson St

Hillel Ha'zaken St
Gedera St
Rabbi Meir St
Manla St
HaKovshim St
Daniel St
HaKarmel St
Kappa St
HaTavor St
Shefer St
Rambam St
Mohliver
Kalisher St

Carmelit Bus Terminal

Ha'Yarkon St
Kaufmann St

Charles Clore Park

MANSHIYE
Degania St
Pines St
Ya'akov St
Ha'mared St
Shabazi St
Yafo Rd

NEVE TZEDEK

Lillenblum St

Independence Hall

Montefiore St
Har Sinai St
Nahalat Binyamin St
Ahad

Great Synagogue

Chelouche Gallery

Allenby St
Balfour St
King George St
Almonit Alley
Hasandla
Bialik St
Tchernikovsky St
Pinsker St

Cemetery

Suzanne Dellal Centre

Tourist Information

HaTachana (Old Railway Station)

Comfort St
Arbanael St
Frenkel St
Vittal St
Florentine St
Shelomo Rd

Rokach St
Rokach St
Wolffsohn St
Herzl St
Shocken St

Yefet St
Tirtza St
Auerbach St
Elifelet St

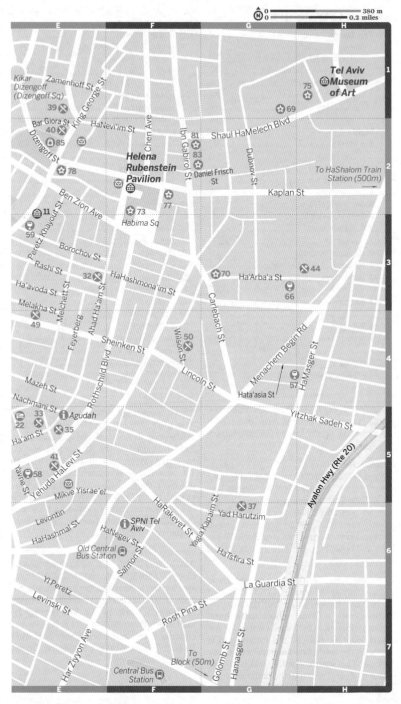

0 380 m
0 0.2 miles

Tel Aviv Museum of Art

75

69

Kikar Dizengoff (Dizengoff Sq)

Zamenhoff St

King George St

HaNevi'im St

Chen Ave

Ibn Gabirol St

Shaul HaMelech Blvd

Dubnov St

To HaShalom Train Station (500m)

39

Bar Giora St

40

85

Dizengoff St

78

81

83

Daniel Frisch St

Helena Rubenstein Pavilion

Kaplan St

Ben Zion Ave

Peretz Khayout St

11

59

Borochov St

73

77

Habima Sq

Rashi St

32

HaHashmona'im St

70

Ha'Arba'a St

44

Ha'avoda St

Melakha St

49

Melchett St

Feyerberg

Ahad Ha'am St

Sheinken St

Rothschild Blvd

Wilson St

50

Carlebach St

66

Mazeh St

Lincoln St

Menachem Begin Rd

HaMasger St

Nachmani St

Agudah

33

22

35

Ha'am St

Hata'asia St

57

Yitzhak Sadeh St

41

Yavne St

58

Yehuda HaLevi St

Mikve Yisrae'el

Levontin

HaHashmal St

SPNI Tel Aviv

HaNegev St

Salmon St

HaRakevet St

Yagia Kapaim St

Yad Harutzim

37

HaTsfira St

Avalon Hwy (Rte 20)

Old Central Bus Station

Yl Peretz

Levinski St

La Guardia St

Har Ziyyon Ave

Rosh Pina St

Golomb St

Hamasger St

To Block (50m)

Central Bus Station

South City Centre

restaurants, bars and Bauhaus buildings, while its shaded central strip becomes a stage for live bands and street entertainers at night.

Chelouche Gallery   GALLERY
(Map p120; ✆03-620 0068; www.chelouchegallery. com; 7 Mazeh St; ⊙11am-7pm Mon-Thu, to 2pm Fri & Sat) This contemporary art gallery spread over three floors is set in a 1920s corner mansion built by architect Joseph Berlin. Downstairs there is a Book Worm cafe and bookshop, great for an intellectual espresso.

Suzanne Dellal Centre   ARTS CENTRE
(Map p120) At the southern end of Shabazi St in Neve Tzedek, you'll find the Suzanne Dellal Centre, a former school and cultural centre, which now serves as a venue for festivals, exhibits and cultural events, and is home to the world-famous Bat Sheva dance troupe. The square outside makes a nice place to sit and recharge the batteries.

FREE Discover Tel Aviv Centre   MUSEUM
(Map p120; ✆03-510 0337; www.migdalshalom. co.il; 9 Ahad Ha'am St; ⊙8am-7pm Sun-Thu, to 2pm Fri) Housed in the Shalom Tower, Israel's first skyscraper built in 1965, Discover Tel Aviv has a permanent exhibition on the city's short history and offers various guided tours (40NIS). While here, check out the free art gallery on the 1st floor and the huge mosaic wall painted by Nachum Gutman.

Nachum Gutman Museum of Art   MUSEUM
(Map p120; ✆03-516 1970; www.gutmanmuseum. co.il; 21 Rokach St; adult/child 24/12NIS; ⊙10am-4pm Sun-Thu, to 2pm Fri, to 3pm Sat) Found on a quiet street, this museum displays 200 lively and fanciful works by the 20th-century Israeli artist. From 1907 to 1914 it housed the editorial board of the newspaper of HaPoel HaTzair (Young Worker), a socialist Zionist political movement.

Home of Shimon Rokach
GALLERY

(Map p120; ☎03-516 8042; www.rokach-house.co.il; 36 Rokach St; admission 10NIS; ☺10am-4pm Sun-Thu, to 2pm Fri & Sat) The former home of the man who founded Neve Tzedek, this house, dating from 1887, displays a small collection of strange antiques and sculptures in its courtyard and rooms.

Hassan Bek Mosque
MOSQUE

The Hassan Bek Mosque near the seafront was built in 1916 by Jaffa's Ottoman governor of the same name. Due to its location, the mosque has always had serious symbolic significance for Jaffa's Arab population (though it stood derelict for many years), being scheduled for demolition then saved on many occasions.

Across the road is the one-time Dolphinarium nightclub, the site of a Palestinian suicide bombing that killed 21 teenagers in 2001.

Etzel Museum
MUSEUM

(Map p120; ☎03-517 7180; Kaufmann St; adult/child 10/5NIS; ☺8am-4pm Sun-Thu) The struggle of the Etzel (Irgun) to expel the British from Palestine and defend the country during the 1948 Arab–Israeli War is covered by the Etzel Museum, in an attractive smoked-glass structure built within the remains of an old Arab house close to the sea. The right-wing Etzel, along with the left-leaning Haganah (90% of the Jewish fighting forces in 1948) and the far-right Lechi, were joined together to form the Israel Defence Force (IDF).

Charles Clore Park
PARK

The Charles Clore Park, originally opened in 1974 and redeveloped in 2010, is a large area of grass at the southern end of Tel Aviv's promenade. It includes the continuation of the bicycle lane that runs from Tel Aviv, via Jaffa, to Bat Yam and has an outdoor gym. On weekends, the park is mainly used as a spot for family barbecues.

TEL AVIV'S BAUHAUS HERITAGE

Tel Aviv has more sleek, clean-lined Bauhaus (International Style) buildings than any other city in the world, which is why it was declared a Unesco World Heritage Site in 2003.

Tel Aviv's White City heritage (www.white-city.co.il) is easy to spot, even through the modifications and dilapidation of the past 70 years. Look for structures characterised by horizontal lines, curved corners (eg of balconies), 'thermometer stairwells' (stairwells with a row of vertical windows to provide light) and a complete absence of ornamentation.

Founded by the architect Walter Gropius and later led by Ludwig Mies van der Rohe, the 'Bauhaus school' – active in the German cities of Weimar, Dessau and Berlin from 1919 to 1933 – had a huge influence on modernist design. The Nazis detested the Bauhaus style, considering it 'cosmopolitan' and 'degenerate' and forced the school to close when they came to power.

The ideas and ideals of Bauhaus were brought to Palestine by German-Jewish architects fleeing Nazi persecution. As Tel Aviv developed in the 1930s (following a street plan drawn up in the late 1920s by the Scottish urban planner Sir Patrick Geddes), some 4000 white-painted Bauhaus buildings – the quintessence of mid-20th-century modernism – were built.

Today, many of these buildings are in need of a lick of paint, but several hundred have already been renovated and each year more are being restored to their former glory. Superb examples of the Bauhaus style include the Cinema Hotel (Dizengoff Sq), Soskin House (12 Lillenblum St) and many of the structures along Rothschild Ave.

The Bauhaus Centre (Map p116; ☏03-522 0249; www.bauhaus-center.com; 99 Dizengoff St; ◷10am-7.30pm Sun-Thu, to 2.30pm Fri) sells a variety of architecture-related books and plans of the city, along with postcards of Tel Aviv in its Bauhaus heyday, and runs a walking tour starting at its shop every Friday at 10am. A free English-language guided Bauhaus tour departs from 46 Rothschild Blvd every Saturday at 11am.

Florentine
NEIGHBOURHOOD

Florentine is the city's artistic up-and-coming shabby-chic neighbourhood, home to designers, musicians, photographers and a few talented graffiti artists (see Street Wise, p119). Head to a bar or cafe on Vittal St to hang out with the hipsters.

NORTHERN TEL AVIV

TOP CHOICE Beit Hatefutsoth
MUSEUM

(Beit Hatefutsoth; off Map p110; ☏03-745 7800; www.bh.org.il; 2 Klausner St, Matiyahu Gate, Ramat Aviv; adult/child 40/30NIS; ◷10am-7pm Sun-Thu, 9am-2pm Fri) Otherwise known as the Diaspora Museum, Beit Hatefutsoth has been revamped and recreated as the Museum of the Jewish People. Located on the leafy campus of Tel Aviv University in the wealthy suburb of Ramat Aviv, the museum undertakes the challenge to tell the epic story of the Jewish exile and global Diaspora. With an excellent collection of films, photographs, models, dioramas and presentations, its innovative exhibitions represent all aspects of Jewish life, festivals and culture. Special attractions in the museum include the Feher Jewish Music Centre, the Douglas E Goldman Jewish Genealogy Centre (where visitors can register their family tree) and a Visual Documentation Centre, the largest database of Jewish life in the world.

A testament to the faith and courage that has preserved Judaism for centuries, Beit Hatefutsoth is one of Israel's most comprehensive museums and visitors need a few hours to get about.

To get here take bus 25 from the Dizengoff Center, or take bus 127 from the central bus station. Get off at the university, either Matatia Gate No 2 or Frenkel Gate No 7.

Park HaYarkon
PARK

Joggers, cyclists, in-line skaters, footballers, barbecuers and frisbee-throwers should head for the stretch of grassy parkland (Map p110) ranged along the Yarkon River, which makes up the city's largest green space. The further inland you go (towards Ramat Gan), the more the park opens up with duck ponds, a small farm and wider spaces.

Aside from being a great place for a picnic, Park HaYarkon also encompasses the popular Sportek, which has basketball courts, a skate park and trampolines. Also part of Sportek, the Olympus Climbing Wall (☏03-699 0910;

Rokach Ave; admission 50NIS; ⊘5-10pm Sun-Thu, 3-9pm Fri, 11am-10pm Sat) offers climbing lessons on its walls. East of Sportek, across Namir Rd, the young and the young at heart will enjoy Mini Golf (☎03-699 0229; per round 30NIS; ⊘4-8pm Sun-Thu, from noon Fri & from 10am Sat).

To reach the Sportek from Dizengoff St, take any bus headed for Ramat Aviv. Without traffic, a taxi will cost around 30NIS.

Eretz Israel Museum　　MUSEUM
(Land of Israel Museum; off Map p110; ☎03-641 5244; 2 Chaim Levanon St; www.eretzmuseum.org.il; adult/child 42/28NIS, incl planetarium 74/32NIS; ⊘10am-4pm Sun-Wed, to 8pm Thu, to 2pm Fri & Sat) The Eretz Israel Museum actually consists of 11 linked, small museums built around an archaeological site, Tel Qasile. Among other things, the museum complex is made up of a planetarium (⊘11.30am-1.30pm Sun-Thu), a glass museum, a folklore pavilion, a reconstruction of a medieval bazaar, a ceramics museum and a couple of halls that house temporary exhibitions. To get here, take Dan bus 25 or Egged bus 86.

Palmach Museum　　MUSEUM
(off Map p110; ☎03-643 6393; www.palmach.org.il; 10 Haim Levanon St; adult/child 30/20NIS; ⊘9am-5pm Sun, Mon & Wed, to 8pm Tue, to 2pm Thu, to 1pm Fri) Dedicated to the elite Haganah-affiliated strike force that played a critical role in the 1948 Arab–Israeli War, the Palmach Museum is a high-performance exhibition presented in a multimedia format, which leads visitors through several chambers that collectively describe the rise of the Palmach, their training and triumphs. It's about 200m past the Eretz Israel Museum; visits must be booked in advance.

Yitzhak Rabin Centre　　MUSEUM
(off Map p110; ☎03-745 3313; 14 Chaim Levanon St; www.rabincenter.org.il; adult/child 50/25NIS; ⊘9am-5pm Sun, Mon & Wed, to 7pm Tue & Thu, to 2pm Fri) A modern complex overlooking Park HaYarkon, the Yitzhak Rabin Centre is best known for the Israeli Museum. Opened in 2005, it has over 150 films and 1500 photographs telling the story of modern Israel's struggle for peace with its neighbours, interwoven with the biography of former Prime Minister Yitzhak Rabin.

The Olympic Experience　　MUSEUM
(☎03-795 5900; www.olympic.one.co.il; 6 Shitrit St; admission 45NIS; ⊘10am-5pm Sun-Thu) This short audiovisual show is set in the Olympic building in the Hadar Yosef neighbourhood. In just over an hour, it goes on a whirlwind trip through the history of the ancient Greek games and Israeli Olympic medal triumphs, and peeks into the future of sport.

EASTERN TEL AVIV
The further east you head in Tel Aviv, the more businesslike the city becomes. Ibn Gabirol St basically marks the eastern border of downtown. Beyond it, you are heading into a world of wide boulevards, tony residential side streets, glassy skyscrapers and suburbs in Ramat Gan.

Azrieli Observatory　　TOWER
(Map p110; ☎03-608 1179; 132 Menachem Begin Rd; adult/child 22/17NIS; ⊘9.30am-8pm Sun-Thu, to 6pm Fri in summer; to 6pm daily in winter) Comprising three striking skyscrapers (one square, one triangular and one round), the Azrieli Centre is one of the symbols of modern Tel Aviv. Finished in 1999, the round tower was the tallest building in the city but was quickly eclipsed in 2001 by the Moshe Aviv Tower across the Ayalon Expressway in Ramat Gan. The Azrieli Observatory, on the 49th floor, offers panoramic views of TLV's ever-changing skyline and admission includes use of an audio guide (in English or Hebrew) that describes the various buildings and landmarks.

Be sure to call ahead to check that the observation deck is open – it's frequently closed for private functions. To reach the towers, take bus 55 from Ibn Gabirol, 60 from the central bus station or 40 from Jaffa. The elevator to the observatory is situated on the 3rd floor of the round tower shopping centre.

Beaches

When the weather is warm Tel Avivians (or Tel Avivim) flock en masse to the city beach, a long golden stretch of sand divided into individual sections, each with its own character. You'll find young and old soaking up the Mediterranean rays, swimming and playing fierce games of *matkot*.

The beaches are safe and clean, and there are changing rooms and freshwater showers scattered along its length. Swimmers, however, must heed lifeguard warnings when conditions become rough; a black flag means that swimming is forbidden; a red flag means that swimming is dangerous and a white flag means that the area is safe.

The main beaches are packed in high season and especially on Saturdays, when crowds descend early to pick a prime spot.

At and after sunset is a great time for a quiet stroll down beside the water's edge.

Here's a rundown of Tel Aviv's beaches, from north to south.

Metzitzim Beach
FAMILY

Named after a 1972 comedy film, *Hof Metzitzim* (Peeping Beach) is now a rather family-friendly bay with a small kids play area. It is the northernmost beach before the Old Port.

Nordau Beach
RELIGIOUS

This is the city's religious beach, where men and women are segregated. Women can use the beach on Sunday, Tuesday and Thursday, while it's the men's turn on Monday, Wednesday and Friday. It's open to everyone on Saturday, when observant Jews don't go to the beach.

Hilton Beach
GAY

Hilton is the city's unofficial gay beach, named after the nearby hotel. Here you'll also find dog walkers (it's the only beach where dogs are officially allowed), lots of buff bodies and keen surfers catching the waves.

Gordon & Frishman Beaches
CENTRAL

South from Hilton, busy Gordon and Frishman Beaches are popular with Tel Aviv teens, tourists and toddlers. Well equipped with sun lounges, beach bars and restaurants, this is also the place to play beach volleyball.

Jerusalem Beach
PARTY

At the start of Allenby St, loud teenage groups characterise this nice, but plain, stretch of sand, further south from Frishman.

Banana Beach
CHILL-OUT BEACH

Named for its resident cafe, Banana's laid-back, mellow vibe attracts a 20- and 30-something crowd, equipped with books, weekend newspapers and *matkot* racquets. Look out for free, open-air film screenings here on summer evenings.

Alma Beach
ALTERNATIVE BEACH

The place for in-the-know young couples and local celebrities, this little beach is tucked just beneath the Manta Ray restaurant, near the Charles Clore Park. At weekends, a mix of young Israelis descend to sunbathe or smoke a nargileh pipe.

Activities

Tel Avivim are an active lot and are usually found running towards the nearest park, biking to the beach or heading off to the gym. Park HaYarkon is the centre for sport but you'll also find volleyball courts and an outdoor gym on Gordon Beach. Here is a rundown of some of the best activities to stay in shape after all that feasting on felafel and suchlike.

Gordon Swimming Pool
SWIMMING

(Map p116; ☑03-762 3300; Tel Aviv Marina; adult/child 62/52NIS; ☺6am-9pm Mon-Thu, to 7pm Fri, 7am-6pm Sat, 1.30-9pm Sun) Originally opened in 1956, the outdoor Gordon Swimming Pool was rebuilt in 2009. Next to the marina, it has a 50m saltwater pool whose water is frequently changed plus childrens and toddler pools. Pay extra and you can also use the sauna or jacuzzi, or get a massage.

DON'T MISS

DESIGN MUSEUM HOLON

The ultrahip and uberimpressive **Design Museum Holon** (☑03-073 215 1500; www.dmh.org.il; 8 Pinhas Eilon St; adult/child 35/30NIS; ☺10am-4pm Mon, Wed & Sat, to 8pm Tue & Thu, to 2pm Fri) opened its doors in March 2010 and has quickly become an icon of modern Israel. Designed by world-renowned Israeli architect Ron Arad, it's worth a visit just to see the building – a huge red swirl made of concrete and steel ribbons. Inside, there's a world of design to discover with temporary exhibitions spanning digital installations to far-out fashion and weird furniture. Many of the exhibits are interactive and special audiovisual tours can be arranged. The museum occasionally closes between exhibitions, so best to call before you go.

Although Holon is a rather dreary extension of Tel Aviv, the museum represents the city's goal to transform itself into a centre of culture. It's in the east of town near the library, cinema and Holon Institute of Technology. Holon is just 6km south of Tel Aviv and the museum can be reached by Egged bus 71 (every 20 minutes) from the Arlozorov Terminal. Get off at Weizman St, near Hoofien St, and it's a short walk to the museum, behind the cinema. Alternatively, take a 15-minute taxi ride from the centre.

Ella Yoga
YOGA

(off Map p116; ☎03-544 4881; www.ellayoga.co.il; Hangar 4, Old Port) A great place to salute the sun or arrange your asanas, Ella Yoga at the Old Port offers a range of classes, from ashtanga to kundalini. Call to register and inquire about drop-ins.

Lev Yam
WATER SPORTS

(Map p116; ☎03-524 2139; www.levyam.co.il, in Hebrew; ⊙10am-5pm) If you want to try windsurfing or kayaking, head to the Lev Yam club on Hilton Beach. It offers an hour of windsurfing with an instructor for 150NIS, 220NIS without. Plus you can hire kayaks from 160NIS an hour.

Danit Tours
SAILING

(Map p116; ☎052 340 0128; www.danit.co.il) Budding yachtsmen may want to contact Danit Tours, which runs sailing and motorboat trips from Tel Aviv Marina. For a group of up to 11 people it charges 1090NIS for two hours at sea. Smaller groups can sail for 880NIS.

Walking Tours

The municipality runs four guided walking tours in the city and it's worth joining at least one of them while you are in town. All four tours are free of charge and there is no need to make an advance booking.

Fans of Tel Aviv's Bauhaus architecture shouldn't miss the 'White City' walking tour; see p124 for details.

A second tour walks around Old Jaffa, its archaeological sites and the flea market. It meets at 10am Wednesday at the tourist office in Jaffa on 2 Marzuk & Azar St, near the clock tower.

The third tour studies the art and architecture of Tel Aviv University. It meets at 11am Monday (except holidays) at Dyonon bookstore at the university campus entrance.

The fourth tour, 'Tel Aviv by Night', departs every Tuesday at 8pm from the corner of Rothschild Blvd and Herzl St, exploring nighttime activities with stories and anecdotes.

For a tasty tour of Tel Aviv and Jaffa call **Delicious Israel** (☎052-699 499; www.deliciousisrael.com), which offers guided culinary walks including 'hummus crawls', as well as gourmet cooking workshops, yoga and boutique shopping experiences.

Courses

Tel Aviv University Ulpan
LANGUAGE COURSE

(☎03-640 8639; www.international.tau.ac.il) An academic-level *ulpan* (Hebrew-language

---

DON'T MISS

DRUMMING INTO SHABBAT

Every Friday as the sun goes down Drummers' Beach (near Banana Beach) comes alive with hypnotic tribal rhythms and freestyle dancers. Situated next to the old Dolphinarium nightclub, the spot of the tragic 2001 suicide bomb attack, this is where Israelis, Africans and tourists jam their way into Shabbat.

---

school), offered twice a year at Tel Aviv University's School for Overseas Students. Consult the website for more details and application tools. The university also runs summer Hebrew and Arabic language programs.

Ulpan Gordon
LANGUAGE COURSE

(Map p116; ☎03-522 3095; www.ulpangordon.co.il; 7 LaSalle St) The most popular *ulpan* in Tel Aviv charges around 700NIS per month for tourists.

Ulpan Or
LANGUAGE COURSE

(☎03-566 1493; www.ulpanor.co.il; 4 Kaufman St) Small centre offering online and off-line Hebrew courses.

Kabbalah Centre
SPIRITUAL

(Map p116; ☎03-526 6800; www.kabbalah.com; 14 Ben Ami St) A favourite of Madonna, the Kabbalah Center has its own California-inflected take on Jewish mysticism. If you want to know more, stop by the centre just off Dizengoff Sq, which offers English-language workshops, drop-in prayer sessions and breakfasts, and has a bookshop.

⚑ Festivals & Events

Tel Aviv has plenty of year-round festival fun, including the Tel Aviv Jazz Festival (www.jazzfest.co.il) in February, the DocAviv documentary festival (www.docaviv.co.il) in May and the Gay Pride Parade (www.lovepa rade.co.il) in June. Plus, thousands of revellers spill out onto the streets of Florentine for fancy-dress parties celebrating Purim in March and there is free all-night music on Laila Lavan (the White Night) in June.

⌂ Sleeping

Tel Aviv accommodation ranges from top-end chain hotels mostly set in towers on the seafront to hostels ranging in quality and price. Recently, a new crop of boutique

TEL AVIV COURSES

TEL AVIV FOR CHILDREN

Most children will be entertained for hours on Tel Aviv's generous beach, which is well lifeguarded and equipped with ice-cream vendors and beach cafes. But if it's a grassy expanse you're after, try Park HaYarkon, equipped with a small zoo, pedal boats and playgrounds. Nearby, there are plenty of rides at the Luna Park (☏03-642 7080; www.lunapark.co.il; admission 98NIS, children under 2 free), a roller-coaster park next door to the Israel Trade Fairs & Convention Center on Rokach Blvd. Opening hours change by the month, so call ahead. Calmer rides are to be had at the good playground at Gan Meir Park on King George St. The wide wooden boardwalk at the Old Port is perfect for a child-friendly wander.

A haven for smaller people and their parents, Dyada (Map p116; ☏1 700 700 815; www.dyada.co.il; 75 Ben Gurion Ave) is a childrens centre hosting all kinds of regular activities, with a cafe downstairs and a well-stocked mother-and-baby shop. Call or drop in to reserve a place for some toddler tumbling. Many shopping malls, including Gan Ha'ir (Ibn Gabirol St just north of City Hall) and Dizengoff Centre, have hugely popular play areas (mischakiyot) for toddlers and young children.

Just outside town, commune with the natural world at the Ramat Gan Safari (☏03-630 5328; www.safari.co.il, in Hebrew; Ramat Gan; per person 49NIS), part of which is a conventional zoo and the other a drive-through safari. Check the website for opening hours and a driving map.

Back in the city, dining with children, at all times of the day, couldn't be easier. Few restaurants, cafes and bars will turn away tiny clients and most of these establishments are well equipped with high chairs and meal options for children. It's common to see kids dining with their parents well into the night, especially since Israel's public smoking ban left restaurants completely smoke-free.

---

hotels has been added to TLV but, as in most internationally minded cities, be prepared for high prices. Book ahead, too, especially during July, August and festival periods such as Sukkot, Rosh Hashana, Hanukkah and Passover, when people from overseas (and especially France) flock to the Holy Land.

Many of the big hotels are found on HaYarkon St, but it's worth noting that the area close to Allenby St can be dirty and noisy. So, for calmer climes, sacrifice that sea view for a more peaceful tree-lined avenue. If Tel Aviv's mix of hostels and hotels doesn't float your boat, you can try a Jaffa hostel or choose from a range of holiday apartments.

Most hotels offer laundry services, but if you are going DIY, there are numerous, nameless self-serve laundrettes (washing machine 12NIS, dryer 5NIS; open 24 hours) about town, particularly common on Ibn Gabirol St, Ben Yehuda St and King George St.

CENTRAL CITY CENTRE

Brown TLV BOUTIQUE HOTEL $$$
(Map p120; ☏03-717 0200; www.browntlv.com; 25 Kalisher St; s/d from US$160/180; ❄☎) Go back in time to the glam of the 1970s with this new chic hotel. Marketed as an 'urban hotel', Brown is within close walking distance of the Carmel Market, Neve Tzedek and Rothschild Blvd. The interior design is a departure from the usual boutique minimalist approach, with the owners preferring eye-catching modern art and plenty of dark brown retro furniture. It offers 30 rooms, some with jacuzzi and balcony, plus a slick meeting room, sundeck and spa. Brown is great for business travellers or those aspiring to be James Bond.

HaYarkon 48 Hostel HOSTEL $
(Map p120; ☏03-516 8989; www.hayarkon48.com; 48 HaYarkon St; dm without/with air-con 98/115NIS, r without/with bathroom 330/385NIS; ❄☎) Just two blocks from the beach, this yellow-painted hostel has decent facilities including a communal kitchen, reliable showers and a very basic breakfast. The common room has a pool table, computers, a TV and it's a good place to hook up with other travellers. If you can, take a look at a room before booking.

Art Plus Hotel BOUTIQUE HOTEL $$$
(Map p120; ☏03-797 1700; www.atlas.co.il; 35 Ben Yehuda St; s/d from US$194/213; ❄☎) One of the latest hotels from the Atlas group, Art Plus deserves special mention for its creative

design and attention to detail. The artistic vibe is set from the entrance, off Ben Yehuda St, with Zadok Ben-David's *Evolution* sculpture depicting the stages of man. Murals from different local artists feature on each floor; breakfast is served in the library and it has a pleasant roof terrace, though you'll probably prefer lazing on the nearby beach.

Galileo
HOTEL $$

(Map p120; ☎03-516 0050; www.sun-hotels.co.il; 8 Hillel Ha'zaken St; s/d from 300/360NIS; ✳🛜) Part of the Sun Hotels chain of Tel Aviv addresses, Galileo is a cute, 12-bedroom hotel just on the edge of the Yemenite Quarter. Its rooms might be on the small side but they're comfortable and tastefully decorated with art and some lavish carpets. Don't miss drinks in the atmospheric bar downstairs or on the roof terrace.

Hotel De La Mer
HOTEL $$$

(Map p120; ☎03-510 0011; www.delamer.co.il; 2 Ness Ziona St, cnr HaYarkon; s/d US$159/179; ✳🛜) Fancifully branding itself a 'feng shui hotel', the De La Mer gets top marks for its airy pastel-shaded rooms, great spa, personal attention and sea views. The big breakfast, too, comes highly recommended and is sure to start your day merrily.

Sky Hostel
HOSTEL $

(Map p120; ☎03-620 0044; www.sky1hostel.com; 34 Ben Yehuda St; dm 80NIS, s without/with bathroom 160/240NIS, d 270/320NIS; 🛜) One of the better budget options in the centre of town, Sky has simple rooms, some with air-conditioning and others with fans. Guests get coffee and cake in the morning and can use the big backpack-size lockers for free.

Lusky Suites
HOTEL $$$

(Map p120; ☎03-516 3030; www.luskysuites-htl.co.il; 84 HaYarkon St; s/d from US$150/180; ✳🛜) A smart lobby leads up to clean, well-appointed rooms with large windows letting in lots of light, and deluxe doubles (US$210) with balconies. Some rooms offer kitchenettes and flat-screen TVs, and drivers will appreciate the free parking.

Sun City Hotel
HOTEL $$

(Map p120; ☎03-517 7913; www.sun-hotels.co.il; 42 Allenby St; s/d 420/500NIS; ✳🛜) Another of the Sun Hotels chain, this friendly little no-frills hotel is on the corner of Yona Hanavi St, right in the middle of town, but somehow it remains quiet inside. Rooms are a touch small but the location is handy for the beach.

NORTH CITY CENTRE

Cinema Hotel
HOTEL $$$

(Map p116; ☎03-520 7100; www.atlas.co.il; 2 Zamenhoff St; s/d from 700/750NIS; ✳🛜) A classic Bauhaus building on Kikar Dizengoff, the Cinema manages to be charming and individual, complete with old bits of projectors, cinema posters and vintage stage lighting. Like the Center Hotel, as with many of the city's best options, it's actually part of a chain. If both the Center and the Cinema are full, try the City, Melody or Shalom, all part of the same reliable, characterful Atlas brand.

TOP CHOICE Center Hotel
HOTEL $$$

(Map p116; ☎03-526 6100; www.atlas.co.il; 1 Zamenhoff St; s/d from US$194/215; ✳🛜) Built in the Bauhaus style, the Center Hotel retains a boutique feel despite its chain affiliations, thanks to the small number of rooms and distinctive decor – hardwood floors, bright-white paintwork and colourful murals in the bedrooms. Wi-fi is free, as is bike hire and the buffet breakfast is served across the walkway at the Hotel Cinema. This is a nice address if you prefer a quiet hotel away from the beach.

HI Tel Aviv Youth Hostel
HOSTEL $$

(Map p110; ☎02-594 5655; www.iyha.org.il; 36 B'nei Dan St; dm/d 162.50/410NIS; ✳🛜) Also known as the Bnei Dan Guest House, this is by far the cleanest and most peaceful of Tel Aviv's hostels. It is in the north, opposite the leafy Park HaYarkon and is within walking distance of the buzzing Old Port, though you may need to take a sherut or bicycle to get into the centre of town.

Hotel Metropolitan
BUSINESS HOTEL $$$

(Map p120; ☎03-519 2727; www.hotelmetropolitan.co.il; 11-15 Trumpeldor St; s/d US$150/198; ✳🛜🏊) Geared towards the business traveller, this centrally located place has 228 rooms and 23 suites, many catching sea views. Other facilities include a business lounge, fitness centre, sauna, bar, restaurant, a decent outdoor pool, gym, sauna and sundeck.

Alexander Suites
LUXURY HOTEL $$$

(Map p110; ☎03-545 2222; www.alexander.co.il; 3 Havakuk St; ste from US$295; ✳🛜) A superb choice for families, the suites at the Alexander (which sleep either three or four) offer plenty of space, kitchenettes and big bathtubs. There's also a well-equipped gym, business centre and a presidential penthouse suite with its own pool, if you're feeling extravagant. It's right near the Old Port and Gan Ha'Atzmaut (Independence Park).

Renaissance
LUXURY HOTEL $$$

(Map p116; ☏03-521 5555; www.renaissancehotels. com; 121 HaYarkon St; s/d 900/1200NIS; ❄️🛜🏊) Set amid other high-rise hotels, this one identifies itself among the crowd with its great beachside location, superbly comfortable beds and great executive-floor facilities. All of its 342 rooms have a balcony, and there is an indoor pool and health club.

Gordon Hotel
HOTEL $$$

(Map p116; ☏03-520 6100; www.gordontlv.com; 2 Gordon St; ste from US$220; ❄️🛜) The Gordon is housed in a refurbished, plush white Bauhaus building on the corner of busy Ha-Yarkon St. Its 12 light and airy rooms offer flat-screen TVs, classic photos of TLV, stylish furnishings and some have balconies ($300). The ground-floor bistro, Salt, is good value and you're never far from the Mediterranean blue here.

Port Hotel
HOTEL $$

(Map p110; ☏03-544 5544; www.porthoteltelaviv. com; 4 Yirmiyahu St; s/d from US$137/149; ❄️🛜) The latest addition to the Sun Hotels chain, the Port offers 21 designer rooms and has a small roof terrace. As the name suggests, it is close to the Old Port and just a short walk up from Yirmiyahu St's trendy cafes.

Leonardo Basel
HOTEL $$$

(Map p116; ☏03-520 7711; www.leonardo-hotels. com; 156 HaYarkon St; s/d from US$160/175; ❄️🛜🏊) Formerly the Basel Hotel, this place is now part of the Leonardo chain that also runs the Herods, City Tower and Leonardo Boutique hotels. Recently renovated, it has 120 decent rooms with all mod cons, an outdoor pool, bar and kosher restaurant.

Gordon Inn
HOSTEL $

(Map p116; ☏03-523 8239; www.hostelstelaviv. com; 17 Gordon St; dm 90NIS, s/d 380/410NIS, without bathroom 380/280NIS; ❄️🛜) This hostel has a great location, bang in the centre, close to the beach and the lively Ben Yehuda St. Yet rooms are basic, small and without any creature comforts. Guests get a coupon for breakfast in the La Mer restaurant, a good 10-minute walk away on the beach.

Ben Yehuda Apartments
APARTMENT $$

(Map p116; ☏03-522 9393; www.tel-aviv-rental.co.il; 119-121 Ben Yehuda St; apt from US$142-329; ❄️🛜)

Two buildings with self-catering apartments, from studios to a three-bedroom duplex.

SOUTH CITY CENTRE

Hotel Montefiore
BOUTIQUE HOTEL $$$

(Map p120; ☏03-564 6100; www.hotelmontefiore. co.il; 36 Montefiore St; d US$380-420; ❄️🛜) A real boutique hotel set in a unique 1920s (pre-Bauhaus) building; this is the hottest address in town to splash out on a night of luxury in one of its 12 deliciously decadent rooms. Dine in style downstairs with its Vietnamese-style cuisine, then retreat upstairs to your bookcase-filled bedroom, through corridors decked out with cool modern photographic art.

Sun Aviv Hotel
HOTEL $$

(Map p120; ☏03-517 4847; www.sun-aviv.co.il; 9a Montefiore St; s/d 350/380NIS; ❄️🛜) Operated by the same company as the Galileo and Sun City, Sun Aviv is well placed for the cafes and bars on Rothschild Blvd. The rooms may be small, but each is individually styled with colourful wallpaper, artworks and simple furnishings.

Neve Tzedek Hotel
BOUTIQUE HOTEL $$$

(Map p120; ☏054 207 0706; www.nevetzedekhotel. com; 4 Degania St; d US$280-800; ❄️🛜) An unassuming building on a quiet Neve Tzedek street, its five luxurious and romantic suites feature modern art, antiques and natural wooden sculptures.

Florentine Hostel
HOSTEL $

(Map p120; ☏03-518 7551; www.florentinehostel. com; 10 Elifelet St; dm 77NIS, s/d 200NIS; ❄️🛜) One for young hipsters, the Florentine is a small hostel with one dorm and a few private rooms. It has a funky Sinai-style roof garden, but due to its 'sababa' laid-back alternative vibe, the hostel imposes an age restriction of 18 to 40 years old.

EASTERN TEL AVIV

Crowne Plaza City Centre Hotel
BUSINESS HOTEL $$$

(Map p110; ☏03-539 0808; www.afi-hotels.com; Azrieli Towers, 32 Menachem Begin Rd; d from US$292; ❄️🛜🏊) A Manhattan-style 13-floor hotel, located in Azrieli's 'square tower', this is a hit with business travellers. Free espressos in the lobby, a steak house, sushi bar and all the usual comforts, along with the advantage of stellar views out over the city, make up for the distance from the beach. Rates also include access to the Holmes Place gym and spa.

TEL AVIV & SHABBAT

If you've already experienced the hush that descends on Jerusalem as Shabbat is welcomed in – and wondered what on earth you're going to do with no ATMs, restaurants, shops or sights in operation for a full 24 hours or so – don't despair: simply go to Tel Aviv and spend Shabbat the secular way.

Here, many shops and felafel stalls close on Friday afternoon and don't open again until Saturday evening or Sunday morning, but that seems to be the extent of the city's nod to the holy day of rest. On Friday evening, bars, restaurants and clubs are packed to the rafters until the dawn. Saturdays see locals thronging to the beach, lazing at cafes with the Friday newspapers, and generally being active throughout the day. Simply head outside to the city's streets and you'll easily be able to find a frothy *cafe hafuch* (cappuccino), schnitzel sandwich or bowl of pasta. Plus, there are AM:PM mini-supermarkets (open 24/7) dotted all over the city in case you forgot to pick something up.

You will notice less noise on the streets as there are no buses, but there are sheruts and taxis if you need to get around.

🍴 Eating

Tel Aviv is like one giant cafe and eating out is a daily occurrence for many of its residents. In fact, at any hour its restaurants and cafes are so busy with chatty clientele that it causes one to wonder if anybody in Tel Aviv (apart from the waiters) is actually working at all.

There is no shortage of choice for the hungry (indeed, we could fill this entire book with Tel Aviv's eating options). With places old and new, from budget to blowout, Tel Aviv's restaurant scene is the most exciting and constantly metamorphosing of any in Israel, if not the Middle East.

Coinciding with the boutique makeover that's sweeping all over TLV, there is a rising crop of 'chef restaurants' and swanky, minimalist bistros. But don't worry if you are on a budget; there are still plenty of cheap street food booths offering felafel, hummus, sabich (Iraqi-style felafel lookalike with deep-fried eggplant and potatoes instead of chickpea balls), shwarma, fresh-squeezed fruit juice, pizza by the slice, frozen yoghurt and *bourekas* (stuffed Turkish-style savoury pastries). So follow the crowds and your nose, and don't be afraid to deviate from our suggestions to find your own culinary marvel.

Prices are generally equivalent to, or slightly below, the UK or USA: a snack costs around 20NIS per person, while a two-course dinner, with a drink or two, at one of Tel Aviv's top-end affairs could run to around 300NIS.

If you're self-catering, the best fresh fruit and vegetables in town are sold at the Carmel Market. Convenience supermarkets are found all over Tel Aviv – most belong to the two small chains of AM-PM and Tiv Taam in the city, which offer a good selection, almost-reasonable prices (considering this is Tel Aviv) and late-night hours.

CENTRAL CITY CENTRE

Sonia Gatzel Shapira　　　CAFE **$$**
(Map p120; 1 Almonit Alley; meals from 35NIS; ⊘9am-late Mon-Thu, 8am-6pm Fri, 11am-late Sat; 🖊) Named after the woman this alleyway was originally built for, Sonia is a cute cafe decked out in vintage furniture, grooving to jazz or R&B music. It has a large sunny patio garden out the back and a mainly vegetarian menu, featuring pastas and sandwiches. Try its *shakshuka* (egg and tomato stew) or Moroccan bread.

Carmella Ba'Nachala　　INTERNATIONAL **$$$**
(Map p120; ☑03-516 1417; 46 Har Tavor St, cnr Rambam St; mains 70-120NIS; ⊘noon-midnight Sun-Thu, 10am-midnight Fri & Sat) Tucked away in an old colonial-style white building near the Nahalat Binyamin market you'll find this chic oasis of silver cutlery and starched white tablecloths. The menu changes frequently, utilising herbs, spices and pomegranate seeds to spice up fish and meat dishes. The daily business-lunch menu, served from Sunday to Thursday between noon and 5pm, gives you the chance to sample the chef's delights with a reduced price tag.

Orna and Ella　　　　CAFE **$$**
(Map p120; ☑03-525 2085; 33 Sheinken St; dishes from 58NIS; ⊘10am-midnight Sun-Thu, to 5pm Fri, 11am-midnight Sat; 🛜) Decorated in stark white design, this Tel Aviv institution serves homey gourmet cuisine and is famed for its delicious desserts. It uses the freshest ingredients brought straight from the market and

everything is made from scratch. The menu changes weekly, but you can count on the seared salmon, smoked duck, sage-infused pasta and sweet potato pancakes.

HaKosem
ISRAELI $

(Map p120; 1 Shlomo HaMelech St; felafel from 16NIS; ☉9am-11.30pm Sun-Thu, to 3pm Fri; ✐) The friendliest felafel stall in town, HaKosem (the Magician) is a popular snack-stop on the corner of King George St. Aside from its trademark green, fried chickpea balls in pita, it also offers *shakshuka,* schnitzel and shwarma (kebabs). If you're lucky, you'll get a free felafel ball straight from the pan while you queue: magic.

Brasserie M&R
FRENCH $$

(off Map p116; ✆03-696 7111; 70 Ibn Gabirol St; mains from 60NIS; ☉8am-5am) Wannabe French maîtres d' (complete with surly attitude) serve up mouth-watering steak, chicken and seafood dishes, in a dimly lit leather banqueted brasserie. Set on Rabin Sq, it still maintains a bustling neighbourhood atmosphere, serving classic breakfasts and cocktails long into the night from its Hebrew and French menu.

Mitbachon
ISRAELI $$

(Map p120; Rabbi Akiva St, cnr Gedera St; mains from 38NIS; ☉8am-2am Sun-Fri, 9am-2am Sat) With a friendly, neighbourhood vibe, this place is tucked down a small lane on the edge of the Yemenite Quarter. It offers what could be called market cuisine. Serving soups, schnitzel, meat balls and salads, it's a great choice when you're in need of some hearty home-cooked food.

Agadir
BURGERS $$

(Map p120; www.agadir.co.il; 2 Nachalat Binyamin St; burgers from 49NIS; ☉noon-4am Sun-Thu, to 5am Fri, to 3am Sat; ☎) Locals swear by one of the best burger and beer joints in town, which sees prime beef patties of varying sizes sizzled up with choose-your-own toppings. Located on the pedestrianised Nahalat Binyamin St, it's the perfect place for a lunchtime pint. Now a chain, it also has a branch on the Old Port (Hangar 3).

Tchernikovsky 6
BISTRO $$

(Map p120; ✆03-620 8729; 5 Tchernichovsky St; mains from 68NIS; ☉noon-midnight Mon-Fri, noon to 6pm Sat & Sun; ☎) If it's a cool, calm night out you're after, you can't go wrong with this lovely local bistro. There's a good wine list and a delicious menu that changes almost

daily; carnivores will melt at the 'butcher's cuts', while vegetarians will delight in gorgonzola salad, homemade gnocchi or polenta with grilled asparagus.

Felafel Gabai
ISRAELI $

(Map p120; 25 Bograshov St; felafel 16NIS; ☉10.30am-10.30pm Sun-Thu; ✐) In a city where every felafel stall claims to be the best, Gabai is a strong contender for the title. Like most stalls, its crispy balls of felafel come with as much salad, pickles and tahina sauce as you can squeeze in a pita bread, but it also does a fine *shakshuka* and schnitzel.

Cafe Noah
CAFE $$

(Map p120; 93 Ahad Ha'am St; light meals from 32NIS; ☉8am-11pm Sun-Thu, to 5pm Fri; ☎✐) Popular with writers, poets, pundits and other folk desperately attempting to avoid a nine-to-five job, Noah has well-worn wooden floors, a small library and dozens of dusty old *National Geographic* mags. The menu offers salads, sandwiches and all-day breakfasts.

Joz ve Loz
FUSION $$

(Map p120; ✆03-560 6385; 51 Yehuda HaLevi St; mains from 65NIS; ☉6pm-1am; ✐) Unusual fish, meat and vegetarian dishes are concocted at this hidden, artsy hang-out, next to a petrol station. Popular with Tel Aviv bohemians and the gay community, it has a cute, eclectic little dining room and overspill outdoor courtyard. The portions might be slightly small (though perfectly formed), but it's worth a visit for some exquisite tastes and a night out.

Moon
SUSHI $$

(Map p120; ✆03-629 1155; 58 Bograshov St; mains from 55NIS; ☉noon-12.30am) Going strong for over 10 years, Moon has the feel of a real Japanese sushi bar, where plates of sashimi go around the blue-lit long bar on a conveyer belt or 'sushi train'. Most of the best sushi has a tuna or salmon base, but you can also order a juicy Japanese steak.

Kurtosh
BAKERY $

(Map p120 & Map p116; 39 Bograshov St & 178 Dizengoff St; cakes from 25NIS; ☉7am-9pm Sun-Thu, to 4pm Fri, 6pm-10pm Sat; ✐) This Hungarian bakery specialises in long, spiral pastries that look like the hollowed-out cooling tower of a miniature nuclear power plant. But there's no toxic waste here; rather, it exudes an intoxicating aroma of chocolate, cinnamon, nut and halva.

Dizengoff Centre Food Market MARKET **$**
(Map p120; Dizengoff Centre; dishes from 18NIS; ⊙noon-late Thu) On Friday morning, this shopping centre becomes overrun with food stalls, where everything from jacket potatoes to couscous is served up piping hot.

Hummus Abu Dhabi HUMMUS **$**
(Map p120; 81 King George St; portion 20NIS; ⊙11am-midnight Sat-Thu, to 4pm Fri; ☑) A classic combo of reggae music and warm plates of hummus, this place certainly 'stirs it up', Bob Marley-style.

NORTH CITY CENTRE

Goocha SEAFOOD **$$**
(Map p116; ☑03-522 2886; 171 Dizengoff St; mains from 54NIS; ⊙noon-1am Sun-Thu, to 2am Fri & Sat) Goocha is one of TLV's biggest hits – you'll often see crowds of eager diners standing on the corner of Ben Gurion Ave and Dizengoff St waiting for a table. Different styles of calamari, shrimps and fish dominate the menu, but there are a few pasta dishes. The Diner, its sister restaurant (14 Ibn Gabirol St), is more about burgers than sea bass. Booking ahead is strongly advised.

Sabich Stall ISRAELI **$**
(Map p116; 42 Frishman St; per sabich 15NIS; ⊙9am-11.30pm Sun-Thu, to 4pm Fri; ☑) This tiny stall specialises in sabich, an Iraqi-derived snack, consisting of roast aubergine, boiled egg and potato, salad, hummus, pickles and spicy *amba* (mango) sauce, all stuffed into a pita. It's on the corner of Dizengoff and Frishman Sts, just look for the long lines and the felafel stall next door. But beware: it's highly addictive.

TOP CHOICE **Raphael** MEDITERRANEAN **$$$**
(Map p116; ☑03-522 6464; www.raphaeltlv.co.il; 87 HaYarkon St; meals from 88NIS; ⊙noon-4pm & 7-11pm; ☑) For years considered Tel Aviv's finest restaurant, Raphael's still got it in abundance. Combining exquisite, upmarket Mediterranean food with sleek design, a celebrated chef and grand seaside vistas, this is one restaurant that's dressed to impress. Set business lunches with two courses cost 88NIS (115NIS on weekends). Entrance is via the luxurious Dan Hotel.

Fresh Kitchen HEALTH FOOD **$$**
(Map p116; www.freshkitchen.co.il; 37 Basel St; salads from 36NIS; ⊙8am-midnight Sat-Thu, to 6pm Fri; ☎☑) Aptly named, this healthy-eating option is a breath of fresh air. With over a dozen types of salad on the menu, this is the place to get your daily five portions of greens and then some. The menu also has a multitude of muesli, sandwiches, refreshing shakes – and it even lists the calories. There are a few dotted around town, but the Fresh on Basel St is in a great spot.

Thai House THAI **$$**
(Map p116; 517 8568; www.thai-house.co.il; 8 Bograshov St; mains from 62NIS; ⊙noon-11pm; ☑) Dedicated restaurants serving Thai food (aside from Asian-fusion noodle joints) are few and far between in Tel Aviv. So if you're craving green, yellow or red curry, try a dinner at Thai House (Beit Thailandi), a bamboo-laden restaurant on the corner of Ben Yehuda and Bograshov Sts. Its papaya salad, sweet potato curry and tom yum soup with tofu are great for vegetarians.

Tamara FROZEN YOGHURT **$**
(Map p116; 96 Ben Yehuda St; cups from 18NIS; ⊙9.30am-12.30am; ☑) Like felafel stalls, it seems as though there is a yoghurt parlour on every street corner. Tamara, one of the frozen yoghurt experts, offers cups of the white stuff with all kinds of fruit, granola and chocolate toppings. Indulgent, yes, but it's the sweetest way to cool down in the summer months.

Adora BISTRO **$$$**
(Map p116; ☑03-605 0896; 226 Ben Yehuda St; mains from 79NIS; ⊙noon-5pm & 7pm-late Mon-Fri, from 1.30pm Sat; ☑) A chef restaurant that exploded onto the Tel Aviv dining scene, Adora is now one of the city's firm favourites. The food is sumptuous and experimental – think felafel stuffed with meat, aubergine and parmesan or fillet of fish with pistachios and bacon. The tapas-style first courses will also satisfy veggies.

Tapas Bashook TAPAS **$**
(☑03-716 2757; Old Port, Hangar 12; tapas from 25NIS; ⊙8am-11pm Mon-Sat) Delve into tasty tapas and sip Israeli wines at this funky bar, opened in 2011. The menu, scribbled on a blackboard, changes with the weather and the chef's whim. It's adjoined to the indoor Port Market.

Ruben SANDWICHES **$$**
(off Map p116; 32 Yirmiyahu St; sandwiches from 32NIS; ⊙noon-1am Sun-Thu, to 6pm Fri, to 2am Sat; ☎) Nothing to do with Formula 1 racing driver Rubens Barrichello, this place is all about American-style sandwiches. Marketed as the place where 'meat meets bread',

ANTHONY PIDGEON/LONELY PLANET IMAGES ®

1. Jaffa (p146)
It's worth visiting the old areas of Jaffa twice, once in the daytime and once in the evening.

2. Tel Aviv (p108)
Tel Aviv is a city of outdoor cafes, leafy boulevards and long sandy beaches.

3. Carmel Market, Tel Aviv (p112)
Push your way through to the aromatic stalls of fruit and veg, nuts, hot breads, fresh fish, olives and spices.

4. Purim, Tel Aviv (p127)
Thousands of revellers spill out onto the streets of Florentine for fancy-dress parties celebrating Purim.

diners can select from a 200-, 300- or a mighty 400g sandwich, filled with fine cuts of roasted meat.

Dizi
CAFE $$

(Map p116; ☑03-629 4559; www.dizi.co.il; 13 Ben Ami St/Dizengoff Sq; dishes from 36NIS; ☺9am-midnight; ☺) Dizi is a trendy one-stop shop for coffee, laundry, DVD rentals and free wi-fi. Grab a coffee, salad or sandwich, check your emails and walk out with a bag of clean clothes – what more does a traveller need?

Hummus Ashkara
HUMMUS $

(45 Yirmiyahu St; meals 18NIS; ☺8am-late Sun-Thu, to 4pm Fri; ☑) A cheap eat on a trendy street, Ashkara serves up hummus and *fuul* (fava-bean stew) with pita and mountains of chips; a fine filler after all that boutique browsing.

SOUTH CITY CENTRE

24 Rupees
INDIAN $$

(Map p120; 14-16 Shocken St; thalis from 30NIS; ☺noon-midnight Sat-Thu, to 5pm Fri; ☺☑) Head straight to Varanasi at this Indian thali hang-out, which is hidden on the 1st floor of what looks like a residential building. Slip off your shoes, slide onto a floor cushion, and munch on vegetarian food served on tin thali platters. The dhal has that just right creamy consistency and the *gulab jamun* (dough dumplings in syrup) will satisfy all those who've craved it since leaving Delhi. The door downstairs is hard to spot and looks locked – don't worry, it's not.

Benedict
BREAKFAST $$

(Map p116 & Map p120; 171 Ben Yehuda St & 29 Rothschild Blvd; www.benedict.co.il; breakfasts from 53NIS; ☺24hr; ☺☑) Where do you go if you're craving blueberry pancakes or eggs Benedict at five in the afternoon, or, for that matter, in the morning? To this constantly crowded all-night breakfast place on Rothschild Blvd (or its sister branch on Ben Yehuda St). Pastries are baked on site and each table gets a basket of warm bread. Look out for unusual breakfast treats such as Mexican chilli, alongside the thick French toasts and steak-and-eggs combinations.

Hotel Montefiore
FUSION $$$

(Map p120; ☑03-564 6100; www.hotelmontefiore. co.il; 36 Montefiore St; mains from 70-150NIS; ☺noon-1am; ☺) For a romantic, colonial-inspired dining night out, stray no further than the gorgeous boutique Hotel Montefiore, whose regal decor complements an exquisite French-Vietnamese menu. It ain't cheap but it is certainly tasty.

DON'T MISS

HATACHANA

After decades of dereliction, the historic **Old Railway Station** (HaTachana; Map p120; www.hatachana.co.il; Neve Tzedek; ☺10am-10pm Sat-Thu, to 5pm Fri), one-time terminus of the rail line to Jerusalem, has been reopened to the public and transformed into a tourism centre with cafes, restaurants and boutique shops. Popularly known simply as HaTachana (the Station), the complex includes 22 buildings, including an old freight terminal, brick factory, villa and the Jaffa Railway Station, inaugurated in 1892 – the year that marked the beginning of modern transportation in Palestine – and closed in 1948.

At the entrance, you'll find some refurbished railway carriages housing various art exhibitions, **tourist information** (www.visit-tlv.com; Hangar 5) and the **Made in TLV** (Map p120; www.madeintlv.com) shop, selling a range of books, postcards and designer souvenirs celebrating Tel Aviv (we liked the cute mouse mats and pita-bread pencil cases). The complex features a whole host of fashionable boutiques from some of the finest Israeli designers, a bookshop, art gallery and activities for children.

As with anywhere in TLV, you are never short of food options and HaTachana has at least eight eateries spanning Middle Eastern cuisine, Italian cafes and an ice-cream parlour. The hottest name here is **Vicky Cristina** (Map p120; ☑03-736 7272; tapas 25-49NIS; ☺noon-1am daily), an outdoor tapas and wine bar named after Woody Allen's 2008 film. Advance booking is essential as this venue fills up with people sampling mouth-watering dishes such as seafood paella, chorizo and *quezo frito* (fried cheese).

The main entrance is found on the seafront road off Kaufman St and can easily be reached from Neve Tzedek and the Carmelit bus terminal. Dan buses 10, 18, 25 and 100 all stop close by.

Manta Ray
SEAFOOD $$$

(Map p120; ☑03-517 4773; southern Tel Aviv promenade; mains 80-115NIS; ⊘9am-midnight) Officially a fish restaurant, Manta Ray, perched right on Alma Beach in the south, also makes a great place for a breakfast omelette with all the trimmings, (42NIS, served until noon). Fish and seafood mains start at around 80NIS but it's worth it just for the spectacular sea views.

Cafe Tazza D'Oro
CAFE $$

(Map p120; 6 Ahad Ha'am St; mains from 50-70NIS; ⊘7.30am-midnight Sun-Fri, from 9am Sat; ☎) One of the cheaper choices in Neve Tzedek, this cafe has a limited but tasteful mix of breakfasts, pasta, meat and fish. Enjoy the wi-fi inside or sit in the elegant courtyard, which hosts live jazz every Friday afternoon.

Cafe Noir
CAFE $$

(Map p120; ☑03-566 3018; 43 Ahad Ha'am St; mains from 51NIS; ⊘8am-1am Sun-Fri, from 9am Sat; ☎) This light and airy, loosely French-decorated restaurant is known locally for two things: its big breakfasts and its schnitzel with piled-high mashed potatoes. Lunchtime specials tempt in business persons and shoppers alike, imbuing the place with a lively, friendly vibe.

Nanuchka
EASTERN EUROPEAN $$

(Map p120; ☑03-516 2254; 30 Lillenblum St; mains from 52NIS; ⊘noon-late) The weird and wonderful Nanuchka is a highly popular place serving heavy Georgian cuisine; even the salads will leave you as stuffed as the restaurant's peppers. The magic begins, however, as dinner makes way for drinks and Nanuchka becomes an all-out bar, complete with a belly dancer and partygoers dancing on tables.

Radio Rosco
ITALIAN $$

(Map p120; 97 Allenby St; pizzas from 48NIS; ⊘11am-12.30am Sun-Thu, 8.30am-midnight Fri & Sat; ☎) Concealed by some shops on Allenby St, Radio Rosco is all too easy to miss. Comprising a little restaurant and courtyard; it is one of TLV's greatest culinary secrets. Students and locals in-the-know come here for lasagna, chicken scallopini and very unkosher pizza.

Suzanna
FUSION $$

(Map p120; 9 Shabazi St; meals 45-65NIS; ⊘10am-midnight) A long-standing Neve Tzedek favourite, Suzanna offers a Mediterranean mix of dishes, including stuffed vegetables and mezze, some more successful than others (so the 'I'll have what they're having' approach pays off here). Enjoy your meal during summer months on the large open courtyard in the shade of an enormous ficus tree and take in views of quaint Neve Tzedek.

Shisko
BULGARIAN $$

(Map p120; 2 Har Sinai St; pizzas from 48NIS; ⊘noon-midnight Sun-Thu, to 6pm Fri, from 7pm Sat) Shisko ('fat man' in Bulgarian) is in one of the city's newest drinking hot spots, in the square behind the Great Synagogue on Allenby St. Its mad mix of Bulgarian tapas, mini-kebabs, rakia (plum brandy) and klezmer music makes for a merry start to any night out.

Bellini
ITALIAN $$

(Map p120; ☑03-517 8486; www.bellini.co.il; 6 Yechieli St; mains from 60-100NIS; ⊘noon-midnight) With its white-checked tablecloths, huge stone fireplace, excellent pastas, meat and wine, Bellini is Tuscan Tel Aviv at its most rustic. It's next door to the Suzanne Dellal Centre on Neve Tzedek's paved piazza.

Nana Bar
STEAKHOUSE $$

(Map p120; 1 Ahad Ha'am St; mains from 60NIS; ⊘noon-late; ☎) A firm Neve Tzedek favourite, Nana's long bar is permanently propped up at weekends, while its twinkling courtyard garden is perfect for balmy evenings. The menu is generally meaty, the wine list is extensive, and the clientele is Tel Aviv's wealthier young 30-somethings.

Cantina
ITALIAN $$

(Map p120; ☑03-620 5051; 71 Rothschild Blvd; mains from 60NIS; ⊘noon-late; ☎) A favourite with local celebrities, cheerful Cantina dispenses Italian classic dishes from its patio perch on stately Rothschild Blvd. Dig into a pizza and watch the stars of the Israeli small screen meet and greet.

EASTERN TEL AVIV

Messa
INTERNATIONAL $$$

(Map p120; ☑03-685 6859; www.messa.co.il; 19 Ha'Arba'a St; dishes 90-170NIS; ⊘noon-1am) If you're seeking the ultimate Tel Aviv designer dining, Messa's your white minimalist dream come true. Private booths surround a ludicrously long central table and the experimental Middle Eastern and European menu offers tiny, though eminently aesthetic, portions.

Pasta Mia
ITALIAN $$

(Map p120; ☑03-561 0189; 10 Wilson St; pasta from 54NIS; ⊘noon-midnight daily; ☑) The big Italian flag outside this little neighbourhood trattoria gives it away. Pasta Mia produces its own fresh pasta daily and is a tiny, little slice of Tuscany in a grubby Tel Aviv backstreet. It lets you match the pasta of your choice to a variety of tomato, oil-based or creamy sauces and you can wash it down with some great homemade *limoncello*.

OUTSIDE THE CITY CENTRE

Coffee Bar
BISTRO $$$

(Map p120; ☏03-688 9696; 13 Yad Harutzim St; mains from 62NIS; ☺9am-midnight Sun-Fri, from noon Sat) Coffee Bar, from the owners of the Hotel Montefiore and M&R Brasserie, is a classy outfit in an otherwise dingy industrial neighbourhood. The Italian-influenced menu includes pasta, meat, risotto and fish; save space for its heavenly desserts and cakes.

Hudson Brasserie
STEAKHOUSE $$

(☏03-644 4733; www.hudson-tlv.com; Or Towers, HaBarzel St, Ramat HaChayal; mains from 62NIS; ☺noon-midnight) Carnivores will likely love this well-run brasserie in the business district of Ramat HaChayal, a 15-minute taxi ride from the centre of town. The speciality here is sloppy joes (62NIS), those most American of minced beef stews. Expect to pay around 150NIS for a tender sirloin steak.

🍷 Drinking

Tel Aviv seems to have more bars than houses. All over the city, drinking joints are constantly opening up or changing name, but there are a number that have stood the test of time. As a general rule, the hottest bars are usually found in the south, particularly around Lillenblum St, and most bars are open seven days a week. Expect to pay between 22NIS to 28NIS for half a litre of beer, while cocktails and wines by the glass begin at 26NIS.

CENTRAL CITY CENTRE

HaMaoz
BAR

(Map p120; ☏03-620 9458; 32 King George St; ☺8pm-late Sun-Thu, from 2pm Fri, from 6pm Sat; ☎) Locals and tourists love HaMaoz, which has three main areas – an outdoor garden, an indoor bar and a backroom that looks like someone's apartment. Here you can relax on the sofas, play a game of pool or mingle with Tel Aviv's young and beautiful. A great place to see in Shabbat; you can call to reserve an area.

Minzar
PUB

(Map p120; 60 Allenby St, cnr Gedera St; ☺24hr; ☎) A few metres back from the main street and a few hundred miles from the mainstream, the Minzar is that rare thing: a pub without

a closing time. A now legendary drinking hole, you will find Israelis, expats and drifters chatting over a beer outside, enjoying a ham and cheese sandwich or just watching the world pass by.

TOP CHOICE Par Derriere
WINE BAR

(Map p120; 4 King George St; ☺10pm-late) Hidden down a dark alleyway off King George St, this French-owned wine bar has its own secret garden atmosphere and is one of the most romantic spots to enjoy a bottle of cabernet sauvignon.

NORTH CITY CENTRE

Bukowski
BAR

(Map p116; 39 Frishman St; ☺10pm-late) Completely enclosed with soundproof walls and without a sign outside, you could walk past Bukowski a dozen times and never know that there was a party going on behind that closed door. This local bar, on the corner of Dizengoff St, is a dress-down place with a vociferous following, a long list of drinks and a cool soundtrack.

Mike's Place
BAR

(off Map p116; www.mikesplacebars.com; 86 Herbert Samuel Esplanade & 342 Dizengoff St; ☺11am-late; ☎) Both the newer bar on Dizengoff St and the original on the beach next to the US Embassy offer burgers, frothy pints, sports and live rock music. The sizeable menu has grill-style meals, cocktails and beer. Happy hour is 3pm to 8pm daily (11am to 8pm on Saturday).

Mate
PUB

(Map p116; 226 Dizengoff St; ☺4pm-late) This no-frills pub is one of the best for value in the north, offering happy hour daily from 4pm to 8pm. In the winter it feels cosy and warm, in the summer it offers an air-conditioned escape from the heat.

Rosa Parks
PUB

(off Map p116; 265 Dizengoff St; ☺6pm-late) Named after the African-American woman who refused to give up her bus seat for a white passenger, this is a popular pub set on two storeys. It attracts a late-20s to 30-something crowd, so it doesn't descend into an all-out trance party like many other bars.

SOUTH CITY CENTRE

Shesek
BAR

(Map p120; 17b Lillenblum; ☺9pm-late) Shesek is a rough-around-the-edges bar and bohemian haunt well known for pumping out a variety of music (mash-ups and punk to trance

GAY & LESBIAN TEL AVIV

With by far the most vibrant gay community in the Middle East, Tel Aviv plays host to the region's biggest Gay Pride Parade each June. The best place to start for information is **Aguda** (Map p120; ☑03-620 5590; www.gayisrael.org.il; 28 Nachmani St), where you can find out what's going on in the city or **Atraf** (www.atraf.com), Israel's most popular gay social networking site, with options in English. **Tel Aviv Gay Vibe** (www.telavivgayvibe. com) is a useful site with plenty of information, a Tel Aviv gay map and even an iPhone app. The **Gay Center** (Map p120; ☑03-525 2896; www.gaycenter.org.il; Gan Meir Park) off King George St hosts gay- and lesbian-themed events, lectures, sports groups and pot-luck picnics. You should also contact the **Gay Hotline** (☑03-516 7234; ☺7.30pm-10.30pm Sun, Tue & Thu). If you are looking for a gay-friendly hotel, try quaint Galileo.

The current gay-oriented club-night hits include the **Theater Club** (10 Jerusalem Blvd, Jaffa), which hosts pop night Big Boys every Friday from midnight; and **Lima Lima** (Map p120; ☑03-560 0924; 42 Lillenblum St), with its Notorious GAY night on Monday from 11pm.

Meanwhile, **Evita** (Map p120; ☑03-566 9559; 31 Yavne St; ☺noon-late) is a cafe that turns into a gay lounge-bar by night. Its Sunday-night Eurovision parties, Monday-night karaoke contests and Tuesday-night drag shows have made Evita a Tel Aviv institution. Evita is in a quiet alley a half block south of Rothschild Blvd.

Beachgoers might also want to visit **Hilton Beach**, Tel Aviv's unofficial gay beach.

TEL AVIV ENTERTAINMENT

and avant-garde hip-hop), nightly DJs and quality beer (including Taybeh, a microbrew manufactured in Ramallah).

Mish Mish BAR
(Map p120; 17a Lillenblum St; ☺8pm-late) Looking back to an earlier age of cocktails and jazz music, Mish Mish attracts a slightly older crowd of Lillenblum faithful. It's right next door to the more youthful Shesek.

Hudna PUB
(Map p120; 13 Arbanael St; ☺9pm-late) Hudna ('truce' in Arabic) is a student and hipster hang-out offering cheap beers and snacks. It is spread over two ramshackle bars across the street in Florentine and lets up-and-coming local DJs spin the tunes.

Lenny's BAR
(Map p120; 7 Vittal St; ☺8am-1am Sun-Fri, 10am-late Sat) Young and hip, Lenny's is a great little neighbourhood bar in Florentine. Other bars such as Chaser and Mate Florentine are also on this street so you can crawl easily from here.

Norma Jeane PUB
(Map p120; ☑03-683 7383; 23 Elifelet St; ☺6.30pm-late Sun-Fri, from 4pm Sat) A bistro bar named after Marilyn Monroe's given name, but really people come here for the drinks menu. It has a plethora of imported whiskies and one of the best selections of beers on tap. Call ahead to book a table or sit by the bar.

EASTERN TEL AVIV
Dancing Camel BREWERY
(Map p120; www.dancingcamel.com; 12 Hata'asia St; ☺5pm-late Sun-Thu, noon-4pm Fri, from 7pm Sat) Emerging from a run-down industrial area, the Dancing Camel is a creative brewery and pub with an American accent. It's not afraid to use ingredients like date honey, bittersweet chocolate or even cherry vanilla in its pale ales and stouts.

Porter & Sons PUB
(Map p120; ☑03-624 4355; www.porter.co.il; 14 Ha'Arba'a St; ☺noon-late; ☎) A relative newcomer on the pub scene, Porter & Sons is inspired by European boutique bars and offers over 50 kinds of beer on tap. Great for business travellers, it offers beer tasting, comfortable booths and traditional pub food.

☆ Entertainment
Nightclubs
Tel Aviv has the best nightlife in Israel, possibly the whole Middle East, but you need to be prepared for some late nights. In some places doors don't open until midnight and the party really doesn't get going until around 2am.

Most of the big commercial clubs are at the Old Port (HaNamal) in the renovated hangars, or along the seafront, and cater for young tourists and soldiers. For more alternative nights out, head south towards Florentine.

If you're going out in a group, taking a taxi can be easier than waiting for buses. There's rarely a dress code, but most people put on their clubbing best. At the time of writing, Galina (Hangar 19, Old Port), the deliberately misspelled Dizingoff (9 Kikar Dizengoff) and Chin Chin (Hangar 4, Old Port) were hot spots.

TOP CHOICE Block DJ

(off Map p120; www.block-club.com; 157 Shelomo Rd; admission 80NIS; ⏰11pm-late Thu-Sat) Now in its new location, the Block usually hosts big-name DJs playing anything from funk, hip-hop and Afrobeat to drum 'n' bass, house and trance. From Japanese DJs to visuals by Israeli street artists, anything goes.

Comfort 13 DJ

(Map p120; 13 Comfort St; admission 60NIS; ⏰11pm-late) One of Florentine's trendiest clubs; nights span from trashy pop to electronica, as well as occasional live rock bands.

HaOman Tel Aviv CLUB

(Map p120; 88 Arbanael St; admission 100NIS; ⏰1am-late) Sister club to the one in Jerusalem, this is one of the biggest, brashest clubs in the city. It hosts international DJs and has plenty of swank, including an on-site sushi bar, a sunken dance floor and five bars. Come dressed to impress.

Sublet DANCE

(Map p120; 6 Kaufmann St; ⏰9pm-late Mon-Sat) Sublet is mainstream music with a capital M. Every night is cheesy pop night at this rooftop club, popular with younger crowds. Sublet is on the seafront next to the David Intercontinental.

YaYa CLUB

(Map p120; HaMigdalor, 3 Ben Yehuda St; ⏰9pm-4am) This popular party venue is on the top floor of a tower. In the summer Thursday and Friday nights heave but there's plenty of outdoor seating on the roof terrace.

Cinemas

Cinematheque CINEMA

(Map p120; ☑03-606 0800; 1 Ha'Arba'a St; admission 37NIS) This is the flagship in a chain of Israeli cinemas that feature classic, retro, foreign, avant-garde, new wave and offbeat films. It often hosts film festivals; drop by to see what's on.

Lev Tel Aviv CINEMA

(Map p120; www.lev.co.il; Ground fl, Dizengoff Centre)

Rav-Chen Movie Theatre CINEMA

(Map p116; ☑03-528 2288; Kikar Dizengoff)

Theatre & Dance

Cameri Theatre THEATRE

(Map p120; ☑03-606 0960; www.cameri.co.il; 30 Leonardo da Vinci St) Hosts first-rate theatre performances in Hebrew, on some nights with simultaneous English translation or English-language subtitles.

Habima National Theatre THEATRE

(Map p120; ☑03-629 5555; www.habima.co.il; 2 Tarsat St, Habima Sq) Recently rebuilt, Habima is home to Israel's national theatre company and stages weekly performances with English translations.

Zoa Theatre THEATRE

(Map p120; ☑03-695 9341; 26 Ibn Gabirol St) A small theatre with nightly performances in Hebrew. The Yiddish theatre (www.yiddishpiel.co.il) occasionally performs here. It also houses the indoor Martha Bistro and outdoor Pipa Tapas Bar.

Suzanne Dellal Centre DANCE

(Map p120; ☑03-510 5656; www.suzannedellal.org.il; 5 Yechieli St) Stages a variety of performing arts including dance, music and ballet, and plays home to the world-famous Bat Sheva dance company, founded by Martha Graham.

Beit Lessin THEATRE

(Map p116; ☑03-725 5333; www.lessin.co.il; 101 Dizengoff St) It has at least one theatrical performance per week, but few in English.

Tzavta THEATRE

(Map p120; ☑03-695 0156/7; 30 Ibn Gabirol St) This club-theatre has pop and folk Israeli music, as well as Hebrew-language comedy.

Live Music

Alongside the following listings, live bands can be found in bars, cafes and on Rothschild Blvd in the summer. In recent years, big stars such as Madonna, Bob Dylan and Paul McCartney (to name a few) have all added TLV to their tours. The biggest open-air venue is the amphitheatre at the heart of Park HaYarkon, which also hosts a free concert by the Israeli Opera every July. Keep an eye out for posters about town.

Mann Auditorium CLASSICAL MUSIC

(Map p120; ☑03-621 1777; www.ipo.co.il; 1 Huberman St) Home to the Israeli Philharmonic Orchestra, the Mann Auditorium is filled with the sweet strains of classical tunes several times a week.

Goldstar Zappa Club
LIVE MUSIC

(☑03-762 6666; 24 Raul Wallenberg St, Ramat HaChayal) Local and international music luminaries play at this intimate club outside the Tel Aviv city centre (best accessed by car or taxi). Call or look out for listings to find out who's on while you're here.

Felicja Blumental Music Centre
CLASSICAL MUSIC

(Map p120; ☑03-620 1185; www.fbmc.co.il; 26 Bialik St) This regal but intimate 115-seat auditorium hosts classical and chamber music concerts. The centre, dedicated to Polish-born Brazilian pianist Felicja Blumental, is also a music library during the day.

Israeli Opera
OPERA

(Map p120; ☑03-692 7777; www.israel-opera.co.il; 19 Shaul HaMelech St) The grand home of opera, it also stages new works by Israeli composers, ballet from international troupes and world music.

Barby
LIVE MUSIC

(☑03-518 8123; 52 Kibbutz Galuyot St) A Tel Aviv institution, the Barby is at the southernmost point of the city at the end of Shocken St, a favourite venue for reggae, rock and random alternative bands.

Ozen Bar
LIVE MUSIC

(Map p120; ☑03-621 5210; 48 King George St) Known for its music store downstairs (the Third Ear); at night it hosts live guitar bands.

Shablul Jazz Club
JAZZ

(☑03-546 1891; Hangar 13; Old Port) Cool jazz, salsa and world music to keep you finger-wagging, wiggling or jiggling well on into the night.

Sport

Ramat Gan National Stadium
FOOTBALL

(229 Aba Hillel Silver Rd, Ramat Gan) Home to Israel's national soccer team and the UEFA Champions League games of Maccabi Tel Aviv and Haifa, this is the biggest stadium in the country, reached from downtown bus 42 or 67. Tickets can be bought at the stadium or in advance from **Le-an ticket agency** (Map p116; ☑03-524 7373; 101 Dizengoff St).

🔒 Shopping

Tel Aviv has plenty of shopping areas, ranging from streetside flea markets all the way up to designer boutiques and shopping malls.

Bring your credit card and some spare luggage space, and you won't leave disappointed.

Bookshops

Lametayel
BOOKS

(Map p120; ☑077 333 4502; www.lametayel.co.il; Dizengoff Centre; ⊘10am-9pm Sun-Thu, to 2.30pm Fri) Specialist in travel books, Lonely Planet titles and maps. Much more than just a bookshop, it also sells backpacks, hiking gear and tents.

Book Worm
BOOKS

(Map p116; ☑03-529 8490; 9 Rabin Sq; ⊘8.30am-10pm Sun-Thu, to 5pm Fri) Cafe-bookshop with a wide range of titles and occasional poetry readings.

Halper's
BOOKS

(Map p120; ☑03-629 9710; 87 Allenby St; ⊘9am-6pm Sun-Thu, to 4pm Fri) Specialist in used English-language titles.

Steimatzky
BOOKS

(Map p116; ☑03-522 1513; 109 Dizengoff St; ⊘9am-8pm Sun-Thu, to 4pm Fri) This branch of the chain bookstore has a decent array of English-language titles.

Markets

Crafts Market
ARTS & CRAFTS

(Map p120; Nahalat Binyamin St; ⊘9.30am-5.30pm Tue, 9am-4pm Fri) Held on Nahalat Binyamin St, this open-air crafts market makes a great place to walk around and soak up Tel Aviv's exuberant atmosphere. You'll find paintings, ceramics, jewellery and glasswork. Interspersed among the craft sellers you'll spot buskers, mime artists and dancers.

Carmel Market
MARKET

(Map p120; HaCarmel St; ⊘8am-5pm Sun-Fri) The city's main produce market, brimming with food, cheap clothing and loud stallholders; this is a place to experience the scents and sounds of Tel Aviv.

TOP CHOICE Port Market
FOOD & DRINK

(Hangar 12, Old Port; ⊘8am-8pm Mon-Sat) The indoor Port Market is the place to buy fine cheeses, sausages, meats and organic veg, as well as stop by for a coffee or tapas. It hosts a farmers market every Friday from 7am to 3pm and an Artist and Collectors' Fair on Saturdays from 10am to 6pm.

Junk Market
ANTIQUES

(Map p116; Kikar Dizengoff; ⊘Tue & Fri) If old stuff's your thing, sort through the assorted wares on offer at the junk market at Kikar

SHOP AROUND

Here's a list of where's best to head for a good, old-fashioned spending spree.

» **Allenby St** If it's cut-price garb or sort-through underwear stalls you need, Allenby St's got exactly what you're after. Haggle, rummage and score a bargain.

» **Dizengoff St** The more northerly you go along Dizengoff St, the swankier and pricier the shops become. Head here to stock up on clothing by well-known Israeli designers, peruse shoe shops or shop for wildly extravagant wedding dresses at one of scores of bridal shops.

» **Florentine** Go walkabout in the backstreets of Florentine to find little treasure-trove boutiques from up-and-coming designers, hidden among this scruffy but charming neighbourhood.

» **Kikar HaMedina (HaMedina Sq)** This wide circular square, barren and bare in the privately owned middle (there have been plans to build apartments here since 1942), is home to Tel Aviv's slew of designer names, the place to fulfil all your Gucci, Tag Heuer and Versace needs.

» **Sheinken St & around** Wander along Sheinken St, and peruse the narrower streets on either side, to find small, cool boutiques, bikini shops and sunglasses stores as well as a smattering of international chain clothing branches.

» **Neve Tzedek** Centring on Shabazi St, Neve Tzedek's little lanes abound with small, artsy stores selling clothing, trendy toys, jewellery, handmade chocolates and enticing Eastern handicrafts.

» **HaTachana** The redeveloped Old Railway Station near Neve Tzedek is an enclosed complex with Israeli designer boutiques, arts and crafts stalls and some wacky souvenirs.

» **Old Port (Namal)** (www.namal.co.il) Tel Aviv's Old Port bustles, particularly on weekends with bars, restaurants, shops and events galore. Here's where Tel Avivians take lazy Saturday morning brunches, bring their toddlers to practise their cycling skills and shop at big-brand stores such as Castro, Crocs, Nike and Levi's, even on Saturday afternoons.

Dizengoff. Among the detritus you'll find old coins, stamps and other antiques.

Shopping Malls

Dizengoff Centre   MALL
(Map p120; ☑03-621 2400; cnr Dizengoff & King George Sts; ☺9am-midnight Sun-Thu, to 4pm Fri, 8pm-midnight Sat) Israel's first mall, the Dizengoff Centre is filled with cafes, fast-food joints and major retail chains like Zara, Mango and Adidas. It also has a cinema, a supermarket, a fitness centre and an indoor pool. A delicious Israeli cooked-food market is held every Friday before Shabbat from 9am to 3pm.

Azrieli Centre   MALL
(Map p110; 132 Menachem Begin Rd; ☺10am-10pm Sun-Thu, to 4pm Fri, 8pm-midnight Sat) The first three floors of the Azrieli Centre are taken up by a shopping mall and cinema. There is a mixed bag of upmarket shops and chain retail outlets, plus an average food court.

Ramat Aviv Mall   MALL
(www.ramat-aviv-mall.co.il; Ramat Aviv) If you're looking for something slightly swisher, this is Tel Aviv's swankiest mall, just outside the city centre and home to a great selection of top-end designer names. Take bus 42 from the central bus station or a taxi from the centre for around 40NIS (15 minutes).

ℹ Information

The English-language *Tel Aviv-Jaffa Tourist* map is an excellent resource and available from the tourist information centre. Most hotels also have free tourist maps of Tel Aviv.

Emergency
Ambulance (☑101)
Fire department (☑102)
Police (☑100)
Tourist police (☑03-516 5832; cnr Herbert Samuel Esplanade & Geula St)

Internet Access

There are a number of internet cafes about town and increasing numbers of cafes, bars and hotels offering wi-fi. All branches of the Aroma coffee chain offer free wi-fi, as do all Metropoline buses. Look for the 📶 wi-fi icon throughout this chapter.

Log-In (21 Ben Yehuda St; per hr 20NIS; ⊙9am-midnight Sun-Fri, from 4pm Sat)

Surf-Drink-Play (112 Dizengoff St; 90min for 20NIS; ⊙11am-midnight)

Spielman (77 King George St; per hr 17NIS; ⊙24hr)

Cyberlink (20 Allenby St; per hr 15NIS; ⊙24hr)

Beit Ariela Library (☑03-691 0141; 25 Shaul HaMelech St; ⊙10am-6.45pm Sun-Thu, 9-11.45am Fri; 📶) The main city library has free wi-fi, plus books in English, French and Russian.

Sourasky Central Library (☑03-640 8745; Tel Aviv University; admission non-students 30NIS; ⊙9am-7.45pm Sun-Thu, to 12.15pm Fri; 📶) University library with wi-fi and a comfortable reading area.

Medical Services

Tel Aviv has top-quality medical services and hotels can contact a doctor or hospital in case of emergency.

Tel Aviv Sourasky Medical Centre (Ichilov) Hospital (☑03-697 4444; www.tasmc.org. il; 6 Weizmann St) Near the city centre, Ichilov is the city's big central hospital, with 24-hour emergency room and a travellers' clinic (the Malram Clinic) for immunisations.

Tel Aviv Doctor (☑054 941 4243; Basel Heights Medical Centre, 35 Basel St; www. telaviv-doctor.com) For a medical clinic aimed at travellers, tourists and English-speakers in Tel Aviv, call Dr Cohen.

Superpharm (62 Sheinken St, 131 Dizengoff St & 4 Shaul HaMelech Ave) This pharmacy chain has a number of branches in town, also open on Shabbat.

Clalit (☑03-525 9459; Dizengoff Centre; ⊙1-6pm Sun-Thu, 10am-2pm Fri) Clinic on the upper floor of the Dizengoff Centre that provides vaccinations for travellers.

Money

If you're seeking currency exchange bureaux, you'll find no shortage on Allenby and Dizengoff Sts; and elsewhere including Basel St. Keep an eye out for the best rates. Most are open from 9am to 9pm Sunday to Thursday, and until 2pm on Friday.

The best place to change a travellers cheque is at a post office, which will do it with no commission.

You'll have no problem finding ATM machines throughout Tel Aviv, though they sometimes run out of cash on Friday nights and Saturdays, since they're not refilled until Sunday. Here are some handy central branches:

Bank Discount (66, 103 & 164 Ibn Gabirol St, 55 & 191 Dizengoff St, 71 Ben Yehuda St, 66 Sheinken St)

Bank Leumi (19 Herzl St, 43 Allenby St, 50 Dizengoff St)

Post

Post office (www.israelpost.co.il; ⊙8am-6pm Sun-Thu, to noon Fri) North Tel Aviv (☑03-604 1109; 170 Ibn Gabirol St); City Centre (☑03-510 0218; 61 HaYarkon St); South City Centre (☑03-564 3650; cnr Mikve Yisrae'el & Levontin Sts)

Tourist Information

Tourist information office (☑03-516 6188; www.visit-tlv.com; 46 Herbert Samuel Esplanade; ⊙9.30am-5pm Sun-Thu, to 1pm Fri) A very helpful office offering maps, tips and tours.

HaTachana Tourist Information (Hangar 5, HaTachana; ⊙10am-8pm Sun-Thu, to 1pm Fri) Small office in the Old Railway Station complex.

SPNI (☑03-638 8688/8616; www.teva.org.il/english; 2 HaNegev St) Society for the Protection of Nature in Israel office, with information on hikes and nature trails.

Travel Agencies

ISSTA (☑03-521 0555; www.issta.co.il; 109 Ben Yehuda St) Student travel agency that can sometimes come up with very well-priced airline tickets. It's on the corner of Ben-Gurion.

Websites

Tel Aviv City (www.telavivcity.com/eng) Local guide to Tel Aviv.

Tel Aviv Guide (www.telavivguide.net) Entertainment, hotels and restaurant reviews.

Tel Aviv Municipality (www.tel-aviv.gov.il/english) Official website with events listings.

Visit TLV (www.visit-tlv.com) For tourist information.

ℹ Getting There & Away

Air

Most travellers fly in and out of Ben Gurion airport, many on **El Al** (☑03-977 1111; www. elal.co.il; 32 Ben Yehuda St). But **easyJet** (www. easyjet.com) also flies from Tel Aviv to London, Basel and Geneva. **Arkia** (☑03-690 3712; www. arkia.com; 74 HaYarkon St) has daily flights to Eilat (one way from 200NIS) from Sde Dov airport and also offers flights to Europe. The other domestic airline is **Israir** (☑03-795 4038; www. israirairlines.com; 23 Ben Yehuda St).

Airline offices in Tel Aviv:

Air Canada (☑03-607 2104; www.aircanada. com; Azrieli Centre, 132 Menachem Begin Rd)

Air France (☏03-755 5010; www.airfrance. com; 7 Jabotinsky St, Ramat Gan)

Alitalia (☏03-971 1047; www.alitalia.com; Terminal 3, Ben-Gurion airport)

American Airlines (☏03-795 2122; www. aa.com; 29 Ben Yehuda St)

Cathay Pacific (☏03-795 2111; www.cathay pacific.com; 29 Ben Yehuda St)

Lufthansa (☏03-975 4050; www.lufthansa. com; Terminal 3, Ben-Gurion airport) E-ticket counter only at airport.

Qantas (☏03-795 2144; www.qantas.com; 29 Ben Yehuda St)

Royal Jordanian Airlines (☏03-516 5566; www.rj.com; 5 Shalom Aleichem St)

Bus

From Tel Aviv's enormous, confusing and grotty **central bus station** (☏03-638 3945), intercity buses depart from the 6th floor, where there's also an efficient information desk. Suburban and city buses use the 4th floor and some Dan buses depart from the 1st floor. Tickets can be bought from the driver or from ticket booths. Note that during Shabbat you'll have to resort to sheruts (shared taxis).

Egged (☏03-694 8888; www.egged.co.il) buses leave for Jerusalem (Bus 405, 20NIS, one hour, every 15 minutes); for Haifa (Bus 910, 26.50NIS, 1½ hours, every 20 minutes); Tiberias (Bus 830, 835 and 841, 42NIS, 2½ hours) once or twice hourly from 6am to 9pm; Eilat (Bus 390 & 395, 78NIS, five hours), more or less hourly from 6.30am to 5pm (an overnight service departs at 12.30am); and Be'er Sheva (Bus 370, 17NIS, 1½ hours, two or three hourly).

Tel Aviv's second bus station, the open-air **Arlosorov Terminal** (☏03-695 8614; cnr Arlosorov & Namir Rd), adjoins the Tel Aviv Mercaz train station (northeast of the centre). To get there, take bus 61, which goes along Allenby, King George, Dizengoff and Arlosorov Sts. If staying in the centre or north, Egged bus 480 (20NIS, one hour, every 15 minutes) is by far the quickest way to Jerusalem.

For details on other services, see the listing for the city you'd like to go to.

Car

Finding street parking in downtown Tel Aviv can be very difficult. Cars are only allowed to park in spaces with blue-and-white curbs, many which require payment (5.50NIS per hour) during the day and are reserved for residents from 5pm to 7pm. Among the complicating factors: the yellow signs that explain the rules that apply to the side of the street they're on may not be in English; and the only way to pay for parking is with an electronic gadget (EasyPark; www.easypark. co.il, in Hebrew) or through your mobile phone using Cellopark (www.cellopark.com/eng).

Parking at the red-and-white curb is illegal and cars *will* be towed.

Parking lots and garages (often signposted with electronic information on whether they're full) charge upwards of 50NIS per 24 hours of parking. Major car parks can be found on Basel St, on Arlozorov St, by HaBima Sq and at the Reading Terminal. If you're staying in a top-end hotel, free parking is likely to be available.

If you are staying in town for a while it might be worth checking out **Car2Go** (www.car2go.co.il), which offers car rental by the hour at various locations for members.

Most of the main car-rental agencies have offices on HaYarkon St.

Avis Ben-Gurion airport (☏03-977 3200); Tel Aviv (☏03-527 1752; 113 HaYarkon St)

Eldan Ben-Gurion airport (☏03-977 3400; www.eldan.co.il); Tel Aviv (☏03-527 1166; 114 HaYarkon St)

Hertz Ben-Gurion airport (☏03-977 2444); Tel Aviv (☏03-522 3332; 144 HaYarkon St)

Sixt Ben-Gurion airport (☏03-977 3500); Tel Aviv (☏03-524 4935; 122 HaYarkon St)

Sherut (Shared Taxi)

The sheruts (yellow minibus services) outside the central bus station run to Jerusalem (20NIS) and Haifa (25NIS). On Saturday, they leave from HaHashmal St just east of Allenby St and charge about 20% more than the weekday fare.

Train

Tel Aviv has three train stations (☏03-611 7000; www.rail.co.il).

Tel Aviv Merkaz Sometimes called Tel Aviv Savidor, at the eastern end of Arlosorov St.

HaShalom Convenient for the Azrieli Centre.

HaHaganna A five-minute walk from the central bus station.

From Tel Aviv Merkaz, you can travel by train to Haifa (30.50NIS, one hour) via Netanya (15.50NIS, 25 minutes) every 20 minutes from 6am to 8pm Sunday to Friday, and on to Akko (39NIS, 1½ hours) and Nahariya (44.50NIS, 1¾ hours). Heading south, you can travel down the coast to Ashkelon (25.50NIS, one hour) and as far as Be'er Sheva (30NIS, 1¼ hours), both departing hourly. To reach Tel Aviv Merkaz from the centre, take bus 61 north from Dizengoff St to the Arlosorov bus terminal, which is a two-minute walk from the station.

ℹ Getting Around

Tel Aviv needs a good subway or tram service but while there are plans, realisation is still a long way off. Until then, a combination of bus, taxi, bike and your own two feet will have to suffice.

To/From the Airport

The most straightforward method of getting from Ben-Gurion airport into Tel Aviv is by train – the station entrance is outside the international terminal, to the left. Except very late at night, at least two trains run per hour to Tel Aviv Merkaz station (14.50NIS, from 3.30am to 11pm daily). Equally as good, but pricier, are airport taxis. Prices are controlled (and metered); make sure to head outside to the taxi rank. Depending on traffic, the ride into central Tel Aviv takes about 20 minutes and costs around 130NIS (day rate) and 152NIS (night rate).

Bicycle

Bicycle is the quickest and easiest way travel around Tel Aviv, thanks in part to over 100km of dedicated bike paths (see p109) along thoroughfares such as Rothschild Blvd, Chen Ave, Ben Gurion Ave and Ibn Gabirol St. For epic rides, go to Park HaYarkon and head east, or pedal along the 10km coastal promenade.

Bike theft has reached epidemic proportions so whenever you park your wheels (especially at night), use a massive chain lock.

For rentals, try **O-Fun** (☑03-544 2292; 197 Ben Yehuda St; per hr 25NIS, per 24hr 60NIS, weekend 100NIS) or **Pinkys** (☑03-510 5323; 15 Hayarkon St; 3hr 40NIS, per day 50NIS).

Zoombike (☑03-373 1717; Tel Aviv Mercaz train station; per hr 25NIS, per 24hr 75 NIS, weekend 95NIS) offers cool electric bicycles from the train station exit.

Bus

Tel Aviv city buses are operated by **Dan** (☑03-639 4444; www.dan.co.il; single fare 6.60NIS) and follow an efficient network of routes, from 5.30am to midnight, except Shabbat. A one-day pass *(hofshi yomi)*, which allows unlimited bus travel around Tel Aviv and its suburbs (valid from 9am until the end of the day), costs 14NIS. To buy one, you'll need a *Rav Kav* travel card, which can be obtained from a Dan information counter at the central bus station or the Arlozorov Terminal (in a hut near the train station entrance) from 8am to 6pm Sunday to Thursday or until 1pm on Friday.

Metropoline also runs services (its buses have wi-fi) from the Carmelit Terminal to the suburbs of Ra'anana (Bus 47 and 48, 13.50NIS), Kfar Saba (Bus 149, 13.50NIS) and Herzliyya (Bus 90, 10.40NIS).

TEL AVIV GETTING AROUND

WORTH A TRIP

WEIZMANN INSTITUTE OF SCIENCE

The world-renowned Weizmann Institute of Science (☑08-934 4500; www.weizmann.ac.il; ☺9am-4pm Sun-Thu) was named after the first president of Israel, Chaim Weizmann, a leading research chemist and statesman. During WWI, Weizmann's scientific research proved invaluable to the Allied war effort, and the goodwill he generated may have influenced Britain's granting of the Balfour Declaration in 1917. Established in 1934 on *moshav* (cooperative settlement) land, the institute now provides facilities for cutting-edge research in fields such as biology, chemistry, biochemistry, physics and computer science. In 2009 Weizmann professor Ada Yonath shared the Nobel Prize for Chemistry.

The new visitors centre, being renovated at the time of writing, has been temporarily moved to the Wix Auditorium. It includes an overview of the institute, the Solar Tower Observation point, a gift shop and a free film. A highlight is the Clore Garden of Science (www.weizmann.ac.il/garden; adult/child 30/20NIS; ☺10am-4pm Mon-Thu, to 1pm Fri), an outdoor science museum with a glass ecosphere. Its exhibits explore solar energy, water power and other natural phenomena.

Also on the institute's grounds, next to the tombs of Dr Chaim Weizmann and his wife, Vera, is the Weizmann House (adult/child 20/15NIS). Designed by German architect Eric Mendelsohn, a refugee from Nazism, the house was built in 1937. There is a museum inside, displaying his personal collection of photos, books and memorabilia, notably his passport (the first in Israel). Parked outside is the Lincoln limousine given to Weizmann by Henry Ford Jr, one of only two ever made (the other was given to US President Truman). It's best to call in advance for all these attractions.

The campus is in Rehovot, 25km south of Tel Aviv. You can get there by train (15NIS, 25 minutes) from any Tel Aviv station. From the train station it's a 10-minute walk to the institute. You can also catch an Egged bus from the central bus station (Bus 201 or 301, 13.50NIS, 40 minutes, every 10 minutes).

Around Tel Aviv

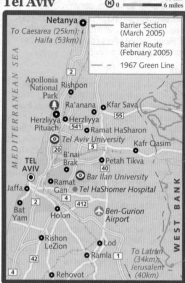

City Tour (Bus 100) Dan also runs a special tourist service in a panoramic open-top bus. It starts at the Reading Terminal and includes stops at all the major museums and Old Jaffa. The two-hour tour costs 45NIS, or a daily pass that allows you to hop on and off at every station costs 65NIS.

Taxi

By law, all taxis must use their meter. Plan on 30NIS for trips anywhere within the central city (if you have a group of four people it becomes more cost-effective than the bus). They operate according to two tariffs: the lower tariff between 5.30am and 9pm and the 25% higher night tariff between 9pm and 5am.

AROUND TEL AVIV

The greater Tel Aviv area, known as the Gush Dan region, is comprised of a web of affluent and not-so-affluent suburbs. The highlight of the region is the long stretches of golden beaches between Tel Aviv and Netanya, particularly nice around the upscale Herzliyya Pituach, but you won't be alone; Israelis flock to the coast, especially on weekends. South from Tel Aviv, historic Jaffa, with its 4000-year-old harbour, is another pleasant break from the hustle and bustle. Among the destinations listed in this section, Jaffa is the only one within walking distance from Tel Aviv; the rest are easy day trips and can be visited by local bus or train from Tel Aviv.

Currently, these are the major Tel Aviv bus routes:

Bus 4 Central bus station via Allenby St and Ben Yehuda St to the Reading Terminal, north of the Yarkon River.

Bus 5 Central bus station, along Allenby St, up Rothschild Blvd, along Dizengoff St, Nordau Ave, Ibn Gabirol St, Pinkas St, Weizmann St and HaMaccabi St and then back. Useful for the HI Hostel, the Egyptian Embassy, HaBima Sq and Kikar Dizengoff.

Bus 10 Central train station via Arlozorov St, Ben Yehuda St, Allenby St, Herbert Samuel Esplanade, Jaffa and on to Bat Yam.

Bus 18 Central train station along Menachem Begin Rd and Shaul HaMelech Ave to Ibn Gabirol St, then Rabin Sq, Dizengoff St, Pinsker St, Trumpeldor St and Ben Yehuda St, Allenby St, Yerushalayim Ave (Jaffa) and on to Bat Yam.

Bus 25 Tel Aviv University via Beit Hatefutsoth Museum, then HaMaccabi St, Ibn Gabirol St and Arlozorov St to King George St, Allenby St and Carmel Market, then on to Jaffa and Bat Yam.

Bus 61 Along King George St, Dizengoff St, Arlozorov St and Jabotinksy St to Ramat Gan.

Bus 129 Dizengoff St, King George St, Carmel Market, then down Allenby St and south to Holon and Rishon LeZion.

Sherut 4 Same route as bus 4 that operates on Shabbat.

Sherut 5 Same route as bus 5 that also operates on Shabbat.

Jaffa يافا יפו

☑ 03 / POP 46,000

With its ancient white fortress walls, tall palm trees and sea views, gentrified Old Jaffa (Yafo) is a firm stop-off for flocks of tourists in the summer. But it wasn't always so. For around 4000 years, while Tel Aviv was nothing more than sand dunes, it was Jaffa that stood as one of the great ports of the Mediterranean. Jaffa's small harbour doesn't get much seafaring traffic these days but its hangars are being transformed into new cafes, shops and art galleries. The town itself, which centres on a bustling flea market, still has the feel of a hectic hub, where Jews, Muslims and Christians intermingle. Compared to its modernised neighbour Tel Aviv, Jaffa can come across as a little shabby (expect the odd pile of rubble and unfinished building work), but this is all part of its unpretentious charm. If staying nearby,

Jaffa is a great little town for strolling, trying some Arabic food or smoking a nargileh pipe.

History

Founded, according to the Hebrew Bible, by Japheth, the son of Noah, the Israelite port of 'Joppa' came to prominence during the time of Solomon, while the temple was being built in Jerusalem. The town was later conquered by the Assyrians (701 BCE), Persians (586 BCE) and the Hellenistic Empire (382 BCE) but was neglected by the Romans, who had their own port at Caesarea.

The city fell to Islamic rule in 640 CE, but when Richard the Lionheart heard that Salah-ad-Din was executing Christians in Jaffa, the Crusaders took the city and ruled until the Mameluke invasion in 1291. The Ottomans then ruled for over 400 years, briefly interrupted in 1799 by Napoleon – at the time, Jaffa was just a small village. Jews began to move here again in the 1820s and by the end of the century, Jaffa had become a major gateway for boatloads of arriving Jewish immigrants. The British General Allenby drove out the Turks in 1917 and tensions between Jewish arrivals and the existing Arab community boiled over into full-blown anti-Jewish riots in 1921, 1929 and 1936, causing most Jews to flee. The decisive fighting of 1948 saw the defeat and subsequent flight of the majority of Jaffa's Arab population. During the 1950s, Old Jaffa became a retrogressive crime area, nicknamed 'the Wasteland'.

Since that time, Old Jaffa has been extensively renovated and developed as a centre of culture with an artists quarter, theatres, craft shops and cafes. The Arab district of Ajami, further south, has lots of Ottoman homes and crumbling charm, though there are a growing number of new apartment buildings in Jaffa catering for the overspill of Tel Aviv.

◎ Sights

OLD JAFFA

While the downtown area of Jaffa was largely constructed during the Ottoman period, the oldest remains of the city, dating back thousands of years, are in the coastal enclave of Old Jaffa. It's worth visiting twice, once in the daytime and once in the evening to savour the fine restaurants and seaside ambience.

HaPisgah Gardens   PARK

The HaPisgah Gardens are a pleasant grassy knoll with a panoramic view of the Tel Aviv seafront as its backdrop. The small **amphitheatre** in the centre of the park hosts the free **Jaffa Nights** music concerts every Saturday in July and August after 9pm. The bizarre white neo-Mayan sculpture on one of the hills depicts the fall of Jericho, Isaac's sacrifice and Jacob's dream. Connecting the gardens to the reconstructed centre of Old Jaffa is the **Wishing Bridge**. If you feel lucky, touch your zodiac sign on the rail,

TEL AVIV JAFFA

WORTH A TRIP

RISHON LEZION

Rishon LeZion (First to Zion), just 20km south of Tel Aviv, makes for a pleasant half-day trip. Founded in 1882 by European Jewish immigrants, the Old City is based on Rothschild St and includes the **Great Synagogue**, built in 1885 and registered as a warehouse because the Turkish authorities wouldn't allow the Jews a place of worship. Across the street from the synagogue the quaint **History Museum** (☑03-959 8862, 1621; 2 Ahad Ha'am St; admission 10NIS; ☺9am-2pm Sun-Thu, to 1pm Fri) is housed in a collection of period buildings that lend insight into the pioneer spirit that drove the early Zionist settlers and the obstacles they faced. Nearby you can stroll around the **Village Park**, passing the large **water tower** (built in 1898) and **village well**. Once famous for the Carmel Winery (now closed to the public), modern Rishon has sprawled out into a large industrial zone, currently home to Israel's only Ikea.

Dan buses run a service from Dizengoff St to Rishon (Bus 129, 6.80NIS) or you can take an Egged bus (Bus 84 or 163, 6.60NIS) from the central bus station. Trains (15NIS) from any of the three Tel Aviv stations also come to Rishon, departing every 20 minutes.

TEL AVIV JAFFA

Jaffa

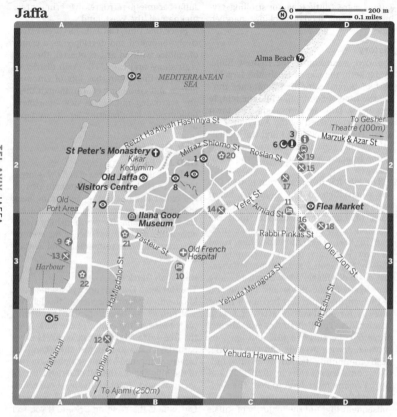

Jaffa

look towards the sea and make a wish; it may come true.

St Peter's Monastery CHURCH
(Kedumim Sq; ⏱8-11.45am & 3-5pm Oct-Feb, to 6pm Mar-Sep) The most prominent building in Jaffa, this beautiful cream-painted Franciscan church was built in the 1890s on the ruins of the Crusader citadel and is still used as a place of worship.

FREE Old Jaffa Visitors Centre MUSEUM
(Kedumim Sq; ⏱10am-6pm Sun-Thu, to 5pm Fri & Sat) Underneath the ground in Jaffa there lies 4000 years of history. So it makes sense that the main visitors centre is actually an archaeological excavation site in a chamber underneath Kedumim Sq. Here, you can view partially excavated remains from the Hellenistic and Roman era, watch a short film on Jaffa and Andromeda, plus learn about Jaffa's colourful past.

Simon the Tanner's House RELIGIOUS
Descending the steps beside the monastery, at the end of a narrow lane is Simon the Tanner's House. This is the traditional site of the house where it is said the Apostle Peter stayed after restoring Tabitha to life (Acts 9:32). In the courtyard you can see a well, believed to have been used in Peter's day, and a stone coffin from the same period.

Clock Tower LANDMARK
(Yefet St) As you are heading in or out of town, take a moment to contemplate the Ottoman clock tower. Funded by residents to mark the 25th anniversary of the reign of Sultan Abdulhamid II (1876–1909), the tower – one of seven built around Ottoman Palestine – was completed in 1903, a time when few of the sultan's subjects had watches. It's a good meeting point for tour groups.

Andromeda's Rock HISTORIC SITE
Beyond the sea wall is a cluster of blackened rocks, the largest of which is named after the goddess Andromeda who, according to Greek mythology, was chained here as a sacrificial victim but was snatched from the jaws of the great sea monster by Perseus on his winged horse. As yet there is no statue on the rocks, but it makes a good backdrop for a photo.

Ilana Goor Museum GALLERY
(☎03-683 7676; www.ilanagoor.com; 4 Mazal Dagim St; adult/child 24/14NIS; ⏱10am-4pm Sun-Fri, to 6pm Sat) This eclectic gallery is set in the labyrinth of stone alleyways named after zodiac signs. Built in the 18th century, it once served as a hostel for Jewish pilgrims arriving at Jaffa. Today it is the private home of artist Ilana Goor, who has turned it into a tasteful museum, with three floors of modern pop and ethnic art, created by artists from Israel and abroad.

Flea Market MARKET
(⏱10am-6pm Sun-Thu, to 4pm Fri) For many visitors, Jaffa's main attraction is not the thousands of years of history but the simple joy of browsing through thousands of antiques. The market (Pishpeshuk in Hebrew) illustrates the fact that there is indeed a fine line between genuine antiques and junk. If you are looking for a Persian rug, Moroccan tea-set, beautiful painting or just an old TV, then it's all here. You can barter for everything at the shuk and there are occasional outdoor auctions, attracting huge crowds. The shuk is between Olei Zion St and Beit Eshul St. Every Thursday night in the summer until midnight, the shuk becomes a stage for outdoor entertainers including jugglers and live bands.

JAFFA PORT
One of the oldest known harbours in the world, the port of Jaffa is mentioned by Hiram, King of Tyre, in conversation with Solomon (II Chronicles 2:16). It is also said to be where Jonah set sail from on the way to his fateful meeting with the whale (Jonah 1:3). For centuries Palestine's main port, Jaffa is where Jewish pilgrims to the Holy Land first arrived en route to Jerusalem.

Today, Jaffa Port, which was nothing but empty warehouses for decades, has recently been renovated, with the hope of injecting the area with a new lease of life. Like much of Israel, progress isn't instantaneous, but cafes, restaurants, galleries and shops are slowly beginning to pop up. One notable addition is the Jaffa Salon (Hangar 2; ⏱11am-6pm Mon-Fri, to 8pm Sat), exhibiting over 200 works of Palestinian art.

AJAMI
It's worth a walk down the hill from Old Jaffa or up Yefet St to the Ajami district, where gentrified Ottoman-era homes still exist side-by-side with tiny, ramshackle fishermen's shacks, for a taste of the real lives of Jaffa's Arab residents. Notorious for crime and drugs, the area featured in the Oscar-nominated 2010 film Ajami.

Ajami's seafront now opens out into a large green park and a boardwalk that connects Old Jaffa to Bat Yam. It makes a great place for a picnic, game of frisbee or a bike ride.

🏃 Activities

Old Jaffa
WALKING TOUR

Every Wednesday, a free guided Old Jaffa walking tour is led by the Association for Tourism, Tel Aviv-Jaffa. Meet in the tourist office on 2 Marzuk & Azar St, near the clock tower at 10am; the tour ends at about noon.

Sea Kayak Club
CANOEING

(☏03-681 4732; www.kayak4all.com; 2hr 150NIS) Offering sea-kayaking trips for experienced and inexperienced rowers, the Sea Kayak Club is on the Old Jaffa Port.

🛏 Sleeping

Old Jaffa Hostel
HOSTEL $

(☏03-682 2370; www.telaviv-hostel.com; 13 Amiad St; dm/s/d 80/210/250NIS; 🛜) In a beautiful old Turkish home, decorated with sepia family photographs, the Jaffa is undoubtedly the most atmospheric option in its price range, in both Tel Aviv and Jaffa. The large bar, common room and communal roof terrace are decorated with historic Arabic furniture, wind chimes and objets d'art. The rooms range from tiny singles with low ceilings to large air-conditioned double bedrooms with small balconies.

TOP CHOICE Beit Immanuel
HOSTEL $

(Map p120; ☏03-682 1459; www.beitimmanuel.org; 8 Auerbach St; dm/s/d 110/220/340NIS; 🛜) Set in a quiet cul-de-sac just off the Jaffa Rd, Beit Immanuel is opposite a tiny but pretty old Anglican church. Built in 1884 by Baron Ustinov, Peter Ustinov's father, this hostel was originally the Park Hotel, in which guise it entertained guests such as Kaiser Wilhelm II of Germany. Nicely renovated, and with a garden, it now comprises a hostel, heritage centre and church for a congregation of Messianic Jews and Arabs. The hostel is a 10-minute walk to either Jaffa or Neve Tzedek, and can be found off Jaffa Rd, where it turns into Eilat St, near the petrol station.

Andromeda Hill
APARTMENT $$$

(☏03-683 8448; www.andromeda.co.il; 3 Louis Pasteur St; apt from $200; ✳🛜🏊) These top-end apartments, with a shared pool, are part of a new complex up the hill from Yefet St.

🍴 Eating & Drinking

Jaffa is a cool dining and drinking destination bursting with high-end eating options rubbing shoulders with its tried and tested bakery joints.

Cordelia
FRENCH $$$

(☏03-518 4668; www.cordelia.co.il; 30 Yefet St; mains from 110NIS; ⏰12.30pm-1am) The home turf of Israeli celebrity chef Nir Zook, cute Cordelia, tucked up an atmospheric alleyway just off Yefet St, is all silver cutlery, mismatched dinner services and sophisticated home cooking. Come here for a romantic night out, or hop to the more relaxed – and substantially cheaper – Noa Bistro, part of the same outfit, whose entrance is just around the back. Bookings are advised.

Said Abu Elafia & Sons
BAKERY $

(7 Yefet St; snacks from 8NIS; ⏰24hr) This is a bakery that has become a legend in Israel. It was Jaffa's first bakery, established in 1880, and four generations down the line the Abu Elafia family is busier than ever and now has branches in Tel Aviv. The main attraction is its giant *sambusas* (filled pastries) or *bourekas* (stuffed breads with sheep's cheese) and a unique Arab oven-baked pizza-like concoction filled with eggs, tomato, cheese and olives.

TOP CHOICE Ali Caravan
HUMMUS $

(1 Dolphin St; hummus portions from 20NIS; ⏰around 7am-2pm Sun-Thu; 🍴) If hummus is a religion, then this could well be its Mecca. Jaffa's diminutive, unassuming Ali Caravan (also known as Abu Hassan) is a tiny restaurant, which you'll spot by its constant queue of locals waiting outside. For a real bowl of manna from heaven, order the 'triple' hummus combo or *masabacha* (chickpeas with warm tahina). Dolphin St is off Yehuda Hayamit St, on the way down to the Port.

Dr Shakshuka
ISRAELI $

(3 Beit Eshal St; meals 40-50NIS; ⏰8am-midnight Sun-Fri; 🍴) If browsing Jaffa's flea market has seen your energy flagging, don't miss a quick, cheap and filling lunch at Dr Shakshuka. The setting is an old Ottoman-era building decorated with hanging lamps, dried chilli peppers and abandoned guitars, but the real highlight is the food. Along with its eponymous *shakshuka*, the Gabso family whips up a range of Libyan and other North African delights.

Yaffo Cafe
ITALIAN **$**

(☑03-518 1988; 11 Olei Zion St; mains from 42NIS; ⊗9am-11pm Sun-Thu, to 4pm Fri, 6-11.30pm Sat; 🔊🍴) This Italian bistro is a welcome sight amid the hustle and bustle of the flea market. With occasional live jazz and an extensive list of Israeli wines such as Tishbi, it has a buzzing vibe at night. Its range of cheesy pastas, pizzas and salads makes it a good choice for vegetarians, while it also does a fine salmon fillet. The homemade ice-cream counter will keep kids and adults happy.

Puaa
CAFE **$$**

(☑03-6823821; www.puaa.co.il; 8 Rabbi Yohanan St; mains from 48NIS; ⊗9am-1am; 🔊) Part retro-style cafe and part antique gallery, this popular place specialises in lunchtime soups and salads, but dabbles in fish and chicken dishes. The beverage selection includes an excellent yoghurt drink with cardamom. Aside from the food, the furniture, paintings and crockery are all up for sale.

Yo'Ezer
STEAKHOUSE **$$$**

(☑03-683 9115; www.yoezer.com; 2 Yoezer Aish Ha'bira St; mains from 88NIS; ⊗12.30pm-1am Sun-Thu, 11am-1am Fri & Sat) Hidden down a dark alleyway near the clock tower, this stone-walled cellar is a carnivore and wine-lover's delight offering quality steak, sausages and vintage wines. Vegetarians won't be at a total loss: plump for the blue-cheese salad and truffle-infused egg noodles. Book a table well in advance at weekends.

Container
FUSION **$$**

(www.container.org.il; Warehouse 2, Jaffa Port; ⊗noon-late Sun-Thu, from 10am Fri & Sat) This renovated warehouse is one of the trendiest hotspots on the port. Part restaurant, late-night bar and art space, the Container serves a mix of seafood, pasta and Israeli-style brunches. Like the food, at night the music is a fusion of world, dub and dance from well-known local DJs.

Saloona
BAR **$**

(Map p120; 17 Tirzta St; ⊗noon-late) Cool, artsy and tucked away, Saloona is one of the area's best bars, equipped with weird and wonderful decor, strong drinks and regular live DJs.

☆ Entertainment

TOP CHOICE **Nalaga'at Centre**
THEATRE

(☑03-633 0808; www.nalagaat.org.il; Jaffa Port) A unique nonprofit organisation set in a renovated shipping hangar, Nalaga'at (meaning 'Do Touch') is the only deaf-blind theatre company in the world. While watching a show here, it's easy to forget that the people on stage cannot see or hear, as the actors tell stories, play musical instruments and even perform choreographed dances. Aside from the theatre, it comprises **Cafe Kapish** (whose ultrafriendly waiters are all deaf) and the **BlackOut** restaurant, where diners eat in darkness, assisted by blind waiters.

Arab–Jewish Theatre
THEATRE

(☑03-681 5554; www.arab-hebrew-theatre.org.il; 10 Mifratz Shlomo St) Two cultures, one stage. This theatre showcases Hebrew and Arabic-language plays that explore genuine coexistence and openly discusses differences between Arabs and Jews.

Mayumana
DANCE

(☑03-681 1787; www.mayumana.com; 15 Louis Pasteur St) Starting out in a Tel Aviv basement in 1996, the Israeli version of *Stomp* is now a huge global hit so you'll need to book well in advance.

Gesher Theatre
THEATRE

(☑03-515 7000; www.gesher-theatre.co.il; 7-9 Yerushalayim Ave) Contemporary Hebrew theatre largely comprising new immigrants from Russia; it sometimes has bilingual plays.

ℹ Information

Tourist office (☑03-516 6188; 2 Marzuk & Azar St; ⊗9.30am-5pm Sun-Thu, to 1pm Fri) The tourist information office is at the entrance of Jaffa, near the clock tower.

ℹ Getting There & Away

From the centre of Tel Aviv, it's a pleasant 2.5km seafront stroll to Old Jaffa. Alternatively, take bus 18 from Tel Aviv Mercaz train station or Dizengoff St, bus 10 from Ben Yehuda St, bus 25 from Ibn Gabirol St or Allenby St and get off at the clock tower. To return to the centre, take bus 10 or 25 from Yerushalayim Ave.

Herzliyya   هرتسليا   הרצליה

☑09 / POP 87,000

Just 20 minutes' drive north of Tel Aviv, Herzliyya is increasingly popular with visitors, especially from the US, due to its fine, clean beaches, marina mall and a string of seafront cafes. Named after Theodor Herzl, the founder of modern Zionism, Herzliyya started as a small farming community in 1924 and now consists of two towns separated by Highway 2. Herzliyya town (east) is mainly residential, while **Herzliyya Pituach** (west towards the sea) is an enclave of huge villas, home to some of Israel's wealthiest residents. *Pituach* (which means 'development') is also home to Israel's blossoming hitech industry; hence modern office blocks are rising up all over the city.

◉ Sights

Apollonia National Park PARK
(adult/child 20/9NIS; ⊗8am-5pm Apr-Sep, to 4pm Oct-Mar, closes 1hr earlier Fri & holiday eves) This picturesque coastal park contains the ruins of a Crusader castle that becomes the venue for open-air concerts during summer weekends. There are some stunning views out over the Mediterranean and nearby you can see the remains of a Roman villa and the well-kept 13th-century Sidni Ali Mosque. The park is north of Herzliyya, just beyond the small town of Nof Yam. It can be reached by a fairly long walk up Wingate St or easily by car from the highway.

Herzliyya Museum of Modern Art MUSEUM
(☎09-955 1011; 4 HaBanim St; admission 10NIS; ⊗10am-2pm Mon, Wed, Fri & Sat, 4-8pm Tue & Thu) If you are in town during its rather sporadic opening hours, this small museum of contemporary art is worth a quick visit.

🏃 Activities

Reef SURFING
(☎09-957 4461; www.reefisrael.com) Located on the beach under the Dan Accadia Hotel, Reef offers private surfing lessons (180NIS, one hour) as well as instructed scuba dives (220NIS, one hour).

🛏 Sleeping & Eating

As you would expect from such an affluent area, Herzliyya accommodation consists of luxury spa hotels, but there are many restaurants for all budgets around the marina and on the beach.

Okeanos HOTEL $$$
(☎09-961 6222; www.okeanos.co.il; 50 Ramat Yam St; s/d/ste US$215/285/335; ❈🔊🐾) Bang in the middle of Ramat Yam, the main seafront road, Okeanos is a luxury hotel with all mod cons. It may be slightly smaller than the other hotel towers in Herzliyya, but its rooms have panoramic sea views and there is a good-sized outdoor swimming pool.

TOP CHOICE Derby Bar SEAFOOD $$
(☎09-951 1818; Arena Mall; dishes 69-89NIS; ⊗noon-midnight) This well-known restaurant serves mouth-watering dishes such as sea bream, shrimps and crabs, along with as many complimentary salads as you like. Part of the Arena shopping mall, Derby overlooks the expensive yachts on the marina.

Benedict BREAKFAST $$
(☎09-958 0701; www.benedict.co.il; 1 Haetzel St; breakfasts from 52NIS; ⊗24hr) It's always breakfast time at this fine cafe, directly opposite the Okeanos Hotel, offering the same menu as its sister branches in Tel Aviv. Diners can fill up on eggs Benedict, *shakshuka* or any other morning munch.

ℹ Getting There & Away

Metropoline bus 90 runs every 20 minutes to and from Tel Aviv (10.40NIS, 30 minutes). Trains run every 20 minutes from Tel Aviv (9NIS, 15 minutes), Netanya (12.50NIS, 15 minutes) and Haifa (28.50NIS, one hour). The station is quite far from the beach, so take a taxi or bus 29 to the marina.

Netanya نتانيا נתניה
☎09 / POP 183,200

Netanya offers 11km of the finest sandy beaches in Israel, while the town itself exudes a rather strange, time-warp sort of feeling, like an out-of-season French seaside resort. It's popular with retirees from France and the UK; grandparents and children can be seen enjoying the spacious seaside promenade with its parks, flower beds and water features. The European flavour continues on the lively main street, which is lined with a mix of cafes, crêperies and Judaica souvenir shops. The beaches remain popular with visiting French and Russian tourists but are far less crowded than those of Tel Aviv.

🏃 Activities

Beaches SWIMMING
Israelis come from all over to enjoy Netanya's expansive golden beaches. There are lifeguards on duty, plus changing rooms, showers, lounge chairs and umbrellas. HaRishonim Promenade, the cliff above the beach, is great for strolling and sea views. From here you can even take an **elevator** down to the beach.

Ranch
HORSE RIDING

(☑09-866 3525; www.yellowgreenfarm.co.il, in He-brew; 1hr 120NIS) Horse riding is available at the Ranch, on the northern edge of Netanya. It offers daytime and moonlight rides on the beach.

Folk Dancing
DANCING

If you are in town on Shabbat you might spot folk dancing around Ha'atzamaut Sq.

🛏 Sleeping & Eating

Unless you're looking for a sleepy 1970s-style French resort, there's probably not much point basing yourself in Netanya. Still, if you are intending to stay overnight, check the **Netanya Hotel Association** (www.netanya hotels.org.il) for options.

King Solomon
HOTEL $$$

(☑09-833 8444; www.inisrael.com/kingsolomon; 18 Hamapilim St; s/d US$155/170; ❄🎧🛜) With-out doubt the best (and priciest) of the Netanya bunch. An eye-catching red lobby leads to stark white rooms with new carpets and balconies offering sea views. All rooms come with flat-screen TV and fridge and there is access to a jacuzzi, gym, sauna and outdoor pool.

TOP CHOICE Shtampfer
CAFE $

(6 Shtampfer St; dishes 43-50NIS; ⊙9am-2am; 🎧) Veering away from Netanya's usual batch of family restaurants, Shtampfer (named after one of the founders of Petach Tikva) attracts a livelier crowd, chatting away on the large patio as funky music plays. The menu runs from fruit shakes and salads to pastas and stir-fries. In the evening it turns into a bar.

Marrakesh
MOROCCAN $$

(☑09-833 4797; 5 David Hamelech St; dishes from 60NIS; ⊙noon-midnight Sun-Thu, to 4pm Fri, 8pm-midnight Sat) Tuck into tasty tagines, couscous and meat dishes in this kosher Moroccan restaurant near the seafront. The whole restaurant is shaped like a giant tag-ine pot with its splendid domed ceiling; in-side it is decorated with exotic lanterns and comfy cushions.

ℹ Information

Tourist office (☑09-882 7286; www.gon etanya.com; Ha'Atzmaut Sq; ⊙8.30am-4pm Sun-Thu, 9am-noon Fri) Housed in a kiosk at the southwest corner of Ha'Atzmaut Sq.

WORTH A TRIP

RISHPON

Just off the coastal Hwy 2, a few kilo-metres north from Herzliyya, you'll find the sleepy village of Rishpon. This is where many Tel Avivians come on Friday mornings, to sip a cappuccino in one of its little cafes, buy flowers from its well-known flower shops and just relax away from the noise of the city.

On the other side of the highway is the **Shefayim Water Park** (☑09 959 5756; www.waterpark.co.il; admission 98NIS; ⊙9am-5pm Sat-Thu May-Oct). Part of the Kibbutz Shefayim holiday village, it is Israel's biggest water park, boast-ing 22 slides and three large pools. Opening hours can change, so visitors are advised to call ahead.

ℹ Getting There & Away

Egged buses run roughly every 15 minutes to and from Tel Aviv (Bus 641, 18NIS, 30 minutes), and every half hour to and from Haifa (Bus 947, 24NIS, one hour) and Jerusalem (Bus 947, 30NIS, 1¼ hours). To reach Caesarea, Megiddo, Nazareth or Tiberias, change buses in Hadera. Sheruts (13NIS, 20 minutes) and the train are the quickest ways to get to Tel Aviv.

Ramla   الرملة   רמלה

☑03 / POP 65,800

With its bustling market, underground pools and crumbling Islamic architecture, Ramla makes for an interesting half-day trip from Tel Aviv. It's not quite as old as nearby Jaffa – history here stretches back 'only' 1300 years – but the town is notewor-thy as the only one in Israel founded and originally developed by Arabs.

Established in 716 CE by the Umayyid caliph Suleiman, Ramla (spot of sand) was a stopover on the road from Egypt to Da-mascus. Prior to the arrival of the Crusaders in the 11th century, Ramla was Palestine's capital and it maintained its importance in the Middle Ages as the first stop for the Jerusalem-bound pilgrims who came ashore at Jaffa. Following the 1948 Arab–Israeli War the majority of the Arab population fled and they were replaced by poor Jewish im-migrants, mainly from Asia (eg India) and North Africa.

Ramla

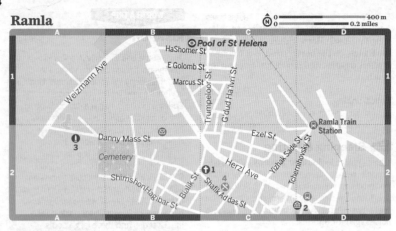

Ramla

ⓞ Top Sights
Pool of St Helena B1

ⓞ Sights
1 Church of St Nicodemus &
   St Joseph of Arimathea C2
2 Ramla Museum D2
3 White Tower A2

⊗ Eating
4 Samir Restaurant C2

Although just 20km southeast of Tel Aviv, Ramla's handful of Islamic and Christian monuments and friendly mixed population of Arabs (20%) and Jews (80%) make it worth a visit, especially for the Wednesday market.

⊙ Sights

Ramla Museum   MUSEUM
(☏03-929 2650; 112 Herzl Ave; admission 6NIS; ⊙9am-4pm Sun-Thu, to 1pm Fri) The small Ramla Museum, aside from providing a basic overview of the town's history, also acts as Ramla's de facto tourist information centre. For 12NIS you can buy a joint ticket for the museum, the White Tower and the Pool of St Helena. It stands in front of Ramla's market and Great Mosque. The market is busiest on Wednesday.

FREE **Church of St Nicodemus & St Joseph of Arimathea**   CHURCH
(cnr Bialik St & Herzl Ave; ⊙9am-noon Mon-Fri) The Church of St Nicodemus & St Joseph of Arimathea was constructed in the 16th century on what Christians believe to be the site of biblical Arimathea, the hometown of Joseph, who is said to have arranged the burial of Jesus with Nicodemus (John 19:38-39). Owned by the Franciscans, the church's claim to fame is that Napoleon stayed in the adjacent monastery during his unsuccessful campaign against the Turks. The church itself has a distinctive square bell tower and a painting above the altar that is attributed to Titian *(The Deposition from the Cross)*. The entrance to the church is off Bialik St, through the first gate on your left. Ring the bell and one of the nuns living here will let you in.

White Tower   MONUMENT
(Danny Mass St; admission 5NIS; ⊙8am-3pm Sun-Thu, to 2pm Fri, to 4pm Sat) The slightly neglected White Tower is a 14th-century minaret built as an addition to the 8th-century White Mosque (Jamaa al-Abiad), of which only traces remain. The inscription above the door to the tower, dating from 1318, indicates renovations at the site made by Sultan Muhammad Al-Nasir. The site includes three original cisterns and the shrine of Nabi Salih, an ancient prophet mentioned seven times in the Koran. An attendant should be on hand to let you inside the tower.

Pool of St Helena   HISTORIC SITE
(HaHaganah St; admission 8NIS; ⊙8am-3pm Sun-Thu, to 2pm Fri, to 4pm Sat) Set in pleasant gardens, the Pool of St Helena is an atmospheric underground 8th-century reservoir. Although the name refers to the mother of

the Roman emperor Constantine, in Arabic it's called the Pool of Al-Anazia and Breichat Hakeshatot (the Pool of Arches) in Hebrew. Visitors can row a boat, admiring the shadowy arches and shafts of daylight.

Eating

TOP CHOICE Samir Restaurant   KEBAB **$**
(7 Kehlat Detroit St; dishes 25-35NIS; ☺8am-8pm) The clock turns back several centuries in historic Samir, an old Arab family-run restaurant emerging from a dusty backstreet behind the market and set in a refurbished Turkish house. It has an English menu and serves various meat kebabs, hummus and salads.

ⓘ Getting There & Away

There are trains to Ramla (14NIS, 20 minutes) from Tel Aviv departing every 20 minutes throughout the day. Buses and sheruts to Tel Aviv (14NIS, 40 minutes) run every 20 minutes, with slightly less-frequent services to Jerusalem (24NIS, 75 minutes). While buses to Tel Aviv depart until around 10pm, the last Jerusalem bus is at 8pm.

Haifa & the North Coast

Best Places to Eat

» Mayan Habira (p169)
» Fatoush (p169)
» Doña Rosa (p175)
» Uri Buri (p186)

Best Places to Stay

» Port Inn (p168)
» Beth Shalom Hotel (p168)
» HI – Knights Hostel & Guest House (p185)
» Akkotel (p185)

Why Go?

Israel's north coast is a tranquil stretch of the Mediterranean punctuated with old farms, quaint seaside towns and historical sites.

The principle city is Haifa, a mixed Jewish-Arab city that often surprises visitors with its openness and tolerance. Sprawling across Mt Carmel, Haifa has stunning views, a wealth of museums and the magnificent Baha'i Gardens. Redevelopment has created a thriving nightlife and arts scene.

Haifa is the starting point for a journey north to the historic port of Akko and the spectacular grottoes of Rosh HaNikra. In the other direction, Herod's port at Caesarea and the ancient civilizations of Megiddo should be on the radar of any history buff. Also in the area, Ein Hod and Zichron Ya'acov are both fine destinations for anyone with a taste for art, wine and homemade beer. After your travels, take some time to chill out on the beaches around Nahariya and Akhziv.

When to Go
Haifa

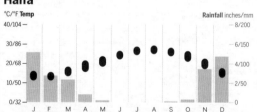

Dec Weekends feature an outdoor carnival in Wadi Nisnas, celebrating the major religious holidays.

Apr–May Temperatures are pleasant and the flowers in the Baha'i Gardens are blooming.

Sep A fine month for road trips, hikes or relaxing days on the beach.

Climate

The north coast sees warm summer temperatures that reach into the low thirties (Celsius) and winter temperatures dip to the low teens. It's one of the wettest parts of the country, with more than 150mm of rain falling in December and January, a fact that allows most of the region to stay green through the year.

ⓘ Getting There & Around

There are plenty of bus and train links from Tel Aviv and Jerusalem to Haifa and the north coast. If you are driving, the usual drive is up Hwy 2 (though Hwy 4 is the scenic route). Note that Hwy 6 is a toll road; if you travel on it your

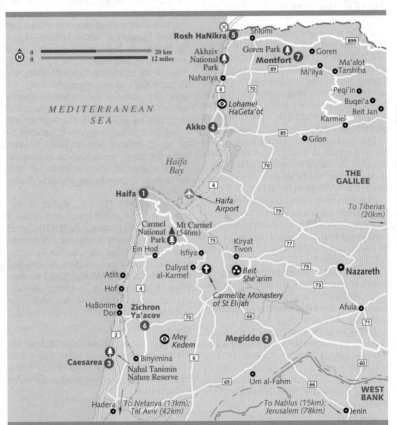

HAIFA & THE NORTH COAST

Haifa & the North Coast Highlights

❶ Stop to smell the roses in the spectacular **Baha'i Gardens** (p158), Haifa's most recognisable site

❷ Wait for Armageddon at **Megiddo** (p180), a biblical site expected to host the end of the world

❸ Explore the impressive ruins at **Caesarea** (p176), Herod's port city

❹ Weave through the underground passages of **Akko** (p181), an extraordinary walled city-on-the-sea

❺ Feel the power of Mother Nature at **Rosh HaNikra** (p188), where the Mediterranean crashes into time-worn grottoes

❻ Sample some wine and cruise the main street of

quirky **Zichron Ya'acov** (p175), home to museums and galleries

❼ Stretch your legs on the mild hike to **Montfort** (p187), an impressive Crusader castle only reached on foot

rental-car company will charge your credit card. There are also bus links to the Galilee region; drivers take Hwy 77 from Tiberias.

The best way around the area is with a car. Otherwise, buses can get you to (or close to) most places, though you may have to put up with some long waits.

Haifa حيفا חיפה

♪04 / POP 264,900

Haifa Bay is the best natural harbour on the Israeli coast and so was destined to be the site of a major port. The graceful contour of the shoreline contrasts with the steep sides of Mt Carmel, which rises majestically to a height of 546m. With sweeping views of the sea, serpentine roads and one of the most beautiful gardens in the world, Haifa is one of the most picturesque cities in the Middle East.

One of Haifa's more unique aspects is its mixed population of Arabs and Jews, living together in visible harmony. Haifans pride themselves on the belief that they can be a model for tolerance in the region.

Haifa's economy was long based on industry and blue-collar jobs but that has changed in recent years with the development of a flourishing high-tech sector thanks in part to the presence of the Technion – Israel Institute of Technology.

Despite Haifa's working-class core, generations of mayors have put significant effort into developing the city's arts and culture community, founding a variety of museums and other cultural institutions.

Haifa's most striking feature is the Baha'i Gardens, an inspired stripe of flower-speckled green running down the flank of Mt Carmel. Visitors interested in the city's religious heritage may also want to visit Elijah's Cave and the neo-Gothic Stella Maris Carmelite Monastery.

Haifa's central location and good transport links make it a useful base from which to explore the Galilee. With a car, it's possible to reach all the sites in this chapter – and quite a few places covered in the Lower Galilee & Sea of Galilee chapter – on day trips.

History

The city's name first appeared in 3rd-century Talmudic literature and although its origin remains obscure, it's been suggested that 'Haifa' is related to the Hebrew words *hof yafe,* which means 'beautiful coast'.

A thousand years ago, Haifa was an important Arab town, but early in the 12th century it was destroyed in battles with the Crusaders. Nearby Akko soon superseded the town in importance, and by the time of the Ottoman conquest of Palestine in the 1500s Haifa was an insignificant village.

By the early 19th century, Haifa's Jewish community had begun to grow, and in the late 1800s German Templers settled here, but the city's modern revival really got under way in 1905 with the opening of a railway line linking Haifa with Damascus and Medina. During the British Mandate, Haifa rapidly became Palestine's main port, naval centre and oil terminal.

As the country's principal port, Haifa was the first sight of the 'Promised Land' for many ship-borne Jewish refugees. Shortly before the British withdrawal from Palestine, Haifa became a Jewish stronghold and it was the first major area to be secured by the newly declared State of Israel in 1948. Today, the mostly secular Jewish community enjoys a generally good relationship with the city's Arab population, which is mainly Christian.

In recent years Haifa has shifted its economic centre of gravity from heavy industry to high-tech. An IT park near Hof HaCarmel bus station is home to divisions of Google, Intel, IBM and other international IT heavyweights. The techies work through thick and thin – during the 2006 war with Lebanon, when Haifa was hit by 93 Hezbollah rockets, they continued to write code while hunkered inside bomb shelters.

Maps

Free street maps are available at most hotels and the Haifa tourist office. The tourist office also sells a glossy map (4NIS) with a backside containing information on sights and activities.

◉ Sights

Haifa's premier attraction is the Baha'i Gardens. Museums are scattered around Wadi Nisnas, Hadar and Carmel Centre – all can be reached by foot and by the Carmelit subway. The maritime museums, Elijah's Cave and the Stella Maris Carmelite Monastery are a few kilometres northwest and are best reached by bus 114.

FREE Baha'i Gardens   GARDENS
(Map p162; ♪04-835 8358; www.ganbahai.org.il; ⊙9am-5pm Thu-Tue) With every tree trimmed to perfection and every blade of grass seem-

Haifa

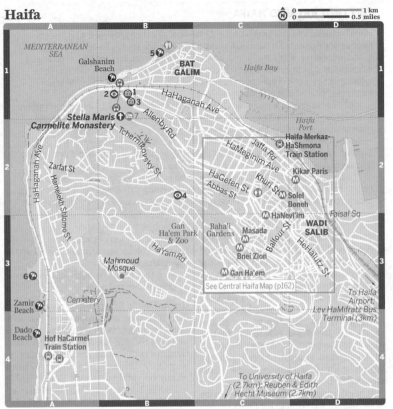

ingly cut to the exact same height, the 19 terraces of the Baha'i Gardens are a sight to behold. In 2008 the gardens and associated shrines and monuments were given World Heritage status by Unesco.

The gardens are one of the two great holy places for members of the Baha'i faith. Baha'ullah, the religion's second leader, visited Mt Carmel four times and announced to his son that this would be the final resting place of the remains of the Bab, his spiritual predecessor who was executed in Persia in 1850.

The Bab's remains were brought to Haifa in 1909 and interred in the golden-domed **Shrine of the Bab** (⊙9am-noon), which combines the style and proportions of European architecture with designs inspired by the Orient. Truly an international building, it was designed by a Canadian architect and built with Italian stone and Dutch tiles.

GETTING AROUND HAIFA

Haifa is divided into three main tiers, with levels of affluence growing the further you head up the slopes of Mt Carmel. Travellers arriving from Tel Aviv or Jerusalem by bus or train are set down at Hof HaCarmel, which is about 5km south of the city – you'll need to change to a local train or bus to reach Haifa Merkaz, the port area, which is within walking distance of the downtown area. Note that some buses do terminate at Lev HaMifratz, located east of downtown.

A familiar landmark is Kikar Paris (Paris Sq), the lower terminal of the city's miniature subway line (the Carmelit). One kilometre west of Kikar Paris is Ben-Gurion Ave, the main thoroughfare of the trendy German Colony.

About a half-kilometre hike uphill from Kikar Paris is Hadar HaCarmel (Glory of the Carmel) area, or Hadar for short. Hadar is the city's traditional commercial centre, with a heavy concentration of shops, offices and restaurants.

The Carmel district occupies the higher slopes of the city, where exclusive residences benefit from cool breezes and magnificent views. The main street, HaNassi Ave, has several excellent restaurants and a youthful – if somewhat *Yekke* (prewar German-Jewish) – vibe.

The tomb, which was completed in 1953, is considered one of the two most sacred sites for the world's five million Baha'is (the other site is the tomb of Mirza Hussein Ali outside nearby Akko). Visitors to the shrine must remove their shoes and be modestly dressed (no shorts or bare shoulders).

Higher up the hill, behind the shrine, stands the **Universal House of Justice** (closed to the public), a domed, colonnaded neoclassical structure from which the Baha'is' spiritual and administrative affairs are governed.

While the gardens right around the Shrine of the Bab were laid out in the 1960s, the terraces both below and above the gold domed-domed structure were laid out between 1987 and 2001, at a cost of some US$250 million. Pilgrims solemnly tread uphill, soothed by the sounds of the lapping water as it flows past the steps. The 19 terraces have a distinctly classical feel, with wrought-iron gates opening up to stone balustrades, sculptures, fountains and impossibly steep walls of grass. One hundred full-time gardeners are on hand to maintain the site.

Access to the Baha'i Gardens is limited. There is one tour per day (except Wednesday) departing at noon; be sure to arrive at 11.30am as its first-come first-served and only 60 people are allowed in daily. Meet at the appointed time at Ye'fe Nof St at the top of the garden (and a little down to the left, look for the sign). Baha'i pilgrims can organise individual entry. Rain usually closes the tours.

The best way to get here is by taking the subway to the top of the mountain and then walking to the top of the gardens. From the German Colony you can take bus 23 up the mountain.

Note that it's a one-hour walk in the sun so bring water and a hat.

Ursula Malbin Sculpture Garden GARDENS
(Map p159; www.malbin-sculpture.com; Gan HaPesalim, HaZiyonut Blvd; ⊙6am-6pm) Further downhill on Ye'fe Nof St, west of the Baha'i Gardens, is this small park filled with contemporary bronze sculptures focusing mainly on children at play. Ursula Malbin is a Berlin-born sculptor who fled Nazi Germany in 1939. Since 1967 she has split her time working in Ein Hod and Switzerland.

University of Haifa UNIVERSITY
(off Map p159; www.haifa.ac.il; Mt Carmel) One of Israel's premier places of higher learning, University of Haifa, 5.5km south of Carmel Centre, covers all areas of academia, but specialises in the liberal arts. There is another spin on 'higher learning' here as the university is perched spectacularly on the summit of Mt Carmel with views of Haifa and far beyond. The best place to take in the panorama is from the observation deck of the 27-storey **Eshkol Tower**, which was designed by the renowned Brazilian architect Oscar Niemeyer.

The basement of the Eshkol Tower houses the impressive **Reuben & Edith Hecht Museum** (off Map p159; http://mushecht.haifa.ac.il; admission free; ⊙10am-4pm Sun-Mon & Wed-Thu, to 7pm Tue, to 1pm Fri, to 2pm Sat), which houses a fine collection of archaeological artefacts relating to Jewish history before the Diaspora. There is plenty of ancient pottery, weapons and even a pair of 2100-year-old petite-sized sandals on display. The museum highlight is a 5th-century-BCE Greek ship found near Caesarea in 1984. It has been carefully re-built and placed in a specially designed an-nexe of the museum. An art wing upstairs contains sections on French Impressionist and Jewish art from the 19th and 20th cen-turies. Among the works are paintings by Monet, Pissarro and Van Gogh.

Near Eshkol Tower, check out the open-air museum, a collection of ancient build-ings brought here from other parts of Israel and reconstructed. There are several build-ings from the Negev and an oil press from Kastra, on the Carmel coast.

Tours of the university can be made, but by advance booking only; call ☏04-824 0097 to make a reservation.

To get to the university take bus 37a from outside the Carmel Centre or bus 46 from the Hof HaCarmel train station.

CARMEL CENTRE

As Haifa quickly rose up Mt Carmel during its great expansion in the early 20th century, real-estate speculators banked on the top of the hill. Not only were the views great, but the hilltop enjoyed a pleasant breeze and was always a few degrees cooler than the port area. Carmel Centre (Merkaz HaKarmel), as it became known, was soon home to a clutch of five-star hotels plus a quaint main drag lined with cafes and boutiques. Cultural life is centred on a cinematheque that screens art-house films.

Mane Katz Museum MUSEUM
(Map p162; 89 Ye'fe Nof St; adult/child 30/20NIS; ⊙10am-4pm Sun-Mon & Wed-Thu, 2-6pm Tue, 10am-1pm Fri, to 2pm Sat) As you stroll behind the hotels you'll spot the entrance for the Mane Katz Museum. Mane Katz (1894–1962), an influential member of the group of Jewish Expressionists based in Paris early in the 20th century, was given this home by the Haifa city authorities in return for the bequest of his works to the city. Mane Katz was a collector of Judaica and much of this is on display. The exhibits change every six months so if you have been here before it's worth a second look. A ticket here is good for the Tikotin Museum (for one day).

THE BAHA'I

Founded in the middle of the 19th century, the Baha'i faith (www.bahai.org) believes that many prophets have appeared throughout history, including Abraham, Moses, Buddha, Krishna, Zoroaster, Jesus and Mohammed. Its central beliefs include the existence of one God, the equality and unity of all human beings, and the unity of all religion.

The origins of the Baha'i faith go back to Ali Muhammad (1819–50), a native of Shiraz, Iran. In 1844 he declared that he was 'the Bab' (Gate) through which prophecies would be revealed. The charismatic Ali was soon surrounded by followers, called Babis, but was eventually arrested for heresy against Islam and executed by firing squad in Tabriz.

One of the Bab's prophecies concerned the coming of 'one whom God would make manifest'. In 1866, a Babi named Mirza Hussein Ali proclaimed that he was this messianic figure and assumed the title of Baha'ullah, having received divine inspiration while im-prisoned in Tehran's infamous Black Pit.

As with the Bab, Baha'ullah's declarations were unwelcome in Persia and he was ex-pelled first to Baghdad, and then to Constantinople, Adrianople and finally the Ottoman penal colony of Akko. Sitting in his cell in Akko he dedicated himself to laying down the tenets of a new faith, the Baha'i, whose name is derived from the Arabic word baha (glory).

Among his writings, Baha'ullah stated that one could not be born into the Baha'i faith; at the age of 15, a person chooses whether or not they want to take on the obligations of being Baha'i. He also spoke of gender equality, the oneness of mankind, world peace, the need for universal compulsory education and harmony between religion and the sciences.

The Baha'i faith now has an estimated five million followers worldwide. Only a hand-ful reside permanently in Israel, site of the Baha'i World Centre (the religion's global headquarters), whose gardens and institutions, on Haifa's Mt Carmel, are staffed by volunteers from around the world. In part to assuage Jewish sensibilities about proselyt-ising, Baha'is do not seek converts in Israel and Israeli citizens are not permitted to join the faith. Tradition dictates that a Baha'i who is able should make a pilgrimage (https://bahai.bwc.org/pilgrimage) to Akko and Haifa.

Central Haifa

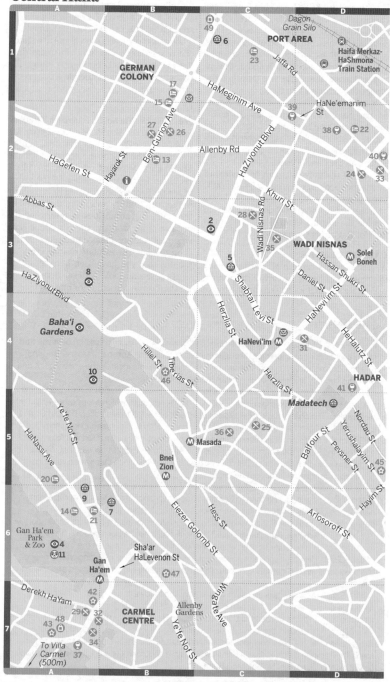

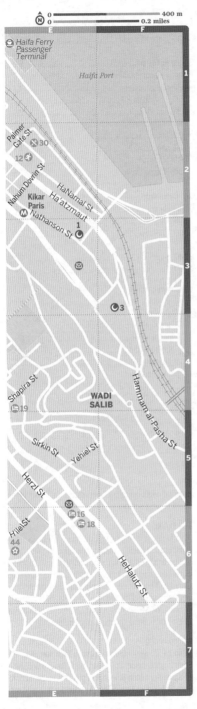

Tikotin Museum of Japanese Art   MUSEUM

(Map p162; www.hms.org.il; 89 HaNassi Ave; adult/child 30/20NIS; ⊙10am-4pm Mon-Wed, 4-9pm Thu, 10am-1pm Fri, 10am-4pm Sat) The somewhat incongruous Tikotin Museum of Japanese Art puts on excellent exhibits of artwork from Japan. Founded by Felix Tikotin in 1957, it features everything from 14th-century Buddhist scroll art to pottery, metal work and newer exhibits on Japanese animation and even Pokémon. A ticket here is good for the Mane Katz Museum (for one day).

Gan Ha'Em   PARK

(Map p162) On the crest of Carmel, across from the upper Carmelit subway station, is Gan Ha'em (Mother's Park), a cool swath of greenery with an arcade of shops and cafes, and an amphitheatre that hosts summer evening concerts.

Zoo   ZOO

(Map p162; admission 30NIS; ⊙9am-6pm Sat-Thu, to 2pm Fri) The northern area of Mother's Park is given over to an attractive small zoo, which sports an aviary, a reptile house and microhabitats that are home to bears, lions, monkeys and other creatures. There are also a few rogue peacocks that bolt past unsuspecting visitors (watch out!). Within the grounds of the zoo you can also enter the M Stekelis Museum of Prehistory, the Biological Museum and the Natural History Museum. Hours for the museums are the same as the zoo and one ticket is good for all the sites.

From downtown, take the Carmelite subway to the zoo.

GERMAN COLONY

At least once during your stay in Haifa, walk up Ben-Gurion Ave from Jaffa Rd and enjoy the splendour that is the German Colony, looked over by the cascading greenery of the Baha'i Gardens. The colony (really just this street), was renovated in the 1990s into the city's premier neighbourhood for shopping and dining, with many of its buildings restored and given plaques describing their colourful history.

The colony was established in 1869 by the Templers (not to be confused with the Knights Templar), a German Protestant sect that sought to hasten the Second Coming by settling in Palestine. In the latter decades of the 1800s, the Templers built seven colonies in Palestine and are credited with introducing improved methods of transport, technology and agriculture.

Central Haifa

The German Colony consists of attractive stone houses with German-language quotes from the Bible over the doors and steep red-shingled roofs. It impressed Baha'ullah, the founder of the Baha'i faith, and was visited by Germany's Kaiser Wilhelm II in 1898. Germans continued to live in the colony until 1939, when the British interned them as enemy aliens and later deported them to Australia.

Haifa City Museum   MUSEUM
(Map p162; 11 Ben-Gurion Ave; adult/child 30/20NIS; ◎10am-4pm Mon, Wed & Thu, 4-8pm Tue, 10am-1pm Fri, 10am-3pm Sat) Near the bottom of Ben-Gurion Ave is the Haifa City Museum, which displays revolving exhibitions by local artists. The building in which it is

housed was once a conference hall and later served as a school.

HADAR

The busiest area of commerce in Haifa, Hadar HaCarmel (Hadar for short) features shops and restaurants covering a low foothill between the port and, high above, Carmel Centre. Thanks to a heavy Russian presence, pedestrianised Nordau St feels like a mini version of Moscow's Arbat. A few streets have been converted to bus-only traffic.

Madatech   MUSEUM
(Map p162; www.madatech.org.il; Technion Bldg, 25 Shemaryahu Levin St, Hadar; adult/child 75/65NIS; ◎10am-4pm Mon & Wed, to 7pm Thu, to 2pm Fri, to 6pm Sat, noon-4pm Sun) A standout building

in the area is the elegant National Museum of Science, Technology & Space, commonly called Madatech. Completed in 1913, it served as the first home of the Technion – Israel Institute of Technology, which is why Albert Einstein visited in 1923. Today it's a museum specialising in interactive science exhibits spread over two buildings. Admission fees are steep but the redesigned exhibits are impressive and if you have kids it's a must-see.

WADI NISNAS

One of the oldest neighbourhoods in the city, Wadi Nisnas retains the feel of the old Middle East, with narrow lanes, sandstone architecture and a bustling street market. To get a feel for the place, walk downhill from the Haifa Art Museum and through the souq, stopping off to enjoy a felafel or a chat with some locals. In December and January there is a unique ongoing festival called Holiday of the Holy Days (www.haifahag.co.il, in Hebrew) here that celebrates Hanukkah, Christmas and Ramadan.

Public Art   PUBLIC ART

The Wadi has lots of public art, more than 100 pieces. Some of the works are large and eye-catching (particularly around the top of Wadi Nisnas Rd). Other pieces are small so you need to keep your eyes peeled as you walk through the backstreets. Beit HaGefen Arab–Jewish Centre has prepared a walking tour and map for visitors; you can pick one up in the office between 8am and 4pm weekdays. Some signage is in English but most of it is in Hebrew and Arabic.

Haifa Art Museum   MUSEUM

(Map p162; www.hms.org.il; 26 Shabtai Levi St; adult/child 30/20NIS; ☺10am-4pm Mon, Wed & Thu, 4-8pm Tue, 10am-1pm Fri, 10am-3pm Sat) This modern-art museum is home to temporary multimedia displays created by local artists.

Beit HaGefen Arab–Jewish
Centre   COMMUNITY CENTRE

(Map p162; ☎04-852 5252; 2 HaGefen St) This community centre sponsors joint Arab-Jewish social and cultural activities and could be worth a visit – check to see if there are any social events or lectures during your stay. The centre is on the 2nd floor behind a huge anonymous metal door.

DOWNTOWN & PORT AREA

After years of neglect, downtown Haifa is experiencing a mini-renaissance with shops, restaurants and nightlife opening up. Jaffa Rd is also worth a wander in daylight (most places shut their doors by 5pm). The best time to visit is on Friday afternoons when a craft market at Kikar Paris draws artists from around the region. Tuesday rockabilly night at Mayan Habira is legendary.

Al-Kebir & Esteklayl Mosques   MOSQUES

(Map p162) About 100m east of Kikar Paris you'll spot the dilapidated Al-Kebir Mosque (Great Mosque), which has a curiously un-Islamic minaret resembling nothing so much as a provincial English town clock tower. A short distance away is the better maintained, typically Ottoman Esteklayl Mosque (Independence Mosque), still in use for worship.

MARITIME MUSEUMS & ELIJAH'S
CAVE

Across the road from Bat Galim, and around 2km west of the German Colony, are a couple of maritime museums as well as Elijah's Cave, Haifa's holiest Jewish site. To reach these sites take bus 114 from downtown.

Clandestine Immigration & Naval
Museum   MUSEUM

(Map p159; 204 Allenby Rd; adult/child 15/10NIS; ☺8.30am-4pm Sun-Thu) The name may sound a bit ho-hum but this place is actually quite fascinating as it deals with the Zionist movement's desperate attempts to infiltrate Jewish refugees from Europe into British-blockaded Palestine in the 1930s and '40s. The centrepiece of the museum (quite literally – the building has been constructed around it) is a WWII landing craft rechristened the *Af-Al-Pi-Chen* (the name means 'nevertheless' in Hebrew), whose hold carried 434 refugees to Palestine in 1947. The boat was intercepted by the British and its passengers were forced into internment

---

HAIFA MUSEUM TICKET

If you plan on visiting more than one museum in Haifa, it's best to buy a combination ticket (single/family 45/120NIS) that gets you into five Haifa museums, including the National Maritime Museum, Mane Katz Museum, Tikotin Museum of Japanese Art, Haifa Art Museum and the Haifa City Museum. Note that the family ticket is good for two adults and two children. The combination ticket can be purchased at any of the five museums.

camps on Cyprus. Other exhibits tell of the famed *Exodus,* a vastly overloaded 1947 ship that carried over 4500 Holocaust survivors to Palestine but was forced by the British to return to Germany (of all places); and the *Struma,* which was sunk by a Soviet submarine off the coast of Istanbul in 1942, killing all but one of its 769 passengers, Jewish refugees from Romania.

Note that you need to have your passport to visit this site (it's run by the Ministry of Defence).

National Maritime Museum   MUSEUM

(Map p159; 198 Allenby Rd; adult/child 30/20NIS; ☺10am-4pm Sun-Thu, 10am-1pm Fri, 10am-3pm Sat) This recently renovated museum shows off the history of shipping in the Mediterranean area. The collection contains old maps, models of ancient ships, navigation equipment, Hellenistic terracotta figures and bits and pieces of sunken ships.

FREE Elijah's Cave   RELIGIOUS

(Map p159; ☺8am-5pm Sun-Thu, to 12.45pm Fri) A holy place for three faiths, Elijah's Cave is where the prophet Elijah is believed to have hidden from King Ahab and Queen Jezebel after he slew the 450 priests of Ba'al (Kings 1:17-19). It is said he established a school here upon his return from exile. There is also a Christian tradition that the Holy Family sheltered here on their return from Egypt, hence the Christian name, Cave of the Madonna.

Enter the cave in modest dress. Note that there are separate sections for men and women.

Although prior to 1948 the cave was a mosque dedicated to Al-Khidr (the Green Prophet) – sometimes seen as an Islamic version of Elijah, or as his companion – these days the rock chamber is usually crammed full of praying Haredim. Outside, the garden is a favourite picnic spot for local Christian Arabs.

The cave is over the road from the National Maritime Museum and up a narrow string of steps. The path running by Elijah's Cave leads up a steep ascent to the Carmelite Monastery (but it's best to do it in reverse so you can walk downhill).

STELLA MARIS CARMELITE MONASTERY & CABLE CARS

The Carmelites are a Catholic order that originated in the late 12th century when a band of Crusaders, inspired by the prophet Elijah, opted for a hermetic life on the western slopes of Mt Carmel (hence the name). However, the desired solitude was rarely granted as, over the centuries, the Carmelites suffered Muslim persecution, frequently having to abandon their monasteries. Occasionally, the Carmelites did have a hand in their own misfortune, as in 1799 when they extended their hospitality to Napoleon during his campaign against the Turks. The French lost their battle for the region and the Carmelites lost their monastery.

The present monastery and church, built over Elijah's Cave, dates from 1836 after the previous buildings were destroyed in 1821 by Abdullah, pasha of Akko.

Stella Maris Carmelite Monastery   CHURCH

(Map p159; ☺6am-noon & 3-6pm) The beautifully painted ceiling inside the main church portrays Elijah and the famous chariot of fire (in which he is said to have ascended to heaven), King David with his harp, the saints of the order, the prophets Isaiah, Ezekiel and David, and the Holy Family with the four evangelists below. A small adjoining museum contains ruins of former cloisters dating from Byzantine and Crusader times. In the garden by the entrance to the church is the tomb of French soldiers, commemorating those who died during Napoleon's campaign.

To reach the monastery take bus 115 from Hadar, or 99 from Carmel Centre. It's possible to walk here from Elijah's Cave along a well-defined path. If you prefer an easier way up, cross the highway to Bat Galim beach and take the cable car (one way/return 19/28NIS; ☺10am-6pm), which whisks you up to the monastery in a few minutes.

🏃 Activities

Bat Galim Beach   BEACH

(Map p159; www.batgalim.org.il) It's not Pipeline but surfers can surely catch some waves at Bat Galim beach. The westernmost break, called Galshanim Beach, is popular with windsurfers and kiteboarders. It's near the bottom of the Stella Maris Cable Car. Surf House (☎09-957 4522; www.surfhouse.co.il; ☺9am-5pm Mon-Sat) is a small surf shop at Galshanim that rents windsurf boards (100NIS per hour). The best bus for Bat Galim is bus 108, which runs past Paris Sq.

Hof HaCarmel Beach   BEACH

Located near the Hof HaCarmel train station in the south of the city, this beach has an inviting promenade with a number of

WHAT TO DO ON SHABBAT IN HAIFA

With a little planning, the Shabbat shutdown shouldn't crimp your style during a visit to Haifa. To begin, things do not shut down entirely as one quarter of the city's residents are Arabs whose commercial activities carry on as usual. The municipality makes things easier by keeping many sights open and running some public transport, though it has a late starting time of around 9.30am.

Saturday is as good a day as any for a visit to the Baha'i Shrine of the Bab and Baha'i Gardens, a museum or the zoo. The souq and grocers in Wadi Nisnas stay open, as do some of the felafel merchants, the bakeries and the cafes along HaNevi'im and HeHalutz Sts in Hadar. At Kibbutz Galuyot, 300m east of Kikar Paris, the locals host a flea market, great for browsing.

A road trip out of town is not a bad idea. Hire a car on Friday morning and head south to Caesarea, Zichron Ya'acov and Ein Hod, or to Nazareth. The only problem here is that the museums in Zichron Ya'acov will be closed.

Alternatively, head east to visit the Druze village of Daliyat al-Karmel, where you'll find Israelis shopping in the vast outdoor furniture market that lines the streets. While in the area you could also visit Mukhraqa's Carmelite Monastery of St Elijah, plus nearby Beit She'arim and Megiddo.

It's a bit easier to get to Akko as it's connected to Haifa by sherut (shared taxi).

If all else fails, grab a bottle of strong sunblock and hit the beach at Dor or Akhziv. The Hof HaCarmel beach is also popular on Saturday and folk dancing is held here to close the Shabbat.

restaurants and cafes. Folk dancing (⊙11am Feb-Jun, 7pm Jul-Jan) is held here on Saturday. Trains from Haifa Merkaz come here every 20 minutes for 5NIS. Zamir and Dado beaches north of Hof HaCarmel are also quite clean.

HaNemala (The Ant) ARTIST STUDIO
(Map p162; ☎052-567 0505; shaharsivan@gmail.com; HaNemal St) Artsy folk, bohemians and socialites meet up at this studio in the port once a week to draw nude portraits. If you're comfortable in this sort of crowd, it's a great place to mingle with young locals and discover the local scene. The event usually happens on Monday and visitors are welcome to join. Drinks are available to purchase and 10NIS is charged as a cover fee. On Tuesday, the same group of artists meet at their private bar, the Bartagnian (51 HaNemal; ⊙9pm-midnight Tue) near the studio. The bar has cheap beers (15NIS) and excellent home-cooked meals (15NIS to 20NIS). Contact Shahar Sivan for details on both events.

Courses

University of Haifa Ulpan HEBREW LANGUAGE
(☎04-824 0766; www.uhaifa.org; University of Haifa) Charges US$850 for a four-week intensive Hebrew language course at the university, 5.5km south of Carmel Centre.

Matnas Hadar ARABIC LANGUAGE
(☎050 562 8039, 04-850 7785; tveria15@gmail.com; 15 Tiberias St) Offers three-month-long Arabic language classes for 390NIS. Classes are held once a week for two hours. Contact Yaron Hadar.

Ulpan Aba Hushi HEBREW LANGUAGE
(Map p162; ☎04-856 7630; ulpanhaifa@gmail.com; 131 HaMeginim Rd) Intensive five-month Hebrew courses for 3000NIS. Classes are held five days a week and the Ulpan has dormitories.

Tours

The two main tour operators in Haifa are Jacob Tours (☎052 247 6333, 050 533 0997; www.jacobtours.com) and Guy Tours (☎04-810 0999, 050 532 1169; www.guytours.com). Either can shuttle you around the north coast for around US$100 a day for a standard tour, either north to Akko, Rosh HaNikra and Tzipori or south to Caesarea and Megiddo. In winter the trips are only private tours by appointment but in summer they offer regularly scheduled day trips.

Sleeping

Haifa has plenty of high-end accommodation in the Carmel Centre but budget options are a little spread out and not too plentiful. For anywhere you want to stay, call ahead and reserve a room, especially in July and August, when sudden waves of Baha'i pilgrims can make accommodation scarce.

PORT AREA & DOWNTOWN

TOP CHOICE Port Inn — GUESTHOUSE $$

(Map p162; ☑04-852 4401; www.portinn.co.il; 34 Jaffa Rd; dm without/with breakfast 90/130NIS; s/d/tr/q 290/375/495/615NIS; ✳@🛜) The Port Inn is a magnet for budget and mid-range travellers coming to Haifa, and for good reason. The guesthouse has a helpful staff, a comfortable lounge, kitchen facilities and laundry service. The dining room is a great place to meet other travellers over a breakfast of cereal, tuna, cheeses and fresh fruit (prepared by the friendly proprietor Rachel and her husband, Rami). Rooms are clean and simply furnished, with neat bedding and spotless bathrooms. Self-contained apartments across the street cost 535/660/780NIS for three/four/five people (breakfast not included). It's about 300m west of Paris Sq.

St Charles Hospice — HOSPICE $

(Map p162; ☑04-855 3705; www.pat-rosary.com; 105 Jaffa Rd; s/d/q 180/300/390NIS; ✳@🛜) Owned by the Latin Patriarchate and run by the Catholic Rosary Sisters, St Charles is housed in a beautiful building with a lovely garden out back. Rooms are simple but comfortably furnished and come equipped with private showers. The gate is often locked so you'll need to ring the bell to enter. Curfew is at 11pm so send an email if you plan a late check-in.

GERMAN COLONY

Colony Hotel Haifa — HOTEL $$$

(Map p162; ☑04-851 3344; www.colony-hotel.co.il; 28 Ben-Gurion Ave; s/d/tr US$176/195/268; ✳@🛜) The Templar building served as a hotel in the early 20th century, closed for a couple of decades then reopened in grand fashion in 2009. The original flooring is still prevalent throughout but everything else has been updated in tasteful fashion. Bathrooms are large and some are equipped with jet tubs. Make use of the spa in the basement and take in the excellent views of the Baha'i Gardens from the roof.

Haddad — HOTEL $$

(Map p162; ☑077 201 0618; www.haddadguesthouse.com; 26 Ben-Gurion Ave; s/d 320/380NIS; ✳🛜) This 11-room micro-hotel has small, tidy rooms with a perfect downtown loca-

tion. On the downside, it's not a great option for non-smokers as we've spotted the staff sneaking puffs on their breaks. Discounts are available if you stay more than seven nights.

Baloutin Rosa — HOMESTAY $

(Map p162; ☑054 746 8844; 49 Ben-Gurion Ave; s/d/tr 150/250/350NIS; ✳@) The proprietors of this German Colony homestay let out an extra room in their home. It's a bit drab but it has a great location on this trendy street near the Baha'i Gardens. The door is upstairs in the back of the building. Husband Walid speaks English and French.

CARMEL CENTRE

Molada Guest House — GUESTHOUSE $

(Map p162; ☑04-838 7958; www.rutenberg.org.il; 82 HaNassi Ave; s/d/tr 250/350/520NIS; ✳🛜) Run by the Ruthenberg Institute for Youth Education, this bare-bones guesthouse has large rooms with single beds, a desk and hot-water showers. It's designed to house students so there's a distinct college-dormitory feel, with a kitchen and living room. Reception (open 9am to 3pm Sunday to Thursday) is at the Beth Ruthenberg building (77 HaNassi Ave), just down the street. After hours, ring the doorbell and somebody will let you in. It's best to call (or email) ahead to make a reservation. It's hidden down a driveway, opposite the Dan Carmel Hotel.

Beth Shalom Hotel — HOTEL $$

(Map p162; ☑04-837 7481; www.beth-shalom.co.il; 110 HaNassi Ave; s/d/tr US$95/125/155; ✳🛜) In the Carmel Centre district, this is a basic but comfortable Lutheran 'evangelical guesthouse'. Each of the 30 rooms is brightly lit, spotless and nicely renovated with hardwood floors. It's a homey place with a garden and a small library. There is a comfortable lounge, and complimentary hot and cold drinks are served throughout the day. From downtown take the subway.

Villa Carmel — BOUTIQUE HOTEL $$$

(off Map p162; ☑04-837 5777; www.villacarmel.co.il; 30 Heinrich Heine St; r US$250; ✳@🛜🏊) This gorgeous 16-room boutique hotel has a peaceful location on the mountaintop, set amid pine and cypress trees. Rooms are ultra-modern with big flat-screen TVs and computerised jet showers. The hotel also has some well-placed amenities, such as a rooftop Jacuzzi and sauna. It's a 10-minute walk from Carmel Centre so it has good access to restaurants and shops.

Nof Hotel
HOTEL **$$**

(Map p162; 📞04-835 4311; www.inisrael.com/nof; 101 HaNassi Ave; s/d from US$132/147; ❄@🛜🅿) The Nof is one of several clunky-looking hotels that dominate the top of the mountain. While it's a little short on elegance, it does offer unbeatable views from the upper floors down to Haifa Bay. Note that prices listed here are for the older rooms. Renovated rooms cost about 20% extra.

STELLA MARIS AREA

Stella Maris Hospice
HOSPICE **$$**

(Map p159; 📞04-833 2084; stelama@netvision.net.il; Carmelite Monastery; s/d US$65/100; ❄@🛜) It's not the most convenient place to stay in Haifa, but the Stella Maris Hospice does offer plenty of old-world charm and some great views over the bay. The hospice is run by the Carmelite order and geared towards Christian pilgrims, but there is plenty of room for independent travellers, so long as they don't mind the simple rooms, sombre atmosphere and 11pm curfew. Wi-fi is available for US$2 per day. Bus 115 stops near the hospice. You'll need to ring the bell at the gate to get inside.

HADAR

Gallery Hotel
HOTEL **$$**

(Map p162; 📞04-861 6161; www.haifa.hotelgallery.co.il; 61 Herzl St; s/d US$120/140; ❄@🛜) Bringing a bit of style into Hadar, this new hotel features modern rooms with tasteful touches of art (created by Haifa-based artists). Rooms are a tad small but otherwise pleasant and nicely furnished.

Hotel Theodor
HOTEL **$$**

(Map p162; 📞04-867 7111; www.theodorhotel.co.il; 63 Herzl St; s/d/tr US$94/110/154; ❄@🛜) Newly renovated in 2011, the Theodor is a local landmark, rising 17 stories above Hadar. Rooms are small and tidy with flat-screen TVs and great views from every angle. The price includes an Israeli breakfast and free wi-fi. Buffet dinner is US$22.

Louis Boutique Hotel
HOTEL **$**

(Map p162; 📞04-432 0149; louishotelapartments@gmail.com; 35 HeHalutz St; s/d US$50/80; ❄🛜) This 12-room hotel has simple, clean rooms with small bathrooms offered at competitive prices. The 1950s-era building is underwhelming but some effort has been made to spruce up the interior, with art on the walls and wood-framed beds. Breakfast is not included.

🍴 Eating

Haifa's restaurant scene has matured in recent years, thanks mostly to the transformation of Ben-Gurion Ave into a local nightspot. The Carmel Centre is also a good place to wander and look for a place that suits your taste. Useful supermarkets are at Paris Sq and in the Carmel Centre.

PORT AREA & DOWNTOWN

In this area you'll find some long-standing restaurants mixed with a few up-and-comers. The problem is that many places in this area are only open for lunch so it can be pretty dead after dark.

TOP CHOICE Mayan Habira
JEWISH **$$**

(Fountains of Beer; Map p162; 4 Nathanson St; mains 40-60NIS; ⏰10am-5pm Wed-Mon, to midnight Tue) Come to Mayan Habira to experience some Jewish 'soul food', classic Eastern European dishes like jellied calf's foot, gefilte fish, chopped liver and *petshai* (boiled calf's leg). You can also try *kreplach,* a meat-stuffed dumpling known affectionately as a 'Jewish wonton'. Don't miss the party held here every Tuesday, when a rockabilly band brings the house down, starting at around 9pm.

HaNamal 24
ITALIAN **$$$**

(Map p162; 24 HaNamal St; mains 50-100NIS; ⏰noon-midnight Mon-Sat) The interior of this popular restaurant resembles the courtyard of an Italian villa, a striking contrast to the warehouses and railway tracks outside. Grab a seat in the main hall or relax into one of the comfy sofas in the cigar lounge, then try some gourmet options, like the delicious goat's-cheese-stuffed portobello mushrooms, or more standard choices like grilled fish and pastas.

Angus
SHWARMA **$**

(Map p162; 27 HaMeginim Ave; shwarma plate 26NIS; ⏰11am-11pm) Carnivores will delight in this tasty and hygienic shwarma joint. Upstairs is a proper sit-down restaurant that has a bigger menu.

GERMAN COLONY

The best concentration of high-end restaurants is on Ben-Gurion Ave in the German Colony; just stroll around for a bit and choose the one that suits your mood.

Fatoush
MIDDLE EASTERN **$$**

(Map p162; 38 Ben-Gurion Ave; mains 40-70NIS; ⏰8am-1am; 🛜) Atmospheric Fatoush is dressed up like a medieval Arabic house, complete with burgundy cushions, nargileh (water pipes) and candle lamps. The Middle Eastern menu includes *aroos al-wadi* (pride of the valley), baked bread topped with minced calf meat and some delectable tasty seafood dishes. Portion sizes are generous. Live music is sometimes played on Thursdays in summer.

Douzan
FRENCH, ARAB $$$

(Map p162; 35 Ben-Gurion Ave; mains 50-98NIS; ☺9am-2am) Decorated with old clocks, musical instruments, antique furnishings and velvet cushions, owner Fadi Najar has created a harmonious atmosphere and is proud that both Arabs and Jews dine together under his roof. The home-cooked meals, prepared by Fadi's mother Leila, are a fusion of French and Arab recipes, with specials such as calamari (60NIS), lamb ribs (95NIS) and some unexpected treats such as *sfeeha* (small meat pie topped with feta cheese and pine nuts).

CARMEL CENTRE

The Carmel Centre has a nice mix of upscale cafes, ethnic restaurants and takeaway joints.

Mandarin
SANDWICHES, PASTA $$

(Map p162; 129 HaNassi Ave; mains 40-55NIS; ☺8am-1am; ☎) Step off busy HaNassi Ave, down past a gardenlike entrance with the sign 'Mandarin' and you'll assume you're headed for a Chinese restaurant. Where you actually end up is a quaint cafe with a wooden deck and cosy interior set to a soundtrack of funk and blues. The menu features soups, salads, big sandwiches and pastas.

Meat
STEAKHOUSE $$$

(Map p162; 129 HaNassi Ave; mains 62-175NIS; ☺noon-11pm; ☎) As the name indicates, this place serves up hearty steaks and burgers and some tasty appetizers, including steak carpaccio and chorizo sausages. The open kitchen allows you to spy on the chef while he grills up your dinner.

Greg Coffee
CAFE $$

(Map p162; 3 Derekh HaYam St; mains 40-60NIS; ☺7am-midnight; ☎) Homey cafe offering excellent coffee and brownies, plus some low-calorie menu options. On Friday it's open all night.

MASADA

Puzzle Café
CAFE $$

(Map p162; 21 Masada St; mains 25-45NIS; ☺11am-late; ☎) The name of this small cafe is a reflection of the clientele; an odd collection of pieces that, when placed together, forms a complete picture. It's popular with scenesters, students and Haifa's small gay community. Live music is played here on Friday afternoon in summer.

Cafe Masada
CAFE $$

(Map p162; 16 Masada St; mains 25-45NIS; ☺8am-late; ☎) Like talking politics over your java? This is a politically charged cafe that attracts a mixed Arab–Jewish crowd. Everyone here seems to be in the far-left pro-peace camp and no one is shy in expressing ideas. It's a great place to mingle with locals and chat with the friendly owner, Eran Prager.

WADI NISNAS

The market in Wadi Nisnas is overflowing with fresh fruit and vegetables, making this the best spot in town for self-caterers. Allenby Rd, near the corner of HaZiyonut Blvd, has a few good places for shwarma.

Nadima
HUMMUS $

(Map p162; souq; ☺7am-3pm; ☑) A Wadi Nisnas institution, Nadima serves up delicious local fare such as hummus and fuul (20NIS) and a rice-and-meat platter (20NIS). A veggie plate is 40NIS.

Felafel Hazkenim
FELAFEL $

(Map p162; Wadi Nisnas Rd; ☺8am-9pm; ☑) Another pillar of the community, this felafel joint has been operating since 1962. Owner Afif Sbait greets every customer with a smile and felafel ball dipped in hummus. A half felafel is 8NIS and full is 14NIS.

HADAR

Around the HaNevi'im St end of HeHalutz St (in Hadar), you'll find a wide range of excellent felafel and shwarma, as well as bakeries selling sweet pastries, sticky buns and other delights.

Kafe Nitsa
CAFE $

(Map p162; 2 Herzl St; snacks 12-20NIS; ☺6.30am-4pm; ☎) This 60-year-old coffee shop retains its classic feel, decorated with old photos on the walls and a devoted crowd of regulars. It's a fine place for a coffee and light sandwich.

Drinking

For an evening out, locals head for the trendy bars and cafes along Moriah St and the environs of Carmel Centre. A handful of bars and nightclubs are clustered around downtown.

Bear
BAR

(Map p162; 135 HaNassi Ave; ⊙5pm-late Sat-Wed, 11am-late Thu-Fri) The Bear is a popular Irish pub and is regarded as the city's main expat hang-out. For main dishes (35NIS to 75NIS), you can choose between salads, sandwiches, chicken, steak and seafood, washed down with your choice of 12 different draught beers.

Eli's
BAR

(Map p162; 35 Jaffa Rd; ⊙9pm-late) Owner Eli likes travellers so introduce yourself and he'll find you a nice spot at his bar. The place really rocks on Monday (jam sessions), Wednesday (jazz), and Saturday (open-mic night) when local bands play here.

Syncopa
BAR

(Map p162; 5 Khayat St; ⊙8pm-late) Injecting some life back into the downtown area, this bar on the corner of Nathanson St is a double-decker nightspot with a bar downstairs and dance floor above. A cream-coloured interior glows with the soft lighting and the whole place grooves to a funk beat. Live music on Thursday, Saturday and Sunday. It's popular with Haifa's GLBT crowd.

Li Bira
BAR

(Map p162; 21 HaNe'emanim St; ⊙7pm-late Mon-Sat) Grab a seat at the bar and order a 'beer tasting', which gets you four types of beer for 18NIS (each glass is 100mL). The owner Leonid Lipkin uses his own secret recipes for some beers and it's all non-filtered and non-pasteurised, so you know it's fresh. The kitchen prepares some tasty tapas designed to complement the beers.

Tichon
BAR

(Map p162; ☎054 934 9237; 2 Balfour St; ⊙7pm-late Mon-Thu, noon-late Fri & Sat) Owners Suzan and Yoni (a unique Arab–Jewish business partnership) promote indie rock bands (including Arab alternative rock) at this gritty nightspot. They sometimes hold seminars on music, fashion, philosophy and other genres. Live music played three times a week usually drags in Haifa's nascent community of artists, poets and hipsters. It's in Hadar above McDonalds.

Sleek
BAR

(Map p162; 124 HaNassi Ave; ⊙7pm-late) A mainstream hang-out for 20-somethings, Sleek starts as a restaurant and becomes a singles bar later in the evening. If you plan to eat, come before 9.30pm and get 25% off. It's reached through a parking garage.

☆ Entertainment

Nightclubs charge between 50NIS and 70NIS cover charge; don't bother turning up until around 1am.

Beat
LIVE MUSIC

(Map p162; ☎04-810 7107; www.beat.co.il; 124 HaNassi Ave; admission 50-120NIS; ⊙9pm-late Thu & Sat) This smoke-free venue is the best place to hear live music in Haifa. Call to find out what's on.

Loft 124
CLUB

(Map p162; www.loft124.co.il; 124 HaNassi Ave; admission 10-30NIS; ⊙10pm-late Thu-Fri) Dress smart and hit this popular nightclub in the Carmel Centre; it's in the same building as Beat.

Cinematheque
CINEMA

(Map p162; ☎04-835 3521; www.haifacin.co.il; 142 HaNassi Ave; admission 33NIS) Shows avant-garde, off-beat and foreign films. The phone number is just a recording in Hebrew asking you to leave a call-back number (an English-speaking staff member should get back to you soon).

Haifa Municipal (Meirhoff) Theatre
THEATRE

(Map p162; ☎04-860 0500; www.ht1.co.il; 50 Pevsner St) Stages concerts and Hebrew-language theatre. Tickets cost around 160NIS. Buses 21, 23, 24, 28 and 37 go to the theatre.

Matnas Hadar
LIVE MUSIC

(Map p162; ☎050 562 8039, 04-850 7785; tveria15@gmail.com; 15 Tiberias St) Community centre with a regular schedule of amateur concerts and Hebrew-language performances. You can usually hear live music on Saturday night in summer. It also has a small library, book exchange and art gallery. Lots of interesting people from different ethnic and religious backgrounds hang out here. To find it, walk out of Masada St subway, turn left and stay on the same level as it makes several curves (the name of the street changes from Masada to Tiberias). From the Madatech it's a 10-minute walk.

Morrison
LIVE MUSIC

(Map p162; 111 Ye'fe Nof St; ⊙7.30pm-late) This booming bar and live-music venue has bands on weekends and karaoke on Mondays. The crowd is a nice mix of students and young professionals. The entrance is down a flight of steps next to the Crowne Plaza Hotel.

Martef 10
LIVE MUSIC

(Basement 10; Map p162; ☑04-824 0762; www.martef10.com; 23 Yerushalayim St; ☺10pm-late) 'Basement 10' is a nonprofit student club that hosts live-music shows most nights of the week from 10pm. During the school year it's closed Tuesday and Saturday. During the summer it's closed Saturday and Monday. It's very informal – cushions on the floor make up the seating and dress is casual.

 Shopping

Auditorium Mall
MALL

(Map p162; 153 HaNassi Ave; ☺10am-10pm) Located in the Carmel Centre next to the Cinematheque. It contains a Steimatzky bookshop, supermarket and pharmacy.

City Centre
MALL

(Map p162; 6 Ben-Gurion Ave; ☺10am-10pm Sun-Thu, 9.30am-2pm Fri, 8-10.30pm Sat) Located in the German Colony, this trendy mall has a modern feel inside while retaining the Templer architecture facade. Brand-name shops, cafes and restaurants are inside.

❶ Information

Emergency
Ambulance (☑101)
Fire (☑102)
Police (☑100; 28 Jaffa Rd)

Internet Access
Gan Ha'em (122 HaNassi Ave; per hr 30NIS; ☺9am-midnight Sat-Thu, to 5pm Fri) At the top of the stairs at Gan Ha'em subway stop.

Laundry
Self-service laundry (34 Jaffa St; per load 15NIS; ☺8.30am-9pm) Located next to the Port Inn.

Medical Services
Rambam Medical Centre (☑1 700 505 150; Bat Galim) One of the largest hospitals in the country.

Money
The main branch of Bank Leumi is on Jaffa Rd, and you'll also find branches with ATMs along most city streets. Exchange bureaus are likewise common; in the Carmel Centre there is one at the corner of Wedgewood and HaNassi. The post offices marked on our map will change travellers cheques.

Post
Main post office (19 HaPalyam Ave; ☺8am-12.30pm & 3.30-6pm Sun-Tue & Thu, 8am-1pm Wed, to noon Fri) Located in the port area, 300m southeast of Kikar Paris. There are also branches in the German Colony (27 Ben-Gurion Ave) and Hadar (corner HaNevi'im and Shabtai Levi Sts).

Tourist Information
Haifa Tourism Development Association
(☑04-853 5606; www.tour-haifa.co.il; 48 Ben-Gurion Ave; ☺9am-4.30pm Sun-Thu, 8am-1pm Fri, 10am-3pm Sat) Near the foot of the Baha'i Gardens, this tourist office distributes several useful publications, including *A Guide to Haifa Tourism* and a city map (4NIS), which outlines four themed walking tours.

Travel Agencies
Diesenhaus (☑04-852 3082; www.deasy.co.il, in Hebrew; 104 Haatzma'ut St) Books air tickets.

Websites
www.haifa.muni.il Official website for the municipality.

www.tour-haifa.co.il Official website for the tourist board. Contains updates on what is happening around the city.

❶ Getting There & Away

Air
Arkia (☑5758; www.arkia.com) connects Haifa with Eilat three or four times a week (US$84 to US$113). **Haifa airport** (HFA; ☑04-847 6170) is in the industrial zone east of Haifa; a taxi will cost around 40NIS. They have no office in Haifa so book over the phone or use a travel agent.

Bus
Arriving from the south, passengers are dropped off at the Hof HaCarmel bus station (adjacent to the train station of the same name), from where you can take bus 103 downtown to the port area. Buses to Akko, Nahariya and the Galilee use the eastern bus terminal at Lev HaMifratz.

During the day, buses depart from both locations every 20 minutes for Tel Aviv (Bus 910, 26.50NIS, 90 minutes), while there's an hourly service to Jerusalem (Bus 940 or 960, 40NIS, two hours). The 940 leaves from Hof HaCarmel and the 960 departs from Lev HaMifratz.

Heading north, bus 272 (express) goes to Nahariya (17.20NIS, 45 to 70 minutes) via Akko, and bus 251 stops at Akko (13.50NIS, 30 to 50 minutes). Eastbound, bus 430 goes to Tiberias (26.50NIS, 90 minutes). Bus services are subject to change; when you buy your ticket ask for any express service to your destination.

For Nazareth, take bus 331 (17.20NIS, 45 minutes), operated by **Nazarene Tours** (☑04-862 4871) and departing from outside the Haifa Merkaz-HaShmona train station. Once you reach Nazareth you can buy a separate ticket to carry on to Jordan, also from Nazarene Tours.

Car

You can cover a lot of territory in northern Israel by hiring a car for a couple of days. It allows you to easily visit off-the-beaten-track places like Montfort, Megiddo and Ein Hod. In Haifa, most of the car-rental agencies are on HaHishtadrot, near the Lev HaMifratz Bus Terminal, including **Avis** (☑04-861 0444; 39 HaHishtadrot Ave).

Ferry

Ferry services to Cyprus have been cancelled.

Sherut (Shared Taxi)

Most sheruts (service or shared taxis) depart from different spots in Hadar. The sherut to Akko (weekday/Shabbat 12/15NIS) and Nahariya (weekday/Shabbat 15/18NIS) leaves from the corner of Herzl and Balfour. In addition you can take a sherut to Akko and Nahariya from downtown Sunday to Thursday from near the post office.

The sherut to Tel Aviv (weekday/Shabbat 28/40NIS) departs from 10 HeHalutz St. A sherut to the airport (87NIS) requires a one-day advanced booking; call ☑04-866 2324.

Train

Haifa effectively has three train stations. The southernmost is Hof HaCarmel (good for getting to the beach from the city centre). The second is Haifa Merkaz HaShmona, near the port and downtown (most useful for tourists). Lev HaMifratz, in the eastern part of the city, is close to the Lev HaMifratz bus station, where you'll end up if you've taken a bus from Akko. However, note that Lev HaMifratz train station closes around 10.30pm.

From Haifa Merkaz HaShmona, trains depart roughly hourly for Tel Aviv (29.50NIS, 90 minutes) via Netanya (26NIS, one hour), and north to Nahariya (19NIS, 45 minutes) via Akko (15NIS, 30 minutes). There are also direct trains to Ben-Gurion Airport (38.50NIS, 90 minutes).

For questions about train schedules, dial ☑5770.

❶ Getting Around

Bus

The Carmelit will only get you up and down the mountain; for getting east to west you'll need to take the **bus** (☑information 04-854 9131; single trip 6.40NIS). Tickets are valid for 90 minutes on any bus line. Handy bus routes include:

Bus 37 Bat Galim train station along HaMeginim Ave, Herzl St (Hadar), Carmel Centre, University of Haifa.

Bus 103 Hof HaCarmel bus station to Lev HaMifratz bus station via Merkaz-HaShmona (central) train station and downtown.

Bus 114 Hof HaCarmel bus station, Allenby Rd (Maritime Museum), cnr Allenby St & Ben Gurion Ave (German Colony), Kikar Paris (downtown), Herzl St (Hadar), Lev HaMifratz bus station.

Bus 115 Hof HaCarmel bus station, Krieger Cultural Centre, Stella Maris Carmelite Monastery, HaZiyonut Blvd, Herzl St (Hadar), Lev HaMifratz bus station.

Bus 108 Bat Galim Beach, Ha'azmaut Rd, Lev HaMifratz (returns to Bat Galim via HaMeginim Ave).

Metro

Israel's only metro (subway), the **Carmelit** (☑04-837 6861; single trip 6.40NIS; ☉6am-midnight Sun-Thu, to 3pm Fri, 8pm-midnight Sat) connects Kikar Paris with Carmel Centre, via the Hadar district. Visitors can ride to the top and see the city sights on a leisurely downhill stroll. A packet of 10 tickets can be purchased for 51.20NIS.

Daliyat al-Karmel
داليـة الكرمل   דלית אל-כרמל

☑04 / POP 13,000

The largest Druze settlement in Israel, Daliyat al-Karmel is a sprawling town on the southern spur of Mt Carmel, 15km south of Haifa. Although still referred to as a village, don't arrive thinking you'll be among stone houses and wheat fields – years of growth have sent Daliyat washing over the neighbouring hills and have nearly fused it with the smaller Druze village of Isfiya (Usfiyeh), just to the north.

Despite its growth, Daliyat's commerce is still concentrated on its lone main street, a 100m stretch of food stands, jewellery shops and stalls cluttered with brightly coloured shawls and trousers, metalwork and factory-manufactured tabla drums, pottery and paintings: bargains for one and all. Tucked into the back of a shop on the north side of the street is the Druze Heritage Centre (admission free; ☉10am-5pm). It's crammed with old photos, baskets and traditional clothing, though nothing is in English. You'll need to poke around a bit for it, as there is no sign.

Following the road due west from the T-junction, about 800m along is a square little building, fronted with Jerusalem stone and topped with a small red dome. This is the Mausoleum of Abu Ibrahim, which serves as a local mosque. Heads must be covered to enter, but you can glance in from the doorway.

About 600m further down the road is Beit Oliphant (signposted as Beit Druze), which was the home of the Christian Zionist Sir Lawrence Oliphant and his wife between 1882 and 1887. The Oliphants were among the few non-Druze to have a close relationship with the sect, and did much to help the community. In the garden is a cave where they hid insurgents from the authorities. The house has been converted to a memorial to Druze members of the Israel Defence Forces (IDF) killed in action. The house faces a modern sports hall, outside which stands a tank and artillery piece with an 18m-long wall mural depicting the 1973 Arab–Israeli War and the signing of the Camp David peace treaty.

For eating, Andarin (mains 50-90NIS; ⊘9am-9pm; 🖉) is right on the main street and is a classy little restaurant that has a takeaway shwarma bar and a sit-down menu. Don't order too much because one main dish will come with a bunch of side salads so you fill up quickly. Try the tasty *gamba* (40NIS), peppers stuffed with mushrooms and cheese. Directly opposite, Halabi Bros (🖉04-839 3537; mains 30-70NIS; ⊘10am-10pm) is a more informal hummus and shwarma place. A takeaway felafel costs 10NIS.

🛈 Getting There & Away

The Druze villages are a half-day trip from Haifa. Take bus 37א (6.40NIS, one hour) which departs from downtown and makes a stop in the Carmel Centre. Because the 37א makes such a circuitous route up the mountain, it's more pleasant to take the subway to Carmel Centre and then change to the 37א at the top (a combined ticket is 10.20NIS). The bus passes through Isfiya en route between Haifa and Daliyat al-Karmel. It also makes a stop at the University of Haifa.

Carmelite Monastery of St Elijah מוחרקה مخرقة

About 4km south of Daliyat al-Karmel is one of the most renowned viewpoints in Israel, the Carmelite Monastery of St Elijah (admission 3NIS; ⊘9am-4.30pm), built to commemorate Elijah's showdown with the 450 prophets of Ba'al (Kings 1:17-19). Climb to the roof of the monastery to enjoy the great views across the patchwork of fields of the Jezreel Valley.

There is no public transport to the monastery, so you have to walk from Daliyat al-Karmel, or take a taxi (10NIS round trip). Bear left at the signposted junction or you'll end up miles away and be part of the view you are meant to be admiring.

Atlit עתלית عتليت

The old Haifa–Hadera coastal road passes Atlit, a settlement 16km south of Haifa. The main reason to stop here is to visit the Atlit Illegal Immigrants Camp (🖉04-984 1980; adult/child 18/15NIS; ⊘9am-5pm Sun-Thu, to 1pm Fri), which from 1940 to 1945 served as a detention centre for thousands of Jews – refugees fleeing Nazi-controlled Europe and, after the war, Holocaust survivors – captured by the British as they tried to enter Palestine in contravention to British policy.

On 10 October 1945, the Palmach (Special Forces unit of the Haganah) broke into the camp and released 200 prisoners. The daring infiltration, led by a young Yitzhak Rabin, caused the British to close the camp. After that, Jews arrested for illegally entering Palestine were sent to camps on Cyprus.

A one-hour tour of the camp includes a short film and a guided tour of the barracks, reconstructed based on prisoners' accounts. You'll see their living quarters and a dreadful wash house where new arrivals were stripped of their clothing and disinfected with DDT.

Atlit has an impressive Crusader castle. Known in Latin as Castrum Pergrinorum and in French as Château Pèlerin (Pilgrims' Castle), it was built by the Crusaders around 1200 and fell to Arab armies in 1291. Sadly, the castle is off-limits to visitors, as it is part of a naval installation.

Ein Hod עין הוד عين هود

Dadaist painter Marcel Janco happened upon Ein Hod in 1950 and fell in love. The Arab village had been abandoned two years earlier during the 1948 Arab–Israeli War and Janco saw the empty homes as the perfect place to set up his workshops. Others followed and today the village is home to around 140 artists and their families.

◉ Sights

There are various working studios and Israelis come here to learn such skills as ceramics, weaving and drawing. The studios are mainly closed to casual visitors but around the centre of the village you can visit the various galleries. For more information on Ein Hod, check the website www.ein-hod.info.

Janco-Dada Museum
MUSEUM

(www.jancodada-museum.israel.net; adult/child 20/10NIS; ⊙9.30am-5pm Sun-Thu, to 2pm Fri, 11am-3pm Sat) Exhibits collages, drawings and paintings by Marcel Janco himself. From the museum's top-floor porch you can appreciate the kind of view that inspired Janco to settle here.

FREE Beit Gertrude Gallery
GALLERY

(⊙11am-2pm Sat Sep-Jun) Next to the Doña Rosa restaurant, this gallery is dedicated to Gertrude Krause, a co-founding member of the colony. The museum contains local artwork and hosts occasional concerts, lectures and other cultural events.

Nisco Museum
MUSEUM

(adult/child 20/10NIS; ⊙9.30am-4.30pm Mon-Thu & Sat) Among other offbeat exhibits in Ein Hod is the Nisco Museum, a collection of mechanical music instruments, some of the items dating back to the 19th century.

Roman Amphitheatre
AMPHITHEATRE

Occasional Friday evening concerts are held at the restored Roman amphitheatre, up the road from Beit Gertrude.

Ain Hud
VILLAGE

The Arabs who fled the fighting in 1948 didn't go far, settling on a hilltop about 4km past Ein Hod. There is little to see in the new village, called Ain Hud, but the HaBait restaurant is worth visiting for a classic Arab meal.

🛏 Sleeping

The Carob Inn
B&B $$

(☑054 728 3311; noahere@bezeqint.net; s/d 400/450NIS; 🅿) This gorgeous family-run guesthouse offers one room accessed by a private entrance, and has views of the sea. It's close to the Art Bar. Contact Noa Brosh.

🍴 Eating & Drinking

Doña Rosa
STEAKHOUSE $$

(☑04-954 3777; www.dona-rosa.israel.net; steaks 65NIS; ⊙noon-9.30pm) Israelis from all over the country save their appetite on the drive to Ein Hod, anticipating a feast of meat at this Argentinean steakhouse. No expense is spared as all the ingredients are imported from Argentina, including the meat, charcoal and wine. You can enjoy your meal on the balcony or in the rustic interior of this old wood-and-stone building. It gets busy so call ahead.

TOP CHOICE HaBait
MIDDLE EASTERN $$$

(☑04-839 7350; set meal 90NIS; ⊙noon-8pm) The Arab family that runs this place takes great pride in their cooking and insists on gathering only local ingredients including herbs plucked from nearby Mt Carmel. It's just about the most authentic Arab cooking you can get in Israel and everything tastes great. Plan on coming on a weekday when it's less crowded; in any case call ahead to see if they can accommodate you. It's in Ain Hud, the Arab village 4km past Ein Hod.

TOP CHOICE Art Bar
TAVERNA $

(☑052 836 2498; ⊙11am-3pm & 9pm-midnight) Danny Schlyfestone is the village beermeister and one of the local characters. He brews up fresh stouts and ales in his home; don't leave town without downing a bottle or two.

ℹ Getting There & Away

Buses 202, 222 and 921 link Haifa's Hof HaCarmel bus station with Ein Hod junction, on the old Haifa–Hadera road (Rte 4). Buses are fairly frequent and the trip takes about 20 minutes. From the junction, walk along the road for about 2km (20 minutes), and the village is on the right.

Zichron Ya'acov
زخرون يعقوب   זכרון יעקב

☑04 / POP 9000

With fine food, great wine, country air and throngs of holiday makers, Zichron Ya'acov looks like a slice of the Napa Valley transported to the Middle East.

◉ Sights

The town, one of Palestine's first Zionist settlements, was established in 1882 by Jews from Romania. Nowadays Zichron Ya'acov is best known for its role in Israel's wine industry and, more recently, its attractive old town and upper-middle-class neighbourhoods.

Carmel Winery
WINERY

(☑04-629 0977; www.carmelwines.co.il; ⊙8.30am-3.30pm Sun-Thu, to 1pm Fri) Visitors are welcome at the Carmel Winery, founded in 1895. Guided tours in English (15NIS) need to be arranged in advance. From the northern end of HaMeyasdim St, its 350m to the east.

HaMeyasdim St
PEDESTRIAN STREET

Two blocks west of the winery, this cobblestone street is lined with 19th-century stone houses that have been restored to perfection, many of them converted into boutique shops, cafes and ice-cream parlours. It makes for pleasant walking and is at its most bustling on the Shabbat.

Aaronsohn House Museum
MUSEUM

(www.nili-museum.org.il; 40 Hameyasdim St; adult/child 15/12NIS; ⊙9am-4pm Sun-Thu, to noon Fri) The end of the *midrahov* (pedestrian mall) is marked by the Aaronsohn House Museum, named after a noted agronomist and botanist who lived in Zichron Ya'acov. He and his family were also leaders of NILI (the acronym of 'Netzah Yisrael Lo Yeshaker', meaning 'the eternity/strength of Israel will not lie' – Samuel 1: 15-29), a network of British agents who spied on the Turks during WWI, and so the museum not only houses his collection of Palestinian plants but also tells a riveting spy story. Tours of the museum in English are conducted every 90 minutes.

First Aliya Museum
MUSEUM

(2 Hanavid St; admission 15NIS; ⊙9am-2pm Sun-Thu) In the early days, the town owed its survival to donations from Baron James de Rothschild, who funded the establishment of the vineyards, the synagogue and other buildings, including the Administration House. The latter is now a museum commemorating the Jewish pioneers who came to the Land of Israel between 1882 and 1904. A multimedia presentation describes the trials and tribulations of those heady days.

Tishbi
WINERY

(☑04-638 0223) Located down the hill on the road towards Binyamina, Tishbi winery is another popular Israeli label. Tours (15NIS) of the vineyard, which include a sampling of the wines, are held at 10am, noon and 2pm. The winery also has a wonderful restaurant if you're in the mood for some fine dining. It's 2.5km south of Zichron Ya'acov on Rte 252.

🍽 Sleeping & Eating

Bet Maimon
HOTEL $$

(☑04-639 0212, 629 0999; www.maimon.com; 4 Zahal St; s/d 342/428NIS; ✳🛜🌊) This pleasant, family-run hotel has 25 spacious rooms, each with TV and modern decor. The patio and garden have some spectacular views

towards the coast (especially at sunset) and there are welcome amenities such as a sauna and Jacuzzi. The restaurant serves up Mediterranean and Sephardic dishes in a rustic setting. Pay wi-fi is available. From Hwy 4 bear right at the first fork in the road, then take the second left as you head uphill and another left at the roundabout.

Haneshika
MEDITERRANEAN $$

(37 HaMeyasdim St; mains 40-60NIS; ⊙12.30-3.30pm & 7-11.30pm Tue-Sat, 7-11.30pm Mon) Charming Haneshika is an old farmhouse and garden, taking you back to Zichron Ya'acov's days of yore. Inside the cosy dining hall, you can sample some fine Provençal cuisine, including excellent appetisers like potato gnocchi with mozzarella and country-style sausages. For a main course you might want to order the lamb casserole with aubergine or the pork stew.

ℹ Getting There & Away

Zichron Ya'acov is about 5km southeast of Dor, accessed by Hwy 652. Buses travel here from Tel Aviv (bus 872, 26.50NIS, 1¾ hours, eight daily) and from Hof HaCarmel (buses 202 or 222, 15.40NIS, 30 minutes, every 60 to 90 minutes).

Mey Kedem مي قيديم מי קדם

This Byzantium-era archaeological site includes a 6km-long ancient tunnel once used to transport water to the port of Caesarea. A 300m section of the tunnel (☑04-638 8622; www.meykedem.com; admission adult/child 24/18NIS; ⊙9am-5pm Mar-Nov) is now open to exploration, provided you don't mind wading through knee-deep water. Bring a torch (flashlight), a change of clothes and suitable footwear for walking in water. Admission includes a one-hour guided tour. This is a great activity if you've got kids. To get there from Binyamina, take Rte 652 (towards Pardes Hanna) to Rte 653 (towards Givat Ada), turn left on Rte 654 and then right at Hwy 6533. It's 4km down Hwy 6533. Note that Mey Kedem is one sight within the larger Alona Park.

Caesarea قيسارية קיסריה

☑04 / POP 3400

Caesarea (pronounced kay-*sar*-ee-ya in Hebrew) was one of the great cities of antiquity, rivalling great Mediterranean harbours such as Alexandria and Carthage. Despite efforts by various conquerors to keep the city alive, time and warfare eventually had their way and by the 14th century most of Caesarea had disappeared under the shifting dunes. Major excavations have been made over the past 60 years and Caesarea is now one of the country's most impressive archaeological sites. Facilities include a visitor centre with a dynamic multimedia display. Cafes and restaurants add to the scene and even after the park closes you can still dine al fresco by the sea.

A modern, gated Caesarea of shopping malls and mansions has developed outside the archaeological area.

History

This place was a small Phoenician settlement in the 3rd or 4th century BCE. Herod inherited the site and set about building his city in 22 BCE. Dedicating it to his patron, the Roman emperor Augustus Caesar, Herod apparently aimed to build the most grandiose city imaginable. For several years, hundreds of builders and divers worked around the clock to complete the project. To create the two lofty breakwaters which stretched for 540m on the southern side and 270m on the north, 230 cu metres of stones were lowered into the open sea.

In the pursuit of his desire, Herod became increasingly tyrannical and those who questioned, let alone disobeyed, his orders were often executed. Following Herod's death (sighs of relief all round, no doubt), Caesarea became the local Roman capital. Pontius Pilate resided here as prefect from CE 26 to 36 – his name even appears on an inscription found in the ruins of the theatre. According to the New Testament (Acts 10), a Roman centurion serving at the garrison here was the first Gentile to be converted to Christianity, baptised by Peter.

Following the Great Jewish Revolt (CE 66 to 70), in which the Jews rose up against – and were crushed by – the Romans (and expelled from Jerusalem), thousands of captives were executed in Caesarea's amphitheatre. Some 65 years later, after the Romans put down the Bar Kochba Revolt, the amphitheatre again became an arena of cruelty as 10 Jewish sages, including Rabbi Akiva, were publicly tortured.

The city was seized by the Arabs in CE 640 only to fall into disrepair. In 1101 the Crusaders took Caesarea from the Muslims and discovered in the city a hexagonal, green-glass bowl that they believed to be the Holy Grail, the vessel from which Jesus drank at the Last Supper. It is now kept at the Cathedral of St Lorenzo in Genoa. The Crusaders favoured Akko and Jaffa as their principal ports and therefore only a part of Herod's Caesarea was rehabilitated.

The city was to change hands between Arabs and Crusaders four times until King Louis IX of France captured it in 1251. That same year he added most of the fortifications visible today. They proved totally inadequate under the onslaught of the Mamluk sultan Beybars, who in 1261 broke through the Crusader defences and devastated the city.

The ruins remained deserted and over time were swallowed by shifting wind-blown sands. In 1878 a group of Muslim refugees from Bosnia were installed here by the Turks but driven out during the 1948 war.

It was only with the establishment of Kibbutz Sdot Yam in 1940 that ancient Caesarea began to re-emerge. While tilling the land, farmers found bits and pieces of the old city and archaeologists soon followed.

◎ Sights

From the ticket office of **Caesarea National Park** (www.parks.org.il; adult/child 38/23NIS, entrance to harbour only 13NIS; ◎8am-6pm Apr-Sep, to 4pm Oct-Mar) a short path leads to the main sights around the harbour. The ticket price includes a movie and a multimedia tour at the harbour.

Once you are inside the park everything is well signposted. When you buy your ticket, pick up a park brochure and a free map with five colour-coded walking tours.

Note that in addition to the main gate there is a second entrance about 800m to the south. Tour groups usually get dropped off at one gate and picked up at the other gate. If you are travelling on your own, it's best to enter at the main gate and then double back to this gate after your tour. The order of the following sites assumes you start your tour at the main gate.

Crusader City   ARCHAEOLOGICAL SITE

King Louis IX of France built the fortifications and moat that surround the Crusader City. The **wall** was 900m long, 13m high and enclosed the harbour and the city, which during Crusader times was much smaller than Herod's Caesarea. There were 16 towers and a moat that is still largely intact. The French monarch actually spent a year here overseeing the construction. Once inside you should follow the marked route to

Caesarea

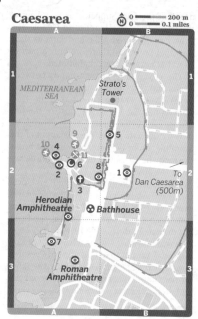

N

0 — 200 m
0 — 0.1 miles

MEDITERRANEAN
SEA

Strato's
Tower

To
Dan Caesarea
(500m)

Herodian
Amphitheatre

Bathhouse

Roman
Amphitheatre

the left, which takes you along the **vaulted street** to the remains of a Crusader-era **church**, built over the site of Caesar's temple and destroyed by the Arabs in 1291. Down by the harbour and easily identifiable is the **mosque** constructed by the Turks for the Bosnian refugees in the late 19th century.

Caesarea Experience
& Crusader Citadel   ENTERTAINMENT COMPLEX

As you walk out on the jetty, the long building on your left is the Caesarea Experience, which starts off with a 10-minute movie (in English at appointed times) dramatising the history of the city from birth to destruction. A second room contains computer-animated holographs of King Herod and co, designed to answer your every question.

The two-storey building behind the Caesarea Experience is the **Time Tower**, also known as the Crusader Citadel. The top floor contains the third segment of the multimedia experience, a computer-generated show that allows you to see the city at different periods of its existence. It helps you to understand the layers of history in the archaeological park. From the Time Tower you get a view of the harbour. The dark blotches are actually the foundations of the enormous breakwater constructed by Herod.

Herodian Amphitheatre
& The Bathhouse   HISTORIC SITE

The U-shaped dirt plaza near Promontory Palace is the Herodian Amphitheatre, also known as the hippodrome, where chariot races and other sporting events took place. The theatre is 250m long and 50m wide, with enough seating for 10,000 spectators. Because the chariots tended to crash when going around the turns, seats at each end of the amphitheatre were most prized. Next to the amphitheatre are the remains of a bathhouse. Well-preserved mosaics are protected from the elements by a temporary roof.

Promontory Palace   HISTORIC SITE

Beyond the amphitheatre is a rocky point with the ruins of the Promontory Palace, a colossal structure built in Roman times. Its western portion contains a pool believed to have been used as a fish market.

Roman Amphitheatre   HISTORIC SITE

The original Herodian structure of the amphitheatre has been modified and added to over the centuries. The semicircular platform behind the stage is a 3rd-century addition, and the great wall with the two towers is part of a 6th-century Byzantine fortress built over the ruins. A great deal more reconstruction has gone on in more recent times to transform the amphitheatre into a spectacular venue for concert performances. The following sites are outside the national park:

Byzantine Street (Cardo)   HISTORIC AREA

Outside the city walls and across the street is a fenced-in excavated Byzantine street (Cardo) with two large 2nd- or 3rd-century CE statues. Some steps lead down to the street, which is attributed in an inscription in the mosaic floor to Flavius Strategius, a 6th-century mayor. The statues originally belonged to temples and were unearthed by the ploughs of local kibbutzniks. The white marble figure is unidentified but the red porphyry one is most probably the Emperor Hadrian holding an orb and sceptre.

Kibbutz Sdot Yam & the Caesarea Museum   MUSEUM

(admission 10NIS; ☺10am-4pm Sat-Thu, to 1pm Fri) Kibbutzniks from nearby Kibbutz Sdot Yam to the south have spent the past seven decades digging up the history of Caesarea. Many of the relics from the ancient city have ended up at the kibbutz in the on-site Caesarea Museum. Among the relics here is a replica of an inscription mentioning Pontius Pilate by name. The plaque is of enormous historical significance as it's the only archaeological evidence that the man whom the Bible says ordered Jesus's crucifixion actually existed. The original is on display at the Israel Museum in Jerusalem.

🏃 Activities

Caesarea Beach Club   BEACH

(adult/child 25/20NIS) The Caesarea Beach Club is the small slice of shoreline fringing Herod's harbour. The price includes the use of lounge chairs, umbrellas and showers. There are also kayaks available to hire. At the time of research the beach was closed due to damage caused by the surf but may re-open by the time you read this. Another option is the beach at the Roman aqueduct. There is no charge but you get what you pay for as there are only basic facilities.

Old Caesarea Diving Centre   DIVING

(☏04-626 5898; www.caesarea-diving.com) Scuba divers will get a kick out of diving in the harbour, where your dive master will give you a guided tour of Herod's breakwater. It is organised by the Old Caesarea Diving Centre, which has a dive shop on the jetty, just behind the Time Tower. A group dive

with equipment costs 165NIS per person. Lessons are available for beginners.

🛏 Sleeping

Grushka B&B   B&B $

(☏04-638 9810; www.6389810.com; 28 Hameyasdim St, Binyamina; s/d 300/335NIS, plus per child 125NIS; ❄@🛜) This friendly Dutch- and Israeli-run B&B offers several comfortable rooms as well as a quiet cottage and a fully equipped villa for families. It's just a seven-minute walk from the Binyamina train station; or call for a pick-up. It makes a good base if you want to explore Caesarea and nearby Zichron Ya'acov.

Dan Caesarea   HOTEL $$

(☏04-626 9111; www.danhotels.com; s/d 500/520NIS; ❄@🏊) Colourfully decorated rooms have balconies, some of which have sea views. Around the hotel you can walk in landscaped gardens, or even play a round of golf at the attached 18-hole course. Other amenities include a gym, spa and tennis courts.

🍴 Eating

Port Cafe   EUROPEAN $$

(mains 48-75NIS; ☺noon-10pm) Offering a range of sandwiches, salads, pastas and a kids menu, this is a good place to fill up after exploring the ruins. It is at the beginning of the jetty.

ℹ Getting There & Away

The best way to visit Caesarea is with a hired car – getting here with public transport is a pain in the bum. If you don't have your own car there are a few options.

From Tel Aviv, take a bus to Hadera and then switch to bus 76, which departs Hadera at 8.20am, 11.25am, 1.10pm and 2.45pm Sunday to Thursday and 9.05am, 11.05am, 12.40pm and 3.05pm Friday.

From Haifa you could travel to Hadera to catch bus 76 or you could go to Or Akiva junction and wait for bus 76 to pass (wait at the bus stop near the shopping mall, 100m west of the junction). The bus will pass about 10 to 15 minutes after the above times.

A final option is to take bus 947 or 910 to Or Akiva Intersection (different from Or Akiva junction), originating at Hof HaCarmel. From the intersection it's a 2km walk to Caesarea (walk in a westerly direction, away from the highway). This option is only for adventurous travellers who don't mind getting dropped off on the side of the highway (and don't mind the 2km walk).

WORTH A TRIP

BEIT SHE'ARIM

An ancient city and later a Jewish necropolis, Beit She'arim (adult/child 20/9NIS; ☺8am-5pm, entrance until 3pm) is now a shady park and a key destination for archaeology hounds.

For part of the late 2nd century CE, Beit She'arim was the meeting place of the Sanhedrin (the era's Jewish supreme court), headed at the time by Rabbi Yehuda HaNassi, who took on responsibilities both secular and religious and handled political affairs between Jews and the Roman overlords. He called together Jewish scholars and compiled the Mishnah (the earliest codification of Jewish law) at Tzipori but asked to be buried here, inspiring others to do the same.

During the 4th century the town was destroyed by the Romans, presumably in the process of suppressing a Jewish uprising. During the following 600 years the many tombs were looted and covered by rock falls. Archaeologists stumbled upon the remains of Beit She'arim in 1936.

As you drive towards the entrance of the park, the ruins of a 2nd-century synagogue are off to the left. At the park itself there are 31 catacombs and a small museum in an ancient rock-cut reservoir. The largest catacomb contains 24 separate chambers with more than 200 sarcophagi. Note the variety of symbols and inscriptions carved onto the coffins, including epithets written in Hebrew, Aramaic, Palmyran and Greek. Some of the dead, it is believed, had come from as far away as Persia and Yemen.

Beit She'arim is 19km southeast of Haifa. With your own car, take Hwy 75 to Hwy 70, then take Hwy 722 north and turn left at the sign that says 'Qiryat Amal'. The entrance to Beit She'arim is a further 400m.

If you don't have a car, take bus 301 from Haifa (Lev HaMifratz station) to Kiryat Tivon (13.50NIS, 30 minutes). Tell the driver you want to go to Beit She'arim and he will let you off one stop past the main intersection (you'll see the large brown sign to Beit She'arim). Walk past the roundabout, down the hill and after 700m turn right and then right again to the park.

Megiddo (Armageddon)

מגידו   مجيدو

☑04

Better known as Armageddon (in Hebrew Har Megiddo, meaning 'Mt Megiddo'), the site that St John predicted would host the last great battle on earth (Revelation 16:16) is now preserved in Megiddo National Park (☑04-659 0316; adult/child 27/14NIS; ☺8am-5pm Sat-Thu, to 4pm Fri).

Although nothing too apocalyptic has happened yet, Megiddo has been the scene of important and bloody battles throughout the ages. Details of the first blood to be spilt at the site come from hieroglyphics on the wall of Karnak Temple in Luxor, which describe the battle that Thutmose III fought here in 1468 BCE. Megiddo remained a prosperous Egyptian stronghold for at least 100 years, holding out against the Israelites (Judges 1:27) and probably only falling to David. Under his son, Solomon, Megiddo became one of the jewels of the kingdom, known as the Chariot City – excavations

have revealed traces of stables extensive enough to have held thousands of horses.

For a while Megiddo was a strategic stronghold on the important trade route between Egypt and Assyria, but by the 4th century BCE the town had inexplicably become uninhabited. However, its strategic importance remained, and among those armies that fought here were the British in WWI. On being awarded his peerage, General Edmund Allenby took the title Lord Allenby of Megiddo. Jewish and Arab forces fought here during the 1948 war.

Excavations of Tel Megiddo have unearthed the remains of 26 or 27 distinct historical periods, from 4000 BCE to 400 BCE, but it takes some stretching of the imagination to see in the modern-day site any traces of its former grandeur. Help is given through an introductory film, some excellent models in the visitors centre museum, and by informative signs planted around the site sketching out the relevance of the earthen hummocks and depressions. The most tangible aspect of the excavations is the preserved

9th-century-BCE water system. This consists of a shaft sunk 30m through solid rock down to a 70m tunnel. This hid the city's water source from invading forces, rather like Hezekiah's Tunnel in Jerusalem. There is no water to slosh through here, though. Save the tunnel until last as it leads you out of the site, depositing you on a side road some distance away from the visitors centre.

ℹ Getting There & Away

The archaeological site is 2km north of Megiddo junction, which is the well-signposted intersection of Rte 66 (Haifa–Jenin) and Rte 65 (Afula–Hadera). Ask the driver to let you off at Megiddo junction and then walk or hitch a lift the last 2km. From Haifa (Lev HaMifratz bus station), bus 302 departing at 6.55am stops near the gate.

Akko (Acre)   עכו   عكا

📷 04 / POP 52,000

Marco Polo passed through Akko around 800 years ago and, quite frankly, the place hasn't changed much since then. Through the centuries Akko has remained a wonderfully preserved city of stone, sited on a narrow spit of land that pokes into the Mediterranean. It seduces visitors with narrow alleys, slender minarets, secret passageways, subterranean vaults and impressive ramparts. While other historic towns in Israel are busy packaging their heritage for the benefit of tourists, Akko has taken a more modest approach, leaving its homes for families, not artists, and its souq (market) for fishers, not souvenir hawkers. The city was awarded Unesco World Heritage status in 2002.

Akko is the Acre of the Crusaders, and as the capital and port of the Latinate Kingdom of Palestine, it received ships from Amalfi, Genoa, Pisa and Venice. The modern visitor can get a real sense of Akko's history by wandering its streets. It's easily visited from Haifa on a day trip but there are a few places to spend the night if you want to catch a glimpse of the town by moonlight.

All the places of interest are firmly enclosed within the walls of Old Akko, so you really only need to get to know a small, albeit confusing, area. Coming out of the train station, turn right on Herzl and then take the first left on Derekh Ha'Arba'a. Walk past the bus station (which is on your left) and walk one block to the traffic lights and turn right onto Ben Ami St. After walking

through the pedestrianised shopping precinct *(midrahov)*, turn left onto Weizmann St and you'll see the city walls ahead. All up, it's a 20-minute walk; you can make things easier on yourself by taking a taxi.

History
Long before it played host to the royalty of medieval Europe, Akko could boast a distinguished and colourful history. It received mention in Egyptian sacred texts of the 19th century BCE and it's reputedly the place where Hercules, the Rambo of Greek mythology, took refuge to heal his wounds.

Akko was always an important port, and Alexander the Great established a mint here in 333 BCE, which operated for 600 years. After Alexander's death, Akko was taken by the Egyptian Ptolemites. In 200 BCE they lost it to the Syrian Seleucids, who struggled to keep it until the Romans, led by Pompey, began two centuries of rule.

In CE 636 Akko fell to the Arabs, who enjoyed a fairly untroubled reign until the coming of the Crusaders. The arrival of the Christian armies heralded the most turbulent period in Akko's history. The Crusaders seized the town and established it as their principal port and lifeline. They lost it to Saladin (Salah ad-Din) for a time, but it was retaken during the Third Crusade by armies under the command of Richard the Lionheart and King Philip of Spain.

In 1291 the Mamluks appeared with an army that outnumbered the defenders 10:1. After a two-month siege, during which most of Akko's inhabitants escaped to Cyprus, the town fell. It was pounded to rubble by the Mamluks and remained in ruins for the next 450 years.

Surprisingly, the rebirth of Akko was undertaken by an Albanian mercenary, Ahmed Pasha al-Jazzar, known as 'the Butcher' *(jazzar* in Arabic) because of his cruelty in suppressing revolts. Taking advantage of the weak and corrupt Ottoman administration, Al-Jazzar established a virtually independent fiefdom and bullied the port back into working order. Old Akko, as it exists today, was shaped by the decrees of Al-Jazzar. By 1799 the city had become important enough for Napoleon to attempt its capture, but he was repelled by Al-Jazzar with some help from the English fleet.

Akko remained in Ottoman hands until the British captured Palestine in 1917. They set up their headquarters and built port facilities in Haifa, and Akko's importance dwindled, although its citadel was maintained as Palestine's main prison. During the 1930s, Akko was a hotbed of Arab hostility towards Jewish immigration but Jewish forces captured the town fairly easily in 1948.

Today Akko, like Haifa, is a mixed city – about 67% of the residents are Jews and 25% Arabs. The population of the Old City is about 95% Arab. In recent decades Arab families from around the Galilee have been moving into the city's historically Jewish neighbourhoods. Residents from both communities generally coexist peacefully, though the city was shaken by several days of rioting in late 2008.

Dangers & Annoyances

Akko shuts down after dark and while most people feel comfortable walking around, some women walking alone in the Old City have been subject to unwanted attention and occasional sexual harassment. Women can reduce such attention by dressing modestly.

⊙ Sights

Walls & Gates   FORTIFICATIONS

As you approach Old Akko on Weizmann St, you first come to the wall and moat built by Al-Jazzar in 1799 after Napoleon's retreat. Today they serve as a very physical division between the predominantly Arab Old Akko and the sprawl of the modern, mostly Jewish town to the north.

Heading west along Al-Jazzar's wall brings you to Burj al-Kuraijim (Vineyard Tower), also known as the British Fortress. From here, the 12th-century sea wall (refaced in the 18th century by Al-Jazzar with stones scavenged from the Crusader castle at Atlit) runs due south before looping around to the harbour. In the shadow of the sea wall is HaHaganah St, which terminates in a car park beside the lighthouse at the southernmost tip of Old Akko.

Back at the point where Weizmann St breaches Al-Jazzar's wall, some stairs to the east ascend to the Land Wall Promenade and the Burj al-Kommander, the squat bastion that anchors the northeastern corner of Old Akko. From the platform atop the tower there are great views across the bay to Haifa and over the exotic skyline of Akko before you. The promenade terminates 200m south at the 12th-century Land Gate, once the city's only land entrance – the only other way in was via the Sea Gate in the harbour, now occupied by the Abu Christo restaurant.

Al-Jazzar Mosque   MOSQUE

(admission 10NIS; ⊙8am-5pm Sat-Thu, 8-11am & 1-5pm Fri) A little bit patchy up close, from a distance the large green dome and slender pencil minaret of Al-Jazzar Mosque form a beautiful ensemble. The mosque was built in 1781 in typical Ottoman Turkish style with a little local improvisation in parts; the columns in the courtyard, for example, were 'adopted' from Roman Caesarea. Around by the base of the minaret, the small twin-domed building contains the sarcophagi of Al-Jazzar and his adopted son and successor, Süleyman. The mosque stands on the site of a former Crusader cathedral, the cellars of which were put into use by the Turks as cisterns.

Festival Garden   GARDENS

From the mosque, backtrack a few steps towards the city wall and turn left into the car park next to the police station. Walk through the lush Festival Garden and turn right into the tourist office. Here you can watch a short introductory film about Akko and look over a model of the city. The helpful staff will be able to provide advice on how to tackle the city. Detailed maps are available for 3NIS.

Outside the tourist office is a kiosk where you purchase mix-and-match combination tickets to the attractions in the city. The best ticket gets you into the Subterranean Crusader City, the Hammam al-Pasha (Turkish Bath), the Okashi Art Museum, the Templars Tunnel, the Treasures in the Wall Museum and Rosh HaNikra for 75/65NIS per adult/child. A separate kiosk passes out audio headsets (free with admission) that lead you through the subterranean city. The exhibits are open 9am to 5.15pm Saturday to Thursday and 9am to 2.15pm Friday. From November to March the sites close one hour early.

Museum of Underground Prisoners   MUSEUM

(adult/child 15/10NIS; ⊙8.30am-4.30pm Sun-Thu, to 1.30pm Fri) Before exploring the Knights' Halls climb up the stairs behind the ticket kiosk to the top of the Akko Citadel, a rambling structure built by the Turks in the late 18th century on 13th-century Crusader foundations. At the top of the stairs, turn left to reach the Museum of Underground Prisoners, dedicated to Jewish armed resistance during the British Mandate. The inmates imprisoned here by the British included Revisionist Zionist leader Ze'ev Jabotinsky in 1920 and 1921. Among the exhibits are memorials to the nine Jewish un-

Akko (Acre)

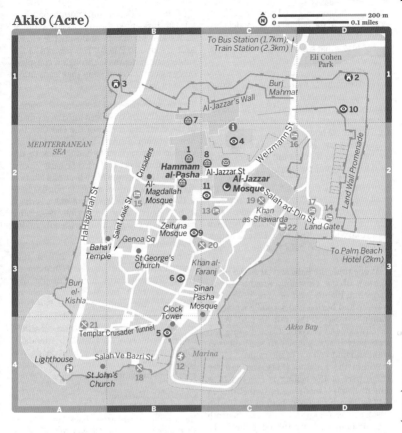

Akko (Acre)

◎ Top Sights

Al-Jazzar Mosque	C2
Hammam al-Pasha	B2

◎ Sights

1	Akko Citadel	B2
2	Burj al-Kommander	D1
3	Burj al-Kuraijim	B1
4	Festival Garden	C2
5	Khan al-Umdan	B4
	Knights' Halls	(see 1)
6	Kurdi & Berit	B3
7	Museum of Underground Prisoners	B1
8	Okashi Art Museum	C2
9	Souq	B3
10	Treasures in the Wall Museum	D1
11	Turkish Bazaar	C2

◎ Activities, Courses & Tours

12	Sailing Around the Walls	B4

◎ Sleeping

13	Akko Sand Hostel	C2
14	Akkotel	D2
15	Effendi's Palace	B2
16	HI – Knights Hostel & Guest House	C2
17	Walied's Akko Gate Hostel	D2

◎ Eating

18	Doniana	B4
19	Elias Dieb & Sons	C2
20	Hummus Said	C3
21	Uri Buri	A4

◎ Drinking

22	Leale al-Sultan	C3

HAIFA & THE NORTH COAST AKKO (ACRE)

derground fighters executed here (the gallows room is open to the public) and a model illustrating the Etzel's (Irgun's) daring mass breakout of 1947 – that scene in the movie version of *Exodus* was filmed here.

For the Baha'i the room upstairs is a holy place. Baha'ullah, founder of the Baha'i faith, was imprisoned here in the late 19th century. Later, his third son Mírzá Mihda fell through a skylight in the roof while meditating. He died 22 hours later.

Note that the Ministry of Defence runs the museum so if you want to enter you'll need to show your passport.

Subterranean Crusader City   HISTORIC SITE
(adult/child 25/22NIS) Buy tickets for the Subterranean Crusader City from the kiosk outside the tourist office. Head across the lawn to the entry to the Knights' Halls, a haunting series of vaulted halls that lie 8m below the street level.

At one time, the halls served as the headquarters of the crusading Knights Hospitallers but, like the rest of Acre, it was laid to waste and buried under rubble when the Mamluks breached the walls in 1291. When the city came to be reconstructed some 450 years later it was simpler to start all over again and build on top of the ruins.

Within the Knights' Halls, you can see where part of the ceiling is covered by a cement patch – this plugs a tunnel dug in 1947 by Jewish prisoners held in the British prison above. Not knowing what lay beneath in the dark halls, they returned to their cells to plot a more successful escape route. Today the halls are occasionally used for concerts, and the annual Akko Fringe Theatre Festival is, aptly enough, staged here. Ongoing reconstruction work may impede your path in places, but most of the area remains open.

The Knights' Halls lead out to an open courtyard. Enter one of the doors to the left to access the Refectorium (dining hall). It's possible that Marco Polo dined in this room when he visited Acre. Opposite the entrance you can see a fleur-de-lys, an emblem of the kings of France.

Next to the entrance to the dining hall is a stairwell that leads to a long and claustrophobic underground sewer that most likely doubled as an escape route through which knights could abandon the halls and make their way to the harbour.

The tunnel continues to a crypt that contains, among other things, the tombstone of the last bishop of Nazareth. Past the crypt is the Crusaders' Domus Infirmorum, or hospital. The Turks used the area as a post office, so it's also known as Al-Bosta (the closest Arabic sound to P is B). The way out of the subterranean depths is through a conspicuously placed souvenir shop that leads into a Turkish bazaar.

Treasures in the Wall Museum   MUSEUM
(adult/child 15/12NIS) Wedged into the ramparts in the northeast corner of the Old City, this new museum displays a wealth of ethnographic items primarily dating back to the 19th century, most of it used by early Zionist farmers. The museum has a beautiful location and has some curious artefacts but has little to do with the grand history of Akko. Perhaps its best feature is the wonderfully descriptive commentary you get from the friendly guides.

Hammam al-Pasha   MUSEUM
From the end of the Turkish Bazaar, turn right and look out for the Hammam al-Pasha (Turkish Bath), housed in the 1780 bathhouse built by Al-Jazzar, which remained in use until the 1940s. The hammam now contains a worthwhile 30-minute multimedia show (adult/child 25/21NIS) called 'The Story of the Last Bath Attendant'. The creatively designed exhibit leads you from the dressing room through the steamy rooms, all brilliantly lit with coloured glass.

Okashi Art Museum   MUSEUM
(adult/child 10/7NIS) Around the corner from the Hammam al-Pasha (back towards the Crusader City) is the Okashi Art Museum, a gallery devoted to the works of Avshalom Okashi (1916–80), an influential Israeli painter and a resident of Akko for the last half of his life.

Souq   MARKET
From the Turkish Bathhouse, head away from the Crusader City and follow your nose to Akko's small but bustling souq. Here fresh hummus is boiled in giant vats while nearby fresh-caught fish flop off the tables. As carts trundle past, children shuck corn and vendors hawk fresh fruit, all to the soundtrack of tinny Arabic music playing from battered radios. As you browse the stalls, visit Kurdi & Berit (◷9.30am-6pm), a tourist-friendly shop that ships herbs and spices worldwide.

Khan al-Umdan & the Harbour   HISTORIC BUILDINGS
Old Akko has several large khans (an inn enclosing a courtyard, used by caravans for

accommodation), which once served the camel caravans bringing in grain from the hinterland. The grandest is the Khan al-Umdan, down by the harbour. Its name means 'Inn of the Pillars', and it was built by Al-Jazzar in 1785. The pillars that give the khan its name were appropriated from Caesarea. It's a two-storey structure and the ground floor would have housed the animals, while their merchant owners would have slept upstairs. It's fairly run down for the moment but there are plans to convert the khan into a hotel.

The harbour's marina is still very much in service and if you are around early enough, you can watch the fishing boats come in and unload the day's catch.

Templars Crusader Tunnel TUNNEL
(adult/child 15/12NIS) Near the lighthouse car park at the southern tip of Akko, look out for the amazing Templar Crusader Tunnel, an underground passageway that connected the port to a Templar palace. The tunnel was found by accident in 1994 after a complaint made by a local woman about a blocked sewer led a plumber to the underground shaft. The tunnel was investigated and opened to tourists. You can enter at either end of the tunnel (near the lighthouse or the Khan al-Umdan).

🏃 Activities

Sailing Around the Walls BOAT TOUR
(☑050 555 1136, 04-991 3890; per person 20NIS) From 10am to 6pm, this outfit runs trips from the end of the breakwater and makes a 30-minute cruise around the walls. The boat leaves whenever a sufficient number of passengers comes aboard. In summer it may run daily but the rest of the year it tends to only work on weekends.

🛏 Sleeping

The ultra-luxurious boutique hotel **Effendi's Palace** (☑054 457 0719) should be ready by 2012. It should be a great option, but not a cheap one at US$350 a night.

HI – Knights Hostel
& Guest House HOSTEL $
(☑1 599 510 511; www.iyha.org.il; 2 Weizman St; dm/s/d US$32/48.50/97; @ 🖤) This gorgeous new IYHA building has 76 rooms spread over three floors. Like other IYHA places it's very clean and institutional but does have some unique features, including an ancient aqueduct running through it and ruins in

the courtyard. Prices include continental breakfast.

Akkotel HOTEL $$$
(☑04-987 7100; www.akkotel.com; Salah ad-Din St; s/d US$145/180; @ 🖤) Embedded inside the walls of the Old City, this unique hotel gives you a perspective on Akko like no other. The 16 rooms all have arched ceilings, flat-screen TV and modern bathrooms. They don't get much sunlight, but that's expected from a hotel that's squeezed inside the city walls.

Palm Beach Hotel HOTEL $$$
(☑04-987 7777; www.palmbeach.co.il; s/d/tr US$136/172/268; @ 🖤🏊) Located 2km east of the old city, the Palm Beach is a mini resort with a pool, sauna, health spa, beach access and water sports. Book through the internet for a 10% discount. It's great if you like kids, but 'peace and quiet' is unknown terminology here.

Walied's Akko Gate Hostel HOSTEL $
(☑04-991 0410; www.akkogate.com; Salah ad-Din St; dm/s/d 75/200/250NIS; @ 🖤) This long-running hostel has a friendly owner and good location. Rooms are simply furnished and a little dated and dark but fine for travellers with low expectations. Rooms on the street side can get some noise at night and it can be chilly in the winter months. The kitchen is too basic to do any serious cooking. Breakfast costs an extra 25NIS. Owner Walied can arrange trips to the Golan Heights (250NIS) and Rosh HaNikra (50NIS) when there is enough demand. Call for a free pick-up from the station.

Akko Sand Hostel GUESTHOUSE $
(☑04-991 8636, 050 908 3402; akko.sand.hostel@gmail.com; Turkish Baazar; dm/s/d 80/150/250NIS; @ 🖤) This new budget guesthouse is squeezed between buildings behind Al-Jazzar Mosque and the Turkish Bazaar. Travellers cook meals together in the atmospheric common area and upstairs there are nine small rooms with wood floors and metal bunk beds. There are decent views from the upper levels and wi-fi in the common areas. On the downside travellers have reported bungled reservations and unreliable service when problems occur. To find it, stand at the western end of Salah ad-Din St then walk through the arched tunnel in the corner (as if you're headed to the covered market). After the tunnel look for the sign pointing right to the Sand Hostel.

✗ Eating & Drinking

For cheap eating, there are several felafel places around the junction of Salah ad-Din and Al-Jazzar Sts. Self-catering supplies are available at Elias Dieb & Sons (Salah ad-Din St), a little cave-like supermarket opposite Souq al-Abiad; there's no English sign.

Leale al-Sultan   COFFEEHOUSE $
(Khan as-Shawarda; snacks 20NIS; ⊘24hr) Traditional Middle Eastern coffeehouse sporting sequined cushions, colourful wall hangings and backgammon tables. A Turkish coffee costs 5NIS while a nargileh is 15NIS. It's popular with locals.

Hummus Said   HUMMUS $
(snacks 15NIS; ⊘6am-2.30pm; ✐) Deeply entrenched in the souq, this place has become something of an institution, doling up that much-loved Middle Eastern dip to throngs of visitors from around the country. For 15NIS, you'll get salads, pickles, pita and a big glob of hummus with fuul (fava bean paste) or garlic.

Doniana   SEAFOOD $$$
(Pisan Harbour; dishes 60-100NIS; ⊘noon-midnight) Excellent seafood and stunning sea views make this a great option for fine dining in Akko. For 90NIS you can get a seafood stew, good for two people, plus side salads for an additional 29NIS. Salad refills are free. Other main dishes include grilled fish, calamari, mussels or crab. Meat lovers may prefer the tender, marinated steak, complemented by a Golan wine.

Uri Buri   SEAFOOD $$$
(✐04-955 2212; HaHaganah St; mains 88-114NIS, half portions 49-62NIS; ⊘noon-11pm) You could easily walk right past Uri Buri and not have a clue that it is one of the most renowned restaurants in Israel. Enter and be greeted by the eccentric owner, Uri, a man of many talents who has at times done everything from spear fishing to diffusing bombs. Today he makes award-winning seafood dishes and is always tinkering with new recipes. Unique and recommended options include the crab with seaweed, sashimi-with-wasabi ice cream, and steamed fish casserole. The end result is sublime and delicious. Ask Uri about his tasting menu (170NIS), which includes arak sorbet, used to clean the palate between dishes. Call ahead to reserve a spot.

❶ Information

Money (cnr Weizmann & Al-Jazzar Sts; ⊘9.30am-6.30pm) Money-changing outlet changes US dollars and euros. Banks with ATMs can be found in the new city. You can also change money at the post office at 49 Ben Ami.

Police (✐04-987 6736; Weizmann St) The police are in the car park near the tourist office.

Post office (Al-Jazzar St; ⊘8am-12.30pm & 4-6pm Sun-Mon & Wed-Thu, 8am-1.30pm Tue, to 1pm Fri) Branch post office that might be able to change travellers cheques. The main post office is in the new city at 49 Ben Ami.

Tourist information (✐04-995 6707; www.akko.org.il; 1 Weizmann St; ⊘8.30am-6.30pm Apr-Oct, to 4.30pm Nov-Mar; @) Located north of the Festival Garden, inside the Crusader citadel. Free internet access is available.

❶ Getting There & Away

Akko's bus terminal and train station lie about a 20-minute walk from the main entrance to the Old City. From Haifa (13NIS, 30 to 50 minutes), the fastest buses are 272 and 252 (avoid any and all local buses, which are horribly slow). From Akko, hop back on bus 272 north to Nahariya (8.80NIS, 15 to 25 minutes).

Sheruts (shared taxis) wait outside the Akko bus station and depart when full, to Haifa (weekday/Shabbat 12/15NIS) and Nahariya (weekday/Shabbat 9/12NIS).

The most pleasant way to travel between Akko and Haifa (15NIS, 25 minutes) or on to Nahariya (8NIS, 15 minutes), however, is by train along the scenic beachfront railway. Trains pass in both directions three times an hour. You will find an automatic ticket machine inside the station.

❶ Getting Around

There's no need for transport within Old Akko; you can walk from the train station in about 20 minutes. There is a bus to the Old City from platform 16 at the bus station, but it only runs once or twice an hour. If you manage to catch it, the bus will drop you off on Weizmann St beside Al-Jazzar's wall. From the train station, a taxi costs around 25NIS.

Around Akko

BAHJE HOUSE & BAHA'I GARDENS

The Bahje House and the Baha'i Gardens (https://bahai.bwc.org/pilgrimage; admission free; ⊘9am-4pm) constitute the holiest site of the Baha'i faith. This is where Baha'ullah, a follower of the Bab and the founder of the faith, lived after his release from prison in Akko and where he died in 1892. His tomb is in lovely gardens, similar in style to those in Haifa. The shrine, known as Bahje House (admission free; ⊘9am-noon Fri-Mon), contains a small museum.

The gardens are about 3km north of the town centre on the main Akko–Nahariya road. Take bus 271 and get off at the stop after the main gate to the gardens, which you should see off to the right, 10 minutes out of the station. Unless you're a Baha'i, you'll have to use the entrance about 500m up the side road to the north of the main gate.

OTTOMAN AQUEDUCT

On your right as you go north on the Nahariya road is a long Roman-style aqueduct. Built by Al-Jazzar in about 1780, it supplied Akko with water from the Galilee uplands.

KIBBUTZ LOHAMEI HAGETA'OT

Just north of the aqueduct is Kibbutz Lohamei HaGeta'ot, established in 1949 by Jews who spent WWII fighting the Nazis in the forests and ghettos of Poland and Lithuania and somehow survived. The Beit Lohamei HaGeta'ot Museum (www.gfh.org.il; adult/child 20/18NIS; ☺9am-4pm Sun-Thu) commemorates the ghetto uprisings, Jewish WWII partisans and Allied assistance during the Holocaust. Despite the depressing theme, it presents a hopeful picture of this tragic period.

Your ticket is also good for the adjacent Yad Layeled (☺9am-4pm Sun-Thu), a moving memorial to the 1.5 million children who perished in the Holocaust. As you descend into the circular structure, haunting voices tell the tales of the victims, and TV monitors play testimonies of the survivors. It culminates at a memorial in the bottom of the building.

The kibbutz is on the road between Akko and Nahariya; just ask the bus driver to let you off.

Nahariya נהריה نهريا
☏04 / POP 51,000

As the main resort town on Israel's northern coast, Nahariya seems to lie in a perpetual state of Shabbat. Numerous hotels line its quiet streets, ice-cream vendors do brisk business on the promenade and families soak up the sun on its gorgeous beaches. There are no major sites here but there are a few reasonably priced hotels around town if you want to use Nahariya as a base to explore the coast or the inland Galilee.

Nahariya started life as a rough frontier town for German–Jewish immigrants during the fifth Aliya, in the 1930s. Early attempts at agriculture failed due to poor soil quality but Nahariya later became an industrial centre

and hometown of Iscar metal works (now owned by Warren Buffet). Located just 10km from the Lebanese border the town has suffered period rocket attacks - during the 2006 Israel–Lebanon war more than 800 Katyusha rockets fell on the city.

In summer (June to August) folk dancing is held on the beach promenade at 9pm every Wednesday and Saturday. In autumn and spring (September to November and March to May) this is held on Saturday at 9pm. In winter (December to February) it is on Saturday morning.

🛏 Sleeping & Eating

Hotel Frank   HOTEL **$$**
(☏04-992 0278; www.hotel-frank.co.il; 4 Ha'Alia St; s/d US$110/140; 🌢@🛜) This hotel has a bland 1970s style but rooms are clean and staff is friendly. It's a couple of blocks from the beach.

Carlton   HOTEL **$$$**
(☏04-900 5555; 23 HaGa'aton Blvd; www.carlton -hotel.co.il; s/d US$150/180; 🌢🛜☒) The Carlton is the most stylish place in town and it's a bargain compared to similar places in Haifa. It has a modern feel and an accommodating staff but the views are nothing special. It's halfway between the bus station and beach.

❶ Getting There & Away

One or two trains per hour head south to Akko (8NIS), Haifa Merkaz HaShmona (19NIS) and beyond.

Bus 272 (express) runs roughly every 20 minutes (until 10.30pm) to Akko (8.80NIS, 15 to 25 minutes) and to Haifa (17.20NIS, 45 to 70 minutes). Do not take any local buses (eg bus 271), which stop every mile to pick up and drop off passengers.

North of Nahariya

MONTFORT מונפורט مونفورط
Montfort is not the most impressive of Israel's Crusader castles, but it is interesting and a visit here involves a pleasant hike. Originally built in 1226 by the French Courtenays, the castle's name was changed from Montfort (Strong Mountain) to Starkenburg (Strong Castle) when they sold it to the Teutonic knights, the Templars and the Hospitallers. They modified the castle, which became their central treasury, archives and Holy Land headquarters, although it had no real strategic value. In 1271 the Muslims, led by the Mamluk sultan Beybars, took the

WORTH A TRIP

ROSH HANIKRA

The tense and volatile border between Israel and Lebanon comes to an appropriately rugged and menacing head at Rosh HaNikra, a frontier-straddling bluff where jagged white cliffs plunge into the sea and waves crash into a series of grottoes. Turn on a radio here and half the stations will be from Cyprus, a corner of the European Union just 250km to the northeast.

The 10km road from Nahariya ends at the Rosh HaNikra Tourist Centre (☎073 271 0100; www.rosh-hanikra.com) from where a cable car (round trip ticket child/adult 35/43NIS; ⏱9am-4pm Sep-Mar, to 6pm Apr-Jun, to 11pm Jul-Aug) descends steeply to the grottoes.

The caves, their white walls lit by the luminescent blue of the Mediterranean, are explored via a meandering path that lets you experience the collision of waves with stone in all its tempestuous glory, especially if the sea is seething. At the northern end, a tunnel leads you into a small theatre, slap-bang on the Lebanese border, where you can watch a 12-minute film on the history of the Haifa–Beirut railway, whose tunnels were excavated by British army engineering units from New Zealand and South Africa in 1941 and 1942. Unsurprisingly, the line has been out of commission since 1948.

Other than the caves, you can grab a bite at a reasonably priced self-service restaurant and peer through the closed gate marking the border between Israel and Lebanon. A few kilometres north is the Naqoura base of the 12,000-member United Nations Interim Force in Lebanon, which has been patrolling the border since 1978. It's also possible to hire a bike at the site to ride 5km south to Betzet Beach. The bike alone is 50NIS, or a combined ticket for the grottoes and the bike is 72NIS.

From Nahariya, Nateev Express buses 20 and 32 run several times daily (9.30am, 2.30pm, 4pm, 5.30pm, 6.30pm) to Rosh HaNikra (7.40NIS, 15 minutes). Once these buses arrive in Nahariya they turn around and head back (so if you arrive on the 2.30pm bus you could take the 4pm bus back). If you're stuck for a lift on the way back it shouldn't be too hard to hitch or hop in a shared taxi.

castle after a previous attempt (five years earlier) had failed. The Crusaders retreated to Akko and the castle was razed.

Little except the view can be seen today. To the right of the entrance is the governor's residence, with the tower straight ahead. The two vaulted chambers to the right are the basement of the knights' hall; next to them is the chapel.

❶ Getting There & Away

The best way to reach Montfort is by car. From Rosh HaNikra take Hwy 899 to Goren Park (it is 7.8km from the Hanita junction). Drive 2km to a car park where you can see Montfort in the distance. The area is poorly signposted so you may need to ask around. From the car park it will take around 40 minutes to hike to Montfort.

If you are coming from the south, there is road access from Mi'iliya on Hwy 89. Travel 3km through town; at the end of the paved road on the right, is a car park. Trail markers painted on rocks point the way. The hike from here is also about 45 minutes.

AKHZIV אכזיב الزيب شاطئ

The short stretch of coastline between Nahariya and Rosh HaNikra on the Lebanese

border is known as Akhziv. Once one of the towns of the Asher tribe in ancient Israel, it was also a Phoenician port, and Bronze Age remains have been found here.

AKHZIV NATIONAL PARK

About 4km north of Nahariya, Akhziv National Park (adult/child 33/20NIS; ⏱8am-7pm Apr-Sep, to 4pm Oct-Mar) has a pleasant beach – with changing rooms, sunshades, showers and snack bar – and costs 14NIS to use.

Just a little further north is an area of well-manicured parkland on the site of an 'abandoned' Arab village. You can see traces of a Phoenician port and use the beach. There are changing rooms and a snack bar.

Around the corner from the park is Akhzivland, self-declared micronation run by old-timer Eli Avivi and wife Rina. They have rooms in a run-down hostel (☎04-982 3250; s/d/tr 200/450/600NIS), which has more than a whiff of Robinson Crusoe to it. They also have campsites (100NIS), which give you access to the basic facilities. There's also a modest museum (admission 20NIS) housing artefacts that date from the Phoenician, Roman, Byzantine and Akhzivland periods.

Lower Galilee & Sea of Galilee الجليل الاسفل وبحيرة طبريا
הגליל התחתון והכינרת

Best Places to Eat

» Havat HaYatzranim (p203)

» Rida Café (p196)

» Abu Ashraf (p196)

» Yisrael's Kitchen (p211)

» Tchelet (p221)

Best Places to Stay

» Fauzi Azar Inn (p195)

» Al-Mutran Guest House (p200)

» Scots Hotel (p210)

» Arbel Guest House (p210)

» Pilgerhaus Tabgha (p215)

Why Go?

Blessed with ancient stone synagogues, archaeological sites associated with Jesus's ministry, and rugged hills cloaked in wildflowers in spring, the Lower Galilee – the part of northern Israel south of Rte 85 (linking Akko with the Sea of Galilee) – is hugely popular with hikers, cyclists, Jewish and Arab Israeli families on holiday, Tel Aviv epicureans and, of course, Christian pilgrims. Green, lush and chilly in winter (the perfect time for a hot-spring dip) and parched in summer (you can beat the heat in the Sea of Galilee), this is where Jesus of Nazareth is believed to have lived, preached and have performed some of his most famous miracles. But these days even Nazareth is much more than a place of Christian pilgrimage – it now boasts one of Israel's most sophisticated dining scenes. The shimmering Sea of Galilee (in Hebrew, the Kinneret), too, juxtaposes holiday pleasures with archaeological excavations linked to Jesus's ministry.

When to Go
Nazareth

Dec–Mar Mt Gilboa is carpeted with daffodils, red poppies and, in March, purple Gilboa irises.

Jul–Sep Oppressively hot at the Sea of Galilee and in the Beit She'an Valley.

Early Dec & early May The twice-yearly Jacob's Ladder Festival brings music to Ginosar.

REALLY, REALLY HOT

The hottest temperature ever recorded anywhere in Asia, a sizzling 53.9°C (129°F), was registered at Kibbutz Tirat Tzvi (8km south of Beit She'an) on 21 June 1942.

Visiting Jenin

» The Gilboa Regional Council, in the Jezreel Valley, and the municipality of the West Bank city of Jenin are working together to improve cross-border 'peace tourism', especially for Christian pilgrims. For details, see http://hagilboa -tour.com/en/gilboa-jenin.

West Bank Crossing

» To travel through the Separation Fence between the Lower Galilee and Jenin, use the Israel Defence Forces (IDF, the national army) Jalameh (Gilboa) Crossing (www.cogat.idf. il/1362-en/Cogat.aspx), 10km south of Afula along Rte 60.

Resources

» Regional Council Tourism Information: www.ekin neret.co.il

» Ministry for the Development of the Negev and the Galilee: www.gogalilee.org

» Travelujah: www.travelu jah.com

» BibleWalks.com: www. biblewalks.com

The Red Line

In newspapers, on the radio and on TV, Israelis follow the water level of the Sea of Galilee at least as closely as they do stock-market indexes. As winter rains flow into the lake, news reports follow its progress towards full capacity (208.8m below sea level), while in summertime, the lake's descent towards (and sometimes even below) the 'red line' (213m below sea level) – beyond which pumping may adversely impact water quality – generates news flashes and, at times, screaming, doomful headlines.

To find out the current state of the lake, stop by the Water Level Surveyor (Medid; southern end, Yigal Allon Promenade; ⊙24hr), a 5m-high sculpture shaped like the land surrounding the Sea of Galilee. The digital readout is accurate to 1cm.

THE JESUS TRAIL

The 65km Jesus Trail (www.jesustrail.com) takes walkers from Nazareth's Church of the Annunciation to Tabgha and Capernaum on the Sea of Galilee. Along the way, it passes through Jewish, Christian, Muslim, Bedouin and Druze communities and a gorgeously varied landscape: rugged hills, olive groves, forests and clifftop lookouts. Highlights include Christian holy sites, ancient synagogues, a Crusader-era battlefield and Nebi Shu'eib, the Druze religion's most important shrine.

Walking the entire trail, which is marked with orange blazes, usually takes four days, but shorter sections can be enjoyed as day hikes. Provided you have decent shoes and plenty of water, the route is suitable for all ages and abilities. Camping is an option, and there are plenty of accommodation options along the way, ranging from B&Bs to top-end hotels. The itinerary and GPS waypoints are available on the excellent website, or you can purchase two first-rate guides: *Hiking the Jesus Trail* by Anna Dintaman and David Landis, and *Jesus Trail and Jerusalem* by Jacob Saar.

Sea of Galilee Stats

» Surface area when full: 170 sq km

» Length of shoreline: 53km

» Maximum depth: 44m

» Volume of water when full: 4.3 cu km

» Average surface water temperature in February: 14.7°C

» Average surface water temperature in August: 28.6°C

» Supplies one-quarter of Israel's water needs

» Elevation of the 'upper red line' (above which there's a danger of flooding): 208.8m below sea level

» Elevation of the 'lower red line' (below which water quality and lake ecology may be compromised): 213m below sea level

Nazareth الناصرة נצרת

04 / POP 73,000

Believed to be the site of the Annunciation and Jesus's childhood home, Nazareth (al-Naasira in Arabic, Natzrat or Natzeret in Hebrew) has come a long way since its days as a quiet Jewish village in Roman-ruled Galilee, so if you're expecting bucolic rusticity be prepared for a surprise. These days, Israel's largest Arab city is a bustling mini-metropolis with shop-lined thoroughfares, traffic jams, blaring car horns

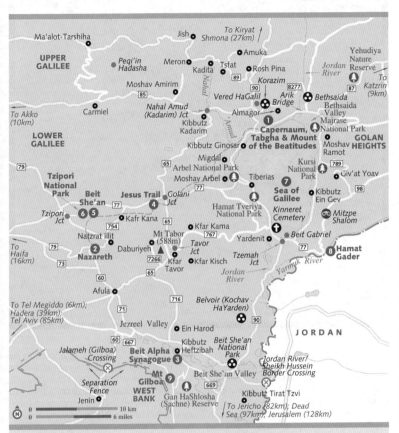

Lower Galilee & Sea of Galilee Highlights

1 Take a quick trip back to the time of Jesus's ministry at **Capernaum** (p214), **Tabgha** (p213) and **Mount of the Beatitudes** (p214).

2 Dine in the Arab-fusion restaurants of **Nazareth** (p196), Israel's new gastronomic star

3 Identify the animals, Jewish symbols and biblical personages depicted on the mosaic at 6th-century **Beit Alpha Synagogue** (p205)

4 Hike from Nazareth to the Sea of Galilee along the **Jesus Trail** (p190)

5 Imagine what Roman-era life was like as you explore the colonnaded streets of ancient **Beit She'an** (p203)

6 Admire the brilliant mosaics of **Tzipori National Park** (p201)

7 Take a dip in the refreshing waters of the **Sea of Galilee** (p209) on a scorching summer's day

8 Loll about in the hot, steaming sulphur pools of **Hamat Gader** (p223) on a cold winter's day

9 Get lost among the spring wildflowers atop **Mt Gilboa** (p204)

Nazareth

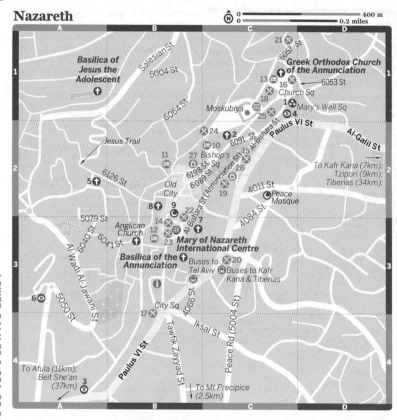

and young men with a penchant for wild driving. The Old City, its stone-paved alleys lined with crumbling Ottoman-era mansions, is currently reinventing itself as a sophisticated cultural and culinary destination.

Nazareth makes an ideal base for exploring the Lower Galilee, especially on Shabbat, when everything here is open for business. On Sunday, on the other hand, while attractions and pastry shops are open, stores and most restaurants are not.

History

According to the New Testament, it was in Nazareth that the Angel Gabriel appeared to Mary to inform her that she would conceive and give birth to the Son of God, an event known as the Annunciation (Luke 1:26-38).

Like Capernaum, Nazareth and its residents were treated rather dismissively in the Gospels. The dismissive words of Nathanael of Cana, 'Nazareth! Can anything good come

from there?' (John 1:46) are believed to reflect most Nazarenes' lack of enthusiasm for their town's most famous preacher.

In the 6th century, Christian interest in Nazareth was rekindled by reports of miracles, but a century later the Persian invasion brought massacres of Christians. After the arrival of Islam in 637 CE, many locals became Muslims but a significant Christian minority remained.

The Crusaders made Nazareth their Galilean capital in 1099 but were driven out a century later by Saladin (Salah ad-Din). In the mid-1200s the Mamluk Sultan Baybars banned Christian clergy and by the end of the century Nazareth was no more than an impoverished village.

Churches were re-established in Nazareth in the 17th and 18th centuries. Napoleon Bonaparte briefly captured the town in 1799. By the end of the Ottoman period, Nazareth had a sizeable Christian community and a

Nazareth

growing array of churches and monasteries (today there are about 30).

Today about 30% of the population of Nazareth is Christian (the largest denominations are Greek Orthodox, Melkite Greek Catholic and Roman Catholic), down from about 60% in 1949. Tensions between Christians and Muslims occasionally result in flare-ups. At research time, City Sq – almost adjacent to the Basilica of the Annunciation – was festooned with anti-Christian Islamist slogans.

◉ Sights & Activities

Basilica of the Annunciation   CHURCH
(☑04-565 0001; www.basilicanazareth.org; Al-Bishara St; admission free; ☺8am-6pm) Dominating the Old City's skyline is the lantern-topped cupola of this Roman Catholic basilica, an audacious modernist structure that's unlike any building you've ever seen. Built from 1960 to 1969, it's believed by many Christians to stand on the site of Mary's home, where many churches (but not the Greek Orthodox) believe the Annunciation took place.

In the dimly lit lower church, a sunken enclosure shelters the Grotto of the Annunciation (☺5.30am-6pm, for silent prayer 6-9pm), the traditional site of Mary's house, and remnants of churches from the Byzantine (4th century) and Crusader (12th century) eras.

The upper church, its soaring dome shaped like an inverted lily, 'glorifies Mary as the Mother of God'. With lovely mid-20th-century flair, the bare cast concrete is adorned with indented dots.

The walls of the courtyard and the upper church are decorated with a series of vivid mosaic panels, donated by Catholic communities around the world, depicting Mary and the infant Jesus in styles so diverse that they may leave you open-mouthed with wonder.

Confessions can be made in a variety of languages from 8.30am to 11.30am and 3pm to 5pm. Weekly events:

Marian Prayer 8.30pm Tuesday
Eucharistic Adoration 8.30pm on Thursdays
Candlelight Procession 8.30pm on Saturdays

Free brochures in a dozen languages – and shawls to cover immodestly exposed shoulders and knees (deposit required) – are available at the Pilgrims Office (☺9am-noon & 2-6pm Mon-Sat), 20m to the left of the basilica's main gate.

THE GOSPEL TRAIL

In late 2011, Israel's Ministry of Tourism inaugurated the Gospel Trail, another track from Nazareth (actually, from Mt Precipice) to Capernaum. Marked by upright boulders bearing the trail's logo (an anchor) in mosaic, the 62km trail – intended for hikers, cyclists and horse riders – largely avoids built-up areas. Perplexingly, the opening of the Gospel Trail was heralded by the mysterious disappearance of the Jesus Trail from Ministry of Tourism maps.

St Joseph's Church
CHURCH

(Al-Bishara St; ☺7am-6pm) Across the courtyard from the upper level of the Basilica of the Adoration, this neo-Romanesque church, built in 1914, occupies a site believed by popular tradition to be that of Joseph's carpentry workshop. It was built on top of the remains of a Crusader church. Down in the crypt, signs explain in situ archaeological discoveries.

Greek Orthodox Church of the Annunciation
CHURCH

(St Gabriel's Church; Church Sq; ☺7am-noon & 1-6pm) According to Greek Orthodox tradition, the Annunciation took place while Mary was fetching water from the spring situated directly under this richly frescoed, 17th-century church (other denominations hold that she was at home during the Annunciation). The barrel-vaulted crypt, first constructed under Constantine (4th century), shelters Nazareth's only year-round spring, a place visited everyone in the village obviously often visited. Check out the centuries-old graffiti carved around the outside doorway.

Synagogue-Church
CHURCH

(☺8am-4pm or 5pm) Hidden away in an alleyway off the souq, this humble Crusader-era structure stands on the site of the synagogue where it is believed that the young Jesus quoted Isaiah (61:1-2 and 58:6) and revealed himself as the fulfilment of Isaiah's prophesy (Luke 4:15-30).

The adjacent Greek Catholic Church (☺Sun morning), with its magnificent dome and two bell towers, was constructed in 1887 for by the local Melkite Greek Catholic community.

Mensa Christi Church
CHURCH

(6126 St) The faux-marble walls and painted dome of this Franciscan chapel were built in 1860 in a French style utterly typical of the period. The structure shelters a large slab of rock known in Latin as Mensa Christi (Table of Christ), believed to be the dining table used by Jesus and his disciples after the Resurrection. Note the graffiti left by pilgrims over the centuries.

To borrow the key (a giant brass sceptre), go up the stairway directly opposite the church gate and knock on the brown wooden door of the first apartment on the right; Mary Danielle, keeper of the key, is happy to help every day except before 10am on Sunday. Be sure to leave a small donation.

Mary's Well
SPRING

(Mary's Well Sq) Eastern Orthodox Christians believe that this spring – whose true source lies under the nearby Greek Orthodox Church of the Annunciation – was the site of the Annunciation (al-Bishara in Arabic). Reality check: the current structure is a modern reconstruction and the water does not actually come from Mary's Spring. The litter, however, is genuine.

Ancient Bathhouse
ARCHAEOLOGICAL SITE

(☏04-657 8539; Mary's Well Sq; www.nazarethbathhouse.com; tour 120NIS, 5 or more 28NIS per person; ☺9am-6pm or 7pm Mon-Sat, later in summer) When Elias Shama and his Belgian-born wife Martina set about renovating their shop in 1993, they uncovered a network of 2000-year-old clay pipes almost identical to ones found in Pompeii – and then, under the floor, an almost perfectly preserved Roman bathhouse once fed by water from Mary's Well. The 30-minute tour, which draws you into the excitement of serendipitous discovery, ends with refreshments.

Cave of the 40 Holy Monks
CAVE

(6198 St; donation requested; ☺tours 9am-4pm Mon-Sat) Under the compound of the Greek Orthodox Bishopric, this network of caves is named after 40 monks killed here by the Romans in the 1st century. Opened to the public in 2011.

Mary of Nazareth International Centre
RELIGIOUS

(☏04-646 1266; www.cimdn.org; Al-Bishara St; recommended donation 50NIS; ☺9am-6pm Mon-Sat, last entry 5pm) Opened in 2011, this stunning complex – almost across the street from the Basilica of the Annunciation – was built by

Chemin Neuf, a Roman Catholic community based in France, as a venue for ecumenical work among Christians and inter-religious dialogue. A four-room multimedia presentation illustrates highlights of the biblical period, ie from Creation through the Resurrection, with an emphasis on the lives of Mary and Jesus. The peaceful rooftop gardens, landscaped with plants mentioned in the Bible, afford 360-degree panoramas, while in the basement there are in situ ruins from as far back as the First Temple. Films in about 20 languages are shown; some can also be watched on www.netforgod.tv. Prayers are held at 6pm daily. Wheelchair accessible.

White Mosque   MOSQUE
(Al-Jaami' Al-Abyad; 6133 St; ◷9am-7.30pm except during prayers) Built in the late 1700s by Sheikh Abdullah al-Fahum – his tomb can be seen through a glass door off the sanctuary – this mosque is known for its longstanding support of harmony between Nazareth's different faith communities. The interior and the courtyard, with a fountain for ablutions, are mostly modern. The colour white symbolises simplicity, purity, unity and peace. You can leave your shoes on, except on the rugs.

Nazareth Village   FARM
(☑04-645 6042; www.nazarethvillage.com; Al-Wadi Al-Jawani St/5050 St; adult/child 50/22NIS; ◷9am-5pm, last tour 3pm Mon-Sat) Run by an ecumenical NGO, this recreation of a 1st-century Galilean farmstead is great at helping visitors imagine Nazareth and its economic life in the time of Jesus. The winepress and vineyard terraces are authentically ancient, but everything else – the threshing floor, the burial cave, the olive press, the carpenter's and weaver's studios, the synagogue – are recreations that accurately portray 1st-century life. Crafts are demonstrated by actors and volunteers in period costume. Call ahead to find out when guided tours (1¼ hours), available in nine languages, are scheduled to depart.

Basilica of Jesus the Adolescent   CHURCH
(☑04-646 8954; Salesian St/5004 St; ◷2-6pm Sun-Fri, 8am-6pm Sat) Built between 1906 and 1923, this neo-Gothic church, with commanding views of Nazareth, has a clean, almost luminescent limestone interior whose delicate arches and soaring vaults can only be described as 'very French'. It owes its name to the fact that Jesus spent much of his early life in Nazareth.

The church, on the Jesus Trail and a steep 20-minute walk from the Old City, is inside École Jésus Adolescent, a school run by the Salesians of Don Bosco, a Catholic religious order. From the gate to the parking lot, head left up the stairs and, at the top, enter the door to your right; the church is at the end of the hall. If possible, call ahead before visiting.

☞ Tours

Fauzi Azar Inn   WALKING
(☑04-602 0469; www.fauziazarinn.com; ◷9.15am) Offers free, daily, two-hour tours of the Old City to guests and nonguests alike.

Sharif Sharif-Safadi   GUIDED
(☑04-601 3717, 054 541 9277; sharifla@zahav.net.il; 3- 4hr tour for up to 10 people US$200) An expert on the preservation of historic monuments, Sharif offers excellent tours of the 'hidden city', including the interiors of Old City mansions normally closed to the public.

🛏 Sleeping

The places listed below are open to members of all religions. They're situated in the Old City (between Mary's Well and the Basilica of the Annunciation) unless otherwise noted.

TOP CHOICE Fauzi Azar Inn   GUESTHOUSE $$
(☑04-602 0469; www.fauziazarinn.com; dm 90NIS, d 350-500NIS; @☎) Hidden away in a gorgeous, two-century-old stone house in the heart of the Old City, this place has oodles of charm – and so do the staff. The 14 rooms are simple but tasteful, though they're no match for the lounge's arched windows, marble floors and 5m-high frescoed ceiling. A great place to meet other travellers – or to volunteer (see website). Anyone with a passport stamp from Syria or Lebanon gets the first night free. Winner of a Virgin Holidays Responsible Tourism Award in 2011.

ⓘ GET LOST

You are going to get lost in the maze of alleyways that make up the Old City so you may as well relax and enjoy! Complicating matters is the lack of street signs – though given that most street names are four-digit numbers, it should come as no surprise that locals don't use them.

TOP CHOICE Al-Mutran Guest House GUESTHOUSE $$

(☎04-645 7947; www.al-mutran.com; Bishop's Sq; d/ste US$128/220; ✻@🤶) Adjacent to the residence of Nazareth's Greek Orthodox *mutran* ('bishop' in Arabic), this family-run gem occupies a gorgeous, 200-year-old mansion with 4.5m-high ceilings, Ottoman arches and antique floor tiles. Nonguests are welcome to drop by the stylish lobby for a coffee.

Villa Nazareth HOTEL $$

(☎04-600 0569; www.villa-nazareth.co.il; Church Sq; d/q US$110/190; ✻🤶) Opened in late 2011 this 18-room hotel, run by a young local architect and his Jaffa-born wife, mixes old-time touches – the building was once a public school named for the poet Jubran Kahlil Jubran – with ultramodern, minimalist styling. The rooms are as spacious as the hallways are wide. Wheelchair accessible.

Rida Café B&B $$$

(☎04-608 4404; 21 Al-Bishara St; d/q 800/1000NIS; ✻) High atop an Ottoman mansion stands a vast, all-wood studio apartment with breathtaking views. Unbelievably romantic!

Sisters of Nazareth Guest House GUESTHOUSE $

(☎04-655 4304; accueilnasra@live.fr; 6167 St; dm/s/d/tr 85/215/280/385, without breakfast 60/190/230/310) Set around a flowery courtyard with archaeological excavations underneath, this 47-room establishment, in a building that dates from 1855, is run by a French Catholic order. Dorm beds (18 for men, six for women) are in spotless, barracks-like rooms. The gate is locked for the night at 10.30pm sharp.

Abu Saeed Hostel GUESTHOUSE $

(☎04-646 2799; www.abusaeedhostel.com; 6097 St; dm without breakfast 70NIS, d 350NIS, with hall bathroom 250NIS; 🤶) Staying here is like being the guest of a local family in their slightly chaotic, 350-year-old house, outfitted with two ancient cisterns, hand-me-down furniture, a family 'museum' and a plant-filled courtyard whose residents include a land turtle, goldfish and lovebirds. Showers are basic.

🍴 Eating & Drinking

Connoisseurs around Israel and beyond know that Nazareth's dining scene has recently become so drop-dead delicious that it's worth staying the night (or weekend)

for. The buzzword is 'fusion', with European-inspired dishes pimped with local seasonings and then served – with an extra helping of Arab hospitality – in atmospheric Old City mansions. Traditional Levantine specialities, tweaked for the Nazareth palate, are another speciality. Portions are copious.

Also famous are Nazareth's hummus joints, Oriental sweetshops, tahina (look for Al-Arz brand) and Kewar, the local arak (anise liqueur).

Friday is Nazareth's big night out so booking ahead is a good idea; restaurants may also be crowded on Thursday night and Saturday (lunch and dinner). Locals tend to eat late, often beginning dinner at 9pm or even 10pm. Wine, beer and spirits are widely available.

Many of Nazareth's trendiest spots for dining and sipping can be found at or around Church Sq, focal point of the town's flourishing nightlife zone.

TOP CHOICE Rida Café ARAB, FUSION $$$

(Alreda; ☎04-608 4404; 21 Al-Bishara St; mains 60-128NIS; ⏰1pm-2am Mon-Sat, 7pm-2am Sun; 🍴) On the ground floor of a 200-year-old Ottoman-era mansion, this atmospheric restaurant – the songs of Umm Kalthoum are on high rotation after 8pm – serves traditional Nazareth recipes with a Mediterranean twist. Specialities include seasonal dishes made with okra *(bamya)* and wild thistle *(akub)* and fresh artichoke hearts filled with chopped beef and pine nuts (owner Daher Zeidani loves nuts of all sorts). Guests are encouraged to share portions.

Méjana LEVANTINE $$

(☎04-602 1067; Al-Bishara Bldg, St Gabriel's Church Sq; mains 47NIS-110NIS; ⏰11am-11pm or later Mon-Sat) Serves superb fusion-style meat, fish and seafood, seasonal salads, and a rotating roster of Levantine dishes such as *shushbarak* (meat dumplings cooked with yoghurt, garlic and mint leaves; 55NIS). Sometimes has live music. Reservations recommended on Friday and Saturday.

Abu Ashraf HUMMUS $

(Diwan al-Saraya; 6134 St; mains 20NIS; ⏰8am-8pm Mon-Sat, noon-3pm or 4pm Sun; 🍴) This old-time hummus joint and coffeehouse (the beans are roasted on the premises) is famous all over town for its *katayef* (sweet pancakes folded over Umm Ashraf's goat's cheese or cinnamon walnuts and doused with geranium syrup; three for 12NIS).

Ebullient owner Abu Ashraf loves to share stories about Nazareth with visitors. Near the White Mosque.

Sudfeh
FUSION $$

(☏04-656 6611; 6083 St; mains 39-115NIS; ☺noon-midnight Mon-Sat, may open Sun evening) European dishes with local touches, Arab favourites and original creations such as shrimp baked with tahina, onions, ginger and arak – made with only the finest ingredients – are served either in an enchanting inner courtyard or under Ottoman-era arches and vaults. *Sudfeh* means 'coincidence', a reference to the serendipity of encountering new people, unfamiliar music and undreamt-of tastes. Has live music on most Thursday nights from 8.30pm.

Olga
FUSION $$

(☏04-656 7755; 6057 St, No 57; ☺11am-11pm or later) Opened in 2011, this modern, airy establishment serves European, American and Arab dishes in a 200-year-old former school in which the legendary Olga served as principal for 42 years. Has garden seating and, upstairs, a sleek, modern bar with floor-to-ceiling windows.

Misk
LEVANTINE $$

(☏077 203 1811; 22 Al-Bishara St; mains 49-159NIS; ☺6pm-11.30pm Mon-Thu, 1pm-11.30pm Fri & Sat) A stylish little restaurant-bar, opened in 2010, serving fusion food, including a good selection of meat dishes and a very creative mushroom cocktail. Often has concerts on Thursday and hosts guest musicians on Friday from 9.30pm.

Tishreen
MEDITERRANEAN $$

(☏04-608 4666; 56 Al-Bishara St; mains 49-99NIS; ☺noon-midnight; ☑) This homey restaurant, its adobe-encrusted walls adorned with antiques and wine bottles, has an autumnal atmosphere. The wood-fired oven turns out Mediterranean-inspired dishes such as aubergine stuffed with pesto and cheese, as well as excellent *muhammar*, an Arab pizza topped with chicken and onion. Also worth trying is *freekeh* (cracked green wheat), a traditional Galilean dish.

Mahroum Sweets
PASTRIES $

(www.mahroum-baklawa.com; cnr Paulus VI & Al-Bishara Sts; ☺8.30am-11pm) Run by the same family since 1890, this is one of the best places in Israel for baklava and other syrup-soaked Arab pastries, as well as *kunafeh* (a syrupy, cheese-based pastry) and Turkish delight.

Muhtar Sweets
PASTRIES $

(Paulus VI St; ☺9am-midnight) A brightly lit sweets emporium that could be in Beirut or Cairo. Has a huge selection of baklava and superb *kunafeh* (10NIS).

Al-Taboun
SHWARMA $

(Paulus VI St; ☺8am-10pm Mon-Sat; ☑) The decor is unspeakably tacky but the shwarma (24NIS), hummus (20NIS) and veggie salad spread (25NIS for two people) are excellent.

Felafel Abu Haani Jabali
FELAFEL $

(St Gabriel's Church Sq; felafels 13NIS; ☺10am-midnight Mon-Sat, 5pm-midnight Sun; ☑) Super-fresh felafel since 1968.

Souq
MARKET $

(Market Sq & along 6152 St; ☺8am or 8.30am-4pm Mon-Sat) Fruit, veggies, bread and even pita pizzas (6NIS) are on sale along the narrow, winding alleys of Old City's market.

🛍 Shopping

TOP CHOICE **Elbabour**
FOOD

(Galilee Mill; www.elbabour.com; Al-Bishara St; ☺8.30am-7 or 7.30pm Mon-Sat) The otherworldly aroma inside this basement spice emporium, run by the same family for four generations, has to be inhaled to be believed. Shelves, sacks, bins and bottles display more than 1500 different products, from exotic spice mixtures (including Pierina's Nazareth Spice Mixture, based on a secret recipe passed down by owner Tony's mother) to herbal teas, and from dried fruits to aromatic oils. The name is the local pronunciation of *al-vapeur* ('the steam' in Arabicised French), the name given a century ago to the company's infernally noisy flour mill (Arabic lacks both the B and V sounds).

TOP CHOICE **Shababik**
CRAFT

(☏04-608 0747; 6198 St; ☺10am-4pm Mon-Wed, to 8pm Thu-Sat, to later Jul, Aug & Christmas) Sells one-of-a-kind handmade crafts from Nazareth and nearby villages, local Musmar pottery, embroidery from Ramallah and Bethlehem, and handmade jewellery, some made with Roman glass. The name means 'windows', as in 'windows open to the world'. If the door is locked, enquire at nearby Al-Mutran Guest House – someone will be happy to come by and open up.

Cactus Gallery
CRAFT

(Mary's Well Sq; www.nazarethcactus.com; ☺9am-6pm or 7pm Mon-Sat, to later summer) The shop

HANAN ISACHAR/LONELY PLANET IMAGES ©

HANAN ISACHAR/LONELY PLANET IMAGES ©

PHOTOSTOCK-ISRAEL/ALAMY ©

1. Mount of the Beatitudes (p214)

This hillside church stands where Jesus is believed to have delivered his Sermon on the Mount.

2. Sea of Galilee (p212)

The shores of Israel's largest freshwater lake are lined with great places to relax.

3. Dalton Winery, Ramat Dalton (p237)

Israeli wines are attracting attention on the world wine scene.

4. Basilica of the Annunciation, Nazareth (p193)

Dominating Nazareth's skyline is the lantern-topped cupola of this Roman Catholic basilica.

above Nazareth's sensational Roman-era Ancient Bathhouse sells creative modern jewellery and gorgeous Palestinian embroidery.

❶ Information

Al-Mutran Guest House (Bishop's Sq; internet per hr 15NIS) Visitors are welcome to use the internet here.

ATMs There are several near the Basilica of the Annunciation. Bank HaPoalim is on Paulus VI St, while Bank Discount is at City Sq.

Currency exchange Cash and travellers cheques can be changed at the post office (on 6089 St a block southwest of Mary's Well) and at several exchange places on Paulus VI St.

Ministry of Tourism Information (☑04-657 0555; www.goisrael.com; Casanova St; ⏲8.30am-5pm Mon-Fri, 9am-1pm Sat) Has brochures about Nazareth and the Galilee in seven languages.

Nazareth Cultural & Tourism Association (www.nazarethinfo.org) Has a useful website. Publishes *Nazareth Today*, a free monthly magazine with feature articles and listings; Arabic, Hebrew and English versions are available in hotels and restaurants.

Police (☑emergency 100; 6089 St) In the Moskubiya, a Russian pilgrims hostel built in 1904.

❶ Getting There & Away

Bus

Most intercity **buses** (www.bus.co.il) can be picked up along Paulus VI St, at stops on either the northbound or the southbound side. Destinations include the following:

» Akko (Egged bus 343; 29NIS, two hours, eight daily except Saturday)

» Haifa's Palmer Sq (Nazareth Tourism & Transport bus 331; 17.20NIS, twice an hour seven days a week)

» Jerusalem (Egged bus 955; 40NIS, 2¼ hours, twice in the morning Sunday to Thursday, one on Friday, two on Saturday night)

» Tel Aviv (Egged bus 823; 36NIS, 3¼ hours, every hour or two except Friday night and Saturday before midafternoon)

» Tiberias via Kafr Kana (Nazareth Tourism & Transport bus 431; 19NIS, 40 minutes, hourly except Friday evening and Saturday)

To get to Kfar Tavor and the base of Mt Tabor you have to change in Afula.

For details on buses to Amman run by **Nazarene Tours** (☑04-601 0458; Paulus VI St), see p28.

Sherut (Shared Taxi)

To find a **sherut** (☑04-657 1140) to Tel Aviv's central bus station (32NIS, 1½ hours, departures from 6am to 4pm), head to tiny 4066 St, just off Paulus VI St.

One daily **sherut** (☑052 285 4640) goes all the way to Jenin (25NIS, 40 minutes, departure at 8am) in the West Bank, via the Jalameh (Gilboa) crossing 10km south of Afula. Call ahead to reserve.

Taxi

Cabs can be ordered from **Mary's Well Taxi** (☑04-655 5105, 04-656 0035).

Kafr Kana כפר כנא كفر كنا

☑04

About 7km northeast of central Nazareth on the road to Tiberias (and the Jesus Trail), the Arab town of Kafr Kana (Cana) is believed to be the site of Jesus's first miracle (John 2:1-11), when he changed water into wine at a wedding reception. About 10% of the population is Christian.

◉ Sights

Cana Catholic Wedding Church CHURCH (⏲8am-noon & 2-5pm, to 6pm during daylight savings) This late-19th-century Franciscan church, topped by a green dome, stands on the site believed by Catholics to be that of the wedding miracle. In the basement is an ancient jar that may have been among the six used by Jesus when he turned water into wine. Under the church floor, through a glass floor tile, you can see an ancient Jewish inscription in Aramaic.

The church is situated 250m up the slope from the main road through town (Rte 754); look for a special bus parking lane on the east side of the main street.

Cana Greek Orthodox Wedding Church CHURCH (First Miracle Church; Rte 754; ⏲8am-3pm Sun-Thu, to noon Sat & Sun) Situated between the main road and the green-domed Catholic church up the slope, this richly decorated, late-19th-century church – topped by a copper-brown dome – shelters two ancient jars believed to have been used by Jesus to perform the wedding miracle.

🛏 Sleeping

Cana Guest House GUESTHOUSE $ (☑04-651 7186, 052-409 8001; www.canagu esthouse.com; dm/d/tr/q without breakfast

120/300/430/500NIS; @🖥️🕐) Four one-time apartments have been turned into 12 basic bedrooms, many of them tiny, some with private bathroom. Guests can use the kitchen and hang out in the lemon-tree-shaded courtyard. Situated around behind the Cana Catholic Wedding Church compound.

❶ Getting There & Away

Lots of short-haul buses connect Kafr Kana with Nazareth, including buses 24, 26, 27, 30 and 31. Nazareth Tourism & Transport's bus 431 (hourly except Friday evening and Saturday) links the town with both Tiberias (19NIS) and Nazareth (8.80NIS).

Tzipori صفورية ציפורי

🗓️04

Today one of Israel's most impressive archaeological sites, Tzipori National Park (Zippori, Sepphoris; www.parks.org.il; adult/child 27/14NIS; ⏱️8am-5pm Apr-Sep, to 4pm Oct-Mar, to 3pm Fri, last entry 1hr before closing) was, in ancient times, a prosperous and well-endowed city with stone-paved roadways (rutted over time by wagons and chariots), an amazing water-supply system (including a 260m-long cistern), a marketplace, bathhouses, synagogues, churches and a 4500-seat theatre. For many modern visitors, though, the star attraction is a mosaic portrait of a contemplative young woman nicknamed the Mona Lisa of the Galilee, one of several superb early-3rd-century mosaics discovered here in the 1980s.

In the 2nd and 3rd centuries CE – a generation or two after the Bar Kochba Revolt (132 to 135 CE) against Rome – Tzipori was one of the most important centres of Jewish life in the Land of Israel. It was here that Rabbi Yehuda HaNassi is believed to have redacted the Mishnah (the earliest codification of Jewish law), and later on Tzipori scholars contributed to the Jerusalem (Palestinian) Talmud.

🛏️ Sleeping

Zipori Village Country Cottages   B&B $$
(🗓️04-646 2647; www.zipori.com; Moshav Tzipori; d without breakfast from 400NIS; ❄️🖥️🕐) Run by the knowledgeable Suzy and Mitch, the spacious cottages here come with gorgeous Galilean views, comfortable cane furniture, cheerful decoration and a jacuzzi. The well-equipped kitchenettes are kosher dairy. Breakfast costs 100NIS for two.

❶ Getting There & Away

The village of Tzipori and Tzipori National Park are 11km northwest of Nazareth via Rte 79. There's no public transport.

Mt Tabor Area
אזור הר תבור   منطقة جبل التابور

🗓️04

Rising from the Jezreel Valley like a giant human breast, the remarkably symmetrical Mt Tabor (588m) dominates the area between Nazareth and the Sea of Galilee.

MT TABOR הר תבור جبل التابور

You don't have to be a Christian pilgrim to enjoy the beauty of Mt Tabor, the traditional site of the Transfiguration of Jesus (Matthew 17:1–9, Mark 9:2-8 and Luke 9:28–36), in which 'his face became as dazzling as the sun; his clothes as radiant as light' and he spoke with the prophets Moses and Elijah. Two compounds crown the mountain, one Catholic (Franciscan), the other Greek Orthodox (closed to the public)

According to the Hebrew Bible, Mt Tabor was where the Israelites, led by the prophetess Deborah, defeated a Canaanite army under the command of Sisera (Judges 4).

The mountain was much contested in the Crusader period. These days, it's often used to launch hang-gliders.

◉ Sights & Activities

Franciscan Monastery & Church   CHURCH
(⏱️8-11.30am & 2-5pm) An avenue of cypresses leads through this Catholic compound to a monastery, home to three Franciscan monks; a small garden of plants from around the world; the ruins of a Byzantine-era monastery; and the Roman-Syrian-style **Basilica of the Transfiguration**, one of the Holy Land's most beautiful churches. Consecrated in 1924, it is decorated with lovely mosaics and has a crypt reached by 12 broad steps. Women are asked to dress modestly (no sleeveless shirts or miniskirts).

Up to the right from the entrance to the church, a **viewing platform** offers spectacular views of the Jezreel Valley's multicoloured patchwork of fields.

Hiking Trails   HIKING
The **Israel National Trail** goes up and over Mt Tabor, intersecting two marked trails that circumnavigate the mountain: **Shvil HaYa'aranim** (the Foresters' Trail) and, up near the summit, **Sovev Har Tavor** (Mt

Tabor Circuit). The topographical map to have is SPNI Map No 3 (*HaGalil HaTachton HaAmakim v'HaGilboa*).

ⓘ Getting There & Away

Mt Tabor is just off Rte 65 about midway between Tiberias and Afula. From Rte 7266, which goes all the way around the base of the mountain, connecting the Arab villages of Shibli and Daburiyeh with Rte 65, it's a teeth-clenching, 3km ride (16 hairpin turns) up to the summit.

KFAR TAVOR   كفر تابور   כפר תבור

Founded in 1901, the village of Kfar Tavor is the area's main commercial and tourism hub.

◎ Sights & Activities

Tabor Winery   WINERY
(☎04-676 0444; www.twc.co.il, in Hebrew; Kfar Tavor Industrial Zone; ◎9am-5pm Sun-Thu, 9am-4pm Fri) Known for its merlot and cabernet sauvignon, this well-regarded winery produces 1.5 million bottles a year. Offers free tastings and sales.

From late July to August, Tabor Winery runs two-hour grape harvests (admission 30NIS; ◎10am Sun-Fri) for children. After using pruning shears to pick bunches of grapes, the kids stomp on them (yes, with their feet and yes, feet are washed first!) to turn them into juice, which they then bottle. Reserve ahead.

John Deere Land   MUSEUM
(www.jdland.co.il; adult & over 3yr 44NIS; ◎9am-5pm, to 3pm Fri, closed Mon) A love poem to the humble tractor. Children will have a ball playing on the 25 vintage farm tractors, the oldest from 1934 (all are in working order); tooling around on miniature pedal-tractors; and trying out the full-sized hydraulic tractor simulator. Situated at the eastern edge of Kfar Tavor towards Tabor Winery. Look for a hangar-sized building painted – what else? – green and yellow.

Trails   HIKING, CYCLING
Kfar Tavor and nearby villages such as Kfar Kisch make a great base for hiking along the Israel National Trail and a spur of the Jesus Trail – for instance northeast to the Yardenit baptism site on the Sea of Galilee or west up Mt Tabor. Sections of both trails are cyclable. For cyclists there's also a single track through Beit Keshet Forest and some fine routes on the Sirrin Heights.

Road, mountain and tandem bikes and trailers for kids can be rented from HooHa Cyclists' House (☎077 708 0524; www.hooha.

co.il; 7 HaHaruvim St; per day 120NIS), which can help you plan your ride and also arrange drop-offs and pick-ups (4NIS per kilometre).

⌑ Sleeping

HooHa Cyclists' House   B&B $$
(☎077 708 0524; www.hooha.co.il; 7 HaHaruvim St; dm/d incl breakfast 180/680NIS Thu & Fri, without breakfast 150/480NIS Sat-Wed; ✲@ ⼈☀) Run for cyclists by cyclists – people who understand sore bums and aching muscles – this four-bedroom villa has a laundry room, a good supply of cycling maps and a swimming pool and hot tub in the backyard. When it's full, owner Dror is happy to recommend nearby options.

✕ Eating

Cafederatzia   CAFE $$
(82 HaMeyasdim St; mains 36-46NIS; ◎8.30am-12.30am Sun-Thu, to 4.30pm Fri, 9.30am-12.30am Sat; ✐) Opened in 2011, this stylish boutique cafe serves a variety of light meals, including salads, pasta and gourmet sandwiches, many made with locavore ingredients sourced from the immediate vicinity. Also offers homemade baked goods and local wines by the glass (from 25NIS). Breakfast costs 36NIS to 49NIS. Situated 300m south of Kfar Tavor's horse-statue roundabout.

ⓘ Getting There & Away

A variety of Egged buses, including bus 835 (twice hourly), link Kfar Tavor and Tavor Junction (at the intersection of Rte 65 and Rte 7266, a bit south of Mt Tabor) with Tel Aviv (36NIS, 1¾ hours), Tiberias (17.20NIS, 50 minutes) and Afula (15.40NIS, 20 minutes), from where frequent buses (eg Kavim lines 354 and 356) go to (or at least near) Nazareth's Old City.

KFAR KISCH   كفر كيش   כפר קיש

Surrounded by open fields where gazelles are a common sight, this moshav (cooperative settlement), 6km southeast of Kfar Tavor, is on both the Israel National Trail and a spur of the Jesus Trail.

⌑ Sleeping

Tabor Land Guest House   B&B $$
(☎050 544 1972; www.taborland.com; Kfar Kisch; dm/d without breakfast 170/420NIS) You're ensured a warm welcome at this two-storey villa, built in 2010. The four bedrooms (one with direct bathroom access) are homey, and the spacious living room will make you feel like a guest at a friend's house. An Israeli breakfast costs 40NIS per person. Owner Sarah is happy to take travellers on walking or 4WD tours of the area. Situated 6km east of

Rte 65 in Kfar Kisch's new neighbourhood, out past the petrol pump; call ahead for pick-up at the Gazit Junction bus stop.

✖ Eating

TOP CHOICE **Havat HaYatzranim**   CHEESE **$$**
(☎04-662 0788; www.shiratroim.co.il, in Hebrew; cheese meals for 2 118NIS, cheese per kg 195NIS; ◷9.30am-sundown Fri, Sat & holidays) This award-winning cheese shop and restaurant astounds even veteran foodies, leaving them gasping for superlatives. Inbar, delicately flavoured with rosemary; Kinneret, an unbelievable blue; Nirit, sprinkled with chestnut ash – all of them may leave you speechless. Also offers free tastings of varietal olive oils, the best sun-dried almonds you've ever encountered and four boutique wines so exclusive that only one barrel (300 bottles) of each is made per year. Housed in a one-time chicken coop.

Sirrin   FRENCH **$$$**
(☎04-676 0976; mains 75-130NIS; ◷noon-9.30pm or later Sun & Tue-Fri, from 9am Sat) Inspired by a long-ago meal in Paris' St-Germain-des-Prés, this classy, family-run restaurant specialises in French-influenced steak and fish dishes. Children's portions cost 30NIS to 45NIS. Three-course meals are available for the price of a main dish from noon to 5pm from Sunday to Thursday. Breakfast is available on Saturday.

KFAR KAMA   כפר קמא   كفر كنا
As the Russian Empire expanded southward in the mid-1800s, at least half-a-million Circassians, a Caucasian people of the Muslim faith, were forced out of their homes in the northern Caucasus – between the Black and Caspian Seas, around Mt Elbrus (5642m) – and found refuge in the Ottoman lands. In 1876 some of them settled in Kfar Kama (population 2900), one of only two Circassian villages in Israel (the other is Reyhaniye). The Circassians have always enjoyed good relations with their Jewish neighbours, and all Circassian men – long famed as fierce warriors – are drafted into the IDF. Signs around the prosperous town are in Hebrew, Circassian (spoken at home and taught in school) and English.

◉ Sights

Circassian Heritage Center   MUSEUM
(☎050 585 7640; www.circassianmuseum.co.il; adult/child 25/20NIS; ◷9am-5pm) Housed in a complex of century-old basalt houses, this

modest museum features a 20-minute film (in Hebrew, Arabic and English), traditional Circassian clothing and antique agricultural implements. Admission includes a tour in English. To get there from the eastern entrance to Kfar Kama (on Rte 767), follow the signs to 'Shami House'.

✖ Eating

Cherkessia   CIRCASSIAN **$$**
(☎04-676 9608, 050-261 9996; Rte 767; set meals 55NIS; ◷noon-8pm; ⊘) Specialities at Israel's only Circassian restaurant, run by a mother-and-son team, include *haluzh* (a deep-fried crêpe filled with homemade Circassian cheese) and *mataza* (boiled ravioli stuffed with Circassian cheese and green onion). Situated in a private house 100m west along the frontage road from the western entrance to Kfar Kama (on Rte 767); look for a Cyrillic sign reading Ресторан.

Jezreel & Beit She'an Valleys   مرج ابن عمار ومرج ببيسان   עמק יזרעאל ועמק בית שאן
☎04
Stretching for about 45km from a bit west of Nazareth southeast to the Jordan River, these two valleys – Jezreel Valley, also known as the Plain of Esdraelon, largely agricultural and, Beit She'an Valley, part of the Great Rift Valley – are bounded on the south by Mt Gilboa.

The listings below are ordered from southeast to northwest. For details on Megiddo see p180, and for Beit She'arim see p180.

BEIT SHE'AN   בית שאן   بيسان
Founded sometime in the 5th millennium BCE, Beit She'an – strategically situated at the intersection of the Jezreel Valley and the Jordan Valley – is best known for having the most extensive Roman-era ruins in Israel. The city was levelled in the massive earthquake of 749 CE. The struggling modern town (population 17,000) has little to offer the visitor.

◉ Sights

TOP CHOICE **Beit She'an National Park**   ARCHAEOLOGICAL SITE
(☎04-658 7189; adult/child 38/23NIS; Rte 90; ◷8am-4pm mid-Oct–Mar, to 5pm Apr–mid-Oct, closes 1hr earlier Fri) Beit She'an's extraordinary Roman ruins are the best place in Israel to

get a sense of what it might have been like to live, work and shop in the Roman Empire. Colonnaded streets, a 7000-seat theatre (with public bathrooms nearby), two bathhouses and piles of rubble from the 749 CE earthquake evoke the aesthetics, grandeur, self-confidence and decadence of Roman provincial life in the centuries after Jesus.

Towering over the Roman city, known in Greek as Scythopolis, is Tel Beit She'an, created by the superimposition of no fewer than 20 layers of settlement. The viewpoint atop the tel offers near-aerial views of the Roman ruins.

The site's new entrance is on Rte 90 just south of the roundabout next to the McDonald's sign. Visitors begin in Beit She'an's Ottoman-era Saraya (government administrative HQ) and continue either by minitrain or on foot past a Crusader fortress (closed to the public) and a 4th-century Roman amphitheatre, originally built to host horse and chariot races. The train has several stops around the periphery of the main excavations. It's wheelchair accessible.

To beat the summer heat, you can visit the ruins by night. She'an Nights (Leilot She'an; ☑04-648 1122, *3639; adult/child 50/40NIS; ☉sundown Mon, Wed, Thu & Sat approx Apr–mid-Nov), an after-dark multimedia spectacular, does a good job of simulating life in Roman times. Visitors stroll among the ruins at their own pace. Call ahead for reservations.

🛏 Sleeping

Beit She'an Guest House   HOSTEL **$$**
(☑02-594 5644; www.iyha.org.il; 129 Menahem Begin Ave/Rte 90; s/d 345/460NIS, additional adult/child 145/113NIS; @🛜🐾) Within easy walking distance of Beit She'an's antiquities, this 62-room hostel has very attractive public areas and a great rooftop patio. Rooms are practical and clean and have five beds. Individual dorm beds are not available. Situated across the street and 100m south from the central bus station. Wheelchair accessible.

❶ Getting There & Away

Egged bus 961 (at least seven daily Sunday to Thursday, six on Friday) goes north to Tiberias (20NIS, one hour) and south via the Jordan Valley to Jerusalem (40NIS, two hours). At least hourly, Kavim bus 411 (and the much slower 412) serves Afula (one hour), from where frequent buses (eg Kavim lines 354 and 356) go to (or at least near) Nazareth's Old City.

Travellers headed to Jordan can make use of the Jordan River/Sheikh Hussein Border Crossing (see p27), 10km east of town.

BELVOIR   כוכב הירדן   كوكب الهوا
Set on a hilltop 550m above the Jordan River, this Crusader fortress (☑04-658 1766; www.parks.org.il; adult/child 21/9NIS; ☉8am-5pm Apr-Sep, to 4pm Oct-Mar, closes 3pm Fri), 20km south of the Sea of Galilee, consists of concentric ramparts, gates, courtyards and towers that afford spectacular views of the Jordan and Jezreel Valleys and Jordan's Gilead Mountains. Measuring an impressive 110m by 110m, it is the only such castle in Israel to have been fully excavated.

Built by the Knights Hospitaller starting in 1168, Belvoir ('beautiful view' in French; the Hebrew name, Kochav HaYarden, means 'star of the Jordan'; Arabic name, Kawkab al-Hawa) was finally forced to surrender to Muslim forces in 1189 after a year-and-a-

---

WORTH A TRIP

OFF THE BEATEN TRACK – MT GILBOA

The rugged, 18km-long ridge known as Mt Gilboa (highest point 536m), which runs along the southern edge of the Jezreel Valley, makes for a great nature getaway. After the winter rains (December to March or April), the area is carpeted with wildflowers, including the purple Gilboa iris (blooms in late February and early March). According to the Bible, this was where King Saul and his son Jonathan were slain in battle with the Philistines (1 Samuel 31:1-13).

For a lovely hilltop drive with stupendous views of the Jezreel Valley (in the other direction, you can see the Palestinian villages around Jenin and, in the foreground, the Separation Fence between Israel and the West Bank), take 28km-long Rte 667, which links Rte 675 (a short highway connecting Rte 71 with Rte 60 at a point 8km southeast of Afula) with Rte 90 in the Jordan Valley.

For a hearty, country-style meal made with local ingredients, stop by Herb Farm on Mt Gilboa (☑04-653 1093; www.herb-farm.co.il, in Hebrew; Rte 667; mains 49-124NIS; ☉noon-10pm Mon-Sat), on Mt Gilboa's northwestern slopes.

SOCIALIST PASSIONS

Life at Kibbutz Ein Harod, midway between Afula and Beit She'an (about 14km from each), carried on in relative tranquillity from its founding in 1921 until the very early 1950s. That was when an ideological dispute over Israeli Prime Minister David Ben-Gurion's strategic preference for the capitalist United States over Stalin's Soviet Union flared into a full-fledged ideological conflagration. Complicating matters was the fact that at the time, Stalin was staging anti-Semitic show trials in which prominent Jews were being accused of trumped-up counter-revolutionary crimes – and then executed. Stalin's fervid devotees at the kibbutz, who were of the 'you can't make an omelette without breaking a few eggs' school of hard-line socialism, stood by their man.

Passions flared – these were, after all, people who lived by their socialist ideology – and soon barricades went up in the dining hall, good friends stopped speaking to each other, fisticuffs were exchanged and couples broke up. Finally, Ein Harod split into two separate kibbutzim, Ein Harod Meuchad, run by the Stalin loyalists, and Ein Harod Ichud, under the control of the Ben-Gurionists (both *meuchad* and *ichud* mean 'united').

Resentments smouldered for decades, and even today some old-old-timers are angry about their rivals' craven betrayal of socialist principles. It was only two decades ago that the first 'mixed' Ichud-Meuchad couple tied the knot, and just 15 years ago that agricultural and cultural cooperation between the two kibbutzim resumed. Today, Kibbutz Ein Harod Ichud is still a traditional 'collective' kibbutz while Kibbutz Ein Harod Meuhad, controlled by the hard left 60 years go, has chosen the route of privatisation.

half siege. The defenders were permitted to retreat to Tyre unharmed, in acknowledgment of their courage.

At the entrance stands a **sculpture garden** of works by the award-winning Israeli artist Yigal (Igael) Tumarkin (b 1933).

BEIT ALPHA SYNAGOGUE
بيت الفا   בית הכנסת בית אלפא

No one was more surprised than the members of Kibbutz Heftzibah when they went out to dig an irrigation channel in 1928 and uncovered a stunning, Byzantine-era (6th-century) mosaic floor. Further excavation revealed the rest of the **Beit Alpha Synagogue** (adult/child 21/9NIS; Kibbutz Heftzibah; ⏰8am-5pm during daylight savings, 8am-4pm rest of year, closes 1hr earlier Fri), whose extraordinarily well-preserved mosaics are among the most evocative ever found in Israel.

The three mosaic panels depict traditional Jewish symbols such as the Torah ark, menorah (seven-branched candelabra) and *shofar* (ram's horn) alongside a spectacular, 12-panel **zodiac circle**, a pagan element if there ever was one. A 10-minute film (in four languages) provides an introduction to the site, which is wheelchair accessible.

Members of the Makoya, a Japanese Christian sect, built a lovely little **Japanese garden** up the hill from the synagogue, beyond the swimming pool.

❶ Getting There & Away

Kibbutz Heftzibah is 8km west of Beit She'an along Rte 669. Kavim bus 412 (at least hourly except Friday night and Saturday) goes both to Afula and to Beit She'an.

EIN HAROD   عين حرود   עין חרוד

Ein Harod is actually two kibbutzim, torn apart 60 years ago by their shared socialist ideology (see the boxed text).

◉ Sights

Museum of Art, Ein Harod   MUSEUM
(Mishkan Le'omanut; www.museumeinharod.org.il; Kibbutz Ein Harod Meuchad; adult/child 26/13NIS; ⏰9am-4.30pm Sun-Thu, to 1.30pm Fri, 10am-4.30pm Sat) As remarkable for its building (inaugurated in 1948, with additions from the 1950s) as its outstanding art collection (over 16,000 works, mainly by Jewish and Israeli artists), this pioneering museum has a permanent exhibition of Judaica and puts on highly regarded temporary exhibits (explanatory sheets available in English) in its 14 halls. To get there, follow the signs to 'Museums'.

⏢ Sleeping

TOP CHOICE **Ein Harod Guest House**   GUESTHOUSE **$$**
(☎04-648 6083; www.ein-harod.co.il; Kibbutz Ein Harod Ichud; d from 460-660NIS, chalets 880-1300NIS; ❄@☎☲) Perched on a hilltop with

THE MONGOLS WERE HERE

The year was 1260, the place very near present-day Kibbutz Ein Harod. The belligerents were the mighty Mongol Empire and the Egyptian Mamluks. In a cataclysmic clash known to history as the Battle of Ein Jalut, the Mongols were decisively and enduringly defeated for the first time in their history, bringing their expansion into the Middle East to a screeching halt.

clear-day views of Mt Carmel, Mt Hermon and the Mountains of Gilead in Jordan, this 42-room guesthouse offers both traditional kibbutz rooms and romantic wooden 'Iris' chalets with 50 sq m of luxury. Discounts are available if you stay two or more nights.

Tiberias طبريا טבריה

04 / POP 42,000

Tiberias is one of the tackiest resorts in Israel, its lakeside strip crammed with 1970s monstrosities. But it's also one of the four holy cities of Judaism, burial place of venerated sages, and a very popular base for Christians visiting nearby holy sites. So not for the first time, the sacred and the kitsch – plus beaches and hot springs – coexist side by side in a whirl of hawkers, hedonism and holiness.

If you've got a car, the Golan, the Galilee Panhandle, Beit She'an, Nazareth and even Akko are an hour or less away.

History

Tiberias' 17 hot springs have been luring pleasure seekers since well before 20 CE, when Herod Antipas, son of Herod the Great, founded the town and named it in honour of the Roman emperor Tiberias (14–37 CE).

After the Jews' disastrous Bar Kochba Revolt, Tiberias became one of the most important centres of Jewish life in the Land of Israel, playing a central role in the redefinition of Judaism after Temple sacrifices in Jerusalem were halted by the Roman victory of 70 CE. Some of the greatest post–Second Temple sages, including Yehuda HaNassi, coordinating editor of the Mishnah, lived here, and much of the redacting of the Jerusalem (Palestinian) Talmud also seems to have taken place in Tiberias. From the late 2nd century, the Sanhedrin (ancient Israel's supreme

court) was based in the town. The system still used today to indicate vowel sounds in written Hebrew was developed in – and named after – Tiberias.

The Crusaders took Tiberias in 1099, building a massive fortress a bit north of the town's Roman-Byzantine centre. In 1187 Saladin captured the town and shortly thereafter devastated the Crusader forces at the nearby Horns of Hattin (just west of Arbel).

In 1558 the newly arrived Ottomans granted tax-collecting rights in the Tiberias area to Dona Gracia (www.donagraciaproject.org), a Lisbon-born Converso (outwardly Catholic but secretly Jewish) woman who had found refuge from the Inquisition in Istanbul.

In the early 1700s a Bedouin sheikh named Daher al-Omar established an independent fiefdom in the Galilee, with Tiberias as its capital, and invited Jewish families to return to the town. By the end of the Ottoman period, Jews constituted the great majority of Tiberias' 6500 residents.

Tiberias was almost completely demolished in the great earthquake of 1837.

⊙ Sights

Hamat Tveriya National Park   SPRING
(Eliezer Kaplan Ave/Rte 90; adult/child 14/7NIS; ⊙8am-5pm daylight savings time, to 4pm rest of year, closes 1hr earlier Fri) Back in Roman times the fame of Tiberias' hot springs was such that in 110 CE the Emperor Trajan struck a coin dedicated to them – depicting Hygeia, the goddess of health, sitting on a rock and enjoying the water. Today, you can get a bit of a sense of Roman-era Tiberias at this grassy hillside park, whose star attraction is a 4th-century synagogue with a beautiful zodiac mosaic. Situated 2.5km south of the centre; served by buses 5 and 28 and sheruts.

Yigal Allon Promenade   BOARDWALK
Most of Tiberias' sights are along the boardwalk (of sorts) that runs along the lakefront. Parts are kitschy and faded, and the area can feel forlorn in winter, but the views of the Sea of Galilee and the Golan never get old. The following sights are listed from north to south.

At the northern end, a few metres west of the ship sculpture, is the **Tiberias Open Air Museum** (HaYarden St), a new pedestrian park decorated with creative modern

Tiberias

Tiberias

sculptures. Look for the tile blow-up of a 1950s one-lira banknote.

The roof of **St Peter's Parish Church** (☎077 308 8296; Yigal Allon Promenade; ⊗visits 8.30am-noon & 2.30-5.30pm Mon-Sat, Mass in English 6.30pm Mon-Sat, 8.30am Sun) is shaped like an upturned boat – a nod to Peter, a Sea of Galilee fisher. This rare Crusader church is administered by Koinonia John the Baptist, a Catholic community based in Italy. The interior paintings date from 1902. A replica of the Vatican's famous statue of St Peter stands in the courtyard near the carved-stone Monument to the Virgin of Czestochowa, erected in 1945 by Polish soldiers who were billeted here during WWII.

On the upper floor of a 1970s monstrosity, the Galilee Experience (☏04-672 3620; www.thegalileeexperience.com; admission US$8; ⊙8.30am-10pm Sun-Thu, to 2pm Fri, may open Sat night) screens a 36-minute film in a dozen languages on the history of the Galilee.

When the basalt Al-Bahr Mosque (Sea Mosque) was built in the 18th century, it had a special entrance for the faithful who arrived by boat.

Near the southern end of the promenade, the Tiberium (☏04-672 5666; admission free; ⊙after dark daily), a jumbo-sized light, laser and music show projected onto a wall of water jets brings a bit of Las Vegas–style razzmatazz to these sedate shores. A bit further south is the Water Level Surveyor (see the boxed text, p190).

At the southern terminus of the promenade is the Greek Orthodox Church & Monastery of the Apostles (⊙8am-4pm Mon-Sat). From the peaceful, flowery courtyard, steps lead down to the church, its air of mystery enhanced by gilded icons, brass lamps and elaborately carved wood. The three chapels are dedicated to the 12 disciples, Saints Peter and Paul, and Mary Magdalene. To see if a monk is available to show you around, ring the bell high up on the right side of the red door 10m west of the overhead pedestrian bridge.

Jewish Sages' Tombs   CEMETERY

Many of Tiberias' Jewish visitors are drawn to the city at least partly by the desire to pray – and ask for divine intercession – at graves believed to be those of some of Judaism's most eminent sages. If you were assembling an all-star team of the most influential Jewish thinkers of all time, the four rabbis mentioned below would certainly be on it.

The tomb of Rabbi Meir Ba'al Hanes (⊙6am-10pm or later Sun-Thu, 6am-1½hr before sundown Fri), a 2nd-century sage often cited in the Mishnah – ba'al ha-nes means 'master of miracles' – is inside a hillside complex 300m up an asphalt road from Hamat Tveriya National Park. The burial site is accessible through the domed Ashkenazi synagogue, situated just up the slope from its Sephardic counterpart, also topped with a dome. Rabbi Meir's hilula (a celebration held by Hasidim on the anniversary of a sage's death) is just three days before that of Shimon Bar Yochai, who is buried at Mt Meron, so some pious Jews pull a spiritual two-fer, travelling to the Galilee to take in both hugely popular events.

The tomb of the Rambam (Ben Zakkai St; ⊙24hr) – 'RaMBaM' is the acronymic nickname of Rabbi Moshe Ben Maimon – is two blocks northeast of the central bus station. Also known as Maimonides (1135–1204), this Cordova-born polymath, famous for his rationalist approach to religion and life (he was fond of quoting Aristotle) wrote the Mishneh Torah, the first systematic codification of Jewish law; the Guide to the Perplexed, a work of theology, written in Arabic, that is still studied today; and various books on medicine. He served as the personal physician of the sultan of Egypt, where he spent last decades of his life. The nearby Maimonides Heritage Center (⊙10am-3pm Sun-Thu) has exhibits on the sage's life and works.

A few metres away from the Rambam's grave is the tomb of Rabbi Yohanan ben Zakkai (Ben Zakkai St; ⊙24hr), Judaism's most eminent 1st-century sage, who played a central role in replacing animal sacrifices – the raison d'être of the Temple in Jerusalem, destroyed in 70 CE – with prayer.

The dome-topped tomb of Rabbi Akiva (HaGevura St; ⊙24hr) is on the hillside about 1.5km west of the town centre. Akiva, a very prominent Mishnaic sage (and teacher of Meir Baal Hanes), played a major role in establishing rabbinic (ie post–Second Temple) Judaism. He was tortured to death by the Romans because of his support for the Bar Kochba Revolt – indeed, his enthusiasm for resistance to the Romans was such that he declared Bar Kochba to be the Messiah.

Al-Amari Mosque   MOSQUE

(Ha-Banim St) With its black basalt walls and white dome, this mosque looks a bit lost squeezed between all the eateries and shops. Built by Daher al-Omar in 1743, it has not been used since Tiberias' Arab minority was evacuated by the British in April 1948.

🏃 Activities

Most of Tiberias' activities are centred on the lake, but there are also some outstanding hiking trails in the vicinity, eg at Arbel National Park.

Hot Springs

Tiberias Hot Springs   SPRING

(Hammei Tveriya; ☏04-672 8500; www.chameytveria.co.il, in Hebrew; Eliezer Kaplan Ave/Rte 90; adult/3-12yr 70/40NIS; ⊙8am-8pm Sun, Mon &

Wed, to 10pm Tue & Thu, 8.30am-3.45pm Sat) For the sort of relaxing soak and *shvitz* (steam bath) so appreciated by the Romans, head to this modern spa, operated by the Rimonim hotel chain. Emerging from the ground at 52°C, the mineral water gets cooled down a bit before it's piped into six pools. You can also hang out in two saunas (one wet, one dry) and in a heated outdoor swimming pool (open year-round), or indulge with a Swedish massage (150NIS for 25 minutes) or a mud wrap (120NIS for 20 minutes). A locker costs 10NIS. Situated 2.5km south of the centre of town, across the street from Hamat Tveriya National Park; served by buses 5 and 28 and sheruts.

Water Sports

Along the Yigal Allon Promenade, several operators offer motorboat rental (120NIS for 30 minutes) and, in summer, water skiing. Two options are: Tiberias Water Sports (☏052 269 2664) and Water Sport Center (☏052 349 1462). Closed on cold, rainy days and on Shabbat.

Cycling

The Sea of Galilee is great cycling territory. Completely circumnavigating the lake (60km) takes about six hours; for much of the distance you can follow the Kinneret Trail (see p213), though for now part of the ride has to be done on highways. For a half-day ride, you can head to Yardenit (see p221), 8km south of Tiberias, from where an 8km circuit follows the Jordan River.

Start early to beat the heat and take plenty of water. When riding on roads, make sure you're highly visible and stay on the verges/shoulders, as far as possible from the traffic. Do not ride after sundown.

Aviv Hostel   CYCLING
(☏04-672 0007; 66 HaGalil St; per day 70NIS; ☉8am-6pm) Has 400 bicycles, most of them quality 24-speed mountain bikes. Prices include helmet, lock and maps. Staff are happy to provide information on itineraries and routes. If your bike has mechanical problems, they'll come out and do repairs.

🏊 Beaches

Most of the beaches right around Tiberias have been fenced off by private operators (including hotels), which is very problematic from the point of view of public access (theoretically guaranteed by law). Tiberias' only free beach is Music Beach, at the northern

end of the Yigal Allon Promenade. Another good bet is Hof Ganim, 1.5km south of the centre, which is run by the municipality.

Pay beaches in or very near Tiberias include Hof HaTchelet (admission 28NIS), a bit north of the centre; and South Beach, unsurprisingly, south of the centre.

Further afield, there are plenty of unguarded stretches of coastline along Rte 90. Beaches with amenities situated north of Tiberias, such as around Migdal (hometown of Mary Magdalene, ie Mary from Magdala/Migdal), include Hawaii, Ilanot and Tamar. South of Tiberias you'll find lots more beaches, including Berniki, Tzinbari and Tzemah.

Buses 26, 28 and 51 follow Rte 90 south around the lakeshore. All buses bound for Rosh Pina and Kiryat Shmona follow the shoreline north of town.

Gai Beach Water Park   BEACH
(☏04-670 0713; admission over 3yr 70NIS; ☉9.30am-5pm Passover-Oct) Has a fine beach, giant water slides (including one at a terrifying 70-degree angle), a wave machine and a special section for small kids. Situated about 1km south of the town centre.

Sleeping

Tiberias has some of the Galilee's best-value dorm beds – as well as one of northern Israel's most luxurious hotels. Boisterous domestic tourists all but take over in July and August, when the weather is too hot for all but the hardiest foreign visitors.

It's possible to camp at many of the beaches that ring the Sea of Galilee, including the municipal Hof Ganim (Rte 90), 1.5km

---

ℹ PUBLIC BEACHES

Environmental organisations and local authorities are waging a legal battle to claw beachfront land around the Sea of Galilee – which by law belongs to the public – back from the clutches of various private operators. A few beaches offering special facilities – lifeguards, security, changing rooms, showers, lawns, chairs, water slides and the like – are still authorised to charge per-person entry or per-car parking fees.

Camping is permitted at most beaches, public and private, around the Sea of Galilee.

south of the centre of Tiberias. If you don't have a car – for instance, if you're cycling – entry at many privately run beaches is free.

☆ Scots Hotel   LUXURY HOTEL $$$

(☎04-671 0710; www.scotshotels.co.il; 1 Gdud Barak St/Rte 90; d weekday/weekend from US$340/415; ✵@☼≋) Built in the 1890s as a hospital, this sumptuously restored complex – still owned by the Church of Scotland – is graced by landscaped gardens, breezy courtyards and a dazzling lake-view pool (open whenever it's warm enough). A spa is set to open in late 2012. Reservations for the 67 rooms can only be made by phone; discounts are often available. Nonguests can visit the gorgeous, tranquil gardens from Sunday to Wednesday.

☆ YMCA Peniel-by-Galilee   GUESTHOUSE $$

(☎04-672 0685; www.ymca-galilee.co.il; Rte 90; s/d 250/450NIS; ✵≋) Built in the 1920s as a holiday home for the founder of the Jerusalem YMCA, this guesthouse is a real gem. Set on a secluded section of shady lakeshore, it has a clean pebbly beach, a natural pool fed by a warm spring and a lobby with a distinct Mandate-era vibe. The 13 rooms are forgivably simple, but some have kitchenettes. Excellent value. Situated on the east side of Rte 90 about 3km north of Tiberias; served by all buses heading north from Tiberias.

Arbel Guest House   GUESTHOUSE $$

(☎04-679 4919; www.4shavit.com; Moshav Arbel; dm/d without breakfast 100/350NIS, Fri, Aug & holidays 120/560NIS; ✵☼≋) Moshav Arbel is just 5km (10 minutes' drive) northwest of the hustle of central Tiberias, but this tranquil B&B feels miles away when you're lazing in a hammock under bougainvilleas by the pool or strolling among no fewer than 60 different kinds of fruit tree. The six two-room units, each with space for four or five, are eclectically decorated, and all have new mattresses, jacuzzi and kitchenette. The absolutely superb breakfasts cost 40NIS. Arbel is 80m above sea level, so it's cooler than Tiberias in summer and warmer than the Golan in winter. Hosts Sara and Yisrael Shavit offer a discount of 20% if you stay three or more nights.

Rimonim Galei Kinnereth   LUXURY HOTEL $$$

(☎04-672 8888; www.rimonim.com; 1 Eliezer Kaplan St; d from US$200; ✵@☼≋) A favourite of David Ben-Gurion back in the 1950s, the doyen of the Tiberias hotel scene – opened in 1946 – retains some of its late-Mandate-era charm. Modern amenities include a private beach, a fabulous spa and a kids club for children aged five to 10. See if you can identify some of the hotel's more famous guests in the mural behind reception. There's a small exhibition on the hotel's storied history in the Hermon Room (2nd floor).

Aviv Hotel & Hostel   HOSTEL $

(☎04-672 0007; www.aviv-hotel.co.il; 66 HaGalil St; dm 70NIS, d without breakfast 200-350NIS; ✵@☼) Run by the same family for three decades, this welcoming hostel has 30 clean, slightly scuffed rooms with practical furnishings, proper spring mattresses, make-'em-yourself beds, fridges and balconies. Dorm beds are all nonbunk; women-only dorm rooms are available. Lift-equipped. Breakfast costs 30NIS. Also has modern, spacious, good-value 'holiday flats'.

Tiberias Hostel   HOSTEL $

(☎04-679 2611; www.tiberiashostel.com; Rabin Sq; dm 75-85NIS, s/d 250/350NIS; ✵@☼) An easy walk from the bus station, this place has 110 dorm beds – all of them double-decker bunks – in rooms for four to 10 people. The sparkling-new section upstairs, opened in 2011, has bathroom blocks that give the place the feel of an old-time hostel. The seven doubles are smallish and a bit scuffed. Breakfast is toast and jam.

Berger Hotel   HOTEL $

(☎04-671 5151; bergerhotel@bezeqint.net; 27 Neiberg St/Rte 77, Kiryat Shmuel; d US$70) A modest, good-value tourist hotel whose 45 simple, spacious rooms come with fridges; most also have kitchenettes and balconies. Lift-equipped and wheelchair accessible. Situated 1km northwest (up the hill) from the centre along Elhadif St, ie Rte 77; served by frequent buses (2.80NIS from town) and sheruts.

✗ Eating & Drinking

The Yigal Allon Promenade is lined with places to grab a bite or sip a beer, as is the perpendicular Midrahov (a pedestrian mall) and a nearby section of HaBanim St.

Only a handful of in-town eateries are open on Shabbat, making Friday night a great time to check out Nazareth's dazzling dining scene.

Decks   STEAKHOUSE $$$

(☎04-671 0800; Lido Beach, Gdud Barak St; mains 75-155NIS; ☺noon-11pm Sun-Thu, noon to

1hr before sundown Fri, opens after sundown Sat)
Legendary for its grilled meats – including
filet mignon, baby lamb and goose liver (not
force-fed) – which are prepared outdoors
over a mixture of five kinds of wood: olive,
lemon, cherry, walnut and eucalyptus. Oc-
cupying a hangar-like space built out over
the sea; tables offer unmatched views. Has
an excellent wine list. Kosher.

TOP CHOICE Yisrael's Kitchen   ISRAELI **$$$**
(⊘04-679 4919; Arbel Guest House, Moshav Arbel;
mains 76-132NIS; ⊙8-10am & 6.30-9.30pm) Ten
minutes by car from Tiberias, this rustic,
family-run restaurant features local produce
and warm, from-the-heart country cooking.
Specialities include lamb and veal served in
terracotta casseroles, baked St Peter's fish
and scrummy desserts, including home-
made ice cream. Particularly jolly on Friday
nights. Ring ahead to let them know you're
coming.

Guy   ISRAELI **$$**
(⊘04-672 3036; HaGalil St; mains 38-70NIS;
⊙noon-9pm or 10pm Sun-Thu, 11.30am-1hr before
sundown Fri; ⊅) Popular with locals, the menu
here features home-style grilled meats,
soups (17NIS to 22NIS) and a delicious array
of stuffed vegetables as well as Ashkenazi-
style chopped liver and Iraqi-style *kubbeh*,
a pocket of *burghul* (cracked wheat) dough
stuffed with chopped meat and fried.

Galei Gil   FISH **$$**
(⊘04-672 0699; Yigal Allon Promenade; mains
62-92NIS; ⊙10am-10.30pm or later) On a long
wooden deck overlooking the waterfront –
an unbeatable location. Eight kinds of fish
are available either grilled or fried.

Little Tiberias   INTERNATIONAL **$$**
(⊘04-679 2806; HaKishon St; mains 59-145NIS;
⊙noon-midnight or later) Serves fish (grilled,
baked or fried), meat, seafood and pasta – on
solid pine tables – seven days a week.

Big Ben   PUB **$$**
(Midrahov; mains 48-95NIS; ⊙9am-2am; ☏)
Decked out like an English-style pub, this
old-timer serves meat and fish dishes, pizza,
pasta and sandwiches, as well as Illy coffee
and four beers on tap (including Murphy's).
Screens international footy matches.

Felafel stalls   FELAFEL **$**
(HaGalil St; mains 17NIS; ⊙8 or 8.30am-10.30pm
Sun-Thu, 8am-1hr before sundown Fri) Four stalls
occupy temporary digs while Gan Shimon

Park – now a huge hole – is turned into an
underground parking garage (this is likely to
take a while).

Hummus Issa   HUMMUS **$**
(7 Ben Zakkai St; mains 20-30NIS; ⊙8am-7pm
Sun-Thu, 8am-4pm Fri; ☏⊅) Very popular.

Fruit & Veggie Market   MARKET **$**
(⊙5am-9pm Sun-Thu, to 1hr before sundown
Fri) Some of the stall owners may be a bit
uncouth but their produce is top quality
and cheap.

Supersol Sheli   SUPERMARKET **$**
(HaBanim St; ⊙7.30am-9pm Sun-Thu, to 2pm Fri)
For picnic supplies.

ⓘ Information

Tiberias' main commercial thoroughfare is
HaGalil St.

ATMs can be found at **Bank Discount** (cnr
HaYarden & Gdud Barak Sts), **Bank Leumi** (cnr
HaBanim & HaYarden Sts), **Bank HaPoalim**
(HaBanim St) and **Beinleumi Bank** (Rabin Sq).

Magen David Adom (⊘04-671 7611; cnr
HaBanim & HaKishon Sts; ⊙first aid 7pm-
midnight Sun-Thu, 2pm-midnight Fri, 10am-
midnight Sat, ambulance 24hr) Provides
after-hours first aid and can arrange house
(and hotel) calls by doctors.

Poriya Hospital (Baruch Padeh Medical
Center; ⊘emergency ward 665 2540; www.
poria.health.gov.il; Rte 768) Tiberias' govern-
ment hospital is 8km southwest of the city
centre. Served by hourly bus 39.

Post office (HaYarden St) Foreign exchange.

Solan Express (3 Midrahov; internet per hr
20NIS; ⊙9am-10pm Sun-Thu, to 3pm Fri, opens

AROUND THE LAKE BY BUS

In July and August and during the Rosh HaShanah and Sukkot holidays, the free **Kav Sovev Kinneret bus** (☑*55477; www.kineret.org.il, in Hebrew) circumnavigates the Sea of Galilee every two hours from 10am to 8pm. Check the website for dates and times.

after Shabbat Sat) Cybercafe and international phone office. Also sells prepaid SIM cards and changes foreign currency.

Tiberias Hotels Association (www.tiberias -hotels.co.il) Publishes a monthly events guide, *B'Tveriya* (Hebrew only), and has a moderately useful website.

Tourist office (☑04-672 5666; Archaeological Garden, HaBanim St; ⊙8.30am-3.45pm Sun-Thu, to 11.30am Fri) Run by the municipality. Has free brochures and maps of Tiberias and the Galilee.

❶ Getting There & Away

Bus

Most intercity buses pass by the rather forlorn **central bus station** (www.bus.co.il; HaYarden St); some short-haul lines also stop along HaGalil St. Certain lines operate on Saturday after sundown.

Destinations served at least hourly (unless otherwise indicated) include the following:

» Beit She'an (Veolia bus 28; 14.90NIS) via the Sea of Galilee's southwest coast (also served by Veolia bus 26)

» Haifa's Merkazit (Lev) HaMifratz bus station (Egged bus 430; 26.50NIS, 1½ hours)

» Jerusalem (Egged buses 961, 962 and 963; 40NIS, three hours) via Beit She'an

» Kfar Tavor (Veolia bus 30; 10.80NIS, four daily Sunday to Thursday, two on Friday)

» Kiryat Shmona (mainly Egged bus 841; 29NIS, 1¼ hours) via Rosh Pina

» Nazareth via Kafr Kana (Nazareth Tourism & Transport bus 431; 19NIS, 40 minutes)

» Tel Aviv (mainly Egged bus 835; 40NIS, twice an hour, 3½ hours)

» Tsfat (Veolia bus 450; 14.90NIS, one hour)

Katzrin-based Rama has services to Katzrin (bus 52; five a day Sunday to Friday, one Saturday night) and Hamat Gader (bus 24; 6NIS, one daily Sunday to Friday).

Car

Tiberias is the best place in the Galilee to hire a car. Among the rental companies with local offices:

Avis (www.avis.co.il; cnr HaYarden St & Ha-Amakim St)

Eldan (www.eldan.co.il; HaBanim St)

Sherut (Shared Taxi)

Sheruts (☑057 899 4001; ⊙5am-7pm Sun-Thu, to 2pm Fri) link the parking lot adjacent to the central bus station with Tel Aviv (40NIS, two hours) and occasionally Haifa (20NIS, one hour).

Sheruts to Beit She'an (15NIS, departures 6am to 9pm Sunday to Thursday, to 4pm Friday) – via the Sea of Galilee's southwest coast and Yardenit (7NIS) – leave from HaGalil St, across the street from the Paz petrol station.

Taxi

Tiberias' taxi stations include **Moniyot Tveriya** (☑04-655 5550).

Sea of Galilee

יم כנרת   بحيرة طبريا

The shores of the Sea of Galilee (in Hebrew, Yam Kinneret or HaKinneret), by far Israel's largest freshwater lake, are lined with great places to relax: beaches, camping grounds, cycling trails and walking tracks.

Jesus spent most of his ministry around the Sea of Galilee. This is where he is believed to have performed some of his best-known miracles (the multiplication of the loaves and fishes, walking on water), and it was overlooking the Kinneret that he delivered the Sermon on the Mount.

The Jordan River flows into the Sea of Galilee near the ruins of the ancient city of Bethsaida, providing three-quarters of its annual intake, and exits the lake, on its way to the Dead Sea, next to the Yardenit baptism site, at the lake's far southern tip.

NORTH OF TIBERIAS

As you drive, cycle or walk north from Tiberias, Hwy 90 and the parallel Kinneret Trail (Shvil Sovev Kinneret) curve around the northwestern shore of the lake, passing some of Israel's most significant New Testament sites.

The places in this section are listed from southwest to northeast.

◉ Sights

Arbel National Park   HIKING
(☑04-673 2904; adult/child 21/9NIS; ⊙8am-5pm during daylight savings, 8am-4pm winter, closes 1hr earlier Fri) Towering above the Sea of Galilee

and offering mesmerising views of the Golan Heights and Mt Hermon, Arbel Cliff is 181m above sea level, making it 390m above the vast blue lake below. It is on both the Israel National Trail and the Jesus Trail.

For great views, you can walk to the Carob Tree Lookout (30 minutes return) and, a few minutes further along the ridge, the Kinneret Lookout. A three-hour circuit that requires some cliff clambering with cables and hand-holds takes you past the Cave Fortress, apparently built by a Druze chieftain in the 1600s. It's also possible to do a circuit (five to six hours) that heads down to the Arbel Spring and then back up to park HQ via the ruins of a 6th-century synagogue – the latter is 800m towards Moshav Arbel along the park's sole access road.

In 1187 Saladin inflicted a devastating defeat on the Crusaders at the Horns of Hattin, the ridge a few kilometres west of Arbel Cliff.

For details on sleeping and eating in nearby Moshav Arbel, see p210 and p211.

The park is 8.5km northwest of Tiberias via Rte 77, Rte 7717 and then the Moshav Arbel access road, whence a side road leads northeast for 3.5km.

TOP CHOICE Ancient Boat HISTORIC SITE
(☏04-672 7700; www.bet-alon.co.il; Kibbutz Ginosar, Rte 90; adult/child 20/15NIS; ⊗8.30am-5pm Sun-Thu, to 4pm Fri, to 5pm Sat) In 1986, at a time when the level of the Sea of Galilee was particularly low, a local fisherman made an extraordinary discovery: the remains of a wooden boat later determined to have plied these waters in the time of Jesus's ministry. The 8.2m fishing vessel, made of 12 different kinds of (apparently recycled) wood, can be seen inside Kibbutz Ginosar's Yigal Alon Center. Wall panels and two films (one five minutes long, the other 17) tell the fascinating story of its discovery and preservation (so does the website).

Another part of the complex houses a museum (open Sunday to Thursday) dedicated to the settlement of the Galilee by Zionist pioneers. Check out the photos of the Sea of Galilee in the early 1900s – the area is almost entirely devoid of trees. There's a viewing platform with fine views up on the 5th floor. Outside, the lovely shoreline site is surrounded by expanses of waving reeds and a garden of sculptures by Jewish and Arab artists.

The cafeteria has free, if slow, internet computers.

Tabgha CHURCH
Two churches a few hundred metres apart occupy the stretch of Sea of Galilee lakefront known as Tabgha (an Arabic corruption of the Greek *hepta pega*, meaning 'seven springs'). An attractive walkway links Tabgha with Capernaum, a distance of about 3km.

The austere, German Benedictine Church of the Multiplication of the Loaves & Fishes (⊗8am-4.45pm Mon-Fri, to 2.45pm Sat), built in 1982, stands on the site of a 5th-century Byzantine church whose beautiful mosaic floor, depicting flora and feathered fauna, can still be seen. (Original tiles are in vivid colours; repaired sections are in shades of grey.) The rock under the altar is believed by some to be the 'solitary place' where Jesus laid the five loaves and two fishes that multiplied to feed 5000 faithful listeners (Mark 6:30-44). Excellent brochures (1NIS) are available along one wall. The church is wheelchair accessible.

A bit to the east, a shady, fragrant garden leads down to the water's edge and the Franciscan Church of the Primacy of St Peter (⊗8am-4.50pm), a chapel – lit by the vivid colours of abstract stained glass – built in 1933. The flat rock in front of the altar was known to Byzantine pilgrims as Mensa Christi (Christ's Table) because it was believed that Jesus and his disciples breakfasted on fish here (John 21:9). On the side of the church facing the lake, a few steps cut out of the rock are said by some to be where Jesus stood when his disciples saw him (on the other hand, the steps may have been cut in the 2nd or 3rd century, when the area was quarried for limestone). Just west of the church, a path leads to three serene

KINNERET TRAIL

Part of an energetic campaign by environmentalists to ensure unrestricted, fee-free public access to the entirety of the Sea of Galilee shore, this trail – known in Hebrew as the Shvil Sovev Kinneret – will eventually make it possible to walk or cycle all the way around the lake, a distance of about 60km. For now, about 35km – including the northeastern corner of the lake, from Capernaum almost to Ein Gev – are trail-marked (with purple and white blazes) and ready for use.

ⓘ MODEST DRESS

The Christian sites along the Sea of Galilee's northern shore require that visitors dress modestly (no tank tops or shorts above the knee).

---

outdoor chapels surrounded by the reeds and trees that grow along the lakeshore.

TOP **Mount of the Beatitudes**　CHURCH
CHOICE

(☎04-671 1225; admission per car 10NIS; ⊘visits 8-11.45am & 2-4.45pm, Mass hourly 8am-3pm except noon & 1pm) This hillside Roman Catholic church, built in 1937, stands on a site believed since at least the 4th century to be where Jesus delivered his Sermon on the Mount (Matthew 5-7), whose opening lines – the eight Beatitudes – begin with the phrase 'Blessed are...'. The sermon also includes the Lord's Prayer and oft-quoted phrases such as 'salt of the earth', 'light of the world' and 'judge not, lest ye be judged'.

Inside the octagonal church, looked after by Franciscan nuns, the Beatitudes are commemorated in stained glass just below the dome, while the seven virtues (justice, charity, prudence, faith, fortitude, hope and temperance) are represented around the altar. The balcony and tranquil gardens have breathtaking views of the Sea of Galilee.

Monte delle Beatitudini (as it's known in Italian), situated on the Jesus Trail, is a 3.1km drive up the hill from Tabgha's Church of the Multiplication of the Loaves & Fishes. Walking is also an option – from just outside the Mount's entrance booth, a 1km path leads down the hill to Tabgha, hitting Rte 87 at a point about 200m east of the Church of the Primacy of St Peter.

Capernaum　ARCHAEOLOGICAL SITE

(Kfar Nachum, Kfar Nahum; admission 3NIS; ⊘8am-4.50pm, last entry 4.30pm) The New Testament relates that the prosperous lakeside village of Capernaum (estimated population 1500), situated on the imperial highway from Tiberias to Damascus, was Jesus's home base during the most influential period of his Galilee ministry (Matthew 4:13, Mark 2:1, John 6:59). It is mentioned by name no fewer than 16 times: this is where Jesus is believed to have preached at the synagogue (Mark 1:21), healed the sick – including Peter's stepmother (Mark 1:29-31) and the centurion's servant (Luke 7:1-10) – and recruited his first disciples, local fishers Peter, Andrew, James and John and Matthew the tax collector.

The Franciscan friars who run the site, dressed in brown cassocks with a white rope around the waist, are happy to answer questions. An explanatory sheet is available at the ticket window.

Capernaum's renowned synagogue, whose facade faces south towards Jerusalem, consists of two superimposed structures. The reconstructed structure that can be seen today, known as the 'White Synagogue' because it's made of light-coloured limestone, was built in the late 4th century atop the dark basalt foundations of the 'Synagogue of Jesus', which – despite its name – appears to have been built at least a century *after* the Crucifixion.

On the other side of the tree-shaded benches from the synagogue, 10m to the right of the olive press, a menorah decorates the upper lip of a column. A nearby column bears a 5th-century inscription in Hebrew commemorating a donation made by someone named Alpheus son of Zebidah.

A modern, glass-walled church (1991), used for hourly Masses in a variety of languages, is dramatically suspended over the ruins of an octagonal 5th-century church that partly obscure St Peter's House, where Jesus is believed to have stayed.

At the entrance to the site, along the fence to the right of the statue of St Peter, is a row of impressive stone lintels decorated with fruits and plant motifs but, in accordance with Jewish tradition, no images of people or animals.

Capernaum is 16km northeast of Tiberias and 3km northeast of Tabgha. Hwy 87 has three signs indicating turn-offs to Capernaum – to get to the archaeological site, take the westernmost of the three.

Monastery of the Twelve Apostles　CHURCH

(⊘9am-about 5pm, to about 6pm summer) Peacocks strut around the verdant, deeply shaded garden of this Greek Orthodox site, a few hundred metres (2km by road) northeast of the Capernaum synagogue at the eastern edge of the ancient city. The chapel-sized church, its distinctive red domes visible from afar (including Mount of the Beatitudes), dates from 1925, but the whole complex – from the grape trellises to the rich interior iconography (redone for the Millennium) – casts a very Byzantine spell.

Korazim National Park ARCHAEOLOGICAL SITE

(adult/5-18yr 21/9NIS; ☺8am-5pm during daylight savings, to 4pm rest of year, closes 1hr earlier on Fri, last entry 1hr before closing) On a hillside overlooking the Sea of Galilee, Korazim is a good place to get an idea of the layout of a prosperous, midsized Galilean town in the time of Jesus and the Talmud (3rd to 5th centuries). The site – especially the synagogue – is known for its extraordinary basalt carvings, which depict floral and geometric designs – permitted by Jewish law – as well as Hellenistic-style representations of animals, humans (eg people stomping on grapes) and mythological figures (Medusa!). Two extraordinary objects were found inside the synagogue: a richly decorated column thought to have held up the table used to read the Torah; and an armchair bearing an inscription in Aramaic. The originals are now in the Israel Museum in Jerusalem (in situ you can see replicas). The people of Korazim – along with the inhabitants of Capernaum and Bethsaida – were denounced by Jesus for their lack of faith (Matthew 11:20-24).

Korazim is on Rte 8277 2.5km east of Rte 90 (Korazim Junction, ie Vered HaGalil) and 8km west of the ruins of Bethsaida (in Park HaYarden). There is no public transport.

Bethsaida ARCHAEOLOGICAL SITE

(☎04-692 3422; www.parkyarden.co.il, in Hebrew; Rte 888 just north of Rte 87; admission per car 55NIS; ☺24hr) These excavations, inside Ha-Yarden Park Nature Reserve (Jordan River Park), are believed to be those of the ancient fishing village of Bethsaida, where Jesus is said to have fed 5000 people with just five loaves of bread and two fish (Luke 9:10-17), walked on water (Mark 6:45-51) and healed a blind man (Mark 8:22-26) – and where he also rebuked (Luke 10:13-15). In ancient times, the Sea of Galilee, now 2km away, probably came up to the base of the tel.

Two walking circuits are trail-marked in black: a 500m route around the basalt ruins, which don't look like much to the untrained eye (signs help visitors imagine the original structures); and a 1km route down to the spring and back. The site is surrounded by old Syrian trenches and minefields.

The Bethsaida Excavations Project (www.unomaha.edu/bethsaida) is based at the University of Nebraska at Omaha.

Bethsaida is in the far northeastern corner of the Sea of Galilee, about 6km from Capernaum.

☂ Activities

Vered HaGalil Stables HORSE RIDING

(☎04-693 5785; www.veredhagalil.co.il; cnr Rte 90 & Rte 8277; 1/2hr ride 128/250NIS, half-day 500NIS) A sign reading 'Shalom y'all' greets visitors to this Western-style ranch, which offers rides on ponies or full-size horses (minimum age: 10 years) as well as five-/10-minute introductory rides for children for NIS20/35 (minimum age three years). It's a good idea to book ahead on Saturday and Jewish holidays. Situated 6.7km (by road) up the hill from Tabgha.

To get there from Tiberias, take any bus linking to Tsfat, Rosh Pina or Kiryat Shmona.

Abu Kayak KAYAKING

(☎04-692 1078/2245; www.abukayak.co.il, in Hebrew; HaYarden Park Nature Reserve, Rte 888; per person 80NIS; ☺trips 9am-4.30pm Sun-Thu, to 3pm or 4pm Fri approx late Mar–Oct) At Abu Kayak you can float down 3km of the Jordan River (1½ hours) in inflatable two-person kayaks, six-person rafts and inner tubes – a lovely way to spend an afternoon, especially for older children (minimum age 3½ years, for inner tubes 12). Has showers and changing rooms. To get free admission to the nature reserve, explain to the guard you're heading to Abu Kayak. Situated just north of the Sea of Galilee's northeastern tip.

☙ Sleeping

Camping is possible at public beaches.

TOP CHOICE Pilgerhaus Tabgha GUESTHOUSE $$$

(☎04-670 0100; www.heilig-land-verein.de; s/d €98/136; ✽@🛜) Opened in 1889, this 70-room German Catholic guesthouse – geared towards Christian pilgrims but open to all – is a tranquil place with glorious gardens, right on the shores of the Sea of Galilee. Sumptuously renovated in 2001, it's an ideal place for meditation and reflection. Reserve well in advance from March to May and mid-September to mid-November. Wheelchair accessible. Situated about 500m from Capernaum Junction.

Frenkels B&B B&B $$

(☎04-680 1686; www.thefrenkels.com; Kfar Korazim, off Rte 8277; s/d 400/550NIS; ✽🛜) Run by welcoming, easy-going immigrants from the US, this sweet *tzimmer* (B&B) has three homey suites, including one that's wheelchair friendly. Breakfast includes homemade goodies, served in a light, airy

(Continued on page 220)

LOWER GALILEE & SEA OF GALILEE SEA OF GALILEE

Religious Sites

Since the time of Abraham the Holy Land has played host to many biblical events and modern visitors can lift the stones and touch the earth where the distant prophets once stood. Each of the three monotheistic faiths can find places of monumental religious importance but even the non-religious cannot help but be moved by these time-honoured sites.

Via Dolorosa

1 Threading through the Old City of Jerusalem, 'The Way of Sorrows' (p58) is a fascinating and spiritual journey passing by the 14 biblical spots associated with Jesus' final march to Calvary.

Dome of the Rock

2 The awesome spectacle of the golden Dome of the Rock (p47) is the centrepiece of Jerusalem and the third-holiest spot in the Muslim world. It contains the rock upon which Mohammed was launched to heaven during his famed Night Journey.

Mt Sinai

3 The craggy mount (p364) in the Sinai Desert is the place where Moses reputedly received the Ten Commandments from God. Make the hike in the pre-dawn to watch a stunning sunrise over a biblical desert landscape.

Mount of Olives

4 A walk over the Mount of Olives (p71) brings pilgrims past gold-topped churches on holy Christian sites and a vast cemetery filled with souls awaiting Judgment Day. Contemplate the scene from the stunning promenade at the top of the mount.

Jericho

5 The world's oldest city (p274) is best known in the Bible as the place where Jesus was tempted by the Devil and where he was baptised by John the Baptist. Ride the cable car up the Mount of Temptation for views of the Moab Mountains.

Clockwise from top left
1. Third Station of the Cross, Via Dolorosa **2.** Sacred stone, Dome of the Rock **3.** Descending Mt Sinai **4.** Cemetery on the Mount of Olives.

Church of the Holy Sepulchre

6 The dim lighting, hushed prayers and shuffling feet inside this ancient building (p55) cast a solemn mood that is most appropriate for Christianity's holiest place. Visit at various points of the day to soak in the ebbs and flows of pious pilgrims.

Mt Zion

7 As the location of King David's tomb and the Room of the Last Supper, this corner of Jerusalem (p65) is sacred to both Jews and Christians.

Tomb of the Patriarchs

8 Walk solemnly into the Ibrahimi Mosque (p279) and marvel at the ancient grandeur of the patriarch tombs. This deeply moving site is the final resting place of Abraham and his brood. Centuries later it remains an all-important spiritual destination for Jews and Muslims.

Western Wall

9 Press your hands against the most holy place in Judaism (p49) and feel an other-worldly spiritual connection to generations of faithful Jews who have prayed here for centuries. It's best to visit on Shabbat when hundreds gather to celebrate the arrival of the Sabbath.

Church of the Nativity, Bethlehem

10 The imposing facade of this church (p260) is meant to instil humbleness before visiting the site of Jesus' birth. Duck through the narrow entrance and make your way into the bowels of the building to pray at the site of the venerated manger.

Tabgha

11 The Bible describes how Jesus miraculously multiplied five bread loaves and two fish in order to feed a congregation of 5000 devotees. Visit the place where the miracle is said to have occurred at Tabgha (p213), a beautiful head of land on the shores of the Galilee.

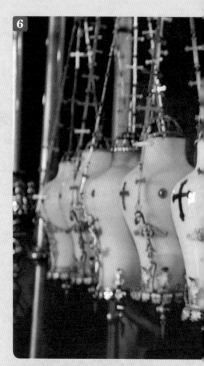

Clockwise from top left

6. Lamps, Church of the Holy Sepulchre 7. King David's Tomb, Mt Zion 8. Cenotaph of Sarah, Ibrahimi Mosque

7

(Continued from page 215)

breakfast room. Situated 8km north of Capernaum Junction.

Sea of Galilee Guesthouse
GUESTHOUSE $$
(☑04-693 0063; www.seaofgalileeguesthouse.com; Moshav Almagor, off Rte 8277; dm/d/tr without breakfast 100/550/650NIS; ✿@🖥️) Lovely gardens with panoramic sea views surround the simple, cheery rooms of this friendly, 28-bed guesthouse. Serves great breakfasts (extra charge). Cooking facilities available. If you've got a tent, you can camp. Situated 4km east of Korazim National Park in Moshav Almagor.

Kadarim Galilee B&B
GUESTHOUSE $
(☑04-698 6300; www.bbkadarim.com, in Hebrew; Kibbutz Kadarim, Rte 65; dm 100NIS, d 1/2 nights 340/500NIS; ✿) The 22 chintz-free rooms and jacuzzi-equipped cabins can sleep up to five, ideal if you're bringing the kids. Rooms are modest, practical and spotless. Has native English speakers on staff. Good value. Situated 20km northwest of Tiberias and a bit over 1km south of Nahal Amud Junction (the intersection of Rtes 65 and 85). To open the yellow gate, roll over the yellow stripe and phone.

Nof Ginosar Hotel
HOTEL $$$
(☑04-670 0300; www.ginosar.co.il; Kibbutz Ginosar, Rte 90; d 520-840NIS; ✿@🖥️♨️) Redolent with '70s charm, this well-run kibbutz old-timer has 236 hotel and cottage rooms, flowery grounds and its very own Sea of Galilee beach. Situated 200m from the Ancient Boat and 8km north of Tiberias.

HI – Karei Deshe Guest House & Youth Hostel
HOSTEL $$
(☑02-594 5633; www.iyha.org.il; dm/d US$32/120; ✿🖥️) Seriously upgraded a few years back, this sparkling-white facility, right on the lake, has 82 double, family and dorm rooms (with four or six beds), a sandy beach and lots of trees and grass. It's often full at the weekend. The nearest bus stop, on Rte 90 next to the Sapir water-pumping station (3km southwest of Capernaum Junction), is served by all buses heading north from Tiberias; it's a 1.2km walk to/from the hostel.

HaYarden Park Nature Reserve
CAMPGROUND
(Jordan River Park; ☑04-692 3422; www.parkyarden.co.il, in Hebrew; Rte 888; admission per car 55NIS; ⏰24hr) You can pitch a tent almost anywhere in this riverside park, which includes splash pools and the ruins of ancient Bethsaida. Amenities include showers, toilets, lighting and water taps. Renting a simple but comfortable room-sized tent with four/five beds costs 500/570NIS. If the gate is unstaffed, pay when you exit. It's just north of Rte 87.

✖️ Eating

🟦TOP CHOICE Ktze HaNahal
LEBANESE $$
(☑04-671 7776; Rte 90; mains 65-125NIS; ⏰noon-about 8.30pm, last order 7pm or 7.30pm; 🐾) From the outside you'd never guess that this unassuming restaurant serves up an incredible, sumac-accented Lebanese feast. After a parade of 11 different mezze (28NIS), you might want to try *shishbarak* (meat-stuffed dough balls cooked in sour goat's milk, 70NIS) or Antabli kebab with pita and roasted tomatoes (70NIS). Situated 400m south of the entrance to Kibbutz Ginosar, next to the Delek petrol station.

Ein Camonim
CHEESE $$
(En Kammonim; ☑04-698 9894; Rte 85; meals 88NIS; ⏰9am-8pm, to 11pm Fri) Surrounded by Galilean brushland, this 'goat cheese restaurant' serves up a gourmet feast that includes 10 kinds of goat's cheese, freshly baked bread, salads and wine that you can enjoy outside in the shade. Has a few kids (baby goats) for the kids (children) to pet. It's a good idea to reserve ahead on Friday and Saturday. Situated 20km northwest of Tabgha, just off Rte 85 at a point 4.8km east of Nahal Amud Junction.

ℹ️ Getting There & Around

All the buses that link Tiberias with Tsfat, Rosh Pina and Kiryat Shmona – ie take Rte 90 north – pass by Migdal, Ginosar, Capernaum Junction (Tzomet Kfar Nahum, which is a short walk from Tabgha but about 4km west of Capernaum) and the access road (1km long) to Mount of the Beatitudes.

Rama bus 52 (seven daily except midafternoon Friday to sundown Saturday), which links Tiberias with the Golan town of Katzrin (1¼ hours), continues from Capernaum Junction east along the northern edge of the lake (Rte 87), passing by Capernaum and not far from Bethsaida.

SOUTH OF TIBERIAS

The places mentioned in this section are listed from north to south.

◎ Sights

Kinneret Cemetery
CEMETERY
(Rte 90; ⏰24hr) Shaded and serene, this luxuriantly green lakeside cemetery, established

in 1911, is the final resting place of socialist Zionist pioneers such as Berl Katznelson (1887–1944), famous for being at the centre of a celebrated love triangle (his grave is flanked by those of this first and second wives), and Shmuel Yavnieli (1884–1961), who worked to bring Yemenite Jews to Israel.

Also buried here is the Hebrew poet Rachel (Rachel Bluwstein; 1890–1931); books of her hugely popular poems – many of which have been set to music – can be found in a stainless-steel container attached to her grave. In 2011 the Bank of Israel decided to portray Rachel on new banknotes set for release in 2014.

In the spring of 1917 the Ottomans expelled the entire population of Tel Aviv and Jaffa. Of the 2000 Jewish refugees who found refuge in the Galilee, 430 died and 10 are buried here, commemorated by 10 anonymous gravestones and a stone plaque, erected in 2003, bearing their names.

The cemetery is situated 9km south of Tiberias, 300m south of Kinneret Junction.

Yardenit   SPIRITUAL
(www.yardenit.com; admission free; ⊙8am-6pm, to 5pm Dec-Feb, to 4pm Fri) This hugely popular, eucalyptus-shaded baptism site, run by Kibbutz Kinneret, is 100m south of the Jordan River's exit from the Sea of Galilee. This may not have been exactly where Jesus was baptised, but groups of Christian pilgrims line up here – praying and singing – to be baptised in white robes (rental/purchase US$10/23, including towel and certificate). Use of the changing rooms and showers costs US$2; the toilets cost 2NIS.

Those furry rodents paddling around the fish-filled Jordan are nutrias (coypus), natives of South America. The site has a restaurant and a large religious souvenir shop. In the garden you can see an olive tree planted by the controversial American conservative Glenn Beck in 2011.

Yardenit is situated 10km south of Tiberias and 1km northwest of Kibbutz Degania Alef, the world's first-ever kibbutz (founded in 1910).

Bet Gabriel   CULTURAL BUILDING
(☑04-675 1175; www.betgabriel.co.il; Rte 92; ⊙closed Sun) Built in 1993, this lakeside cultural centre – one of Israel's most beautiful buildings – is known for its art exhibitions, first-run cinema and restaurant. In November 1994 it served as the venue for a ceremony reconfirming the peace treaty between Israel and Jordan. King Hussein's red-and-white keffiyeh and a sword given to Shimon Peres by Yasser Arafat can be seen in the Peace Room (⊙free tours 10-11.30am Tue), whose mirrors ensured that everyone, no matter where around the six-sided, eight-seat table they sat, could see the Sea of Galilee. Situated 300m east of Tzemah Junction.

🛏 Sleeping

HI – Poriya Guest House
& Youth Hostel   HOSTEL $
(Poriya Taiber Youth Hostel; ☑02-594 5720; www.iyha.org.il; dm/s/d US$33/90/110, additional adult/child US$29/23; ❄@🛜) Perched on a hillside high above the Sea of Galilee, the gorgeous new Poriya (Poria) campus, opened in 2011, boasts a glass-walled lobby with spectacular views, 58 rather spartan rooms, and proximity to the Switzerland Forest. Dorm rooms have six beds. Also offers tile-roofed wooden cabins. Situated 9km south of Tiberias, a steep 4km up Rte 7877 from Rte 90. No public transport.

🍴 Eating

Tchelet   FRENCH, ISRAELI $$
(☑04-670 9200; www.betgabriel.co.il; Bet Gabriel, Rte 92; mains 30-95NIS; ⊙11am-10pm Mon-Sat) Perfect for a full meal or just a drink, this French-inflected restaurant and cafe has one of the loveliest views of the Sea of Galilee anywhere. The reasonably priced menu includes meat, fish, pasta and salads. Gourmet sandwiches are another option (except after 5pm on Friday and before 5pm on Saturday). Kids mains cost 40NIS. Situated inside the Bet Gabriel cultural centre, 300m east of Tzemah Junction.

ℹ Getting There & Around
Rte 90 between Tiberias and Tzemah Junction (at the Sea of Galilee's southern tip; 30 minutes) is served by all Tiberias–Beit She'an buses as well as some short- and medium-haul lines such as Veolia bus 26 (six daily Sunday to Thursday, four on Friday).

EASTERN SHORE
As you cross Arik Bridge and continue towards the eastern shore, the main road verges away from the Kinneret and runs around the edge of the beautiful Bethsaida Valley, Israel's largest natural wetlands. Moshav Ramot is 3km up the hill from Rte 92 (officially, it's on the Golan).

The places below appear from north to south.

ALL ABOARD FOR DAMASCUS!

From shortly before WWI until 1948, you could hop on the legendarily slow Jezreel Valley Railway in Haifa at 8am and pull into Hamat Gader at 11.45am – or Damascus at 7.47pm. Or you could transfer to the Hejaz Railway in the Syrian town of Daraa, 60km east of Hamat Gader, and roll south. (Daraa is where the popular rebellion against Syria's Assad regime began in 2011.) Until the Hejaz Railway was knocked out of commission during WWI by Lawrence of Arabia and his Bedouin fighters, you could take the train all the way to Medina, now in Saudi Arabia.

In the 1930s, the Jezreel Valley Railway helped carry construction materials for the 942km Kirkuk–Haifa Pipeline that, until 1948, carried crude oil from Iraq to the refineries of Haifa Bay. Remains of the pipeline can still be seen on the Golan Heights. Regional peace would make rebuilding the pipeline very attractive both economically and strategically – and turn Haifa into the major Mediterranean port the British intended it to be.

Proposals to place the Jezreel Valley Railway back into service have been mooted for decades, but in 2011 Israel Railways finally started issuing tenders. The planned standard-gauge line (the Ottoman tracks were narrow-gauge) will link Haifa with Bet She'an and, at a later stage, with Irbid, Jordan, allowing the Hashemite Kingdom to take advantage of Haifa's Mediterranean port facilities.

For details on cycling the 150km route of the original Jezreel Valley Railway, pick up a copy of the guidebook *Shvil Rakevet HaEmeq* by Aharon Brindt (in Hebrew).

◉ Sights & Activities

Majrase
PARK

(☏04-679 3410; adult/child 27/14NIS; ◷8am-5pm during daylight savings, to 4pm rest of year, last entry 1hr before closing) Located in the northeast corner of the Sea of Galilee, this nature reserve's spring-fed streams and jungle-like natural swampland are a great place for a 'water hike'. The 'wet route' (there's also a dry one), open only in the warm season, takes 40 to 60 minutes and is usually suitable for kids over the age of five – but be prepared for water that's up to hip-high (1.2m deep in the late spring). In winter, when the reserve is very quiet (and the admission price may drop), you've got a better chance of seeing the local fauna. The lagoons near the lake are off-limits, to allow fish to breed. Changing rooms are available.

Kursi National Park
ARCHAEOLOGICAL SITE

(www.parks.org.il; Rte 92; adult/child 14/7NIS; ◷8am-4pm Oct-Mar, to 5pm Apr-Sep, to 4pm Fri, last entry 1hr before closing) Mentioned in the Talmud as a place of idol worship, this Roman-era Jewish fishing village is where Jesus is believed to have cast a contingent of demon spirits out of two men and into a herd of swine (Mark 5:1-13, Luke 8:26-39). The beautifully conserved ruins feature an impressive 5th-century Byzantine monastery. Wheelchair accessible.

Ofen Harim
CYCLING

(☏04-673 2418, 052 851 5058; booki@zahav.net.il; Moshav Ramot; per day 60NIS; ◷8am-3pm or later) Rents mountain bikes (free if you stay at its B&B) and can recommend off-road trails. Call ahead to reserve.

🛏 Sleeping

Leafy Moshav Ramot (www.ramot4u.co.il, in Hebrew), a favourite with domestic tourists, has several dozen upmarket *tzimmerim* (B&Bs).

TOP CHOICE Genghis Khan in the Golan
HOSTEL $

(☏052 371 5687; www.gkhan.co.il; Giv'at Yoav, Golan; dm/6-person tent 100/590NIS, linen & towel 30NIS; ❄) Inspired by the yurts (*gers*) used by the nomads of Mongolia, Sara Zafrir designed and handmade five colour-coded yurts, each of which sleeps 10 on comfortable foam mattresses. Powerful air-con units make sure you stay cosy in winter and cool in summer. In the kitchen, the pans, plates and fridge space are, like the tents, colour-coded, and guests can cook with fresh thyme, lemongrass and mint grown in the herb garden (a row of recycled tyres). The Golan Trail is just one of the hiking paths that pass by here.

Situated in the Golan Heights village of Giv'at Yoav, on Rte 789 13km southeast of Rte 92's Kursi (Kursy) Junction. Bus 51 links Giv'at Yoav with Tiberias (eight daily Sunday to Thursday, six on Friday, one on Saturday night); Sara is happy to pick up guests at the stop.

Ramot Resort Hotel   HOTEL $$$

(☑04-673 2636; www.ramot-nofesh.co.il; Moshav Ramot, Golan; d 540-980NIS, chalets 1080-1600NIS; ✻☞🏊) Affording incredible views of the Sea of Galilee, this elegant, 123-room, hillside establishment will coddle you with its 25m outdoor pool (open mid-March to November), kiddie pool and weight room. It's near a number of hiking trails. Suitable for families with children. Situated 2km towards Moshav Ramot from Rte 92.

Ein Gev Holiday Resort   HOTEL $$$

(☑04-665 9800; www.eingev.com; Kibbutz Ein Gev, Rte 92; d US$180-240; ✻@☞) From 1948 to 1967, when most the Sea of Galilee's eastern coast was under Syrian control, the only way to get to Kibbutz Ein Gev was by boat. Today, the seaside kibbutz owns banana, mango and lychee orchards, a cowshed and this well-managed, 166-room hotel, which boasts the Sea of Galilee's only natural sand beach. Options include sunny beachfront family units (US$220 to US$420) that can sleep five. Situated about 1.5km south of the kibbutz entrance.

✖ Eating

Moshbutz   STEAKHOUSE $$$

(☑04-679 5095; www.moshbutz.com; Dalyot St, Moshav Ramot; mains 62-92NIS, steaks per 100g 28-52NIS; ☺6pm-about 10.30pm, opens at 1pm Sat & during school holidays) This cosy restaurant serves up fabulous steaks, juicy burgers and creative salads as well as starters such as grilled aubergine with spicy goat's-milk yoghurt – complemented by boutique Golan wines, charming service and great views down to the Sea of Galilee. Almost all the ingredients, including the meat, are local. Situated behind a cowshed – to get there, follow signs featuring six white Hebrew letters on a bright red background.

Hamat Gader   الحمة   חמת גדר

A favourite of the Romans, whose impressive 2nd-century bath complex can still be seen, this 42°C natural hot spring (☑04-665 9965/99; www.hamat-gader.com; adult/child from 1m height to 16yr 88/66NIS, after 5pm 60NIS; ☺8.30am-10.30pm Mon-Fri, to 5pm Sat & Sun Oct-May, 8.30am-5pm Mon-Sat Jun-Sep) – elevation 150m below sea level – is hugely popular (except in the summer heat) with both Jewish and Arab Israelis. Has picnic facilities and two restaurants. You generally need to book ahead for spa treatments. It's wheelchair accessible.

Kids will love the splash pool (open in summer); the small zoo, which has baboons, ibexes, ostriches and an 8m-long reticulated python named Monica; the cuddly rabbits in the petting corner; and a troupe of performing parrots (shows at 11am, 1pm and 3pm).

Hamat Gader, part of British-mandated Palestine, was occupied by the Syrians in 1948 and captured by Israel in 1967.

❶ Getting There & Away

Hamat Gader is 10km southeast of Tzemah Junction along Rte 98, which affords close-up views into Jordan across the Yarmuk River, a major tributary of the Jordan.

Rama bus 24 links Tiberias with Hamat Gader once a day except Saturday; departures are at 9.15am from Tiberias and 2.30pm from Hamat Gader.

Upper Galilee & Golan
الجليل الاعلى والجولان
הגליל העליון והגולן

Why Go?

The rolling, green hills of the Upper Galilee (the area north of Rte 85) and the wild plateaux and peaks of the Golan Heights offer an incredible variety of activities to challenge the body and the soul – and nourish the stomach and the mind. Domestic tourists flock to the area – some come looking for luxurious *tzimmerim* (B&Bs), boutique wineries and gourmet country restaurants, others in search of superb hiking, cycling and horse riding through dazzling carpets of spring wildflowers, white-water rafting and even skiing. Yet other visitors are attracted by some of the world's best birdwatching and the spiritual charms of Tsfat, the most important centre of Kabbalah (Jewish mysticism) for over five centuries. The entire region, its summits refreshingly cool in summer, is just a short drive from the Christian sites and refreshing beaches of the Sea of Galilee.

Best Places to Eat

» Dag Al HaDan (p243)

» Misedet HaArazim (p236)

» HaBokrim Restaurant (p250)

» Villa Lishansky (p242)

» Rishikesh (p236)

Best Places to Stay

» Villa Tehila (p239)

» Villa Lishansky (p242)

» Ohn Bar Guesthouse (p235)

» Golan Heights Hostel (p252)

When to Go
Tzfat

°C/°F Temp

40/104 —
30/86 —
20/68 —
10/50 —
0/32 —

Rainfall inches/mm

8/200
6/150
4/100
2/50
0

J F M A M J J A S O N D

Dec–Mar
Skiing on Mt Hermon – if there's enough snow.

Dec–Aug
Spring flowers bloom earliest in Hula Valley, latest on Mt Hermon.

Feb–mid-Jun
Adventure rafting on the wild Yarden Harari (Mountainous Jordan River).

Upper Galilee & Golan Highlights

❶ Gaze into the burbling, spring-fresh water below the Suspended Trail at **Banias Nature Reserve** (p251)

❷ Get lost in the mysticism and ancient stories of Tsfat's **Synagogue Quarter** (p226)

❸ Breathe in the crisp alpine air high atop **Mt Hermon** (p253)

❹ Visit award-winning wineries on **Ramat Dalton** (p237 and the **Golan** (p244 and p251)

❺ Hike the canyons and waterfalls of the **Yehudiya Nature Reserve** (p247)

❻ Get a close-up view of migrating cranes from the

Safari Wagon at **Agamon HaHula** (p240)

❼ Stay at a luxury B&B in a flowery old stone house in **Rosh Pina** (p238)

❽ Go **horse riding** (p250) with a genuine Israeli cowboy from Kibbutz Meron Golan – up a volcano

❶ Getting There & Around

The best way to explore the region is by car – distances are relatively short and having your own car gives you unmatched flexibility. There's a rental agency in Kiryat Shmona but you'll probably be better off hiring a vehicle in Tiberias, Haifa, Tel Aviv or Jerusalem.

The main bus hub is Kiryat Shmona.

Although not recommended, many Israelis hitchhike their way around, especially on the Golan.

THE UPPER GALILEE

الجليل الاعلى

הגליל העליון

Tsfat (Safed)   צפת   صفد

✏️ 04 / POP 30,300

The mountaintop city of Tsfat is an ethereal place to get lost for a day or two. A centre of Kabbalah (Jewish mysticism; see p377) since the 16th century, it's home to an otherworldly mixture of Hasidic Jews and devout-but-mellow former hippies, many of them American immigrants.

In the old city's labyrinth of cobbled alleys and steep stone stairways, you'll come across ancient synagogues, crumbling stone houses with turquoise doorways, art galleries, artists' studios and Yiddish-speaking little boys in black kaftans and bowler hats. Parts of Tsfat look like a *shtetl* (ghetto) built of Jerusalem stone, but the presence of so many mystics and spiritual seekers creates a distinctly bohemian atmosphere.

On Shabbat (Friday night and Saturday until sundown), commerce completely shuts down. While this may be inconvenient if you're looking for a bite to eat, the lack of traffic creates a meditative, spiritual Sabbath atmosphere through which joyful Hasidic tunes waft from hidden synagogues and unseen dining rooms.

In July and August and during the Passover and Sukkot holidays, Tsfat is packed with tourists – both Israeli and foreign – and the city's restaurants and cafes buzz until late at night. Winter, on the other hand, is very quiet, giving the city's many artists a chance to get some work done.

History

Founded in the Roman period, Tsfat was fortified by Yosef ben Matityahu (later known as Josephus Flavius), commander of Jewish forces in the Galilee in the early years of the Great Jewish Revolt (66–70 CE). According to the Jerusalem Talmud, Tsfat was the site of one of the hilltop fire beacons used to convey news of the sighting of the new moon in Jerusalem.

The Crusaders, led by King Fulk of Anjou, built a vast citadel here to control the highway to Damascus. It was later captured by Saladin (1188), dismantled by the Ayyubids (1220), rebuilt by the Knights Templar (1240) and expanded by the Mamluk Sultan Beybars (after 1266).

During the late 15th and 16th centuries, Tsfat's Jewish community increased in size and importance thanks to an influx of Sephardic Jews expelled from Spain in 1492. Among the new arrivals were some of the Jewish world's pre-eminent Kabbalists. During this period, Tsfat was an important stop on the trade route from Akko to Damascus and was known for its production of textiles. A Hebrew printing press – the first such device anywhere in the Middle East – was set up in Tsfat in 1577.

In the late 1700s, Tsfat welcomed an influx of Hasidim from Russia.

Tsfat was decimated by the plague in 1742, 1812 and 1847, and devastated by earthquakes in 1759 and 1837. The latter disaster killed thousands and levelled all but a handful of buildings.

In 1948 the departing British handed the town's strategic assets over to Arab forces, but after a pitched battle Jewish forces prevailed and the Arab population fled. These days, many of Tsfat's residents are American Jews who turned to mysticism in a 1960s-inspired search for spirituality and transcendental meaning.

Israel's fifth medical school, run by Bar Ilan University, opened in Tsfat in 2011.

◉ Sights

Most of Tsfat's sights are in the Synagogue Quarter or the adjacent Artists' Quarter.

SYNAGOGUE QUARTER

Tsfat's long-time Jewish neighbourhood spills down the hillside from HaMaginim Sq (Kikar HaMaginim; Defenders' Sq), which dates from 1777. All of Tsfat's historic Kabbalist synagogues are a quick (if often confusing) walk from here. If you're short on time, the two to visit are the Ashkenazi Ari and Caro synagogues.

Synagogue hours tend to be irregular and unannounced closings are common. Visitors should wear modest clothing (no shorts or bare shoulders); kippas/yarmulkes are provided for men. Caretakers expect a small donation. Synagogues are closed to tourists on Shabbat and Jewish holidays.

Ashkenazi Ari Synagogue

SYNAGOGUE

(Najara St; ⏰9.30am-afternoon prayers Sun-Thu, to 12.30pm Fri) Founded in the 16th century by Sephardic Jews from Greece, this synagogue stands on the site where the great Kabbalist Yitzhak Luria (Isaac Luria; 1534–72) – often known by the acronym Ari – used to greet the Sabbath. In the 18th century, it came to serve Tsfat's Ashkenazi Hasidic community – thus the name. Incidentally, the Jerusalem-born Ari had a Sephardic mother and an Ashkenazi father.

Destroyed in the 1837 earthquake, the synagogue was rebuilt in the 1850s. High atop the 19th-century holy ark (where the Torah scrolls are kept), carved and elaborately painted according to the traditions of Galicia (Poland), the lion has a human-like face that worshippers speculate may be that of the Ari (the Hebrew word *ari* means 'lion').

In 1948, the synagogue was packed with worshippers when an Arab mortar round slammed into the courtyard, sending shrapnel crashing into the side of the *bimah* (central platform) facing the door. Miraculously, say locals, there were no casualties. The hole is now stuffed with Western Wall–style entreaties to God.

From Sunday to Thursday, the synagogue closes for the day when afternoon prayers begin, which is sometime between 3.15pm (in December) and 7.30pm (in June). It closes at 1.30pm on Fridays in summer.

Caro Synagogue

SYNAGOGUE

(☑04-692 3284), 050-855 0462; Beit Yosef St; ⏰8.30 or 9am-4 or 5pm Sun-Thu, closes earlier Fri) Named (like the street it's on) in honour of the author of the *Shulchan Aruch* (the most authoritative codification of Jewish law), Toledo-born Yosef Caro (1488–1575), this synagogue was founded as a house of study in the 1500s but rebuilt after the earthquakes of 1759 and 1837 – and again in 1903. The ark contains three ancient Torah scrolls from Spain, Iraq and Persia.

In the 16th century, Caro, the head of Tsfat's rabbinical court, was the most respected rabbinical authority not only in all of Palestine but in many parts of the Jewish Diaspora as well. According to tradition, an angel revealed the secrets of Kabbalah to Caro in the house below the synagogue.

Abuhav Synagogue

SYNAGOGUE

(Abohav Synagogue; Abuhav St; ⏰generally open 9am-4pm Sun-Thu, to 11am Fri) Named after the 15th-century Spanish scholar Rabbi Yitzhak Abuhav, this synagogue was founded in the 16th century but moved to its present location after the 1759 earthquake. The ornately carved courtyard, restored in the late 20th century, is used for weddings.

Inside, the four central pillars represent the four elements (earth, air, water and fire) that, according to Kabbalists (and ancient Greeks such as Aristotle), make up all of creation. The oval dome has 10 windows, one for each of the Ten Commandments; representations of the 12 Tribes of Israel; illustrations of the musical instruments used in the Temple; pomegranate trees (whose fruit is said to have the same number of seeds as there are Jewish commandments, 613); and

UPPER GALILEE & GOLAN TSFAT (SAFED)

LOST ON THE WAY TO ETERNITY

Ask a local for directions, explaining that you're lost, and you may be told, 'You're not lost, you're in Tsfat!'.

If you're headed to a specific place within Tsfat, providing details on where you're going is likely to elicit the desired directions – the locals, though otherworldly in their spiritual yearnings, are generally a friendly and helpful lot (and many are native English speakers).

Even the geographically gifted visitor is almost sure to get lost in the old city's tangle of alleyways. Most have names (or at least Hebrew-letter designations), but signs are few and far between and in any case few locals use – or even know – the official street names. Making matters worse is the fact that street numbers, where they exist, are not always sequential.

Note: the signs pointing the way to various landmarks are designed to provide directions for cars, not pedestrians.

Tsfat (Safed)

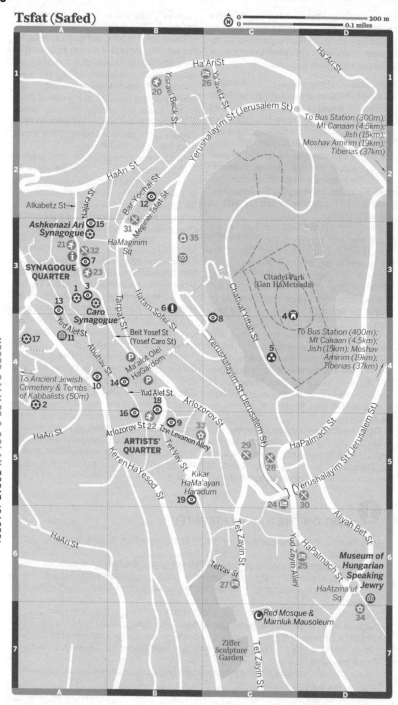

N

0 ——————— 200 m
0 ——————— 0.1 miles

Ha'Ari St

Ha'Ari St

Yisrael Beck St

Ya'avetz St

20

26

Yerushalayim St (Jerusalem St)

To Bus Station (300m);
Mt Canaan (4.5km);
Jish (15km);
Moshav Amirim (19km);
Tiberias (37km)

HaAri St

Alkabetz St →

Bar Yochai St

Meginei Tsfat St

12

35

**Ashkenazi Ari
Synagogue**

15

31

21

32

7

HaMaginim
Sq

Citadel Park
(Gan HaMetsuda)

**SYNAGOGUE
QUARTER**

23

1

3

13

**Caro
Synagogue**

Hatam Sofer St

6

8

Chativat Yiftah St

4

Tarpat St

Yud Alef St

11

17

Beit Yosef St
(Yosef Caro St)

5

To Bus Station (400m);
Mt Canaan (4.5km);
Jish (15km); Moshav
Amirim (19km);
Tiberias (37km)

Abuhav St

Ma'alot Olei
HaGardom

10

14

Yud Alef St

18

Arlozorov St

16

22

9

33

Arlozorov St

Tzvi Levanon Alley

2

To Ancient Jewish
Cemetery & Tombs
of Kabbalists (50m)

HaAri St

**ARTISTS'
QUARTER**

Tet Vav St

29

HaPalmach St

Yerushalayim St (Jerusalem St)

28

Keren HaYesod St

Kikar
HaMa'ayan
Haradum

19

24

30

Aliyah Bet St

HaAri St

Tet Zayin St

TetVav St

27

25

HaPalmach St

Yud Zayin Alley

**Museum of
Hungarian
Speaking
Jewry**

HaAtzma'ut
Sq

34

Tet Zayin St

Red Mosque &
Mamluk Mausoleum

Ziffer
Sculpture
Garden

the Dome of the Rock, a reminder of the Temple in Jerusalem. Note the synagogue is sometimes closed in the morning on Mondays and Thursdays.

Sephardic Ari Synagogue — SYNAGOGUE

(Ha'Ari St; ☉irregular hours, sometimes 10.30-11am Sun-Thu) Tsfat's oldest synagogue – it is mentioned in documents from as far back as 1522 – was frequented by the Ari, who found inspiration in the panoramic views of Mt Meron and the tomb of Shimon bar Yochai. The small alcove on the left in the back is where he is said to have studied mystical texts with the prophet Elijah. Despite its ancient appearance, the present structure is largely the result of rebuilding after the earthquake of 1837.

HaMeiri Museum — MUSEUM

(☎04-697 1307; www.bhm.org.il; 158 Keren Ha-Yesod St; adult/child 6-18yr 20/13NIS; ☉8.30am-2.30pm Sun-Thu, 9.30am-1.30pm Fri) Housed in a 150-year-old building that once served as the seat of Tsfat's rabbinical court, this museum illustrates Jewish life in Tsfat during the 19th and early 20th centuries. Exhibits include unique household and Jewish ritual objects made by local tinsmiths using empty kerosene cans – some even incorporate the Shell logo into the design! Upstairs is a re-creation of a one-room apartment inhabited by a family with six children. The mother got to sleep in the one bed; the shower consisted of a hanging bucket made of reused tin with a showerhead welded to the bottom. Signs are in English. Visitors are asked to check backpacks so they don't knock anything over.

HaMeiri Dairy — DAIRY

(☎04-692 1431; www.hameiri-cheese.co.il; Keren HaYesod St; ☉9am-3pm Sun-Thu, to 1.30pm Fri) Each year this small dairy, run by the same family for six generations, turns about 50,000 litres of sheep's milk into delicious cheeses, including soft and creamy Bulgarian cheese (aged for a full year) and a variety of *gvina Tzfatit* (Tsfat-style cheese; aged for six months) that's harder, saltier and sheepier than the supermarket variety. The dairy sells cheeses – most of which are made from January to June – and runs tours (adult/child 20/15NIS) at noon on Friday; a cafe is planned. Situated 100m to the left as you exit the HaMeiri Museum.

Tsfat (Safed)

Kadosh Dairy
DAIRY

(☎04-692 0326; 34 Yud Alef St; ☺8am-8pm Sun-Thu, to 1hr before sundown Fri) Run by the Kadosh family for seven generations, this microdairy produces minuscule quantities of deliciously sharp, salty *gvina Tzfatit* as well as a variety of other cheeses, including blue cheese. A sampler plate with 10 different cheeses and bread – enough for a meal – costs 30NIS. You can usually watch cheese being made on Sunday, Tuesday and Thursday from 8am to 3pm. To get there from the Synagogue Quarter, follow the signs down the hill to 'Tzefat Cheeze'.

Ma'alot Olei HaGardom
HISTORIC SITE

Leading southwest from the Mandate-era police station on Yerushalayim St, this broad, arrow-straight stairway was built by the British in the late 1930s to serve as a buffer between the Arab community (living mainly in what's now the Artists' Quarter) and the Jewish community (inhabiting the Synagogue Quarter). Much of the rioting of 1929 took place on what is now Tarpat St, which is about halfway down the hill. From the top, look at the rooftop directly across Yerushalayim St and you'll see an old British searchlight.

ARTISTS' QUARTER

The neighbourhood south of the Ma'alot Olei HaGardom stairway used to be Tsfat's Arab quarter, but after the 1948 war the area was developed as an artists' colony. To help things along, the government declared that any artist who was willing to live in Tsfat for at least 180 days a year would be given a free house and gallery.

In the '50s and '60s some of the country's most celebrated painters (Moshe Castel, Yitzhak Frenkel, Simcha Holtzman, Arieh Merzer and Menahem Shemi), inspired by Tsfat's stunning landscapes and mystical traditions, opened studios and held exhibitions in the town. Art-lovers escaped the heat of Tel Aviv and spent their summers holidaying in the city's two dozen hotels.

Most of the galleries and studios around the quarter are open to visitors, with many artists happy to talk about their work and even happier to make a sale. For details on some of the more interesting galleries here and in the Synagogue Quarter, see p226.

General Exhibition
GALLERY

(Ta'arucha Klalit; ☎04-692 0087; Arlozorov St; ☺10am-5pm Sun-Thu, to 6pm daylight savings time, to 2pm Fri & Sat) Opened in 1952, this group gallery – housed in the white-domed, Ottoman-era Market Mosque – displays

(and sells) works by about 50 artists, including some very talented immigrants from the former Soviet Union. If you find yourself intrigued, ask for directions to the particular artist's studio.

ANCIENT JEWISH CEMETERY

The weed-covered, rock-strewn jumble of sun-baked graves below the Synagogue Quarter doesn't look like much, but for followers of Jewish mysticism, the spirits of the great 16th-century Kabbalists buried here make this hillside an exceptional place to connect with the divine spark through prayer and meditation.

A wander through the area is a bit otherworldly at any time, but it's particularly magical in the early evening, when you can walk in the flickering glow of memorial candles, often to the haunting echoes of chanted prayers and psalms.

Anyone who was remotely famous has had their stones painted 'Tsfat blue', a light hue that reminds passers-by that the Kabbalists' spiritual role is to connect the heavens and the earth.

To avoid impure thoughts among the pious men who come to pray in Tsfat's ancient Jewish cemetery, Hebrew signs direct women to separate walkways and platforms. But it's not always clear where you're supposed to go, and even strictly Orthodox people often ignore the contradictory signage, part of a growing trend among some ultra-Orthodox groups to separate the sexes to a degree unprecedented in Jewish history.

If you can't read Hebrew, all you need to know to keep the signs straight is that the word for 'women' (*nashim*, written נשים) includes the letter *Shin*, which looks like a three-branched candelabra.

As at any holy site, visitors should dress modestly.

Ari's Mikveh
RELIGIOUS

(south of the southern end of Ha'Ari St; ☺24hr) A boldface Hebrew sign on the gate reads 'entry for men only' but here the reason is not gynophobia but the fact that inside there are naked men taking a quick, ritually purifying dip in the icy waters of a natural spring. Once used by the Ari, the site is run by the Breslov (Bratzlav) Hassidic movement.

Tombs of the Kabbalists
CEMETERY

(below Ha'Ari St; ☺24hr) The graves of many of Tsfat's greatest sages and Kabbalists are about one-third of the way down the slope, just below a solitary pine tree in an area

TSFAT'S GALLERY SCENE

A retreat and inspiration for Israeli artists since the 1950s, Tsfat is home to one of Israel's largest collections of artists' studios and art galleries, making it the best place in the country (along with Jerusalem) to shop for Judaica (Jewish ritual objects). You'll find jaw-dropping original art, commercial semi-kitsch and everything in between, but almost all the works – illuminated Hebrew manuscripts, jewellery, glasswork, sinuous modern sculpture, oil paintings – are imaginative and upliftingly colourful. Most, in the mystical Hasidic tradition, is also joyous.

Galleries can be found in the Synagogue Quarter along Alkabetz St (stretching south from the Ashkenazi Ari Synagogue) and its southern continuation, Beit Yosef St (Yosef Caro St). More galleries, as well as artists' studios, are hidden away in the Artists' Quarter along the alleys around the General Exhibition, including Tet Vav St.

The galleries mentioned below are listed from north to south.

Kabbalah Art (✆04-697 2702; www.kosmic-kabbalah.com; 38 Bar Yochai St, Synagogue Quarter; ⊙9am-7pm Sun-Thu, to 2hrs before sundown Fri) The art of Denver-born David Friedman uses the mysteries of the Hebrew alphabet, Kabbalistic symbols such as the Tree of Life, and the universal language of colour and geometry to create striking visual representations of Kabbalah. David is happy to give visitors a short introduction to Kabbalah. Situated about 100m northwest of HaMaginim Sq.

Safed Candles (Najara St, Synagogue Quarter; ⊙9.15am-6.45pm Sun-Thu, 9.15am-12.30pm Fri, to 1.45pm Fri in summer) If you've ever wondered how Chanukah and Shabbat candles decorated with stripes, braids and textured layers are made, drop by the candle emporium from 9.15am to 4pm Sunday to Thursday to watch an expert candlemaker at work. Other highlights include the world's largest braided Havdalah candle (it's got 180 strands!) and a gloriously gory mini-diorama showing David holding aloft the severed head of Goliath – a masterwork of kitsch! Situated 50m down an alley from the Ashkenazi Ari Synagogue.

Fig Tree Courtyard (22 Alkabetz St, Synagogue Quarter; ⊙9am-5.30pm or later Sun-Thu, 9am-2pm or 3pm Fri) Set around a centenarian fig tree and a 9m-deep cistern (visible through a glass floor panel), this collection of galleries, opened in 2009, is one of Tsfat's classiest. It's well worth climbing two flights of stairs to the rooftop patio, where you can see half the Galilee, from Mt Meron all the way south to Mt Tabor, with the cliffs of Amud Stream (Nahal Amud) in the depths below. Restrooms available.

Canaan Gallery (www.canaan-gallery.com; 49 Beit Yosef St, Synagogue Quarter; ⊙9am-6pm or later Sun-Thu, 9am-2pm or 3pm Fri) Continuing Tsfat's centuries-old textile tradition, begun by Jews fleeing the Inquisition, Orna and Yair Moore's studio produces richly textured tapestries, wall hangings and Jewish ritual objects made from cotton and chenille. You can see weavers at work from 9am to 5pm Sunday to Thursday. The gorgeous view takes in Amud Stream.

Safed Craft Pottery (✆04-697 4970, 054-434 5206; www.haaripottery.blogspot.com; 63 Yud Alef St, Artists' Quarter; ⊙10am-6pm Sun-Thu, to 3hrs before sundown Fri) UK-born potter Daniel Flatauer works in the English studio pottery tradition, producing tableware, kitchenware and Judaica that is both functional and extraordinarily beautiful. He has the only salt kiln in Israel – if you're not sure what that means, ask him!

Sheva Chaya Gallery (✆04-699 9687; www.shevachaya.com; 7 Tet Vav St, Artists' Quarter; ⊙9am-5pm Sun-Thu, to 2pm Fri) Denver-born painter and glass-blower Sheva Chaya Shaiman represents Kabbalistic concepts and women's themes in Judaism in her art. She does glass-blowing demonstrations most days in July and August (and for groups the rest of the year). Across the street from the General Exhibition.

Tzfat Gallery of Mystical Art (✆04-692 3051; www.kabbalahart.com; 35 Tet Vav St, Artists' Quarter) Avraham Loewenthal, who hails from Detroit, is happy to explain the symbolism of his colourful, abstract works, which are based on Kabbalistic concepts. Situated across the street from HaMa'ayan HaRadum Sq.

where the converging double walkways are covered with transparent roofing. If you can't read Hebrew, ask passers-by for help in finding the tombs of Yitzhak Luria (Isaac Luria; born in Jerusalem in 1534, died in Tsfat in 1572), aka HaAri, the father of modern Jewish mysticism (Lurianic Kabbalah); and Shlomo Alkabetz (born in Thessalonica c 1500, died in Tsfat in 1580), best known for composing the hymn 'Lecha Dodi'.

Yosef Karo (born in Toledo in 1488, died in Tsfat in 1575), the most important codifier of Jewish law, is buried about 100m further down the hill.

ELSEWHERE AROUND TOWN

Citadel Park　　　　　　　　　PARK
(Gan HaMetsuda; Chativat Yiftach St; ⊘24hr) The highest point in Tsfat (834m), now a breeze-cooled park, was once part of the largest Crusader fortress in the Middle East (its outer walls followed the line now marked by Jerusalem St). The ruins of one of the inner walls can be seen along Chativat Yiftach St, near the park's southern tip. Footpaths lead up to the ridge line, which affords panoramic views in all directions.

Yerushalayim Street　　　　HISTORIC SITE
(Jerusalem St) Tsfat's main commercial thoroughfare, lined with shops and eateries, was the scene of intense Arab–Jewish fighting in the spring of 1948.

About 50m south of City Hall, the Davidka Monuments recalls the role played by the ungainly, notoriously inaccurate Davidka mortar in sowing panic among the Arab population, possibly because of rumours that its 40kg warhead was an atomic bomb. Nearby, a free audio guide tells the dramatic tale of the battle for Tsfat in 1947 and 1948 – from the Israeli perspective, of course.

Across the street is the former British police station, riddled with bulletholes from 1948.

Museum of Hungarian Speaking Jewry　　　　　　MUSEUM
(☑04-692 3880; www.hjm.org.il; HaAzma'ut Square; admission 15NIS, incl tour 30NIS; ⊘9am-2pm Sun-Thu, to 1pm Fri) The museum has a rich collection of evocative artefacts, photographs and documents that do a masterful job of evoking the lost world of pre-WWII Hungarian-speaking Jewry. A 17-minute film provides context. If you're interested, museum co-founder (with her husband) Chava Lustig will tell you about the Budapest ghetto, which she survived as a 14-year-old. The museum has extensive archives for those interested in doing family research. Signs are in Hebrew, Hungarian and English.

Courses

A variety of organisations work to connect Jews – and, in some cases, non-Jewish travellers as well – with Jewish mysticism and traditional Hasidic life. For a list of options, see the Learning Centers section of http://safed.co.il.

Note that some places have an agenda (turning secular Jews into Orthodox ones) that they're not completely above-board about, so while questioning is ostensibly encouraged, those in search of frank, truly open give-and-take may be disappointed.

Tzfat Kabbalah Center　　　KABBALAH
(International Center for Tzfat Kabbalah; www.tzfat-kabbalah.org; 1st fl, Fig Tree Courtyard, 18 Alkabetz St, Synagogue Quarter; ⊘9am-6pm Sun-Thu, to 1pm Fri) Adherents of all religions, or none at all, are welcome to drop by for an introduction to Jewish mysticism and on-the-spot meditation. Hour-long personalised workshops with Eyal Riess, who lectures around the world on the Tsfat Kabbalah tradition, cost 100NIS to 200NIS. Screens films (15NIS) on Tsfat in Hebrew, English, Spanish and Russian.

Livnot U'Lehibanot　　　　JEWISH
(☑052-429 5377; www.livnot.com; Alkabetz St, Synagogue Quarter) Offers young Jewish adults classes, hikes, inexpensive accommodation and community service opportunities. Orthodox-run but low-pressure. The name means 'to build and be built'.

Ascent Institute of Safed　　KABBALAH
(☑04-692 1364; www.ascentofsafed.com; 2 Ha'Ari St; ⊘classes at 9.15am, noon & 8.30pm Sun-Thu) Offers Jews interested in 'spiritual discovery' drop-in classes on the Torah and Jewish mysticism. Run by members of the Chabad Hasidic movement.

☞ Tours

While it's easy to float around Tsfat on your own little trip, it's a town where stories and secrets run deep. If you don't take a tour, you might want to pick up a copy of Yisrael Shalem's *Safed: Six Guided Tours in and Around the Mystical City*, available at Eliezer's House of Books (p234).

Baruch Emanuel Erdstein　　WALKING
(☑052-251 5134; www.safedexperience.com; per hr 180NIS) Offers spiritual walking tours, generally of three to five hours. Baruch, a

storyteller and musician who grew up near Detroit, describes Tsfat as having a 'tremendous gift' to offer, a place that 'opens people up to themselves, to their potential and to beginning to understand the meaning of their lives and of creation'.

Path of the Heart
WALKING

(B'Shvil HaLev, Tzfat Experience; ☏04-682 6489, 050 750 5695; www.shvilhalev.co.il; 20 Yud Zayin St, Artists' Quarter; 2hr tour 550NIS) Runs experiential walking tours of the old city accompanied by tales of the Kabbalists and an exploration of their spiritual message. Call at least two hours ahead.

Aviva Minoff
GUIDED

(☏04-692 0901, 050-540 9187; minoff@netvision.net.il; 2½hr tour from 200NIS) New York-raised Aviva, a fully licensed, veteran guide who's active in Tsfat's Conservative synagogue, tailors her tours to individual interests such as archaeology, history and mysticism.

✦ Festivals

Tsfat Klezmer Festival
MUSIC

(www.klezmerf.com) The squares and alleys of the old city come alive with Eastern European Jewish soul music. It's open from 8am until late for three days in August. Accommodation is in short supply so book way ahead.

🛏 Sleeping

Carmel Hotel
HOTEL $$

(☏04-692 0053; 8 Ha'Ari St, ie 8 Ya'avetz St; s/d/q US$75/100/150; ❄@🛜) Thanks to owner Shlomo, who may insist that you try his etrog (a type of citron) confiture and limoncello liqueur, staying here is like having the run of a big, old family house. The 12 smallish rooms aren't romantic but they're clean and practical; all but one have a glass-enclosed balcony. Don't miss the century-old grapevine on the lobby balcony.

Ruth Rimonim
HOTEL $$$

(☏04-699 4666; www.rimonim.com; Tet Zayin St, Artists' Quarter; d 850-1350NIS; ❄@🛜🛁) Housed in part in a converted Ottoman-era post house, this hotel has stone-walled common areas with wrought iron furnishings and fresh-cut flowers, a spa and 78 elegant, modern rooms with sparkling marble bathrooms.

Artist Quarter Guest House
B&B $$

(☏077-524 0235, 050-410 7469; www.artistquarterguesthouse.com; 43 Yud Zayin Alley, Artists' Quarter; d 400NIS; ❄🛜) The two stone-walled units

run by Northern Californians Joy and Evan mix 19th-century charm with modern mod-cons, including fridges and kitchenettes. Women's Swedish massage available. Rates are higher (double 450NIS) on Fridays.

Beit Yosef Suites
B&B $$$

(☏04-692 2515; www.beityosef.co.il; d without breakfast 650NIS, additional person 100NIS; ❄🛜) Dotted throughout the old city, these eight family-friendly suites and one three-bedroom house – run by a family from Los Angeles – are cosily decorated in a mix of French provincial and Middle Eastern boho. Reserve by phone or online; when you arrive, someone will meet you with the key.

Adler Apartments
STUDIO APARTMENTS $

(☏052-344 7766; office at 88 Yerushalayim St; badler@013.net.il; d without breakfast 300NIS, Fri night & all day Sat 350NIS; ❄) Ten clean rooms with kitchenette and fridge (some also have a Jacuzzi) in or near the centre of town.

MT CANAAN

Back before air-conditioning, 950m-high Mt Canaan (Har Kna'an) – now a neighbourhood of Tsfat – offered a welcome escape from the summer heat. The area is about 4.5km from the city centre.

TOP CHOICE Safed Inn
GUESTHOUSE $$

(Ruckenstein B&B; ☏04-697 1007; www.safedinn.com; cnr HaGdud HaShlishi St & Merom Kna'an St; dm/s/d/q without breakfast 100/300/400/500NIS, deluxe 400NIS; ⏱reception open 8am-8pm; ❄@🛜) A world away from the old city, this popular guesthouse – a great place to meet other travellers – is surrounded by lush gardens, where you'll find a sauna and outdoor hot tub (open 6.30pm to 11pm). Rooms here good-quality mattresses and linens; deluxe rooms come with Jacuzzi. Riki and Dov are affable hosts who get rave reviews for their local knowledge and tasty Continental/Israeli breakfasts (25/50NIS). Bike hire is available for 40NIS. If you don't have a car, there's not much to do out here on Shabbat. Call ahead if you'll be arriving after 8pm. To get here from the centre, take local bus 3 (4.40NIS; once or twice an hour until 9pm, no buses from 2.30pm Fri until Sunday morning) and get off at 'HaPikud'. A daytime taxi from the centre of town should cost about 25NIS.

🍴 Eating

Fast food is easy to find. On the edge of the Synagogue Quarter, tiny eateries selling pizza, felafel and shwarma can be found at HaMaginim Sq; several more are strung out along Yerushalayim St.

All of central Tsfat's restaurants close on Shabbat, so other than self-catering, your only option is to reserve (and pay in advance) for a kosher meal at a hotel restaurant, like Ruth Rimonim Hotel, where a buffet lunch or dinner costs 130NIS.

For picnic supplies, head to **Pashut Zol Supermarket** (102 Arlozoroff St; ⊘7.30am-8pm Sun-Wed, to 9pm Thu, to 2pm Fri).

Gan Eden
ITALIAN $$$

(☑04-697 2434; 33 HaGdud HaShlishi St, Mt Canaan; mains 69-87NIS; ⊘9am-10.30pm Sun-Thu, to 2.30pm Fri) It's worth the 3km ride from the centre (about 20NIS by taxi) for the scrumptious antipasti and oven-baked fish, prepared under the supervision of chef Rafi; and the fabulous desserts (35NIS), many of them chocolate-based, made by his wife, pastry chef Yael. Occupies an early-20th-century house with a lovely garden and views to Mt Meron. Kosher-dairy.

Maximilian
CAFE $$

(2 Arlozoroff St, Artists' Quarter; mains 39-80NIS; ⊘7am-7pm Sun-Thu Oct-Mar, to midnight Apr-Sep, to 1/2hr before sundown Fri; 🛜) Serves a range of tasty pastas, quiches (48NIS), salads and freshly squeezed juices as well as creative fare such as figs (fresh when in season) filled with local goat's cheese and topped with a berry sauce. Has a sunny courtyard. Situated right next to the General Exhibition.

Tree of Life Vegetarian Cafe
VEGETARIAN $$

(HaMaginim Sq, Synagogue Quarter; mains 38-48NIS; ⊘9am-10pm Sun-Thu, to midnight or later in summer, to 2hrs before sundown Fri; 🥗) If you're in the mood for something very healthy – portobello mushroom quiche, for instance, or quinoa pilaf, or whole-grain desserts sweetened with organic date syrup – LA-raised Feiga and her tiny, partly-vegan eatery may be the perfect destination. Some dishes are gluten-free.

HaAri 8
ISRAELI $$

(☑04-692 0053; 8 Ha'Ari St; mains 48-118NIS; ⊘noon-10pm or 11pm Sun-Thu, closed Fri, opens after sundown Sat) Serves grilled meats, fish and veggie burgers under stone arches; also has a good selection of vegetarian side dishes. Situated under the Carmel Hotel.

Yemenite Food Bar
YEMENITE $

(18 Alkabetz St, Synagogue Quarter; mains 25-33NIS; ⊘8.30am-7pm or 8pm Sun-Thu, to midnight May-early Sep, to 2hrs before sunset Fri) Decked out in a gown and kaftan that Abraham might have worn, Ronen flips pan-fried 'Yemenite pizza' called *lachuch*.

Felafel Ta'amim
FELAFEL $

(85 Yerushalayim St, Artists' Quarter; felafel 10NIS) Cheap and tasty.

Rafi Laffa
SHWARMA $

(Yerushalayim St, Artists' Quarter) One of two shwarma places underneath the Palmach St overpass.

☆ Entertainment

Back in the 1970s Tsfat had half-a-dozen nightclubs, but these days the city goes to bed fairly early, except in summer when tourists keep the old city's streets and cafes lively until late.

Almost everything is closed on Shabbat – except, of course, for the synagogues, some of which sing their prayers in the tradition of **Shlomo Carlebach** (http://carlebach.intzfat.info) or hold Chabad-style *farbrengen* (joyous community gatherings).

🔝CHOICE Khan of the White Donkey
CULTURAL EVENTS

(☑077-234 5719; www.thekhan.org, www.halevav.org; 5 Tzvi Levanon Alley, Synagogue Quarter) This pluralistic cultural centre hosts a variety of cultural, environmental and health-oriented community activities, including concerts (30NIS to 90NIS) or open-stage jam sessions on Thursday at 8pm or 8.30pm; yoga classes in English and Hebrew three mornings a week; and a low-cost holistic medicine clinic on Monday night and Tuesday. The hot tub may be available for underwater childbirth. The alternative vibe attracts a mix of hippies, backpackers and strictly observant Jews. It occupies a 700-year-old khan (caravanserai), beautifully restored with all-natural materials in 2009, that can be visited Sunday to Thursday from 9am to 4pm.

Yigal Alon Cultural Centre
CULTURAL EVENTS

(☑04-686 9600/1; HaPalmach St, Artists' Quarter) Hosts occasional cultural events and concerts. Renovations should be completed by mid-2012.

🛍 Shopping

Eliezer's House of Books
BOOKS

(37 Yerushalayim St, Synagogue Quarter; ⊘9.30am-2pm Sun-Thu, to 1pm Fri) Sells books on Judaism in Hebrew, English, French, Spanish and

UPPER GALILEE & GOLAN TSFAT (SAFED)

Russian. If you don't have room for the entire Zohar in your suitcase, they ship worldwide.

ℹ Information

Adler Internet (88 Yerushalayim St; per hr 15NIS; ⊙10am-1am Sun-Thu, to 1½hr before sundown Fri) Tsfat's only cybercafe has four computers. Can also change money. Situated under the Palmach St bridge.

ATMs Can be found at banks along Yerushalayim St, at Nos 34, 35 and 72.

Kappell Visitors Centre (☏04-692 4427; laurie@livnot.com; 17 Alkabetz St, Synagogue Quarter; ⊙8.30am-4pm Sun-Thu) English-speaking Laurie is happy to provide information on visiting Tsfat and on local volunteering opportunities. There's a 10-minute video on the history of the city, and you can explore the 500-year-old rooms and ritual bath discovered under the centre. Run by Livnot U'Lehibanot (www.livnot.com), an organisation that seeks to bring young Jewish people closer to their heritage.

Post office (37 Yerushalayim St)

Rivka Ziv Hospital (Sieff Hospital, Ziv Medical Center; ☏04-682 8811; www.ziv.org.il; HaRambam St; ⊙emergency 24hr) Founded in 1910, this large government hospital is 3km southwest of the central bus station. Served by buses 6 and 7.

Safed.co.il (www.safed.co.il) Informative website covering history, things to see, accommodation, study options and some colourful local personalities.

ℹ Getting There & Away

The **central bus station** (www.bus.co.il; HaAtzma'ut St), situated about 700m west of the Synagogue Quarter, is linked to Tiberias (Veolia bus 450; 14.90NIS, one hour), Jerusalem (Egged bus 982; 40NIS, seven daily Sunday to Thursday, two on Friday morning), Haifa (Egged bus 361; two hours, twice an hour) and Kiryat Shmona (mainly Nateev Express bus 511; 20.70NIS, 40 minutes, a dozen daily Sunday to Thursday, eight on Friday) via Rosh Pina (10.20NIS, five minutes) and the Hula Valley.

Tellingly, there are a lot more direct buses to the ultra-Orthodox Tel Aviv suburb of Bnei Brak than to Tel Aviv itself (Egged bus 845; three hours, two daily Sunday to Thursday, one on Friday morning). In fact, to get to Tel Aviv it's faster to take Egged bus 361 to Akko and then hop on a train.

Mt Meron Area

West of Tsfat, antenna-topped Mt Meron (1204m), Israel's second-tallest peak (after Mt Hermon), looms over the Dalton Plateau and scattered Jewish, Druze and Arab villages.

Until recently, the area was planted with deciduous fruit trees such as pear and apple, but more and more land is being given over to grapevines for the thriving wineries of Ramat Dalton, sometimes called (with some exaggeration) the 'Israeli Napa Valley' or 'Israel's Tuscany'.

MOSHAV AMIRIM اميريم אמירים

Founded in 1958 by pioneers of the Israeli vegetarian movement, Amirim (elevation 600m) is still 100% veggie – no one here cooks, eats or serves meat, fowl or fish. Set on the southeastern slopes of Mt Meron, the moshav is known for its excellent organic food and rustic guesthouses – a beautiful place to bliss out. Everything here is well signposted.

◉ Sights & Activities

Walking around Amirim is like wandering into a fairy tale, with gingerbread-looking houses and cosy restaurants tucked into the woods at the end of lantern-lit paths. Even the swimming pool (open July and August) is situated in an enchanting canyon. Trails lead into the nearby Mt Meron Nature Reserve.

Artists' galleries are dotted around the village and there's a sculpture park in the centre of the moshav.

Many locals are as passionate about alternative medicine as they are about vegetarianism, and yoga teachers, shiatsu practitioners and naturopaths abound.

☐ Sleeping

Amirim has about 160 *tzimmer* (B&B) rooms.

TOP CHOICE **Ohn Bar Guesthouse** GUESTHOUSE $$
(☏04-698 9803; www.amirim.com; d without breakfast 290-1050NIS, additional child 50NIS; ✳@⊛) A US-trained architect with an interest in green design, Ohn – an excellent source of information on the area – warmly welcomes guests. Perched on a terraced hillside, his 14 wooden units come with balcony, Jacuzzi and fully-equipped kitchenette. Outside, hammocks swing among the fruit trees and there's an organic vegetable garden. Breakfast costs 100NIS per couple. Discounts are offered if you stay three or more nights, are a student or arrive by public transport. Wheelchair accessible.

Campbell Family Guest Rooms B&B $$
(☏04-698 9045; alitamirim@hotmail.com; d from 400NIS; ✳) Friendly British-expat Phillip

Campbell and his wife Alit rent out four rooms, two with Jacuzzi. In addition to being a good source of information on Amirim and surrounds, they function as something of a clearing house for local sleeping options. Let them know your specific requirements or preferences – rustic, luxury, romantic – and they'll be happy to put you in touch with local B&B owners.

✖ Eating

Amirim has half-a-dozen strictly vegetarian and vegan restaurants. Having breakfast/dinner delivered to your B&B generally costs 100/200NIS per couple.

Rishikesh   INDIAN $$

(☎052-578 4114; set meal 65NIS; ☺2-11pm; ✔) Chef Sono, who hails from the vegetarian city of Rishikesh in India's far north, cooks up tasty pappadam, dhal, biryani with cashew nuts, and lots of vegetable dishes made with spices he brings back from India. Small and cheerful.

Dalia's Restaurant   VEGETARIAN $$

(☎04-698 9349/3; breakfast 45NIS, brunch 60NIS, lunch & dinner menu 65-100NIS; ☺8am-9pm; ✔) Dalia serves a hearty set menu featuring soups, stuffed vegetables, 'meatballs' made of almonds and peanuts, and delicious salads. With its sunny terrace overlooking the Sea of Galilee, it's a relaxing place for a long meal. Children under six eat for free.

Stupp's   VEGETARIAN $$

(☎04-698 0946; mains 46-57NIS; ☺9am-10pm Sun-Thu, to 2hr before sundown Fri; ✔) Situated in a log cabin near the entrance to Amirim, this *mehadrin* (extra strict) kosher restaurant – run by a woman who grew up in Arnprior, Ontario – serves a variety of creative dishes. If you're not in the mood for a veggie cheeseburger (57NIS), try the 'meal-in-one' (stir-fried veggies with brown rice, tofu and a homemade soy burger). Breakfast (110NIS per couple) is served until noon.

☆ Entertainment

Hemdat Yamim   MUSIC

(☎04-698 9423; www.hemdatyamim.com, in Hebrew; Moshav Shefer) A much beloved music venue, with frequent concerts of Israeli pop, jazz, Western classical etc, especially on Thursday, Friday and Saturday. Situated across Rte 866 from Amirim.

❶ Getting There & Away

Egged 361 (twice hourly) links Amirim with Haifa's Bay Center Intercity Terminal (26.50NIS,

1-1/4 hours) and Tsfat (15.40NIS, 20 minutes). To get to Tel Aviv, take bus 361 to Akko's train station and continue by rail.

JISH   الجش   גוש חלב

The only village in Israel with a Maronite (Eastern Catholic) majority, the serene, hillside village of Jish (population 3000) was settled by migrants from Lebanon in the 18th and 19th centuries. Today, it is the site of a pioneering effort to revive the use of Aramaic, the language of Jesus and an important source of identity for Maronites.

During the Great Jewish Revolt (66–70 BCE), Jish – then, as now, known in Hebrew as Gush Halav – was the last place in the Galilee to fall to the Romans, according to Josephus Flavius.

◉ Sights & Activities

Near the entrance to the village, you can visit a large, modern Maronite church and the tombs of Shamaiya and Avtalion, Jewish sages who served on the Sanhedrin in Jerusalem during the 1st century BCE. In a small valley 2km east of the village, hikers can explore the remains of an ancient synagogue (3rd or 4th century) amid gorgeous fig and olive groves.

A paved, 2.5km hiking and cycling path known as the Coexistence Trail (wheelchair accessible) links Jish with Moshav Dalton via Dalton Reservoir.

Local farmers let visitors pick their own cherries (May) and apples (late August to October).

✖ Eating

Several restaurants serve authentic Lebanese cuisine.

TOP CHOICE Misedet HaArazim   LEBANESE $$

(☎04-698 7762; Rte 90; mains 52-98NIS; ☺10am-10pm or 11pm; ✔) Scrumptious offerings include 10 kinds of hummus, stuffed grape leaves (45NIS), grilled meats and *shishbarak* (meat dumplings in goat yoghurt sauce; 50NIS). A selection of 20 different veggie salads costs 40NIS per person (30NIS if you order a main dish; minimum two people). Situated at the entrance to Jish; the sign features a green cedar of Lebanon.

Baladna   GALILEE ARAB $$

(☎04-699 1151; mains 40-70NIS; ☺10am-2am) An atmospheric restaurant, ensconced in two 19th-century stone houses, which specialises in Galilee-style Arab cuisine, including *shishbarak* (40NIS). Also serves pork

WINERY TOURS

Israeli wines are attracting growing attention on the world wine scene – and winning top international awards. Among those that are kosher, the best are not *mevushal* (flash pasteurised), a process that can devastate a wine's delicate nuances.

The country now has about 220 wineries, 90 of them within a 40-minute drive of Rosh Pina. The Golan, with its well-drained volcanic soils, cool breezes, varied elevations and microclimates, is home to 27 of them.

Quite a few Galilee and Golan wineries are happy to welcome visitors. To create your own 'wine route', you could visit (listed alphabetically):

Adir Winery (p237)

Bahat Winery (p249)

Bazelet Hagolan Winery (p250)

Dalton Winery (p237)

Golan Heights Winery (p245)

Odem Mountain Winery (p251)

Wine connoisseurs might want to look out for two excellent wine guides: *The Ultimate Rogov's Guide to Israeli Wines* (Daniel Rogov, 2012) is a comprehensive guide by Israel's premier wine critic, who died in late 2011, and *The Wine Route of Israel* (Yaron Goldfisher and Eliezer Sacks, 2006), with a new edition rumoured to be in the works.

Useful websites covering the Israeli wine scene include www.wines-israel.co.il and www.israelwines.co.il (in Hebrew).

Shiri Bistro & Wine Bar (p239) in Rosh Pina is a great place to taste hard-to-find boutique vintages. It also offers wine tours.

schnitzel (50NIS) and seven cocktails (35NIS to 40NIS). Situated 600m up the main street from the town entrance.

🛏 Sleeping

Ruah Glilit　　　　　　　　　　　　B&B $$

(☑04-698 7240, 052-281 0433; swojish@yahoo.com; d 450NIS) George Samaan, a well-known musician (you can see him on YouTube) who often appears with Ehud Banai, and his wife Eva offer guests a warm, musical welcome in a cosy sitting room outfitted with an upright piano, an old gramophone and a wood-burning stove. The three upstairs rooms feature wooden balconies and gorgeous views. Situated 600m up the main street from the entrance to town.

❶ Getting There & Away

Jish is 13km northeast of Tsfat, right where Rte 89 does a 90 degree turn.

RAMAT DALTON

The area around Moshav Dalton, known as Ramat Dalton (Dalton Plateau), produces some highly regarded wines. Several wineries do their thing in the Ramat Dalton Industrial Park, 4km northeast of Jish on Rte 886.

🏃 Activities

Dalton Winery　　　　　　　　　　　WINERY

(☑04-698 7683; www.dalton-winery.com; Ramat Dalton Industrial Park; admission 15NIS; ⊙9am-5pm Sun-Thu, to 2pm Fri, to 3pm in summer) Using cabernet sauvignon, merlot, petit syrah, shiraz and zinfandel grapes, this winery produces about one million bottles a year. It has a log-cabin-style tasting centre across the car park from the modern production facilities. Offers 45-minutes tours (call ahead if you can).

Adir Winery　　　　　　　　　　　　WINERY

(☑04-699 1039; www.adir-winery.com; Ramat Dalton Industrial Park; ⊙9am-5pm Sun-Thu, to 3pm Fri, closes later in summer) At the all-white visitors centre, you can sample Adir's award-winning wines (25NIS; free if you buy a bottle); production is just 80,000 bottles a year. It also has a cheese shop that serves sublime frozen yoghurt (5NIS to 20NIS for a cup) and ice cream made with goat's milk. Breakfast (100NIS for two), based on goat cheeses, is served from 9am to 1pm.

Butterfly　　　　　　　　　　　　BREWERY

(☑04-699 1079; www.bfbeers.com, in Hebrew; Ramat Dalton Industrial Park; ⊙8am-5pm Sun-Thu, 10am-2pm Fri, to 4pm or 5pm in summer) A

Belgian-style microbrewery that offers tours and tastings (15NIS) of its sunset (wheat), brown (toasted oats), blond (oats) and pink (pomegranate-fortified) premium ale beers.

BAR'AM بِرعم ברעם

Site of a well-to-do village from the 1st to the 7th centuries CE, **Bar'am National Park** (☏04-698 9301; adult/child 14/7NIS; ☉8am-5pm Apr-Oct, to 4pm Nov-Mar, closes 1hr earlier Fri) is best known for its impressive Talmudic period synagogue, solidly built of finely hewn limestone around the year 400 CE. It is surrounded by fields and a grove of cypress trees.

At the top of the hill stands a church that's still used by the former residents of the Maronite village of Bir'am, evacuated by the Israeli army 'for two weeks' during the 1948 war.

Nateev Express bus 367 (every two hours), which links Tsfat with Nahariya, stops at Hiram Jct, 3km south of here.

TOMB OF THE RASHBY هر ميرون ميرون جبل הר מירון

Authorship of the *Zohar*, the most important work of Kabbalah, is traditionally credited to the 2nd century CE Jewish sage Rabbi Shimon bar Yochai, who is often known by his acronym, the Rashby (Rashbi). (Scholars believe the work was compiled in Spain in the 13th century.) By tradition, the **tomb of the Rashby** (Rte 866; ☉24hr) is 5km northwest of Tsfat on the slopes on Mt Meron, somewhere under a rigorously sex-segregated complex that appears to date, in part, from the Crusader period. Since his precise burial place is unknown, there is no actual tomb, just a *tziun* (marker) – inside a multialcove synagogue – above which candles flicker behind opaque glass.

Other important sages some believe are buried in the immediate vicinity include the Rashby's son Rabbi Elazar; the renowned 1st-century BCE sage Hillel the Elder, who summed up Judaism with the single commandment 'What is hateful to thee, do not unto thy fellow man'; and Hillel's great rival in legal disputations, Shammai.

On the eve of the holiday of Lag BaOmer, tens of thousands of mostly Haredi pilgrims flock to the tomb of the Rashby, spending the whole night in fervent prayer, with singing and dancing around bonfires. Some pilgrims perform a ceremony known as Upsherin in Yiddish and Halaaka in Judeo-Arabic, at which three-year-old boys are given their first haircuts.

The Rashby's blue-domed grave complex, situated inside the Orthodox Moshav Meron (gate locked on Shabbat and Jewish holidays), is run rather chaotically by squabbling Haredi groups. Adding to the hair-trigger atmosphere is the fact that the complex serves as a place of refuge for homeless people (some with psychiatric issues), criminals recently released from prison and even people on the run from the police. To get to the tomb you have to run a gauntlet of beggars. Non-Jews, as well as anyone who's not modestly dressed or who arrives on Shabbat, may encounter hostility, as did Madonna, who had rocks thrown at her. The situation is unlikely to improve until the Israeli government implements a plan – mandated by the courts but opposed by some Haredi factions – to take over management of the site.

KADITA

The tiny, out-of-the way settlement of Kadita has an ecological philosophy and a hippy vibe.

Artsy, rustic **Bikta BeKadita** (☏04-692 1963; www.kadita.co.il; cabins US$130-462; ❄) has five eclectic cabins for two to four people. It's full of dogs, cats, chickens and highly vocal frogs and has incredibly friendly hosts who serve up lavish homemade breakfasts. There's also wine from Kadita's own vineyard. It's perched high on a hillside 4.5km northeast of Meron Jct.

Rosh Pina راس بينه ראש פינה

☏04 / POP 2700

Rosh Pina's 19th-century stone houses, oozing with charm, were discovered years ago by Tel Aviv chicsters. The town now plays host to artists' studios and some of the most upscale sleeping and dining in the Upper Galilee.

◉ Sights

Rosh Pina Pioneers
Restoration Site   HISTORIC SITE

Settled in the 1870s by Jews from Tsfat and from 1882 by immigrants from Romania, Rosh Pina's old town – just three short cobblestone streets, one of them, with Henry Jamesian pretension, called HaBlvd – has been turned into a pedestrian zone. Visitors can explore the quiet lanes, lined with pretty, restored (and unrestored) stone houses, visit the old synagogue and pop into about 15 galleries (☉10am-5pm, later in Jul & Aug) selling jewellery, ceramics and paintings. In **Professor Mer's House** (1887) there's a small museum with exhibits on Rosh Pina's early years.

Follow the signs to the Baron's Garden (founded 1886), across HaRishonim St from Shiri Bistro; and the Old Cemetery (via Ben Arich St).

The Pioneers Restoration Site is at the upper edge of Rosh Pina at the top of HaRishonim St, which heads up the hill from the roundabout on Old Rte 90,

Nimrod Lookout　　　　　　　VIEWPOINT
(☉24hr) At the top of town, next to an ancient fig tree, this memorial elevation (503m) offers fantastic views. It was established in memory of Nimrod Segev, a 29-year-old computer programmer killed in the Second Lebanon War. Like other Israeli memorials for war dead, it is highly personal – an audio guide tells his story. At dusk you can often hear the cries of jackals.

🛏 Sleeping

Rosh Pina's 500 B&B rooms, easy to find online, have created a market glut so prices have dropped a bit in recent years.

Villa Tehila　　　　　　　B&B $$$
(☏04-693 7788; www.villa-tehila.co.il, in Hebrew; HaHalutzim St; d from 630NIS; ❄@🖥🌊) You're likely to spot a few old-time Israeli celebrities at this fabulous B&B, whose shaded, 19th-century stone courtyards shelter bubbling fountains, glittering fairy lights, stained glass, a veritable menagerie, a cosy bar – and, during the British Mandate, a secret weapons cache. Villa Tehila has 11 rooms, all of them exquisite. Book well ahead. Situated 150m down the hill from the Restoration Site.

Pina BaRosh　　　　　　　B&B $$$
(☏04-693 6582; HaHalutzim St; www.pinabarosh.com; d weekday/weekend from 550/700NIS; ❄🖥) Arrayed around the central courtyard of a one-time livestock yard, with seven atmospheric rooms (there's also a luxury villa) featuring vaulted ceilings, Jacuzzis and exposed stone- and brickwork. Breakfast is served until 1pm.

Hotel Mizpe Hayamim　　　　RESORT $$$
(☏04-699 4555; reservations 1-800-555 666; www.mizpe-hayamim.com; d incl half-board US$430-610; ❄@🖥🌊) One of Israel's most exclusive hotels, this plush hillside establishment is set in 15 hectares of gorgeous gardens. Amenities include a spa offering saunas, Jacuzzis, massages and beauty treatments; a 25m heated indoor pool; and an acclaimed French gourmet restaurant, Muscat, that uses mostly home-grown organic ingredients. The 96 rooms are as comfortable as they are romantic – in both cases, very. Mobile phone use is prohibited in public areas. Situated 3km towards Tsfat from Rosh Pina along Rte 8900.

🍴 Eating & Drinking

Rosh Pina has about 50 places to eat. Some are hidden away behind the old houses of the Pioneers Restoration Site, others are 1.5km down the hill in the modern Centre HaGalil mall along Rte 90.

Shiri Bistro & Wine Bar　　BISTRO $$$
(☏04-693 6582; www.pinabarosh.com; Pina BaRosh B&B, HaHalutzim St; mains 65-135NIS; ☉8.30am-11.30pm; 🗪) Fresh-cut flowers, white tablecloths and flickering candles in red glass holders greet you at this Mediterranean-inflected French bistro, named after the chef, whose great-great-great-great-grandparents built the place in the late 1870s. Blessed with spectacular views, this is an excellent place to sample rare Israeli boutique wines – at least 40 Galilee and Golan wines are available by the glass.

Amburger　　　　　　　BURGERS $$
(☏04-680 0044; Centre HaGalil mall, Rte 90; mains 41-159NIS; ☉11.30am-midnight; 🗪) An excellent choice for burgers (41NIS to 61NIS), steaks (porterhouse will set you back 159NIS) and other meaty dishes, most of them made with aged Golan-raised meat (though the entrecôte is from Uruguay). Has pasta for vegetarians.

Tangerine　　　　　　　　BAR
(☉8pm-2am or 3am) Down a stairway from the Pioneers Restoration Site, this vaulted pub – run by local blokes – has live concerts twice a month, usually on Saturday night.

ℹ Information

The Centre HaGalil mall on Rte 90 at the entrance to the town has several banks with ATMs, a pharmacy, a Steimatzky bookshop and two petrol stations.

ℹ Getting There & Away

All long-haul buses to/from the Hula Valley and Kiryat Shmona (eg from Tiberias) pass by the entrance to Rosh Pina on Rte 90, from where it's 1.5km up the hill to the Pioneers Restoration Site.

Nateev Express bus 511 (a dozen daily Sunday to Thursday, eight on Friday), which takes Rte 8900 and thus passes near the outskirts of Pioneers Restoration Site, goes up the hill to Tsfat (10.20NIS, five minutes), and north to Kiryat Shmona via the Hula Valley.

Around Rosh Pina

TEL HATZOR

At **Tel Hatzor** (Tel Hazor; 04-693 7290; adult/child 21/9NIS; 8am-5pm during daylight savings, to 4pm rest of year, last entry 30 min before closing) – a Unesco World Heritage site since 2005 – archaeologists have uncovered no less than 21 layers of settlement from the 3rd millennium BCE to 732 BCE, when the Israelite city, whose 10th-century BCE gate, which may have been built by Solomon, was destroyed by the Assyrians. In times of siege, the supply of water was ensured by an extraordinary underground system whose 40m-deep shaft is accessible via a spiral staircase. Signage is excellent.

The tel is 7km north of Rosh Pina on Old Rte 90. From Rte 90, get off at Ayelet HaShahar; the access road is about 400m south of the kibbutz, site of the **Hazor Museum** (Fri, Sat & holidays), which displays finds from Tel Hatzor.

Hula Valley

وادي الحوله   עמק החולה

The swamps of the Hula Valley were once notorious for malaria, but a massive drainage program completed in 1958 got rid of the malarial anopheles mosquitoes – and destroyed one of the country's most important wetlands, a crucial stopping point for many of the estimated 500 million birds that pass through Israel on their way from Europe to Africa and vice versa. In recent years about 10% of the old lake has been restored.

The Society for the Protection of Nature in Israel (SPNI) was founded in 1953 by people galvanised into action by the draining of the Hula.

Sights & Activities

TOP CHOICE **Agamon HaHula**   PARK
(04-681 7137; www.agamon-hula.co.il; admission 3NIS; 9am-dusk Sun-Thu, from 6.30am Fri & Sat, last entry 1hr before closing) In the 1990s, the Hula's cotton fields were converted to

growing peanuts – the soil here is ideal and Israel needs a massive supply of peanuts to produce Bamba, Israeli children's favourite junk food. Unfortunately (or fortunately, depending on how you look at it), cranes love peanuts as much as Israeli kids love Bamba, so conflict between the birds, protected by law, and local farmers was inevitable.

But an elegant solution was found. It turns out that the best way to encourage the birds to continue on their way to Ethiopia and Sudan is to feed them – if they can't find nibblies, they stick around longer and end up munching even more peanuts. Or they may stop migrating altogether – 35,000 cranes have already decided to become wintertime couch potatoes. One big field is now given over to supplying the migrating birds with six to seven tonnes of daily corn, delivered by tractor.

Seeing cranes upclose is fiendishly difficult because cranes are skittish creatures – normally, if anyone comes near, the entire flock will fly off en masse, landing in the safety of a neighbouring (peanut) field. A local farmer noticed that the one moving mass that the cranes showed no fear of was their great benefactor, the corn tractor. Then he had a brilliant idea: the corn tractor could be used to bring not only corn but also birdwatchers very near the flock – without the cranes paying any attention. That's how the 50-seat **Safari Wagon** (Aglat Mistor; per person 53NIS; hourly 9am-1hr before dark late Sep-Apr, often also at 6am) was born. Camouflaged and pulled by the utterly unremarkable (from a crane's point of view) John Deere tractor, it offers visitors unparalleled crane-watching opportunities – you can see the birds without even having to crane your neck! Reserve ahead if possible.

Other birds that can be seen here seasonally including **pelicans** (Sep-Oct & Mar–mid-Apr), 65,000 of whom fly between the Danube Delta in Romania and the Blue Nile and Lake Victoria in Africa, and **storks** (Aug-Sep & Apr-May), 500,000 of whom pass by here twice a year.

To cover the 8.5km path around the restored wetlands, you can either walk or rent a bicycle (52NIS), four-wheeled pedal cart (175NIS for up to five people), seven-seat 'conference bike' (45NIS per person) or golf cart (145NIS for two people). Don't expect to see many birds in the summer. Wheelchair accessible.

Call ahead to coordinate a visit to the site's banding (ringing) station.

By road, Agamon HaHula is 7.5km north of the Hula Nature Reserve, and 1.2km off Rte 90.

TOP CHOICE Hula Nature Reserve   PARK

(☑04-693 7069; www.parks.org.il; adult/child 32/20NIS; ☺8am-5pm Sun-Thu, to 4pm Fri, last entry 1hr before closing) Migrating birds flock to the wetlands of Israel's first nature reserve, founded in 1964. Over 200 species of small waterfowl mingle happily with cormorants, herons, pelicans, raptors, storks and cranes, while water buffalo roam certain areas of the reserve, their grazing patterns helping to preserve the open meadows. The visitors centre offers an excellent **3D film** on bird migration and informative dioramas on Hula wildlife. The main 1.5km trail, which passes by birdwatching hides, is wheelchair accessible. In the lake, which is just 2m or 3m deep, you may spot fur and fins rather than feathers – these would be attached to nutrias, otters and catfish weighting up to 20kg. Renting binoculars costs 10NIS.

Situated 15km north of Rosh Pina, 2km west of off Rte 90.

Kiryat Shmona & Tel Hai
قريات شمونه وتل حاي
קרית שמונה ותל חי

☑04 / POP 23,300

Once regularly in the news for being the target of hundreds of Katyusha rockets fired from Lebanon, Kiryat Shmona is a sunbaked, hardscrabble 'development town' with little to offer the visitor except a faded, grungy bus station. It is almost completely shut on Shabbat. The name, which means 'Town of the Eight', honours eight Zionist pioneers, including Josef Trumpeldor, killed in 1920 at Tel Hai, 3km to the north.

◉ Sights & Activities

Open Museum of Photography   MUSEUM

(☑04-681 6700; www.omuseums.org.il; Tel Chai, east side of Rte 90; adult/child 3-18yr 18/14NIS; ☺8am-4pm Sun-Thu, 10am-5pm Sat, also 10am-2pm Fri Jul & Aug) Temporary exhibitions, by renowned local and international photographers, change three times a year. This is a good place to teach your kids about the 'ancient' technologies of pre-digital photography.

Situated inside the high-tech Tel Hai Industrial Park, next to an attractively landscaped sculpture garden. To get there from the centre of Kiryat Shmona, head north on

Rte 90 for 3km and follow the signs to 'Photography'.

☞ Tours

Oren Fuchs (☑04-695 3344, 052-239 9188; www.etz-oren.co.il, in Hebrew) A knowledgeable local tour guide; offers personalised English-language visits to the Galilee and Golan.

⊨ Sleeping

HI – Tel Hai Youth Hostel   HOSTEL $

(☑02-594 5666; www.iyha.org.il; Tel Chai, east side of Rte 90; dm 119NIS, s/d 225/310NIS,; ❋@☞) The modern, well-kept facilities were built in 1998. Dorm rooms have four to six beds and are excellent value. Rates are higher on Fridays (single/double 275/353NIS). From the vehicle gate of the Open Museum of Photography, follow the signs to 'Guest House'.

⊕ Getting There & Away

Bus

Kiryat Shmona is the major bus junction in the Galilee Panhandle. Destinations include:

Jerusalem (Egged bus 963; 47NIS, four hours, twice a day except Shabbat)

Majdal Shams (Rama bus 58; 30 minutes, five daily Sunday to Thursday, three on Friday, one on Saturday afternoon) and sites along Rtes 99 and 989, including the Banias Nature Reserve, Nimrod Fortress and Neve Ativ

Tel Aviv (Egged buses 841, 842 and 845, 47NIS, 3¾ hours, at least hourly except Shabbat)

Tiberias (mainly Egged bus 841; 29NIS, 1¼ hours), which goes via Rosh Pina

Tsfat (Nateev Express bus 511; 20.70NIS, 40 minutes, a dozen daily Sunday to Thursday, eight on Friday), which goes via the turn-offs for Agamon HaHula (12.40NIS), the Hula Nature Reserve (13.70NIS) and Rosh Pina.

Car

The area's only car rental agency is run by **Eldan** (☑04-690 3186; www.eldan.co.il; 4 Tzahal St).

Taxi

For a taxi based at Nehemia Mall (at the intersection of Rte 90 and Rte 99), call ☑1-800-304 141. For taxis based at the bus station, call ☑04-694 2333/77.

Metula   מטולה   مطوله

☑04 / POP 1600

Situated at the Galilee's northernmost tip, this picturesque, hilltop village – surrounded on three sides by Lebanon – was founded in

ⓘ KATYUSHAS

While the Northern Galilee feels peaceful, it still occasionally comes under fire from Katyusha rockets launched from southern Lebanon, either by Hezbollah or another radical armed faction. First fielded by the Soviet Union during WWII (thus the name, which is the diminutive form of Yekatrina, ie Catherine), these notoriously inaccurate rockets take a mere 30 to 40 seconds from launch to impact.

1896 with help from the French branch of the Rothschild family. In 1920, its existence was crucial in determining that the Galilee Panhandle was included in the British mandate of Palestine instead of the French mandate of Lebanon. Today, the economy is based on tourists in the mood for a Swiss alpine vibe, and on fruit orchards (kiwi fruit, apricots, apples, nectarines, peaches and cherries).

⊙ Sights & Activities

Strolling up and down Metula's quaint main street, you'll pass lots of solid stone houses built a century or more ago, some with ceramic panels explaining their history.

Dado Lookout   VIEWPOINT

Perched high atop the hill southwest of HaRishonim St – the one with the red-and-white antenna tower on top – this lookout offers spectacular, often windy views south towards the Hula Valley, east to the Golan (including Mt Hermon and the twin volcanoes of Avital and Bental) and north into Lebanon. In the foreground is the Ayoun Valley; on the horizon it's easy to spot the Beaufort, a Crusader fortress where the Israel Defence Forces (IDF) unit featured in the 2007 Israeli film *Beaufort* was stationed.

To get to the lookout, follow the signs – it's about 1km above the centre. A bit past the turn-off is the site of the Good Fence, where southern Lebanese used to cross into Israel to work and for medical care. The area is now off-limits except for local farmers and their Thai field hands (that's why some of the signs are in Thai).

TOP CHOICE Nahal Iyyun Nature Reserve   HIKING

(☑04-695 1519; www.parks.org.il; adult/child 27/14NIS; ⊙8.30am-5pm Apr-Sep, to 4pm Oct-Mar) One of the Galilee's loveliest creek-side trails

follows the Iyyun (Ayun) Stream from its crossing from Lebanon into Israel through a cliff-lined canyon to four waterfalls, including the 31m-high Tanur (Chimney) Waterfall. The latter is accessible from both of the park's well-signposted entrances – it's about a 1½ hour (2.5km) walk downstream from Metula's northeastern corner, just 100m from the border fence (last entry 1½ hours before closing); or a 30 minute circuit from the lower car park (last entry 30 minutes before closing), on Rte 90 3km south of town. A wheelchair-accessible trail is being constructed from the lower entrance.

Canada Centre   ICE SKATING

(☑04-695 0370; www.canada-centre.co.il; Rte 90; ⊙10am-8pm Mon-Thu, 10am-6pm Fri & Sat) This modern sports complex, a bit down the hill (south) from the village centre, houses Israel's largest ice rink (adult/child 92/72NIS; ⊙10am-4pm Sun-Thu, to 5pm Fri & Sat), a big indoor pool with water slides, a 10-lane bowling alley (⊙11am-4pm), a spa and an impressive fitness centre.

🍽 Sleeping & Eating

The historic houses along HaRishonim St are home to a number of rustic restaurants and a few places to stay.

TOP CHOICE Villa Lishansky   HISTORIC HOTEL $$

(☑04-699 7184; www.rest.co.il/lishansky, in Hebrew; 42 HaRishonim St; d 550NIS) Built in the Bauhaus style in 1936 by the family of a famous WWI spy, this place – still owned by the Lishanskys – retains the original floor tiles, mouldings and lamps. Hearty beef, lamb, chicken and fish dishes are prepared with Galilean herbs and spices in the hotel's restaurant (mains 86-125NIS; ⊙9am-3.30pm & 6pm-midnight). Upstairs, the three very spacious guest rooms connect to a sitting room that's straight out of the 1930s.

HaBayit Mool HaBeaufort   B&B $$$

(☑04-953 0232; www.mula-bo-4.co.il; 22 Hanarkis St; d from 800NIS; ❄) This pretty B&B, high above the town centre, has three serene suites and great views of the Beaufort, a Crusader fortress across the border in Lebanon. The friendly owners are an excellent source of information on local hikes and attractions.

HaTachanah   STEAKHOUSE $$$

(☑04-694 4810; 1 HaRishonim St; mains 65-179NIS; ⊙noon-10pm or later) Modern and airy, with wood-panelled walls and panoramic views, this restaurant serves first-rate steaks as well as hamburgers, pasta, soups, salads and lamb chops. A 1L pitcher of German beer costs 39NIS. Kiddie portions available (of the mains, not the beer). Call ahead on Thursday night, Friday, Saturday and holidays, and in August.

Luissa BISTRO $$
(www.rest.co.il/luissa, in Hebrew; 21 HaRishonim St; mains 59-107NIS; ☺10am-10pm Mon-Sat) Run by a young couple with three generations of restaurant experience, this homey place, decorated with antiques, serves hearty, French- and Italian-inspired home-style cooking, including steak, fish and pasta.

ℹ Getting There & Away

Metula is linked to Tel Hai and Kiryat Shmona (11NIS, 20 minutes) by Egged buses 020 and 021 several times a day.

East of Kiryat Shmona

Heading east from Kiryat Shmona, Rte 99 passes by a number of worthwhile sites on its way to the Golan.

For details on the Banias Nature Reserve, 5km east of the Tel Dan Nature Reserve, see p251.

◉ Sights & Activities

Tel Dan Nature Reserve PARK
(☑04-695 1579; adult/child 27/14NIS; ☺8am-5pm during daylight savings, to 4pm rest of year, closes 1hr earlier Fri, last entry 1hr before closing) This half-square-kilometre reserve, 1.6km north of Rte 99, boasts two major attractions. The first, a lush, forested area is fed by year-round springs gushing eight cubic metres of water per second into the Dan River, the most important tributary of the Jordan. The second is the remains of a grand city inhabited by the Canaanites in the 18th century BCE and the Israelites during the First Temple period (12th century BCE).

You can explore the reserve on three trails, parts of which are virtual tunnels through the thick brambles and undergrowth. All pass by a 40cm-deep wading pool, a great place to cool your feet (swimming is prohibited elsewhere in the reserve). A section of the Short Trail is wheelchair accessible.

Because the reserve is a meeting place of three ecosystems, it supports a surprisingly varied selection of flora and fauna, including the Indian crested porcupine and the en-

dangered fire salamander, a speckled orange and black critter with five toes on its back feet but only four on its front feet! Some of the reserve's eucalyptus (gum) trees, obviously a non-native species, are being selectively cut to allow native species to grow.

The Tel Dan Stele, found by an archaeology team from Hebrew Union College in 1993, is a fragment of a 9th-century BCE tablet in which the king of Damascus boasts (in Aramaic) of having defeated the 'king of Israel' and the king of the 'House of David'. This is the earliest known reference to King David from a source outside the Bible. The original is at the Israel Museum in Jerusalem.

Galil Nature Center MUSEUM
(Beit Ussishkin; ☑04-694 1704; adult/child 20/15NIS; ☺8am-4.30pm Sun-Thu, 8am-3pm Fri, 9.30am-4.30pm Sat) This first-rate regional museum has two sections. In the old-fashioned but informative (and, in its own way, beautiful) natural history room, you can get a close-up look at (stuffed) butterflies, birds and mammals that you're not likely to encounter in the wild. The archaeology section focuses on nearby Tel Dan and includes a copy of the Tel Dan Stele. It screens a film on the Golan in eight languages and is well worth a stop.

The 940km Israel National Trail, which goes all the way to the Red Sea, begins in the parking lot. The Syrian tank on the nearby lawn was knocked out by kibbutz members at the beginning of the 1967 Six-Day War.

The museum is situated on the edge of Kibbutz Dan, 300m off the road linking Rte 99 with Tel Dan Nature Reserve.

Mifgash HaOfanayim CYCLING
(Bike Place; ☑04-689 0202; www.bikeplace.co.il; Rte 9888, Kiryat Shmona; per half-/full day 50/85NIS; ☺8am-8pm) Rents and repairs bikes and can supply you with route tips and cycling maps. The matron of the house is American. Situated 2km south of Rte 99.

🛏 Sleeping

Area villages such as Moshav Beit Hillel are filled with signs for B&Bs, most of them in Hebrew.

Good camping options for the warm season include:

Dag Al HaDan CAMPGROUND $
(04-695 0225; www.dagaldan.co.il; adult/child 70 NIS/60NIS) At the entrance to Moshav Beit Hillel.

Chenyon Yarok CAMPGROUND $

(📞054-950 6445; adult/child 60/50NIS; ☺Apr-Nov; 🛜) A grassy, family-friendly site in Moshav Beit Hillel, on the banks of the Hatzbani River (no swimming). For an extra 15NIS per person you can stay on mattresses in a tepee (bring a sleeping bag).

Eating

There are several decent restaurants, including Focaccia (Italian) and Klompus (American-burger), at the Gan HaTzafon shopping mall, on Rte 99 4km east of Rte 90 (Kiryat Shmona). There's also a McDonald's with wi-fi.

Restaurants in the Galilee Panhandle cater to weekend vacationers so it's a good idea to reserve ahead on Friday night and Saturday.

TOP CHOICE **Dag Al HaDan** FISH $$$

(📞04-695 0225; www.dagaldan.co.il; off Rte 99; mains 86NIS; ☺noon-10.30pm, from 8.30am Fri, Sat & daily in Aug) One of Israel's best fish restaurants, this place is renowned for its grilled trout (86NIS) – raised in ponds (open to visitors) just 50m away – served with superb roasted potatoes and first-rate starters such as asparagus and roasted garlic. Also has a few pastas for vegetarians. From Passover to September, diners sit outside with the cold, clear waters of the Dan burbling by. Situated north of Rte 99, across the highway from Kibbutz HaGoshrim.

Nehalim BISTRO $$$

(📞04-690 4875; www.rest.co.il/nehalim, in Hebrew; Gan HaTzafon shopping mall, Rte 99; mains 79-129NIS, set lunch menus 69-109NIS, dinner menus from 330NIS; ☺11am-11pm) Tucked away unobtrusively in the corner of a strip mall, this elegant 'chef's restaurant', with white tablecloths and sparkling crystal, has been acquiring a reputation as serving some of the Galilee's best French-inspired meat, seafood and fish. Specialities include trout in orange and ginger sauce, and lamb T-bone with thyme sauce.

THE GOLAN HEIGHTS

لجولان العالي الجليل

רמת הגולן

Offering commanding views of the Sea of Galilee and the Hula Valley, the volcanic Golan plateau is dry and tan in the summer, and lush and green – and carpeted with wildflowers – in the spring. Its fields of basalt boulders – and, on its western edge, deep canyons – are mixed with cattle ranches, orchards, vineyards and small, friendly communities. The area is a favourite destination for holidaying Israelis. Accommodation – mostly B&Bs – tends to cost more than in the Galilee.

Israel captured the Golan Heights from Syria during the 1967 Six Day War, when 90% of the inhabitants fled or were expelled. In the bitterly fought 1973 Yom Kippur War, Syrian forces briefly took over much of the Golan before being pushed back to the current lines. All around the Golan – unilaterally annexed by Israel in 1981 – you'll see evidence of these conflicts: abandoned Syrian bunkers along the pre-1967 front lines; old tanks, left as memorials, near the battlefields of 1973; and ready-for-action Israeli bunkers facing the disengagement zone staffed by the blue-helmeted soldiers of the UN Disengagement Observer Force troops (Undof).

❶ Getting Around

Bus services around the Golan and down to Kiryat Shmona, Hatzor HaGlilit (near Rosh Pina) and the entire shoreline of the Sea of Galilee (including Tiberias) are run by Katzrin-based **Rama** (📞*3254, *8787; www.bus.gov.il, www.golanbus.co.il, in Hebrew). The main lines run four to 10 times a day from Sunday to Thursday, one to six times on Friday until midafternoon, and once on Saturday afternoon or evening.

Katzrin قتسرين קצרין

📞04 / POP 6700

The 'capital of the Golan', founded in 1977, is the region's only real town. The lively little commercial centre, a classic 1970s complex, has a bank, some eateries and a first-rate museum; the nearby Lev Katzrin mall has a supermarket. About 1.6km east of there you can visit Byzantine-era excavations; the tourist information office and the renowned Golan Heights Winery; more eateries are a bit further east in the Katzrin Industrial Zone. Everything, except two excellent restaurants in the Industrial Zone, closes on Shabbat.

☉ Sights & Activities

TOP CHOICE **Golan Archaeological Museum** MUSEUM

(📞04-696 1350; www.mpkatzrin.org.il, in Hebrew; Katzrin town centre; adult/child 17/14NIS, incl Ancient Katzrin Park 26/18NIS; ☺9am-4pm Sun-Thu,

RAFTING THE JORDAN

First-time visitors may be surprised at the Jordan's creek-sized proportions, but first-time rafters are often bowled over – sometimes into the soup – by how powerful its flow can be. Three excellent outfits offer rafting and kayaking down the Jordan – competition is as fierce as the current, which means standards of service and safety are high.

All the places listed below have changing rooms, so you can put on your bathing suit, and lockers for valuables (10NIS or 20NIS); they'll hold your car keys and perhaps your mobile phone for no charge. Unless you're told otherwise, assume that you'll get either wet or drenched. Discounts are often available on the internet and from locally distributed coupon books.

The wildest bit of the river, a 13km stretch known as the Yarden Harari (Mountainous Jordan), runs from B'not Ya'akov Bridge (on Rte 91) to Karkom (about 6km north of Rte 87's Arik Bridge).

For details on rafting near the northeastern corner of the Sea of Galilee, see p215.

Jordan River Rafting (☎04-900 7000; www.rafting.co.il; Rte 918) Situated 15km north of the Sea of Galilee, this veteran operation offers both family-friendly paddles and wild white-water rafting along the legendary Yarden Harari. The regular route (one to 1½ hours, minimum age five), which operates (depending on the weather) from late March or April until September or October, costs 79NIS per person in a two-person inflatable kayak (you'll get wet) or a raft with room for three to eight (you can stay dry if you try). You can take on the Yarden Harari (16km in three to five hours) from about February to mid-June; the cost is 345NIS per person (minimum age 16). Other activities here include cycling (80NIS; not available when the track is too muddy) along a 1½-hour route (not including swimming time); and a zipline (45NIS). Camping costs 20NIS per person; amenities include security, showers, toilets and barbeque pits. Jordan River Rafting is on Rte 918 about 4km north of B'not Ya'akov Bridge, which takes Rte 91 over the Jordan.

Kfar Blum Kayaks (☎04-690 2616; www.kayaks.co.il; ◷10am-3 or 4pm, to 5 or 6pm in summer, open Passover-Sukkot or first rains) In an inflatable kayak (two people) or rafts (for up to six), a tame, 4km (1¼-hour) route costs 80NIS, while a more challenging 8km (2½-hour) route costs 112NIS. Both start on the Hatzbani River and end on the Jordan. Also has an 'active amusement' park with a fantastic zipline into the river (30NIS), a 15m climbing wall (30NIS), a kids rope-bridge park (26NIS), archery (30NIS) and bike rental (80NIS for two hours). To get there from Rte 99, take the turn-off to Beit Hillel (Rte 9888).

HaGoshrim-Ma'ayan Kayaks (☎04-681 6034/5; www.kayak.co.il; Kibbutz Ma'ayan Baruch; ◷Apr-Oct) Based up near the Lebanese border at the entrance to Kibbutz Ma'ayan Baruch (a bit north of Rte 99), this veteran outfit – run by two neighbouring kibbutzim – offers trips in inflatable kayaks (for two people) and rafts (for up to six). The Family Route costs 80NIS per person; the wilder Challenge Route is 100NIS. Runs begin from 9am to 4.30pm or 5pm in the summer, to 2.45pm in spring and autumn.

to 2pm Fri) This small museum of artefacts unearthed on the Golan is a real gem. Highlights include extraordinary basalt lintels and Aramaic inscriptions from 30 Byzantine-era Golan synagogues, coins minted during the Great Jewish Revolt (66–70 CE), a model of Rujum al-Hiri, a mysterious Stone Age maze, 156m across and built some 4500 years ago, and a film (available in English) that brings to life the Roman siege of Gamla. Wheelchair accessible. Situated 100m west of Katzrin's commercial centre, next to the library.

Golan Heights Winery   WINERY
(☎04-696 8409/8435; www.golanwines.co.il; Katzrin Industrial Park; tasting 10NIS, incl tour 20NIS; ◷8.30am-6pm Sun-Thu, to 1.30 Fri, last tour 4.30 or 5pm Sun-Thu, noon or 12.30pm Fri) This outstanding winery, winner of many international awards, offers guided tours of its cellar (advance reservations preferred) and wine-tasting. We particularly liked the slightly sparkling moscato (6% alcohol). The shop sells 40 wines bottled under its Yarden, Gamla, Golan and Galil Mountain labels. All

ℹ MINEFIELDS

Some parts of the Golan Heights – particularly those near the pre-1967 border and the 1974 armistice lines – are still sown with antipersonnel mines. For more information, see p424.

wines are kosher but they're not *mevushal* (flash pasteurised).

Ancient Katzrin Park
ARCHAEOLOGICAL SITE
(☑04-696 2412; http://parkqatzrin.org.il, in Hebrew; adult/child 24/16NIS, incl Golan Archaeological Museum adult/child 26/18NIS; ⊗8am-4pm Sun-Thu, 9am-2pm Fri, 10am-4pm Sat) To get a sense of local life during the Talmudic period (3rd to 6th centuries), when the Golan had dozens of Jewish villages, drop by this partly restored Byzantine-era village, whose highlights include a basalt synagogue and an audiovisual presentation on Talmudic luminaries (not shown on Saturday). On some Jewish holidays, it has animations with actors in period costumes. Admission is cheaper on Saturdays (adult 16NIS); closing times are usually later in August. Situated 1.6km east of the main entrance to Katzrin.

Kesem HaGolan
VISITORS CENTRE
(☑04-696 3625; www.magic-golan.co.il; Hutzot HaGolan Mall, Katzrin Industrial Zone; adult/child 25/18NIS; ⊗9am-5pm Sat-Thu, to 4pm Fri) An excellent introduction to the Golan, this centre can take you on a half-hour virtual journey around the region, projected on a 180-degree panoramic screen (in English hourly on the half hour). Also has a 1:5000-scale topographic model of the Golan. Situated in the shopping mall 2km east of the main entrance to Katzrin, next to the Industrial Zone.

🛏 Sleeping

SPNI Golan Field School
HOSTEL $$
(☑04-696 1234; www.teva.org.il; Zavitan St; d 405-490NIS, additional child 87-112NIS, adult 131-167NIS; ❄🛜) An unpretentious, 1970s complex on the edge of town, this place makes a convenient base for exploring the Golan. The 33 simple rooms, all with fridge, can sleep up to seven – a good option for families and groups of friends. Sometimes offers free group hikes. Situated 1km from the main entrance to Katzrin – head down Daliyot St and then turn left on Zavitan St; follow the signs to 'Field School'.

🍴 Eating & Drinking

Fast food (shwarma and the like) is available in Katzrin's commercial centre – except on Shabbat, when your eating options shrink to two excellent restaurants 2km or 3km east of town in the Industrial Zone.

For picnic supplies, head to **Mister Zol** (Lev Katzrin Mall; ⊗8am-9pm Sun-Thu, 7am-2.30 or 3pm Fri) supermarket.

TOP CHOICE Golan Brewhouse
BREWERY $$
(☑04-696 1311; www.beergolan.co.il; Hutzot HaGolan Mall, Katzrin Industrial Zone; mains 48-126NIS; ⊗11.30am-11pm; 🅿) This pub-restaurant, with a circular wooden bar and panoramic windows, serves red meat, chicken, fish, soup, salad, veggie mains and some damn fine beer. The Brewhouse Beer Sampler (13NIS) gets you a whisky tumbler of each of its four beers (an amber ale, a pilsner, a Doppelbock and a wheat beer), brewed in the copper vats in the corner. For 44NIS you can sample 200mL of each one and munch on olives and sauerkraut. Staff are happy to answer questions about brewing techniques.

Hummusila
YEMENITE $
(commercial centre; mains 22-35NIS; ⊗10am-8pm Sun-Thu, to 3pm Fri; 🅿) This tiny place serves up hummus (22NIS), tabouleh (14NIS), soups (meat, lentil or bean) and delicious Yemenite specialities such as *jachnun* (heavy, slow-cooked dough; 15NIS) and *melawah* (pancakes eaten with schug hot sauce, grated tomato sauce or honey; 15NIS).

MeatShos
STEAKHOUSE $$
(☑04-696 3334; www.meatshos.co.il, in Hebrew; Katzrin Industrial Zone; mains 55-155NIS; ⊗noon-11pm Mon-Sat) Renowned for its flavoursome steaks, chops, kebabs and hamburgers, all made with Golan-raised kosher calf and lamb, this cutting-edge meatery also serves rare Salokiya boutique wine (per glass 34NIS). Situated next to the fire station at the far northern end of the Industrial Zone, 1km past the Golan Heights Winery.

Pub Safta
PUB
(Ancient Katzrin Park; ⊗9pm-late Sat-Thu) Inside the archaeological site, this beer pub is popular with locals and young Israelis travelling in the area.

ℹ Information

Franchuk (Lev Katzrin Mall; ⊗8am-8pm Sun-Thu, 7am-3pm Fri) A bakery and cafe with free wi-fi (ask for the access code).

Information Centre (☎04-696 2885; www.tourgolan.org.il; ☉9am-4pm Sun-Thu, to 1pm Fri) Run by the local council, this tourist information office has brochures and free maps in Hebrew, English and Russian, and can supply information on accommodation, hiking and winery visits. Bus maps are available from the nearby Rama bus company office. In the shopping centre 2km east of Katzrin's main entrance, behind the round fountain next to Kesem HaGolan.

SPNI Hiking Information (☎04-696 5030; www.teva.org.il; SPNI Golan Field School, Zavitan St; ☉8am-4pm or later Sun-Thu) Free consultations about Golan hiking with experienced SPNI guides. You can also phone with questions.

ℹ Getting There & Away

Katzrin is the Golan's public transit hub. **Rama buses** (☎*8787, *3254; www.bus.co.il, www.golanbus.co.il, in Hebrew) head to virtually every part of the Golan, as well as to Tiberias, Hatzor HaGlilit (near Rosh Pina) and Kiryat Shmona. To get to Neve Ativ, Majdal Shams and the other three Druze villages, change in Kiryat Shmona. See individual listings for bus details.

Egged runs one morning bus a day (except Saturday) from Tel Aviv's Central Bus Station to Katzrin (bus 843; 3½hours) via the east coast of the Sea of Galilee.

South of Katzrin

The southern Golan – the area between Katzrin and the Sea of Galilee (see p212) and the hills overlooking the Sea of Galilee from the east – has some excellent hiking.

For details on Moshav Ramot and staying in Giv'at Yoav, see p222.

YEHUDIYA NATURE RESERVE

שמורת טבע יהודיה · منتزه يهودية

One of the most popular hiking areas in all of northern Israel, the 66-sq-km Yehudiya Nature Reserve (☎Yehudiya entrance 04-696 2817, Meshushim entrance 04-682 0238; adult/child 21/9NIS; ☉8am-5pm during daylight saving, to 4pm rest of year) offers walks suitable for casual strollers as well as experienced hikers, including those who aren't averse to getting very wet. Mammals you might encounter include gazelles and wild boar; cliffs are home to birds of prey as well as songbirds.

Most of the trails follow three cliff-lined wadis, with year-round water flow, that drain into the northeastern corner of the Sea of Galilee. Wadi Yehudiya and Wadi Zavitan are both easiest to access from the Yehudiya Parking Lot, which is on Rte 87 midway between Katzrin and the Sea of Galilee.

Wadi Meshushim, easiest to get to from the Meshushim Parking Lot, is situated 2.8km along a gravel road from Rte 888, which parallels the Jordan River. The parking lot is 8km northeast of the New Testament site of Bethsaida (p215).

The rangers at both entrances to Yehudiya (pronounced yeh-hoo-*dee*-yah) are extremely knowledgeable and will be able to point you in the right direction, as well as register you, for your own safety. The only map you'll need is the excellent colour-coded one provided at ticket booths. At both entrances, snack counters sell sandwiches and ice cream.

ℹ HIKING MAPS & SAFETY

The Golan's most visited nature reserves issue excellent trail maps when you pay your admission fee, but if you'll be hiking further afield, the map to get – if only to avoid the area's many minefields (see p424) and firing zones – is the Hebrew-only, **SPNI Map 1** (see p431), a 1:50,000-scale topographical trail map which covers Mt Hermon, the Golan and the Galilee Panhandle (the Hula Valley and surrounds).

In nature reserves with entry fees, up-to-the-minute details on trail conditions are available at information offices. For certain routes you'll be asked to register, possibly by leaving a card on your dashboard so if rangers find your car after dark they'll know where to send the rescue teams.

Other safety tips:

» Bring plenty of water.

» Wear a hat and sturdy shoes.

» Never dive into the pools of water often found at the base of waterfalls (every year people are killed when they hit underwater boulders).

» Make sure you get back by nightfall.

SPRING WILDFLOWERS

The fields, hills and wadis of the Golan plateau burst into bloom from about February to mid-May (the exact dates depend on the rains). The higher up Mt Hermon you go, the later the wildflowers bloom.

Stick to marked trails – people have fallen to their deaths while attempting to negotiate treacherous makeshift trails, and there's an army firing zone southeast of Wadi Yehudiya.

Sights & Activities

Upper Yehudiya Canyon Trail HIKING
The most popular walk in the park, this four-hour circuit is great for competent hikers and swimmers – but is definitely not for those with vertigo. Don't take along anything that's not waterproof as it's bound to get wet.

At press time, the section of the trail past Yehudiya waterfall was closed due to a cliff collapse. By mid-2012 park management hopes to reopen the entire loop, which includes some precariously steep bits, a 9m-high ladder affixed to the cliff face, and a 30m pool you have to swim across, holding your backpack above your head like a character in a war film.

The trail, marked with red blazes, begins at the basalt ruins of the one-time Syrian village of Yehudiya, built on the remains of an ancient Jewish settlement. To get there from the Yehudiya Parking Lot, cross the highway via the new tunnel (in the lot's southern corner).

Upper Zavitan Canyon Trail HIKING
This three- or four-hour circuit offers great views of 27m-high Zavitan waterfall, spectacular after a rainy winter. The descent begins at the ruins of the Arab village of Sheikh Hussein, northeast of the Yehudiya Parking Lot. An easy trail, with red blazes, the path heads downstream to link up with the Lower Zavitan Canyon Trail and Meshushim (Hexagons) Pool. If you begin hiking after 11am, don't plan on doing the entire circuit.

Branches of the Upper Zavitan Canyon Trail can be picked up near Katzrin and on Rte 9088 between Katzrin and Katzrin Darom Jct.

Meshushim (Hexagons) Pool HIKING
Surrounded by extraordinary, six-sided basalt pillars (thus the name), this chilly (19°C), 7m-deep pool makes for a refreshing dip, though remember that there is no lifeguard, and jumping and diving are absolutely forbidden (people have died here from hitting their heads). Walking to the pool involves a delightful, 20-minute downhill walk from the Meshushim Parking Lot, which has changing rooms; getting back up takes 30 to 40 minutes. The new Stream Trail, which hits Wadi Meshushim farther upstream (and has a 3m cliff ladder), takes 40 or 50 minutes downhill. Begin these routes before 2pm (3pm during daylight savings).

It's possible to hike down to Meshushim Pool from the Yehudiya Parking Lot (four to six hours) but transiting from Wadi Zavitan to Wadi Meshushim involves a steep ascent and then an equally steep descent; and getting back up to your car (assuming you have one and parked it at Yehudiya) could be a problem. This route cannot be started, in either direction, after 11am.

Sleeping

Yehudiya Camping Ground CAMPGROUND $
(Orchan Laila; ☑04-696 2817; www.campingil.org.il; Yehudiya Parking Lot; per person incl next-day reserve admission 50NIS; ⊙24hr) Open year-round, this camping area is securely fenced and well-lit at night, and has hot showers, barbecue pits and shade constructions. If there's no one around, just make yourself at home and pay in the morning. Bags can be left at the information desk (when it's open); nearby there are lockers (10NIS) for valuables.

Getting There & Away

Rama bus 51 (seven or eight daily Sunday to Thursday, six on Friday), which connects Katzrin with Tiberias, stops at the Yehudiya Parking Lot. Egged bus 843, which links Tel Aviv's Central Bus Station (3¼ hours) with Katzrin once a day (except Saturday), also passes this way. A bus schedule is posted to the right of the Yehudiya snack counter.

GAMLA NATURE RESERVE
שמורת גמלא • منتزه جمال
The site of a thriving Jewish village during the late Second Temple period, Gamla (☑04-682 2282; www.parks.org.il; adult/child 27/14NIS; Rte 808; ⊙8am-5pm Sat-Thu, to 4pm Oct-Mar, to 3pm Fri, last entry 1hr before closing) – perched atop a rocky ridge shaped like a camel's back (*gamla* is the Aramaic word for camel) – dared to defy the Romans during

the Great Jewish Revolt (66–70 CE) and as a result was besieged by Vespasian's legions. The 1st-century CE historian Josephus Flavius recorded the seven-month siege (in 67 CE), the defenders' valiant stand and the bloody final battle, and reported a Masada-like mass suicide of thousands of Jews. After it was identified in 1968 based on Josephus' precise descriptions, excavations unearthed an enormous quantity of Roman siege weaponry (some can be seen in Katzrin's Golan Archaeological Museum, p244) as well as one of the world's oldest synagogues, believed to date from the 1st century BCE.

Gamla is also known for the dozens of Griffon vultures that nest in its cliffs and soar majestically over the valley below. Sadly, they are becoming rarer, victims of poisoned carrion that ranchers set out – illegally – to kill wolves.

The park also has Israel's highest perennial waterfall, which drops 51m to a pool. It can be visited by a strenuous trail that passes a field full of dolmens (basalt grave markers created by nomads 4000 years ago).

Gamla is 20km south of Katzrin.

ANI'AM ARTISTS VILLAGE

This quiet moshav, 9km southeast of Katzrin (and about 1km off Rte 808), is home to about a dozen lovely ateliers and galleries, most open on Shabbat. The artists – including ceramicists, a painter, a woodcarver and a New York–born goldsmith, Joel Friedman of Golan Gold (www.golangold.co.il) – are happy to tell visitors about their crafts. There's also a relaxing fish spa (70NIS for 20 minutes), where tiny fish eat the dead skin off your feet. Most places are open Sunday to Thursday from 10am to 4.30pm or 5pm (7pm in summer); Friday and Saturday hours tend to be 10am to about 3pm (4pm in summer).

Ani'am has plenty of B&Bs and two restaurants. Suzana Bistro Bar (mains 49-109NIS; ◎noon-10.30pm Sun-Thu, to 2.30pm Fri) serves kosher old favourites such as schnitzel, steak, burgers, couscous and meat stew in a wood-plank dining room that looks like a cross between a Swiss chalet and a Western saloon.

North of Katzrin

The north-central Golan includes several nature reserves and the twin volcanoes of Avital and Bental, which tower over the UN disengagement zone. Sites in the section are listed more or less from south to north.

EIN ZIVAN   عين زيوان   עין זיוון

Kibbutz Ein Zivan, 19km northeast of Katzrin, was the first kibbutz in the country to undergo privatisation.

For details on a nearby pick-your-own orchard, see p250.

A true boutique operation, Bahat Winery (☑04-699 3710; www.bahatwinery.co.il, in Hebrew; tour adult/child 20/10NIS; ◎9am-5.30pm Sun-Thu, to 3.30pm Fri) produces just 8000 bottles of cabernet sauvignon and pinot noir a year. Short tours of the one-room production facilities, in Hebrew and English, leave every half-hour and end with a tasting session. Kids can learn how wine bottles are corked (30NIS).

Kids will love the 25-minute tour of De Karina's artisanal Chocolate House (☑04-699 3622; www.de-karina.co.il; tour adult/child 22/18NIS, incl workshop 59/49NIS; ◎9am-5pm Sun-Thu, to 3pm Fri, last tour 1hr before closing) and the chocolate-making workshop.

🛏 Sleeping

Rooms are simple but comfortable at Lan BaGolan (☑04-699 3612; www.enzivan.co.il; d 490-520NIS, cabin 910NIS); the all-wood cabins come with a Jacuzzi and sauna. Discounts apply if you stay two or more nights. Or try the spartan 12-bed rooms at Khan (☑050-757 8444; www.enzivan.co.il, in Hebrew; dm adult/child 2-14yr 90/70), a bucolic site in the middle of Ein Zivan's vineyards and apple orchards, midway between Mt Avital and the UN's Quneitra crossing to Syria. Situated 1.5km northeast of Zivan Jct (the intersection of Rtes 91 and 98).

QUNEITRA VIEWPOINT

مرقب القنيطرة   תצפית קוניטרה

From high atop Mt Avital, IDF electronics peer deep into Syria, but even the volcano's lower flanks offer fine views into the territory of Israel's northern neighbour. This viewpoint and memorial (an audio guide narrates the 1973 battles here) overlooks Quneitra, the one-time Syrian 'capital of the Golan' that was destroyed by Israel in the 1967 war and has been in the UN buffer zone since 1974.

At the end of the Six Day War, Quneitra, at the time a garrison town defending Damascus (60km to the northeast), was abandoned in chaos by the Syrian army after Syrian government radio mistakenly reported that the town had fallen. It changed hands twice during the 1973 Yom Kippur War, which Israel began with just 177 tanks against the attacking Syrians' 1500.

PICK YOUR OWN FRUIT

The Golan Heights is Israel's prime deciduous fruit-growing region, and from about May to September or October some orchards open their gates to visitors who want to pick their own. There's generally a small admission cost (around 25NIS), which allows for all-you-can-eat fruit while you pick; you pay per kilo for what you want to take home. Some sites have other attractions for kids, including animals. Call to find out what's ripe.

Tempt your taste buds at **Bustan HaGolan** (☑04-696 1988; Rte 98; adult/child 30/25NIS; ☺9am-4pm May-late Sep). In addition to picking raspberries, apples, pears, nectarines, grapes, figs and/or cherries, this place has a little zoo, pony rides (15NIS), a snack bar and great spots for a picnic. Kids can pick an apple and then use it to make a cupcake-sized apple pie. Situated 22km northeast of Katzrin, on Rte 98 2.3km north of Zivan Jct.

Just beyond the apple orchards and vineyards of Kibbutz Ein Zivan, you can see the only **crossing** between the Golan and Syria, used by the Undof, established to implement the Syrian–Israeli ceasefire that ended the Yom Kippur War; Golan Druze students and brides heading to Syria to study and/or get married (the subject of the 2004 Israel film *The Syrian Bride*), and – in an example of what could be called 'fruit diplomacy' – Druze-grown Golan apples being exported to Syria.

The viewpoint, and the adjacent **geological park** (situated in an old quarry), are next to a small parking lot on the eastern side of Rte 98, 1.3km north of Zivan Jct.

MEROM GOLAN מרום גולן مروم جولان

Nestled at the base of Mt Bental, this kibbutz was the first Jewish settlement on the Golan Heights established after the 1967 Six Day War.

Head into them thar (volcanic) hills with th*e bokri*m (cowboys) of the Golan. **Havat HaBokrim** (☑057 851 4497; 1hr ride 135NIS; ☺10am-5pm) offers horse-riding opportunities.

Rest your saddle-weary body at **Merom Golan Resort Village** (☑04-696 0267; www.meromgolantourism.co.il; d 490-680NIS; chalets 650-1050NIS; ✳☎☒). The 40 wood and basalt chalets and 32 guestrooms, most with Jacuzzi, are surrounded by lovely gardens, giving the place the feel of a small, prosperous village. It is wheelchair accessible.

[TOP CHOICE] HaBokrim Restaurant (☑04-696 0206; mains 65-131NIS; ☺noon-10pm Sun-Thu, to 3pm & 7-10pm Fri) serves mouth-watering, Golan-raised steaks, lamb and hamburgers. Opened in 1990, this veteran meatery also has fish, pasta and a good selection of

childrens portions. Local wines cost 21NIS per glass. Food is kosher, so Friday dinner is pre-prepared.

MT BENTAL הר בנטל جبل بنتل

This inactive volcano sports fantastic views from the top (elevation 1165m) where, from an old Syrian bunker, you can see Syria, Lebanon, the Hula Valley, Mt Hermon and Mt Avital – allegedly a 'spy mountain' with a high-tech underground nerve centre. Signposts on the top direct you to Damascus (60km), Amman (135km), Baghdad (800km) and Washington DC (11,800km).

Named in honour of former UN Secretary General Kofi Annan, once in charge of the UN troops on patrol down below, **Coffee Annan** (☑04-682 0664; www.meromgolantourism.co.il; sandwich 27NIS; ☺9am-sundown) serves sandwiches, salads, frozen yoghurt and breathtaking views of Syria. In Hebrew, the name means 'cafe in the clouds'.

WASSET TOURISM CENTER

מרכז וואסט مفرق وسط

Situated at Wasset Jct (the intersection of Rtes 959 and 978), this grassy **visitors complex** (www.waset.co.il), opened in 2011, has an **art gallery**, a fantastic **spice shop**, a **sculpture garden** (across Rte 959) and a wine bar run by the boutique **Bazelet Hagolan Winery** (www.bazelet-hagolan.co.il; tasting 25NIS), whose annual production is just 80,000 bottles.

If you're hungry, head to **Yogichef** (☑04-689 3630; www.yogichef.co.il; mains 59-89NIS; ☺12.30pm-about midnight Thu-Mon). This new, seven-table restaurant, which sources most of its ingredients (including first-rate steaks) from Golan suppliers, is getting great reviews. Boutique Golan wines cost 22NIS to 38NIS per glass.

ODEM

This small moshav is 12km north of Wasset Jct.

Kids age two to 12 will love Ya'ar HaYe'elim (☑050-522 9450; www.yayalim.co.il, in Hebrew; child 2-12yr/adult 45/30; ☺9am-5pm), a hillside ranch that's home to deer from Scotland, India and Japan, ibexes, mini-ponies you can ride, a petting zoo, a trampoline and a rope park with a 15m zipline.

For the adults, try Odem Mountain Winery (☑04-687 1122; www.harodem.co.il; ☺10am-4 or 5pm Sun-Thu, to 1hr before sundown Fri). You're assured a warm welcome at this family-run boutique winery, which makes just 80,000 bottles a year. Tasting one/three/five wines costs 10/20/30NIS. Call ahead for a tour (10NIS).

For a different sort of sleeping experience, head to Khan Har Odem (☑050-567 4072; www.hanharodem.co.il, in Hebrew; per person over 2yr without breakfast 130NIS; ☎). Think of it as luxury camping – up to 50 guests sleep on mattresses on the floor of a large hall, subdivided with curtains like a medieval French charity hospital. Full kitchen facilities are available. A sleeping bag or blankets can be rented for 5NIS. For cheap sleeps in simple tin huts, head to Ya'ar HaYe'elim (☑050-522 9450; www.yayalim.co.il, in Hebrew; per person without breakfast 90NIS).

Northern Golan

The area along and north of Rte 99 includes some superb nature reserves and towering Mt Hermon, with four Druze villages on its southern slopes. Places in this section are listed from west to east.

For details on the Tel Dan Nature Reserve, 5km west of Banias Nature Reserve, see p243.

BANIAS NATURE RESERVE

منتزه بنياس שמורת הבניאס

The gushing springs, waterfalls and lushly shaded streams of Banias Nature Reserve (☑lower entrance 04-695 0272, upper entrance 04-690 2572; www.parks.org.il; Rte 99; adult/child 27/14NIS, incl Nimrod Fortress 38/25NIS; ☺8am-5pm during daylight savings, to 4pm rest of year) form one of the most beautiful – and popular – nature spots in Israel. The park has two entrances on Rte 99 that are about 2.5km apart. Last entry is one hour before closing.

Many sections of the park's four trails (trail map provided) are shaded by oak, plane, fig and carob trees. The new Suspended Trail, a boardwalk cantilevered out over the rushing Banias (Hermon) Stream, provides a glimpse of Eden. A bit upstream is the 10.5m Banias Waterfall, with its sheer, thundering drop into a deep pool. Tempting as it may look, swimming is sadly prohibited here.

Near the upper entrance are the excavated ruins of a palace complex built by Herod's grandson, Agrippa II. The name 'Banias' derives from Pan, Greek god of the countryside, to whom the area was dedicated.

Both entrances are served by Rama bus 58 from Kiryat Shmona to Majdal Shams (see p241).

NIMROD FORTRESS قلعة الصبيبة מבצר נמרוד

Built by the Muslims in the 13th century to protect the road from Tyre to Damascus, Nimrod Fortress (☑04-694 9277; www.parks. org.il; Rte 989; adult/child 21/9NIS; ☺8am-5pm Apr-Sep, to 4pm Oct-Mar) towers fairy-tale-like on a long, narrow ridge (altitude 815m) on the southwestern slopes of Mt Hermon. The work that went into building such a massive fortification – 420m long and up to 150m wide – on the top of a remote mountain ridge boggles the mind. If you're going to visit just one Crusader-era fortress during your trip, this should be it.

Background on the fortress' colourful medieval history, including its destruction by the Mongols, can be found in the excellent English map-brochure given out at the ticket booth. Highlights include an intact 13th-century hall, complete with angled archers slits, in the Northern Tower.

The castle, visible from all over the Hula Valley, is protected by near-vertical cliffs and vertiginous canyons on all sides but one. South of Nimrod is Wadi Sa'ar, which divides the Golan's basalt plateau (to the south) from the limestone flanks of Mt Hermon (to the north).

The fortress is served by Rama bus 58 from Kiryat Shmona to Majdal Shams (p241). Last entry is one hour before the park closes.

EIN KINYA

The smallest and quietest of the Golan's Druze villages is in a valley just up the hill from Nimrod Fortress, 2km south of Rte 989.

Opened in 2010, Snabl (Druze Tourist Center; ☑050-577 8850; snabl.tal@gmail.com; d from 550NIS) is a great place for families. It offers Druze-style luxury hospitality and fine views of Nimrod Fortress; the name is pronounced *snah*-bel. It is situated in a chocolate-brown house with Jerusalem stone trim on the northern side of town, up the hill from the main street; to get there follow the signs.

NEVE ATIV נווה אטי''ב نوه اتيف
04 / POP 150

An alpine-style mountainside moshav on the flank of mighty Mt Hermon, Neve Ativ is a good base for hiking in summer and skiing in winter.

When you're ready to rest, Rimonim Hermon Holiday Village (04-698 5888; www.rimonim.com; Rte 989; d 560-720NIS; ❄️🛜🏊) has 44 two-storey, A-frame chalets that can sleep up to eight, a large indoor swimming pool, a spa and a sauna. Elevation is 960m. It offers ski packages in winter and sometimes has a four-night minimum.

Particularly cosy in winter and very popular with families is the B&B Chez Stephanie (04-698 1520; upper section of Naftali St; d 550NIS; ❄️). Owners Reine and Maurice were born in Marseille but the log-built chalets, which can sleep up to six, feel like Chamonix.

Neve Ativ is 4km west down Rte 989 from Majdal Shams. Served by Rama bus 58 from Kiryat Shmona to Majdal Shams (see p241).

NIMROD בימרוד نيمرود
04

This isolated hilltop hamlet off Rte 98 (and on the Golan Trail), with its staggering views and winter snows, is home to only six families but it has some interesting places to stay.

TOP CHOICE Golan Heights Hostel (Chalet Nimrod Castle Hostel; 04-698 4218; www.bikta.net; camping per person 45NIS, dm 110NIS, cabins 600-1000NIS) has 10 rustic rooms built of recycled wood surrounded by an organic cherry orchard. For dinner you can order a meat or veggie stew cooked in a casserole on an open fire. The hostel accepts volunteers interested in ecological construction techniques. Call ahead for a dorm bed. Camping is possible.

For hippyish hillside accommodation in three tepees, a Mongolian-style tent and some shacks, head to Ohel Avraham (Abraham's Tent; 04-698 3215, 052-282 1141; camping per person 50NIS; tepee 100NIS plus per person 60NIS; ☺Passover-Sukkot). It's a great spot to chill out. Bring a sleeping bag or blankets. It may be open in the off-season – call to find out.

Nimrod is surprisingly served by Rama bus 58, which links Kiryat Shmona with Majdal Shams (see p241).

MAJDAL SHAMS מג'דל שמס مجدل شمس
04 / POP 9800

The largest of Golan's four Druze towns – big enough, in fact, to have traffic jams – Majdal Shams serves as the commercial and cultural centre of the Golan Druze community. Druze flags, which sport five horizontal stripes (blue, white, red, yellow and green), flutter in the wind, and you often see men with elaborate curling moustaches sporting traditional Druze attire, including a black *shirwal* (baggy pants) and a white fez.

🅾 Sights

Shouting Hill   HISTORIC SITE

Druze families separated by the conflict between Israel and Syria long used megaphones to communicate with relatives and friends assembled on the far side of a small, UN-controlled ravine. In recent years Skype and cellphones have pretty much replaced this ritual, which featured prominently in the award-winning 2004 film *The Syrian Bride*.

In May and June 2011, crowds of Palestinian protesters from Syria tried to breach the fence here. Israeli troops opened fire, killing several people. Both Israelis and Palestinians suspected that the incident was an attempt by Syria's beleaguered Assad regime to divert attention from the country's domestic opposition.

The Shouting Hill is on the eastern outskirts of town. From the easternmost of the two traffic circles with heroic statues in the middle, head down the hill (southeast) for 700m.

🛏 Sleeping

Narjis Hotel   HOTEL $$

(Malon Butik Narkis; 04-698 2961; www.narjishotel.com; Rte 98; d 500-600NIS; @🛜) Opened in 2009, this stylish, locally owned hotel has 21 huge, romantic rooms with modern decor, Jacuzzi and balcony. Situated on the road up to Mt Hermon.

🍴 Eating & Drinking

There's a strip of shops selling felafel, shwarma, Druze pita with labaneh (15NIS) and baklava along Rte 98 between the intersection of Rte 989 and the traffic circle.

Nisan   DRUZE $$

(Rte 98; mains 25-65NIS; ☺10am-midnight; 🛜🍴) A brightly lit, modern place, opened in 2011, that serves both Druze favourites (hummus, kebab and salads) and Western standards (pasta, pizza and something called a

THE GOLAN TRAIL

Marked with blue, white and green blazes representing the Sea of Galilee, the snows of Mt Hermon and the Golan's springtime greens, the 130km Golan Trail (www.golan.org.il/shvil, in Hebrew) meanders through the eastern part of the Golan Heights, extending from Mt Hermon in the north to Ein Taufiq in the south. The beautiful trail has 15 segments (ranging from 5km to 12km) that follow streams, traverse nature reserves and pass by ruins and a hilltop wind farm. The ends of each segment are accessible by car (seasoned hikers could cover two segments in one day), or you can hike the whole trail, camping along the way. You can walk in either direction, but it's of course easier to head south from Mt Hermon. Don't attempt the walk without SPNI topographical map No 1 (see p431). Or you can pick up a Hebrew trail guide, Shvil HaGolan – HaMadrich by Ya'akov Shkolnik and Yisrael Eshed (97NIS).

'California salad'). Wheelchair accessible. Situated 400m up the hill from the Narjis Hotel.

Undefined Restaurant & Bar   BAR $$
(Rte 98; ☺10am or 11am-midnight) Though opened in 2010, this place feels like the 1980s – but the sliced-log bar is a simpatico spot for a beer or a bite. Situated 50m east of the Narjis Hotel.

❶ Information
Majdal Shams' banks have ATMs.

❶ Getting There & Away
Majdal Shams is 30km east of Kiryat Shmona. Served by Rama bus 58 from Kiryat Shmona (see p241), which passes by Neve Ativ, Nimrod Fortress and Banias Nature Reserve.

MT HERMON   הר חרמון   خبل الشيخ
Israel's only ski station (☎24hr 1-599-550 560, 03-606 0640; www.skihermon.co.il; Rte 98; adult/child winter 49/44NIS, summer free; ☺8am-4pm, last entry 3.30pm, may open 7am in winter) is situated at the far northern tip of the Golan, high atop Mt Hermon, known for its crisp mountain air, delicate alpine plants and unpredictable snowfall. The mountain's 2814m summit is in Syrian territory; the highest point controlled by Israel is 2236m.

The facilities at Mt Hermon look like a low-altitude, low-budget ski station in the Alps, circa 1975; visitors are greeted by cheesy giant styrofoam snowmen. In a good year, there are 30 to 40 ski days between December and March – not enough to meet demand so the pistes are often extremely busy.

In winter, there's usually 3m or 4m of snow at the top of Mt Hermon; the record, set in 1992, was 10m! Details on ski conditions are available by phone or online.

The site has three blue (easy) runs, seven red (difficult) runs and two runs rated black (very difficult). The longest is 1248m, with a vertical drop of 376m; the highest begins at 2036m. To get you uphill, there are 11 lifts, including five chair lifts and five T-bars.

Hitting the slopes of Mt Hermon can be pricey – but for Israelis, it's a lot cheaper than flying to Austria (before 1948, Palestinian Jews with a passion for winter sports used to head to Lebanon). After you pay for a ski pass (all-day/afternoon 245/200NIS), you'll probably have to rent skis (adult/child 150/135NIS) or a snowboard (170NIS), plus hire ski clothing (120NIS).

If you decide to ski, make sure your travel insurance covers 'high-risk' sports and includes evacuation.

In the warm season, there's access to the summit – and its riot of alpine wildflowers (the blooming season up here lasts from late May to August) – on Lifts 1 & 3 (adult/child 3-12yr 49/44NIS). The price includes a 1½-hour guided walk (☺departures 11am & 1pm Jun-Sukkot) that takes a look flora, flowers and local military history. For the walk, get to the lift a half hour ahead.

Adventure cyclists can rent specially equipped downhill bikes (per bike 150-250NIS, safety equipment 80NIS; ☺Apr-Nov or Dec, only Fri & Sat at start & end of season) underneath the pedestrian bridge to Lift 1. There are four scary-steep routes, the longest 3700m. A lift pass for cyclists costs 130/85NIS for the day/afternoon.

Edibles are available at a number of food bars, greasy spoons and a cafeteria.

The ski station is about 9km up the hill from Majdal Shams along Rte 98. Admission fees, when applicable, are paid at toll booths. The Israel Ski Club (☎03-641 3066; www.skiclub.co.il, in Hebrew; membership 30NIS) offers bus transport from Tel Aviv.

UPPER GALILEE & GOLAN NORTHERN GOLAN

West Bank الضفة الغربية
יהודה ושומרון

Best Places to Eat

» Qaabar (p264)

» Zamn (p271)

» Pronto Resto-Cafe (p270)

» Abu Mazen (p279)

Best Places to Stay

» Dar Annadwa (p263)

» Arab Women's Union (p263)

» Cinema Guesthouse (p283)

» Al-Yasmeen Hotel (p281)

Why Go?

Pocket-sized West Bank is jam-packed with history, bustling souqs and some of the friendliest people you'll ever meet. Sadly, it's also the Middle East poster child for strife, violence and failed peace agreements.

Despite the West Bank's troubled past and uncertain present, its doors are open to tourists. Amid the rolling hills, olive groves and chalky desertscapes you can visit traditional villages and biblical sites galore, from the birthplace of Jesus to the last resting place of Abraham. Palestinian capital Ramallah is a surprisingly vibrant place, with gourmet restaurants and a lively cultural scene. Offbeat sites include Jenin's Freedom Theatre and a cable car strung over Jericho.

Perhaps most appealing is the chance to meet strong, determined and hopeful Palestinians. You'll be spellbound by their decades-long quest for recognition and independence, which always seems tantalisingly close. The West Bank is not the easiest place in which to travel but the effort is richly rewarded.

When to Go
Bethlehem

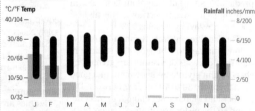

Oct There's a festive air as city dwellers return to their native villages for the olive harvest.

Nov A harvest festival is held at Burqi'in in early November.

Late Dec Bethlehem is electric, with lights, decorations, carolling and Christmas Eve Mass.

Times & Dates

The West Bank day of rest is Friday, but in Bethlehem and Ramallah, Sundays might also see some shops shut, due to Christian ownership. During the Muslim holy month of Ramadan, shopkeepers scale back opening hours, as do some attractions; food isn't on the menu during the daytime, except in Christian establishments: it's unlikely you'll go hungry in Bethlehem or Ramallah.

ONE-WEEK ITINERARY

Most of the West Bank can be reached from Jerusalem on a day trip. However, Jerusalem makes a lousy base because returning each day involves dealing with time-consuming checkpoints and rush-hour traffic. By staying overnight you'll be pumping much-needed shekels into the West Bank economy.

Get in a full day of sightseeing around **Bethlehem** before a day trip to **Hebron**. From Bethlehem take a service taxi to **Jericho**, tour the city and surrounding desert sites. Next travel to **Nablus** (via the Qalandia checkpoint or Ramallah) for a city tour and much-needed visit to the bathhouse. Next travel to **Jenin** to see the Freedom Theatre and Burqi'in. Finally, head back south to spend a day around **Ramallah** and **Taybeh**.

Areas

» The West Bank is divided into three different Areas: A, B and C, designating the amount of civil and military power Israelis and Palestinians respectively exercise in each.

» Area A (around 17% of the West Bank): under full Palestinian civil and military control; you'll see Israeli signs forbidding Israelis from entering. Includes the cities of Ramallah, Nablus, Tulkarem, Jenin, Qalqilya, Bethlehem, Jericho, parts of Hebron and some other small towns.

» Area B (around 24% of the West Bank): includes many rural Palestinian areas. Under Palestinian civil control but Israeli military control.

» Area C (about 59% of the West Bank): under full Israeli control. Includes many sparsely populated areas, outskirts of towns and villages, and the highway network running through the West Bank.

MEDIA

This Week in Palestine (www.thisweekinpalestine.com) is a free monthly booklet with listings, articles, events and maps related to the West Bank.

Basic Costs

» **Shared taxi between cities** 10–20NIS
» **Can of juice** 3NIS
» **Budget hotel room** US$60–90
» **Museum admission** 10–20NIS
» **One-hour taxi hire** from 50NIS
» **Shwarma** 10–14NIS

Travel Warning

In recent years, the West Bank has proved a largely safe and trouble-free destination for Western visitors, but circumstances can change quickly. It's important to keep an eye on the news and heed local and embassy advice while travelling. On a first visit it's a good idea to have a knowledgeable guide who can explain the political and security situation as you go.

Resources

» Palestine Hotels (www.palestinehotels.com)
» Holy Land Tour Operators (www.holylandoperators.com)
» Visit Palestine (www.visitpalestine.ps)
» Palestine News Network (http://english.pnn.ps)
» EnglishPAL (www.englishpal.ps)

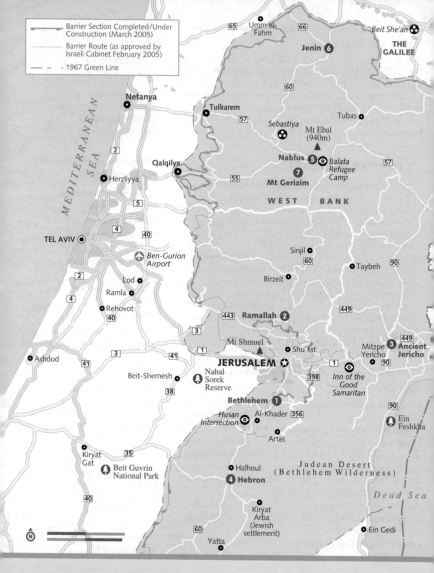

West Bank Highlights

1 Wander the serene stone streets of **Bethlehem** (p260), from the Old City to Manger Sq and the Church of the Nativity

2 Keep cool over cocktails in one of **Ramallah**'s in-the-know gathering spots (p271)

3 Dangle aloft in a cable car above **Ancient Jericho** (p275),

the sandy remains of the oldest continuously inhabited civilisation on earth

4 Visit the troubled city of **Hebron** (p278) and its contentious resting place of the monotheist patriarchs

5 Come clean at a soap factory and Turkish bath in **Nablus** (p281)

6 Meet the inspiring actors at the world-renowned **Freedom Theatre** in Jenin (p282)

7 Clamber up to the platform on **Mt Gerizim** (p280), believed by Samaritans to be God's first creation on Earth

History

The West Bank, as a geographical designation, was a creation of the 1948 Arab–Israeli War, which resulted in areas north, east and south of Jerusalem – the 22% of Mandatory Palestine now known as the West Bank – falling under Jordanian control. The name is derived from the area's position on the western bank of the Jordan River (the Hashemite Kingdom of Jordan is sometimes known as the East Bank).

Historically, Jews have called the area Judea (Yehuda) and Samaria (Shomron), in reference to the West Bank's southern and northern lobes, respectively. Contemporary use of this expression – the preferred nomenclature among Jewish settlers and right-wing Israeli governments – is contentious since it suggests a belief that contemporary Israeli policy should be based on the biblical boundaries of the Land of Israel. You may also hear the terms 'the Occupied Palestinian Territories' or 'the Territories'; or, as used throughout this book, 'the Palestinian Territories'.

West Bank Palestinian culture still bears the stamp of 400 years of Ottoman Turkish rule, during which the area was part of the Ottoman province of Syria. Shorter occupations, such as the post-WWI British Mandate (1917–48), have also left their mark. (English is still taught widely in Palestinian schools.)

Although small in numbers, Jews maintained a presence in the West Bank (particularly in Hebron) throughout the Ottoman period. In the late 19th and 20th centuries large numbers of Jews immigrated from Russia, Yemen and other countries to Palestine but few settled in the mountainous parts of Palestine that would later become the West Bank.

During the 1948 Arab–Israeli War, Jordan captured (and later annexed) the West Bank, only to lose control of the area to Israel in the 1967 Six Day War.

In the years since 1967, Israel has not annexed the West Bank – under Israeli law, the area (including, theoretically, Jewish settlers) has always been under military administration – for demographic reasons: giving citizenship to the area's two million-plus Arab residents would endanger Israel's Jewish majority. During the 1970s and 1980s Jordan sought to reunify the West Bank with the East Bank but relinquished all claims to the Palestine Liberation Organisation (PLO) in 1988.

In the wake of the First Intifada (Arabic for 'uprising' or 'shaking off') from 1987 to 1993, the 1993 Oslo Accords set the stage for the eventual creation of a Palestinian state in the West Bank and Gaza. Under the accords, some areas (such as Jericho, Ramallah and Jenin) were handed over to Palestinian Authority control (see p255).

During the Second Intifada (2000–05), the West Bank served as a staging post for scores of suicide bombings inside Israel. In response to hundreds of civilian deaths, Israel constructed a sophisticated security fence, sealing off the West Bank from Israel (see p268). West Bank Palestinians could no longer travel to jobs in Israel or to Muslim religious sites in Jerusalem, and Israeli settlers found themselves living in places that most Israelis considered to be outside their country's de facto borders.

In 2006 Hamas, an Islamic militant-turned-political group, swept parliamentary elections and international aid was promptly scaled back (since many countries considered Hamas a terrorist organisation). With financial lifelines squeezed, the isolated Hamas leader lost power in the West Bank after a coup by Fatah leader Mahmoud Abbas.

Today the situation in the West Bank is relatively calm but bleak for the Palestinian inhabitants. Most Israeli military checkpoints within the West Bank have been dismantled, making travel around the territory somewhat easier. But travelling out of the territory is difficult for locals (the Palestinians clogging the Qalandia and Bethlehem checkpoints are mainly residents of East Jerusalem).

But Palestinians have not given up hope. Across the cities of the Fatah-ruled Palestinian Authority, you'll spot big banners proclaiming the Palestinians' right to a seat at the United Nations – a symbolic chair has even been placed in the centre of Ramallah. Violent clashes with the Israeli army are now relatively rare (less rare are clashes between Palestinians and radical settlers, and between radical settlers and the Israeli army) but Palestinians' discontent simmers as the Israeli government continues to expand Jewish settlements (see p258). In the meantime, the Palestinians continue to build their institutions and economy – and dream of an independent homeland.

Climate

Where you're located in the West Bank determines the climate: Bethlehem, like

JEWISH SETTLEMENTS

Israeli Jewish colonies set up in the Palestinian Territories are most often referred to as 'settlements'. Some 296,700 Israeli settlers currently live in more than 100 Jewish settlements in the West Bank, with around another 192,800 Jews living in parts of Jerusalem captured by Israel in 1967.

Settlements range in size from a collection of caravans on a remote hilltop to large urban areas, such as Ma'ale Adumim near Jerusalem, home to tens of thousands of Israelis and now effectively a suburb of Jerusalem. There are a variety of reasons cited by settlers for their choice to live on the West Bank: most commonly, cheaper housing prices than in Israel and, among the religious, the fulfilment of biblical prophecy and an extension of the will of God.

Under most interpretations of international law, which forbids the transfer of civilians to land under military occupation, all Israeli settlements on the West Bank are illegal. The Israeli right disputes this interpretation of international law. Palestinians complain that Jewish settlements often occupy private Palestinian land (as opposed to state-owned land), divert precious water resources from surrounding Palestinian cities, towns and villages and, most significantly, fragment the territory of the West Bank, making the establishment of a coherent, contiguous and viable Palestinian state impossible.

Under the final status maps proposed by both Israel and the Palestinians, major blocks of settlements, home to up to 80% of settlers, would be annexed to Israel; the Palestinian state would be compensated elsewhere with an equal amount of pre-1967 Israeli territory. The many scattered settlements located outside these areas would be evacuated. In 2008 negotiations, Israeli Prime Minister Ehud Olmert proposed that 6.3% of the land of the West Bank be annexed to Israel under this formula; Palestinian President Mahmous Abbas was willing to accept 1.9%.

The USA and European Union have declared the settlements an obstacle to peace and have pressured Israel to stop further building. Israeli Prime Minister Binyamin Netanyahu has officially endorsed a two-state solution to the Israeli–Palestinian conflict, but his

---

Jerusalem, can receive snow in winter and enjoys cooler climes in the midst of the otherwise sweltering summer. Balmier Jericho, meanwhile, is the place to escape chillier winter days, and can be oppressively hot during the summer months. If you're considering doing some hiking around Wadi Qelt or elsewhere, spring and autumn are the times to plump for – though if you're seeking Yuletide spirit, bring your woolly jumper and don't miss out on a crisp, cold Bethlehem Christmas.

☞ Tours

If visiting the West Bank solo seems daunting, a great way to get a first taste of the region is by taking an organised tour; see p440 for details (Green Olive Tours, p440, is particularly recommended).

See the boxed text p266 for a list of insider organisations, many of whom organise day trips within the region. For active travellers, the Beit Sahour–based Siraj Center for Holy Land Studies runs cycling and walking trips:

Bike Palestine (☎02-274 8590; www.bikepal estine.com) Seven-day bike tour from Jenin to Jerusalem.

Walk Palestine (☎02-274 8590; www.walk palestine.com) Brings tourists on walking tours that last three to 14 days, staying with locals in villages en route. This route makes up part of the Abraham Path (www.abrahampath.org).

ℹ Getting There & Around

Transport options include private (special) taxis, cheaper shared service (pronounced ser-*vees*) taxis and buses of various shapes and sizes. When going through checkpoints by bus all the passengers get off the bus, go through security and reboard the same bus (in Bethlehem the soldiers ask that foreign tourists stay on the bus).

If you're considering self-driving, it's worth bearing in mind that most Israeli rental-car agencies won't allow you to take their cars into Palestinian-controlled areas. **Green Peace** (☎02-585 9756; www.greenpeace.co.il; Shu'fat, East Jerusalem) is one notable exception.

right-wing coalition government has continued to construct housing in West Bank settlements and East Jerusalem, announcing plans in late 2011 to build another 1000 homes.

In recent years, extremist settlers have responded to Israel Defence Forces (IDF, the national army) efforts to dismantle outposts deemed illegal by Israel's Supreme Court with 'price tag' attacks. Among them are the 'hilltop youth', young religious nationalists – some of them living in remote hilltop settlements – enraged by Israel's 2005 evacuation of all 21 Gaza settlements and four settlements in the Jenin area. Their actions have included the destruction of private property in Palestinian villages, chopping down Palestinian-owned olive trees and even setting fire to mosques. They have made themselves particularly unpopular in Israel by using violence against Israeli soldiers who disrupt their activities. Palestinian violence against settlers, too, has sometimes flared up.

One of the most contentious settler enclaves is in Hebron, where several hundred settlers occupy small settlements in the heart of the city. The Israeli army presence here is massive, and Palestinians are unable to cross through settler-occupied areas to reach other parts of town. International human rights organisations keep 'observer' groups in town to monitor breaches of human rights law in Hebron. The settlers have not made themselves popular with many of the soldiers sent to protect them – see the website of Breaking the Silence (www.breakingthesilence.org.il), an organisation set up in 2004 by Israeli combat veterans disillusioned by their service in Hebron.

A 2009 study by Tel Aviv University suggests that Israeli public opinion is less than enthusiastic about the settlements, with two-thirds of respondents saying the settlements are more a liability than an asset. The settlers themselves are aware of this sentiment and feel unappreciated, misunderstood and betrayed by the country they believe they've dedicated – and risked – their lives (and their children's live) to serve.

To find out more about Jewish settlement activity on the West Bank, visit the websites of the left-wing Israeli organisations Peace Now (Shalom Achshav www.peacenow.org.il) and B'Tselem (www.btselem.org). For a right-wing religious-nationalist perspective, see www.ahavat-israel.com.

Since distances are short (and local knowledge of roads essential) a better idea is to hire a taxi to take you to the place you want to visit. Ask a tour operator to set you up with a reliable driver. Most taxi drivers in Bethlehem are used to the needs of tourists and can run ad hoc day trips all over the West Bank. They hang around Bab iz-Qaq or the entrance to the Bethlehem checkpoint.

Israeli licence plates are yellow, while Palestinian plates are green and white. Yellow-plated cars, while fine to drive throughout most of the West Bank – especially in more peaceful times – might cause you to be mistaken for an Israeli or Jewish settler. To play it safe, place a keffiyeh on the dashboard. Remember to remove it when stopped at an Israeli checkpoint, or it may become an inadvertent conversation piece for bored Israeli soldiers.

Since roadblocks, settlement construction and security-wall building work are all ongoing, accessibility and roads can change quickly. It pays to buy an up-to-date road map (maps bought in Israel cover the West Bank, too) before travelling around the region. GPS users can purchase the most up-to-date road maps with satellite coordinates at the Educational Bookshop (p98) in East Jerusalem.

Bethlehem בית לחם بيت لحم

♻ 02 / POP 27,800

Most visitors come to Bethlehem with a preconceived image – a small stone village, a manger and shepherds in their fields – thanks to a childhood crèche, perhaps, or a drawer full of fading Christmas cards.

The reality is quite different. Bethlehem positively hums with activity, its winding streets congested with traffic and its main square filled with snap-happy tourists scrambling to keep up with their guides.

Churches now cover many of the holy sites – the most famed is the Church of the Nativity on Manger Sq – but there is plenty to see and do for even for the non-religious. There's a lively Old City and bazaar, plus sites around town including the incredible Herodium. There are numerous cultural centres where you can critique local art, watch performances and talk politics.

Most travellers come on a day trip but to get the most out of your visit it's best to stay overnight – accommodation and food are both cheaper here than what you'll get in Jerusalem.

History

Built along ancient footpaths, the little town where Mary and Joseph went for a census and returned with a son has had residents since as far back as the Palaeolithic era. The town is thought to have first developed in the 14th century BCE as a city state named Beit Lahmu, after Lahmu, goddess of protection, and later took the Hebrew Bible name, Ephrata.

Then in 313 CE, three centuries after the birth of Jesus, the Roman Emperor Constantine made Christianity the official state religion. Bethlehem soon became a popular, well-to-do pilgrimage town, with flourishing monasteries and churches. In 638 the city was conquered by Muslims, but a treaty was signed guaranteeing Christians property rights and religious freedom, and Bethlehem continued to prosper for the next millennium or so.

Bethlehem's numbers then swelled after the 1948 Arab–Israeli War, when Palestinian refugees from the newly created State of Israel poured into town. Many continue to live, along with their descendants, in the refugee camps of Aida, Dheisheh and al-Azzah on the edges of town.

Today Bethlehem continues to rely – as it has for the last 1700 years or so – on the tourist and pilgrim trade. It is easily the most visited city in the West Bank, especially around Christian holidays, with crowds still flocking here for Easter and for the traditional Christmas Eve midnight Mass.

◉ Sights

From Bab iz-Qaq (where bus 121 from Jerusalem stops) walk up Pope Paul VI St for five minutes to Cinema Sq, from where it's a 10-minute walk to Manger Sq. If you took the bus to the checkpoint, there are taxi drivers waiting to bring you into the city for around 10NIS to 20NIS.

If you get a taxi to Manger Sq, then saunter from here up along bustling Pope Paul VI St (taking in the souq to the left), then take a right to loop around and return down charming Star St for an atmospheric taste of the Old City.

Most of the city's other sights are within walking distance of the town centre; pick up a taxi down on Manger St or on Manger Sq itself to venture out to Shepherds' Field, Mar Saba Monastery or Herodium.

Manger Square & Old City   HISTORIC SITE
The narrow limestone streets and exotic storefronts are a scene from another age, particularly Pope Paul VI St, Star St and the narrow alleys connecting the two. Visit on a Sunday to experience some church services. Most in attendance will be Palestinians and resident monks and nuns from across the world, but visitors are welcome to attend or stop in for a few moments of contemplation.

To sample a few services, spend a Sunday morning dropping discreetly in and out of the following. Set out at 9am to the 19th-century Lutheran Christmas Church (Pope Paul VI St, Madbasseh Sq) to experience a Lutheran service. Then head towards Manger Sq to the more modern St Mary's Syrian Orthodox Church (☉9am-5pm), where 9am Sunday Mass is held in Syriac. Descend the stairs to Manger Sq and enter the Church of the Nativity to find a Greek Orthodox service in session. Tiptoe through the cloisters around to the left and through a passage to St Catherine's Church for a Roman Catholic Mass.

And finally, don't miss a visit to the little souq (☉8am-6pm Mon-Sat), known to locals as the Green Market. This souq – with its range of fruit and vegetables, meat and fish, junk, shoes and some mighty tasty snacks – was established in 1929.

Church of the Nativity   CHURCH
(☉5am-8pm, to 6pm winter) Though sceptics argue over whether X (or in this case a star) really does mark the spot, the Church of the Nativity nevertheless makes an imposing marker for the birthplace of Jesus. Also called the Basilica of the Nativity, it's the oldest continuously operating church, commissioned in 326 CE by Emperor Constantine. To really get the most out of a visit to the church, negotiate a price for a tour from one of the handful of milling tour guides you'll find outside (around 50NIS per hour is a decent price): they know all the nooks and crannies intimately, and may even introduce you to some of the resident priests and monks.

You might be surprised, if you've never seen pictures, to find that the facade of the church is only a tiny Ottoman-era front door, aptly named the Door of Humility. Watch your head as you bow through (originally the entrance was much larger, but the Crusaders reduced its size to prevent attackers from riding in; later, either during the Mamluk or Ottoman period, the portal was made

KICKING IT IN BETHLEHEM

The Beautiful Game is alive and kicking in Bethlehem. It is here that members of the Palestinian Women's National Soccer Team practise their dribbles and passes at schoolyards around the city.

Though they have little in the way of resources – without even a grass pitch to train on – and some of the team's members are in inaccessible Gaza – the team won't be daunted. And despite checkpoints and permits, they've competed so far in Abu Dhabi and Amman, among other Middle Eastern locations. They may have yet to win a tournament, but the team members see their very existence as a victory against their current circumstances.

Another newcomer to the local sports scene is Palestine's first professional rugby side, the Beit Jala Lions (www.beitjalalions.com), who have already embarked on tours to Cyprus and Jordan. Follow the guys on their website, or their Facebook page.

If you feel like participating in some local sport, regular basketball matches are held at the Ibdaa Cultural Centre in Dheisheh (see the boxed text, p275).

even smaller – you can still see the outline of the original 6th-century doorway and, within it, the pointed Crusader-era arch), and proceed on to the cavernous nave. Renovations over the centuries have included a new floor here, beneath which lies Constantine's original 4th-century mosaic floor, rediscovered in 1934 and now viewable through wooden trapdoors in the central aisle.

The 6th century saw the church rebuilt almost entirely by Emperor Justinian, after the majority was destroyed in a Samaritan revolt. The mammoth red-and-white limestone columns that still grace the nave are probably the only surviving remnants of the original structure, their stone quarried from nearby. Some of them are decorated with frescos of saints, painted by Crusaders in the 12th century. To the right of the Door of Humility, a doorway leads to the Armenian Monastery, these days housing just six monks to service the needs of Bethlehem's 300-strong Armenian congregation. The Armenians flourished during the 1600s, when they were noted for their transcribed and illuminated versions of the Bible.

At the front of the nave, descend the stairs to enter the Grotto of the Nativity. It's popular with tour groups, so try to time your visit over lunchtime midweek, and you'll likely have the grotto entirely to yourself (come on a weekend and you may have to stand in line for an hour or more).

Atmospherically lantern-lit and redolent with mystery, this is where Jesus is said to have been born, the 14-pointed silver star marking the spot. The Chapel of the Manger or 'the Crib' to one side of the grotto represents the scene of the nativity, while the chapel facing it houses the Altar of the Adoration of the Magi, which commemorates the visit of Caspar, Balthazar and Melchior. The Persians spared the church and grotto when they sacked Palestine in 614 CE, ostensibly because they saw a depiction of the magi in their own native costume.

Though all might seem serene down here, conflict has actually rocked this cradle for ages. The 14-pointed star was stolen in 1847, each of the three Christian communities in residence (the Greek Orthodox, the Armenians and the Catholics, who have bitterly and ceaselessly fought for custodianship of the grotto) blaming the others. A copy was subsequently supplied to replace it, but the fights didn't end there, and administrative domination of the church changed hands repeatedly between the Orthodox and Catholics. To this day, management of the church is divvied up metre for metre between the Orthodox, Catholic and Armenian clerics (see p376 for more on this system of management for holy places, known as the 'status quo'). Take the grotto lanterns for example: six belong to the Greek Orthodox, five to the Armenians and four to the Catholics.

St Catherine's Church
CHURCH

Midnight Mass at the pink-toned St Catherine's Church, next door to the Church of the Nativity, is broadcast across the world on Christmas Eve, but there's nothing like being there in person for an atmospheric – if rather lengthy – Christmas experience. Access the church via the Church of the Nativity to first wander through the Crusader-era Franciscan cloister with a statue of St Jerome.

Bethlehem

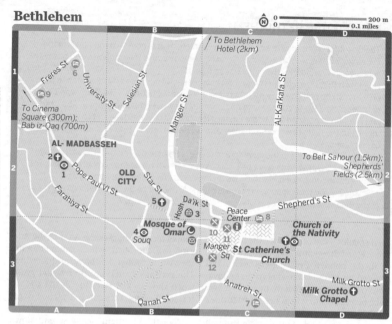

N
0 ____ 200 m
0 ____ 0.1 miles

Bethlehem

Milk Grotto Chapel   CHURCH

(Milk Grotto St; ⊘8-11am & 2-6pm) A short walk from Manger Sq is the lesser-known Milk Grotto Chapel. The white rock inside this stony chapel is said to bring milk to a mother's bosom and enhance fertility in women who swallow a morsel of the chalky substance. Legend has it that Mary and Joseph stopped here to feed the baby during their flight to Egypt; a drop of milk touched the red rock, turning it white.

Mosque of Omar   MOSQUE

On Manger Sq, opposite the Church of the Nativity, is the Mosque of Omar; named after the 2nd Muslim caliph, Omar Ibn al-Khattab, it is the sole mosque in Bethlehem's old city. It was built in 1860 on land granted by the Greek Orthodox Church in honour of Omar, the Prophet Mohammed's father-in-law, who in 637 took Jerusalem from the flagging Byzantines and then stopped for prayer at the Christian Church of the Nativity. He declared, in his Pact of Omar, that the basilica would remain a Christian shrine, and that Christians, even under Muslim rule, would remain free to practise their faith.

Rachel's Tomb RELIGIOUS

(⊙7.30am-4pm Sun-Thu, to 1.30pm Fri) In a desolate corridor created by Israel's security wall, near the main checkpoint into town, stands Rachel's Tomb. Another Bethlehem sojourner during labour, Rachel, wife of Jacob, is said to have died here in childbirth, on the way south to Hebron, after which her husband 'set a pillar upon her grave' (Genesis 35:20). Revered by followers of all three Abrahamic religions – Jews and Muslims in particular – the place has been enshrined and guarded for centuries, from the Byzantine and Islamic eras through to the Crusaders, and during the epochs of the Ottomans and Israelis.

Today the tomb is completely surrounded by the security wall, and visiting the site – situated on the Israeli side of the wall – involves a short drive through an eerie concrete corridor. You cannot walk this section of road, so flag down a private car or bus at the gate to take you the final 300m. The gate is near the main Bethlehem checkpoint, reached on Arab bus 24. Egged bus 163 from Jerusalem's Central Bus Station goes all the way to the tomb.

Once at the tomb there are separate sides for men and women (kippas for men are available at the door). The adjoining Bilal ibn Rabah mosque, long inaccessible to Palestinians, is now off-limits to visitors.

Palestinian Heritage Center CULTURAL CENTRE

(www.phc.ps; Manger St, Al-Qubba; ⊙11am-6pm Mon-Sat) A steadfast sign of life near the separation wall and Bethlehem checkpoint, the Palestinian Heritage Center sits at the crossroads of Manger and Caritas Sts. Have your picture taken in Palestinian folk dress, and learn from the effusive museum owner, Maha Saca, how Palestinian hand-stitched embroidery (also for sale here) identifies wearers according to their village of origin.

Old Bethlehem Museum MUSEUM

(www.arabwomenunion.org; Star St; admission 8NIS; ⊙8am-noon & 2-5pm Mon-Wed, Fri & Sat, to noon Thu) The Old City's Old Bethlehem Museum is located in the dusty basement of a typical Palestinian home of the 19th century. See native costumes, peruse the collection of early-20th-century photos of Palestine, and purchase embroidery produced by the Beth-

lehem Arab Women's Union, at the embroidery centre upstairs.

International Center of Bethlehem (Dar Annadwa) CULTURAL CENTRE

(☎02-277 0047; www.annadwa.org; Pope Paul VI St, Madbasseh Sq; ☎) The Lutheran-run International Center of Bethlehem (Dar Annadwa) puts on concerts, plays, films, English-language documentaries, workshops and lectures. There's also a coffee shop, guesthouse, art gallery and gift shop, known as the Cave (Al-Kahf; thecave@annadwa.org), where local artists show off their work. Attached to the gallery is a small, underground cave dwelling, hence the name of the gallery.

🛏 Sleeping

Most hotel rooms in Bethlehem are rather nondescript, though comfortable nonetheless. Since most cater to a pilgrim crowd, expect to pay 30% to 50% more at Christmas or Easter time, and book your room well in advance.

TOP CHOICE Dar Annadwa GUESTHOUSE $$

(Abu Gubran; ☎277 0047; www.diyar.ps; 109 Pope Paul VI St, Old City; s/d US$65/90; ☎) Each of the 13 tasteful rooms at this little guesthouse, also known as Abu Gubran, is named after a Palestinian village. Students from the International Center's art school provide decor in this very comfortable, Lutheran-sponsored boutique guesthouse with all the amenities.

Arab Women's Union GUESTHOUSE $$

(☎277 5857; www.elbeit.org; Beit Sahour; s/d/tr US$45/60/80; @) The women who run this guesthouse in beautiful Beit Sahour recycle paper, run community programs and produce olive-wood artefacts. The guesthouse has clean and modern rooms and there's a nice balcony where you can relax with a cup of tea.

Bethlehem Star Hotel HOTEL $$

(☎274 3249; www.star-inn-hotels.com; University St; s/d US$45/75; ☎) This place has clean and comfortable rooms with 1980s decor and small TVs. There are good views, free wi-fi and friendly staff. Good value for money.

Bethlehem Hotel HOTEL $$

(☎277 0702; www.bethlehemhotel.com; Manger St; s/d/tr US$55/85/100; @) Rooms are cheery but plain, and this Manger St standard, 1km from the Nativity Church, makes a decent central base, on a portion of street lively with cafes.

Grand Hotel Bethlehem HOTEL $$

(274 1440; www.grandhotelbethlehem.com; Pope Paul VI St; s US$50-60, d US$70-80;) Neat, clean, efficient and in the middle of the action, the Grand Hotel's 107 rooms might not have bags of character, but they're comfy and central. Breakfast is served at the hotel's Mariachi Bar and the coffee shop serves Mexican dishes and seafood daily until midnight. The pricier rooms have been renovated with new furnishings.

Casanova Orient Palace HOTEL $$

(274 3980; www.casanovapalace.com; s/d/tr from US$45/60/90; @) The closest you'll get to sleeping in the manger itself, this perennially popular place offers reasonable rooms and a buzzing atmosphere, particularly around Christmas. The lobby, just off Manger Sq next to the Church of the Nativity, is as much a gathering place for transient tourists and devout dignitaries as it is for hotel guests. The hotel has two sections: a nicer wing closer to the square and a more basic wing around the corner (next to the church).

Bethlehem Youth Hostel HOSTEL $

(274 8466, 059 964 6146; byh@ejepal.org; 66 Anatreh St; dm 60NIS; @) This brand-new hostel consists of three spacious dorm rooms, hot showers and a balcony with distant views of the Herodium. Breakfast costs an additional 20NIS but the owner may offer you a free walking tour of Bethlehem. It's one street below the Milk Grotto.

Ibdaa Cultural Centre Guesthouse GUESTHOUSE $

(277 6444; www.ibdaa48.org; Dheisheh Refugee Camp; dm 50NIS; @) This multipurpose facility on the Jerusalem–Hebron Rd is a lively, happening place, treating travellers to free internet, cheap eats, simple dormitory lodging, a host of ongoing activities and a fascinating window into Palestinian refugee life (see the boxed text, p275).

Eating

For fast food, stroll along Manger St or head up to the small souq just off Pope Paul VI St. Here you'll find fist-sized felafel, sizzling shwarmas and lots of tempting produce for picnics or self-catering.

TOP CHOICE Afteem MIDDLE EASTERN $

(Manger Sq; felafels 6NIS, hummus from 15NIS) A Bethlehem institution for decades; topnotch hummus and *masabacha* (warm hummus with whole chickpeas) are dispensed here to locals' delight, just down the ramp from Manger Sq. For something a little different, go for a delectable bowl of *fatteh* – a sort of soupy hummus topping submerged pieces of pita and finished with roasted pine nuts.

Square MIDDLE EASTERN, WESTERN $

(Manger Sq; mains from 35NIS; 9am-midnight;) A swish lounge-style place right in the heart of Bethlehem, this makes a great respite from a long walking tour around the city. Sip a cappuccino or sup a light lunch (salads and pastas) in the basement dining room. Also available are cocktails, nargilehs (water pipes; on the upper level; try melon, apple or cherry flavours).

Peace Center Restaurant SANDWICHES, ITALIAN $

(Manger Sq; mains 20-45NIS; 9am-6pm Mon-Sat) This spacious, central spot is great for a light snack or something more refined such as Mediterranean salmon or *shish tawooq* (chicken skewers).

Qaabar MIDDLE EASTERN $

(Beit Jala; BBQ 33NIS; 9am-11pm) Get to the old city of Beit Jala, 2.2kn northwest of Manger Sq, and ask for barbecue. Everyone knows Qaabar for the charcoal-grilled chicken and its fabulous aioli – a habit-forming eggless garlic mayonnaise. Smack your lips and use your fingers.

Dar al-Balad INTERNATIONAL $

(Beit Sahour; mains 25-50NIS; noon-midnight) This atmospheric restaurant with arched ceilings and stone walls serves tasty grilled dishes salads and pastas. It's located down a narrow alley, a pleasant find in Beit Sahour's restored old town, 1.2km east of Manger Sq.

ⓘ Information

Peace Center (276 6677; www.peacenter. org; 8am-3pm Mon-Thu & Sat) This information desk gives away city maps and provides helpful hints on accommodation and transport.

Visitor Information Center (275 4235; vic. info.palestine@gmail.com; 8am-4pm Tue & Wed, to 5pm Thu-Sat) Located in the southwest corner of Manger Sq, this is a Vatican-

CHECKPOINTS

Checkpoints (in Hebrew, *machsomim*) control the flow of travellers between the West Bank and Israel. There are also some checkpoints inside the West Bank, although these tend to be less stable, shifting locations, shutting down altogether or popping up in new locations. Most checkpoints are run by the IDF, although some have been outsourced to private contractors. The latter tend to be more troublesome as foreigners are more likely to be questioned and have their bags searched.

Operating hours of checkpoints vary, often depending on whether the primary users are settlers or Palestinians. For example, the checkpoint leading south from Jerusalem on Rte 60 near Bethlehem is open 24/7, while Bethlehem checkpoint 300 (which leads into Bethlehem city) is sometimes closed at night (but not always). Checkpoints used by Palestinians are subject to random closures, especially around Jewish holidays, when the West Bank is sometimes sealed for security reasons.

Checkpoints range in size from small pedestrian-only checkpoints like Abu Dis to larger ones that accommodate vehicles and resemble an international border crossing, such as the Bethlehem 300 checkpoint. 'Flying checkpoints' are temporary IDF road-blocks set up inside the West Bank. Delays depend on the volume of traffic. Checkpoints set up by Palestinian police exist too (for example, near Jericho) but traffic generally flows smoothly through them.

In general, travellers are not checked when going into the West Bank, only when travelling from the West Bank back into Israel.

Foreign-passport holders are allowed to travel through IDF checkpoints into areas under the control of the Palestinian Authority but by military order, Israeli citizens are (theoretically) forbidden from doing so.

There is no cost involved with crossing a checkpoint and foreign-passport holders do not need any special documentation. Just show your passport and put your bags through an X-ray machine. The procedure is generally fast but with waiting time you can expect to be at a checkpoint for 15 to 20 minutes (or longer if lines have formed).

Try to avoid passing through a checkpoint in the early morning (7am to 9am) or on holidays (Muslim or Jewish) due to long lines.

Foreigners can take a vehicle into and out of the West Bank (if you've got a rental car, make sure your insurance policy covers travel to the Palestinian Authority – most don't) but expect delays upon your return to Israel as the soldiers may inspect the vehicle for explosives.

The following are some of the main checkpoints into and out of the West Bank:

Qalandia – Between Jerusalem and Ramallah. Use this checkpoint for Ramallah, Nablus and Jenin. This is one of the busiest checkpoints and it sports some fairly grim metal corrals and locking turnstiles of the sort you'd expect to see at a maximum-security prison. There is actually a checkpoint on both sides of the road – one for pedestrians and the other for bus travellers.

Bethlehem 300 – Located south of Jerusalem at the entrance to Rachel's Tomb. One road leads to the checkpoint for cars and one for pedestrians. This is an indoor checkpoint and the conditions are better than the one at Qalandia, but opening hours are not reliable and the checkpoint is sometimes closed at night.

Bethlehem (highway) – You will go through this checkpoint if you take bus 21 from Bethlehem. It resembles a toll gate and security here is very light. Tourists may remain on the bus during the passport check (Palestinian passengers are asked to line up outside the bus). It's open 24/7.

Jalameh – Located 10km south of Afula, this checkpoint is one of the best in terms of ease and accessibility. However, long lines have been reported here.

Abu Dis – This checkpoint connects East Jerusalem to Abu Dis, from where travellers can connect to Jericho. It is a pedestrian-only checkpoint and is usually closed at night.

For more details on the conditions at individual checkpoints, visit the website of the left-wing Israeli group Machsom Watch (www.machsomwatch.org).

INSIDE THE WEST BANK

To make the West Bank all the more accessible, explore the work of some of the following organisations.

Alternative Tourism Group (☎02-277 2151; www.patg.org; 74 Star St, Beit Sahour) Offers plenty of information, and recommended day tours of Hebron and Bethlehem (every Tuesday, 225NIS, 8am to 6pm).

Holy Land Trust (☎02-276 5930; www.holylandtrust.org) Based in Bethlehem, arranges tours of the Territories, study programs and homestays, and helps organise the annual Palestine Summer Encounter.

Palestine Fair Trade Association (☎04-250 1512; www.palestinefairtrade.org) Organises homestays and voluntary work placements in Palestinian homes and farms, particularly during the annual olive harvest.

Palestinian Association for Cultural Exchange (☎02-240 7611; www.pace.ps) Offers one-day and longer tours of Nablus, Hebron, Qalqilya and around, supports local cooperatives and can arrange lecture programs.

Siraj Center for Holy Land Studies (☎02-274 8590; www.sirajcenter.org) Organises and coordinates plenty of activities and 'encounters' throughout the West Bank.

sponsored tourist office run by international volunteers.

❶ Getting There & Away

Bus 21 from Jerusalem to Bethlehem (7NIS, 30 minutes) departs every 15 minutes between 6am and 9pm (until 6.30pm in winter) from the Damascus Gate bus station. Alternatively, take bus 24 (5NIS) from Jerusalem to the main Bethlehem checkpoint, from where there are taxis into Bethlehem.

The best way to get from Bethlehem to other destinations in the West Bank is by taxi. Negotiate a price per hour (something around the 50NIS mark is standard) and you'll have the freedom to get to the sights out of town or take a trip to one of the other West Bank cities.

Alternatively, it's possible to get shared taxis from the main bus station to Jericho (18NIS) and Hebron (9NIS). Share taxis to Hebron also leave from Bab iz-Qaq.

Around Bethlehem

Bethlehem makes a great base for excursions throughout the West Bank, but there are also some worthwhile sights close to home.

SHEPHERDS' FIELD

If you've always wondered where exactly 'shepherds watched their flocks by night' (Luke 2:8), drop into Shepherds' Field (Map p267), a parklike area just outside Beit Sahour, to see for yourself. While the Beit Sahour Shepherds' Field isn't the only

Bethlehem location earmarked as the exact spot for the lauded visit of the heavenly host to announce Jesus's birth to a group of shepherds, it's certainly the most frequented. As well as the strollable grounds, you'll find a Byzantine cave housing a chapel (often the scene of atmospheric monastic chanting) and the 1953 Italian-designed Church of the Angels, with its lovely, light interior.

To reach Shepherds' Field take a private taxi from Bethlehem (15NIS) or catch Beit Sahour–bound bus 47 (2NIS) from Shepherd's St, just below Manger Sq.

HERODIUM   הרודיון   هروديون

King Herod's spectacular fortress-palace, Herodium (adult/child 27/14NIS; ⏱8am-5pm Apr-Sep, to 4pm Oct-Mar), built between 23 and 15 BCE, was known through the centuries for Arab inhabitants as the Mountain of Paradise.

Even from a distance, you won't miss the site: it rises from the Judean Desert like a flat-topped caricature of a volcano (the top is actually an extension of the natural hill, hollowed out to hold Herod's palace), 9km south of Beit Sahour. The complex features a series of stunning remains of Herod's own personal 'country club' (which included a bathhouse and rooftop pool) and also includes King Herod's own tomb, discovered in 2007. Though it was sacked by the Romans in 71 CE, around the same time as Masada was similarly assaulted, much remains at the site, with still more awaiting further excavation.

Note that Herodium falls under 'Area C' and is thus under full Israeli control (you'll see the military base at the foot of the hill); the site itself is administered by the Israeli Parks and Nature Authority (www.parks.org.il). To get here, take a private taxi from Bethlehem (around 50NIS per hour), and negotiate at least an hour's waiting time. Try to avoid Fridays, when Herodium fills up with tour buses from Israel.

AL-KHADER CHURCH
كنيسة الخضير   כנסיית אלח'דר

Just outside Bethlehem, on the road to Hebron, Al-Khader Church (St George's; Jerusalem–Hebron Rd; ⏰8am-noon & 3-6pm Sun & holidays) is dedicated to St George, famous enemy to dragons and patron saint of travellers and the sick. St George is also known as the patron saint of Palestine, or St George the Green; his feast day is celebrated annually on 5 May with a pilgrimage out to the church, attended by both Christians and Muslims. Someone from the Muslim family entrusted with the keys to the small Greek Orthodox church will perform a chaining ritual at your request, ceremonially chaining and unchaining any visitor desiring to release bad energy, cleanse the soul, cast off illness or prepare for a long journey. It's said that this derives from the practice (thankfully no longer undertaken) of chaining the mentally disturbed to the walls in the hope that St George might cure their insanity. You can take a private taxi from Bethlehem (20NIS) to Al-Khader. Note that the church is only open on Sundays and holidays.

SOLOMON'S POOLS برك سليمان   בריכות שלמה
The more prominent site in the Al-Khader area is Solomon's Pools. During Roman times a system of springs filled three mammoth rectangular reservoirs supplying water via aqueducts to Jerusalem and Herodium. King Solomon enjoyed respite beside their serene shimmer, where he is said to have written the sensuous *Song of Solomon*. The springs were used into the 20th century for irrigating crops in the surrounding fertile valley, while successive armies have also set up camp here. An Ottoman fortress is still evident, the historic last stop for pilgrims on their way to Jerusalem.

Unfortunately, the pools are now fenced off and the water drained, so it's no longer a very picturesque place. Only travellers with a serious interest in history make it this way.

To reach Solomon's Pools from Bethlehem take Dheisheh bus 1 (3NIS) from Manger Sq, or private taxi (20NIS).

Central West Bank

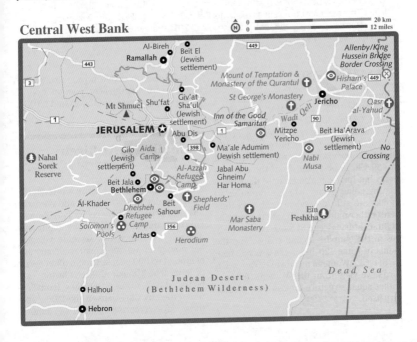

0   20 km
0   12 miles

Al-Bireh
Ramallah
443
3
Beit El (Jewish settlement)
449
Allenby/King Hussein Bridge Border Crossing
Mount of Temptation & Monastery of the Qurantul
St George's Monastery
Hisham's Palace
449
Mt Shmuel   Shu'fat   Giv'at Sha'ul (Jewish settlement)
Jericho
Qasr al-Yahud
1
JERUSALEM
Abu Dis
1
Inn of the Good Samaritan
Wadi Qelt
90
Mitzpe Yericho
Beit Ha'Arava (Jewish settlement)
No Crossing
Gilo (Jewish settlement)
Aida Camp
398
Ma'ale Adumim (Jewish settlement)
Jabal Abu Ghneim/ Har Homa
Nabi Musa
Nahal Sorek Reserve
Beit Jala
Bethlehem
Al-Azzah Refugee Camp
90
Al-Khader
Dheisheh Refugee Camp
Beit Sahour
Shepherds' Field
Ein Feshkha
Solomon's Pools
Artas
356
Mar Saba Monastery
Herodium
Dead Sea
Halhoul
Hebron
Judean Desert (Bethlehem Wilderness)

ISRAEL'S SECURITY FENCE

From 1967 until the Second Intifada (2000–05), there was virtually no physical barrier between the West Bank and Israel. West Bank Palestinians could cross into Israel pretty much whenever they wanted to, and over 100,000 commuted to work inside Israel every day.

But in the mid-1990s and even more so during the Second Intifada, scores of suicide bombers crossed into Israel from the West Bank, killing hundreds of Israeli civilians. Israel responded with military incursions into areas controlled by the Palestinian Authority, and both security experts and the Israeli public called on the government to build a security fence to prevent infiltration (see the somewhat outdated Israeli Ministry of Defence website, www.securityfence.mod.gov.il, for more on this).

Although Jewish settlers were bitterly opposed to such a fence – not wanting to find themselves literally and psychologically outside Israel's de facto borders – the government eventually gave in to public pressure.

The stated goal of the Oslo Accords was the establishment of two separate states. From the point of view of the Israeli left, a border fence would only further that process, along the lines of 'good fences make good neighbours'. Unless you build them through your neighbour's yard, say West Bank Palestinians, who have watched helplessly as Israel has erected fences and concrete barriers through their villages and fields and made access to Jerusalem difficult or impossible. Except in Jerusalem, most of the fence (about 5% of which is a concrete antisniper wall up to 8m high) parallels the Green Line (the 1949 armistice between Israel and Jordan) – but only roughly. Quite a few sections loop and scoop around Jewish settlements, separating Palestinians from their communities, businesses, schools and crops. Palestinians call the security barrier the 'Apartheid Wall' and see it as part of a concerted campaign to grab land wherever possible. Israel – where the barrier is seen as a security success – says that the route of the fence can always be modified, eg if there is a final status accord on borders.

Around Bethlehem, the wall has served as a vast canvas for graffiti artists and activists – you can see some of their work along the road to the checkpoint. Demonstrations are periodically held in other parts of the West Bank where the Wall cuts through villages. These often turn violent as the Israel Defence Forces (IDF) regularly disperses the crowd with tear gas and rubber bullets. As of 2011, more than 20 people had died in antiwall demonstrations.

MAR SABA MONASTERY
دير مار سابا   מנזר מרסבא

A must-see on any architectural journey through the Holy Land is Mar Saba Monastery (☉8am-4pm Sun-Thu), a bleak and beautiful 20km drive east of Bethlehem (beyond Beit Sahour). This phenomenal cliff-clinging copper-domed hermitage, founded in 439 CE, is best seen from the opposite slope, but men can also exercise their privilege by going inside, where a dozen or so monks are still in residence. Also residing here (rather more eternally) are the remains of 5th-century ascetic St Sabas, whose body lies in the church's second chapel, and the skulls of some 120 monks massacred here in 614 CE. Women, meanwhile, can get a bird's-eye view from the Women's Tower, a rather squat structure opposite the monastery itself.

You'll need to take a private taxi out to Mar Saba from Bethlehem; plan on around a three-hour journey, costing around 120NIS to 150NIS.

Ramallah & Al-Bireh
رام الله   רמאללה ואל-בירה
🖉 02 / POP 73,000

Sitting at a lofty 900m above sea level, it's understandable why Gulfites and Jordanians used to cool off here before 1967. Ramallah (the name means God's Mountain) and Al-Bireh were once two separate villages, but now make up one urban conglomerate of around 65,000 people, a mere 10km north of Jerusalem. Though Al-Bireh's history can be traced back to the Canaanites, Ramallah was settled by Christians in the 1500s, and these days comprises a bustling, almost-cosmopolitan city, largely free from dense politics and religious fervour.

Ramallah may lack the plethora of historic sights of Jericho or Bethlehem, but wander the arteries running from central Al-Manara Sq to find snacks, perfumeries and jewellery shops galore, or head down to more sedate Al-Muntazah neighbourhood to rub shoulders with Pekingese-toting ladies and local notables. With polite policemen manning the city's zebra crossings, roaming fez-capped coffee vendors, shoppers, hawkers, and busy, besuited businessmen, Ramallah revels in an air of gleeful sophistication, and makes a terrific place to spend a day.

⊙ Sights & Activities

A good place to start your Ramallah explorations is at busy Al-Manara Sq (Lighthouse Sq). Think Trafalgar Sq in miniature and with a Palestinian twist, complete with columns (though no Nelson), stone lions (bearing Palestinian-flag graffiti), traffic and pigeons. From Al-Manara Sq, wander Al-Ra'eesy St (also known as Main St), or Palestine St on the opposite side, to find coffeehouses and bustle in abundance.

This area is also filled with jewellers, food and pharmacies, so if you're looking for any – or all – of these three, you've come to the right place.

To reach the Al-Muntazah neighbourhood, head down the wider Jaffa Rd; take a right at the HSBC bank (which hosts Ramallah's most reliable ATM machine for foreign cards), and head up Eisah Zeyada St, which has a host of chic cafes and dining destinations.

Crusader Church
CHURCH
Located in Al-Bireh, this church, according to the Crusader story, was built where Mary and Joseph lost their preteen son while on their way to Jerusalem, before relocating him in Jerusalem where he was busy praying and philosophising with the grownups at the Temple.

Muqata'a
HISTORIC BUILDING
(Al-Itha'a St) Those interested in modern history might want to stop by at the now rebuilt Muqata'a, Yasser Arafat's large presidential compound, in which he spent his sunset years, following the Israeli invasion of Ramallah during the Second Intifada. His enormous **cubicle tomb** (⊙9am-9pm), guarded by soldiers and adorned with wreaths, is open to visitors daily; he was buried here in 2004 after he died of unknown causes in a hospital in Paris. Buildings have been restored with the exception of some holes from tank shelling. The Muqata'a is around 1km from Al-Manara on the road to Birzeit and Nablus.

Al-Kamandjati
CONCERT HALL
(☑297 3101; www.alkamandjati.com, in French; Old City) Back in the city centre, Ramallah's Old City is a blink-of-an-eye example of Ottoman architecture, and is home to small Al-Kamandjati conservatory, with the strains of violin and flute wafting over an ancient arch with an edgy, modern copper entryway. It offers intimate concerts and recitals.

🛌 Sleeping

Most foreign visitors to Ramallah, with the exception of aid workers, volunteers and businesspeople, come here for the day, basing themselves in Jerusalem. But if you do want to stay in town, there's a reasonable selection of digs for all pockets.

Royal Court Suites Hotel
HOTEL $$
(☑296 4040; www.rcshotel.com; Al-Muntazah; s 255-310NIS, d 370-450NIS; @) Units have furnished kitchenettes, some with separate bedrooms. There is no wi-fi but rooms do come with a cable that you can hook up to a laptop. Breakfast is substantial. Rooms are tastefully designed, have excellent bathrooms and some come with balconies.

Beauty Inn
HOTEL $$
(☑246 6477; www.beautyinn.ps; Khalil Al Sakakini Cultural Centre St, Al-Muntazah; s/d/ste US$90/110/150; @🛜⚙) Local entrepreneur Andres Dahdal has recently opened this excellent midrange hotel with a number of amenities, including a pool, gym and sauna. Rooms are well equipped and nicely furnished, and if anything is amiss Andres will be quick to correct the problem.

Merryland Hotel
HOTEL $
(☑295 7331; Martyr Nazeeh al-Qourah; s/d 170/260NIS; 🛜) Located inside an older shopping mall, this place does not feel like it was designed to be a hotel. Rooms are bright and filled with an ugly assortment of furniture, but it's fine for a night or two.

Al-Wihdeh Hotel
HOTEL $
(☑298 0412; Al-Nahda St, Al-Manara; s/d/tr 100/120/130NIS; 🛜) Dirt-cheap rooms, free

Ramallah

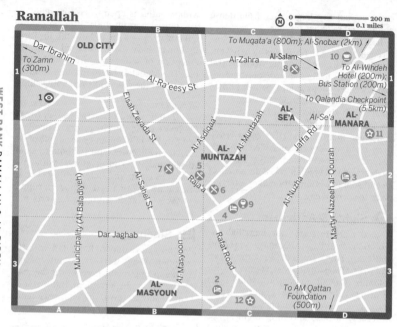

Ramallah

◉ Sights

🛏 Sleeping

✕ Eating

◉ Drinking

✪ Entertainment

wi-fi and a central location, but it's pretty beat up, so only consider it as a backup if you're stuck for the night.

✕ Eating

The area around Al-Manara Sq is packed with hole-in-the-wall eateries and fast-food joints. Heading south you'll find the classier eats congregated along Eisah Zeyada St and Jaffa Rd.

Follow your nose for felafel and shwarma; both are particularly plentiful around Al-Manara Sq.

TOP CHOICE **Pronto Resto-Café**   ITALIAN **$$**

(Al-Muntazah; mains 45-75NIS; ☺7am-11pm) This dark and cosy little trattoria is a popular spot for musicians, filmmakers, professionals and peacemakers. The carbonara is full of smoky bacon and garlic, and the blue-cheese sandwich is a cheese-lover's pungent delight. Top it all off with a glass or two of Palestinian-produced wine.

Zeit ou Zaater   BAKERY, CAFE **$**

(Al-Ra'eesy St; snacks from 10NIS; ☺10am-late; 🛜) Busy for both eating in and takeaway, this atmospheric little place has a whole range of yummy pastries, sandwiches and little pizzas on offer. The owner, Nasser Abdelhadi, is locally famous for once preparing the world's largest tabouleh salad (authenticated by the *Guinness Book of World Records*).

Zamn CAFE $

(Al-Tireh; coffees from 10NIS; mains 35-60NIS; ⏰7am-11pm; 📶) The hippest spot in Ramallah and meeting ground for reporters and NGO workers, Zamn is a fun place for a morning croissant and cuppa or a lunchtime sandwich. Walk down Dar Ibrahim and bear right at the roundabout.

Café de la Paix CAFE $

(Al-Muntazah; coffees from 10NIS, mains 35-75NIS; ⏰9am-late) This swanky, European-style cafe and bakery has great cakes and coffee, leather chairs and cool jazz. The salads are vast and the cappuccinos frothy. Pancakes with plenty of maple syrup are to be had for 32NIS.

Za'rour Bar BQ BARBECUE $

(Old City; mains 40-70NIS; ⏰noon-midnight) The grilled meats and salads at this local fail-safe place behind the Municipality building offer quality Palestinian staples, which can be topped off with a sweet pastry and a strong coffee. It has a small playground to keep kids busy.

🍷 Drinking

Traditional coffeehouses in Ramallah – offering simple, cheap-thimbleful-of-black-coffee experiences – are everywhere; they're especially plentiful around Al-Manara Sq. Though many are predominantly male hang-outs, visiting women will find a welcome in most. At the other end of the sipping spectrum, there are several cocktail-dispensing bars that stay open till the wee hours.

Sangria's BAR

(☎295 6808; Jaffa Rd, Al-Muntazah; ⏰noon-midnight) Make a reservation for Ramallah's favourite summer bar if it's Thursday or Saturday night. The Mexican and international menu is ambitious, but you're there for the drinks and glamour-garden ambience.

Stars & Bucks CAFE

(Al-Manara; ⏰8am-late) Seeing the Stars & Bucks logo never fails to raise a smile and may even induce a double take. There's not a hazelnut latte in sight but you can get good local coffee and light snacks.

☆ Entertainment

The entertainment listing *This Week in Palestine* will help you navigate cultural offerings; you'll find it on offer at most cafes, restaurants, cultural centres and higher-end hotels.

Al-Kasaba Theater & Cinematheque CINEMA

(☎296 5292; www.alkasaba.org; Al-Manara) A magnet for artists, musicians and film and theatre buffs, it's well worth catching a performance or screening here while you're in town.

Khalil Sakakini Centre CULTURAL CENTRE

(☎298 7374; www.sakakini.org; Al-Muntazah) Hosts art exhibitions by the locally and internationally renowned, along with a whole host of other cultural pursuits. Check the website for upcoming events.

AM Qattan Foundation CULTURAL CENTRE

(☎296 0544; www.qattanfoundation.org; Al-Jihad St, Al-Masyoun) Readings and competitions in poetry, short story, novel and script writing, journalism and plastic arts.

Al-Snobar CLUB

(Pine; ☎296 5571; www.al-snowbar.com; ⏰May-Oct) This entertainment complex is a flashy restaurant, a swimming pool and one of the hottest nightclubs in the city. Note that it's only open in high season. It's located 2km northwest of Al-Manara Sq.

ℹ Getting There & Around

From the old Arab bus station in East Jerusalem take bus 18 (7NIS, 30 minutes) all the way to Ramallah (nonstop service). Some buses will go to Qalandia checkpoint (4NIS), from where you can take a shared taxi another 5.5km to Al-Manara (3NIS per person) – you're there when you see the stone lions.

As a rule of thumb, the smaller buses and service taxis are faster than the big lumbering buses. Buses to/from Ramallah operate from 6am to 9pm in summer or until 7pm in winter but after the buses stop, service taxis and private taxis are available all night (though you may need to change in Qalandia).

Going the other way you'll need to pass through the Qalandia checkpoint: have your passport ready. If you are on a Ramallah to Jerusalem bus hold onto your ticket to show to the driver once you're on the other side of the checkpoint.

Everything within the Ramallah area is 10 minutes or less by private taxi and should cost 10NIS to 20NIS; be sure to agree on the final price with the driver before setting off. To Bethlehem, a private taxi should cost around 70NIS; though it's not very far, the journey takes around 1½ hours, to avoid checkpoints.

3

Nabi Musa (p276)
ere is an annual Muslim pilgrimage
Nabi Musa, which is believed to be
e site where Moses is buried.

2. Nablus (p280)
Nablus is situated in and around a
lush spring valley between Mt Gerizim
and rocky Mt Ebal.

3. Ramallah (p268)
A bustling city that serves as the
de facto administrative capital of
the Palestinian Authority.

Around Ramallah

When a small Christian village is known more for its beer than for its Bible stories, one might think the past is forgotten. But the townsfolk in Taybeh hold fast to their heritage, raising a glass to the place they believe Jesus stayed with his disciples in his final hours (John 11:54). Sample its nectar yourself at the Taybeh Beer Brewery (☑02-289 8868; www.taybehbeer.net); call to arrange a tour, or drop by for its annual two-day Oktoberfest, a must-visit if you are anywhere in the region. Taybeh is around 15km from Ramallah and is situated on a reasonably remote – and very picturesque – hillside. Drive, negotiate a taxi ride or join an organised tour (see p258).

Jericho & Around יריחו اريحا

☑ 02 / POP 20,300

Local authorities proudly call Jericho the 'world's oldest continuously inhabited city.' This is no idle boast as archaeological evidence traces the city's history back over 10,000 years. Despite this staggering statistic, Jericho is better known in popular Western culture for Joshua's trumpet blasts that caused the city walls to come a-tumblin' down.

Jericho has modernised somewhat since the Canaanite period, but not much. Small-scale farming still makes up a significant portion of the local economy, although tourism is making inroads. Though the town is rather scruffy and unkempt, it retains a raffish charm and a smiley demeanour. Most visitors just stay long enough to ascend the Mount of Temptation and marvel at the archaeological remains of Tel al-Sultan (Ancient Jericho).

Though an Israeli military checkpoint remains in place at the entrance to town, it's generally faster-flowing than either Ramallah's Qalandia or Bethlehem's main checkpoints.

For details on visiting the northwestern corner of the Dead Sea, see p294.

History

Settled history in Jericho dates to around 10,000 BCE when hunter-gatherer groups settled here around a spring. Mudbrick buildings were erected at the site and by 9400 BCE it's believed that some 1000 people lived here.

For the biblically astute, Jericho is known as the first city the Israelites captured after wandering for 40 years in the desert: shaken by horn blasts and the Israelites' shouts, the city walls came crashing down (Joshua 6). Following Alexander the Great's conquest of the region in the 4th century BCE, Jericho became his personal fiefdom.

Further waves of occupiers arrived and departed until Jericho fell into the hands of Mark Antony, who gave it to Cleopatra as a wedding gift. Herod later leased it from Cleopatra and improved its infrastructure with aqueducts and a hippodrome. The 1st-century aristocracy of Jerusalem used the city as a winter getaway.

Christians celebrate Jericho as the place where John the Baptist received his own baptism in the Jordan River and where the temptation of Jesus took place on the mountain.

In the 1967 Six Day War Israel captured Jericho from Jordan. After the signing of the 1993 Oslo Accords, it became the first city to be handed over to Palestinian Authority control (see p380). During the Second Intifada, the Israeli army attacked the Palestinian Authority prison and security headquarters in Jericho. Much of the latter still remains in ruins.

Today Jericho has returned its attention to tourism and daily trade, and though you won't find a great many foreign visitors in town, it makes an interesting stop for a night or two.

⊙ Sights & Activities

A gaggle of storefronts and restaurants with colourful bouquets of household products, fresh produce and roasting snack foods spilling into the streets marks Jericho's diminutive and dusty town centre. The Tree of Zacchaeus, nearby on Ein as-Sultan St (a sycamore said to be more than 2000 years old) received its name from the story of the wealthy tax collector who, according to the tale, was too short to see Jesus amid the crowds and thus climbed this very tree to get a better view. Jesus asked the tax collector if he could visit his home, a gesture that so moved Zacchaeus that he decided to dedicate himself to a life of charitable deeds.

Many of Jericho's sights, however, are outside the city, making for good drives, hikes or cable-car rides into the surrounding area. But if four legs are preferable to four wheels, then try the Equestrian Centre of Palestine

VISITING A REFUGEE CAMP

The term 'refugee camp' brings to mind crowded tents, food riots and waterborne disease. But the refugee camps in the West Bank have existed for more than 60 years, time enough to transform them into established neighbourhoods with housing, schools, hospitals and other infrastructure. The camps were developed – and are still run by – the United Nations Relief and Works Agency (UNRWA) but limited funding has only allowed the UN to build the most basic facilities.

Although the camps are not a hotbed of tourism, some visitors are keen to visit them to experience a different side of Palestinian life. While the camps are generally safe, it's best to be aware of the risks, as the security situation can change at a moment's notice. One minute it's all clear and the next minute, when Israeli soldiers arrive, the air is filled with tear gas, hurled stones and rubber bullets.

Israel Defence Forces (IDF, the national army) raids are more likely in Nablus, Hebron and Jenin but have occurred in Bethlehem too. In any refugee camp it's best to visit with a Palestinian guide who understands the security situation.

Aida Refugee Camp

This camp is located in the shadow of Israel's security fence, near Rachel's Tomb. A cornerstone of the community is the Al Rowwad Centre (275 0030; www.alrowwad. org), which offers drama, music, computer and arts training, as well as arranging special classes and workshops for women, the blind and disabled residents. The centre makes a wonderful beacon of hope in a sometimes gloomy landscape. A taxi here from the city centre will cost 20NIS.

Dheisheh Refugee Camp

Located 3km west of Bethlehem, this camp was founded in 1948 to house refugees from 45 different villages around Jerusalem and Hebron. The camp is home to the Ibdaa Cultural Centre (www.ibdaa48.org), the headquarters for a world-renowned youth folk-dance troupe. It also supports a media centre, trade school, women's leadership initiative, basketball league, restaurant and Ibdaa Cultural Centre Guesthouse (p264). The centre has a gift shop where you can purchase bags, clothing and other items produced by residents of the camp. It also runs tours of the camp; payment is by donation (usually 50NIS for a one-hour tour). To get to Dheisheh, catch a private taxi (20NIS) from the city centre, or a service taxi (3NIS) at Bab iz-Qaq in Bethlehem.

(232 5007; per hr 40NIS), it is on Al-Qadisiya St, offering lessons and rides out into the countryside.

Tel al-Sultan (Ancient Jericho) RUIN
(adult/child 10/5NIS; 8am-5pm) The term 'old city' takes on a whole new meaning at the archaeological site of Tel al-Sultan, wherein lies the remains of some of the world's oldest manmade structures, built some 10,000 years ago.

Today you'll see what look like sand dunes and stairways (the oldest known stairways in the world), while the layers of civilisation beneath go back even further into the mists of history. The remains of a round tower, thought to date from 8000 BCE, indicates that Jericho was possibly the world's first fortified city; legend has it that the tower withstood seven earthquakes, and

earthquakes or not it's certainly managed to survive a good deal of history since its creation. Though a large portion of the site remains unexcavated, it's nevertheless worth the trip simply to wander and ruminate on our long-distant ancestors, who made some of the earliest attempts at animal domestication and agriculture on this far-flung spot.

A 20-minute movie at the entrance helps explain the site but you'll need to request that the caretaker show it as he usually just sends you straight into the park. The entrance to the site is located across the street from the cable car.

**Mount of Temptation &
Monastery of the Qurantul** RELIGIOUS
(Map p267; round trip 55NIS; 8am-9pm) If your heart can handle the height more than the hike, take a swingy Swiss-made cable car

from near the ancient city ruins of Tel al-Sultan, up to the place where we're told Jesus resisted. The Mount of Temptation and Monastery of the Qurantul mark the spot where the Devil is said to have tested Jesus, suggesting that after a 40-day fast the Son of God should make a loaf of bread out of a stone (Matthew 4:1-11). The 12th-century Greek Orthodox Monastery of the Qurantul (Monastery of the Forty) clings to a cliff-side overlooking orange and banana trees in the river valley, the Dead Sea to the south and the Jordan Mountains to the east.

There's some stair climbing at the summit if you want to visit the monastery itself. Opening hours for the cave-church are sporadic but it's best to try in the morning. Marwan the curator sometimes locks the door when he is showing visitors around, so you may need to wait a bit. Beware, too, that the cable car can be closed without notice, making for a hefty 400m climb to admire the hilltop views. You can revive at the restaurant just a few minutes' walk from the monastery.

Hisham's Palace   RUIN
(Khirbet al-Mafjar; Map p267; admission 10NIS; ☉8am-5pm) For archaeology-lovers, Hisham's Palace, 3km north of Jericho, is a spot not to be missed. The sprawling winter hunting retreat of Caliph Hisham Ibn Abd al-Malik must have been magnificent on its creation in the 8th century, with its baths, mosaic floors and pillars – so much so that archaeologists have labelled it the 'Versailles of the Middle East'. This was not a Versailles fated to last, however, being largely destroyed by an earthquake soon after its completion.

Don't, therefore, expect a great deal of surviving grandeur. It's worth the trip though, if only to see the exquisite 'tree of life' mosaic – bearing an image of a lion bringing down a deer beneath a tree of red oranges – housed in the entertaining room of the bathhouse. Various interpretations as to its meaning have been proffered; some believe that the peaceful deer grazing to the left, in contrast with the brutal lion to the right, are symbols of good versus bad governance. It's a tempting thought, too, that great swaths of the site are paved with similarly stunning mosaics, hidden just under the sand and soil, ripe for excavation and preservation.

Wadi Qelt & Nabi Musa   HISTORIC SITE
(Map p267) The steep canyon of Wadi Qelt, situated between Jerusalem and Jericho, is a naturalist's treat, where you'll find a

waterfall, wildlife and the remains of Roman-era aqueducts along the way. Among several monasteries established in this area, you'll find the spectacular 5th-century St George's Monastery (Map p267; ☉8am-noon & 3-7pm Sun-Thu, 8am-noon Sat) blending into a rock face. Signs to the Israeli settlement of Mitzpe Yericho, off Hwy 1, will put you on the path, though it's advisable to go with a local guide. If you can get a ride to the end of the access road it's a 20-minute walk down to the monastery from the car park.

Drinking water is available at the monastery for thirsty hikers. You'll see signposts along the way in Wadi Qelt to the springs of Ein Qelt, Ein Farah and Eir Fawwar, but don't drink the spring water. Also, beware of extreme heat in summer and flash floods in winter.

Another side road on the way to Jericho from Jerusalem will take you south to the complex of Nabi Musa (Prophet Moses; ☉8am-sunset). About 10km northeast of the northern end of the Dead Sea, this is where Muslims believe Moses (Musa in Arabic, Moshe in Hebrew) was buried. A mosque was built on the site in 1269, under Mamluk Sultan Baybar (it was expanded two centuries later), and from around this time festive, annual, weeklong Muslim pilgrimages have set out from Jerusalem to Nabi Musa. However, these were eventually banned by the British – who feared them turning into anti-Zionist rallies – in 1937. Pilgrimages are now allowed again; tourists are still welcomed and donations towards the mosque's upkeep are appreciated.

Qasr al-Yahud   RELIGIOUS
(Map p267; ☉9am-4pm daily Apr-Oct, to 3pm Nov-Mar) At an isolated spot on the Jordan River, on the border between Jordan and the West Bank, stands Qasr al-Yahud, the reputed spot of Jesus's baptism by John (Matthew 3). Christian baptism has its roots in the Jewish purification ritual of bathing in a pool called a *mikveh*, usually before prayer. John adapted the *mikveh* concept so that the bath ritually cleansed people of their sins before the coming of the Messiah. He set up his ministry at an important crossroads, where he preached to passing traders, businessmen and soldiers. The baptism marked the start of Jesus's ministry. Several churches are located here but those on the Israeli-controlled side of the border are inaccessible.

Reopened to pilgrims in 2011, Qasr al-Yahud (the name means 'palace of the Jews') is located in a sensitive military area surrounded by barbed wire and minefields. The Jordan River is divided in the middle by a low fence to prevent visitors from wading across to the Jordanian side. However, the site has been fully renovated to handle tourists, and has bathrooms, a gift shop and shaded areas where you can sit and admire the view.

The site is located north of the Dead Sea, just off Hwy 90, which skirts along the eastern side of Jericho.

Inn of the Good Samaritan HISTORIC SITE
(Map p267; adult/child 21/9NIS; ☺8am-5pm daily Apr-Oct, to 4pm Nov-Mar) Located just off the main road between Jerusalem and Jericho, this site is associated with the popular parable told in Luke 10: 25-37. In the story, Jesus describes a man who is robbed, beaten and left for dead on the road between Jerusalem and Jericho. A priest passes by and then a Levite but neither lends a hand to the stricken traveller. Finally a Samaritan stops to help the stranger, dressing his wounds and bringing him to a nearby inn. The story gained fame throughout Christianity and 'Good Samaritan' became a by-word for 'compassionate individual'. However, historians suggest that an 'Israelite' rather than a 'Samaritan' was the original hero the story, a Greek translator having mistakenly swapped the words while compiling the Book of Luke.

Archaeologists have unearthed a Second Temple–era palace, presumably constructed by Herod, which may have been converted to the inn mentioned in the Bible. A church was added under the Byzantines, and during the Crusader period a *khan* (travellers inn) was erected. The ruins you can see today are a confection of foundations and mosaics from the different eras of construction. A collection of mosaics is housed inside a new museum.

🛏 Sleeping

Jericho's accommodation scene is hardly burgeoning, but there is a handful of options for each price category.

Jericho Resort Village RESORT $$
(☏232 1255; www.jerichoresorts.com; s/d US$120/140, bungalows US$180; @🛜🏊) This breezy bamboo-bedecked vacation getaway has big bungalows that sleep four, and standard rooms with tile floors and terraces. The price includes use of the jacuzzi, pool and tennis court. It's situated out near Hisham's

Palace, quite a way away from the Jericho action (such as it is) and can feel almost as desolate as the earthquake-destroyed palace itself.

Hotel Intercontinental Jericho HOTEL $$
(☏231 1200; www.intercontinental.com; s/d US$160/190; ❄@🛜🏊) Just like the Jericho Resort Village, the Intercontinental – while comfortable – largely suffers from a dearth of hotel guests, making it a pleasant but strangely quiet choice. Still, it's got all the perks, with a lovely swimming pool and gardens, and extremely attentive staff. The wi-fi costs US$15 for 24 hours.

Sami Youth Hostel GUESTHOUSE $
(☏232 4220; eyad_alalem@live.com; r 120NIS; 🛜) English-speaking owner Sami has opened this simple guesthouse in the western part of Jericho, near the Hotel Intercontinental Jericho. Rooms are simple but clean and there are kitchen facilities. It's a little isolated but Sami can help arrange transport around town. It's located 3.2km from the town centre and impossible to find on your own, so take a taxi the first time you visit.

Jerusalem Hotel Jericho GUESTHOUSE $
(☏232 2444; www.jerusalemhotel-jericho.com; s/d/tr US$80/110/150; 🛜) A 1970s relic frozen in time, this hotel has dozens of empty rooms just waiting for some guests to turn up. Some rooms have pleasant balconies and all include cable TV. It's located 1.5km east of the town square, on the road to Allenby Bridge.

🍴 Eating

There are lunch (serving the usual grilled meats and mezze combinations) and snack joints scattered across town, though some locals assert that hygiene is dubious in many. Go for the most-crowded options to guarantee that your skewered meats haven't been sitting about for too long.

Green Valley Park MIDDLE EASTERN $
(Ein al-Sultan St; mains 30-60NIS; ☺9am-11pm) One of a jubilant strip of shaded dining patios on this street, for eating in the local style. It specialises in grilled meats and mezze.

Abu Omar MIDDLE EASTERN $
(Ein al-Sultan St; mains 20-50NIS; ☺6am-midnight) Next to the main square, this local favourite serves everything from felafel in a pita (4NIS) up to a half-chicken dinner for two people (50NIS).

❶ Getting There & Away

There are no direct service taxis from Jerusalem to Jericho. If you're not travelling under your own steam, take a service taxi from Al-Musrasa in Jerusalem to Abu Dis (6.50NIS) and then another service taxi from Abu Dis to Jericho (12NIS). Alternatively, a private taxi ride from Jerusalem to Jericho (or vice versa) should cost around 400NIS.

To Ramallah take the bus from just off Jericho's main square (several times per day, 12NIS). Ask around for the bus times, since they vary; they generally take around 90 minutes via a circuitous route to avoid the Qalandia checkpoint.

Remember to bring a passport; you'll need to show it on the way back to Jerusalem.

Hebron الخليل חברון

📝 02 / POP 183,000

For Jews, Christians and Muslims alike, Hebron (Al-Khalil in Arabic) is considered the cradle of organised religion. For thousands of years the major holy site has been the Tomb of the Patriarchs – the collective tomb of Abraham, Isaac and Jacob, along with their wives (except Rachel). In addition, Islamic tradition states that Adam and Eve lived here after being exiled from the Garden of Eden. Sadly, the common thread of beliefs has done little to improve relations between the major monotheistic religions, as Hebron has long been a flashpoint for religious violence.

What distinguishes Hebron from other Palestinian towns is the presence of Jewish settlers within the city centre itself. There are five microsettlements in the city centre, with other, larger ones on the outskirts, effectively dividing the city into two pieces. For the traveller, this causes some inconveniences, as many streets are barricaded and/or off-limits. The security situation in Hebron has created palpable tension and while it is generally calm, visitors should be aware of the potential for confrontations between settlers and soldiers or Palestinians. Obviously, if you see a situation developing, go the other way. Bringing a local guide can help explain the situation in the city (but be aware that Palestinian guides probably won't be allowed in settler areas).

Despite its woes, Hebron continues to flourish as a business leader among Palestinian communities. Situated on a former trade route to the Arabian Peninsula, Hebron is still celebrated for its grapes, its skilled traders

and its artisans' production of blown glass, leather and hand-painted pottery, just as it has been since antiquity.

History

According to the Hebrew Bible, Hebron was founded around 1730 BCE, its biblical name, Kiryat Arba (the Village of Four), perhaps referring to its position on four hills on which four Canaanite tribes settled.

For centuries Hebron had been home to a small Jewish community, but in 1929, Arab nationalists attacked the city's Jews – all of them non-Zionist ultra-Orthodox – and killed 67 of them. The rest of the community fled.

After 1967, Orthodox Jews returned to the city, and a prominent feature of today's Hebron is the presence of Israeli soldiers guarding Jewish enclaves – populated by some of the West Bank's most hard-line settlers – in the town centre. The suburb of Kiryat Arba, now home to over 7000 Jews, was established nearby.

In 1994, during the Muslim holy month of Ramadan and on the Jewish holiday of Purim, Brooklyn-born physician Baruch Goldstein opened fire on Palestinians while they prayed in the Ibrahimi Mosque, killing 29 men and boys and injuring a further 200. Moderate settlers, like the average Israeli, view Goldstein as a cold-blooded killer. However, extremist Jewish settlers, who see local Palestinians as foreign interlopers in the Land of Israel, consider him a hero and his gravesite remains a popular place of pilgrimage.

◉ Sights & Activities

For most travellers, there are three main parts to Hebron. The first is Ras al-Jora (Jerusalem Sq) set on Hebron Rd (also known as Shari'a al-Quds) as it comes in from Bethlehem. The area is a commercial hub with plenty of restaurants and workshops that produce glass and ceramics.

About 3km further along, Hebron Rd becomes Ein Sarah St, which eventually runs into Al-Manara Sq (really just an intersection). From Al-Manara Sq, turn right for about 200m, to reach the bus station, or turn left and walk for 10 minutes to reach Bab al-Zawieh, the entrance to the Old City souq and further to the Ibrahimi Mosque.

The Jewish section of town lies south of the Old City, beyond high walls and barbed-wire fences. You can easily walk there from the Ibrahimi Mosque/Tomb of the Patriarchs. With all the barricades around town,

Hebron feels tense, but as a tourist you shouldn't have any problems. Have your passport handy to cross through checkpoints between the Arab and Jewish parts of town.

Ibrahimi Mosque/Tomb of the Patriarchs

MOSQUE, SYNAGOGUE

(☺8am-4pm Sun-Thu, except during prayers) The focal point of Hebron for most visitors is the Tomb of the Patriarchs (Cave of Machpelah), known to Muslims as the Ibrahimi Mosque (Ibrahim is the Arab name for Abraham). For both Jews and Muslims, the site is second in importance only to Jerusalem's Al-Haram ash-Sharif/Temple Mount. Be aware of the strict security and separate prayer spaces for Jews and Muslims.

When entering the mosque, you will be asked to remove your shoes, and women will be handed a head covering. Looking rather like decorated tents, the mostly Mamluk-era cenotaphs commemorate the patriarchs Abraham, Isaac and Jacob, and their wives, but it's the cave below that both Jews and Muslims believe was chosen by Abraham as the actual final resting place of his family.

You can peer into the cave through a metal grate situated in the corner of the mosque. As you walk into the room that allows viewing of the cenotaph of Abraham, note the small niche near the door where you can see a footprint. The Muslims believe this to be Mohammed's footprint while Jews say Adam created it.

Built by Herod (notice the Herodian stones at the base of the walls), the complex was altered by the Byzantines in the 6th century – they added a church, beside which a synagogue was built. When the Arabs conquered the area in the following century, the church was converted to a mosque but the synagogue remained intact. After the Crusaders left the scene, the Mamluks built another mosque.

Old City

ARCHITECTURE

The Old City's stunning, often crumbling Mamluk-styled Ottoman architecture includes a souq, but merchants have been moved to an outdoor area due to friction with Jewish settlers. The open-air market is a sensual odyssey offering everything from agriculture to art.

Glass & Ceramic workshops

ARTS CENTRE

At the northern entrance to Hebron, in the area called Ras al-Jora, several of Hebron's traditional blown-glass and ceramic factories are open for viewing and shopping. Al-Natsheh and Al-Salam glass factories receive visitors and shoppers, as does the smaller Tamimi Ceramics. All are open between 9am and 7pm daily except during Friday-morning prayers.

🛌 Sleeping

Hotels aren't Hebron's strong point, and since the city makes an easy day trip from Bethlehem, it's not essential to hang about overnight. If you're here, however, contact the Association d'Échanges Culturels Hebron-France (AECHF; ☎222 4811; www.hebron-france.org), which can arrange homestays with local families.

Hebron Hotel

HOTEL $

(☎225 4201; hebron_hotel@hotmail.com; King Faisal St, Ein Sarah; s/d/tr US$35/45/55) An airy lobby gives way to adequate rooms mixing shabby with new. Try to go for one of the front rooms; the ground-floor complex beyond the banquet hall gives way to a weird, deserted vibe, slightly reminiscent of *The Shining*.

Royal Suites Hotel

HOTEL $$

(☎224 4080; Nimra St; s/d 130/180NIS; 🛜) The rooms in this hotel are palatial, as if they were simply converted two-room apartments. It's a tidy place, but furnishings are bit basic.

🍴 Eating

Hebron doesn't boast many top-notch culinary choices, though there are plenty of places for a quick, tasty bite on the go, particularly along Nimra St.

🏆 Abu Mazen

MIDDLE EASTERN $

(Nimra St; mains 25-35NIS; ☺7am-9pm) Understandably crowded from noon to 2pm, Abu Mazen offers great value and tasty home cooking. *Mensef* (lamb on rice served beside a salted broth of lamb stock and dissolved dried yoghurt) is usually a big-event family meal, so this could be your only chance to try it. The lamb melts in your mouth, and the yoghurt-soaked yellow rice is a profusion of authentic flavours. *Kidreh* (a baked casserole of meat, nuts and rice) is a good bet too, and there are plenty of soups and mezze for vegetarian visitors.

Abu Salah

MIDDLE EASTERN $

(Bab-e-Zawi; mains 10-35NIS; ☺7am-10pm) Perched on the edge of Hebron's Old City, this busy restaurant is a good bet for shwarma or a plate of chicken, rice and potatoes served buffet style.

❶ Getting There & Away

To reach Hebron from Jerusalem, first take Arab bus 21 (7NIS) from Al-Musrara (near Damascus Gate) to Husan intersection and change to a service taxi (9NIS). The drive from Husan to Hebron takes about 20 minutes. For a very different perspective – that of Hebron's Jewish settlers – take Egged bus 160 (9.60NIS, every 30 minutes) from Jerusalem's Central Bus Station. It stops right by the Ibrahimi Mosque/Tomb of the Patriarchs.

From the bus station in Hebron, it's possible to catch service taxis to Jericho (30NIS), Bethlehem (9NIS) and Ramallah (27NIS) between 5am and 6pm. Vehicles move when full.

Nablus نابلس שׁכֶם

✍09 / POP 136,000

Situated in and around a lush spring valley between Mt Gerizim (Jarzim in Arabic) and rocky Mt Ebal, Nablus (known as Shechem in Hebrew) has historically been a significant exporter of olive oil, cotton, soap and carob. Best known these days for its olive-oil

soap factories, olive-wood carving and *kunafeh* (a warm, syrupy cheese-based pastry), the city is layered with millennia of plunder and glory.

The northern West Bank is still known to Jews as Samaria, from which the term 'Samaritan' is derived. Among the most fascinating elements of the Nablus area is its tiny Samaritan community (see p392).

History

After the 12 tribes of Israel split into two rival kingdoms in the 10th century BCE, Shechem was briefly the capital of the northern faction, ie of the 10 tribes who would eventually be lost to history.

In 70 CE the Romans obliterated ancient Shechem and set up Flavia Neapolis (New City), whose name the Arabs would later pronounce as Nablus. Graeco-Roman cults developed, only to be destroyed in 636 CE when the city was conquered by Arab forces. Christian shrines were converted to Muslim mosques, and Nablus developed the character it still displays today. The Old City dates back to Ottoman times, though relics from as long ago as the Roman occupation can still be spotted.

DON'T MISS

MT GERIZIM

The Samaritans (members of an ancient religion closely related to Judaism) believe that Mt Gerizim, which overlooks Nablus from the south, was not only the first piece of land ever created, but is also the land out of which Adam was made, the only place spared in the great flood, the place Abraham went to sacrifice his son Isaac (Judaism holds that this event took place on Jerusalem's Temple Mount) and the location chosen by God for the Temple.

One of the world's last communities of Samaritans (there's another in Holon, Israel) lives on the mountain. Learn more about their community at the Samaritan Museum (✍237 0249; samaritans-mu@hotmail.com; admission 15NIS; ⏰9am-3pm Sun-Fri, to 1pm Sat) on Mt Gerizim. From the museum, continue further down the main road to the Good Samaritan Center (admission free; ⏰9am-4pm Sun-Fri, to 1pm Sat), which contains a library and information desk. The director of the library, Priest Husney Cohen, will happily answer any questions you have about the Samaritans.

After a short walk further down the road, take the left fork to reach the Platform (admission 15NIS; ⏰9am-sunset daily), the ancient site of the Samaritan Temple. A guard will need to unlock the gate to let you inside and will give a brief tour of the site. Once at the top, you'll see the lowered floor that Samaritans say was the foundation of their Temple, which was built in the 5th century BCE. It only survived about 200 years before being destroyed by the Maccabees (a Jewish rebel army) in 128 BCE. The remains of a church, first constructed in 475 CE, have also been found here.

From the centre of Nablus, Mt Gerizim can be reached by taxi in around 10 minutes. It's a 50NIS journey including wait time. Taxis have to wait outside the village at a military checkpoint, so be prepared to pay your driver in advance to keep him waiting.

Nablus is now surrounded by some of the West Bank's most hard-line Jewish settlements. On nearby hilltops you'll see Bracha, Itamar, Yitzhar and Elon Moreh, often in the news because local Jewish extremists have clashed either with Palestinians or with Israeli soldiers.

Sights & Activities

For more information on things to do and see, go to www.nablusguide.com.

Al-Qasaba NEIGHBOURHOOD

The focal point for visitors to Nablus is Al-Qasaba (Casbah or Old City), where you'll find an Ottoman-era rabbit warren of shops, stalls and pastry stands, spice sacks and vegetable mounds. Here, amid the clamour, you'll find dozens of contemplative mosques, including the **Al-Kebir Mosque** (Great Mosque), which is built on the site of an earlier Crusader church and Byzantine and Roman basilicas. Bits and pieces of its earlier incarnations have survived; look out for the huge columns and capitals, traces of the Byzantine structure.

Soap Factories SOAP FACTORIES

If cleanliness is next to godliness, then the Old City offers plenty of opportunities for both. Nablus has seven or eight functioning soap factories that produce olive-oil-based suds, carrying on an 800-year-old Nablus tradition. **Mofthen Factory**, on Martyrs Sq, is just one of those happy to receive visitors.

Hammam Al-Hana BATHHOUSE

(Hammam es Sumara; bath 35NIS, massage 10NIS; ☎238 5185; ⏰men 6am-11pm Wed-Mon, women 8am-5pm Tue) This tourist-friendly hammam offers a bath, steam room and massage. It's deeply entrenched in the souq but locals can point the way.

Jacob's Well CHURCH

(donations appreciated; ⏰8am-noon & 2pm-4pm) Near the entrance to Balata (population 20,000), the largest United Nations Relief and Works Agency (UNRWA) refugee camp in the West Bank, you'll find Jacob's Well, the spot where Christians believe a Samaritan woman offered Jesus a drink of water, and that he then revealed to her that he was the Messiah (John 4:13-14). A Byzantine church destroyed in the Samaritan revolt of 529 CE was replaced by a Crusader church, which itself fell into ruins in the Middle Ages. The current church, St Photina the Samaritan, was built in the 1860s by the Greek Orthodox Patriarchate.

About 300m southeast, a compound known as **Joseph's Tomb** has in recent years been a source of considerable friction between Jews, who come here to pray under IDF escort (in coordination with the Palestinian Authority), and local Arabs.

FREE **Sebastiya** RUIN

(Map p267) Located uphill from a village of the same name, Sebastiya is a collection of ruins that includes an **amphitheatre** (which once held 7000, making it the largest in Palestine) and a **Byzantine church**, built upon a site considered to be the grave of John the Baptist. In the mid-4th century the grave was desecrated and the bones were partly burned; surviving portions were taken to Jerusalem and later to Alexandria where they were interred at a Coptic monastery. Sebastiya is 11km from Nablus. A taxi with waiting time will cost around 100NIS. Sebastiya is also a good place for lunch; try the **Holyland Sun Restaurant** (☎09-253 2421; ⏰10am-6pm), which can set a nice table of Middle Eastern salads and *mensef*. It's located near the car park; call ahead to make sure it can arrange lunch.

Sleeping

Nablus isn't blessed with a wide range of accommodation, but the following both make reliable, comfy choices.

TOP CHOICE **Al-Yasmeen Hotel** HOTEL $$

(☎233 3555; www.alyasmeen.com; s/d/tr 180/220/260NIS; ❄📶) Nablus' best hotel and favourite lodging of aid workers and politicos puts you in the middle of it all, at the centre of the Old City. Rooms are clean and well appointed and the staff are extremely helpful and knowledgeable about the West Bank.

Crystal Motel MOTEL $

(☎233 2485; Faysal St; s/d/tr 80/120/150NIS) Good rates at this basic but well-maintained option just outside the Old City.

Eating & Drinking

In addition to confectioners selling Turkish delight, halvah (fruit and nuts covered with a sweet sesame paste, made into a slab and cut into squares) and syrupy pastries, Nablus is full of cafes for sipping and puffing – but the clientele is usually masculine. While

THE LAST PALESTINIAN ZOO

The town of Qalqilya, about 25km west of Nablus and just 15km inland from the Israeli coastal city of Netanya, is largely surrounded by Israel's contentious security barrier. Qalqilya has a couple of claims to fame: first, it was the first town to vote Hamas into power in local elections; second, it's home to the Palestinian Territories' longest-running and last-remaining zoo (admission 5NIS; ⊘9am-4pm).

Charismatic, indomitable and infinitely humorous, head vet Dr Sami Khader has struggled through intifadas, roadblocks and curfews to keep the zoo – one of the only recreational outlets for the area's children – functioning. The zoo today is home to lions, a hippo, zebras and monkeys, among other inhabitants, and while shabby, forlorn and iron-bar clad, it presses valiantly on.

The zoo, and Dr Sami, gladly receive foreign visitors; take a taxi from Nablus (30NIS, 20 minutes) and ask for Qalqilya Zoo. For its full, tragicomic story, and to get to know Dr Sami before you visit, read *The Zoo on the Road to Nablus*, written by Amelia Thomas.

a solo woman will still be served in one of these, she might draw a few stares. A more female-friendly place is the Zeit ou Zaatar restaurant at Al-Yasmeen Hotel, which also has one of the city's only functioning bars (hence its popularity with visitors). Anywhere in the market, try *kunafeh*, warm, elastic cheese and syrup-soaked wheat shreds, a local favourite.

Assaraya   MIDDLE EASTERN $
(Hitten St; mains 40-70NIS; ⊘10am-10pm) Around the corner from the Al-Yasmeen Hotel, this classy restaurant does excellent grilled meats, *mensef* lamb and salads. Enjoy your meal on soft couches under black-and-white photos of old Nablus. It's somewhat hidden down an alley, so you may need a local to point the way.

⊕ Getting There & Away

There is no direct bus service to Nablus from Jerusalem. You will need to change at either Qalandia checkpoint or Ramallah, where a service taxi will cost 17NIS.

Jenin جنين ג׳נין

⊉04 / POP 54,000

The northernmost city in the West Bank, Jenin is home to religious sites, a bustling souq, a unique performing-arts scene and the Arab-American University, but its isolation has left it well off the tourist trail.

The recent opening of the Jalameh (Gilboa) Border Crossing (p190), just 10km south of Afula, may improve the situation and allow travellers to make day trips from Nazareth or Haifa.

⊙ Sights

Masjid Jenin al-Kabir
& Downtown   MOSQUE, NEIGHBOURHOOD
With its unmissable green roof, **Masjid Jenin al-Kabir** (Jenin Great Mosque), was built in 1566 on the orders of Fatima Khatun, then wife of the Governor of Damascus. Cross the street and enter a dense network of alleys that form the **Old City**, today largely occupied by furniture makers, barbers and machinists. Two blocks south of the mosque is King Talal St, which leads to Jerusalem Sq, the main bus station and the **Jenin Cinema**. North of King Talal St it's fun to wander into the **souq**, which is absolutely bursting with activity.

Freedom Theatre   THEATRE
(⊉250-3345; www.thefreedomtheatre.org; ⊘9am-6pm Sun-Thu) This is a world-renowned theatre group that has persevered under difficult circumstances (the director of the group and several actors have been assassinated under various circumstances). The theatre lies on the edge of Jenin's refugee camp, which suffered enormous damage in 2002 during IDF incursions. The people living in the camp are friendly but it's still a sensitive area so you'd be wise to bring an Arabic-speaking guide if you want to tour the camp (enquire at the Freedom Theatre or Cinema Guesthouse). It's a 15-minute walk from the Cinema to the Freedom Theatre; alternatively, hop in a passing service taxi for 3NIS.

Greek Orthodox Church
of St George   CHURCH
Located in Burqi'in village, this church was built upon the site where Jesus healed 10 lepers (Luke 17: 11-19). It's said to be one of the

world's oldest surviving churches (dating to the 4th or 5th century CE) and contains the cave that sheltered the lepers. Service taxis (3NIS) go here from a station about 300m west of the Masjid Jenin. The church is often locked but the caretaker family should be able to unlock the gates for you.

Canaan Fair Trade FACTORY
(☎243-1991; www.canaanfairtrade.com; ☺8am-5pm Sat-Thu) Located 2km beyond Buqi'in, this newly built olive-oil factory practises fair-trade policy with its olive farmers. A tour of the factory (40NIS) includes a free bottle of olive oil and if you want to get to know the olive farmers, they can set you up with a homestay.

🛏 Sleeping & Eating

Cinema Guesthouse GUESTHOUSE $
(☎059 931-7968; www.cinemajenin.org; 1 Azzaytoon St; dm/s/d 75/125/250NIS; @☎) A quiet spot in the heart of chaotic Jenin, the Cinema Guesthouse is a great place to meet other travellers (or NGO workers, journalists, activists and the like) and unwind for a day or two. It has three spacious dorm rooms, a couple of tiny private rooms and

a nice kitchen for cooking communal meals. Breakfast is an extra 10NIS. The English-speaking manager is a font of information on the area. It's opposite the central bus station.

North Gate Hotel HOTEL $$
(☎243 5700; www.northgate-hotel.com; Palestine St; s/d US$45/70; @☎) This new hotel is the best Jenin can offer, a brand-new facility with spacious rooms and a big grassy patio.

Awtar WESTERN, MIDDLE EASTERN $
(Cinema Circle; dishes 20-40NIS; ☺8am-midnight) This popular restaurant serves grilled meats, Arabic breakfast and some Western dishes in a flashy dining hall. It's located around the corner from the Jenin Cinema.

❶ Getting There & Away

There are frequent buses during the day to/from Nablus for 10NIS. From the north (Nazareth or Haifa), it's possible to take a direct share taxi from Nazareth (see p200) or Afula (10NIS) to Jenin, passing through the Jalameh border crossing. Expect a long delay if you are passing through with your own car.

The Dead Sea
ים המלח   البحر الميت

Best Places to Stay

» Shkedi's Camplodge (p302)

» Ein Gedi Kibbutz Hotel (p291)

» Masada Guest House (p297)

Best Family Hikes

» Wadi David (p289)

» Wadi Arugot (p290)

» Wadi Bokek (p298)

Why Go?

The lowest place on the face of earth, the Dead Sea (elevation 425m) brings together breathtaking natural beauty, compellingly ancient history and modern mineral spas that soothe and pamper every fibre of your body. The jagged bluffs of the Judean Desert, cleft by dry canyons that turn into raging tan torrents after a cloudburst, rise up from the cobalt-blue waters of the Dead Sea, heavy with salt and oily with minerals. In oases such as Ein Gedi, year-round springs nourish vegetation so lush it's often compared to the Garden of Eden. Atop the bluffs is the arid moonscape of the Judean Desert, while down below, human beings have been at work for millennia, creating Masada and Qumran (where the Dead Sea Scrolls were found) in ancient times and, more recently, hiking trails, bike paths, kibbutzim, luxury hotels, sandy beaches and even a world-famous botanical garden.

When to Go
Ein Gedi

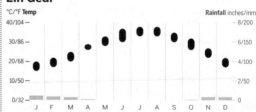

| | Nov–Apr Warm and sunny. Judean Desert cloudbursts cause spectacular flash floods in wadis. | Jul–mid-Sep Oppressively hot. Record temperature: 49.2°C. Begin hikes at dawn. | Passover & Sukkot Holidays Completely booked with domestic tourists. |

Preparing for a Dead Sea Dip

The waters of the Dead Sea have some fantastic healing powers, but unless you respect their bromines and chlorides you may find yourself in significant pain – or even danger. As a result, a few preparations are in order before you slip into the slimy brine. First off, don't shave the day before you swim or you may find out more than you'd like to know about the meaning of the phrase 'to have salt rubbed into your wounds'. Other nicks and cuts – whether you realised you had them or not – are also likely to call attention to themselves.

SOOTHING, HEALTHFUL & BRACING

The water of the Dead Sea contains 20 times as much bromine, 15 times more magnesium and 10 times as much iodine as the ocean. It is, in effect, 33% solid substance. Bromine, a component of many sedatives, relaxes the nerves; magnesium counteracts skin allergies and clears the bronchial passages; and iodine has a beneficial effect on certain glandular functions – or so it's claimed.

If this were not enough, the Dead Sea's extremely dense air – the area has the world's highest barometric pressure – has 10% more oxygen than sea-level air. Other healthful properties, especially for people with breathing problems, include high temperatures, low rainfall, low humidity and pollen-free air.

Tours

Several companies offer rather pricey day tours that take in Masada, a float in the Dead Sea and a walk through Ein Gedi.

Abraham Tours TOUR
(☎02-566 0045; www.abrahamtours.com; per person not incl admission fees 245NIS; ☺Sat-Thu) Minibus tours run by Abraham Hostel that on some days include Masada at sunrise (departure at 3am).

Bein Harim Tourism TOUR
(☎03-542 2000; www.beinharim.co.il; per person from Jerusalem US$92, from Tel Aviv US$99; ☺daily) Standard day circuit.

United Tours TOUR
(☎03-617 3333; www.unitedtours.co.il; per person from Jerusalem US$92, from Tel Aviv US$99; ☺daily) Standard day circuit.

NATURAL SUNBURN PROTECTION

The Dead Sea's dense, low-elevation air naturally filters the sun's harmful ultraviolet rays, making it much harder to get sunburnt than at sea level – despite scorching temperatures.

Hiking Maps

» SPNI topographical trail maps (1:50,000-scale) are on sale for 82NIS at two places at Ein Gedi: the SPNI Field School and the Wadi Arugot entrance to the Ein Gedi Nature Reserve.

Health Benefits

» The Dead Sea Medical Research Centre (www.deadsea-health.org), affiliate with Ben Gurion University of the Negev, conducts scientific analyses of the Dead Sea's health benefits.

Internet Resources

» Dead Sea Tourist Information: www.deadsea.co.il

» Tamar Festival: www.tamarfestival.com

» Ein Gedi International Semi-Marathon: www.deadsea-race.co.il

» Mt Sodom International Bike Race: www.desert challenge.co.il

Dead Sea Highlights

1 Float in the briny, soothing waters of the Dead Sea at sandy **Ein Bokek Beach** (p298)

2 Ascend **Masada's Snake Path** (p296) before dawn and watch the sunrise from up top

3 Take a refreshing dip in the waterfall-fed plunge pools of **Ein Gedi Nature Reserve** (p289)

4 Soak in a hot sulphur pool and glop on black mud at **Mineral Beach** (p296)

5 Imagine life among the defenders of Roman-besieged Masada at the evocative **Masada Museum** (p296)

6 Cycle one of the wide wadis around **Neot HaKikar** (p301)

7 Descend **Wadi Daraja** (p295) with the help of ropes and the breast stroke

8 Shoot the breeze around the campfire at **Shkedi's Camplodge** (p302) in Neot HaKikar

9 Pamper yourself at one of the hotel day spas at **Ein Bokek** (p298)

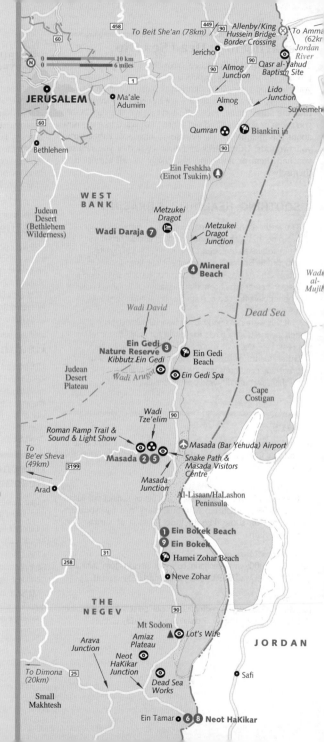

History

Human awareness of the Dead Sea's unique qualities goes back to at least the 4th century BCE; such luminaries as Aristotle, Pliny and Galen all made mention of the sea's physical properties. The Nabataeans collected bitumen from the surface of the water and sold it to the Egyptians, who used it for embalming.

In general, however, the Dead Sea – today shared by Israel, Palestinians and Jordan – has generally been regarded as unhealthy (popular wisdom had it that no bird could fly over its waters without dropping from the sky) and hence shunned. This made the area a favoured retreat of religious ascetics and political fugitives – the future King David, King Herod, Jesus and John the Baptist all took refuge along its shoreline or in nearby mountains and caves.

Because it was seen as the 'Sea of the Devil', the area remained uncharted until it was finally explored by a team from the United States Navy in 1848. The Palestine Potash Company (now the Dead Sea Works) was established in 1930 by Moshe Novomeysky, a Siberian-born engineer and Zionist pioneer. The 1948 war left Israel with a quarter of the Dead Sea's shoreline and Jordan with the rest. Israel captured the lake's northwestern shore in 1967.

In 2011 Israel, the Palestinian Authority and Jordan joined forces in an attempt to get the Dead Sea selected – by popular, worldwide vote – as one of the Seven Natural Wonders of the World. The briny lake made it to the 14-member semi-finals but not into the final seven.

Geography

The Dead Sea (Yam HaMelach, ie the Salt Sea, in Hebrew), whose surface is now about 425m below sea level, is the lowest point on the face of the earth. Connected to the Mediterranean Sea until about two million years ago, it forms part of the 6000km-long Great Rift Valley (Syrian–African Rift), which stretches from Mozambique to Syria and includes the Red Sea and the Sea of Galilee.

About 65km long and 18km across at its widest point, the Dead Sea is fed mainly by the Jordan River, supplemented by underground springs, seasonal wadis and flash floods. With no outlet, the inflow has historically been balanced, more or less, by evaporation. Water arrives with normal mineral concentrations (mainly magnesium, sodium, calcium and potassium chlorides) – but, over the millennia, evaporation has removed vast quantities of H_2O but left behind everything else, causing mineral concentrations in the lake to rise dramatically. Almost nine times more saline than the ocean, the Dead Sea's salt concentration is about 30%, making human beings so buoyant that you'll find it a cinch to lie on your back and comfortably read this book.

Because some 95% of the water of the Jordan River basin is now diverted to agriculture in Israel, Jordan, Syria and Lebanon, the Dead Sea is drying up. Every year its surface drops by approximately 1.2m, and the shore, depending on its gradient, recedes by up to 5m. A plan to reconnect the Dead Sea with the Mediterranean, generating electricity by taking advantage of the 400m drop, was proposed in the 1980s, but the Med-Dead Project (http://meddead.org) was eventually shelved. These days, Israeli, Jordanian and Palestinian policy-makers and environmentalists – such as Friends of the Earth Middle East (www.foeme.org) – are engaged in a spirited debate over the virtues and risks of the proposed 180km-long 'Red-Dead Canal', which would refill the Dead Sea with seawater from the Red Sea.

The Dead Sea's shores are dotted with springs and oases, which provide water for 90 species of birds, 25 species of reptiles and amphibians, and 24 species of mammals, as well as more than 400 species of plants, some of them at the extreme northern or southern edge of their natural distribution.

These days the Dead Sea is in fact two separate lakes connected by an artificial channel. The larger northern basin (fronting Mineral Beach and Ein Gedi Beach) is a proper – if shrinking – lake whose deepest point is about 375m below the surface. The shallow southern section (fronting Ein Bokek) – actually an expanse of artificial evaporation pools – would be completely dry if not for the water pumped in by the Dead Sea Works. Whereas the level of the northern lake is dropping, that of the southern section is actually rising – to the point of threatening the Ein Bokek hotels – due to the accumulation of salt deposits on the bottom of the evaporation pools. The two lakes are separated by a peninsula that juts out from the Dead Sea's eastern shore and is known as HaLashon in Hebrew and Al-Lisaan in Arabic (both names mean 'the Tongue').

SWIMMING SAFELY

Staying safe while bobbing and paddling requires a bit more caution than at the sea shore.

» Do not under any circumstances dunk your head! If water gets in your eyes, it will sting horribly and temporarily blind you. Do not thrash around – calmly get out of the water and ask someone to help you rinse your eyes under a tap or shower.

» Swallowing just a few gulps of sea water – or inhaling it – is extremely dangerous and can even be fatal. Seek immediate medical attention (eg from lifeguards) if this happens.

» Drink *lots* of water – not only will the heat dry you out, but also the water of the Dead Sea is so saturated with minerals that it will suck out your body's fluids like a thousand leeches. Remember what happened in high school physics class when you learned about osmosis by putting a slice of potato in saltwater?

» The Dead Sea can be so relaxing that some people don't notice when westerly winds gently blow them out towards the middle of the lake (ie towards Jordan). Broadsheet readers are in special danger – a newspaper makes an excellent sail!

ⓘ Getting There & Around

The most convenient way to tour the Dead Sea area is with a car, which for two or more people can work out cheaper than taking buses (and much more cost-effective than a tour).

BUS

It's possible, though a bit fiddly, to explore the Dead Sea by public bus. To avoid hanging around wilting under the sun, it's a good idea to plan your itinerary in advance.

Egged buses (www.bus.co.il) link sites along Rte 90 (including, from north to south, Qumran, Ein Feshkha, Metzukei Dragot junction, Mineral Beach, Ein Gedi Nature Reserve, Ein Gedi Beach, Kibbutz Ein Gedi, Ein Gedi Spa, Masada, Ein Bokek, Neve Zohar and, for some lines, Neot HaKikar) with:

» Jerusalem (buses 421, 444 and 486; 40NIS to 45NIS, 11 daily Sunday to Thursday, seven on Friday until mid-afternoon, three on Saturday evening)

» Eilat (bus 444; 75NIS, about three hours, four daily Sunday to Thursday, three on Friday, one or two on Saturday evening)

» Tel Aviv (bus 421; 45NIS, departs Tel Aviv at 8.40am and Neve Zohar at 2pm Sunday to Friday, 3½ hours) Departs from the Central (Arlozoroff/Savidor) train station.

» Be'er Sheva (bus 384; 40NIS, 2¼ hours, four daily Sunday to Thursday, two on Friday).

All of these lines can be used for travel north and south along Rte 90 (which runs along the Dead Sea's western short), eg from Masada to Ein Gedi Beach.

Except on Saturday, Egged bus 321 does a morning circuit from Dimona (departure at 7.45am) to Neot HaKikar, Ein Bokek, Masada and Ein Gedi Spa, and an afternoon circuit in the other direction (departure from Ein Gedi Spa at 4pm). More locally, bus 21 (three times daily Sunday to Thursday) links Kibbutz Ein Gedi and Ein Gedi Spa with Ein Bokek.

If you're short on time, it's possible to do a one-day circuit from Jerusalem on weekdays (Sunday to Thursday). Take bus 444 from Jerusalem to Masada (first departure at 7am); after visiting Masada, hop on any northbound bus to Ein Gedi Nature Reserve; walk over to Ein Gedi Beach for a dip; and finally take bus 444 back up to Jerusalem (last bus at about 8pm).

CAR

Only one car rental company (Hertz) has an office at the Dead Sea (at Ein Bokek), so your best bet is to hire a car in Jerusalem or Tel Aviv.

The Dead Sea's western coast is served by Rte 90 (Israel's longest highway, it continues north to the Lebanese border and south to the Red Sea). There's an army roadblock about 14km north of Ein Gedi at the junction below Metzukei Dragot.

The Dead Sea is served by three east–west highways:

» **Rte 1** – Thanks to this modern, divided highway (and Rte 90), Ein Gedi is only 75km from Jerusalem. Rte 1 passes through the West Bank but is quite safe. For Jerusalem-bound traffic, there's an army roadblock between Ma'aleh Adumim and Jerusalem.

» **Rte 31** – Connects Arad with Rte 90 at a point very near Ein Bokek. To get to the back (western) side of Masada, turn onto Rte 3199.

» **Rte 25** – Passes through Be'er Sheva and Dimona on its way to the Dead Sea's southern tip, near Neot HaKikar.

Trying to drive from the Dead Sea direct to Hebron, via the Judean Desert, is a very bad idea.

Locals recommend that you arrive in the Dead Sea area with a full tank as the only petrol stations are (from north to south) at Lido junction (40km north of Ein Gedi near Jericho), Ein Gedi Beach, Neve Zohar junction and Arava junction (11km west of Neot HaKikar).

Most of the hikes mentioned in this chapter are circuits, so you end up where you began. For one-way hikes, you can arrange (for a fee) to be dropped off and picked up, eg by the kind folks in Neot HaKikar.

Ein Gedi עין גדי عين غدي

♫ 08 / POP 520

Nestled in two dramatic canyons that plunge from the arid moonscape of the Judean Desert to the shores of the Dead Sea, **Ein Gedi** is one of Israel's most magical desert oases. The area's freshwater pools, cool streams, Eden-like waterfalls and luxuriant vegetation, fed by four year-round springs, are a haven for wildlife such as the majestic Nubian ibex (*ya'el* in Hebrew) and the boulder-dwelling hyrax (*shafan sela* in Hebrew; also known as a dassie or rock rabbit), both of which you're very likely to encounter. Ein Gedi is the northernmost natural habitat of a number of plants that are more usually found on the savannahs of East Africa, thousands of kilometres south along the Great Rift Valley.

Ein Gedi (literally 'Spring of the Kid', as in 'young goat') was first settled during the Chalcolithic Age (5000 years ago), when people just out of the Stone Age built a temple here. In the Bible, David fled to Ein Gedi to escape the wrath of Saul (I Samuel 23:29). The oasis crops up again in the love poetry of the Song of Songs (1:14): 'My beloved is to me as a cluster of henna blossoms in the vineyards of Ein Gedi'. More recently, the erotic waterfall scene in one of Brooke Shields worst movies, *Sahara* (1983), was filmed at Ein Gedi.

◉ Sights & Activities

Ein Gedi Nature Reserve　　　RESERVE
This **reserve** (♫08-658 4285; www.parks.org. il; adult/child incl Ein Gedi Antiquities 27/14NIS) consists of two roughly parallel canyons, **Wadi David** and **Wadi Arugot**, each of which has its own entrance complex and ticket office.

The key to a successful hike in the reserve is the excellent colour-coded **map-brochure** given out when you buy your tickets. It has invaluable details on the area's many trails (indicated with the same colours as the trail markings), how long each route takes, and the times by which you need to begin and finish each circuit.

Park rangers make sure that visitors do not enter the park before it opens or stick around after closing time (theoretically, they can fine violators 730NIS). The reason: desert animals such as the wolf, jackal and fox need some people-less peace and quiet in order to search for food and drink (the reserve has the only year-round water sources in the entire area).

The last time a critically endangered Arabian leopard (*Panthera pardus nimr*) was spotted in the Ein Gedi area – carrying off Kibbutz Ein Gedi house pets for dinner – was in 2006. The species is now presumed to be extinct here.

The reserve's trails, or parts of them, may be closed when the weather gets too hot or there is a danger of flash flooding.

Eating is not allowed in the reserve.

Wadi David　　　HIKING
(Nahal David; ◷8am-5pm during daylight savings, 8am-4pm rest of year, until 3pm Fri, last entry 1hr before closing) Ein Gedi's most accessible – and popular – pools and waterfalls are situated along **Lower Wadi David** (Nahal David Tachton), ie the area downstream from **David's Waterfall** (Mapal David; one hour return). This part of the reserve can get very crowded, especially on Jewish holidays and on days when raucous coach loads of schoolkids are around. The first 400m of the trail is fully accessible to wheelchairs.

The entrance pavilion has free drinking water (if you don't have an empty bottle, ask staff for one that's on the way to being recycled) and lockers. The refreshments counter sells sandwiches and drinks, including espresso.

To get to **Upper Wadi David** (Nahal David Elyon), which is significantly less crowded, head up the trail that climbs the south wall of the canyon. A bit past tiny **Shulamit's Spring** (Ma'ayan Shulamit) is a T-junction. Go right and you'll head down the slope to the section of Wadi David above David's Waterfall, including **Dodim Cave** (Lovers' Cave); hanging a left takes you to a **Chalcolithic Temple** (3000 BCE), the pools of **Ein Gedi Spring** (most of whose water is

SAFE HIKING

A few tips on staying safe and healthy in the Dead Sea's unique climate and geography:

» Don't hike without a 1:50,000-scale **SPNI topographical trail map** (82NIS; not necessary at Ein Gedi unless you climb up to the plateau above the wadis). The maps to have – available only in Hebrew – are No 11 *(Ein Gedi v'Daroma)* for Ein Gedi and places south of there; and No 8 *(Tzfon Midbar Yehuda v'Yam HaMelach)* for Ein Gedi and points north. Both can be purchased at the Ein Gedi Field School and the Wadi Arugot entrance to Ein Gedi Nature Reserve.

» Bring along *lots* of **water** – at least 5L per person per day.

» To **beat the heat** of summer, hit the trail shortly after dawn. If you're still out at midday, you're unlikely to run into anyone other than 'mad dogs and Englishmen'.

» **Flash floods** can turn the dry canyons above the Dead Sea into raging torrents. In the late autumn, winter and spring, keep an eye on the weather reports and stay well away from narrow channels (eg those along Wadi Daraja) if there's any chance of a cloudburst up in the Judean Desert.

» Temperatures can drop precipitously at night so bring along a fleece jacket to avoid **hypothermia** in case you get stuck.

» Keep away from areas (eg south of Ein Gedi Beach and across Rte 90 from Ein Gedi Youth Hostel) where signs warn of **sinkholes** *(bol'anim)*, which can open up under your feet with no warning and swallow you alive (yes, this has happened to people!). Caused by the dissolution of underground salt deposits, sinkholes – 1700 of them up to 25m across and 20m deep – have been found at 30 different sites around the Dead Sea.

» Stay out of the area's caves, all of which (including the famous Flour Cave) are closed to the public because various geological factors, including high salt content, make them susceptible to sudden collapse.

---

diverted and bottled by Kibbutz Ein Gedi) and, near the base of Wadi Arugot, an archaeological site known as Tel Goren (7th to 8th century BCE).

Wadi Arugot   HIKING

(Nahal Arugot; ☺8am-5pm during daylight savings, 8am-4pm rest of year, until 3pm Fri, last entry 2hr before closing) Generally less crowded but no less lovely than Wadi David, Wadi Arugot offers a number of excellent trails, some of them quite challenging. The ticket office complex, a 20-minute walk or a five-minute drive from the Wadi David car park, has free lockers, a small refreshment counter and a shop that sells SPNI 1:50,000-scale trail maps.

Hikers must leave Upper Wadi Arugot (Nahal Arugot Elyon), where you'll find the Hidden Waterfall (HaMapal HaNistar) and the Upper Pools (HaBreichot HaElyonot), by 2pm (3pm during daylight savings time).

The reserve's most difficult hike (six to eight hours), marked by black blazes, links Wadi Arugot with Wadi David via the Desert Plateau, Ein Gedi Lookout (Mitzpeh Ein Gedi) and Ein Gedi Spring.

Desert Plateau Hikes   HIKING

The plateau above Ein Gedi – the eastern edge of the Judean Desert – is about 200m above sea level, ie 625m above the Dead Sea. Five trails head up to the plateau and its spectacular panoramas, taking you well away from the madding crowds. From north to south, they are: the Yishay Ascent (from Ein Gedi Field School); the Ein Gedi Ascent (from Ein Gedi Spring, on the hillside between Wadi David and Wadi Arugot); Bnei HaMoshavim Ascent (an especially difficult route that begins at the upper section of Wadi Arugot); Ha'Isiyyim Ascent (from near the top of Wadi Arugot); and the Tzruya (Zeruya) Ascent (from near Kibbutz Ein Gedi). A 1:50,000-scale SPNI trail map (82NIS), sold at the entrance to Wadi Arugot and the Ein Gedi Field School, is a must for all these routes, which are sometimes closed on especially hot days.

For details on half- and full-day routes that combine several trails, enquire at one of the nature reserve's ticket offices or the Ein Gedi Field School. Before heading out, let park staff know your route.

Ancient Synagogue ARCHAEOLOGICAL SITE
(Ein Gedi Antiquities National Park; adult with/without nature reserve 27/14NIS, child 14/7NIS; ⊘8am-5pm during daylight savings, 8am-4pm rest of year, until 3pm Fri) Situated about midway between the Wadi David and Wadi Arugot ticket offices, this 5th-century CE synagogue sports a superb mosaic floor decorated with the 12 signs of the zodiac and three Aramaic inscriptions, one of which calls down a curse on anyone who is quarrelsome, slanderous or larcenous.

Ein Gedi Beach BEACH
(Rte 90; ⊘24hr) This hugely popular but unpleasantly stony public beach (bring plastic flip-flops) fulfils the bare requirements of those seeking a Dead Sea float in that it has toilets and changing rooms (per entry 2NIS; ⊘8am-3.25pm) and a 24-hour snack bar. Renting a towel costs 10NIS (plus a 10NIS deposit). Situated 1km south (a 20-minute walk) along Rte 90 from the Ein Gedi Nature Reserve turn-off.

Ein Gedi Botanical Garden GARDENS
(☑08-658 4444; www.ein-gedi.co.il; Kibbutz Ein Gedi; admission 26NIS; ⊘8am-4pm Sat-Thu, 8am-2pm Fri) These famous botanical gardens are home to a thousand species of indigenous and exotic plants, from near-mythological biblical species such as frankincense and myrrh to the highly poisonous Sodom apple, and from gargantuan baobab trees to tiny plants that can survive with minuscule quantities of water. By the time you read this, visitors with difficulties walking should be able to rent golf carts. Situated 3km south of Ein Gedi Nature Reserve.

Ein Gedi Spa SPA
(☑08-659 4813; www.ein-gedi.co.il; Rte 90; Sun-Fri without/with lunch 69/119NIS, child 5-12yr 40/89; ⊘8am-6pm during daylight savings, 8am-5pm rest of year, closes 1hr earlier Fri) Owned by Kibbutz Ein Gedi, this unpretentious spa is a popular place to catch a float and get coated with invigorating natural black mud. The shoreline has receded 1.2km since the spa opened in 1984 but beach-goers can take a little train to the water's edge. The spa has six sulphur pools and a freshwater pool and offers a range of natural beauty and massage treatments. There's also a coffee shop and a meat restaurant (⊘11.30am–half-hour before spa closing time). Wheelchair accessible. Situated 6km south of Ein Gedi Nature Reserve.

🛌 Sleeping
The field school and hostel are often full (Friday night is booked out months ahead) so don't show up without reservations.

Ein Gedi Kibbutz Hotel HOTEL $$$
(☑08-659 4222; www.ein-gedi.co.il; d from US$182-272; ❄@🛜🏊) A step up from most kibbutz guesthouses, this low-rise campus, lushly planted with exotic trees and plants (including two immense baobab trees), offers a new on-site spa and five categories of very comfortable rooms, some with space for two adults and two children. The bar attracts a mix of tourists and *kibbutznikim* (kibbutz members). The Rte 90 turn-off to Kibbutz Ein Gedi is 2.3km south of Ein Gedi Nature Reserve.

SPNI Field School HOSTEL $$
(☑08-658 4288; near Ein Gedi Nature Reserve; www.teva.org.il; dm/s/d 115/345/385NIS, additional adult/child 7-14yr 129/89NIS; ❄🛜) The 50 rooms, each with five to seven beds, are not as swish as at the youth hostel, but this is an excellent launching point for early hikes. Guests are greeted by a sign – not a joke – reading 'please don't feed the ibex'. Dinner (53NIS, on Friday 63NIS) is served almost daily. Reception sells hiking maps. Situated 800m up the hill from the Rte 90 turn-off to Ein Gedi Nature Reserve and the bus stop.

Ein Gedi Youth Hostel HOSTEL $
(Beit Sarah; ☑02-594 5681; www.iyha.org.il; Rte 90, near Ein Gedi Nature Reserve; dm/s/d 118/276/352NIS, additional adult/child 2-17yr 103/81NIS; ❄@🛜) The sensational setting and the clean, contemporary rooms, with up

THE FOUR EIN GEDIS
The area known as Ein Gedi stretches for 6km along Rte 90, with separate turn-offs (and bus stops) for (from north to south):

» **Ein Gedi Nature Reserve** – This is the turn-off to use for Wadi David, Wadi Arugot, the Ein Gedi Youth Hostel and the Ein Gedi Field School

» **Ein Gedi Beach** – 1km south of the nature reserve

» **Kibbutz Ein Gedi** – 3km south of the nature reserve

» **Ein Gedi Spa** – 6km south of the nature reserve

1

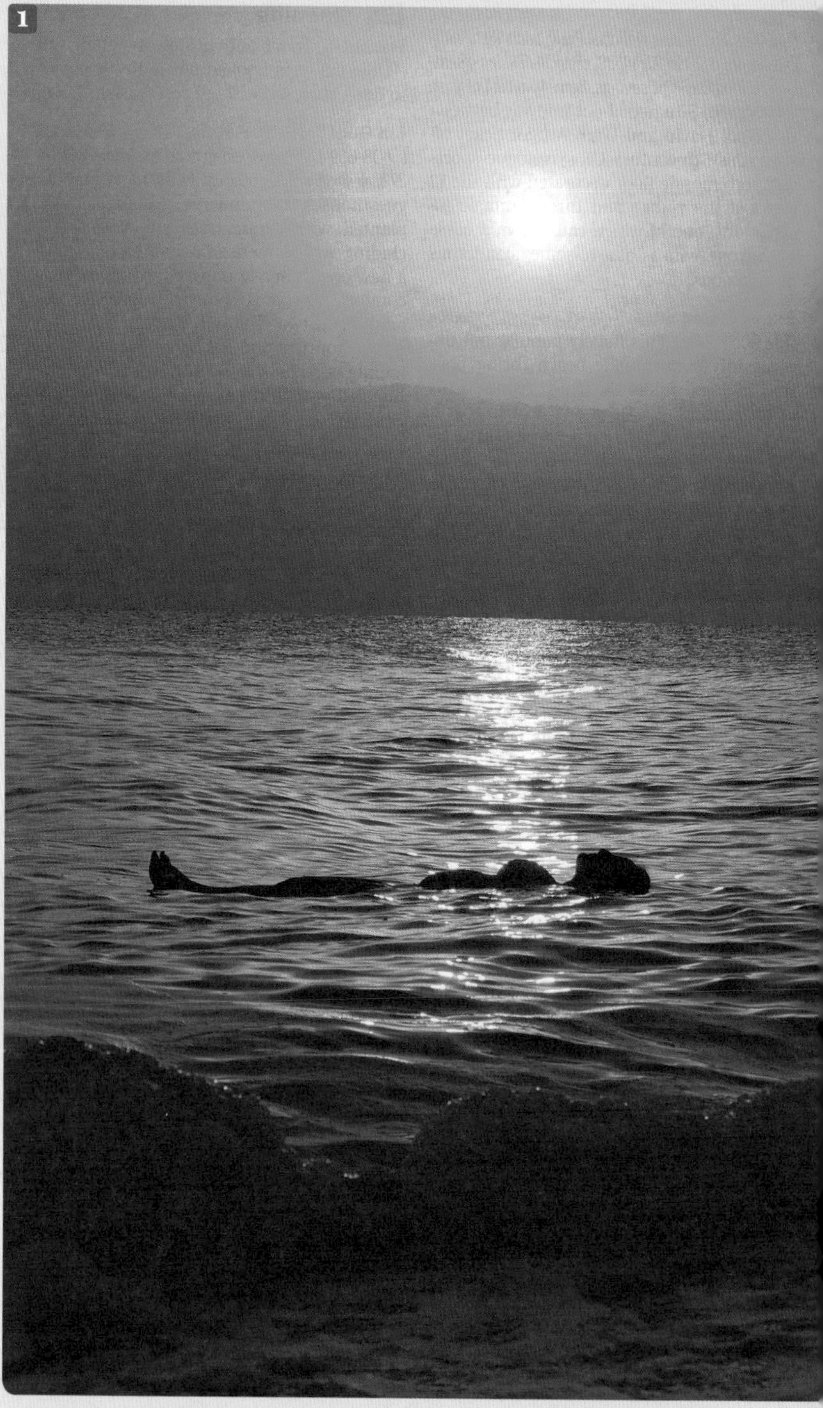

1. Ein Gedi Beach (p291)
Float in the waters of the Dead Sea, which are 33% solid matter, at Ein Gedi Beach.

2. Ein Gedi Nature Reserve (p289)
A desert oasis of freshwater pools, cool streams, Eden-like waterfalls and luxuriant vegetation.

3. Masada (p296)
Site of the legendary last stand of the Jews against the Romans, atop a desert mesa.

4. Dead Sea (p284)
Salt pools fringing the Dead Sea, whose waters have fantastic healing powers.

to six beds, make this 68-room hostel madly popular. Offers discounts to various area attractions. Dinner is 54NIS (64NIS on Friday). Situated 200m up the slope from the Rte 90 turn-off to Ein Gedi Nature Reserve and the bus stop.

FREE **Ein Gedi Beach** CAMPGROUND **$**

(Rte 90; toilet & changing rooms per entry 2NIS; ⊘beach & toilet 24hr, changing rooms 8am-3.25pm) Camping is free. There's a 24-hour snack bar in the car park. Bring flip-flops and a torch. Situated 1km south of the Ein Gedi Nature Reserve turn-off from Rte 90.

✕ Eating

There are few dining options in the Ein Gedi area so arrive with picnic supplies and consider having dinner at your hotel or hostel.

Pundak Ein Gedi Kiosk SANDWICHES **$**

(Ein Gedi Beach; sandwich 17-19NIS; ⊘24hr) Serves pre-packaged sandwiches, ice cream and beer. Across the car park from the entrance to the beach.

Pundak Ein Gedi CAFETERIA **$$**

(✆08-659 4761; Ein Gedi Beach; main with 2 side dishes 52NIS; ⊘11am-3.30 or 4pm; ✺) For lunch you might try this bland but blessedly air-conditioned self-service cafeteria next to the petrol station. Offers uninspiring meat dishes and non-meat side dishes but the salad bar (small/large plate 22/35NIS) is fresh and tasty.

Kolbo GROCERY **$**

(Kibbutz Ein Gedi; ⊘7.30-9am & 11.30am-7pm Sun-Thu, 7.30am-9am & 10.30am-2pm Fri, 12.30-2pm Sat) The only proper food shop in the area.

❶ Information

ATM Inside the Ein Gedi Kibbutz Hotel; takes only four-digit PIN codes.

SPNI Field School (✆08-658 4288; www.teva.org.il, www.mokedteva.co.il, in Hebrew; ⊘8.30am-2.30pm Sun-Thu, sometimes staffed Fri) Free consultations by expert staff on area hikes, including family-friendly Wadi Mishmar and Wadi Tze'elim. Sells 1:50,000-scale SPNI topographical trail maps (82NIS). Situated 800m up the hill from the turn-off to the Ein Gedi Nature Reserve from Rte 90.

❶ Getting There & Away

For information on bus services to the Dead Sea, see p288. Bus schedules are posted at the both entrances to the Ein Gedi Nature Reserve.

North of Ein Gedi

Highlights along the Dead Sea's north-western corner include the Qumran Caves, where the Dead Sea Scrolls were discovered, and some wild, unspoilt nature sites. Captured by Israel from Jordan in 1967, this almost uninhabited corner of the West Bank is just a short drive from Jericho.

Listings here appear from north to south.

QUMRAN NATIONAL PARK

גן לאומי קומראן   قمران

(✆02-994 2235; Rte 90; adult/child 21/9NIS, incl entry to Ein Feshkha 39/19NIS; ⊘8am-5pm during daylight savings, 8am-4pm rest of year, until 3pm Fri, last entry 1hr before closing) World-famous for having hidden the Dead Sea Scrolls for almost 2000 years, Qumran was the site of a small Essene settlement around the time of Jesus, ie from the late 1st century BCE until 68 CE, when it was destroyed by the Romans. The ruins are not that extensive, but from an elevated wooden walkway you can clearly make out the aqueduct, channels and cisterns that ensured the community's water supply. Elsewhere are ritual baths (the Essenes were zealous about ritual purity); the refectory, in which communal meals were eaten; and the scriptorium, where some of the Dead Sea Scrolls may have been written. One of the caves where the scrolls were discovered is open to visitors. The small museum (and its seven-minute multimedia program) will give you a good potted history of the site. Wheelchair accessible.

Qumran is 35km east of Jerusalem and 35km north of Ein Gedi. All Jerusalem–Dead Sea buses pass by here.

EIN FESHKHA (EINOT TSUKIM)

עינות צוקים   عين فشخة

(✆02-994 2355; Rte 90; adult/child 27/14NIS, incl entry to Qumran 39/19NIS; ⊘8am-5pm during daylight savings, 8am-4pm rest of year, closes 1hr earlier on Fri, last entry 1hr before closing) These spring-fed freshwater pools and the lush greenery around them were a favourite holiday spot of Jordan's King Hussein in the 1950s and 1960s. Today, the oasis and its veritable forest of salt-resistant plants, including tamarisks, reeds and grass, are an agreeable place to take a cooling dip, though the pools tend to become quite murky and can be crowded at weekends. They are particularly popular with large groups of young men; women may not feel comfortable swimming solo.

THE DEAD SEA SCROLLS

Few discoveries in the history of archaeology have elicited as much enduring worldwide fascination as the Dead Sea Scrolls, accidentally found in 1947 at Qumran inside earthenware jars hidden in a cliffside cave – by a Bedouin shepherd boy searching for a stray goat. Eventually, about 950 different parchment and papyrus documents written during the Second Temple period and the earliest years of Christianity (200 BCE to 68 CE) were found in 11 caves. Most of the documents, which include the oldest known manuscripts of the Hebrew Bible, texts that didn't make it into the Bible and descriptions of life in Judea around the time of Jesus, are in Hebrew, while some are in Aramaic and a few are in Greek. Many are in tiny fragments, making the process of reassembling and deciphering long and arduous.

The scrolls are believed to have belonged to the Essenes, a separatist, ascetic Jewish sect – mentioned by Josephus Flavius – that moved to the desert to escape the decadence they believed was corrupting their fellow Jews.

In 2011 the Israel Museum in Jerusalem, where some of the scrolls are on display, and Google launched the **Dead Sea Scrolls Digital Project** (http://dss.collections.imj.org.il), whose goal is to make searchable, high-resolution images of the scrolls available to the general public.

For some interesting facts on the scrolls, see www.centuryone.com/25dssfacts.html.

There is no access to the rapidly receding Dead Sea shoreline – note the sign, almost 2km from the water's edge, reading 'The sea was here in 1967'. However, you can see a Second Temple-period **farm** where the Essenes of Qumran worked the land and raised sheep and goats.

The southern **Hidden Reserve** is off limits – for reasons of conservation – unless you join a one-hour **guided tour** (⊙10am & noon Fri, 10am, noon & 2pm Sat mid-Sep–Jun).

Ein Feshkha is 3km south of Qumran.

METZUKEI DRAGOT

מצוקי דרגות   متسوقي درجوت

Perched on a cliff 600m above the Dead Sea – the views are truly spectacular – this no-frills, hippyish **holiday village** (✐reservations 1-700-707 180, 02-994 4777; www.metzoke.co.il; dm adult/child 100/85NIS, d in tent with common bathroom 250NIS, d 400-520NIS, basic q 400NIS; ⊙reception staffed 8am-8pm; ﹡) is like a quick trip back to the 1970s, with barebones infrastructure, nicked furnishings and very basic bathrooms. There are 50 basic rooms and hundreds of sleeping spots in large tents that can be subdivided to keep members of a family or group together. You can pitch your own tent for 50NIS per person (90NIS including an excellent Israeli breakfast). Sleeping bags can be rented. If you want to cook, bring your own food. Dinner is available for 85NIS (55NIS for kids aged three to 12). If you arrive after 8pm, call the phone number posted on the yellow vehicle gate. Situated 18km north of Ein Gedi, a steep 5.5km up the hill (it may be possible to hitch) from the army roadblock on Rte 90, where you can ask any Jerusalem–Dead Sea bus to stop.

WADI DARAJA

נחל דרגה   وادي درجة

(Wadi Darga) One of the more difficult hikes in the area, this steep canyon descent (five to six hours not including stops) requires you to climb down about two dozen waterfalls (30m climbing rope required) and swim across year-round pools up to 4m deep – all your kit will get wet so leave those mobile phones and cameras somewhere safe. Wear proper shoes (which you don't mind getting wet), not sandals. The minimum age is 10.

The Israel Nature and Parks Authority has an **information booth** (www.parks.org.il; ⊙Fri, Sat & Jewish holidays) right outside Metzukei Dragot, which is 1.5km from the trailhead; schematic maps are available there or at the Metzukei Dragot reception desk. Begin this hike no later than 9am (10am during daylight savings) – and don't begin it at all if there's any chance of rain in the Judean Desert. The bottom of the trail intersects Rte 90 near Kibbutz Mitzpe Shalem.

Several circular, family-friendly hikes (which don't require you to get soaked) start at the same point. These include the **Wadi Tekoa Circuit** (five hours) and the **Mashash-Murba'at Circuit** (three hours), which passes by caves in which letters personally signed by Bar Kochba (leader of the Bar Kochba Rebellion of 132 to 135 CE) were found in 1952.

MINERAL BEACH חוף מינרל شاطئ مينرال (02-994 4888; www.dead-sea.co.il; adult/child 50/30NIS, on Sat 60/35NIS; 9am-6pm during daylight savings, until 5pm rest of year, opens 8am Fri & Sat) Run by Kibbutz Mitzpe Shalem, this is one of the nicest of the Dead Sea beaches. After having a float and glopping on black mud, you can soak in naturally sulphurous spring water (39°C) or indulge in a Tibetan or Swedish massage (160NIS for 30 minutes). Lockers and towels each cost 10NIS (plus a 10NIS deposit). By the time you read this, there should be a restaurant and a mini-train to take bathers down to the receding water line. Wheelchair accessible. Camping is not permitted.

'Mineral' is where contemporary artist Spencer Tunick (www.nakedsea.info) took a series of stunning photos of 1200 naked Israelis in 2011.

Masada מצדה مصاده

08

After the Romans conquered Jerusalem in 70 CE, almost a thousand Jews – men, women and children – made a desperate last stand atop Masada (08-658 4207/8; adult/child 27/14NIS), a desert mesa surrounded by sheer cliffs and, from 72 CE, the might of the Roman Empire's Tenth Legion. As a Roman battering ram was about to breach the walls of their fastness, Masada's defenders chose suicide over enslavement. When Roman soldiers swarmed onto the top of the flat-topped mountain, they were met with silence.

Until archaeological excavations began in 1963, the only source of information about Masada's heroic resistance and bloody end was Josephus Flavius, a Jewish commander during the Great Jewish Revolt (66 to 70 CE) who, after being captured, reinvented himself as a Roman historian. He writes that as the Roman siege ramp inched towards the summit, the defenders – Zealots known as Sicarii (Sikrikin in Hebrew) because of their habit of assassinating their (Jewish) rivals using a curved dagger (sica in Greek) hidden under their cloaks – began to set fire to their homes and possessions to prevent their falling into Roman hands. Ten men, who would have the task of killing everyone else, were then chosen by lot. Nine of the 10

were then executed by one of their number before the last man alive committed suicide. When the Romans broke through everyone was dead – except for two women and five children, who had survived by hiding.

Over the last century, Masada has become Israeli shorthand for the attitude that 'they'll never take us alive'. During WWII, before the British stopped Rommel's German divisions at El Alamein (Egypt) in 1942, some Palestinian Jews made plans for a last stand atop Mt Carmel, and a number of Israeli army units hold their swearing-in ceremonies here, vowing that 'Masada shall not fall again'. Less apocalyptically, the Israeli air force has been known to send groups of officers up top do yoga at sunrise!

Masada has been a Unesco World Heritage Site since 2001.

Sights & Activities

TOP CHOICE Masada Museum MUSEUM
(Visitors Centre; admission incl audioguide atop Masada 20NIS; 8.30am-4pm, last entry 3.30pm) A really excellent introduction to Masada's archaeology and history, this museum combines 500 evocative artefacts unearthed by archaeologists (and five replicas) with introductions to Masada personalities – eg Herod the Great, who built a palace here in the 1st century BCE, and Josephus Flavius – to make the dramatic events of 73 CE seem close enough to touch. Objects on display include Roman arrowheads; a leather sandal once worn by a Roman legionnaire; the remains of Roman-era dates, wheat, barley and olives; and 11 pot shards that – as Josephus writes – may have been used to select those who killed everyone else as the Romans neared breached the ramparts. Visitors receive an audio headset (available in six languages).

Snake Path HIKING
This famously serpentine footpath winds its way up Masada's eastern flank, starting from near the Visitors Centre. Walking up takes about 45 minutes; count on spending 30 minutes to come back down. If you'd like to watch sunrise from the summit, get to the base an hour before the sun comes up. On particularly hot summer days, park authorities sometimes close the trail at 10am or 11am.

Ramp Trail HIKING
The Romans wimped out and so can you – the path up the spine of their siege ramp takes only about 15 minutes to climb. The catch is that the ramp (ie western) side of

the mountain is accessible only from Arad (ie the west), a 68km drive from the Visitors Centre via Rte 31 and then Rte 3199.

If you'd like to watch sunrise from the summit, get to the base of the ramp an hour before the sun comes up.

Cable Car
AERIAL TRAMWAY

(return/up only/down only incl admission fee adult 72/54/27NIS, child 41/28/14/NIS; ⊙every 10 min 8am-5pm during daylight savings, 8am-4pm rest of year, closes 1hr earlier on Fri, last trip up 1hr before closing) Whisks you from the Visitors Centre to the top in Swiss comfort in just three minutes. Each car holds 65 people. Wheelchair accessible, as is the summit (except for the Northern Palace).

Atop Masada
ARCHAEOLOGICAL SITE

The plateau atop Masada, which measures about 550m by 270m, is some 60m above sea level – that is, it's about 485m above the surface of the Dead Sea. Look down in any direction and chances are you'll be able to spot at least one of the Romans' eight military camps and their siege wall. The effort put into the siege by the Roman Legions is mind-boggling – no surprise, then, that they commemorated their victories over the rebels of Judea by erecting a monumental victory arch, the Arch of Titus, in the centre of Rome.

Visitors are given an excellent map-brochure of the ruins. Similar information can be had from an audioguide (incl admission to the Masada Museum 20NIS). Both are available in Hebrew, English, French, German, Spanish and Russian. On the ruins, lines of black paint divide reconstructed parts (above) from original remains (below).

Drinking water available so bring a bottle to refill. Eating atop Masada is forbidden.

TOP CHOICE Trails Around Masada
HIKING

Paths link the remains of the eight Roman military encampments that still encircle Masada, making it possible to circumnavigate the mesa in part or in full.

From the Visitors Centre, a trail heads west up Mt Eleazar to Camp H (30 minutes). From up here, Roman legionnaires could peer down at Masada, gathering aerial intelligence on the Zealots' activities. The path continues down to the bottom of the siege ramp on Masada's western side.

Alternatively, you can walk north from the Visitors Centre, following the siege wall on a trail known as Shvil HaRatz (the Runner's Trail). It, too, goes to the siege ramp.

Another trail links Camp D (north of Masada) with the eminently hikeable Wadi Tze'elim, 4km to the north.

Sound & Light Show
SOUND & LIGHT

(☑08-995 9333; adult/child 45/35NIS; ⊙8.30pm Tue & Thu Mar-Oct) This dramatic, open-air recounting of the history of Masada is meant to be watched from the base of the Roman siege ramp (ie on Masada's western side). The narration is in Hebrew but you can rent earphones (15NIS) for simultaneous translation into five languages. Access is via Arad and then Rte 3199; from the Visitors Centre, it's a 68km drive.

Scenic Fights & Parachuting
ADVENTURE SPORTS

For a thrilling view the Romans and the Zealots could only dream about, take a 20-minute flight over the Masada area with Sunair (☑for Haviv 054-581 8883; www.sun-air.co.il, in Hebrew; 3-/5-passenger light plane 700/1200NIS). Or try a tandem parachute jump with Masada Skydive (☑1-700-504 031; www.masadaskydive.com, in Hebrew; per person US$275); instructors are USPA rated and have all made at least 3500 jumps. Both companies operate from the southern end of Masada's 1.2km-long airstrip (Bar Yehuda Airfield), which parallels Rte 90 1.5km north of the Masada turn-off (look for a sign reading 'Flightseeing').

🛌 Sleeping

Some visitors, especially those heading to the Ramp Trail, stay up in Arad.

TOP CHOICE Masada Guest House
HOSTEL $

(☑08-594 5622; www.iyha.org.il; dm/s/d 138/285/388NIS; ❋@🛜🏊) This 280-bed hostel, whose six-bed, single-sex dorm rooms border on luxurious, is ideal if you'd like to see sunrise from atop Masada. Staff do their best to separate travellers from the packs of noisy schoolkids. The swimming pool is open from Passover to Sukkot; the basketball court is available year-round. Dinner (54NIS, on Friday 64NIS) is served most nights until 8pm. Frequently full, especially on Friday, so reserving is a must. Situated a few hundred metres below the Visitors Centre.

Camping Zones
CAMPGROUND $

If you'd like to camp near Masada, ask the guards at Chenyon HaDekalim (the bus parking area next to Masada Guest House) for permission to pitch your tent. If they're not in the mood, head to the signposted parking area situated on the Masada access road at a point 1km west of the junction with Rte 90. There are no amenities; bring a torch.

Another option is to pitch your tent next to the Bedouin-style tent at the southern end of the Masada airfield (📞for Haviv 054-581 8883; per tent 100NIS), just east of Rte 90 at a point 1.5km north of the Masada turn-off. Or you can sleep inside the Bedouin tent (per person 60NIS), used during the day to fold parachutes. Toilets and showers available.

✖ Eating & Drinking

Free drinking water is available atop Masada.

Visitors' Centre Food Court FOOD COURT
(⊙until 5pm during daylight savings, until 4pm rest of year; 📞) Has a cafeteria (felafel 24NIS, mains 55NIS to 65NIS, cold beer from 22NIS), an ice-cream and frozen yoghurt joint, a Cup O' Joe cafe and a McDonald's. Downstairs from the ticket windows.

ⓘ Getting There & Away

Masada's Visitors Centre, on the eastern side of the mountain, is 21km south of the Ein Gedi Nature Reserve; the access road from Rte 90 is 3km long. The Roman siege ramp, on Masada's western side, is accessible from Arad (via Rte 3199). As the crow flies, the Visitors Centre is a bit over 1km from the siege ramp; by car the distance is 68km!

For details on bus services, see p288. Bus times are posted at the Visitors Centre's ticket windows.

Ein Bokek עין בוקק عين بوقيق

📞08

Sandwiched between the turquoise waters of the southern Dead Sea and a dramatic tan bluff, Ein Bokek's strip of luxury hotels – by far the region's largest tourist zone – rises out of the desert like a mini-Eilat. Even if you're not staying here, Ein Bokek (also spelled En Boqeq) offers the Dead Sea's nicest free beaches.

Ein Bokek is the Dead Sea's main centre for treating ailments such as psoriasis, arthritis and respiratory conditions with naturally occurring minerals and compounds.

The three most commonly heard languages here are Hebrew, Arabic and Russian because the area is hugely popular both with Israelis (Jews and Arabs) and with Russians (immigrants and tourists).

Unlike beaches further north, Ein Bokek fronts evaporation pools (kept full by Dead Sea Works pumps) rather than the open sea, which is why the lakeshore is not receding here.

⊙ Sights & Activities

A 3km-long pedestrian promenade links Ein Bokek's two hotel zones, Ein Bokek (the northern one) and Neve Hamei Zohar.

TOP CHOICE Ein Bokek Beach BEACH
(admission free; ⊙24hr) This broad, clean beach, in the middle of Ein Bokek's main (northern) hotel zone, is gloriously sandy. Has lifeguards, shade shelters, beach showers, changing rooms and bathrooms (closed at night). Camping is permitted – this is a much more comfortable option than Ein Gedi Beach. Wheelchair accessible.

FREE Hamei Zohar Beach BEACH
(⊙24hr) Situated in Ein Bokek's southern hotel zone, near three Leonardo-branded hotels. Amenities include beach showers and a snack bar. Has men- and women-only sections for Orthodox Jewish and traditional Muslim families. Camping permitted. Wheelchair accessible.

Wadi Bokek HIKING
One of just three wadis on the Dead Sea's western shore fed year-round by spring water (the other two are at Ein Gedi). The narrow gorges, lush vegetation and waterholes make for an easy and refreshing hour-long hike. Access is through a tunnel under Rte 90 (between the Le Meridien David and Leonardo Inn hotels).

Day Spas SPA
Almost every Ein Bokek hotel boasts a spa with multiple pools, saunas, jacuzzis, a long menu of treatments and an army of predominantly Russian therapists. Most places charge non-guests a reasonable 80NIS to 120NIS to use their facilities for the day, not including special treatments (eg massages). Deals that include meals are also available – for instance, for an adult/child aged three to 13, the Crowne Plaza (📞08-659 1919; www.h-i.co.il) charges 180/140NIS (230/180NIS on Saturday).

☞ Tours

Getting off-road is a great way to explore the wadis, hills and plateaus around – and especially south of – Ein Bokek.

Giora Eldar   ADVENTURE TOUR
(☑052-397 1774; eldarara@netvision.net.il) Of-
fers a full day of 4WD off-roading (1400NIS
for six to eight people) as well as rappelling
(1400NIS for up 15 people). Also available
for hiking and mountain biking pick-ups
and drop-offs.

🛏 Sleeping

Unless you camp on the beach (free), there's
no budget (or even midrange) accommodation in Ein Bokek's two hotel zones. But if
you're up for a splurge there are loads of
options – the area's dozen hotels offer gloriously air-conditioned facilities (a life-saver
during the summer), gorgeous swimming
pools, state-of-the-art spas and buffet bo-
nanzas. Significant discounts are often available on the web.

All the hotels, except three of the four
places branded as Leonardo (www.fattal.co.il),
are in Ein Bokek's northern zone.

Hod Hamidbar   HOTEL **$$$**
(☑08-668 8222; www.hodhotel.co.il; d US$233-
300; ✳@�⊠) On its own private beach,
this 203-room, non-chain hotel – one of Ein
Bokek's smaller establishments – is known
for its high-quality service. The swimming
pool overlooks the sea and the swanky glass-
enclosed spa offers sulphur pools, hydro-
therapy and dry and wet saunas.

Crowne Plaza   HOTEL **$$$**
(☑08-659 1919; www.h-i.co.il, d US$265; ✳@�\奈⊠)
Highlights include a beachfront swimming
pool, a luxurious spa and lots of activities
for adults and kids. Some of the 304 spacious rooms can sleep two adults and two
children.

Le Meridien David   HOTEL **$$$**
(☑08-659 1234; www.fattal.co.il; d 890-1250NIS;
✳@☈⊠) Its lobby decked out like a mar-
ble Ein Gedi, complete with two-storey
waterfalls and a grove of fake palm trees,
this hotel offers two swimming pools and a
children's club. The sprawling Mineralia Spa
is great for Dead Sea salt scrubs and mud
wraps. The plush, well-appointed rooms
come with balconies. Tuktuks ferry guests to
the private beach.

✗ Eating & Drinking

Most of Ein Bokek's restaurants are inside
hotels and cannot be described as inexpen-
sive. There are few budget options around,
but there's a McDonald's (with wi-fi) in the

ⓘ WHAT TO WEAR – AND NOT TO WEAR

When swimming in the Dead Sea con-
sider the following:

» Do not wear jewellery – silver will
turn jet black (don't worry, it can be
cleaned) and other metals (including
gold that isn't 24 carat) may also be
affected.

» Wear waterproof sandals to protect
your feet from the sharp stones both
on shore and in the water, and from
burning the soles of you feet on sun-
baked sand.

Petra Shopping Centre. Both Sky Blue Mall
and Petra Shopping Center have mini-
markets but little proper food is on offer. Ein
Bokek doesn't have much nightlife.

Taj Mahal   GRILLED MEAT **$$**
(mains 35-95NIS; ☉noon-2am) Completely
unconnected with anything Indian, this
restaurant – a Bedouin tent with rugs and
low couches – serves Middle Eastern grilled
meats, nargilehs (water pipes; 25NIS) and
East Jerusalem baklava (25NIS). A belly
dancer gyrates on Friday from 11pm. Situated on the grounds of the Leonardo Inn
Hotel, at the end facing Isrotel Ganim.

Aroma Espresso Bar   CAFE **$**
(Petra Shopping Center; sandwiches 18-18NIS;
☉8am-11pm; 奈☏) Serves salads, sandwiches
and pastries.

MixMarket   GROCERY
(Sky Blue Mall; ☉8am-10.30pm) Sells ice cream,
snacks, yoghurt and Russian Baltika beer.

🛍 Shopping

The Sky Blue Mall, next to the beach in the
northern zone, is the best place in the country to buy Dead Sea beauty products. Other
shops sell beach footwear, vital if you'll be at
any rocky beaches.

ⓘ Information

ATMs There are several at the Sky Blue Mall
and one in the Petra Shopping Center (inside
the Minimarket).
Currency Exchange Bureaux (Petra Shopping
Center & Sky Blue Mall) Rates are poor.
Dead Sea Tourist Information (☑08-997
5010; www.deadsea.co.il; ☉9am-4pm Sun-
Thu, 9am-3pm Fri) A good source of maps and

information on hotels, B&Bs, restaurants and outdoor activities in the area south of Ein Gedi. Situated inside the Solarium-400 complex.

Internet Access The Dead Sea Tourist Information office has a free internet computer. Four pay terminals are inside the Sky Blue Mall, at the far end of the hall next to Café Café. Solarium-400 has free wi-fi.

ⓘ Getting There & Away

For bus information, see p288.

The Dead Sea's only car rental agency is run by **Hertz** (☑1-700-507 555; www.hertz.co.il; inside Solarium-400). Pick-up or drop-off here may involve surcharges.

Sodom سدوم סדום

By tradition, this area is the site of Sodom and Gomorrah, the biblical cities that were destroyed in a storm of fire and brimstone, punishment from God because of their people's depravity (Genesis 18-19). These days, Sodom is much better known for its desert hiking and cycling trails than for sodomy.

◉ Sights & Activities

Mt Sodom   HIKING, CYCLING

Mt Sodom, 11km long and up to 2km wide, is one of the world's stranger geological formations. Start with the fact that it's made almost entirely of rock salt, a highly soluble material that in any other climate would have melted away. In fact, over the millennia the area's rare rainfalls *have* dissolved some of the salt, creating deep in the bowels of the mountain a maze of caves (closed to the public) up to 5.5km long. Many are connected to the surface by shafts that hikers need to make sure they don't fall into, and some are filled with delicate, eerie salt stalactites. And then there's the matter of Mt Sodom's summit. A respectable 250m above the surface of the Dead Sea – the views of Jordan's Moab Mountains are gorgeous – it also happens to be 176m below sea level.

Two trails head down the steep flanks of Mt Sodom from a lookout point, reachable by 4WD, whose views are at their best in the late afternoon. Ma'aleh HaSulamot (Ladders Ascent; 1½ hours to walk down), named after its many stairs, connects with Rte 90 across the highway from the remains of the Dead Sea Works' first workers' camp, built in 1934. Another descent to Rte 90 is Shvil HaDagim (Fishes Trail; 1½ hours

down), so named because of the many fossilised fish you can see in the rocks.

West of Mt Sodom, Wadi Sodom is ideal for mountain biking. If you start at the top (accessible by 4WD), it's about two hours, mostly downhill, to the Neve Zohar area. A round-trip circuit that connects with beautiful Wadi Pratzim (Wadi Perazim) whose upper reaches pass by the famous Flour Cave (closed to the public), is another option.

Lot's Wife   ROCK FORMATION

About 11km south of the southern end of Ein Bokek, high above the west side of Rte 90, a column of salt-rich rock leans precariously away from the rest of the Mt Sodom cliff face. It is popularly known as Lot's Wife because, according to the Bible, Lot's wife was turned into a pillar of salt as punishment for looking back to see Sodom as it burned (Genesis 19:17 and 19:26).

Dead Sea Works   INDUSTRIAL COMPLEX

(DSW; Rte 90; www.iclfertilizers.com) Israel's only major natural resource – other than sunlight and the newly discovered gas fields off the Mediterranean coast – is the Dead Sea, from which products ranging from magnesium chloride and anhydrous aluminium chloride to table salt and cosmetics are extracted. Founded in the 1930s, the DSW is now the world's fourth-largest producer of potash, an important component in agricultural fertiliser.

By day, the rusty (from the salt air) smokestacks, pipes and holding tanks of the DSW complex look like a mid-20th-century industrial dystopia, but by night, when it's lit up by thousands of yellowish lights, the site has a certain raw beauty.

'The Situation of Man'   SCULPTURE

(Rte 90) Atop a bluff overlooking the Dead Sea Works stands a modern sculpture called 'The Situation of Man', a rusty steel column with old steel railway ties striving to climb it like desperate worms.

Next to the sculpture, a viewpoint looks out over a crazy juxtaposition of smoke-spewing heavy industry, electric blue evaporation pools, green farm fields over in Jordan and the wild, tawny beauty of the desert. Views are best in the late afternoon, when the setting sun turns the mountains of Moab a reddish gold.

The 600m-long access road intersects Rte 90 250m north of the main entrance to the Dead Sea Works. Ignore the yellow 'no trespassing' sign and instead follow the green signs marked (in Hebrew) *LaMitzpeh* (to the scenic lookout). Beyond the sculpture, a 4WD road continues on to the Amiaz Plateau.

🛌 Sleeping

The Mt Sodom area has several well-marked camping zones *(chenyonei layla)* without facilities, including one up on Amiaz Plateau and another at Wadi Tze'elim.

Neot HaKikar ناؤت هاكيكار
נאות הכיכר

📞 08 / POP 410

Snuggled up against the Jordanian border in one of Israel's remotest corners, this agricultural moshav (population 75 families) is the perfect base for exploring the wadis, plateaux and bluffs of the southern Dead Sea. Tranquil and laid-back, Neot HaKikar and its sister moshav, Ein Tamar, have some excellent sleeping options and all sorts of options for mountain biking, hiking, birdwatching and exploring the desert by jeep. The nearest beach is 20 minutes away at Ein Bokek. Because of the intense summer heat, some places close down from July to mid-September.

The moshav's main source of income is agriculture, with 70% of the produce destined for export. Crops – grown with the help of some 500 Thai farm-workers, in salty soil using saline well water – include red, green, yellow and orange peppers, winter-ripened vegetables and melons (watermelons in winter!), and organic medjool dates. The latter are sorted using the world's most advanced sorting machine – eight digital cameras take portraits of every single date, which air guns shuttle to this or that box according to a sophisticated algorithm. Back in the 1960s, Neot HaKikar was the site of some of the earliest experiments with modern drip irrigation.

👁 Sights & Activities

Neot HaKikar's remote desert location makes it a great base for exploring the wild wadis and crumbly, untamed mountains south and southwest of the Dead Sea.

Hikeable and cyclable wadis *(nechalim)* within a 20-minute 4WD drive of here include Arava, Tzin (Zin), Amatzya (Amazyahu), Peres, Tamar, Tzafit and Ashalim. Other great places to pedal or hoof it include Mt Sodom and the Amiaz Plateau. The Small

Makhtesh – the smallest of Israel's erosion craters – is a 25-minute drive west. Your place of lodging can arrange to have someone take you out to the trailhead by 4WD (for a fee).

Birdwatchers from around the world flock to Neot HaKikar in search of exotic birds such as the bee-eater and the Nubian nightjar.

The moshav has a tennis court, a basketball court, a children's playground and a public swimming pool (adult/child 30/15NIS; ⊗Apr-Sukkot).

Several local artists produce pottery, sculptures and handmade furniture.

Jeep Tours
ADVENTURE TOUR

Tooling along wadis, up hills and around cliffs in the company of a knowledgeable local guide is a great way to get acquainted with the desert, its flora and – if you're lucky – its fauna. Operators include Gil Shkedi (📞052-231 7371; www.shkedig.com; per person 150NIS; minimum 4; ⊗year-round), owner of Shkedi's Camplodge, who has been running excellent desert tours – in an air-con Land Rover – since 1996; one-time camel expert Barak Horwitz (📞052 866 6062; barakhorwitz@gmail.com); and B&B owner Ya'akov Belfer (📞08-655 5104, 052-545 0970).

Desert Cycling
CYCLING

Mountain biking is a fantastic way to experience the wild wadis that drain into the Syrian–African Rift around Neot HaKikar. A wide variety of off-road circuits, including one called HeCharitz ('the slit') and another that follows Wadi Sodom to Wadi Pratzim, can be found within a 30-minute drive of Neot HaKikar. Mountain bikes can be rented from Cycle Inn (📞052 899 1146; www.cycle-inn.com; per day 50NIS); Uzi is happy to supply you with maps and the low-down on area trails.

🌱 Greenhouse & Field Visit
AGRICULTURAL TOUR

(📞052-368 7442; raz.zabar@gmail.com; per person 50NIS, minimum 3; ⊗Oct–mid-May) An affable tour guide and organic date grower, Raz Zabar offers walking tours (one to two hours) that may include the option of picking your own veggies.

🛌 Sleeping

Neot HaKikar has about 40 B&B units, none of which offer breakfast unless you special-order it (100NIS per couple).

Shkedi's Camplodge TENTS, CABINS $
(Khan Shkedi; ☑052-231 7371; www.shkedig.com; dm/d/q with shared bathroom & without breakfast 90/300/400NIS; ☺closed Jul–mid-Sep; 🕾) A wonderful place to linger for a couple of days, this desert retreat is especially enchanting at night, when guests hang out around the campfire or sip beers in the chill-out tent before heading to one of the cosy dorm tents, equipped with mat floors and quality mattresses. The clean, modern bathroom block feels vaguely Mexican. Has a well-equipped kitchen. Inform owner Gili Shkedi ahead of time if you need to be picked up from the bus stop on Rte 90.

Belfer's Dead Sea Cabins B&B $$
(☑08-655 5104, 052-545 0970; www.tzofit.co.il/id/6555104; d 450NIS; ❄) Has three cosy, all-wood cabins that sleep up to five.

Korin's Home B&B $$
(☑050-680 0545; www.korins.co.il; d/q without breakfast 500/800NIS) Like having your own three-room apartment; each unit sleeps up to six. Opened in 2011.

Melach HaAretz B&B $$
(☑050-759 4828; http://madmonynh.com; d without breakfast 500NIS) Studio apartments off a garden adorned with owner Asaf's stone, wood and metal sculptures.

Mul Edom B&B $$
(☑052-395 1095; muledom@gmail.com; d/6 people US$130/180; 🕾) Welcoming, jacuzzi-equipped accommodation in the old hillside neighbourhood of Ein Tamar.

Nof Tamar B&B $$
(☑052-899 1170; www.noftamar.co.il; in Hebrew; d 450NIS, Thu & Fri NIS650, additional person 50NIS) All-wood suites with two rooms at the highest point in Ein Tamar, with views of the Jordanian villages of Fifa and Safi.

Eating

Neot HaKikar has two grocery stores, one of which is even open for two hours on Saturday morning. Lunch and dinner can be ordered a day ahead from local families for 65NIS to 110NIS per person.

Information

ATM There's one inside one of the grocery stores.

Information centre Being built next to one of the roundabouts on the access road.

Getting There & Away

Neot HaKikar is 8km southeast of Rte 90's Neot HaKikar junction and 11km southeast of Arava junction, where Rte 25 from Dimona and Be'er Sheva intersects Rte 90.

All buses to Eilat, Be'er Sheva, Jerusalem and the northern Dead Sea (see p288) stop at Neot HaKikar junction (accommodation owners are usually happy to pick you up); some also drive into the moshav.

The Negev النقب הנגב

Best Places to Eat

» Neot Semadar Inn (p323)

» Haksa (p320)

» Ginger Asian Kitchen & Bar (p330)

» Last Refuge (p330)

» Chez Eugene (p320)

Best Places to Stay

» Green Backpackers (p319)

» Kibbutz Lotan Guesthouse (p322)

» Desert Lodge (p315)

» Orchid Reef Hotel (p328)

» Kfar Hanokdim (p305)

Why Go?

The Negev Desert, often bypassed by travellers hurrying to Eilat, is much more than just sand. Look closely between the rocks of the wadis (valleys) and you will find water and even wine. The Negev Highlands region is also home to so many vineyards that it now has its own wine route. Today, ecologists from all over the world come to the kibbutzim of Sde Boker and the Arava to study solar energy and water treatment. But this isn't new. Two thousand years earlier, the Nabataeans cultivated grapes and practically invented desert irrigation, which can still be seen at the ancient ruins of Shivta, Mamshit and Avdat.

This region, comprising 62% of Israel's land mass, may seem sparse but it offers a world of adventure, including mountain hikes, camel treks, 4WD desert drives and Red Sea diving. Yet perhaps the biggest secret of the Negev is Makhtesh Ramon, a crater-like wilderness, which feels like another planet.

When to Go
Eilat

°C/°F Temp
Rainfall inches/mm
40/104 —
— 8/200
30/86 —
— 6/150
20/68 —
— 4/100
10/50 —
— 2/50
0/32 —
— 0
J F M A M J J A S O N D

Mar–May, late Sep–Nov The best time for desert treks; sunny at daytime but cold at night.

Aug The Red Sea Jazz Festival adds coolness to a sweltering Eilat summer.

Dec–Feb A rare rainstorm can cause fleeting waterfalls to appear at Wadi Zin, Sde Boker.

The Negev Highlights

1 Step back more than 2000 years by exploring the Nabataean hilltop ruins of **Avdat** (boxed text, p314)

2 Trek across the Wadi Zin desert valley to the freshwater spring of Ein Akev near **Sde Boker** (p313)

3 Sample some fine Negev merlot on the **Wine Route** (p307) in the Negev Highlands between Be'er Sheva and Mitzpe Ramon

4 Witness millions of years of evolution beneath your feet from the lookout at **Makhtesh Ramon** (p316)

5 Learn about ecodesign, try water shiatsu and go birdwatching on the Arava sand dunes at **Kibbutz Lotan** (p321)

6 Sleep in a *tukul* (Ethiopian-style tepee) at the foot of the ruined city of **Mamshit** (boxed text, p314)

7 Jump and splash on the Red Sea waves as you try kitesurfing in **Eilat** (p326)

Arad عراد ערד

📞 08 / POP 23,400

Situated on a high plateau, between Be'er Sheva and the Dead Sea, Arad itself doesn't offer too much to do but is a popular place to stay for those visiting nearby Masada (p296).

Directly opposite the tall birds of prey sculptures at the entrance to Arad, the Es-het Lot Artists' Quarter is in an abandoned industrial zone 2km southwest of town. The highlight here is the small Glass Museum (📞08-995 3388; www.warmglassil.com; 11 Sadan St; ⊙10am-1pm Sun-Wed, 10am-2pm Thu & Sat) opened by artist Gideon Friedman.

🛏 Sleeping & Eating

TOP CHOICE Kfar Hanokdim   LODGE $$

(📞08-995 0097; www.kfarhanokdim.co.il; s incl breakfast & dinner 413NIS; d 500NIS; ❄) A sprawling palm-tree oasis in the stark Ju-dean Desert, about 10km from Arad on the road to Masada, this joint Bedouin–Jewish venture offers sleeping in stylish cabins or in an authentic Bedouin tent. Travellers can drop by for traditional Bedouin meals and coffee; there's also drumming, yoga and belly-dancing activities. There's no need to worry about cold desert nights as the tents are heated. Larger groups of around 10 people can stay in a Bedouin tent for 80NIS each.

Yehelim   BOUTIQUE HOTEL $$$

(📞077 202 8126; www.yehelim.com; 72 Moav St; d 650NIS, deluxe ste with balcony 750NIS; ❄🛜) Get pampered in peace at Yehelim, a bou-tique hotel with 10 rooms, many of which give breathtaking views of the Dead Sea and, with clear skies, of Jordan. It's located in a residential area on the eastern side of Arad. All the materials used for the decor were sourced locally, the staff are friendly and it has a spa treatment room offering massages, reflexology and aromatherapy.

HI – Blau Weiss Hostel   HOSTEL $$

(📞08-995 7150; arad@iyha.org.il; 34 Atad St; s/d 260/360NIS; ❄) Set in a quiet, green part of Arad near the local football fields, this hostel offers 45 clean and comfortable rooms. Most rooms come with a fridge and TV. To find it walk east from the bus station up Yehuda St, and follow the signs before turning right on HaPalmach St.

Inbar Hotel   HOTEL $$

(📞08-997 3303; www.inbar-hotel.com; 38 Yehuda St; s/d440/550NIS; ❄🛜❄) A big hotel in a small town, the Inbar sticks out like a sore thumb, but it gets top marks for friendly service. It has 103 comfy rooms with cable TV, a wi-fi area in the reception and a spa featuring a reinvigorating Dead Sea pool and black-mud treatments.

Muza   PUB $$

(www.muza-arad.co.il; Rte 31; mains 49NIS; ⊙noon-2am) Tucked behind the Alon petrol station, this big sports-oriented pub serves hearty pub food such as salads, pasta, grilled sand-wiches and towering burgers.

ℹ Information

Arad Tourist Office (📞08-995 4160; ⊙9am-5pm Thu-Sat) Located behind the Paz petrol station; has information on activities in the Dead Sea and surrounding area.

ℹ Getting There & Away

To get to Arad, take Egged bus 384 or 385 from Be'er Sheva (18NIS, 45 minutes) at 9.40am, 12.15pm or 3pm. From Arad, bus 384 leaves to Be'er Sheva from the central bus terminal on Yehuda St at 9.20am, 1.40pm, 4.40pm and 7.40pm, and for Ein Gedi (34NIS, 1½ hours) at 10.15am, 1pm and 3.45pm.

To access the sound and light show at Masada (30-minute drive; see p297) take Rte 3199 from the back of Arad.

Be'er Sheva بئر السبع באר שבע

📞 08 / POP 194,300

As you approach Be'er Sheva (Bear Share-Vah) from the north, the green fields merge into desert and you begin to notice that green blades and leaves are at a premium. Be'er Sheva was developed in the '60s and is still rapidly expanding. For many travellers it's just a convenient stop used for its trans-port connections; but it is also the fourth-largest city in Israel, the 'capital of the Negev', and home to the region's major hos-pital and the pioneering Ben-Gurion Univer-sity, with over 20,000 students. The student population is so important here that locals joke that if Tel Aviv is a city with a university, then Be'er Sheva is a university with a city.

Today the young, educated population is starting to stay on after graduation, and high-tech research is big business here. Al-though most of the city hangs out in the air-conditioned malls, you should head to

DON'T MISS

TEL ARAD

Founded in the 3rd century BCE, Tel Arad is the country's best example of an early Bronze Age city. Mentioned in the Hebrew Bible (Numbers 21:1–3, 33:40; Joshua 12:14), ancient Arad was an important fortress guarding the southern approaches to the country.

The site covers several hectares and consists of a lower and an upper city. The upper city is called the 'hill of fortresses' and was settled during the Israelite period (1200 BCE). Archaeologists have found an Israelite temple with a sanctuary and a small room that served as the Holy of Holies.

Tel Arad National Park (adult/child 14/7NIS; ☉8am-5pm Sun-Thu Apr-Sep, to 4pm Oct-Mar) is 8km west of Arad. Take any bus towards Be'er Sheva, get off at the Tel Arad junction (6NIS) and walk the final 3km to the site on Rte 80.

the Old Town for Be'er Sheva's best felafel and coffee.

History

Be'er Sheva has a rich history, receiving mention in the Bible (Judges 20:1; I Samuel 3:20; II Samuel 3:10, 17:11, 24:2), though little of that is detectable today. The one surviving ancient monument, a well on Hebron Rd, attests to the town's association with the story of Abraham (Genesis 21:25–33), in which the name Be'er Sheva is given as meaning 'the well of the oath', though it could also derive from the 'seven wells' of Isaac. In fact, until the Turks developed the town in the late 19th century, Be'er Sheva remained little more than a collection of wells used by local Bedouin.

During WWI the small town fell to Allenby's allied forces after a charge by units of the Australian Light Horse. The Egyptian army conquered Be'er Sheva after the State of Israel was declared, but in October 1948 the Israel Defence Forces (IDF) regained the town and a new era of immigration began.

◉ Sights

Tel Be'er Sheva   ARCHAEOLOGICAL SITE
(adult/child 14/7NIS; ☉8am-5pm Apr-Sep, to 4pm Oct-Mar) Some 5km east of the city, Tel Be'er Sheva is one of three biblical tels (hilltop ruins) declared a Unesco World Heritage site in 2005.

The archaeological digs of the tel reveal a meticulously planned city protected by enormous fortress walls with impressive gates, castles, temples, storage rooms, stables and water cisterns.

At Tel Be'er Sheva archaeologists have uncovered two-thirds of a settlement dating from the early Israelite period (10th century BCE), when a fortified administrative city was built on the hill. The best-preserved parts are

the well-engineered cisterns and a 70m well, the deepest in Israel. There are great views to be had from the observation tower.

The site is 5km east of Be'er Sheva on the Shocket Junction road, near the Bedouin settlement of Tel Sheva.

**Negev Palmach Brigade
Memorial**   MONUMENT
On a windswept hill 3km northeast of town is a stark, modern tribute to the Israeli soldiers killed while taking Be'er Sheva from the Egyptians in 1948. Designed by Israeli artist Dani Karavan in 1963, the Negev Palmach Brigade Memorial (known as the Andarta, ie memorial, for short) offers excellent views of the city and the surrounding desert.

The memorial is difficult to reach by public transport. Near the Arad road, you can get off bus 388 and walk the 750m, or take local bus 4 to the Tzafon (North) train station and cut across the tracks to reach the hill.

Negev Museum of Art   MUSEUM, GALLERY
(60 Ha'Atzmaut St; adult/child 15/10NIS; ☉8.30am-3.30pm Sun, 10am-4pm Mon, Tue & Thu, noon-7pm Wed, 10am-2pm Fri & Sat) This small art gallery is housed in the elegant Ottoman governor's mansion, which was built in 1906. The building has been beautifully restored into a superb configuration of stone and glass, creating an intimate space for the four halls that house works from Israeli artists as well as travelling exhibitions. The Turkish-era mosque next door has been renovated and occasionally houses small archaeological exhibitions.

FREE Negev Artists' House   GALLERY
(www.b7omanim.com; 55 Ha'Avot St; ☉10am-1.30pm & 4-7.30pm Mon-Thu, 10am-1.30pm Fri, 11am-2pm Sat) Originally built in 1933, this grand colonial-style building is now a

compact but impressive art gallery displaying diverse works by artists from all over the Negev.

Ethiopian Jewish Handicrafts Centre
ARTS CENTRE

(☎08-623 5882; 50 Arlozorov St; ⏰9am-1pm Sun-Wed) Preserving the unique culture of the Ethiopian Jews, this arts and crafts centre, near the Soraka Medical Centre, has a small exhibition, shop and holds pottery workshops. To get here, continue up Yitzhack Rager St past the hospital, turn right on Ben-Gurion Blvd and again onto Arlozorov St, or take bus 5 from Ha'Atzmaut St in the Old City.

Bedouin Market
MARKET

(⏰7am-4pm Mon &Thu) Every week a car park in the southeast of town is transformed into a Bedouin market attracting both Arab and Jewish bargain hunters from all over the Negev. Not to be confused with the city market on the same road, this was traditionally where hundreds of the Negev's Bedouin came to town to sell their livestock, carpets, clothes and jewellery. Today the camels have been replaced by car boots, where cut-price 'designer' shoes, bags and perfumes are sold. There are also stalls offering olives, nuts, dates and fruit, but other than that it's not especially enticing to visit.

It's a 10-minute walk south of the Kenyon HaNegev shopping centre on the main Eilat Rd.

🏃 Activities

Skykef Skydiving Centre
SKYDIVING

(☎1 700 705 867; www.skykef.co.il) Thrill seekers should check out Skykef Skydiving Centre at Sde Teiman Airport, the largest parachute centre in Israel. Every Friday and Saturday it offers tandem skydiving (1090NIS) and it has a course of eight jumps (9500NIS). As you can imagine, there are spectacular desert views and a good chance of blue skies. The airport is 15km northwest of Be'er Sheva.

🛏 Sleeping

Despite its size, Be'er Sheva has an extremely limited selection of accommodation.

TOP CHOICE HI – Beit Yatziv Hostel
HOSTEL $$

(☎08-627 7444; www.beityatziv.co.il; 79 Ha'Atzmaut St; s/d/ste 250/350/400NIS; ❄🛜🏊) Not too dissimilar to college dorms, it's not surprising that this hostel is mainly used by visiting academics and school groups. The rooms in the old building are small but each comes with a fridge, TV and wi-fi. If not on a tight budget, it is worth paying the extra 100NIS for one of the newer 'deluxe' rooms. The pleasant gardens and swimming pool (open June to August) are a blessed relief on a scorching desert day. Take bus 12 or 13 from the bus station and look for the three large radio antennae.

THE NEGEV BE'ER SHEVA

WORTH A TRIP

THE WINE ROUTE

In recent years the number of vineyards in the valleys and northern hills of the Negev has grown significantly. These vineyards mark the first attempts to nurture grapes in the desert since the ancient Nabataean winepresses of Shivta and Avdat. Using innovative computerised watering methods (such as drip irrigation), winegrowers have converted arid areas of dust into fertile land. Calling ahead is advised before visiting any of these wineries.

Located on the road to Tel Arad (Rte 80) the Yatir Winery (☎08-995 9090; www.yatir.net) has had meteoric success since its first wine was released in 2004, and is known for its sauvignon blanc and cabernet merlot. Note that the Yatir Forest, however, is better reached from Rte 60, north of the Shocket Junction, then right towards Shani.

Heading south on Rte 40, just before Sde Boker, the Boker Valley Vineyard (☎052 682 2930; www.israeldesertlodge.com) has an excellent wine lodge restaurant, as well as a farm store selling wines and olive oil.

The Sde Boker Winery (☎050 757 9212; www.sde-boker.org.il/winery) was established in 1999 by Zvi Remak from California and specialises in handcrafted, barrel red wines from Zinfandel and Carignan grapes. It's next to the Ben-Gurion Desert Home (p312).

Continuing south on Rte 40, just before the Avdat ruins, the Carmey Avdat Winery (☎08-653 5177; www.carmeyavdat.com) is a family-run ecological farm that produces fine merlots with a unique desert aroma. It also offers accommodation in cabins.

Be'er Sheva

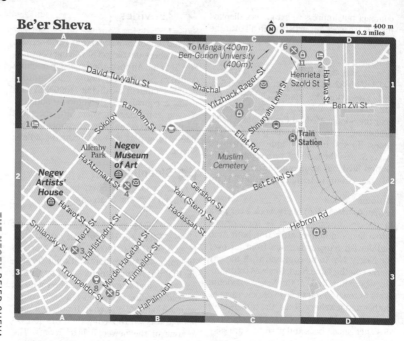

Be'er Sheva

◉ Top Sights
Negev Artists' House.............................A2
Negev Museum of Art B2

🛌 Sleeping
1 HI — Beit Yatziv Hostel A1
2 Leonardo Negev.................................D1

✕ Eating
3 Arabica A3
4 Beit Ha-Ful B2

5 Gecko A3
6 Grandpa Jebetto's.............................C1

☕ Drinking
7 Pitput..B1
8 Smilansky..A3

🛍 Shopping
9 Bedouin Market.................................D3
10 Kenyon HaNegev...............................C1
11 Lametayel..D1

Leonardo Negev   HOTEL $$$
(☎08-640 5444; www.leonardo-hotels.com; 4 Henrietta Szold St; r from 700NIS; ❄🐾☲) The only hotel in the centre of Be'er Sheva, the Leonardo (formerly the Golden Tulip) comprises 250 spacious rooms all with minibar and cable TV, as well as two luxury presidential suites. Primarily designed to host business conferences and to accommodate wedding or bar mitzvah guests attending the five-star venue next door, Leonardo boasts a pool, gym, courtyard dining area and a giant bar with funky furniture.

Eating

Beit Ha-Ful   ISRAELI $
(cnr Herzl & Ha'Atzmaut Sts; mains from 15NIS; ☺8am-8pm Sun-Thu, to 2pm Fri; ☑) For a quick bite in the Old Town you can't beat what locals say is the best fuul (fava bean paste) joint in town. Dig into some decent felafel or *sabich* (a felafel alternative with roast aubergine, boiled egg and potato, salads and spicy mango sauce) in hot pita while you're at it – stand up or sit down, inside or out.

Grandpa Jebetto's
SANDWICHES $$

(Yitzhack Rager St; mains 38NIS; ⊙9.30am-midnight Sun-Thu, to 4pm Fri, 7pm-late Sat) Supposed to be named after the grandpa of Pinocchio (Geppetto), this cafe is famous locally for its supersized, super-tasty sandwiches. Tucked away in the Rusko City pedestrian mall, Jebetto's several menu pages attest to the myriad fillings and sauces on offer. Try the roast-beef sandwich with all the trimmings; non-meat eaters should sample the Bulgarian cheese with aubergine salad.

TOP CHOICE Arabica
FUSION $$

(☑08-627 7801; www.arabica-rest.co.il; 12 Herzl St; mains from 50NIS; ⊙11.30am-late Sun-Thu, to 4pm Fri; 7pm-late Sat) The slick and stylish Arabica restaurant is adjoined to the Youth Art Centre – an ugly building with a slanted roof covered with green felt. The food is perhaps more Americana than Arabica; expect juicy burgers, chicken wings and steaks. Noodles, pastas and curries add a touch of exoticism, and it also has a good selection of cocktails, salads and children's meals.

Gecko
CAFE $$

(13 Smilansky St; dishes from 35NIS; ⊙8am-midnight, to 4pm Fri; ☑🛜) The best place for a Be'er Sheva brunch, Gecko is also known for its gourmet coffee. It offers a mainly dairy menu with salads, pasta and sandwiches. Try the *shakshuka* (a rich egg-and-tomato breakfast dish served in a frying pan) and a slice of the to-die-for cheese cake.

Drinking

Manga
BAR

(87 Yitzhak Rager St; ⊙8pm-late Sat-Thu, closed Fri; 🛜) Be'er Sheva's most popular student bar is in the Teachers Centre not far from the university campus, opposite Soraka Medical Centre. The covered outdoor area is for relaxing with friends and sampling plates of sushi, while inside the music is pumped up loud as the young crowd check each other out.

TOP CHOICE Smilansky
BAR

(23 Smilansky St; ⊙5pm-2am Sun-Thu, noon-2am Fri & Sat; 🛜) With a wide selection of draught beers, wines and cocktails, this dimly lit bar in an old Turkish-era building is the place to come if you fancy a pint of Guinness with your carpaccio. Plates of tapas start at 34NIS and beers cost 25NIS.

Pitput
CAFE

(122 Herzl St; ⊙8am-12.30am Sat-Thu, to 4pm Fri) A charming little cafe at the start of the Old Town, Pitput has tables outside where you can enjoy a good coffee, mint tea or ice shake. It also has an excellent selection of Israeli wines from the Golan and the Negev.

Shopping

Lametayel
BOOKS, OUTDOOR EQUIPMENT

(www.lametayel.co.il; 8 Henrietta Szold St; ⊙10am-8pm Sun-Thu, to 2pm Fri) Stock up on travel books, maps and hiking gear before heading into the Negev.

Kenyon HaNegev
MALL

(cnr Yitzhack Rager St & Eilat Rd; ⊙9.30am-10pm Sun-Thu, to 3pm Fri, 7-11pm Sat) Be'er Sheva's main air-conditioned mall houses a food court and big chain stores.

Information

Emergency
Police station (☑08-642 6744; Herzl St) At the northern end of Keren Kayemet Le-Y'Israel St in the Old Town.

Money
There are banks in the Kenyon HaNegev shopping centre as well as the following:
Bank Discount (Henrietta Szold St)
Bank Hapoalim (cnr Ha'Atzmaut & HaHalutz Sts) In the Old Town.

Post
Main post office (cnr Yitzhack Rager & Ben Zvi Sts) Just north of the central bus station.
Old Town post office (cnr HaHistradrut & Hadassah Sts) Conveniently located in the Old Town.

Tourist Information
Tourist information office (☑08-646 4900; Municipality, Menachem Begin Sq) Cross the road opposite the train station and walk up HaTikva St to the municipality complex.

Getting There & Away
Bus
The central bus station is like a mini marketplace usually filled with soldiers chomping on felafels bought from the stalls that line the platforms. On business days Egged buses run every 30 minutes to Tel Aviv (bus 370, 17NIS, 1½ hours), at least half-hourly to Jerusalem (buses 470 and 446, 32.50NIS, two hours) and every 30 minutes for Dimona (bus 48, 11.80NIS, 30 minutes). Egged services for Eilat (bus 392 or 397, 55NIS, 3½ hours) depart more or less every 90 minutes and run via Mitzpe Ramon (30NIS, 1½ hours).

Buses to Masada and Ein Gedi (bus 384; 42NIS, 2¼ hours, four daily Sunday to Thursday, two on Friday) pass through Arad (18NIS, 45 minutes). Metropoline also operates bus services to Tel Aviv (bus 380) and Mitzpe Ramon (bus 60) for the same fares as Egged.

Car
Budget (☏08-935 0077; 1 Shazar Blvd)
Eldan (☏08-643 0344; www.eldan.co.il; 4 Leonard Cohen St) Order online to get the best car-rental deal.

Sherut (Shared Taxi)
Moniot Ayal (☏08-623 3033) operates sherut (shared or service taxi) services to Tel Aviv (30NIS), but there's nothing running on Saturday and you have to wait until they fill up. They operate from a booth just outside the central bus station.

Train
Northbound trains from Be'er Sheva's central **train station** (www.rail.co.il) start at 5.38am and run hourly until 9.38pm, stopping at Be'er Sheva Tzafon (Ben-Gurion University), Lahavim-Rahat, Lod, Tel Aviv (29NIS, 1½ hours), Haifa, Akko and terminating at Nahariyya. There are no services after 11.29am on Friday until 7pm Saturday.

🛈 Getting Around
You can easily walk from the central bus station to the Old Town and the market. Otherwise, buses 12 and 13 depart every 20 minutes for the Beit Yatziv HI Hostel.

Around Be'er Sheva
◉ Sights

🖋 **Museum of Bedouin Culture** MUSEUM
(☏08-991 3322; www.joealon.org.il; admission 25NIS; ⊙9am-4pm Sat-Thu, to 2pm Fri) With the fast-paced social and technological changes of the 21st century, preservation of Bedouin culture is becoming increasingly important. The idea for this museum came from Jews and local Bedouin interested in promoting Bedouin culture and heritage.

The collection, consisting of traditional clothes, household utensils, tools and jewellery, was amassed at Kibbutz Lahav and at the Bedouin Museum in southern Sinai. After the Israeli withdrawal from Sinai, the two collections were united by anthropologists Orna and Avner Goren.

NEGEV BEDOUIN

Think of Bedouin and the age-old images of nomadic pastoralists roaming the desert, tending flocks of sheep and dwelling in tents spring to mind. But times are changing. Fast.

Many younger Bedouin now refer to themselves as 'Negev Arabs', as the word '*bedû*' (Bedouin) is usually associated with agriculture. Nearly half of the Negev Bedouin now reside in urbanised villages and towns; some even have PhDs or medical degrees.

The truth is nobody really knows how many Bedouin live in the Middle East. Before 1948, 65,000 to 90,000 Bedouin resided in the Negev Desert. Today, there are an estimated 180,000 Bedouin in the area, many in the far-flung clusters of tents that dot the landscape east and south of Be'er Sheva. They speak a mixture of Arabic and Hebrew, and around five to 10 per cent of Bedouin men of draft age serve in the IDF (Israel Defence Forces), often as trackers, though service is not compulsory.

The city of Rahat, 20km north of Be'er Sheva, is the largest recognised Bedouin settlement and has approximately 40,000 residents. An ugly mess of cramped housing, Rahat is an isolated town crippled by poverty and crime, many of its people without job prospects. A visit is not recommended.

In 2011, Israel's cabinet approved a controversial US$335 million plan to relocate 30,000 Bedouin from unrecognised settlements to state-recognised villages in a bid to integrate them with the rest of society. Activists fear that the plan will create socioeconomic conditions like those in Rahat.

Growing numbers of Bedouin are turning towards tourism as a source of income, offering not only camel rides but also accommodation. At camps all over the Negev, visitors can stop by for the traditional three cups of Bedouin coffee and sweet tea for a handful of shekels. As they move frequently, finding a specific Bedouin tent can be difficult.

The Bedouin **Kashkhar Family** (☏050 441 3212/551 3212, dm tents 45NIS) reside just before the Avdat ruins on Rte 40 between Sde Boker and Mitzpe Ramon. Other Bedouin operate joint ventures with Israelis, such as at Kfar Hanokdim (p305) near Arad.

WHAT EXACTLY IS A MAKHTESH?

Usually translated as 'crater' and occasionally as 'canyon', a more accurate definition of a *makhtesh* is an 'erosion cirque' – a large, asymmetrical hole formed by erosion as the Negev made the transition from ocean to desert. Providing a peep into the Earth's crust, the *makhteshim* found in the Negev and Sinai are thought to be unique geological phenomena, because each is drained by a wadi (valley), although similar rock features have been found in Turkmenistan and Iran. Makhtesh Ramon, the largest in Israel, certainly looks like something out of a science-fiction film.

There are two other *makhteshim* in the Negev, Makhtesh HaKatan (Big Makhtesh) and Makhtesh HaGadol (Small Makhtesh). Both are south of Dimona, but neither is accessible by bus. The best option if you want to hike in the area is to hire a car in Be'er Sheva.

Makhtesh HaKatan, almost perfectly circular, can be found off the highway linking Dimona with the Dead Sea (Rte 25). The entrance to HaMakhtesh HaGadol is near the sleepy town of Yeroham (take Rte 204 south from Dimona towards Sde Boker). There is a beautiful drive right through the crater on Rte 225; look out for the coloured sands.

Museum attractions include a video, demonstration of traditional home-making activities such as bread-making and weaving, medicinal garden, archaeological section with a display of local caves throughout the ages, and a hospitality tent where visitors can sit with a local Bedouin, drink coffee and talk.

The museum is part of the Joe Alon Regional & Folklore Centre, which is a combined museum, research institute and field school. Yosef Alon (1929–73) was a pilot who became one of the founders of the Israeli Air Force. Opened in 1985, the centre aims to educate in the fields of folklore, archaeology, nature and coexistence.

The complex stands behind Kibbutz Lahav, near Kibbutz Dvir, 20km north of Be'er Sheva. Both are off a side road that intersects with Rte 31. Bus 42 (13NIS, 50 minutes) runs directly to Kibbutz Lahav at 11.50am daily, but immediately heads back to Be'er Sheva without allowing time for a visit. So the best way to get here is by car.

TOP CHOICE **Israeli Air Force Museum** MUSEUM
(www.iaf-museum.org.il, in Hebrew; admission 30NIS; ⊙8am-5pm Sun-Thu, to 1pm Fri) Even if you don't have a strong interest in military history, this museum is one of Be'er Sheva's most worthwhile attractions. Set in the Hatzerim Israeli Air Force (IAF) base, it displays over 100 aircraft from Spitfires to Phantoms and Hawkeye helicopters.

Highlights include the story of Ron Arad (the Israeli pilot who was captured in Lebanon in 1986) and a rather dusty helicopter that carried Presidents Sadat and Begin for the 1979 Egypt–Israel peace treaty. A film is screened in the Boeing 707 used in Operation Solomon, when 14,000 Ethiopian Jews were airlifted to Israel in 1991. There are also noses from fallen planes from WWII, the Six Day War and other battles. If anything, this museum shows just how many times Israel has had to face war with its neighbours.

Hatzerim (sometimes spelt Khatserim) is 6km west of Be'er Sheva. From the central bus station take bus 31 (8.80NIS, 16 minutes, every hour); the IAF museum is the last stop.

Lakiya Negev Weaving ARTS CENTRE
(☎08-651 9883; www.lakiya.org; ⊙8am-5pm Sun-Thu, 10-4pm Sat) Lakiya was established in 1991 as an income-generating project for Bedouin women living in villages in the Negev. It provides these women with an opportunity to develop the tradition of spinning and weaving, and to acquire new skills in dyeing, production and business management.

You can visit the centre, which is in the Bedouin village of Lakiya, about 6km north of Be'er Sheva off Rte 31. Share a cup of sweet herbal tea and check out the vast range of woven rugs, cushions and bags. A tour (including Bedouin snacks) costs 25NIS and a private weaving lesson is 60NIS.

Sde Boker سده بوك שדה בוקר
☎08 / POP 1200

Israel's first prime minister, David Ben-Gurion, once said, 'The Negev is the cradle of our nation; it lies in a dangerous, vulnerable region, but one of tremendous potential.'

There is no better place to witness this tremendous potential than at Sde Boker, one of the best known of all kibbutzim.

The kibbutz was established in 1952 by young pioneers who planned to breed cattle in the desert; its name is Hebrew for 'Cowboy's Field'. Ben-Gurion joined this lush oasis the following year at the age of 67, to practise what he preached by cultivating the Negev. Only 14 months later he returned to the political scene as minister of defence and went on to serve a second term as prime minister, returning to kibbutz life in 1963.

Sde Boker is well known for its environmental research and education thanks largely to Midreshet Ben-Gurion (www.boker.org.il), a satellite campus of Be'er Sheva's Ben-Gurion University of the Negev. Sde Boker has more than 20 different research and educational institutions, including the Zuckerberg Institute for Water Research, the Institute for Desert Research, the National Solar Energy Centre and an environmental high school.

◉ Sights

Ben-Gurion Desert Home HOUSE

(adult/child 12/9NIS; ☺8.30am-4pm Sun-Thu, to 2pm Fri, 10am-4pm Sat) When Ben-Gurion died in 1973 he asked in his will for his kibbutz quarters to remain exactly as he left them, and that's what you see when you visit the small desert home. A recently made short animation is shown near the entrance about the life of Ben-Gurion, from his birth in Poland to leadership in Israel. The tour of the modest hut where he lived begins in his living room and ends in the private library with some 5000 books. Ben-Gurion read in nine different languages (he taught himself Greek in order to read philosophy). Appropriately, the book left resting on a coffee table is entitled *Let Us Live in Peace and Friendship*.

Ben-Gurion graves MEMORIAL

The graves of David and Paula Ben-Gurion (1892–1968), who once said she wasn't as fond of the desert as her husband, lie in a spectacular clifftop setting overlooking the stunning Wadi Zin and the Avdat plain. Sunrise or sunset, it offers awe-inspiring views of the broad ravine, and a desert flora park has been planted next to the tombs, where wild ibexes wander around.

The graves can be reached from the upper entrance of Ein Avdat National Park, which is just on the southern edge of the Midreshet Ben-Gurion campus, about 3km south of the kibbutz.

Ein Avdat National Park PARK

(adult/child 27/14NIS; ☺8am-5pm Apr-Sep, to 4pm Oct-Mar) Less than 50m from Ben-Gurion's tomb, Ein Avdat National Park is a freak of nature – a pool of icy water in the hot expanse of desert, fed by waters that flow through an intricate network of channels. Dominated by a steep, winding ravine of soft white chalk and poplar trees, the pool is reached via an easy hike through incredible scenery.

There are two entrances to the national park – the southern and northern. The main ticket office is at the northern entrance, next to the Ben-Gurion graves and the beautiful Wilderness of Zin nature trail. The trail leads down a 3km zigzag road, then along the river to the upper entrance, which is 5km south along Rte 40.

Hikers can choose between two trails – a long one-way route (two to three hours) or a short circular route (about one hour round trip).

The longer trail starts from the car park and follows a path that leads off beyond into the rocky creek. About 40 minutes

---

GOURMET GOATS

Aside from camels and migrating birds, the Negev Highlands region has also traditionally been a home for mountain goats. Usually associated with Bedouin herders, a number of new Israeli gourmet goat farms are cropping up along the wine route.

Naot Farm (☎054 421 8788; www.naotfarm.co.il) has 150 goats and runs tours of the farm, offers accommodation in cabins (800NIS with breakfast) and sells *labneh* (thick yoghurt) and other dairy delights in its shop.

Across the highway, **Kornmehl Farm** (☎08-655 5140; www.kornmehl.co.il; ☺10am-6pm) has a restaurant serving cheese platters, goat's-cheese pizzas and homemade yoghurts with syrup. They don't call it the 'land of milk and honey' for nothing!

Both farms offer the chance to see goat-milking and are on Rte 40 between the Telalim and Halukim Junctions near Sde Boker.

HIKING IN THE NEGEV

There are some excellent hikes in the Negev region, taking in a surprisingly wide variety of landscapes. Particularly recommended are those around Sde Boker and Ein Avdat, Mitzpe Ramon and Eilat.

There is a very good SPNI 1:50,000 hiking map of the Eilat mountain region (see p431), as well as individual trail maps for some of the more popular hikes across the region.

The SPNI has field study centres at Sde Boker, Mitzpe Ramon and Eilat, and at Hatzeva, 50km south of the Dead Sea on Rte 90 – these are the places to visit for detailed maps and information, and for recommendations on routes and desert sights. It also runs SPNI Tours (☏03-638 8688/8616; www.teva.org.il/english; private day tour for family with guide from per person 42NIS, group day tour with guide incl bus from Tel Aviv from per person 200NIS) of the Negev region for groups and families, where many of the guides and participants speak English. Tours range from hiking, abseiling and cycling day trips to weekends away snorkelling in Eilat.

Also, check out the official Negev Development Authority (www.gonegev.co.il) website for the latest hikes and tours.

The Negev is a harsh desert, but due to its rapid development visitors can easily be lulled into a false sense of security and forget to follow the safety guidelines. It is best to make an early start, cover your head, drink plenty of water and avoid physical exertion in the middle of the day (noon to 3pm).

THE NEGEV SDE BOKER

later you will see a large cave appear up on your right. Ibexes and gazelles can often be seen along here, too. Simply follow the trickle of water and after another five minutes you will arrive at the freshwater spring.

This is a dead end, so return the way you came and on your left look out for some steps cut into the rock leading up the cliff to reach the top of the ravine. Climb the steps to the paved ledge, where there's a great observation point. The best views are from the steps, rather than at the very top, so take a good look around before the end of the climb.

Carry on walking and after another few minutes you will reach the top of a waterfall, which usually flows more in winter due to seasonal rainfall.

Note that as this is a one-way hike (you are not allowed to go *down* the steps), to return to the lower car park you'll need to hitch or wait for a bus (one every 1½ hours) back to Sde Boker. Check the bus schedule before heading off to help time your hike.

A less ambitious option is to walk from the lower entrance to the Ein Ma'arif pools at the foot of the waterfall, return along the same path and then drive to the upper parking lot where you can admire the view from the observation point and pretend you did the steep climb up the steps.

Ein Akev
SPRING

Another popular trail is to Ein Akev, a freshwater spring on the other side of Wadi Zin. Starting from the car park of Midreshet Ben-Gurion, follow the winding path down to the Wadi Zin valley floor. Follow the blue signs across the valley and you will start ascending a gentle slope until you reach the Akev spring, which has a pool of clear water all year. From the spring, you can go back the way you came or take the higher green-signed path back to the car park, walking above dry waterfalls. The trail is a 12km loop back to the start and takes around six hours.

 Activities

Geofun Desert Cycling
CYCLING

(☏08-655 3350; www.geofun.co.il) Situated in the small Midreshet Ben-Gurion commercial centre, Geofun runs cycling tours of the Negev wineries, Wadi Zin, Sde Boker and beyond. It also offers bikes for hire and sells cycling gear.

Out of the Wilderness
ADVENTURE TOUR

(☏08-653 5053; www.art4tour.com) A real-life *Crocodile Dundee* character who hit his 15 minutes of fame when he wrestled a wild Arabian leopard *(namer)* inside his Sde Boker home, Arthur du Mosch provides horse riding, 4WD excursions and hiking tours in English, Hebrew, German and Dutch.

A SPICE ODYSSEY

Often overlooked in school history lessons, the Nabataeans were ancient Arabs known to have lived in the Negev from the 4th century BCE. They were a nomadic people until Rome became aware of the profitability of the spice route and muscled in on their trade. After the Roman conquest, the Nabataeans took on more 'European' attributes and eventually adopted Christianity. They spoke a form of Aramaic, the lingua franca of the region some 2000 years ago. Despite the hostile desert environment, the Nabataeans developed sophisticated irrigation methods, and their kings lavishly wasted water in front of guests to show off.

At one point, the spice and incense route stretched from India to Rome, passing through Saudi Arabia, Ethiopia, Sudan, Petra and Judea. As a result, the Negev cities of Avdat, Mamshit and Shivta became prosperous, and the desert around them flourished. The ruins of these towns were declared Unesco World Heritage sites in 2005.

Avdat   عبدات   תדבע

A beautifully preserved site, this ancient city upon a hill dominates the surrounding desert skyline. With its impressive ruins, arches and pillars and its incredible vistas, Avdat National Park (adult/child 27/14NIS; ⊙8am-5pm Apr-Sep, to 4pm Oct-Mar) is well worth the steep climb. Parts of the film *Jesus Christ Superstar* were shot here.

Named after the Nabataean monarch Obada, Avdat was built in the 3rd century BCE as a caravan stop on the road from Petra to the Mediterranean. Prosperous throughout the Byzantine period, the city was deserted following an earthquake in 630 CE and the Muslim takeover of the Negev six years later.

The ruins include a Roman bathhouse, catacombs, several 4th-century churches, a pottery workshop and a Byzantine winepress.

On Rte 40, Avdat lies 10km south of Sde Boker and 23km north of Mitzpe Ramon. Bus 60 passes by in each direction about every hour.

Shivta (Subeita)   سبيطى   הטביש

The most isolated of the Nabataean towns, Shivta (admission free; ⊙8am-5pm Apr-Sep, to 4pm Oct-Mar) was founded during the early Roman period (1st century BCE). Most of the findings are from when it was an important Byzantine town (4th to 7th centuries CE) on the caravan route between Egypt and Anatolia.

Shivta's ruins include Byzantine churches, houses and tiled streets and an impressive irrigation system.

Shivta is 58km southwest of Be'er Sheva. From Rte 40 continue from Telalim Junction on Rte 211 for about 15km. At the junction near the petrol station, drive 9km south.

Mamshit   ممشيت   תישממ

Much easier to reach than Shivta, Mamshit National Park (☎08-655 6478; adult/child 21/9NIS; ⊙8am-5pm Apr-Sep, to 4pm Oct-Mar) is the ancient city also known as Memphis or Kurnub. It is the smallest but best-preserved Nabataean city in the Negev.

The Nabataeans built their city in Wadi Mamshit in the 1st century CE; it was later used by the Romans. The excavations include ancient reservoirs, watchtowers, churches and Roman and Byzantine cemeteries. One highlight is the large mosaic floor at the courtyard of the Church of St Nilus.

Mamshit is on Rte 25, about 8km from Dimona. Any of the buses heading to Eilat via Dimona will drop you at the turn-off for the site.

The Nabataean Khan (dm tents 50NIS, tukuls for 5 people 350NIS, bungalows for 5 people 450NIS) is a camping ground at the foot of the site, featuring a *tukul* (Ethiopian-style tepee). The tents have heaters and there are shower cubicles on site.

Shekett   GUIDED TOUR

(☎052 220 1776; www.shekett.co.il) Shekett ('quiet') invites hikers to tread carefully on peaceful desert tours without excessive speaking or 4WDs and with a minimal ecological footprint.

🍽 Sleeping & Eating

Hamburg Guest House   GUESTHOUSE **$$**

(☎08-653 2016; www.boker.org.il; s/d 300/390NIS; ❄) Run by the Sde Boker Field School and located on the very edge of Wadi Zin, Hamburg Guest House has accommodation in spacious and comfortable rooms, all with a TV and fridge. Some of the rooms are big enough for six people and have outstanding views of the valley. A large Israeli breakfast buffet is served in the campus cafeteria.

Desert Lodge   LODGE **$$**

(☎08-657 3483; www.israeldesertlodge.com; s/d 400/450NIS; ❄) This South African-style lodge, part of the Boker Valley Vineyard, offers home comforts for desert travellers. Run by a friendly Israeli-Dutch couple, Moshe and Hilda Zohar, the lodge consists of wooden cabins with small kitchenettes, private bathrooms, picnic tables and outdoor barbecue areas. Groups of up to 16 can sleep in its huge khan (Nabataean caravan) or guest tent, where mattresses are provided. On site there is a magnificent wine lodge restaurant, olive grove and a jacuzzi hut in the middle of the desert valley. It's a 10-minute drive north of Sde Boker on Rte 40, between the Telalim and Halukim Junctions.

Krivine's Guest House   GUESTHOUSE **$$**

(☎052 271 2304; www.krivines.com; d 450NIS) For a more personal atmosphere try this British-run establishment in the residential area of Neve Zin, near the Midreshet. The airy rooms are nicely decorated and guests can also enjoy a three-course dinner with wine (90NIS) in its pretty garden. Speaking both English and French, the friendly Krivine family provides excellent tourist information and transport from the Sde Boker bus. Advance booking is essential.

Sde Boker Field School   HOSTEL **$**

(☎08-653 2016; www.boker.org.il; s/d 290/240NIS; ❄) The Sde Boker Field School runs a youth hostel, which is often filled with noisy school groups but is available for travellers.

Desert Dew   ISRAELI **$$**

(meals from 39NIS; ⊙9am-7pm Sun-Thu) Near the campus supermarket, this small kosher restaurant (Tal BaMidbar in Hebrew) serves big meals including fish, chicken schnitzels and homemade hummus.

ℹ Information

Information office (☎08-656 0430; ⊙9.30am-3.30pm Sun-Thu, to 1pm Fri, 10am-3pm Sat) Information and short film about the kibbutz.

SPNI Field School (☎08-653 2016; www.boker.org.il; ⊙7.30am-4.30pm Sun-Thu, 7.30am-noon Fri) The field school is mainly responsible for nature conservation in the area. The young guides are extremely knowledgeable and will tell you all about the local mammals, reptiles and birds of prey. The guides have all the maps and information about the various hikes in the desert.

ℹ Getting There & Away

From Be'er Sheva, Metropoline bus 60 (14.20NIS, 55 minutes) runs every 30 minutes. Egged bus 392 (24.50NIS, one hour) leaves Be'er Sheva at 8.15am, 9.15am, noon and 3.45pm. The bus makes three separate stops for Sde Boker – the main entrance of the kibbutz, then at the turn-off for the Ben-Gurion Desert Home and, finally, at the turn-off for the university campus, the Ben-Gurion graves and Ein Avdat. Warn the driver in advance where you want to get off.

Mitzpe Ramon

ر امونيمتسئه   מצפה רמון

☎08 / POP 5500

Mitzpe Ramon feels like something out of a sci-fi movie. The lunar landscape here resembles Tatooine (the fictional desert planet in *Star Wars*) and the wide, open spaces, far from city lights, are perfect for a spot of stargazing. Mitzpe is Hebrew for 'lookout'; accordingly, this small desert town is perched above the dramatic Makhtesh Ramon, Israel's very own Grand Canyon. All along this spectacular watchtower you'll find far-ranging views and an extensive network of hiking routes. The Makhtesh Ramon Nature Reserve, which encompasses the crater and the Negev Mountains, is the largest protected area in Israel.

Despite being in the heart of the desert, Mitzpe Ramon is also one of the coldest places in Israel, especially at night, due to its elevation (900m above sea level). Snow falls here more often than in Jerusalem.

Founded as a workers camp in 1951, Mitzpe remained an isolated community for many years. When Rte 90 was opened in the late '60s, traffic to Eilat was able to bypass the town, halting its development.

But today many travellers prefer to take the scenic route south, allowing time to soak up the sights here. The *makhtesh* is now a magnet for an eclectic mix of city-slicking artists, adventurous backpackers and eco-tourists. However, the recent opening of the five-star Beresheet Hotel on the crater's edge is likely to have a galactic impact on this remote town.

◉ Sights

Makhtesh Ramon
LANDMARK, LOOKOUT

Although Israel is a little country, the *makhtesh* is one place where it feels vast. Here the desert landscape opens up and you would be forgiven for thinking you were in Arizona. The *makhtesh* is 300m deep, 8km wide and 40km long and features multicoloured sandstone, volcanic rock and fossils.

Unless you suffer from vertigo, the **lookout**, which juts out over the edge of the crater, is a must. Stop for a while and look out over millions of years of geological evolution and unbelievable rock formations. Just don't look down from the platform if you're faint-hearted as there's nothing between your feet and the bottom of the crater. The lookout is about 300m south of the visitors centre along the *makhtesh* promenade.

A few nature trails have been marked out in the *makhtesh* and detailed hiking maps are available from the SPNI Field School.

Nahal Gewanim-Ein Sharonim Trail

The Nahal Gewanim-Ein Sharonim trail is one of the most popular hikes or 'moon-walks' near Mitzpe. The variety of colours of rock (black, red, yellow and orange) seen along the way is astounding. In winter the stream running from Ein Sharonim can be hundreds of metres long, but it dries up in summer.

The hike takes around 2½ to three hours, plus a 20-minute drive there and back from the town on Rte 40. If you have a car, turn off where the sign says 'Be'erot Camping' and drive up the dirt track for 10 minutes. You start the trail in the middle of the *makhtesh* at the Be'erot camping ground.

Otherwise you can reach the trail by taking the southbound bus (to Eilat) from the

Mitzpe Ramon

petrol station in Mitzpe Ramon and telling the driver you want to get off at the turning for the Be'erot camping ground. Walk up the 4WD track from the road for about 30 minutes, then take the right fork after the electricity pylon.

At the top of the slope follow the green-on-white trail markers on a narrow path that takes you along the ridge. After 15 minutes the path splits into high and low paths. Scramble up the rock face to the top of the ridge for a commanding view of the rock formations and maze of wadis winding through them.

The **Sharonim Stronghold**, a station on the Nabataean Incense Route, sits on top of the hill, though not much remains of this ancient site except a few low-cut walls. If you took the high path, climb down to join the low path, which leads to a wadi (Nahal Gewanim).

Mitzpe Ramon

Follow the wadi and after 25 minutes it narrows considerably, with caves on both sides of the canyon. Follow the blue-on-white trail markers for 20 minutes until you come to a couple of water holes. From here, follow the trail left until you reach the 4WD track and the electricity pylon where you started.

Other hikes, also starting from Be'erot camping ground, include a trek to Nahal Ardon, which is a mostly flat hike that takes 3½ hours to complete and ends with great views of the Ardon Valley, or if you have the stamina you could take the six-hour trek to Mt Ardon on the northeastern edge to give a different view of the crater.

Scenic Pass

The scenic pass is part of the Israel National Trail, a series of hikes that runs the length of the country. It is a leisurely and very scenic two-hour hike that takes you down into Makhtesh Ramon to the Carpenter's Workshop and on to the main road. From the youth hostel, follow the path along the edge of the crater until you see the sign pointing down. Follow the green trail markings and you'll eventually come to the Carpenter's Workshop. Continue to reach the main road, where you can either hitch back to town or flag down one of the infrequent buses.

Carpenter's Workshop

Shortly after the road from Mitzpe Ramon zigzags down into the crater, an orange signpost points to this site of geological interest, 500m to the right. The Carpenter's Workshop is a unique rock formation that has been shaped by pressure and is said to resemble wood.

Follow the 4WD track from the road that ends with a car park. From here take the path up the hill to the left, which leads you around the hill to a wooden observation platform. You can either take the Eilat bus or hitch from Mitzpe Ramon, or stop here on your way down on the Scenic Pass hike.

Visitors Centre MUSEUM

(adult/child 25/13NIS; ⊘8am-4pm Sat-Thu, to 3pm Fri) Perched on the crater rim, the visitors centre was undergoing some major renovations during our visit but is set to become a new museum, featuring different exhibits on desert, geology, archaeology and astronomy. One of the highlights is likely to be an exhibit on Ilan Ramon, the first Israeli astronaut, who died on the fatal *Columbia* mission in 2003. You can also pick up a Makhtesh Ramon Nature Reserve map and information on hikes at the reception. Up on the rooftop lookout there is a sundial and amazing views of the crater.

Bio Ramon WILDLIFE RESERVE

(adult/child 21/9NIS; ⊘8am-5pm Sat-Thu, to 4pm Fri) A tiny desert wildlife park, Bio Ramon shows how nature can find a way to survive even in the harshest desert conditions. It offers an integrated approach to the geology, flora and fauna that represent the six habitats of the Negev's desert residents (insects, mammals and reptiles). Here you will find scorpions, tortoises and snakes among reeds and limestone. Bio Ramon is just down the hill from the visitors centre.

TOP CHOICE Alpaca Farm
FARM

(☑08-658 8047; www.alpaca.co.il; admission 25NIS; ☺8.30am-6.30pm summer, to 4.30pm winter) This is no ordinary farm. It all started when owners Ilan and Na'ama Dvir flew 188 llamas and alpacas to Israel on a specially chartered plane from the South American Andes. Alpaca Farm now has over 400 llamas and alpacas, perhaps the biggest herd in the world, as well as donkeys, goats and ponies. The farm is tucked into a hidden valley about 3km from Mitzpe Ramon down the dirt track at the end of Ben-Gurion Blvd. The animals are being raised for their delicate wool, which comes in many different shades and needs no artificial colouring. Visitors can see such activities as shearing, washing and weaving and the farm also offers horse rides in the desert (150NIS, 1½ hours) or a trail to the Negev Highlands (240NIS, two hours).

Desert Sculpture Park
PARK

The stone sculptures in this park, which were assembled by Israeli artist Ezra Orion, can add another dimension to your desolate desert photographs. The sculptures are a 10-minute walk north of the visitors centre and represent different periods of human life.

INDUSTRIAL ZONE

Mitzpe Ramon's old industrial zone is now a fully fledged tourist zone, where once-abandoned hangars have been turned into alternative art galleries, shops and studios.

Handmade in Mitzpe
ARTS CENTRE

(12 HarBoker St; ☺10am-7pm Sun-Thu, to 2pm Fri) Stop by Handmade in Mitzpe, a studio for local ceramics, jewellery and clothing.

Nature Scent
FACTORY

(www.naturescent.co.il; 22 Har Ardon St; ☺8.30am-7pm Sun-Thu, to 4.30pm Fri) Nature Scent is a factory shop where you can see, touch and smell over 50 types of soaps, all handmade from natural ingredients.

Activities

Desert Archery
ARCHERY

(☑08-658 7274, 050 534 4598; www.desertarchery. co.il) Imagine a game of golf but instead of a club you have a bow and arrow, then you have desert archery. The goal of this fun game is to hit the balloons spread out around the rocky course. It costs 50NIS per person for two hours with a guide and equipment.

Adama
DANCE

(☑08-659 5190; www.adama.org.il; Har Boker St) Adama, which means 'Earth', runs regular workshops on dance, meditation and the language of movement. It also holds monthly dance festivals during summer and accommodation is available.

Tours

Sometimes the best way to see the *makhtesh* is on a guided tour. Many companies run off-road 4WD tours, usually for groups.

Guide Horizon
ADVENTURE TOUR

(☑08-659 5333; www.guidehorizon.com; 27 Har Boker St) One of the most established tour companies in the area, Guide Horizon hires out dune buggies for self-drive or escorted *makhtesh* tours. A three-hour trip, meal and single room costs 300NIS, while an overnight trip plus spa, sauna, lunch and dinner is 850NIS.

Tiyul Acher
GUIDED TOUR

(☑08-659 5192; www.tiyulacher.com; Har Ardon St) Tiyul Acher ('A Different Tour') offers desert tours, with activities ranging from hiking and cycling, to abseiling and wildlife watching.

Sleeping

With its variety of accommodation from desert tents to boutique hotels, Mitzpe Ramon is the best place to be based in the Negev. Rates can be 100NIS cheaper on weekdays.

Succah in the Desert
HUT $$

(Succah BaMidbar; ☑08-658 6280; www.succah. co.il; half board s/d 300/550, weekends 700NIS) If you are searching for silence and seclusion, then this is your place. The only disturbances here are the occasional IAF (Israeli Air Force) jet and your own racing thoughts. Set 7km from town on a very bumpy track, these huts built of stones and palm leaves sit on the rocky hillside. The word *sukkah* (small dwelling) comes from the Bible, and each hut is named after one of the ancient Ten Lost Tribes of Israel. There is one larger *sukkah* that houses a kitchen, lounge and dining area, while the others provide accommodation that's tastefully furnished with rugs and Bedouin-style fabric. Each *sukkah* has its own solar panel. Continue down the road at the end of Ben-Gurion Blvd for 4km until you see a sign for 'Succah in the Desert'. Turn down the dirt track and drive for another 3km.

iBike HOTEL $$

(☑08-653 9393, 052 436 7878; www.ibike.co.il; 4 Har Ardon St; s/d 320/410NIS; ❉☎) The iBike comprises seven spacious rooms with private bathrooms and a large, comfortable communal lounge area. Located in the industrial zone, it has the feel of a dive club or ski club and is a great place to mix with other travellers. Guests can use the spa with a sauna and jacuzzi, as well as get expert advice and tours for all levels of cyclists from helpful hosts Aviva and Menachem. Next door, it also has a cafe serving breakfasts, salads, sandwiches and pasta dishes.

TOP CHOICE **Green Backpackers** HOSTEL $

(☑08-653 2319; www.thegreenbackpackers.com; 10 Nahal Sirpad St; dm 75NIS, d without bathroom 255NIS; ❉@☎) Opened in 2011, this cute, homely hostel with soft carpets and clean rooms meets all the budget backpacker's needs. There is a library of DVDs, secondhand books, travellers' message board and shared recipes in the communal kitchen. It also offers laundry services, hiking gear and free wi-fi. Idiosyncratic touches include a framed painting of Kramer from *Seinfeld* in the hallway and a toilet decorated with old cassette tapes. Located in a quiet cul-de-sac at the end of Nahal Zia St, the hostel is a little hard to find but owner Lee will be happy to direct you.

Silent Arrow CAMPGROUND $

(Hetz BaSheket; ☑052 661 1561; www.hetzbashekt.com; Bedouin tent beds/dome tents per person 80/120NIS) As the name suggests, this is indeed a place for peace and desert tranquillity. The camp is 700m from town, down a dirt track, and the only sound you will hear is that of your own snoring. Guests can choose from a mattress in the communal Bedouin-style tent or a private dome tent. Remember to bring your own sleeping bag. Free coffee and tea are provided in the kitchen and lounge tent area, but breakfast is not provided. It also takes volunteers (one week minimum).

Be'erot Camping CAMPGROUND $

(☑08-658 6713; www.beerot.com; Bedouin tents per person 50NIS, private r for 6 people with shower 500NIS) This remote Bedouin-run camp is the only place to sleep in the *makhtesh*. It is also the starting point for most of the hikes, so it is popular with tour groups and can be busy during the day. Sleeping options include traditional Bedouin tents, as well as

new private rooms with clean bathrooms and a modern shower block. It's 12km south of Mitzpe Ramon on the highway to Eilat, and then 5km down a bumpy access road.

Alpaca Farm B&B B&B $$

(☑08-658 8047, 052 897 7010/11; www.alpaca.co.il; studios per person 100NIS, d 500NIS; ❉) Where else in Israel can you wake up to the sound of birds singing as fluffy llamas and horses quietly munch on their breakfast below? If you love animals, Alpaca Farm is special place to stay. The attractive hillside cabins are decked out with wooden floors, cable TV, kitchenette and a great balcony for enjoying the desert views. There is also a separate studio, where you need your own sleeping bag. It provides electric heaters, a fridge and very clean shower rooms. Just don't leave too much food lying around; as we found out, the animals might want to 'share' it.

Adama HOSTEL $$

(☑08-659 5190; Har Boker St; www.adama.org.il; campsites & dm 80NIS, tepees 175NIS, s/d 275/395NIS, r for 4 people 595NIS) A kind of spiritual and dance retreat set in a large industrial hangar, Adama may not be everyone's cup of herbal tea. But if you dig dreadlocks and have always had a secret love of all things psychedelic, then this could be for you. You can crash on a mattress in one of the airy studios, or for a bit of privacy crawl into one of the tepee-like structures. Those with tents can pitch them in the garden. Guests are welcome to participate in dance and meditation activities.

Chez Eugene BOUTIQUE HOTEL $$$

(☑08-653 9595; www.mitzperamonhotel.co.il; 8 Har Ardon St; ste from 800NIS; ❉☎) This new boutique hotel represents just how far Mitzpe has come in recent years. Each room here is stylishly designed with contemporary art, funky furniture and flat-screen TVs, and all have walk-in showers. Eugene offers a different level of luxury and cuisine, but is pricier than other sleeping options in the industrial zone.

Desert Home B&B $$

(Bait BaMidbar; ☑052 322 9496; www.baitbamidbar.com; 70 Ein Shaviv; d 550NIS, Fri & Sat 600NIS; ❉) On the edge of a quiet residential neighbourhood, this is for travellers who enjoy their creature comforts. The five units are decorated in a minimalist style with bleached-wood floors, locally made furniture, art and photography. There is an on-site treatment room for massage and alternative therapy.

Beresheet
LUXURY HOTEL, RESORT $$$

(☎08-638 7799; www.isrotelexclusivecollec tion.com/beresheet; 1 Beresheet Rd; ste from US$375; ❄️🛜🏊) More of a small town than a hotel, recently opened Beresheet (which means 'Genesis') is unlike anything else in Mitzpe. The 111 ultraluxurious rooms (many with their own pools) are supposed to complement the natural surroundings. Tightly guarded by security staff on golf buggies, it has a lavish gourmet restaurant, piano bar and the ultimate infinity pool overlooking the crater.

Desert Shade
LODGE $

(☎08-658 6229; www.desert-nomads.com; dm/s/d 70/100/200NIS; @🛜) Directly opposite the Desert Sculpture Park, Desert Shade is an ecotourism centre running occasional seminars on peace and ecology. It has incredible views of the *makhtesh* and offers accommodation in Bedouin tents or mud huts, where empty wine bottles are used as windows. It also has wi-fi connectivity in the cushioned communal area.

HI – Mitzpe Ramon Youth Hostel
HOSTEL $

(☎08-658 8443; mitzpe@iyha.org.il; dm/s/d 152/320/450NIS; ❄️🛜) A short downhill walk from the visitors centre, this large hostel is right on the edge of the crater, but unfortunately not all rooms offer views. This hostel can occasionally fill up with tour groups, and during term time you can expect a little noise from the elementary school next door.

Daniella's Residence
B&B $$

(☎050 526 5628; 39-41 Ein Shaviv St; d 400NIS, r for 5 people 650NIS; ❄️) Charming rooms in a quiet residential area; look for the yellow house with cactus plants in the garden.

Ramon Inn
HOTEL $$$

(☎08-658 8822; www.isrotel.co.il; 1 Ein Akev St; s/d 573/675NIS; ❄️@🏊) Run by Isrotel, this hotel was the only luxury option in town until its sister Beresheet came along.

Guide Horizon
LODGE $$

(☎08-659 5333; 27 Har Boker St; s 390NIS, d incl tour 600NIS; ❄️) From outside it looks like a simple warehouse, but inside it has seven rooms, plus a spa, sauna, solarium, jacuzzi, gym, yoga classes, drumming, barbecue area and hammocks.

Har HaNegev Field School
GUESTHOUSE $$

(☎08-658 8615; www.teva.org.il; s/d 345/405NIS; ❄️) Run by the SPNI, these simple but spacious rooms offer front-row views of the *makhtesh*. Popular with groups, it is 2.5km down a dirt track, south of Ben-Gurion Blvd.

🍴 Eating

Self-caterers can stock up at the Super-Sol supermarket in the town centre.

Chez Eugene
EUROPEAN $$$

(www.mitzperamonhotel.co.il; 8 Har Ardon St; mains from 78NIS; ⏱7pm-midnight Sun-Thu, noon-4pm Fri, noon-11pm Sat) Inspired by European cuisine and using only local ingredients, recently opened Chez Eugene is a tasty alternative to the usual desert cuisine. Try succulent steaks, salmon, goose breast and other delights from Israeli gastro-chef Shahar Dabah.

TOP CHOICE Haksa
ISRAELI $

(2 Har Ardon St; dishes from 28NIS; ⏱noon-8.30pm Sat-Thu, 1-8.30pm Fri) Haksa offers real home cooking and has to be a contender for some of the best *labneh* (thick yoghurt) in Israel. The cosy restaurant is set in the owner's home in the industrial area. The menu changes on a daily basis, but specialities include dishes such as meatballs with aubergine and couscous, grilled chicken and beef goulash.

HaHavit
PUB $$

(8 Nahal Zia; mains 58NIS; ⏱8am-2am Sun-Thu, 8.30-4pm Fri) HaHavit ('the Barrel') has been serving up hefty portions of fresh salad, soups, hamburgers, sandwiches and pasta dishes since 1987. Diners can sit inside or out and after eating can enjoy rock classics and a range of beers on tap until late.

Hadasaar
ORGANIC

(23 Har Arif St; ⏱9am-7pm; 🥗) Stock up on organic nuts, granola, dried fruit and more before your desert trip

ℹ️ Information

The **SPNI Har HaNegev Field School** (☎08-658 8615; har@spni.org.il; ⏱8am-4pm Sun-Thu, to noon Fri) on the edge of the crater is worth visiting if you plan any serious hiking.

At the entrance to Ben-Gurion Blvd there is a small commercial concourse with a **Bank Hapoalim** and a **post office**(⏱8am-6pm Sun-Thu, to noon Fri).

❶ Getting There & Away

Mitzpe Ramon lies 23km south of Avdat and 136km north of Eilat. Metropoline bus 60 shuttles hourly to and from Be'er Sheva (16.50NIS, 1½ hours) from 6am to 9.30pm via Sde Boker and Ein Avdat. From Sunday to Thursday Egged buses 392 or 397 travel to Eilat (44NIS, three hours) at 9.53am, 10.53am, 1.38pm and 5.23pm. The only bus to Eilat on Friday is at 9.38am. Catch the bus to Eilat from the petrol station.

The Arava وادي عربة הערבה

⎙ 08 / POP 5200

The Arava is a beautiful, sparsely populated desert that runs from the Dead Sea to the Red Sea, and is part of the Great Rift Valley (which runs north to south for some 5000km from northern Syria to central Mozambique). Wherever you are in the southern Arava, the red mountains of Jordan can be seen. The region is home to Israel's most innovative environmental projects.

◉ Sights

Timna Park
HISTORIC SITE

(www.timna-park.co.il; adult/child 44/39NIS; ⊘8am-4pm Sat-Thu, to 1pm Fri & Sun) About 25km north of Eilat, Timna Park is the site of one of the world's earliest copper mines. The park is dotted with ancient mine shafts, some dug by Egyptians in the 5th century BCE, but it also includes a wonderland of geological phenomena. The most intriguing are the Natural Arch, Solomon's Pillars (two huge columns of granite formed by rainwater some 540 million years ago) and the Mushroom, an eroded monolith in the shape of, you guessed it, a mushroom. Chariots Corner has ancient, childlike wall inscriptions dating from the second millennium BCE.

You could easily spend a whole day hiking here, but the park is so spread out that a hire car is needed. Information about walks is available at the entrance, where visitors can watch a film. There is also a camping area at the lake, where you can pitch your tent for 40NIS per person.

Buses between Eilat and Jerusalem pass the park turn-off, 2.5km from the park entrance.

Yotvata Hai-Bar Nature Reserve
WILDLIFE RESERVE

(www.parks.org.il; adult/child 43/22NIS; ⊘8.30am-5pm Sun-Thu, to 3.30pm Fri & Sat) Located 35km north of Eilat, Yotvata Hai-Bar was created to establish breeding groups of wild animals that are mentioned in the Bible, as well as other threatened species.

The reserve has three parts: a 1.2-hectare penned-in area where you can observe the animals (mainly African asses, addax, ostriches and oryxes); the predator centre, where reptiles, small desert animals and large predators such as wolves and leopards are on display; and the desert Night Life exhibition hall, where night and day are reversed so daytime visitors can observe nocturnal animals such as pygmy gerbils while they're active.

A private car is needed to navigate the reserve's gravel roads and a visit takes about an hour. It's recommended to visit at feeding time; between 11am and 1pm. Visitors can pitch tents near the entrance for 50NIS a night and use the bathrooms.

The reserve is on Rte 90 between Kibbutz Yotvata and Kibbutz Samar.

✍ Kibbutz Lotan
KIBBUTZ

(www.kibbutzlotan.com; Rte 90) Synonymous with an ecological vision known in Hebrew as *tikkun olam* (repairing the world), Lotan has operated for over 25 years. The kibbutz, one of only two kibbutzim in Israel affiliated with the Jewish Reform Movement, has three core centres: Bird Reserve, Creative Ecology (Eco-Kef in Hebrew) and Holistic Desert Health. The Bird Reserve is set in the sandy plain very near the Jordanian border and is dotted with camouflaged viewpoints. Lotan runs regular workshops in alternative building methods, as well as half-day and full-day tours that show visitors how to put environmental theory into practice. The Holistic Desert Health Centre offers sessions in ashtanga yoga, massage, reiki, reflexology and Watsu (water shiatsu). A 50-minute session of Watsu is 280NIS.

Lotan is known for its funky geodesic dome houses, invented by German engineer Walther Bauersfeld in 1922 and later developed by American architect Buckminster Fuller in the '50s. Students or volunteers interested in permaculture can come here and learn about ecodesign and ecoplanning on a six- or 10-week Green Apprenticeship. All buses to/from Eilat stop on Rte 90 near Lotan.

🛏 Sleeping & Eating

Camel Riders
CAMPGROUND $

(⎙08-637 3218; www.camel-riders.com; Shaharut; dm tents 100NIS per person) Camel Riders is located at Shaharut, a remote spot, about

THE NEGEV THE ARAVA

60km north of Eilat and then another 22km off the highway (Rte 12). A Sinai-style retreat, it is popular with Tel Aviv exiles looking to enjoy desert music workshops, massages and, as the name suggests, camel rides. The only accommodation is on a mattress in what they call a 'caravan tent'. If you arrive on bus 392 (between Eilat and Mitzpe Ramon) the owner will pick you up from the Shizzafon Junction.

Kibbutz Lotan Guesthouse   GUESTHOUSE $
(☑08-635 6935; www.kibbutzlotan.com; Rte 90; s/d 270/340NIS; ❋☎☻) If you are after a base for exploring the Arava, then this pleasant ecovillage is a peaceful place to stop for a night or two. The 20 air-conditioned rooms with kitchenette are simply decorated, and outside there are numerous hammocks and shaded areas where guests can mingle with kibbutz members, who will happily discuss local desert hikes and environmental issues, or just point you towards the dining hall, where breakfast and a small dinner are served.

Kibbutz Ketura Country Lodge   GUESTHOUSE $$
(☑08-635 6658; www.keren-kolot-israel.co.il; Rte 90; s/d 350/480NIS; ❋☎☻) Ketura hit the headlines in June 2011 when it opened Israel's first solar field, part of a plan to make the country meet its renewable-energy goals. Remarkably successful in making the desert bloom, Ketura also houses the Arava Institute for Environmental Studies, so the guest rooms are occasionally occupied by groups of students. More like a hotel than a kibbutz, there is a swimming pool, basketball court and football field on site, and the 45 modern guest apartments come with kitchen, wi-fi, balcony or a grass lawn. The kibbutz is on Route 90, just south of the Ketura Junction.

Ashram in the Desert   COMMUNE $
(☑08-632 6508, 052 544 3349; www.deser tashram.co.il; NahalShittim; campsites/dm/d/ private hut 100/150/300/460NIS; ☎) Between Mitzpe Ramon and the Arava, this is not a kibbutz but an Israeli version of an ashram. Founded by followers of Indian mystic Osho, it offers spiritual workshops on yoga, tantra and slightly less spiritual trance parties. Accommodation ranges from tepees to comfortable rooms, and communal vegetarian breakfast, lunch and dinner are provided. Guests wishing to stay longer can also try the WOMP (Work Meditation Program) for

10 days or weeks. Twice a year in spring and autumn it holds the Zorba Festival, where DJs, hedonists and artists descend on the ashram; see the website for details. Take the 392 bus and get off at Shittim; the ashram is a few minutes' walk from there.

Negev Eco Lodge   LODGE $$$
(☑052 617 0028; www.negevecolodge.com; Zukim; d from 600NIS; ☎) With solar-powered cabins made of straw bales and mud, this place is sustainable with a capital 'S'. Inside, the rooms are comfortable and each cabin can easily sleep six people. It may be remote but this lodge offers an artificial desert oasis in the shape of three small circular pools. The homemade breakfast costs an extra 50NIS each. To reach the lodge, turn off Rte 90 at Zukim and after 50m you will see the sign for 'Desert Days'.

Kibbutz Eilot Guesthouse   GUESTHOUSE $$
(☑08-635 8800/8816; www.eilot.co.il; s/d 300/410NIS; ❋☻) Israel's southernmost kibbutz, just 3km north of Eilat, Eilot has 40 rooms in a country-lodge guesthouse surrounded by lawns. There's plenty for kids to enjoy here, including two swimming pools, an animal farm and horse riding. It is a great place to stay if you want to be on the outskirts of Eilat or fancy a trip to Aqaba or Petra.

Neot Semadar Inn   CAFE $$
TOP CHOICE
(www.neot-semadar.com; Shizzafon Junction; mains 38-50NIS; ◷7am-9pm Sun-Thu, to 4pm Fri, 6-9pm Sat; ☎) Definitely worth the drive up here, this cute roadside inn has a beautiful rear garden, worthy of its name (*neot* means 'oasis'). Try the delicious goat's cheese lasagne, *shakshuka*, nectarine juice or plum ice cream. If you eat here you get a 5% discount off the organic olive oil, jams, teas and ice cream produced by Kibbutz Neot Semadar, a young, very alternative community nearby.

Yotvata Restaurant   CAFETERIA $$
(Kibbutz Yotvata, Rte 90; dishes from 32NIS; ◷24hr, closed Fri night) This dairy restaurant and supermarket, run by one of the wealthiest kibbutzim in Israel (despite its remote desert location, Yotvata is famous around the country for its top-quality milk products), is permanently filled with busloads of tourists. It's noisy and overcrowded, but serves the kibbutz's own cheese, chocolate and ice cream.

Eilat אילת ايلات

08 / POP 47,500

A thin wedge between Jordan and Egypt at the southern tip of Israel, Eilat makes a lot of noise for its size. A raunchy resort town set around a lagoon lined with glitzy hotels, this is where Israelis come to have fun.

Thanks to an average winter temperature of 21°C, the place is heaving all year, but come summer the temperature rises to over 40°C, making it one of the hottest places in the country. Luckily, the Red Sea is the ideal antidote and will help cool you off throughout the year.

For many visitors Eilat's real appeal is its proximity to desert mountains and canyons. Eilat has a small coral reef, but serious divers searching for the Red Sea's magical underwater world should head onward to Sinai.

History

Inhabited since antiquity, Eilat is first mentioned in the Book of Exodus, after the Israelites' crossing of the Red Sea. In ancient times on the border of the states of Edom and Midian, it was an important stopping point on the copper and incense trade routes, and in the Roman era a road was built from Eilat to Petra. Trade declined over the centuries, and eventually the Ottomans built a port across the bay in Aqaba.

Eilat remained little more than a small British police station until the modern city was founded in 1951. Rapidly developed for tourism, Eilat is now a popular and, you could say, overcrowded resort town. If the planned new airport in Timna goes ahead, the removal of the present airport could open up acres of city-centre land for development and, no doubt, more hotels.

⊙ Sights

Underwater Observatory
Marine Park   AQUARIUM

(08-636 4200; www.coralworld.com/eilat; Coral Beach, Mitzrayim Rd; adult/child 89/69NIS; ⊙8.30am-5pm Sat-Thu, to 4pm Fri) For as much aquatic action as you can get without getting wet, head to the Underwater Observatory Marine Park, south of Coral Beach. Aside from standard aquarium features such as shark tanks, turtles and stingray pools, highlights include the magical glassed-in observatory, 4.25m below the water's surface, through which you can view the rich marine life of the Red Sea. The accompanying aquarium is outstanding and there's even a pitch-black room for viewing phosphorescent fish. Kids will get a thrill out of the petting pool and the regular feedings that take place between 11am and 3pm.

The Oceanarium submarine is a true theme-park-style ride with jolting seats and a squealing audience. For more seabed cruising jump on the *Coral 2000* (adult/child 35/29NIS), which has 48 underwater windows for optimal marine-life viewing. The 35-minute tour leaves from the observatory at 11am and 1pm Monday to Saturday.

Dolphin Reef   WATER PARK

(Map p324; 08-630 0111; www.dolphinreef.co.il; South Beach; adult/child 64/44NIS; ⊙9am-5pm Sun-Thu) Dolphin Reef is home to a group of bottlenose dolphins consisting of one male (Cindy) and seven females. The dolphins were brought from the Black Sea to the Red Sea in the early '90s. In the observation area, visitors can watch the dolphins maintain their normal routines of hunting, playing and socialising in their 'natural habitat'.

Admission includes the use of the private beach, as well as a screening of a documentary. You can also snorkel with the dolphins (280NIS) or do an introductory dive (320NIS).

Another feature of Dolphin Reef is the gorgeous relaxation pools (150NIS for 1½ hours including refreshments). Surrounded by lush greenery, the three pools (rainwater, seawater and Dead Sea water) are all heated and have underwater music, making for a rather blissful experience!

Advance booking is advised to swim or snorkel with the dolphins and use the relaxation pools.

King's City & Funtasia   AMUSEMENT PARK

(Map p326; 08-630 4430; www.kingscity.co.il; East Lagoon; adult/child 125/99NIS; ⊙9am-1am Sun-Thu, to 5pm Fri, 6pm-1am Sat) Housed inside a giant fake castle, this biblical Disneyland took four years to build and cost US$40 million. King's City is a Middle Eastern theme park with a distinctly American accent. The interactive attractions include mazes, kaleidoscopes, 3D films and a heart-thumping water ride through King Solomon's life. The park now includes the newly opened Funtasia – a more conventional outdoor amusement park with bumper cars, a small roller coaster and carousel. The King's City entrance fee includes three rides in Funtasia; extra rides cost 10NIS each.

Ice Space
FAMILY FUN

(Map p326; www.ice-space.co.il; Spiral Centre, North Beach; adult/child 54/29NIS; ☺10am-11pm Mon-Sat, from 5pm Sun) A strange mix of a vodka bar and a children's attraction, Ice Space features ice sculptures by German artist Chris Funk. The visit starts with a short film about Antarctica and the melting ice caps. Then inside you can check out frozen guitars, pianos and an 18m slide. The temperatures are maintained at a frosty -7°C, so coats and gloves are provided.

Botanical Garden of Eilat
GARDENS

(Map p324; www.botanicgarden.co.il; adult/child 20/15NIS; ☺8.30am-6pm Sun-Thu, to 1pm Fri, 10am-1pm Sat) Displaying over 1000 different types of tropical trees, plants and bushes, this small garden, on the northern hills above Eilat, makes for a pleasant ramble with children. Take the first right as you enter Eilat on Rte 90; the garden is behind the petrol station.

FREE International Birdwatching Centre
WILDLIFE RESERVE

(Map p324; www.eilatbirding.blogspot.com; ☺7am-4pm) Tens of millions of migrating birds pass through the Arava and Eilat en route from Africa to Europe and vice versa. So, if your timing is right and you're lucky, you can spot the odd owl, falcon, dove, buzzard, crane or other sedentary and migratory bird at this lakeside reserve, directly opposite the Arava Border Crossing.

TOP CHOICE Coral Beach Nature Reserve
DIVE SITE

(Map p324; adult/child 33/20NIS; ☺9am-5pm Sat-Thu, 9am-3pm Fri) Away from the crowded town centre on the Taba Rd, this protected beach is by far the best in Eilat. With over 100 types of stony coral and 650 species of fish, the nature reserve is also a utopia for snorkellers. A wooden bridge leads from the shore to the beginning of the reef (which is over 1km in length), where you can follow several underwater trails marked by buoys. The reserve stretches from the Underwater Observatory to the Reef Hotel, and the entrance is opposite the SPNI Field School. Snorkelling equipment can be hired for 16NIS.

☂ Beaches

Eilat's central beaches can be cluttered, so many tourists prefer to hang around their hotel pools. Outside these seaside resorts the coastline is dominated by the port and construction work.

North Beach
CITY BEACH

(Map p326) The main stretch of beach in town, this is great for a drink in the sun and gets quieter the closer you get to Jordan.

Red Rock Beach
CENTRAL BEACH

(Map p326) On the side of the Mall HaYam shopping centre, it has terrific views of the Gulf of Eilat and those red mountains.

Eilat

Eilat

HaDekel (Palm) Beach PEACEFUL BEACH
Map p324) Just south of town, HaDekel is a calmer spot to watch the sunrise or sunset, preferably with a milkshake or cocktail in hand.

Village Beach PARTY BEACH
(Map p324) Nearer Coral Beach, Village Beach has free umbrellas, clean water for snorkelling and a bar hosting loud parties at weekends.

Activities

From diving and snorkelling to hiking and parasailing, there are more than enough fun activities to keep you occupied here. Alternatively, you could just relax on the beach.

Water Sports

The Red Sea offers some of the best diving in the world – and Eilat has no shortage of dive clubs. However, due to the sheer volume of divers, the reef has seen some inevitable damage over the years. Over the past decade, steps have been taken to rehabilitate the coral and thousands of young colonies have been grown in aquariums and attached to the existing reef.

It is true that all you need to do is pop your head underwater in Eilat and you're likely to see all sorts of colourful fish. This accessibility makes it a great place for kids as well as for beginners looking to do a PADI course. There are also a fair number of companies running glass-bottomed boat trips.

Israel Yam BOATING
(Map p326; ☑08-637 5528; Yacht Marina; adult/child 69/49NIS) A popular excursion from the main hotel area is the *Israel Yam*, a glass-bottomed boat that cruises between the Egyptian and Jordanian borders, before heading to Coral Beach. It lasts two hours and leaves at 10.30am, 1pm and 3.30pm.

Manta Diving Club DIVING
(Map p324; ☑08-633 3666; www.redseasports.co.il; Yam Suf Hotel, Coral Beach) A long-term expert in the region, the Manta Diving Club (formerly the Red Sea Sports Club) is connected to Isrotel's Yam Suf Hotel. Manta offers dives in the Red Sea Triangle of Aqaba, Eilat and Sinai including PADI open water courses (2050/3250NIS three/five days) and introductory dives (220NIS, one hour). Manta also run trips on the *Orionia*, a wooden cruiser built in Spain in 1926, to the beaches at Taba or to Coral Island off the Sinai Peninsula (155NIS, four hours).

TOP CHOICE **Aqua Sport** DIVING
(Map p324; ☑08-633 4404; www.aqua-sport.com; Coral Beach) One of the oldest dive companies in Eilat, Aqua Sport has been exploring the Red Sea since 1962. A snorkelling cruise to Sinai costs US$65 and two dives with equipment will set you back US$110. Check the website for details of PADI courses.

Deep Siam DIVING
(Map p324; ☑08-632 3636; www.deepdivers.co.il; Coral Beach) This friendly diving group is one of the best value, with boat trips and dives to Aqaba going for around 270NIS.

Snuba DIVING
(Map p324; ☑08-637 2722; www.snuba.co.il; South Beach) Snuba provides an easier way for non-divers to explore the underwater world. The

Eilat Town Centre

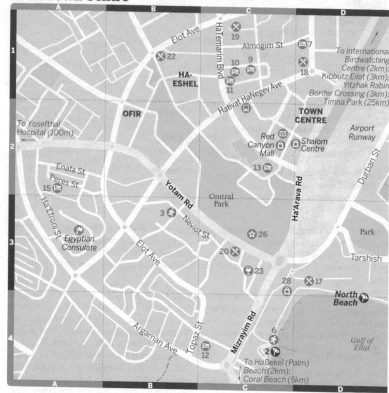

heavy air tank remains on a light inflatable boat while the air comes from an air-line attached by a harness, allowing you to swim deep under the sea. Guides take scuba divers to the Caves reef, considered one of the best in Eilat. It costs 220NIS and includes two hours of snorkel rental after the dive. Its five-day Open Water PADI course costs 1200NIS.

Kite X Eilat
KITE SURFING

(Map p324; ☎08-637 3123; www.kitexeilat.co.ik; Coral Beach) Those looking for some fast and furious kicks should head to the beach next to the Orchid Reef Hotel, where Israeli kitesurfers have set up a new school. After just six hours (split into three lessons), you will literally be flying on water.

Kisuski
WATER SPORTS

(Map p326; ☎08-637 2088; Red Rock Beach) At Kisuski you can rent all the other water toys you hadn't thought of, such as jet skis (180NIS for 10 minutes), banana boats (40NIS per person) and parascending (320NIS for 10 minutes).

Desert Hikes

Although overshadowed by the activities on the beach and underwater, there are some marvellous hiking possibilities in the colourful mountains and valleys just outside Eilat.

When you go hiking in the desert be sure to abide by the safety guidelines: follow a marked path, take sufficient water, cover your head and avoid the Israel–Egypt border area.

Mt Zefahot Circular Trail
MOUNTAIN

This almost circular hike culminates in superb views of the four countries whose borders meet around the Gulf of Eilat/Aqaba: Israel, Egypt, Jordan and Saudi Arabia. Within reach of non-drivers, the three-hour hike is best enjoyed towards the end of the day.

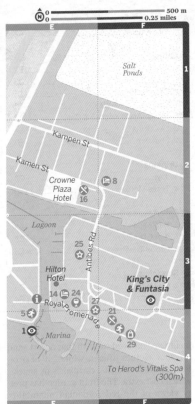

can be beautiful here, hikers are advised not to return after dark as the trail can be difficult to follow. The path ends at the SPNI Field School on the main road.

👉 Tours

Desert Eco Tours
ADVENTURE TOUR

(Map p326; ☎08-637 4259; www.desertecotours.com; Neviot St) A good choice for wilderness tours is the reputable Desert Eco Tours, which runs 4WD, camel and hiking tours in the Negev, Sinai and southwest Jordan. Plan on spending US$247 (plus border taxes) for a full-day trip to Petra and US$400 for two days to Petra and Wadi Rum (including meals).

Holit Desert Tours
DRIVING TOUR

(Map p326; ☎08-631 8318; www.holiteilat.co.il; Chan Centre) Opposite the Dan Panorama Hotel, Holit operates a whole host of tours to Cairo, Jerusalem, Petra and numerous desert safaris. For a bumpy ride in the wadis and mountains outside Eilat, try a two-hour desert buggy tour for US$125.

🎉 Festivals & Events

Red Sea Jazz Festival
MUSIC

(www.redseajazzeilat.com) Going strong since 1987, the Red Sea Jazz Festival is an international four-day jazz festival held annually in the last week of August. Outdoor performances are staged around the Eilat Sea Port. The festival's legendary jam sessions are free and take place poolside each night at the luxurious Yam Suf Hotel on Coral Beach.

Red Sea Classical Music Festival
MUSIC

(www.redsea-classic.co.il) Bringing a touch of class to Eilat, the Red Sea International Classical Music Festival is usually held in January in a hangar at Eilat Port. Check the website for details.

🛏 Sleeping

Eilat's accommodation ranges from the good to the bad to the downright ugly. Occasionally touts offering cheap private rooms wait at the central bus station. It is advisable to view a place before agreeing to stay.

As a resort town, the cost of hotel rooms in Eilat rises by about 25% at weekends and 50% (or more) from June to August. Reserve ahead, particularly during the holiday season.

Camping is illegal on most of Eilat's beaches. Exceptions are the areas towards the Jordanian border and north of the port and the SPNI Field School on Coral Beach.

Take bus 15 from the central bus station and get off by the old Texas Ranch (opposite Coral Beach and near Club Med). Follow the sign pointing to Wadi Shlomo and walk along the dirt road for about 2km past Camel Ranch and head left along Wadi Zefahot (Tzefahot), following the green trail markers. You pass a dry waterfall on your right and after 300m the path forks with a black-marked trail veering off to the right. Keep going straight ahead on the green marked trail for another 200m. It then turns to the left and starts to climb quite steeply. Head up this path and keep climbing for about 15 minutes to reach the **Mt Zefahot** summit at about 278m.

From this vantage point, Sinai is visible to the south, including the Crusader castle on Coral Island, while across the gulf are the Jordanian port city of Aqaba and the Saudi Arabian border. To the northeast is the greenery of Kibbutz Eilot. Although sunset

Eilat Town Centre

If you enjoy outlandish luxury hotels, then Eilat has plenty to choose from. There are more than 40 complexes along North Beach and on the road to Taba.

TOP CHOICE **Orchid Reef Hotel**   HOTEL $$$
(Map p324; ☏08-636 4444; www.reefhoteleilat. com; s/d 480/670NIS; ❈🅦🅢) Part of the Orchid chain of hotels, the Reef is situated on one of the nicest stretches of sand in Eilat, between Village Beach and Coral Beach. It has good snorkelling, a huge pool decked out with sunbeds, plus a gym and a treatment room for massages. The comfortable rooms, all with balcony, are modern and spacious, offering great value. There's also free bicycle hire and a shuttle bus to and from the town during the daytime.

Arava Hostel   HOSTEL $
(Map p326; ☏08-637 4687; www.a55.co.il; 106 Almogim St; dm/s/d 75/170/185NIS; ❈🅦) Within walking distance of the town centre and marina, this is one of the best budget options in Eilat. The rooms are nothing special – most are quite small with old-fashioned decor and a lack of daylight – but this is a good place to meet other backpackers. It has a pleasant reception and dining area with wi-fi connectivity, plus ample kitchen and laundry facilities (you need to wash that desert sand off your clothes after a while). It also offers Israeli breakfasts, cornflakes or snacks, which cost extra. The front garden has pretty views of the red Jordanian mountains, and the staff can advise on desert trips.

SPNI Field School
Eilat   GUESTHOUSE, CAMPGROUND $
(Map p324; ☏08-637 1127/2021; www.teva.org.il/ english; Coral Beach; campsites per person 50NIS, s/d 220/295NIS) This camping ground, open year-round, is a good choice for budget travellers. Bring your own tent and enjoy the clean bathrooms, barbecue areas and an excellent kibbutz-style cafeteria. If there are no groups staying, the spacious and well-equipped rooms are also superb value.

Orchid   LUXURY HOTEL $$$
(Map p324; ☏08-636 0360; www.orchidhotel.co.il; Coral Beach; d from US$290; ❈🅦🅢) One of the last hotels before the Egyptian border, Orchid is a tranquil, Thai-style retreat with peaceful Buddha statues and water features. Beautifully furnished bungalows cling to the hillside and some of the more expensive units have a loft area that is perfect for families. The tropical pool is dotted with palm trees and there's a Thai restaurant and spa on site.

Herod's Vitalis Spa
LUXURY HOTEL $$$

(off Map p326; ☎08-638 0000; www.herodshotels.com; North Beach; d from 980NIS; ❄️📶🏊) This health and lifestyle retreat is a boutique hotel within a hotel. Part of the opulent Herod's Palace complex, the Vitalis offers an exceptional range of spa treatments, a mineral pool, plush rooms with jacuzzis, a gorgeous roof garden and a restaurant serving 'spa cuisine'. If you can't afford to sleep here, visitors can enjoy a 50-minute massage and an hour in the spa for 310NIS.

Royal Beach
LUXURY HOTEL $$$

(Map p326; ☎08-636 8888; www.isrotel.co.il; Royal Promenade, North Beach; ste from 1000NIS; ❄️📶🏊) You cannot miss this gargantuan hotel complex, which has 363 rooms and purports to be one of the most luxurious in Eilat. Owned by Isrotel, it is housed in a huge modern building, where the floors are layered like steps above the vast glass lobby. It has a tastefully decorated terrace for sunset drinks, designer shops and no fewer than three swimming pools, with waterfalls and underwater tunnels.

Villa Kibel
APARTMENT $

(Map p326; ☎08-637 6911, 050 534 5366; www.villakibel.co.il; 18 Peres St; apt from 180NIS; ❄️) Situated in a quiet suburban neighbourhood, Villa Kibel is a private home divided into a collection of clean, self-catering studios and holiday apartments run by a friendly South African couple. The apartments have separate lounge, kitchen and bathrooms, and there is a shared wooden terrace with sea views. Russell, the owner, will happily pick you up from the bus station or airport if given notice.

Aviv Motel
HOSTEL $

(Map p326; ☎08-637 4660; www.avivhostel.co.il; 126 Ofarim Lane; s/d 220/270NIS; ❄️📶🏊) Aviv Motel (otherwise known as Spring Hostel) is in good, clean condition. All rooms have shower, cable TV and air-conditioning, though some rooms are much smaller than others and the decor is rather bland. The stylish lounge, pool table and outdoor pool take it up a notch.

Rio
BOUTIQUE HOTEL $$

(Map p326; ☎08-630 1111; 9 Ha Temarim Blvd; s/d from 250/400NIS; ❄️📶🏊) A boutique hotel with a bargain price tag does sound too good to be true, but the rooms in Rio have been tastefully designed. The small swimming pool can be crowded in summer and the hotel is located on a busy road, but Rio is a welcome addition to a town that mostly offers high-rise hotels or low-budget hostels.

Astral Village
RESORT $$

(Map p326; ☎08-636 6888; www.astralhotels.co.il; Kamen St; d from 399NIS; ❄️📶🏊) A good midrange choice for families, Astral Village is well placed near the marina, King's City theme park and seafront shops. Accommodation is in 182 bungalow-style rooms. Like the other Astral chain hotels in Eilat, it has a swimming pool for adults and toddlers; definitely not for those seeking peace and tranquillity.

Blue Hotel
HOTEL $

(Map p326; ☎08-632 6601; www.bluehotel.co.il; 123 Ofarim Lane; s/d 255/300NIS; ❄️) Formerly the Hotel Pierre, the Blue is now run by the Reef Diving Group. This unassuming hotel is about 10 minutes' walk from the beach, near the central bus station and offers deals on dives. The 34 small but comfortable rooms all have fridges, phones and cable TV.

Corinne Hostel
HOSTEL $

(Map p326; ☎08-637 1472; www.corinnehostel.com; 127 Retamim St; s/d 140/200NIS; ❄️) Eilat's oldest hostel is an atmospheric place with small wooden bungalows out the back. The double rooms in the main block are in the basement, but they are filled with light, and are cool. Breakfast is not included but guests can use the kitchen. Rooms have cable TV and refrigerators, and there is a good common area for meeting other travellers.

Eilat Guesthouse & Youth Hostel
HOSTEL $$

(Map p326; ☎02-594 5611; www.iyha.org.il; Mitzrayim Rd; dm/s/d 160/330/426NIS; ❄️📶) Undergoing renovations at the time of research, this big, grey concrete building facing the sea has rooms and facilities of the high standard visitors have come to expect from the Israeli Youth Hostel Association. The main problem is that it generally attracts huge groups of schoolkids and not all of the rooms offer Red Sea views.

🍴 Eating

A number of small restaurants, cafes and shwarma stands can be found in the New Tourist Centre, opposite the IMAX theatre, as well as all along the North Beach seafront.

Shibolim
BAKERY $$

(Map p326; Eilot Ave; mains 37NIS; ⏰8am-6pm Sun-Fri) This cute rustic bakery is worth hunting down at breakfast time; it makes a variety of interesting breads and pastries that come with homemade jams, salad and dips. Coffee comes with a sample of its biscuits, and the wooden terrace is a pleasant place to relax.

Agadir Resort
BURGERS $$

(Map p326; Kamen St; mains 59NIS; ⊗noon-3am) Like its main rival on the Israeli hamburger scene, Moses, Agadir is a Tel Aviv import that's doing pretty well in Eilat. A lively restaurant, especially at night, it is located on the marina and serves burgers with all kinds of toppings and has a well-stocked bar.

Cafe Optimi
CAFE $$

(Map p326; 10 Pninat Centre; mains 52NIS; ⊗9am-2am; ☑) A departure from the usual seafood and meat restaurants in town, Optimi is the place to come for omelettes, bowls of muesli and huge salads. There is a variety of vegetarian options, including a mighty goat's cheese, eggplant and peppers sandwich or haloumi and pesto ciabatta.

La Cucina
ITALIAN $$

(Map p326; ☑08-636 8932; Royal Promenade, North Beach; mains 49-80NIS; ⊗7-11pm Sun-Fri, from 1pm Sat) Lovers of Italian elegance should head to La Cucina under the Royal Beach hotel, where waiters wear tuxedos and the ceilings are painted with cherubs and heavenly murals. The food is as tasteful as the decor, with highlights being the wonderfully thin pizzas and fresh pasta dishes. Desserts such as panna cotta and tiramisu are certainly worth saving room for.

TOP CHOICE Ginger Asian Kitchen & Bar
ASIAN $$

(Map p326; www.gingereilat.com; New Tourist Centre, Yotam St; mains from 59NIS; ⊗noon-midnight; ☑) Ginger is still one of the top places to eat out in Eilat and offers some of the best Asian food in Israel. Seekers of sushi will be content with this slick restaurant, with black leather banquettes and a wraparound bar, serving Japanese *gyoza* (dumplings) and Asian-infused cocktails. The spicy dishes span the Far East, from Thai curries to Indonesian noodle dishes and seafood tempura.

Last Refuge
SEAFOOD $$$

(Map p324; ☑08-637 2437/3627; Coral Beach; mains from 89NIS; ⊗1-4.30pm & 6-11.30pm) Yitzhak Rabin, Shimon Peres and just about every notable Israeli has eaten at this seafood institution. The cosy but kitsch atmosphere is created by the over-the-top fishing nets and paintings, but the fish here is some of the best

in Eilat. Try the catch of the day grilled over charcoal or the spicy crab speciality, or tuck into bowls of calamari and shrimps. Unless you fancy a stomach-rumbling wait in the foyer, ring ahead, especially on a Friday night.

Eddie's Hide-A-Way
STEAKHOUSE $$

(Map p326; ☑08-637 1137; 68 Almogim St; mains from 60NIS; ⊗6-11pm Mon-Fri, from 2pm Sat) Hidden in the backstreets behind Almogim and Agmonim Sts, Eddie Hertz is a veteran chef who founded his Hide-A-Way in 1979. The menu takes you on a tour of Italy, France, the USA and China, including no fewer than seven kinds of shrimp dishes, eight spaghetti delicacies and heaps of steak. Vegetarians are not excluded, with an excellent meat-free lasagne on the menu as well as soups. Entrance is off Eilot Ave.

Casa do Brasil
STEAKHOUSE $$$

(Map p326; Hativat Golani Ave; mains 148NIS; ⊗noon-late) Definitely one for carnivores, the premise at this popular new Brazilian grill restaurant is to eat as much meat as you can handle for 148NIS. Diners are given a green and red card: as long as it is green, the waiters will keep bringing you cuts of fine steak. The place is busy most nights, but you can sit on the terrace and enjoy the samba music as you wait for a table.

Drinking

Three Monkeys Pub
PUB

(Map p326; Royal Promenade; ⊗7pm-3am) Not surprisingly, there are three large wooden monkeys outside this pub on the promenade. Usually packed with a mixture of tanned Israelis and sunburnt tourists, this has long been the beating heart of Eilat's nightlife. It regularly has live music and if it is not to your liking, you can always sit out on the sand under the fairy-lit palm trees and sample 12 kinds of beer or sip cocktails.

Joya
BAR

(Map p326; New Tourist Centre; ⊗7pm-3am) An expansive circular bar dominates this late-night joint (formerly Unplugged) usually filled with teenagers and 20-somethings. There is an outdoor tented area with picnic tables and a few beer taps.

TOP CHOICE Village
BAR

(Map p324; Village Beach; ⊗noon-late) This lively seafront bar holds a karaoke-style party with a DJ on Fridays (and sometimes Saturdays) from noon. It serves fast food and snacks.

☆ Entertainment

IMAX Theatre
CINEMA

(Map p326; ☑08-636 1000; www.imaxeilat.co.il; Yotam Rd, admission 49NIS; ☺11am-midnight Sun-Thu, to 5pm Fri, 9pm-1am Sat) Come face to face with a great white shark, aliens or even a T-Rex in this family friendly, air-conditioned pyramid-shaped 3D cinema.

TOP CHOICE Isrotel Theatre
THEATRE

(Map p326; ☑08-638 6701; www.isrotel.co.il; Royal Promenade, North Beach) Adjoined to the sprawling Isrotel Royal Garden Hotel, this theatre houses spectacular dance, skating, special-effect and acrobat shows with extravagant sets and costumes. Advance booking is essential.

HaMoadon
CLUB

(Map p326; ☑08-633 3066; 3 Antibes Rd; admission 60-100NIS; ☺11pm-6am) Formerly called Blanco, this is the most popular club in Eilat and it plays host to a wide range of guest DJs. Located in the King Solomon Hotel; expect laser beams, cocktails and lots of beautiful young people.

View
CLUB

(1 HaMalcha St; admission 60-100NIS; ☺11.30pm-late) Slightly away from the centre of town, it is worth the taxi ride out to the View just for the rooftop bar and dance floor. Packed with locals, it hosts various Israeli and international DJs.

🛍 Shopping

Mall HaYam
MALL

(Map p326; Yotam Rd; ☺9.30am-11pm Sun-Thu, 9am-5pm Fri, 11am-midnight Sat) The main shopping centre in Eilat, Mall HaYam is right on the seafront and encompasses big chain stores and a central food court. The whole of Eilat is a duty-free shopping zone, so if in town be sure to pick up some bargains.

Steimatzky
BOOKS

(Map p326; ☺9am-7pm Sun-Thu, to 2pm Fri) Chain bookstore on the Royal Promenade.

ℹ Information

Emergency

Police station (☑100, 636 2444) Located at the eastern end of Hativat HaNegev Ave.

Tourist police (☺10am-3am Sun-Wed, 10-6am Thu-Sat) This station is near the tourist information office at North Beach.

Yoseftal Hospital (☑08-635 8011; cnr Yotam Rd & Argaman Ave)

Money

To change money, you can head for one of the many exchange bureaux in the old commercial centre off HaTemarim Blvd, the post office in the Red Canyon Centre or the following:

Bank Discount (Shalom Centre)

Bank Leumi (Commercial Centre, HaTemarim Blvd)

Post

Post office (Map p326; Red Canyon Mall; ☺8am-6pm Sun-Thu, to noon Fri)

Tourist Information

SPNI Field School (☑08-637 1127, 637 2021; eilat@spni.org.il) Just across from Coral Beach on the coastal road to Taba; has information on hiking and birdwatching in the area.

Tourist information office (Map p326; ☑08-630 9111; eilatinfo@tourism.gov.il; Bridge House, North Beach Promenade; ☺8.30am-5pm Sun-Thu, 8am-1pm Fri) A helpful place with a plethora of maps and brochures.

ℹ Getting There & Away

The Yitzhak Rabin–Wadi Araba border crossing between Israel and Jordan is about 3km northeast of Eilat. For details on crossing over to Aqaba and getting to Petra, see p28 and p352.

Air

Sound and air pollution were probably not great factors when Eilat's municipal **airport** (Map p324; ☑1 700 705 022) was built, as its runway is right in the heart of the town. However, plans are under way for a new airport in Timna, north of Eilat. When completed (estimated in 2014) it will replace the current civil airports in Eilat and the Ovda air-force base.

Both **Arkia** (☑08-638 4888; www.arkia.com; Red Canyon Mall) and **Israir** (☑1 700 505 777; www.israirairlines.com; Shalom Centre) fly several times daily to Sde Dov and Ben-Gurion

THE NEGEV EILAT

SECURITY ALERT

In August 2011 four squads of terrorists entered Israel from Sinai along a 12km stretch of border-hugging Rte 12, about 10km northwest of Eilat, killing eight Israelis, most of them civilians. At the time of research, areas right along the Egyptian border, including Rte 12, were closed to non-military traffic. Before setting out on a hike (eg to Ein Netafim), consult the SPNI Field School tour guides (p332) about the security situation.

airports in Tel Aviv (from US$81), and to Haifa three times per week (from US$84).

Ovda Airport (1 700 705 022) is about 67km north of the centre of Eilat. It serves occasional charter flights from Europe as well as Arkia and El Al flights, but its distance from town means it's not the most convenient landing post.

Bus

The **central bus station** (Map p326; HaTemarim St) offers services to Tel Aviv (bus 393 or 394, 78NIS, five hours), with buses departing hourly from 5am to 10pm and an additional overnight service at 1am. The last Friday bus is at 3pm and the first Saturday bus is at 11.30am. Bus 392 to Be'er Sheva (57NIS, three hours) stops at Ovda (27NIS, 45 minutes) and Mitzpe Ramon (44NIS, 2½ hours). To Jerusalem (bus 444, 78NIS, 4½ hours) there are four buses per day, which pass through Ein Gedi (47NIS, three hours). On Saturday the first bus departs at 4.30pm.

All buses pass by Timna National Park, Yotvata Hai-Bar Nature Reserve and the Yotvata visitors centre. There are no direct buses from Eilat to Cairo. Bus 15 goes from the central bus station to the Taba border crossing (via Coral Beach).

❶ Getting Around

The town centre is walkable, but you'll need a bus or taxi for locations along the Taba road. The hourly Egged bus 15 connects the central bus station with the Egyptian border at Taba (7.50NIS) from 8am to 9pm Sunday to Thursday, to 3pm Friday and 9am to 7pm Saturday. To reach the Rabin border crossing into Jordan, you'll have to get a taxi (30NIS).

Car

You can rent a car by calling any of the following, all located in the Shalom Centre:

Eldan (☎08-637 4027; www.eldan.co.il) Check online for deals.

Hertz (☎1-700 507 555)

Sixt (☎08-6373511)

Taxi

Eilat's taxis can be an inexpensive and comfortable way to get around, especially when there are two or more of you. Although distances are short, much of the town is on a hill and, worn out by the heat, you could well decide to take a smart Mercedes ride rather than walk. A taxi from the town centre to Taba is around 38NIS.

Around Eilat

Eilat is surrounded by jagged, red-rock mountains created by the tectonic movements of the Great Rift Valley (Syrian–African Rift). The desert environment, blazing with glorious colours (especially at sunrise and sunset), is home to a huge variety of wildlife, flora and fauna.

There are also many archaeological sites in the area which show that ancient peoples managed not only to live in these harsh surroundings but also to thrive – among other things, they helped usher humanity out of the Stone Age and into the Bronze Age by smelting copper. Hikers will want to head for the Eilat Mountains, but be sure to pick up a copy of the 1:50,000 SPNI *Eilat Mountains* topographical hiking map (see p431) at the SPNI Field School in Eilat. Any of the following places are accessible on a 40NIS to 60NIS taxi ride from Eilat.

About 20km north of Eilat on the Arava Rd (Rte 90) hikers can follow the Israel National Trail to the spectacular Shehoret Canyon, which takes around three to four hours to hike. Near the mouth of Shehoret (or 'Black') Canyon lie the impressive Amram Pillars, also along the Israel National Trail, where there's an official camping ground (but no water).

An excellent six- to seven-hour hike will take you through the spectacular Nakhal Gishron (part of the Israel National Trail) from Har Yoash to the Egyptian border. Get an early start and carry at least 3L of water per person.

Further north, the 600m-long Red Canyon can be reached off the highway to Ovda (Rte 12). The canyon, which is just 1m to 3m wide, and 10m to 20m deep, is accessible on foot by way of a 1.5km walking track from the car park. It makes a great 1½-hour hike and involves some climbing.

If you want to travel like Lawrence of Arabia, then Camel Ranch (Map p324; ☎08-637 0022; www.camel-ranch.co.il; Nakhal Shlomo) organises 90-minute (135NIS per person) camel treks from its base. Treks include Bedouin snacks such as *labneh* and pita bread. The ranch is less than 2km inland down Wadi Shlomo from the Eilat–Taba road.

The Gaza Strip قطاع غزة
רצועת עזה

Gaza in Numbers

» 1.65 million –
Total population

» 1.1 million –
Estimated refugees

» 360 sq km – Total area

» 17 years – Average age

» 45% – Unemployed

Gaza at a Glance

» 1516–1917: Ottoman
Empire

» 1917–48: British Mandate

» 1948–67: Egyptian
occupation

» 1967–2005: Israeli
occupation

» 2006–present: Hamas
control

Why Go?

Gaza is not on the 'to-do' list for most travellers – for good reason. Since Hamas took control of the territory in June 2007 after a showdown with rival Fatah, Gaza has been blockaded by land, sea and sky by Israel (Gaza's land border with Egypt was sealed by the Mubarak regime until its fall in 2011). Getting out of Gaza can be even harder, and travellers can be detained on both sides of the border for questioning.

So why go to Gaza at all? Well, in times of safety and peace, a visit to Gaza could be one you won't quickly forget. Beyond the poverty and rubble, you might find traces of an illustrious Mediterranean trading history spanning three millennia.

Today's Gaza is a paradox of extreme poverty and privilege. While the vast majority of Gazans rely on international aid, you'll also see spacious villas, the odd Mercedes and a few luxury hotels. Yet, at just 45km long and 10km wide, Gaza is one of the most densely populated areas in the world.

When to Go

Winters in Gaza are temperate and mild, with only occasional rain. If you're there at the end of July, you can see thousands of children fly colourful kites for the Gaza Kite Festival. The height of the heatwave is through August and September, when many Gazans head to the beach.

The Gaza Strip

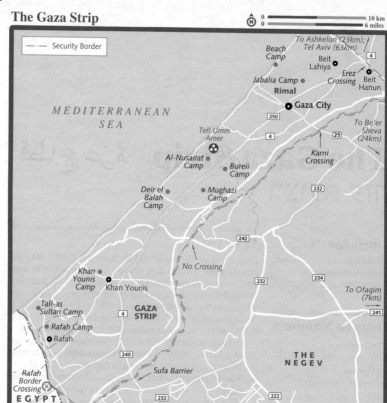

- - - - Security Border

To Ashkelon (23km);
Tel Aviv (63km)

Beach
Camp

Beit
Lahiya

Erez
Crossing

Beit
Hanun

Jabalia Camp

Rimal

MEDITERRANEAN
SEA

Gaza City

250

4

To Be'er
Sheva
(24km)

Tell Umm
Amer

Al-Nusairat
Camp

Bureii
Camp

25

Karni
Crossing

Deir el
Balah
Camp

Mughazi
Camp

232

242

No Crossing

232

234

Khan
Younis
Camp

Khan Younis

To Ofaqim
(7km)

Tall-as
Sultan Camp

GAZA
STRIP

241

THE
NEGEV

Rafah Camp

Rafah

240

Rafah
Border
Crossing

Sufa Barrier

EGYPT

232

232

222

History

COMMERCE AND CONQUERORS

Settlement in Gaza is thought to date back to the Bronze Age, when it was used by the ancient Egyptians as a centre of trade. As far back into antiquity as 1500 BCE, an inscription on the Egyptian Temple of Amun at Karnak noted that Gaza was 'flourishing'. By the time Alexander the Great arrived in 332 BCE, the land had already passed through the hands of the Philistines, the Israelites (under King David and Solomon), the Assyrians and the Persians. In 63 BCE Gaza became part of the Roman province of Judea (later named Syria Palaestina) and was governed by a diverse 500-man senate. In the late 4th century, the Bishop Porphyrius forced Gazans to convert to Christianity and burned down the pagan Temple of Marna to replace it with a church.

Islam arrived in 635 CE, turning churches into mosques, a process that was briefly reversed in 1100 CE by the Crusaders, who built a cathedral that now forms part of the Great Mosque.

During the 14th century, Mamluk rule came to Gaza but the population dwindled due to a deadly plague in the 1340s. In 1516 Ottoman Empire rule began, lasting until the British arrived in 1917.

RECENT EVENTS

During WWI, the British air force under General Edmund Allenby pounded Gaza while taking Palestine from the Turks, reducing much of the city to rubble. Then, in 1927, a huge earthquake finished off much of what was left standing after the war.

Gaza was under British Mandate administration until 1948 when, with the creation of the State of Israel, Palestinian refugees flooded into the area, swelling its population from 35,000 to 170,000 in a matter of months. Egypt immediately responded to the declaration of Israel's independence in

1948 and occupied Gaza. During Egyptian occupation housing projects were expanded but after President Nasser closed the Straits of Tiran in 1967, the Six Day War began and Israel took control of Gaza.

Israeli settlers arrived in the 1970s and growing tensions ignited Palestinian activism and riots. The radical Islamic organisation Hamas was formed in 1987 and the First Intifada began with the throwing of stones and, eventually, hand grenades. A brief period of calm followed the Oslo Peace Accords and, in 1994, the Palestinian Authority (PA) assumed administrative control of Gaza. But talks to transfer permanent control to the PA failed and a Second Intifada began in September 2000, causing a series of Hamas suicide bombings and IAF strikes.

Under international pressure and in a bid to improve Israel's home security, Prime Minister Ariel Sharon ordered Israel's disengagement from Gaza and removed all of the 21 Jewish settlements with their 8000 inhabitants in August 2005. Afterwards, a power struggle within Palestinian ranks began, culminating in the shocking victory of Hamas in the January 2006 PA elections and the withdrawal of much international aid.

In June 2006, Israel Defence Forces (IDF) soldier Gilad Shalit was kidnapped at the Gaza–Israel border. Several days afterwards, Israel launched 'Operation Summer Rains', a series of attacks that killed some 280 Palestinian militants and over 100 Palestinian civilians. In 2007 violent clashes broke out within Palestinian ranks as Hamas took control from Fatah with targeted assassinations and civilian casualties.

Meanwhile, from 2005 to 2008, thousands of Kassam and Grad rockets and mortars were fired on southern Israel from within Gaza, culminating in 87 rockets in just 24 hours on 24 December 2008. In response, Israeli forces launched 'Operation Cast Lead' by air and then by land. The Gaza War resulted in the deaths of 10 Israeli soldiers and three Israeli civilians; in Gaza there were approximately 1400 dead and thousands were made homeless. Many NGOs declared a humanitarian crisis and Israel declared a ceasefire after three weeks of fighting. Rocket attacks from Gaza on southern Israeli cities and towns have continued sporadically since then.

There was further trouble on 31 May 2010, when a flotilla of six ships (three carrying cargo and three filled with activists), heading from Turkey to Gaza, intentionally broke the naval blockade. The flotilla was intercepted by Israeli Navy commandos and, in the course of a violent struggle aboard the Turkish ship *Mavi Marmara,* nine activists were killed, contributing to a serious deterioration in the relations between Israel and Turkey.

In October 2011, after five years and four months in captivity, Israeli soldier Gilad Shalit was released by Hamas in return for

THE GAZA STRIP

TRAVEL WARNING

Following Hamas' armed takeover in 2007, Gaza has remained an unstable place and a source of rocket attacks, bombings and kidnappings. Most countries' foreign ministries advise against all nonessential travel to the Gaza Strip while the political situation remains volatile.

The fragile ceasefire since the end of the Gaza War in January 2009 has been broken numerous times by mortars fired into southern Israel by various Gaza-based Palestinian militant groups and by Israeli air strikes. Raids by the IAF sometimes inadvertently result in civilian casualties; several of the foreigners injured or killed in Gaza during the last decade were victims of Israeli army operations.

The Israeli authorities have made it clear that they will prevent any vessels breaching the naval blockade, so participating in any sort of protest flotilla is not advised. Anyone wishing to send aid to Gaza should do so only through established organisations.

Foreigners of various nationalities have been kidnapped in Gaza with worrying regularity. On 14 April 2011 an Italian activist was kidnapped by radical Islamists and murdered the following day. Following the release of IDF soldier Gilad Shalit in October 2011, there have been reports that extremist Islamist groups are on the lookout for new captives to use as bargaining tools.

If conditions allow, contact trusty locals before your visit to ensure that you've got a guide and someone to pick you up from the Erez Crossing.

Gaza City

Gaza City
0 ——— 400 m
0 ——— 0.2 miles

ment and poverty. In early 2012, Fatah and Hamas agreed to form a unity government, though it is unclear what this means for Gaza's future.

ⓘ Getting There & Away

At the time of writing, access to the Gaza Strip was extremely limited for foreigners due to security reasons. The Erez Crossing is the only potential way for foreigners to enter Gaza from Israel. However, entry is restricted to residents of Gaza, Egyptian nationals and international aid workers (even journalists are restricted, and gates may be shut completely without warning).

In May 2011, following the Arab Spring, the Rafah border with Egypt was reopened, providing a way for Palestinians to travel in and out of Gaza. Under the new Egyptian travel guidelines, Palestinian women, children and men over 40 are no longer required to obtain a visa to enter Egypt. This border is infamous for its arms-smuggling tunnels into Gaza and can also be closed at any time.

Gaza's Yasser Arafat International Airport, which opened in 1998, was closed by the IAF in 2001 during the Second Intifada.

Gaza's single railway line, which used to connect with the Israeli railways, has been out of service since the early 1970s. Train services from Gaza to Cairo, on a line built by the British during WWI, were suspended in 1967.

1,027 Palestinian and Arab prisoners, many of whom were convicted terrorists. The deal gave the Hamas regime, which many Gazans viewed as corrupt, a brief boost. Yet, as the Arab Spring swept through the Middle East, Gaza remained an area of mass unemploy-

Gaza City غزة עזה

◪ 08 / POP 450,000

The exact meaning of the name Gaza has been obscured through time. Some scholars say that it derived from the old Hebrew word for 'stronghold', the ancient Egyptians called it Ghazzat ('the prized city') and Arabs called it 'the treasure'. One of the oldest functioning cities in the world, Gaza has always been considered a treasure for invaders and emperors.

Gaza City is based around the long Omar al-Mukhtar St, which runs north to south from the sea to the main Salah ad-Din St. At the southern end of Omar al-Mukhtar, the town's main focus is Palestine Sq. At the opposite end, the Rimal (Sands) area of town has the swishest houses, the city's beaches and some hotels. Directly to the east of Rimal is the Beach Refugee Camp, also called the Al-Shati Camp.

◉ Sights & Activities

Great Mosque
MOSQUE

(Omar al-Mukhtar St; ⊙closed to non-Muslims Fri) It is said that the Great Mosque was built on the site of the biblical Temple of Dagon, which Sampson pulled down on the Philistines. Subsequently the site has been put to a number of other uses, including as a 5th-century Byzantine church, a 7th-century mosque and a 12th-century Crusader cathedral dedicated to St John the Baptist. Damaged in the British shelling of Gaza in 1917, the mosque was restored in the 1920s and remains one of Gaza's most prominent buildings.

St Porphyrius Church
CHURCH

(Zaytun Quarter, Old City) This Greek Orthodox Church was built in the 5th century by Bishop Porphyrius, though much of the current building dates from the Crusader period and the 19th century. Porphyrius reputedly brought about an end to Graeco-Roman pagan worship in Gaza and ordered the destruction of the Temple of Marna. The church still serves Gaza's Christian community of around 1500 people. If it's locked, you can get the key from the priest who lives above the school opposite the church. Porphyrius himself (who died in 420 CE) is buried in the Byzantine graveyard.

Napoleon's Citadel
FORTRESS

(Daraj Quarter, Old City) This imposing building, also known as the Radwan Fortress and Pasha's Palace, was built by a 13th-century Mamluk sultan for his Gazan wife. In 1799, this was where Napoleon set up camp in Gaza; the Ottoman Empire used it as the governor's house and it served as a police station under the British Mandate. In its most recent incarnation it became a girls' school, though the United Nations Development Programme (UNDP) has restored parts of it as an archaeological museum, housing Hellenistic, Roman and Byzantine artefacts.

Mosque of Said Hashim
MOSQUE

(Yafa St; ⊙closed to non-Muslims Fri) Situated in Gaza's Daraj quarter, the popular Mosque of Said Hashim, off the northern side of Al-Wahida St, was built in 1850. It's famous for the tomb of the Prophet Mohammed's great-grandfather, Hashim, a prominent merchant who died as he was passing through Gaza.

🛌 Sleeping

If you're staying in Gaza, book in advance and ask the hotel to arrange a pick-up service from near the Erez crossing.

Al-Mathaf Hotel
LUXURY HOTEL $$$

(☑285 8444; www.almathaf.ps; Al-Rasheed St; d from US$160; ❋🛏🔊) Al-Mathaf, which means 'the Museum', is a lavish 34-room hotel housed in a complex with an archaeological museum, landscaped gardens and restaurant. Located on the seafront, it is 1km from the city centre, 45km from Rafah and 13km from the Erez border.

⎡TOP⎤ Al-Deira Hotel
⎣CHOICE⎦
HOTEL $$

(☑283 8100; www.aldeira.ps; Al-Rasheed St; s/d US$120/150; ❋@🔊) Undoubtedly the best hotel in town, Al-Deira is a swish, stylish and tightly run place. It is constructed from traditional Gazan red brick and has comfy beds, hot showers and a good sea view from its balconies.

Grand Palace Hotel
HOTEL $$$

(☑284 9498; www.grandpalace.ps; Al-Rasheed St; ste from US$190;❋) Also located on the city's seafront road in the upscale Rimal neighbourhood, the Grand Palace (opened in 2004) has an extravagant entrance hall with chandeliers, modern conference rooms and well-equipped bedrooms. If it is full, the Adam (☑282 3521; www.adamhotelgaza.com; Al-Rasheed St; ❋) and Al Quds International (☑282 3481; Al-Rasheed St; ❋) hotels on the same strip are of a similar price and standard.

🍴 Eating

Aside from felafels, hummus and shwarmas (available from stands all over the city), Gaza has fantastically fresh seafood and heavy meat stews, usually served with rice.

Al Salam Restaurant
SEAFOOD $$

(www.alsalam.150m.com; behind Al-Deira Hotel; mains from 60NIS; ⊙12pm-late) Many locals swear that this family-run restaurant is *the* place for fish and seafood. However, if some fish dishes are temporarily missing from the menu, opt for one of the grilled chicken dishes.

Roots Club
INTERNATIONAL $$$

(✆288 8666; www.rootsclub.ps; Cairo St; mains 70-160NIS; ⊙11am-midnight) Roots is a world away from the poverty found elsewhere in Gaza. Here, VIPs and wealthy businessmen dine on steak *au poivre* and chicken cordon bleu. Spread over four venues, the Roots Club also caters for big events.

❶ Information

There are a few things to see in Gaza City but unsurprisingly there's no tourist office. So your taxi driver, hotel receptionist or host are the best sources of information. Most shops are closed on Fridays, as are mosques to non-Muslim visitors.

Medical Services

Al-Shifa Hospital (Rimal District) Originally a British Army barracks, Al-Shifa is the biggest medical complex in Gaza.

Money

The New Israeli Shekel is the main currency in Gaza, though Egyptian pounds and US dollars may be accepted. It is advisable to arrange currency before arrival.

Websites

UN Relief and Works Agency (www.unrwa. org) Humanitarian programs.

UN Development Programme (www.undp.org) Development programs.

Arab Hotel Association (www.palestinehotels. com) Information on local hotels.

Visit Palestine (www.visitpalestine.ps) Tourist information on Gaza and the West Bank.

Elsewhere in the Gaza Strip

KHAN YOUNIS
خان يونس   חאן יונס
POP 179,900

Once a stopping point on the ancient trade route to Egypt, Khan Younis is primarily a market town and is Gaza's second-largest urban centre. It incorporates the neighbouring Khan Younis refugee camp, home to around 68,000 people. The ruined khan in the square nearby – from which the town got its name – dates back to 1387, and was built by the Mamluks.

The town is 30km south of Gaza City and the only way to get there is by taxi.

TELL UMM AMER
تل ام عمر   תל אום עמר

Located in Al-Nusairat village, 8.5km south of Gaza City, the ruins of this Byzantine site cover around two acres. The site consists of a monastery, church buildings including a chapel, and a hammam. Construction has been attributed to St Hilarion, a young Christian convert from Gaza. A number of beautiful mosaics (thought to date from the 4th and 8th centuries CE) decorate the floors.

To get there, take a taxi from Gaza City, which should cost around 50NIS.

RAFAH
رفح   רפיח
POP 170,000

Rafah is traditionally the gateway between Egypt and the Middle East, but is now infamous for its subterranean network of tunnels – the main route for arms-smuggling into Gaza. According to the United Nations Relief and Work Agency, 99,000 people live in the Rafah and Tall-as-Sultan refugee camps, which are no longer distinguishable from Rafah town. After the Israeli withdrawal in 2005, the Rafah border was monitored by the EU but this ended in 2007, when Hamas took full control. In May 2011 Egypt reopened the border for Palestinians but it can be shut without warning. See p29 for details.

Petra بترا

Best Places to Eat & Drink

» Cave Bar (p351)

» Al-Saraya Restaurant (p350)

» Petra Kitchen (p345)

» Red Cave Restaurant (p351)

» Basin Restaurant (p345)

Best Places to Stay

» Mövenpick Hotel (p349)

» Amra Palace Hotel (p350)

» Petra Palace Hotel (p349)

» Petra Moon Hotel (p349)

» Rocky Mountain Hotel (p350)

Why Go?

It's dawn. The path winds down towards the Siq, the dramatic rift in the land that leads towards the hidden city of Petra. The only sounds are the ringing of hooves on cobblestones as horse carts pass into the narrow gorge. The corridor of stone narrows and the cliffs cast long shadows across the sacred way. At length, the path slithers into sunlight and there, bathed in morning glory, stands the Treasury, a beacon of hope to the ancients and a promise of 'wonderful things' for the modern visitor.

If this sublime experience isn't sufficient inducement to visit Petra, then the spectacle of the 'pink city' tombs at sunset surely will be. Magnificent as they are, however, these dramatic gestures of immortality may prove less memorable than quiet ambles through forgotten tombs, glimpses of outrageously coloured sandstone, or the sense of satisfaction, perched on top of a High Place, of energy well spent.

When to Go
Wadi Musa

Mar–May It's peak tourist season and for good reason, with flowering oleanders and safe hiking.

Mid-Oct–end Nov A last chance to visit Petra in good weather before rains put some routes off-limits.

Dec–Jan Bitterly cold by night and bright blue skies by day, Petra is almost empty in winter.

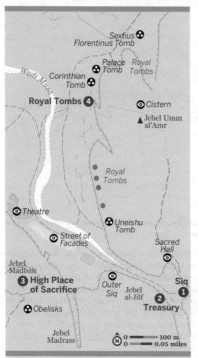

Petra Highlights

❶ Tread the path of history by winding through the **Siq** (p341), the sheer-sided chasm leading to an ancient world

❷ Catch the early morning sun slanting off the pillars of the **Treasury** (p341), the sublime spectacle at the end of the Siq

❸ Climb the processional way to the **High Place of Sacrifice** (p341), pause for tea with the Bedouin and return to the valley floor through a garden of wildflowers

❹ Search the **Royal Tombs** (p341) for spirits, lurking in the rainbow-coloured hollows

❺ Make the pilgrimage to the **Monastery** (p344) and watch the weather-burnished stones catch alight at sunset

❻ Let your soul glide through the Siq's shadows, guided by music and candlelight on tour with **Petra by Night** (p345)

❼ Prepare your own traditional Jordanian supper at **Petra Kitchen** (p345)

❽ Visit **Little Petra** (p352) and enjoy Nabataean tombs and temples in a miniature siq without the company of tour groups

History

Petra was established in the 4th century BCE by the Nabataeans, a nomadic tribe from Arabia. In its heyday, the city was home to around 30,000 people, including scribes and engineers who built a city of sophisticated culture with an emphasis on the afterlife. Around 100 CE, the Romans assumed control, leaving their trademark features such as the colonnaded street.

Earthquakes in 363 and 551 ruined much of Petra and it became a forgotten outpost, known only to local Bedouin who preferred to keep its whereabouts secret. In 1812, a young Swiss explorer, JL Burckhardt, ended Petra's splendid isolation, riding into the city disguised as a Muslim holy man.

During the 1950s, Petra achieved near-mythological statue in Israel and a number of young Israelis risked – and in some cases lost – their lives trying to visit the site surreptitiously.

A Unesco World Heritage Site since 1985, Petra was elected as one of the 'New Seven Wonders of the World' by an international public poll in 2008, proving that its allure has survived two centuries worth of outside scrutiny.

❶ Getting There & Away

It's almost impossible to cover Petra as a day trip from Israel or the West Bank by public transport.

The **Yitzhak Rabin–Wadi Araba border crossing** (☏08-630 0555; ☉6.30am-10pm Sun-Thu, 8am-8pm Fri & Sat) provides the easiest access to Jordan. From Eilat it's a short taxi ride (35NIS) to the border. On the Jordanian side, a taxi to Petra costs around JD50. Alternatively, take a taxi into Aqaba (JD8) and a minibus to Petra (JD5, 2½ hours, 120km); these leave when full between 6.30am and 8.30am, and there is also an occasional afternoon service.

The **Allenby–King Hussein Bridge border crossing** (☏02-548 2600; ☉8am-8pm Sun-Thu, to 2pm Fri & Sat) is handy from Jerusalem (45 minutes), but you must have a pre-arranged visa and it's frustratingly long-winded returning to the Palestinian Territories and Israel through this border. From Jerusalem, a sherut to the border costs around 40NIS. From Amman to Petra, there is a daily JETT (☏962-6-566 4146; www.jett.com.jo, one way/return JD8/16; ☉6.30am, returning at 4pm) bus and regular minibuses (JD5, four hours, 210km); these leave when full from Amman's south bus station between 7am and 4pm. A taxi from Amman costs from JD70 (or JD120 along the spectacular King's Highway).

For details on Jordanian visas and crossing from Israel and the West Bank into Jordan, see p28. For information on the Aqaba–Sinai ferry see p29.

The Ancient City
◎ Sights

There are over 800 registered sites in Petra, including some 500 tombs. From the entrance, a path winds 800m downhill through an area called **Bab as-Siq** (Gateway to the Siq), punctuated with the first signs of ancient Petra.

Beware that Petra is crowned with 'high places' of ancient religious significance. These locations, affording magnificent views, usually involve steep steps to a hilltop where there is no railing or other safety features.

Siq   CANYON
The 1.2km Siq, with its narrow, 200m vertical walls, is technically not a canyon (a gorge carved out by water), but a single block that has been rent apart by tectonic forces. The walk through this magical corridor, as it snakes its way towards the hidden city, is one full of anticipation for the wonders ahead – a fact not lost on the Nabataeans who embellished the processional route with sacred sites. Note the water channels: in some places the 2000-year-old terracotta pipes are still in place. Roman paving was revealed in 1997 after removal of 2m of soil accumulation.

Treasury (Al-Khazneh)   TOMB
Known locally as Al-Khazneh, the Treasury is where most visitors fall in love with Petra. The Hellenistic facade is an astonishing piece of craftsmanship. Although carved out of iron-laden sandstone to serve as a tomb for the Nabataean King Aretas III (c 100 BCE to 200 CE), the Treasury derives its name from the story that an Egyptian pharaoh hid his treasure here (in the facade urn) while pursuing the Israelites. Some locals clearly believed the tale because the 3.5m-high urn is pockmarked by rifle shots. As with all rock-hewn monuments in Petra, the interior is unadorned. The Treasury is at its most photogenic in full sunlight between about 9am and 11am.

Street of Facades   STREET
From the Treasury, the passage broadens into the Outer Siq. Riddling the walls are over 40 tombs and houses built by the Nabataeans in a 'crow step' style reminiscent of Assyrian architecture.

High Place of Sacrifice   VIEWPOINT
The most accessible of Petra's 'High Places', this well-preserved site was built atop Jebel Madbah with drains to channel the blood of sacrificial animals. A flight of steps signposted just before the Theatre leads to the site: turn right at the **obelisks** to reach the sacrificial platform. A donkey to the summit costs JD10 (one way).

Theatre   AMPHITHEATRE
Originally built by the Nabataeans (not the Romans) over 2000 years ago, the Theatre was chiselled out of rock, slicing through many caves and tombs in the process. It was enlarged by the Romans to hold about 8500 (around 30% of the population of Petra). Badly damaged by an earthquake in 363 CE, the Theatre was partially dismantled to build other structures but it remains a Petra highlight.

Royal Tombs   TOMBS
Downhill from the Theatre, the wadi widens to create a larger thoroughfare. To the right, the great massif of Jebel al-Khubtha looms over the valley. Within its west-facing cliffs are burrowed some of the most impressive burial places in Petra, known collectively as the 'Royal Tombs'. They look particularly stunning bathed in the golden light of sunset.

Colonnaded Street   STREET
Downhill from the Theatre, the Colonnaded Street marks Petra's city centre. The street was built in about 106 CE and follows the standard Roman pattern of an east–west

---

FAST FACTS ON JORDAN

Capital Amman

Country code ☎962

Petra area code ☎03

Language Arabic

Money Jordanian dinar (JD); JD1 = 1000 fils; JD1 = US$1.41, E£7.78, 5.28NIS

Visas Most nationalities can get a two-week Jordanian visa free of charge at the Yitzhak Rabin crossing. An exit tax of 101NIS is payable on leaving Israel; it costs JD5 to enter Jordan. The Allenby–King Hussein Bridge border crossing (Israeli exit tax 172NIS) does not issue Jordanian visas.

Petra

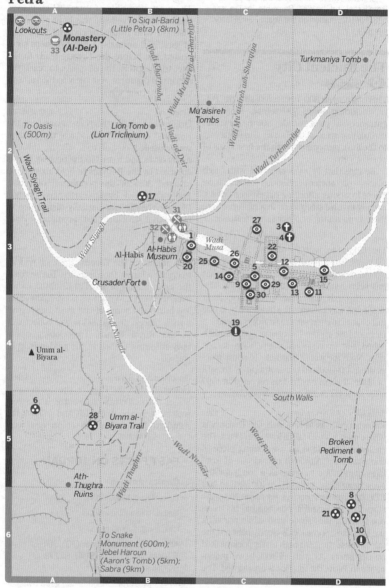

To Siq al-Barid (Little Petra) (8km)

Lookouts

Monastery (Al-Deir) 33

Turkmaniya Tomb

Mu'aisireh Tombs

To Oasis (500m)

Lion Tomb (Lion Triclinium)

Wadi Siyagh Trail

17

31

32

Al-Habis Museum

Al-Habis

Crusader Fort

20

1

25

26

14

9

30

5

29

27

3

4

22

12

15

13

11

Wadi Musa

19

Umm al-Biyara

South Walls

6

28

Umm al-Biyara Trail

Broken Pediment Tomb

Ath-Thughra Ruins

8

21

7

10

To Snake Monument (600m); Jebel Haroun (Aaron's Tomb) (5km); Sabra (9km)

decumanus, but without the normal cardo maximus (north–south axis). Columns of marble-clad sandstone originally lined the 6m-wide carriageway, and covered porticoes gave access to shops.

Qasr al-Bint

TEMPLE

One of the few free-standing structures in Petra, Qasr al-Bint was built in around 30 BCE by the Nabataeans. It was later adapted to the cult of Roman emperors and destroyed around the 3rd century CE. Despite

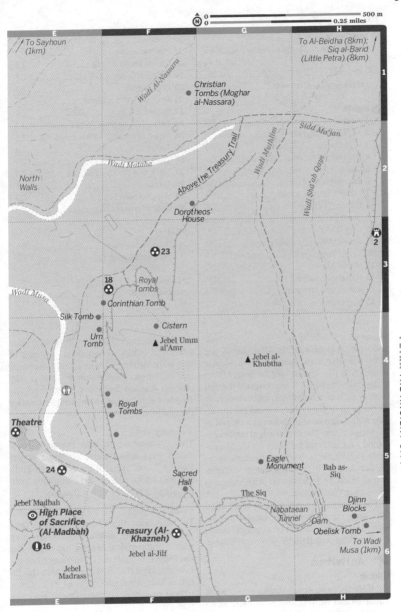

the name given to it by the local Bedouin – Castle of the Pharaoh's Daughter – the temple was originally built as a dedication to Nabataean gods and was one of the most important temples in Petra. It once stood 23m high and its features included marble staircases, imposing columns, a raised platform for worship, and ornate plaster and stone reliefs – examples of which are housed in the modest Nabataean Museum nearby.

Petra

Monastery (Al-Deir)   TOMB
Hidden high in the hills, the Monastery is one of the legendary monuments of Petra. Similar in design to the Treasury but far bigger (50m wide and 45m high), it was built in the 3rd century BCE as a Nabataean tomb. It derives its name from the crosses carved on the inside walls, suggestive of its use as a church in Byzantine times. The cave teashop opposite is a good vantage point for admiring the Monastery's Hellenistic facade – particularly spectacular bathed in mid-afternoon sunlight. A trail leads up to lookouts with stunning views over Wadi Araba.

The ancient rock-cut path of more than 800 steps starts from the Nabataean Museum and follows the old processional route. Donkey rides cost JD10/20 (one way/return).

🏃 Activities

Hiking
Wadi Muthlim to Royal Tombs   HIKING
This 1½-hour canyon hike is an exciting alternative route into Petra if you've already taken the main Siq path. Having a guide is mandatory.

Wadi Farasa   HIKING
Starting from the High Place of Sacrifice, this one-hour hike leads through Wadi Farasa passing magnificent rock formations and wildflower gardens. Features of this walk also include the Lion Monument (an ingenious Nabataean fountain), the elegant Roman Soldier's Tomb and the Garden Triclinium (with unique interior decorations).

Treasury Vista   HIKING
This 1½-hour return hike ascends processional steps about 150m northeast of the Palace Tomb. The stiff climb leads to a hilltop Nabataean cistern and a dramatic lookout about 200m above the Treasury.

Umm al-Biyara   HIKING
The strenuous three-hour hike from Qasr al-Bint to Umm al-Biyara offers stunning mountaintop views. Legend has it that the flat-topped mountain (1178m) was once the Edomite capital of Sela, from where the Judaean king Amaziah (r 796–81 BCE) threw 10,000 prisoners to their deaths over the precipice.

Jebel Haroun   HIKING
This six-hour return hike via Snake Monument starts from Qasr al-Bint. Jebel Haroun (1350m) is thought to be biblical Mt Hor – burial site of Moses' brother Aaron; a white shrine built in the 14th century marks the site.

Horse Riding

It costs from JD30 for a two- to three-hour horse ride around the surrounding hills. Book a ride through a tour agency in town or, for an adventure, ask the animal handlers near the entrance to Petra to take you to their favourite haunt.

Eating

In addition to the two main restaurants below, there are several stalls selling tea, soft drinks and snacks scattered around Petra.

Basin Restaurant INTERNATIONAL **$$**
(lunch buffet JD17, fresh orange juice JD4; ☺11am-4pm; 🅙) Next to the museum, and run by the Crowne Plaza Resort, the excellent buffet sports a healthy selection of salads, fresh felafel and barbecued meats.

Nabataean Tent Restaurant JORDANIAN **$$**
(lunch buffet JD10, drinks JD2; ☺11am-3pm) Similar, with a more modest spread.

ⓘ Information

Ticket Office

The ancient city of Petra is strewn over mountains and wadis, but there's just one main access point by the **Visitor Centre** (📋/fax 03-2156044; ☺6am-4pm, to 6pm in summer – undergoing major reconstruction at the time of research). Although tickets are not sold after 4pm, you can remain in Petra until sunset (5pm in winter). Petra is open every day unless it rains heavily. Sturdy footwear (and a warm coat in winter) is essential.

Entry fees are JD50/55/60 for one-/two-/three-day passes (payable only in Jordanian currency). Multiday tickets are non-transferable. Children under 15 are admitted free. If you are visiting Petra as a day trip from Israel the entry fee is JD90.

An **official guide** (JD50 for 1 to 9 people) is available from the visitor centre to explain the sights between the entrance and the museum. Guided tours are available in English, Spanish, French and Arabic.

ⓘ Getting Around

A return horse ride for the 800m stretch between the main entrance and the start of the Siq is included in your ticket. A tip of JD3 or JD4 is appreciated. Horse carriages, seating two people, travel between the main entrance and the Treasury (2km) for JD25, and to the museum for JD50 per carriage.

Magnificently bedecked camels are available for rides between Qasr al-Bint and the Treasury (about JD15), pausing for a photograph near the Theatre.

Wadi Musa وادي موسى

📋03 / POP 20,000 / ELEV 1150M

The village that has sprung up around Petra is called Wadi Musa (Valley of Moses). The commercial centre of Wadi Musa is Shaheed roundabout, around 3km from the entrance to Petra.

🏃 Activities

A Turkish bath is the perfect way to ease aching muscles after a hard day's sightseeing. The service typically includes steam bath, massage, hot stones and scrubbing. Several hotels offer excellent facilities too. Book in advance; women can request a female attendant.

Petra Turkish Bath BATHHOUSE
(📋03-2157085; JD24; ☺3-10pm) Separate baths with female attendants for women.

Salome Turkish Bath BATHHOUSE
(📋03-2157342; JD24; ☺4pm-10pm) Atmospheric sitting area for relaxing after bathing.

Sella Turkish Bath BATHHOUSE
(📋03-2157170; www.sellahotel.com; JD20; ☺5.30-10pm) Dead Sea products are on sale here.

🥢 Courses

Petra Kitchen COOKERY
(📋03-2155700; www.petrakitchen.com; cookery course per person JD35; 🅙) If you've always wanted to know how to whip up heavenly hummus or bake the perfect baklava, Petra Kitchen, offering nightly cookery courses, is for you. A local chef is on hand to make sure you don't make a camel's ear of the authentic Jordanian dishes. The experience starts at 6.30pm (7.30pm in summer) and the price includes the printed recipes, ingredients and soft drinks.

👉 Tours

Hotels arrange simple day trips around Petra and further afield.

Petra by Night TOUR
(📋03-2154010; www.pntours.com; adult/child under 10 JD12/free; ☺8.30pm Mon, Wed & Thu) This magical candlelit walk through the Siq to the Treasury was introduced in response to numerous requests from visitors wanting to see Petra by moonlight. It starts from Petra Visitor Centre at 8.30pm on Monday, Wednesday and Thursday nights (it doesn't run when it's raining), and lasts two hours.

Petra

WALKING TOUR

Splendid though it is, the Treasury is not the full stop of a visit to Petra that many people may imagine. In some ways, it's just the semicolon – a place to pause after the exertions of the Siq, before exploring the other remarkable sights and wonders just around the corner.

Even if you're on a tight schedule or worried the bus won't wait, try to find another two hours in your itinerary to complete this walking tour. Our illustration shows the key highlights of the route, as you wind through Wadi Musa from the **Siq 1**, pause at the **Treasury 2** and pass the tombs of the broader **Outer Siq 3**. With energy and a stout pair of shoes, climb to the **High Place of Sacrifice 4** for a magnificent eagle's-eye view of Petra. Return to the **Street of Facades 5** and the **Theatre 6**. Climb the steps opposite to the **Urn Tomb 7** and neighbouring **Silk Tomb 8**: these Royal Tombs are particularly magnificent in the golden light of sunset.

Is the thought of all that walking putting you off? Don't let it! There are donkeys to help you with the steep ascents and Bedouin stalls for a reviving herb tea. If you run out of steam, camels are on standby for a ride back to the Treasury.

Treasury
As you watch the sun cut across the facade, notice how it lights up the ladders on either side of Petra's most iconic building. These stone indents were most probably used for scaffolding.

Jebel Madb

Jebel al-Khubtha

To Entrance to Petra

Siq
This narrow cleft in the land forms the sublime approach to the ancient city of Petra. Most people walk through the corridor of stone but horse-carts are available for those who need them.

Down Differently
A superb walk leads from the High Place of Sacrifice, past the Garden Tomb to Petra City Centre.

TOP TIPS

» **Morning Glory** From around 7am in summer and 8am in winter, watch the early morning sun slide down the Treasury facade.

» **Pink City** Stand opposite the Royal Tombs at sunset (around 4pm in winter and 5pm in summer) to learn how Petra earned its nickname.

» **Floral Tribute** Petra's oleanders flower in May.

High Place of Sacrifice

Imagine the ancients treading the stone steps and it'll take your mind off the steep ascent. The hilltop platform was used for incense-burning and libation-pouring in honour of forgotten gods.

Outer Siq

Take time to inspect the tombs just past the Treasury. Some appear to have a basement but, in fact, they show how the floor of the wadi has risen over the centuries.

Street of Facades

Cast an eye at the upper storeys of some of these tombs and you'll see a small aperture. Burying the dead in attics was meant to deter robbers – the plan didn't work.

airs to High Place

5

6

Souvenir shops, teashops & toilets

Wadi Musa

Wadi Musa

To Petra City Centre

7

Jebel Umm al'Amr (1066m)

Royal Tombs

8

Royal Tombs

Head for Heights

For a regal view of Petra, head for the heights above the Royal Tombs, via the staircase.

Urn Tomb

Earning its name from the urn-shaped finial crowning the pediment, this grand edifice with supporting arched vaults was perhaps built for the man represented by the toga-wearing bust in the central aperture.

Silk Tomb

Perhaps Nabataean builders were attracted to Wadi Musa because of the colourful beauty of the raw materials. Nowhere is this more apparent than in the weather-eroded, striated sandstone of the Silk Tomb.

Theatre

Most stone amphitheatres are freestanding, but this one is carved almost entirely from the solid rock. Above the back row are the remains of earlier tombs, their facades sacrificed in the name of entertainment.

PETRA WADI MUSA

Wadi Musa

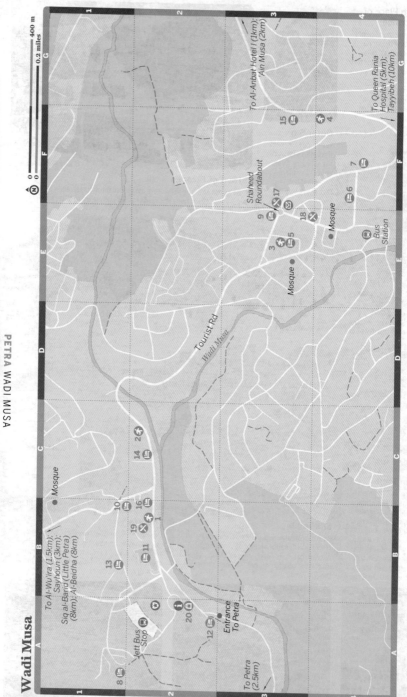

N

0   0.2 miles
0   400 m

To Al-Wu'ira (1.5km);
Sayhoun (3km);
Siq al-Barid (Little Petra)
(8km); Al-Beidha (8km)

Mosque

To Al-Anbat Hotel I (1km);
Ain Musa (2km)

To Queen Rania
Hospital (5km);
Tayyibeh (10km)

Shaheed
Roundabout

Mosque

Mosque

Bus
Station

Tourist Rd

Wadi Musa

Jett Bus Stop

Entrance
To Petra

To Petra
(2.5km)

8

13

10 16
19 1
11

2
14

20

12

3 5
9
17 18

15 4

7
6

At the Treasury, traditional Bedouin music is played and mint tea served. Tickets are available from travel agencies in town, or from Petra Visitor Centre before 5pm.

Petra Moon Tourism Services TOUR
(☑03-2156665; www.petramoon.com) Professional, experienced agency arranging fully supported treks inside and around Petra.

Raami Tours TOUR
(☑/fax 03-2154010; www.raami.tours.com) Based in the Bedouin village of Sayhoun; organises authentic 'Bedouin' treks and home-cooking experiences.

Jordan Travel & Tourism TOUR
(www.jordantours-travel.com) Experienced with international trips to/from Israel, the Palestinian Territories and Syria.

🛏 Sleeping

You can't stay overnight in Petra itself. The prices quoted here are for high-season accommodation with bathroom and breakfast and including taxes.

LOWER WADI MUSA
The following hotels are located within walking distance of the entrance to Petra.

TOP CHOICE **Mövenpick Hotel** HOTEL $$$
(☑03-2157111; www.moevenpick-hotels.com; s/d JD155/170; ❄@🛜⛱🅿) This beautifully craft-ed Arabian-style hotel, 100m from the entrance to Petra, is worth a visit simply to admire the inlaid furniture, marble fountains, wooden screens and brass salvers. A roaring fire welcomes winter residents to the Burckhardt Library (a lounge on the upper floor).

Petra Moon Hotel HOTEL $$
(☑03-2156220; www.petramoonhotel.com; s/d/tr JD60/70/90; ❄@🛜⛱) This newly renovated hotel is a luxurious complex of modern rooms, sumptuous bathrooms, and a rooftop swimming pool with splendid sunset views. Readers' letters indicate it's fast becoming the hotel of choice. Located on the hill behind the Mövenpick Hotel.

Petra Palace Hotel HOTEL $$$
(☑03-2156723; www.petrapalace.com.jo; s/d/tr JD90/120/165; ❄@🛜⛱) An attractive well-established hotel, with palm-tree entrance, big bright foyer and helpful management. The lively bar and restaurant are further drawcards. On the main road in lower Wadi Musa.

Crowne Plaza Resort Hotel HOTEL $$$
(☑03-2156266; www.crowneplaza.com; s/d/tr JD140/170/210; ❄@🛜⛱🅿) A great location (next to the entrance to Petra and overlooking sandstone bluffs) makes this a popular choice, although the rooms are not as luxurious as one might expect for the price.

PETRA WADI MUSA

Wadi Musa

🔵 Activities, Courses & Tours

🔵 Sleeping

🔵 Eating

🔵 Drinking

🔵 Shopping

Petra Guest House

HOTEL $$$

(☑03-2156266; www.crowneplaza.com; s/d/tr JD97/105/130; ❄@☀) You can't get closer to the entrance to Petra without sleeping in a cave – and indeed the hotel's bar (the famous Cave Bar) is located in one. Choose from motel-like chalets or sunny if cramped rooms in the main building.

La Maison

HOTEL $$

(☑03-2156401; www.lamaisonhotel.com.jo; s/d/tr JD70/80/90; ❄) The brass jardinières decorating the foyer set the tone for this good-value hotel with stylish rooms, just uphill from the entrance to Petra.

Silk Road Hotel

HOTEL $$

(☑03-2157222; www.petrasilkroad.com; s/d/tr JD60/70/90; ❄) Hand-painted panels of Bedouin camps stretch across the foyer and restaurant walls of this old favourite, 300m from the entrance to Petra. Ask for a room with a view.

WADI MUSA TOWN CENTRE

The following hotels are near the bus station. Free transport to and from the entrance to Petra is usually offered once a day.

TOP CHOICE Amra Palace Hotel

HOTEL $$

(☑03-2157070; www.amrapalace.com; s/d/tr JD44/72/84; ❄@☀☀) This lovely hotel lives up to its name with a magnificent lobby, marble pillars, giant brass coffeepots and Damascene-style furniture. Most rooms have views across the valley. Services include heated pool, jacuzzi, summer terrace and excellent Turkish bath (JD13 per person). Located downhill from the bus station, with pretty gardens of roses and jasmine, this is undoubtedly one of the best hotels in Wadi Musa.

Rocky Mountain Hotel

HOTEL $

(☑03-2155100; rockymountainhotel@yahoo.com; s/d/tr/q JD25/36/45/56, buffet lunch/dinner JD8; ❄@☀) This delightful hotel has caught the right vibe to make it a successful travellers' lodge. The hotel is 'big on cleanliness' and there's a cosy communal area with free tea and coffee. Located near the junction to Wadi Musa town centre.

Cleopetra Hotel

HOTEL $

(☑03-2157090; www.cleopetrahotel.com; s/d/tr JD20/30/40; ☀) One of the friendliest budget hotels in town, with bright, fresh rooms and communal sitting area. Located uphill from Shaheed Roundabout.

Al-Anbat Hotel I

HOTEL $

(☑03-2156265; www.alanbat.com; s/d/tr JD20/35/45, buffet lunch/dinner JD8; ❄@☀☀) Located some way out of town, on the road between 'Ain Musa and Wadi Musa, this three-storey resort with great views offers midrange quality for budget prices. The same friendly family run the central Al-Anbat III and the budget option next door, Al-Anbat I.

El-Rashid Hotel

HOTEL $

(☑03-2156800; wailln@hotmail.com; s/d/tr from JD20/35/45) This well-run, friendly hotel, off Shaheed Roundabout, has unappealing rooms but an attractive, marble-floored lobby.

✗ Eating

TOP CHOICE Al-Saraya Restaurant

INTERNATIONAL $$$

(☑03-2157111; lunch/dinner JD18/JD22; ❄🖉) Serving a top-notch international buffet in an elegant banquet hall, this fine-dining restaurant offers a quality of dishes that match-

---

FINDING YOUR OWN PACE IN PETRA

Instead of trying to 'see it all' (the quickest way to monument fatigue), make Petra your own by sparing time to amble among unnamed tombs or sip tea at a Bedouin stall.

» **Half Day** (five hours) Stroll through the Siq, savouring the moment of revelation at the Treasury. Climb the steps to the High Place of Sacrifice and take the path through Wadi Farasa, passing a paintbox of rock formations.

» **One Day** (eight hours) Complete the half-day itinerary, but pack a picnic. Visit the Royal Tombs, walk along to Qasr al-Bint and hike the wadi that leads to Jebel Haroun as far as Snake Monument – an ideal perch for a snack and a snooze. Save some energy for the climb to the Monastery, a fitting finale for any Petra visit.

» **Two Days** Spend a second day scrambling through exciting Wadi Muthlim and restore energies over a barbecue at the Basin Restaurant. Sit near the Theatre to watch the Royal Tombs at sunset – the best spectacle in Petra. Reward your efforts with a Turkish bath and a drink in the Cave Bar – the oldest pub in the world.

WALKING TIMES

The following table indicates one-way walking times at a leisurely pace. At a faster pace without stopping, you can hike from Petra Visitor Centre to the Treasury in 20 minutes and the museum in 40 minutes along the main thoroughfare. Don't forget to double the time for the uphill return journey.

DIRECT ROUTE	TIME	DIFFICULTY
Visitor Centre to Siq Entrance	15 minutes	Easy
Siq Entrance to Treasury	20 minutes	Easy
Treasury to Royal Tombs	20 minutes	Easy
Treasury to Obelisk at High Place of Sacrifice	45 minutes	Moderate
Obelisk to Museum (via main thoroughfare)	45 minutes	Easy
Treasury to Museum	30 minutes	Easy
Museum to Monastery	40 minutes	Moderate

es the general opulence of the Mövenpick Hotel in which it's located.

Red Cave Restaurant   JORDANIAN **$$**
(mains from JD5; ☺9am-10pm) Cavernous, cool and friendly, this restaurant specialises in local Bedouin cuisine including *maqlubbeh* (steamed rice with meat). On the main road in lower Wadi Musa, it's deservedly a popular travellers' meeting point.

Oriental Restaurant   JORDANIAN **$$**
(mains JD6; ☺11am-9.30pm) Together with neighbouring **Sandstone Restaurant** (entrees/mains JD2/8), this main street favourite offers simple fare of mixed grills, salad and mezze with pleasant outdoor seating. Located next to Red Cave Restaurant.

Al-Wadi Restaurant   JORDANIAN **$**
(salads JD1, mains JD4-5; ☺7am-late) A lively spot on Shaheed Roundabout offering local Bedouin specialities such as *gallayah* and *mensaf*.

**Cleopatra Restaurant &
Coffee Shop**   JORDANIAN **$$**
(buffet JD6; ☺6am-11pm) Open buffets, with a range of Bedouin specialties off Shaheed Roundabout.

Drinking

TOP
CHOICE ⟩ **Cave Bar**   BAR
(☎03-2156266; beer/cocktails JD6.500/4.500; ☺4pm-11pm; ❄) You can't come to Petra and miss the oldest bar in the world. Occupying a 2000-year-old Nabataean rock tomb, the Cave Bar invites a drink among the spirits, alcoholic or otherwise, and delicious bar food.

Al-Maqa'ad Bar   BAR
(☎03-2157111; ☺6pm-midnight) This Mövenpick hotel bar has a superb Moroccan-style interior: have a cocktail and enjoy the ambience.

Wranglers Pub   PUB
(☎03-2156723; beer JD3-5; ☺2pm-midnight) A simple beer is at its most sociable at the Wranglers Pub run by Petra Palace Hotel and decorated with assorted local memorabilia.

Shopping

The **Wadi Musa Ladies Society** (☺6am-9pm) and the **Society for the Development & Rehabilitation of Rural Women** (☺6am-9pm) both have shops at the visitor centre selling a range of souvenirs, books and crafts.

Made in Jordan   CRAFT
(☎03-2155700; www.madeinjordan.com) This excellent shop sells quality crafts from various local enterprises. Products include olive oil, soap, paper, ceramics, embroidery, nature products, jewellery and camel-hair shawls. The fixed prices reflect the quality and uniqueness of each piece.

Information
Emergency
Main police station (☎03-2156551, emergency 911) In Wadi Musa, adjacent to the Police roundabout.
Tourist police station (☎03-2156441; ☺8am-midnight) Opposite Petra Visitor Centre.

Internet Access
Rum Internet (per hr JD1; ☺10am-midnight)
Seven Wonders Restaurant (per hr JD3.500; ☺9am-11pm)

PETRA WADI MUSA

Medical Services

Queen Rania Hospital High-standard healthcare; open for emergencies without referral. Located 5km from the police roundabout on the road to Tayyibeh.

Wadi Musa Pharmacy Located near the Shaheed roundabout.

Money

The banks on Shaheed roundabout have ATMs. For changing money, banks are open from about 8am to 2pm Sunday to Thursday and (sometimes) 9am to 11am on Friday.

Post

Main post office (⊘8am-5pm Sat-Thu) Located inside a miniplaza on the Shaheed roundabout.

Tourist Information

The best source of information is Petra Visitor Centre. The easiest way to find information about transport is to ask at your hotel or log on to **Jordan Jubilee** (www.jordanjubilee.com).

❶ Getting Around

Wadi Musa bus station is in the town centre, a 10-minute walk uphill from the entrance to Petra. Private (yellow) unmetered taxis shuttle between the two (around JD3).

Siq al-Barid (Little Petra)
(سيق البيضاء) البتراء الصغيرة

Siq al-Barid (Cold Canyon), a resupply post for caravans visiting Petra, is well worth a visit. Nearby camps offer a rural alternative to hotels in Wadi Musa.

◉ Sights

FREE Little Petra Siq   ARCHAEOLOGICAL SITE
(⊘daylight hr) From the car park, an obvious path leads to the 400m-long siq, flanked by a temple, triclinia and the Painted House, reached by some exterior steps and unusual for its interior frescoes. At the end of Siq al-Barid, climb the steps for great views of the wadi beyond.

FREE Al-Beidha   ARCHAEOLOGICAL SITE
(⊘daylight hr) Dating back some 9000 years, these ruins (which require imagination) constitute one of the oldest archaeological sites in the region and pinpoint the transition from hunting to farming.

FREE Al-Wu'ira   CASTLE
(⊘daylight hr) Built by the Crusaders in 1116, the castle was overrun by Muslim forces 73 years later. A bridge leads over the gorge to a gatehouse and the limited ruins.

🛏 Sleeping & Eating

The Rock   CAMP $$
(☑079-777589; www.therockpetra.com; s/d half board in Bedouin tent JD45/JD66) This luxury camp in Ba'ja has a gorgeous location in a wide valley with typical wind-blown rocks for a backdrop. Luxury and goat-hair tents are available.

Ammarin Bedouin Camp   CAMP $$
(☑079-5667771; www.bedouincamp.net; half board per person in tent JD50) A 10-minute walk from Little Petra, this basic camp is hidden in a spectacular amphitheatre of sand and hills. An ethnographic museum spotlights the local Ammarin tribe.

Seven Wonder Bedouin Camp   CAMP $
(☑079-7958641; www.sevenwonderbedouincamp.com; half board per person JD30, B&B JD20; ☑) Relaxed camp, magical at night with open fire and traditional suppers. Accommodation is in simple cabins.

Little Petra Bedouin Camp   CAMP $$
(☑079-5300135,   077-6331431;   www.littlepetrabedouincamp.com; half board per person JD40, minimum 2 people) Secluded complex bringing a touch of urban chic to the rural retreat with beds in army tents.

❶ Getting There & Away

From Wadi Musa, a private taxi costs about JD20 one way or JD30 return, including an hour's waiting time. Alternatively, Little Petra is a pleasant 8km walk following the road.

Sinai (Egypt) سيناء

Best Places to Eat

» Seabride (p363)

» Kitchen (p363)

» Blue House (p363)

Best Places to Stay

» Sawa Camp (boxed text, p357)

» Alaska Camp & Hotel (p362)

» Nakhil Inn (p358)

» Sunrise Lodge (p362)

Why Go?

Rugged and starkly beautiful, Sinai's vast and empty desert heart has managed to capture imaginations throughout the centuries. It has been coveted for both its deep religious significance and its strategic position as a crossroads of empires; prophets and pilgrims, conquerors and exiles have all left their footprints on the sands here.

Today travellers flock to Sinai's seaside resorts, which serve up a medley of sun-drenched holiday fun and offer a springboard to the underwater wonders of the Red Sea. Step away from the buzz of the coast, though, and you'll find Sinai's true soul. Here amid the red-tinged, ragged peaks and endless never-never of sand, the Bedouin continue to preserve their proud traditions while finding ways to cope with the increasing infiltration of modern ways. On a star-studded night, surrounded by the monstrous silhouettes of mountains, you'll realise why Sinai continues to cast a spell over all who visit.

When to Go
Taba

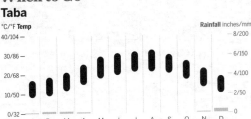

Mar Head into the desert when spring's flurry of life colourfully carpets the sands.

Apr Celebrate all things Sinai at the Dahab Festival.

Oct Shrug off the winter blues by sneaking in some autumn sun along the coast.

Sinai Highlights

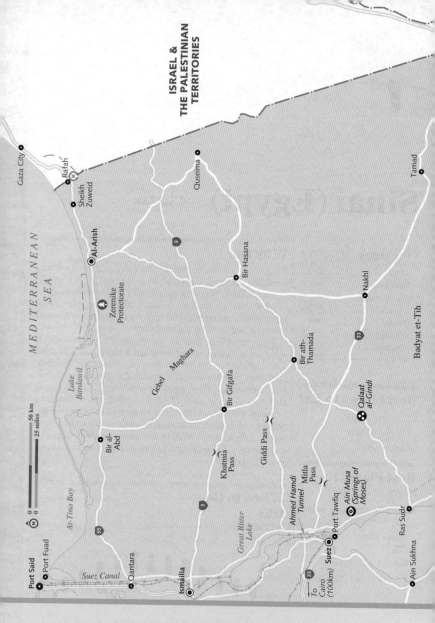

1 Dive in the **Red Sea**, an underwater fantasia of coral mountains and ghostly shipwrecks

2 Follow in the footsteps of prophets and pilgrims along the time-worn Steps of Repentance on **Mt Sinai** (p365)

3 View one of the world's most important collections of early religious art and manuscripts at **St Katherine's Monastery** (p364)

4 Snorkel the Lighthouse Reef then relax with a beer, sheesha (water pipe) and new friends, at a waterfront restaurant in the backpacker vortex of **Dahab** (p359)

5 Escape the crowds to laze on a beach, with a blissful to-do list of nothing,

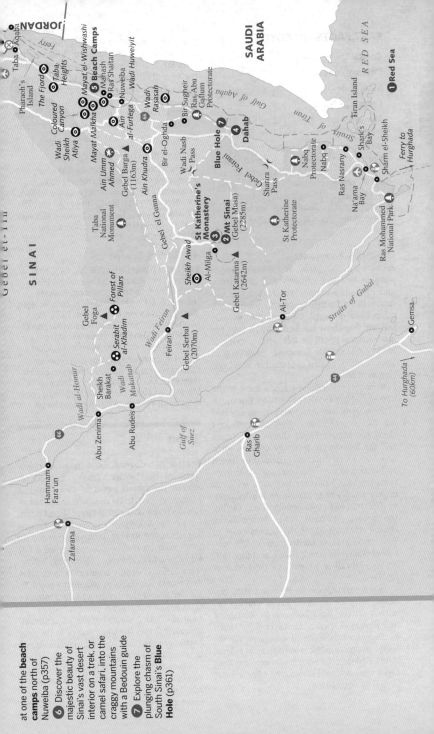

SINAI

JORDAN

Taba ●
Aqaba ●

Pharaoh's Island ●
Taba Heights ○
The Fiord ○
Coloured Canyon ○
Wadi Sheikh Atiya ○

5 Beach Camps

Mayat el-Wishwashi ○
Mahash ●
Ras 'Shaitan ○
Nuweiba ●
Wadi Huweiyit
Mayat Malkha ○
Ain al-Furtega ●
Wadi Rasasah ○
Bir Sugheir ●

6

Ras/Abu Galum Protectorate

7 Blue Hole
4 Dahab

Bir el-Oghda ●
Wadi Nasb Pass
Ain Umm Ahmed ○
Gebel Barga (1163m) ▲
Ain Khudra ○
Gebel el-Gunna
Gebel Feiran

Sharira Pass

Naba Protectorate
Naba ●
Ras Nasrany ●
Na'ama Bay ●
Sharm el-Sheikh ●

Ferry to Hurghada

Shark's Bay ●
Tiran Island
Straits of Tiran

SAUDI ARABIA

RED SEA
Gulf of Aqaba

1 Red Sea

Taba National Monument

St Katherine's Monastery
3
2 Mt Sinai (Gebel Musa) (2285m)

Sheikh Awad
Al-Milga
St Katherine Protectorate
Gebel Katarina (2642m) ▲
Al-Tor ●

Ras Mohammed National Park

Gebel Foga ▲
Forest of Pillars ▲
Serabit al-Khadim ▲

Gebel Serbal (2070m) ▲
Feiran ●
Wadi Feiran

Sheikh Barakat ●
Wadi Mukattab
Abu Zenima ●
Abu Rudeis ●

Wadi al-Homur

Gulf of Suez

Ras Gharib ●

Hammam Fara'un ●

Zafarana ●

Straits of Gubal

Gemsa ●

To Hurghada (60km)

at one of the beach camps north of Nuweiba (p357)

6 Discover the majestic beauty of Sinai's vast desert interior on a trek, or camel safari, into the craggy mountains with a Bedouin guide

7 Explore the plunging chasm of South Sinai's **Blue Hole** (p361)

FAST FACTS ON EGYPT

Capital Cairo

Country code ✆20

Sinai code ✆069

Language Arabic

Money Egyptian pound (E£), E£1 = 100 piastres (pt); US$1 = E£6, €1 = E£7.88

Visas If you are entering Sinai from Israel and only intend to visit the eastern coastal resorts and St Katherine's Monastery, no Egyptian visa is required – you will just need a 14-day pass, which can be issued at the Taba border crossing. For further information, see p29.

Dangers & Annoyances

Because of the Sinai Peninsula's unique position between cultures and continents, and its tourist masses, the region has traditionally had a higher security profile than other parts of Egypt. Over the past decade, the Red Sea coast has been thrust into the international spotlight following a string of high-profile suicide bombings, including at Taba in 2004, Sharm el-Sheikh in 2005 and Dahab in 2006.

Security concerns have again come to the fore since Egypt's 2011 revolution, but much of the activity has occurred far from any Red Sea tourist centre. In August 2011 tensions along the border Egypt shares with Israel and the Palestinian territory of Gaza hit a new high when militants (claimed by Israeli authorities to have crossed into Israel from Gaza through Sinai) carried out a series of deadly attacks near the Israeli border town of Eilat that left eight Israelis dead. During the ensuing gun battle, when Israeli forces chased militants along the border close to Taba, two Egyptian border guards were mistakenly killed by Israeli troops and four others injured (all of whom later died of their injuries).

In a separate issue, in February 2012 two kidnapping incidents aimed at tourists occurred on the road between St Katherine and Sharm el-Sheikh. Hostages were taken by Bedouin tribesmen in a high-profile attempt to pressure the government to release jailed Bedouin. In both instances, the hostages were released unharmed after a short period of negotiation.

Although it is impossible to offer any guarantees regarding the likelihood of future terrorist bombings or kidnappings in Sinai, it is important to remember that the overwhelming majority of travellers to Sinai's Red Sea coast enjoy their visits without incident. That said, it is worth checking your embassy's travel advisory to get an update on the situation before making any plans.

ⓘ Getting There & Away

The Eilat–Taba border is open 24 hours daily and is the only safe and reliable crossing between Israel and Egypt. Israeli departure tax is 103NIS. For information on crossing the border see p29.

There are regular ferry links between Nuweiba on the Sinai coast and Aqaba in Jordan. For details see p29.

ⓘ Getting Around

East Delta Travel Co (✆069-353 0250) has its bus station along the highway about 800m south of the Taba border crossing. Buses to Nuweiba (E£11, one hour) leave at 3pm and 4pm. The 3pm bus carries on to Dahab (E£25, 2½ hours) and Sharm el-Sheikh (E£30, four hours). To Cairo (E£60 to E£80, seven hours) there are two buses every day at 10.30am and 4.30pm.

Taxis and minibuses wait by the border for passengers. Per-person fares are about E£15 to Nuweiba, E£30 to Dahab, E£45 to Sharm el-Sheikh and E£55 to Cairo. Your bargaining power increases if a bus departure is not too far off.

Taba   طابا

✆069

Because of a dispute about the exact placement of the border, Taba – nestled up against the Israeli frontier – was the last portion of Sinai to be returned to Egypt under the terms of the 1979 Egypt–Israel peace treaty. As part of this agreement, Israelis are permitted to visit Taba visa free for up to 48 hours, a provision that sparked a fair bit of hotel development. However, following a series of deadly bomb attacks in 2004 and recent warnings to Israelis to avoid Sinai because of the danger of kidnapping by Gaza-based Palestinian groups, tourism by Israelis – both Jews and Arabs – has virtually ceased. Today the town serves as the only border crossing available for overland travel between Israel and Egypt.

The town centre is home to a couple of banks, a small hospital and various shops. Just inside the border are an ATM and several foreign-exchange booths. Cash and travellers cheques can also be exchanged at the Taba Hilton.

Nuweiba نويبع

🎵 069

Spread out seemingly at random over about 15km of the coast, Nuweiba lacks a defined centre and a cohesive ambience, and functions primarily as a port rather than a travellers' retreat. For a brief period following the Egypt–Israel peace treaty of 1979, a thriving Israeli tourism trade here meant that Nuweiba could claim rivalry to Dahab as Sinai's hippie beach paradise. However, due to the vagaries of the regional political situation, over recent decades Israelis have for the most part shunned Nuweiba. So while Dahab has grown steadily into a low-key resort town, Nuweiba has been left to go to seed. As a result most travellers merely pass through Nuweiba either on their way

to the scenic beach camps further north, or to catch the Aqaba-bound ferry en route to Petra or other places in Jordan.

Although it's perhaps not a tourist destination in itself, some fine sandy beaches, a number of laid-back resorts and backpacker-friendly camps make Nuweiba a pleasant enough place to spend a few days.

🏃 Activities

Snorkelling & Diving

While not as dramatic as those at other resorts on the Gulf of Aqaba, the dive sites here tend to be less busy, with an impressive variety of marine life. There are shallow reefs offshore that are reasonable places to snorkel, but the best snorkelling is the Stone House Reef, just south of town. Listed dive centres offer introductory dives for between €50 and €95, as well as PADI Open Water dive courses for between €275 and €320.

WORTH A TRIP

GO EXPLORE THE OTHER SINAI SHORE

If you're seeking a sandy shore that hasn't succumbed to the restaurant touts and rowdy bar music of the resorts further south, a place where lazing in a hammock is the *de rigeur* activity, then the stunning coastline between Taba and Nuweiba, speckled by simple beach camps, may be for you.

Here are some places to get you started but there are plenty more camps along this stretch if you want to explore. All the camps listed here have restaurants and can help organise desert treks for those who tire of slothing out on the sand. If you don't have your own transport and don't want to hire a taxi, the East Delta buses running between Taba and Nuweiba can drop you anywhere along this shore.

Sawa Camp (☎0111 322 7554; www.sawacamp.com; Mahash area; hut s/d E£50/60) A strip of perfect white beach, hammocks on your hut porch to swing in, solar-powered showers and a restaurant dishing up delicious meals – Sawa is our idea of heaven. Bedouin owner Salama has got all the little touches right. Huts have electricity at night, the communal bathrooms win our award for most spotlessly clean toilets in Egypt, and the service and welcome make you instantly feel at home. Laid-back, family friendly and the perfect de-stress travel stop.

Basata (☎350 0480; www.basata.com; Ras Burgaa area; campsites per person €14, hut s/d €23/42, 3-person chalets €80) Basata ('simplicity' in Arabic) is an ecologically minded settlement that lives by its name – using organically grown produce and recycling its rubbish. There are simple huts sharing facilities, or traditionally designed mud-brick chalets. Self-catering is the norm here, with a communal kitchen and cooking ingredients available to buy. The ambience is very laid-back and family friendly with a New Age twist.

Ayyash Camp (☎0122 760 4668; Ras Shaitan area; hut s/d E£30/60) Located on the rocky point of Ras Shaitan (Satan's Head), Ayyash's stretch of sand is a bit stony and the facilities really are basic. But that doesn't dissuade its fans, who come here to flop out on its hippie vibes and cheap, chilled-out beach-bum living.

Castle Beach (☎0122 739 8495; http://castlebeachsinai.net/home.html; Ras Shaitan area; hut s/d half board E£150/300; ❋) Just north of Ayyash Camp, Castle Beach has more upmarket huts made of palm-thatch and stone on a wide strip of beach.

AWAY FROM THE BEACH – COVER UP!

Once you leave the beach, tourists (including men) should cover up. Traipsing around town in a bikini – or, for the blokes, with beer gut on display – isn't really an acceptable fashion statement in Egypt.

Emperor Divers DIVING
(☑352 0321; www.emperordivers.com; Nuweiba Hilton)

Sinai Dolphin Divers DIVING
(☑350 0879, www.sinaidolphindivers.com; Nakhil Inn, Tarabin)

Camel & Jeep Safaris

With the exception of Dahab, Nuweiba is the best place along the coast to arrange camel or jeep safaris into the interior. All the camps and hotels can organise a custom-designed itinerary for you. See p361 for more information.

🛏 Sleeping

Unfortunately the lack of business in recent years has contributed to a lackadaisical attitude to both beach cleaning and camp repairs; a shame, because if Nuweiba was spruced up a little it could easily be the mellow beach-camp paradise that Dahab was a decade ago.

The camps and hotels listed here all keep their patch of sand clean and are good choices for those seeking a more serene scene than Dahab offers.

TOP CHOICE Nakhil Inn INN $
(☑350 0879; www.nakhil-inn.com; Tarabin; s/d US$46/56; ❇🛜) The friendly Nakhil is a cosy compromise for those who want hotel comforts without the crowds. Local textiles and stained wood have been used in abundance throughout the communal areas, while the charming studio-style wooden cabins exude simple beach-chic. Guests can snorkel the reef just a few metres from the shore, go kayaking or diving, or simply unwind while lazing about in one of the hammocks or shaded seating spots strewn across the private beach. Rates include breakfast.

Petra Camp BEACH CAMP $
(☑350 0855; www.petra-camp.com; Tarabin; hut s/d E£40/80) One of the nicest camps in Tarabin. Huts are simple but well cared for and most come with air-con. The communal bathrooms are clean, and the restaurant serves up a decent selection of Egyptian and international favourites.

Big Dune BEACH CAMP $
(☑0100 610 8731; Nuweiba City; hut E£25) Chilled out to the max, Big Dune is reminiscent of the hippie beach camps of old. Although bare-bones basic, it's the setting that's the drawcard here, with the huts scattered across a wide sweep of golden sand.

Saraya Beach BEACH CAMP $
(☑0109 198 7803; Tarabin; hut/r E£30/80) This well-looked-after Tarabin camp has a wide variety of accommodation ranging from rustic wooden huts with fan through to more expensive air-con rooms (E£100).

Al-Badawi BEACH CAMP $
(☑0122 731 1455; Tarabin; s/d E£60/130, without bathroom E£40/80; ❇) Spartan but spotless rooms in a well-cared-for garden slap in the middle of the Tarabin scene. Management really endeavour to keep everything spick and span and are a friendly bunch.

Helnan Nuweiba RESORT $$$
(☑350 0401; www.helnan.com; Nuweiba City; s/d US$125/160; ❇❇) Although lacking in character, the newly renovated cottages here are comfortable and modern, and the private beach and pool area is attractive. Breakfast included.

🍴 Eating

At the port there is a cluster of fuul (fava bean paste) and ta'amiyya (mashed, deep-fried fava beans; Egyptian variant of felafel) places in the area behind the National Bank of Egypt and before the ticket office for Aqaba ferries.

Cleopatra Restaurant SEAFOOD $
(Nuweiba City; dishes E£20-50) One of the more popular tourist restaurants in Nuweiba City, Cleopatra offers up the bounty of the sea along with a few Western fast-food favourites.

Han Kang ASIAN $
(Nuweiba City; dishes E£20-40) This surprisingly good Chinese restaurant hits the spot, especially if you've been on the road for a while and can't bear to look at another felafel sandwich.

Dr Shishkebab KEBAB $
(Bazaar, Nuweiba City; dishes E£10-30) The place
to head to for filling and tasty kebab meals.

ⓘ Information

Nuweiba is divided into three parts: to the south
is the port, with a bus station, banks and a couple of scruffy hotels; about 8km further north is
Nuweiba City, a small but spread-out settlement
with a small bazaar and several cheap places
to eat; and about a 10-minute walk north along
the beach is the strip of sand lined with beach
camps known as Tarabin.

Emergency
Tourist police (☑350 0231; Nuweiba City;
⊙24hr) Near Helnan Nuweiba Hotel.

Internet Access
Al-Mostakbal Internet Café (Nuweiba City;
per hr E£4; ⊙9am-3am)

Medical Services
Nuweiba Hospital (☑350 0302; Nuweiba City;
⊙24hr)

Money
Banque du Caire (Nuweiba Port; ⊙9am-2pm
Sun-Thu) ATM.
Banque Misr (Nuweiba Port; ⊙8.30am-2pm
Sun-Thu) ATM.

Post
Post office (Nuweiba Port)

ⓘ Getting There & Away

Boat
See p29 for details on the Nuweiba–Aqaba ferry.

Bus
East Delta Travel Co (☑352 0371; Nuweiba
Port) buses depart for Cairo at 9am and 3pm
(E£60 to E£100, seven to eight hours), going
via Taba (E£15); there is also a noon service
to Taba only. Buses to Sharm el-Sheikh (E£25,
three to four hours) via Dahab (E£15, one hour)
leave at 6.30am and 4pm. There are no public
bus services to St Katherine but local transport
initiative **Bedouin Bus** (☑0101 668 4274; www.
bedouinbus.com) runs transport between
Nuweiba and St Katherine every Wednesday
and Sunday (E£50). Check its website for up-
to-date details.

Taxi
Taxis hang out by the port. A taxi to Dahab costs
about E£150 and roughly E£100 to the beach
camps on the Nuweiba–Taba road.
   Expect to pay E£10 to E£20 for a taxi from the
port/bus station to Nuweiba City.

Ras Abu Gallum Protectorate راس ابو جلوم

The starkly beautiful Ras Abu Gallum Protectorate covers 400 sq km of coastline between Nuweiba and Dahab, mixing high
coastal mountains, narrow valleys, sand
dunes and fine gravel beaches with several
excellent diving and snorkelling sites.

There is a designated camping area and
several walking trails in the protectorate,
and you can hire Bedouin guides and camels through the ranger house at the edge of
Wadi Rasasah. While still beautiful, the area
has become an extremely popular destination, overflowing at times with day trippers
from Sharm el-Sheikh and Dahab.

The most popular destinations within the
protectorate include Bir el-Oghda, a now-
deserted Bedouin village, and Bir Sugheir, a
water source at the edge of the protectorate.

Dive centres and travel agencies in
Nuweiba and Dahab offer excursions to
Abu Gallum. The protectorate can also be
reached by hiking in from north of the Blue
Hole near Dahab.

Dahab دهب
☑069

Low-key, laid-back and low-rise, Dahab continues its evolution into the Middle East's
prime beach resort for independent travellers. Meaning gold in Arabic, a reference to
the area's sandy coastline (despite the main
tourist area having no golden sands to speak
of), Dahab is the perfect base from which
to explore some of Egypt's most spectacular
diving and snorkelling.

This is the one town on the South Sinai
Peninsula where independent travellers are
the rule rather than the exception, and Dahab's growth has not destroyed its budget
traveller roots. Reeled in by a fusion of hippie mellowness and resort chic (where good
cappuccino and sushi are as much a part
of the action as cheap rooms and herds of
goats fossicking in the back alleys), many
travellers plan a few nights here and instead
stay for weeks. If Dahab is in your sights,
be forewarned – after a few days of crystal-
clear diving, desert trekking, oceanside dinners and countless sheesha (water pipe) sessions, you might want to cancel the rest of
your itinerary.

Dahab

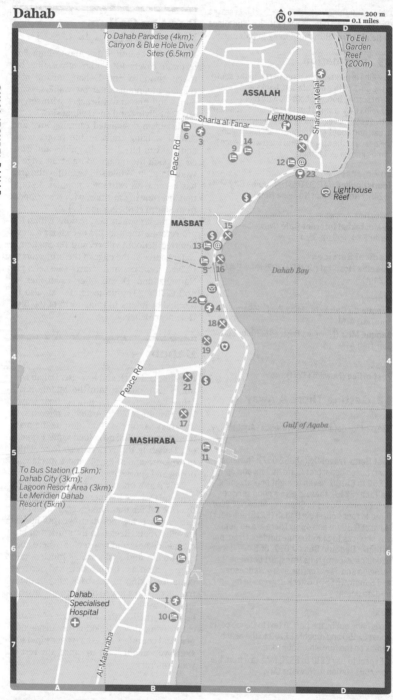

SINAI (EGYPT) DAHAB

N
0   200 m
0   0.1 miles

To Dahab Paradise (4km);
Canyon & Blue Hole Dive
Sites (6.5km)

To Eel
Garden
Reef
(200m)

ASSALAH

Sharia al-Melal

Sharia al-Fanar

Lighthouse

MASBAT

Dahab Bay

Lighthouse
Reef

Gulf of Aqaba

MASHRABA

To Bus Station (1.5km);
Dahab City (3km);
Lagoon Resort Area (3km);
Le Meridien Dahab
Resort (5km)

Peace Rd

Al-Mashraba

Dahab
Specialised
Hospital

Dahab

Sights & Activities

There are two parts to Dahab: the small and newer area of Dahab City to the south, with a smattering of resort hotels at the lagoon, the bus station, post office and a bank; and Assalah, which runs along the beach and is the major tourist stretch. Assalah is further divided into three areas. The northernmost point, and the main local residential area, is still known as Assalah. From the lighthouse the Masbat area begins, made up of a stretch of 'camps', hotels and laid-back restaurants that curve along the bay. To the south, starting roughly at the ruins (no entry) is the slightly more staid Mashraba.

There's no beach to speak of in Assalah itself – instead the rocky coastline leads straight out onto the reef. For the golden sands after which Dahab was named, you'll need to head to the lagoon resorts. Most offer beach use day access starting from E£50, and you can hire pedalos and kayaks as well as take windsurfing and kitesurfing courses.

All the travel agencies and hotels can arrange overnight trips to Mt Sinai and St Katherine's Monastery.

Desert Riders
QUAD BIKING

(📞0111 515 4411; Sharia al-Fanar) Most tours do a loop circuit from town taking in one of either Wadi al-Rayan or Wadi Connexion and the lagoon. A two-hour tour, including helmet, costs E£120.

Blue Beach Club
HORSE RIDING

(📞364 0411; www.bluebeachclub.com; Assalah) This professional-standard stable runs highly recommended hacks and treks. Rates start at about E£100 per hour.

Snorkelling & Diving

Other than just lounging around, snorkelling and diving are the most popular activities in Dahab. The best reefs for snorkelling are Lighthouse Reef and Eel Garden, both in Assalah.

The most popular diving sites are Canyon, Bells and Blue Hole, Islands and Umm Sid. Note that despite the intimidating reputation of the Canyon and Blue Hole dive sites as danger zones for careless divers, the tops of the reefs are teeming with life, making them fine snorkelling destinations too when the sea is calm. Many dive centres also organise snorkelling and dive safaris to the nearby Ras Abu Gallum Protectorate.

Red Sea Relax Dive Centre
DIVING

(📞364 1309; www.red-sea-relax.com; Red Sea Relax, Masbat)

Poseidon Divers
DIVING

(📞364 0091; www.poseidondivers.com; Crazy Camel Camp, Mashraba)

Big Blue Dive Centre
DIVING

(📞364 0045; www.bigbluedahab; Mashraba)

Camel & Jeep Safaris

Dahab is one of the best places in Sinai to arrange camel safaris into the dramatic mountains lining the coast, especially the spectacular Ras Abu Gallum Protectorate. Itineraries – and prices – are generally custom designed, but expect to pay around

E£200 per person for an evening trip into the mountains with dinner at a Bedouin camp, and from about E£300 to E£400 per person per day for a safari, including all food and water.

One of the most popular 4WD safaris is a trip to Coloured Canyon, to the northeast of Nuweiba. The canyon derives its name from the layers of bright, multicoloured stones that resemble paintings on its steep, narrow walls, and is magnificently beautiful. As the canyon is sheltered from the wind, the silence – assuming you aren't there with a crowd – is one of its most impressive features.

Other popular destinations are Ain al-Furtega, a palm-filled oasis 16km northwest of Nuweiba; and Mayat el-Wishwashi, a large cistern hidden between two boulders in a canyon.

All of the hotels, dive centres and travel agencies offer 4WD safaris, though prices vary considerably depending on the time of year, your destination and the size of your party – don't be afraid to shop around and bargain hard.

✷ Festivals & Events

The Dahab Festival (www.dahabfestival.info) takes place every April for one week, combining water sport competitions, Bedouin cultural activities, live bands and beach parties.

🛏 Sleeping

Increased competition has raised the bar in town and there are some excellent rooms to be had for the price of a decent meal back home. Assalah boasts bedding-down options ranging from cell-like cement huts to attractive backpacker palaces with cushioned seating shaded by palm groves, as well as a good mix of more midrange resorts that are still small enough for guests to catch the mellow Dahab vibe. Luxury accommodation is available at the lagoon area.

TOP CHOICE Alaska Camp & Hotel   HOSTEL $

(☑364 1004; www.dahabescape.com; Masbat; r with/without air-con E£200/100; ❋🖵) Easy on the wallet without sacrificing the small comforts, Alaska has a variety of spacious, bright and sparkling-clean rooms with super-comfortable beds. The attractive courtyard garden is a welcoming shady spot to relax and meet other travellers and the central

location means you're just a couple of steps from the Promenade bustle.

TOP CHOICE Sunrise Lodge   GUESTHOUSE $

(☑0109 057 4242; www.sunrisedahab.com; Masbat; r E£120; ❋🖵) Tucked away down a sandy alley just off the Promenade, this welcoming home from home has just five large, spotless rooms (one fan-only room is a cheaper E£80) set around a sandy courtyard shaded by palm trees. There's free tea and coffee, hammocks and a cushion area to lounge in and a small play area for children, and management provides a highly personalised service and can help with any query.

Dahab Paradise   RESORT $

(☑0100 700 4133; www.dahabparadise.com; s/d US$58/68; ❋🖵🏊) This low-key resort on a secluded sweep of bay is the perfect place to get away from it all. Decorated in warm earthy tones with accents of antique wood thrown in for good measure, the charming rooms are a touch of understated beach-chic elegance. It's on the main road to Blue Hole. Rates include breakfast.

Red Sea Relax   HOTEL $

(☑364 1309; www.red-sea-relax.com; Masbat; dm/s/d €8/37/46; ❋@🏊) With rooms wrapped around a glistening pool, Red Sea Relax dishes up a winning formula of resort-like facilities for bargain prices. It's a well-organised set-up with free water fill-ups, a beckoning rooftop bar and an excellent dive centre. Cheap dormitory accommodation means you get all the resort facilities for backpacker costs. Breakfast included.

Seven Heaven Hotel   HOSTEL $

(☑364 0080; www.7heavenhotel.com; Masbat; dm E£20, r with/without air-con E£80/60, without bathroom E£30; ❋🖵) An all-in-one stalwart of the Dahab scene that still offers one of the best-value shoestringer deals in town. The huge range of rooms go up in price as you add extras, and the six-bed dorms that come with air-con and bathroom are a bargain.

Alf Leila   B&B $

(☑364 0595; www.alfleila.com; cnr Peace Rd & Sharia al-Fanar, Masbat; s/d €30/36; ❋🖵) Alf Leila's seven rooms are a daydream of gorgeous tile-work and traditional textiles decorated using lashings of muted earthy colours, stone and wood. The location (on the main road) isn't the best but if you don't mind a walk to the beach, for its sheer uniqueness this place is still worth it.

Le Meridien Dahab Resort
RESORT $$

(☑364 0425; www.lemeridien.com/dahab; Dahab City; s/d/ste from US$125/150/175; ❋☎❄) By far the best of the lagoon resorts, Le Meridien spills over a series of terraces that flow down to a sweep of white sand. This is where to come if you want your Dahab experience served up with oodles of five-star service and comfort. Rates include breakfast.

Dahab Coach House
GUESTHOUSE $

(☑364 1027; www.dahabcoachhouse.dk; Masbat; s/d €38/40; ❋☎) What this place lacks in midrange resort facilities, it more than makes up for with hugely helpful management and a genuine welcoming feel. The rooms are simple but comfortable, and the courtyard is the perfect place to chill out after a long day's diving. Breakfast included.

Nesima Resort
RESORT $

(☑364 0320; www.nesima-resort.com; Mashraba; s/d/ste €47/61/84; ❋☎❄) A lovely compromise if you want resort living without being isolated from town. Set amid a mature garden of blooming bougainvillea, Nesima's cosy cottages have pleasing stone and wood overtones, domed ceilings and dinky terraces. Rates include breakfast.

Ghazala Hotel
HOTEL $

(☑364 2414; www.ghazaladahab.com; Mashraba; s/d E£100/140; ❋☎) Ghazala's cute white-domed rooms surround a narrow courtyard set with colourful mosaic tiles. Some are larger than others, so ask to see a few before you decide. There are a couple of cheaper fan-only rooms as well.

Christina Beach Palace & Christina Pool
HOTEL $

(☑364 0390; www.christinahotels.com; Mashraba; s/d with air-con US$62/83, without air-con US$55/76; ❋☎❄) This small Swiss-run hotel offers a degree of efficiency unmatched in town. Depending on your preference, Beach Palace rooms have lovely sea views, while the recently renovated poolside ones are more luxurious. Breakfast included.

Bishbishi Garden Village
HOSTEL $

(☑364 0727; www.bishbishi.com; Sharia al-Mashraba; s/d without bathroom €5/8; ☎) Classic of the Dahab camp scene, Bishbishi continues to offer a winning mix of easy-on-the-wallet rooms and lots of shaded communal areas for socialising.

✗ Eating

The waterfront is lined with Bedouin-style restaurants where you can relax on cushions while gazing out over the sparkling waters of the Gulf of Aqaba. Unfortunately places serving up quality Egyptian cuisine are thin on the ground, but seafood is on almost all menus, together with a good selection of international dishes.

TOP CHOICE Seabride Restaurant
SEAFOOD $$

(Mashraba; meals E£40-60) Away from the shorefront, this is the locals' favourite haunt for seafood, serving up startling good value. All meals come loaded with fish soup, rice, salad, *baba ghanoug* (purée of grilled aubergines), a delectably tangy tahina and bread. Choose your fish fresh from either the display or from the menu.

Kitchen
INTERNATIONAL $$$

(Masbat; mains E£60-95) With a menu offering a choice of Indian, Chinese, Thai and Japanese and superb service, this is as close as Dahab gets to fine dining. The Indian is the real standout here, with delicious Madras and biriyani dishes, while the sushi plates are as good as any you'll get in Egypt.

Blue House
THAI $$

(Masbat; mains E£35-60) An inspiring selection of authentic Thai cuisine keeps this breezy upstairs terrace packed with diners. Tuck into the flavour-filled curries or the zingy papaya salad and you'll understand why this place has so many fans.

Ali Baba
INTERNATIONAL $$

(Masbat; mains E£30-80) One of the most popular restaurants along the waterfront strip for good reason; this place adds flair to its seafood selection with some inspired menu choices. Great service, comfy sofas to lounge on, stylish lanterns and twinkly fairy lights add to the relaxed seaside ambience.

Fighting Kangaroo
EGYPTIAN $

(Masbat; meals E£15-20) Despite the unfortunate name this narrow waterfront restaurant should be commended for serving up Egyptian-style feasts at bargain-basement prices. Simple and hearty meals (pick from fish, *kofta*, chicken or vegetarian) all come with soup, salad and tahini.

Ralph's German Bakery
BAKERY $

(Sharia al-Fanar, Masbat; sandwiches E£18-25, pastries E£4-15; ⏰7am-6pm) Singlehandedly raising the bar for coffee in Dahab, this place is caffeine heaven and also serves up a range of particularly tempting calorific pastries and excellent sandwiches. There's a second branch at Masbat's Ghazala Supermarket courtyard.

King Chicken
EGYPTIAN **$**

(Sharia al-Mashraba; dishes E£15-25) Always crowded with locals, this cheap and cheerful little place hits the spot for budget chicken-dinner heaven.

Drinking

Most travellers are content with simply sprawling out in any of Dahab's waterfront restaurants and nursing a few cold Stellas after a long day of diving or desert adventure.

Lavazza Cafe
CAFE

(Masbat; coffees E£10-15) Excellent cappuccino and decent espresso make this cafe a good stop for your morning caffeine fix.

Yalla Bar
BAR

(Masbat; beers E£10-12) This popular waterfront bar and restaurant has a winning formula of friendly staff and excellent happy-hour beer prices from 5pm to 9pm.

Information

Emergency

Police (☑364 0213/5; Mashraba) At the main junction near Ghazala Supermarket.

Internet Access

Aladdin Bookstore & Internet (Masbat, per hr E£5)

Seven Heaven Internet Cafe (Seven Heaven Hotel, Masbat; per hr E£5; ⏲24hr)

Medical Services

Dahab Specialised Hospital (☑364 2714; Mashraba) An excellent private hospital with full hyperbaric chamber facilities.

Dr Haikal (☑0100 143 3325; Dahab City) Local doctor whose surgery also has a hyperbaric chamber. At the lagoon.

Money

Banque du Caire (Sharia al-Mashraba; ⏲9am-2pm & 6-9pm Sat-Thu, 9-11am & 6-9pm Fri) ATM. Also in Masbat, near the bridge.

National Bank of Egypt (Sharia al-Mashraba; ⏲9am-2.30pm & 6-8pm Sun-Thu) ATM; another in Masbat, near the bridge.

Post

Main post office (Dahab City; ⏲8.30am-2.30pm)

Getting There & Away

Bus

From the bus station in Dahab City, well south-west of the centre of the action, **East Delta Travel Co** (☑364 1808) has one bus a day heading north at 10.30am to Nuweiba (E£15, one hour) before continuing on to Taba (E£35, two hours). There is a 5.30pm bus to Sharm el-Sheikh (E£15 to E£20, two hours) but all the following listed buses also stop there. Buses to Cairo (E£90, nine hours) leave at 9am, 12.30pm, 3pm and 10pm. There is also a non-air-con service at 7.30pm (E£65). For Hurghada (E£105, 10 hours) and Luxor (E130, 18 hours) there is one bus daily at 4pm.

There are no public buses to St Katherine but local transport initiative **Bedouin Bus** (☑0101 668 4274; www.bedouinbus.com) runs transport between Dahab and St Katherine every Tuesday and Friday (E£50, two hours). Check the website for up-to-date details.

Taxi

Pick-ups charge E£10 between the bus station and Assalah. The standard charge for a taxi to St Katherine is E£250.

St Katherine's Monastery & Mt Sinai

دير سانت كاترين وجبل موسى

⏲069

Sinai's rugged interior is a vast land of barren mountains and wind-sculpted canyons. Against this desolate backdrop some of the most sacred events in recorded human history took place, immortalising Sinai in the annals of Judaism, Christianity and Islam.

◉ Sights

St Katherine's Monastery
MONASTERY

(www.sinaimonastery.com; admission free; ⏲9am-noon Mon-Thu & Sat, except religious holidays) This ancient monastery traces its founding to about 330 CE, when the Roman empress Helena had a small chapel built beside what was believed to be the burning bush from which God spoke to Moses. In the 6th century CE Emperor Justinian ordered a fortress to be constructed around the original chapel, together with a basilica and a monastery, to provide a secure home for the monastic community that had grown here, and as a refuge for the Christians of southern Sinai. Since then the monastery has been visited by pilgrims from throughout the world, many of whom braved extraordinarily difficult and dangerous journeys to reach the remote and isolated site. Today St Katherine's is considered one of the oldest continually functioning monastic communities in the world, and its chapel is one of early Christianity's only surviving churches.

Although much of the monastery is closed to the public, it is possible to enter the ornately decorated 6th-century Church of the Transfiguration, with its nave flanked by massive marble columns and walls covered in richly gilded icons and paintings. High in the apse above the altar is the mosaic of the transfiguration, one of the monastery's most stunning artistic treasures. It's also possible to see what is thought to be a descendant of the original burning bush in the monastery compound.

Don't miss the superb monastery museum (adult/student E£10/25), which has displays of many of the monastery's artistic treasures, including some of the spectacular manuscripts and Byzantine-era icons from its world-famous collection, numerous precious chalices and gold and silver crosses.

When you visit, remember that this is still a functioning monastery, which necessitates conservative dress – no one with shorts is permitted to enter, and women must be sure to cover their shoulders.

Mt Sinai
MOUNTAIN

(guide E£125, camel ride one-way E£125) Known locally as Gebel Musa, Mt Sinai is revered by Christians and Muslims, who believe that God delivered the Ten Commandments to Moses (Musa in Arabic) at its summit. (Judaism does not associate the giving of the Ten Commandments with a particular known location.) The mountain is easy and beautiful to climb, and although you may be overwhelmed by crowds of other visitors, it offers a taste of the magnificence of southern Sinai's high mountain region. For those visiting as part of a pilgrimage, it also offers a moving glimpse into biblical times. All hikers must be accompanied by a guide (hired from the monastery car park), which helps provide work for the local Bedouin.

There are two well-defined routes up to the summit – the camel trail and the Steps of Repentance – which meet about 300m below the summit at a plateau known as Elijah's Basin. Here, everyone must take a steep series of 750 rocky and uneven steps to the top, where there is a small chapel and mosque (although these are kept locked).

Most people make the climb in the predawn hours to see the magnificence of the sun rising over the surrounding peaks, and then return to the base before 9am, when the monastery opens for visitors.

The Camel Trail is the easier route, and takes about two hours to ascend, moving at a steady pace. The trail is wide, clear and gently sloping as it moves up a series of switchbacks, with the only potential difficulty being gravelly patches that can be slippery on the descent.

The alternative path to the summit is the taxing 3750 Steps of Repentance. The steps are made of roughly hewn rock, and are steep and uneven in many places, requiring strong knees and concentration in placing your feet. The stunning mountain scenery along the way, though, makes this path well worth the extra effort, and the lower reaches of the trail afford impressive views of the monastery.

If you want to try both routes, it's easier to take the camel trail on the way up and the steps on the way back down.

🛌 Sleeping & Eating

There are a couple of simple restaurants and several well-stocked supermarkets located around the bus stop.

El-Malga Bedouin Camp
HOSTEL $

(☏0100 641 3575; www.sheikhmousa.com; dm E£25, s/d E£100/150, without bathroom 55/85; 🕾) This popular and friendly camp run by the affable Sheikh Mousa is a backpacker favourite and offers excellent quality for the price. The new-built en suite rooms are large and comfortable, while the cheaper rooms all share excellent bathroom facilities with hot water. It's an easy 500m walk from the bus stop.

Monastery Guesthouse
GUESTHOUSE $

(☏347 0353; St Katherine's Monastery; s/d US$35/60) A favourite of pilgrims the world over, this guesthouse right next to St Katherine's Monastery offers well-kept rooms with heaters and blankets to keep out the mountain chill, and a pleasant patio area with views towards the mountains. Breakfast included.

ℹ️ Information

Banque Misr (⊙10am-1pm & 5-8pm Sat-Thu) ATM. Also changes US dollars and Euros. It's beside the petrol station.

Police (☏347 0046) Beside the St Katherine Protectorate Office.

Nahda Internet (E£5 per hr) Beside Al-Malga Bedouin Camp.

St Katherine Hospital (☑347 0263) Provides very basic care only.

Post office Beside the bakery.

ⓘ Getting There & Away

Bus

East Delta Travel Co (☑347 0250) has its bus station and ticket office just off the main road, behind the mosque. There is a daily bus to Cairo (E£50, seven hours) at 6am.

There hasn't been a public bus service between St Katherine's Monastery and the Sinai coast for well over a year but a local transport initiative, **Bedouin Bus** (0101 668 4274; www. bedouinbus.com), operates a twice-weekly service to Dahab and Nuweiba. To Dahab the bus departs every Tuesday and Friday at 11am and to Nuweiba, at 8am every Wednesday and Sunday. Both cost E£50 and take two hours. The bus leaves from next to the bakery (opposite the mosque).

Many people arrive here on organised tours from Dahab or Sharm el-Sheikh. These tours generally leave at 11pm for the two-hour drive to the base of the mountain, in time to make your way up to the summit for the spectacular sunrise. They usually begin the return journey mid-morning, allowing you time to visit the monastery.

Taxi

Taxis and pick-ups usually wait at the monastery car park for people coming down from Mt Sinai in the morning, and then again around noon when visiting hours end. The rate per car to Dahab is E£250.

Understand Israel & the Palestinian Territories

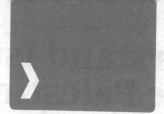

population per sq km

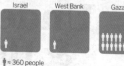

Israel   West Bank   Gaza

ᵢ ≈ 360 people

Israel & the Palestinian Territories Today

Prospects for Peace

Optimism about peace between Israel and her neighbours was widespread among both Israelis and Palestinians in the heyday of the Oslo peace process, in the mid-1990s. But following years of suicide bombings, rocket attacks from Gaza and calls by Palestinian Islamists for Israel's destruction, many Israelis have become pessimistic about the chances for peace. Retaliatory strikes from Israel, continuing Israel Defence Forces (IDF) roadblocks, the right-wing composition of Israel's current government, settlement construction and settler violence have had a similar impact on the assessment of many Palestinians.

The ancestors of about half of Israeli Jews immigrated from Europe (especially Russia, Romania, Poland, Germany and Hungary) and the Americas, the other half from Africa (eg Morocco and Ethiopia) and Asia (especially Iraq, Iran, Yemen and India).

Israeli Prime Minister Binyamin Netanyahu has declared his support for a two-state solution to the Israeli–Palestinian conflict, but since his right-wing coalition government came to power in 2009, it has continued to expand Jewish settlements and offered only vague answers to Palestinian questions about eventual borders, calling into question Netanyahu's commitment to the eventual establishment of a viable Palestinian state next to Israel.

The leadership of the Palestinian Authority may be similarly hamstrung. Although PA President Mahmoud Abbas and his prime minister, Salam Fayyad, have a long record of support for a two-state solution, they too have seemed reluctant to make any bold moves. Instead, Abbas has been putting great effort into having Palestine admitted to the UN General Assembly as a full member state, a campaign that diplomatic manoeuvres by Israel, the US and some European countries has blocked.

Exclusion of Women

Women serve on Israel's Supreme Court and as government ministers (including, from 1969 to 1974, as prime minister – Golda Meir, of course),

Top Non-Fiction

The Anatomy of Israel's Survival (Hirsh Goodman, 2011) Analysis of Israel's internal fissures.
The Unmaking of Israel (Gershom Gorenberg, 2011) Looks at domestic threats to Israeli democracy.

Top Films

Sallah Shabbati (Ephraim Kishon, 1964) Satire about life in a 1950s transit camp.
Waltz with Bashir (Ari Folman, 2008) Haunting, personal look at the 1982 Lebanon War.
Yossi & Jagger (Eytan Fox, 2002) IDF officers, secret love.

Documentaries

The Flat (2011) Filmmaker looks at his German-Jewish roots.
Strangers No More (2010) A South Tel Aviv elementary school takes in refugee children.
Precious Life (2010) A Gaza baby fights for medical treatment in Israel.

if Israel were 100 people

76 would be Jewish
17 would be Muslim
2 would be Christian
2 would be Druze
3 would be Other

if West Bank were 100 people

75 would be Muslim
17 would be Jewish
8 would be Christian

and they head major political parties and large corporations. Women make up 56% of Israel's BA students and over 50% of newly minted PhDs.

But among the Orthodox and, particularly, the ultra-Orthodox (Haredim), the last few years have seen attempts to impose a dramatic new degree of separation between the sexes.

In the name of modesty (ie the fear that the presence of women will cause men to have impure thoughts), supermarkets have been pressured to institute separate shopping hours for men and women, women (even modestly dressed ones) have disappeared from advertising posters (eg on buses and bus stops) due to threats of vandalism from ultra-Orthodox zealots, public buses serving Haredi neighbourhoods have been segregated (women sit in the back), and in Jerusalem's Mea She'arim neighbourhood signs have been put up demanding that women and men use separate footpaths.

The army, in which few Haredim serve, has not been immune from these trends. Some 'national religious' (modern Orthodox) draftees have demanded they be allowed to absent themselves from military ceremonies at which women sing, and refused to be trained by women soldiers. But the response of the IDF brass, at first hesitant, has been made clear: women will continue to train men, serve as pilots and do virtually all army jobs except ground combat – and they will continue to sing in public.

Israel's Supreme Court has ordered that buses be desegregated (only 'voluntary' segregation is allowed) and that the police prevent public spaces such as footpaths from being segregated, but imposing such rulings on insular Haredi groups – that do not recognise the State of Israel, much less its Supreme Court – has proven difficult. Women (including Orthodox feminists) have organised public sing-alongs, demanded that ads for things like organ donation portray women as well as men, and boarded segregated buses where, Rosa Parks–style, they have refused to move to the back.

» Population

» Israel 7.8 million (including 497,000 settlers in the West Bank and East Jerusalem)

» West Bank 2.7 million

» Gaza 1.7 million

Top Jewish Music

Andalusian Mediterranean Orchestra (www.andalusit.org.il) North African liturgical music with a Mediterranean flourish.
Shlomo Bar & HaBrera HaTiveet (www.shlomobar.com) Mizrahi and world music.

Top Sports Teams

Maccabi Tel Aviv (Basketball) Winner of five European Championships.
Maccabi Haifa (Football/Soccer) Seven-time Israeli Premier League champions.

Hapoel Ironi Kiryat Shmona (Football/Soccer) Surprise Premier League powerhouse.
Palestine National Football Team (Soccer) Represents the Palestinian Territories internationally.

Fatah Versus Hamas

Fatah, the Palestinian nationalist movement founded by Yasser Arafat in Kuwait in 1959, has been secular and left-wing from its inception. Its main rival, Hamas (see p385), has had a strongly Islamist orientation since its founding in Gaza in 1987. Both seek to establish a Palestinian state, but whereas Fatah has officially accepted a two-state solution, Hamas calls for the destruction of Israel and the establishment of a strict Islamist state in its place. Both organisations have thousands of armed men at their disposal.

Fatah, especially during Arafat's last years, became mired in corruption. Hamas, on the other hand, entered the 2006 Palestinian legislative elections as an alternative with a reputation for grass-roots engagement and community building – and won a landslide victory, taking 76 seats to Fatah's 43.

After the vote, Fatah military commanders refused to take orders from their rivals and Hamas and Fatah were unable to reach an agreement on sharing power. The two sides were soon engaging in mutual kidnappings, attacks and assassinations. In 2007 Hamas forces ejected Fatah from Gaza in a bloody takeover that saw pitched street battles and party loyalists from both sides executed by their opponents. Fatah responded by cracking down on Hamas activities in the West Bank. Since then, the two discontiguous regions that make up the Palestinian Territories have been ruled by rival governments.

Repeated attempts at reconciliation have foundered due to ideological differences, bitterness over past violence and deep mistrust. It remains to be seen whether the Arab Spring, accompanied by Islamist gains in elections across North Africa, will provide a context in which intra-Palestinian reconciliation becomes possible.

GDP: Israel US$219 billion, West Bank US$13 billion

GDP growth: Israel 4.6%, West Bank 7%

GDP per capita: Israel US$29,800, West Bank US$2900

Modest Dress

At holy sites, don't wear short pants or shirts that expose your shoulders or upper arms. Women are expected to wear skirts at Jewish sites and cover their hair in mosques. Men's heads should be covered at Jewish sites and hatless in churches.

Keeping Shabbat

On the sabbath, Orthodox Jews do not perform 39 'creative activities', including lighting or extinguishing fire, using electricity, travelling by motorised vehicle, writing, cooking, baking, sewing, harvesting, doing business or transporting objects between private and public spaces. Most of these restrictions also apply on the first, and sometimes the final, day of major Jewish holidays.

History

Israel and the Palestinian Territories have been inhabited – and contested – since the dawn of civilisation. A litany of the empires and kingdoms that have ruled the country reads like a Who's Who of Western and Middle Eastern history: there are Egyptians and Canaanites, Israelites and Philistines, Greeks and Samaritans, Romans and Byzantines, Arabs and Crusaders (and, briefly, Mongols), Ottomans and British. Each left behind fascinating evidence of their aspirations and follies for modern-day travellers to ponder.

Ancient Times

The land now occupied by Israel and the Palestinian Territories has been inhabited by human beings and their forebears for some 2 million years. Between 10,000 and 8000 BCE – a little later than in nearby Mesopotamia – people in places such as Jericho switched from hunting to the production of grain and the domestication of animals.

During the 3rd millennium BCE, the area was occupied by seminomadic tribes of pastoralists. By the late 2nd millennium BCE urban centres had emerged, and it is clear from Egyptian documents that the pharaohs had significant interests and influence in the area. Around 1800 BCE, Abraham is believed to have led his nomadic tribe from Mesopotamia to a land the Bible calls Canaan, after the local Canaanite tribes. His descendants were forced to relocate to Egypt because of drought and crop failure, but according to the Bible Moses led them back to the Land of Israel again in about 1250 BCE. Conflicts with the Canaanites and Philistines pushed the Israelites to abandon their loose tribal system and unify under King Saul (1050–1010 BCE) and his successors, King David and King Solomon.

Myth and history intersect on the large, flat rock that now lies beneath Jerusalem's golden Dome of the Rock. Originally an altar to Baal or some other pagan deity, the rock is known to Jews as the Stone of Foundation, the place where the universe began and Adam was created out of dust.

Because the terms BC (Before Christ) and AD (Anno Domini, ie the 'Year of Our Lord') assume Christian belief, this book uses the religion-neutral abbreviations BCE (Before the Common Era) and CE (Common Era), standard practice in most academic writing.

TIMELINE	2 million BCE	9000 BCE	4500–3500 BCE
	Hominids inhabit Tel Ovadia, 3km south of the Sea of Galilee. Around 780,000 BCE their successors set up camp along the Jordan River 13km north of the Sea of Galilee.	Abundant water and good climate attract early Neolithic people to Jericho, where they establish a permanent settlement surrounded by a mud-brick wall, grow food crops and flax, and raise goats.	Chalcolithic (pre-Bronze Age) people inhabit small villages in Jordan Valley and on the Golan, producing pottery and stone tools. Food sources include agriculture and domesticated goats and sheep.

It's also said to be where Abraham bound his son Isaac in preparation to sacrifice him, as a sign of obedience to God. King Solomon built the First Temple (Solomon's Temple) here in the 10th century BCE to serve as the centre of Jewish sacrificial worship.

After Solomon's reign (965–928 BCE), the Jews entered a period of division and periodic subjugation. Two rival entities came into being: the Kingdom of Israel in what is now the northern West Bank and the Galilee; and the southern Kingdom of Judah, with its capital at Jerusalem. After Sargon II of Assyria (r 722–705 BCE) destroyed the Kingdom of Israel in 720 BCE, the 10 northern tribes disappeared from the historical record (even today, ethnic groups around the world claim descent from the 'Ten Lost Tribes').

The Babylonians captured Jerusalem in 586 BCE, destroying the First Temple and exiling the people of Judah to Babylonia (now Iraq). Fifty years later Cyrus II, king of Persia, defeated Babylon and allowed the Jews to return to the Land of Israel. The returning Jews immediately set about constructing the Second Temple, consecrated in 516 BCE.

The earliest extra-biblical mention of Israel is on the Egyptian Museum's Israel Stela (1230 BCE), inscribed with the victory hymn of the Pharaoh Merneptah: 'Plundered is Canaan, carried is Ashkelon, Israel is laid waste.'

Greeks & Maccabees, Romans & Christians

When Alexander the Great died in 323 BCE, Ptolemy, one of his generals, claimed Egypt as his own, founding a line of which Cleopatra would be the last. He also took the Land of Israel, but in 200 BCE the Seleucids, another dynasty descended from one of Alexander's generals, captured it.

The 'Hellenistic' period – so called because of the Greek origin of the Seleucids and the Olympian cults they promoted – was marked by conflict between the Sadducees, mostly urban, upper-class Jews who were open to Greek culture and the refined Greek lifestyle, and the Pharisees, who resisted Hellenisation. When the Seleucid king Antiochus IV Epiphanes banned Temple sacrifices, Shabbat and circumcision, the Jews, led by Judah Maccabee, revolted. Using guerrilla tactics, they captured Jerusalem and rededicated the Temple.

The Hasmoneans – as the dynasty founded by the Maccabees is known – became a useful buffer for the Roman Empire against the marauding Parthians, whose empire was based in what is now Iran. But the

---

ISRAEL BY ANY OTHER NAME

The land on which the State of Israel and the Palestinian Territories are situated has been known by a variety of names. Among the names you may come across are Canaan, the Land of Israel (Eretz Yisra'el) and Judah, in the Hebrew Bible; Judea (Provincia Iudaea) and, after 135 CE, Syria Palaestina, used by the Romans; Ash-Sham (Syria) and Filastin (Palestine), in Arab sources; and the Holy Land (Terra Sancta in Latin) and Palestine, in texts by Christians, Muslims and Jews.

1250 BCE

Estimated date of the Israelites' biblical exodus from Egypt. Archaeologists have found no evidence of Egyptian slavery, desert wandering or conquest and posit that the Israelites originated in Canaan.

10th century BCE

King Solomon, legendary for his wisdom, rules Israel and builds the First Temple in Jerusalem to house the Ark of the Covenant, containing the original Ten Commandments tablets.

» Lithograph of David bringing the Ark to Jerusalem

ARCH OF TITUS

In 82 CE the Romans celebrated Titus' hard-fought victory over Judea by constructing an impressive triumphal arch just off the Roman Forum in Rome. Still standing today, its friezes depict a procession of Roman legionnaires carrying off the contents of the Temple in Jerusalem, including a seven-branched *menorah* (candelabra).

Hasmoneans fought among themselves and in 63 BCE Rome stepped in. The Romans sometimes ruled the area – which became the Roman province of Judea – directly through a procurator, the most famous of whom was Pontius Pilate, but preferred a strong client ruler like Herod the Great (r 37–4 BCE), whose major construction projects included expanding the Temple.

The 1st century CE was a time of tremendous upheaval in the Roman province of Judea, not least between approximately 26 and 29 CE, when it's believed Jesus of Nazareth carried out his ministry. The tension exploded in 66 CE, when the Jews launched the Great Jewish Revolt (the First Jewish–Roman War) against the Romans. Four years later, Titus, the future emperor, crushed the rebels and destroyed the Second Temple, leaving only one outer wall standing, now known as the Western Wall. Masada fell in 73 CE, putting an end to even nominal Jewish sovereignty for almost 2000 years. However, although the Jews were expelled from Jerusalem, a large Jewish population remained in other parts of the Land of Israel.

Just 60 years after Josephus Flavius wrote *The Jewish War,* his first-hand, decidedly pro-Roman account of the Great Jewish Revolt, another one broke out. The Bar Kochba Rebellion (132–35 CE) was led by Simon Bar Kochba, whose guerrillas lived in caves near the Dead Sea and whom some considered to be the Messiah. The Romans, under Hadrian, suppressed the rebellion with difficulty – and with great ferocity, essentially wiping out the Jewish population of Judea.

After his victory, Hadrian sought to erase both Judaism and any traces of Jewish independence: statues of Jupiter and of Hadrian himself were placed on the site of the Temple, Jews were barred from living in Aelia Capitolina (his new name for Jerusalem), and the Roman province of Judea was renamed Syria Palaestina after the Philistines, a people of Mycenaean Greek origin who had been arch-enemies of the Jews for a millennium.

With the Temple destroyed and the elaborate animal sacrifices prescribed in the Torah suspended, Jewish religious life was thrown into a state of limbo. In an effort to adapt to the new circumstances, Jewish sages established academies around Roman Judea and Galilee and set about reorienting Judaism towards prayer and synagogue worship, though the direction of Jewish prayer remained (as it does today) towards Jerusalem.

THE TEMPLE

The Temple in Jerusalem was so central to Jewish life that some scholars estimate only 270 of the 613 Commandments that religious Jews are obligated to perform can actually be carried out in the absence of the Temple's priesthood and animal sacrifices.

Late 10th century BCE	586 BCE	516 BCE	4th century BCE
The northern Kingdom of Israel splits from the southern, Jerusalem-based Kingdom of Judea. The 10 northern tribes are eventually lost to history; today's Jews are descended from the Judeans.	Nebuchadnezzar, King of Babylon, destroys the First Temple and exiles the Jews to Babylonia. Cyrus II, King of Persia, allows them to return to Judea 48 years later.	The Second Temple is consecrated in Jerusalem. Though without the Ark of the Covenant, lost to Nebuchadnezzar, it serves as the focus of Jewish worship though animal sacrifices.	Nabataeans, a nomadic tribe from Arabia, establish Petra, now in Jordan. They wax wealthy from the incense trade between Yemen and the Horn of Africa, and Greece and Rome.

THE JEWISH DIASPORA

During the 3300 or so years since the Children of Israel appeared in Canaan, according to the Bible after the Exodus from Egypt, there have always been Jews in the Land of Israel. But for about two-thirds of that time, most Jews lived outside the Holy Land, dispersed among other nations in communities collectively known as the Jewish Diaspora (from the Greek word for 'dispersion' or 'scattering').

The first major Diaspora community was established in Babylonia (now Iraq) after Nebuchadnezzar destroyed the First Temple and exiled the Jews in 586 BCE. When Cyrus II of Persia allowed them to return to Judea 48 years later, many stayed on in Babylonia.

From the 3rd to the 6th centuries CE, Jewish sages in Palestine and Babylonia vied for supremacy in establishing Jewish law. Babylonia eventually won out.

In the 11th century, the seat of the Jewish world's greatest legal authorities shifted to North Africa (Cairo and Kairouan, Tunisia) and, more improbably, to the Rhineland, in a faraway land that the Jews called Ashkenaz. From the 13th to 15th centuries, many of the greatest sages lived in Spain, known in Hebrew as Sfarad.

Persecuted in Western Europe, Ashkenazi Jews began moving eastward into the Slavic lands from the 14th century, bringing with them a German-Hebrew patois known as Yiddish. By the 17th century the world's main centre of Jewish scholarship was in Lithuania and Poland. By the 1700s, for the first time in Jewish history, more Jews lived in Europe than in North Africa and Asia. The Jews of Eastern Europe were again dispersed in the late 19th century when czarist pogroms forced many of them to flee. The vast majority of European Jews who found themselves under Nazi occupation during WWII died in the Holocaust; most were either shot, their bodies dumped in mass graves, or perished in the gas chambers.

The expulsion of the Jews from Spain in 1492 scattered Sephardic Jews to the lands of the Ottomans (who welcomed the exiles) as well as the Netherlands, from where some eventually went to England. A few Sephardic Jews lived in colonial America before 1776, but most of the American Jewish community is descended from 19th-century Ashkenazi immigrants. Today, the United States and Israel, each with about 6 million Jews, vie for Jewish cultural and religious pre-eminence, just as Babylonia and the Land of Israel did 17 centuries ago.

The 'Rabbinic Judaism' practised today is almost entirely the result of principles, precepts and precedents laid down by sages and rabbis after the destruction of the Second Temple.

In the years following Jesus's crucifixion, which some experts believe took place in 33 CE, Jews who believed him to be the Messiah and those who didn't often worshipped side by side, observing Jewish rituals with equal meticulousness. But around the time the Gospels were being written (late 1st century CE), theological and political disagreements emerged

167–161 BCE	**63 BCE**	**37 BCE**	**c 4 BCE**
Outraged by Seleucid king Antiochus' imposition of pagan sacrifices, the Jews, led by Judah Maccabee, revolt. Their victory, celebrated by the holiday of Hanukkah, establishes the Hasmonean dynasty.	The independent Kingdom of Judea becomes a Roman client state after Pompey captures Jerusalem. Roman proconsuls rule Judea but Temple sacrifices continue.	The Roman Senate appoints Herod the Great as king of Judea. To win popular support, he rebuilds the Second Temple, including the Western Wall. He also constructs a palace atop Masada.	A Jew known to history as Jesus is born in Bethlehem. He grows up in Nazareth, preaches in Galilee and is tried and crucified in Jerusalem by Pontius Pilate.

and the two communities diverged. Christian polemical tracts against the Jewish faith from this period, delivered from a position of weakness – at this time Christianity, but not Judaism, was treated as an illegal sect by the Romans – would be used to justify anti-Semitism in subsequent centuries.

Christianity was generally suppressed by the Romans until 313 CE, when the Roman Empire's Edict of Milan granted tolerance to all previously persecuted religions, including Christianity. Shortly thereafter, Constantine the Great's mother Helena set about identifying and consecrating sites associated with Jesus's life. Many of the most important Christian sites, including the Church of the Holy Sepulchre in Jerusalem and St Katherine's Monastery in Sinai, date from this period.

The Byzantine Empire – the Christian successor to the eastern part of Roman Empire – ruled Palestine from the 4th to the early 7th centuries CE. During this time, there were three revolts – one by the Jews of Galilee and two by the Samaritans – but as can be seen from the opulent ruins of Beit She'an and the Galilee's many beautiful Byzantine-era synagogues, the country was quite prosperous and, for the most part, at peace.

In 611 CE the Persians invaded, capturing Jerusalem, destroying churches and seizing the True Cross. Byzantine rule was restored in 628 CE – but it didn't last long.

> Some Jews believe that when the Messiah comes the Temple will simply reappear on the Temple Mount. In the Old City's Jewish Quarter, you can find artists' renderings of the 'Third Temple'. Muslims, of course, prefer to keep the Dome of the Rock right where it is.

Muslims & Crusaders

Islam and Arab civilisation came to Palestine between 636 and 638 CE, when Caliph Omar (Umar), the second of the Prophet's successors, accepted the surrender of Jerusalem from the Byzantines. This was just six years after the death of the Prophet Mohammed, whose followers had initially been told to pray facing Jerusalem; in 623 they were instructed to face Mecca.

The Temple Mount was holy to the newly arrived Muslims because they believed it to be the site of Mohammed's Night Journey (Mi'raj) to behold the celestial glories of heaven. In the Quran, the ascension is described as happening in a 'faraway place', which Muslims interpret as meaning Jerusalem, Sunni Islam's third-holiest city (after Mecca and Medina).

Omar's successors built Al-Aqsa Mosque and the Dome of the Rock on the Temple Mount, which had been a derelict trash dump during Byzantine times. Jews were again permitted to settle in Jerusalem. With Christianity seen as a valued precursor of Islam, the shrines of previous generations were preserved, although over time many Christians converted to Islam and began using Arabic.

Omar issued a famous promise to the Christians of Jerusalem that 'the security of their persons, their goods, their churches, their crosses' would be guaranteed. That is, until 1009 when the mentally disturbed Fatimid Caliph Al-Haakim destroyed many churches and persecuted Christians and Jews.

66–70 CE	67	73
Jewish anger at Roman oppression sparks the Great Jewish Revolt, crushed by Roman legions under Vespasian and Titus. Jerusalem and the Second Temple are destroyed, ending sacrifices.	Yosef ben Matityahu, commander of the Great Jewish Revolt in Galilee, is captured by the Romans and reinvents himself as the great Roman historian Josephus Flavius.	Three years after the fall of Jerusalem, the desert stronghold of Masada succumbs to the might of the Roman legions, marking the end to all Jewish resistance in Judea.

» Church of the Nativity

Christian pilgrimage to the holy sites in Jerusalem was possible until 1071, when the Seljuk Turks captured the city and travel became difficult and often dangerous due to political turmoil. In 1095 Pope Urban II issued a call for a crusade to restore the site of Jesus's Passion to Christianity. By the time the Crusades began, the Seljuks had been displaced by the Fatimid dynasty, which was quite happy to allow the old pilgrimage routes to reopen. But it was too late for the Christians to turn back. In 1099 the Crusaders overwhelmed Jerusalem's defences and massacred its Muslims and Jews. It would be 200 years before the bloodshed came to a halt.

When the Crusaders took Jerusalem, they founded what even Arab chroniclers acknowledged was a prosperous state with an effective administration, based on the feudal system prevalent back home in Europe. The first King of Jerusalem was Baldwin I (r 1100–18), who saw himself as restoring the kingdom of the biblical David and had himself crowned on Christmas Day in David's hometown of Bethlehem.

In 1187 the celebrated Kurdish-Muslim general Saladin (Salah ad-Din) defeated a Crusader army at the Horns of Hattin in Galilee (near Arbel) and took Jerusalem. Even Saladin's enemies acknowledged his decent treatment of prisoners and the honour with which he observed truces – not something that could be said for the Crusader chiefs.

The final Crusader left the Middle East with the fall of Akko in 1291, but the bloody symbolism of the Crusades lived on. When Britain's General Edmund Allenby entered Jerusalem in 1917 to become its first Christian ruler since Saladin's victory, he declared: 'now the Crusades are over'.

For an alternative, highly readable look at the Christian invasions, try *The Crusades Through Arab Eyes* by Lebanese writer Amin Maalouf.

Ottomans, Zionists & British

The Ottoman Turks captured Constantinople in 1453 and built an empire that extended to the Balkans, the Middle East and North Africa. In 1516 Palestine was added to their territory, and two decades later Sultan Süleyman the Magnificent (r 1520–66) built the present massive walls around Jerusalem's Old City. For most of the 400 years of Ottoman rule, Palestine was a backwater run by pashas more concerned with capricious tax collection than good governance.

The lack of effective administration in Palestine reflected the gradual decline of the Ottoman Empire, which would eventually cease to exist at the end of WWI. But the final decades of the empire saw other forces taking shape in Palestine that remain strong today. Zionism arose largely in response to post-Napoleonic nationalism in Western Europe and a wave of pogroms in Eastern Europe. While at least small numbers of Jews had remained in Palestine continuously since Roman times (eg in the Galilee town of Peki'in) and pious Jews had been immigrating whenever political conditions permitted, organised Zionist immigration to agricultural

132–35	2nd century	313	358
After Hadrian bans circumcision, Bar Kochba leads the catastrophic Bar Kochba Rebellion, leading to a crushing Roman victory and the near-annihilation of the Jewish communities of Judea.	With Jerusalem in ruins and sacrifices halted, centres of Jewish learning are established in Yavneh, Tzipori and Beit She'arim. Oral traditions are written down in the Mishnah and, later, Talmud.	Constantine the Great, the Roman Empire's first Christian emperor, issues the Edict of Milan, granting religious freedom to all religions, including Christianity.	The lunisolar Hebrew calendar still in use today is adopted by the Sanhedrin right before its dissolution. It fits lunar months into the solar year by inserting seven leap months every 19 years.

MYSTIC JUDAISM

The leading thinkers of Spain's illustrious medieval Jewish community were rational philosophers whose interests encompassed both science and medicine. In 1492 Spain's Christian rulers expelled all the country's Jews, causing a crisis of faith to which the rationalists had no answer. (The expulsion, after all, seemed deeply irrational, unless you were the Spanish king and queen, who confiscated property from departing Jews.) As a result, some Jews developed a new, mystical understan7ding of why bad things happened to them. The centre of this new mysticism was the hilltop Galilee town of Tsfat, where a number of eminent Spanish rabbis found a home. Its greatest figure was Jerusalem-born Yitzhak Luria (1534–72), who expanded an old form of mysticism called Kabbalah (pronounced kah-bah-LAH) so that it could provide answers to the vexing spiritual questions haunting Jews after the Expulsion.

Lurianic Kabbalah (the word means 'receiving') was inspired by earlier texts such as the 13th-century *Zohar*, but Luria's adaptations and innovations had such an impact that many are now part of mainstream Jewish observance. Luria left no writings, but his assistant recorded the essence of his teachings. Luria asserted that in order to create the world, the Infinite (the Eyn-Sof) was damaged – to make a space in which to fit Creation. As a result, sparks from the Divine Light fell from their original position and were at risk of being used for evil purposes. Jews, he argued, could restore the Divine Light and repair the Infinite by performing the 613 Commandments (the 10 on Moses' tablets were only the beginning). It gave Jews a way to understand the horror of the Expulsion from Spain and the Inquisition – as well as later persecution – because it asserted that such evil was inherent in the world. It also directed them to look inward to build a higher degree of spiritual awareness, and in so doing to 'repair the world'.

settlements began in 1882; for slightly different reasons, Jews from Yemen began arriving the same year. Known as the First Aliya (the Hebrew word for emigrating to the Land of Israel, *aliya*, literally means 'going up'), this group was joined starting in 1903 by the Second Aliya, made up largely of young, secular-minded socialists. But until after WWI, the vast majority of Palestine's Jews belonged to the old-line Orthodox community, most of it uninterested in Zionism, and lived in Judaism's four holy cities: Hebron, Tsfat (Safed), Tiberias and Jerusalem, which had a Jewish majority since about 1850.

In 1896 the Budapest-born Jewish journalist Theodor Herzl, convinced by the degrading treatment of Captain Alfred Dreyfus (court-martialled in Paris on trumped-up treason charges) that Jews would never achieve equality and civil rights without self-determination, formulated his ideas in *The Jewish State*. The next year, he opened the first World Zionist Congress in Basel, Switzerland. Inspired by political Zionism, young Jews

638	749	1095–99	1187
Just six years after the death of the Prophet Mohammed, Muslim armies capture Jerusalem, bringing Islam, Arab culture and the Arabic language to Palestine.	A massive earthquake destroys Beit She'an and Tiberias. In Jerusalem it kills thousands and seriously damages Al-Aqsa Mosque.	The First Crusade brings Christian armies from Europe to Muslim-ruled Jerusalem, which is defended by both Muslims and Jews. Crusaders massacre Jews in both Europe and the Holy Land.	Saladin (Salah ad-Din) defeats the Crusaders at the hugely important Battle of Hattin, in the Galilee, and captures Jerusalem, allowing Jews to return to the city.

– many of them secular and socialist – began emigrating to Palestine, mostly from Poland and Russia.

In November 1917 the British government issued the Balfour Declaration, which stated that 'His Majesty's Government view with favour the establishment in Palestine of a National Home for the Jewish People'. The next month, British forces under General Edmund Allenby captured Jerusalem.

Immediately after the end of WWI, Jews resumed immigration to Palestine, this time to territory controlled by a British-run mandatory government – approved by the League of Nations – that was friendly, modernising and competent. The Third Aliya (1919–23) was made up mostly of young, idealistic socialists, many of whom established kibbutzim (communal settlements) on marginal land purchased from absentee Arab landlords, deals that sometimes resulted in the displacement of Arab peasant farmers. But the Fourth Aliya (1924–29) was made up largely of middle-class merchants and tradesmen – not exactly the committed pioneers that the Zionist leadership had hoped for. In the 1930s they were joined by the Fifth Aliya, made up largely of refugees from Nazi Germany, many of them from comfortable bourgeois backgrounds.

The rise in Jewish immigration angered Palestinian Arabs, who were beginning to see themselves in Arab nationalist terms and Palestine's growing Jewish population as a threat to Arab interests. Anti-Zionist riots rocked the country in 1921 and 1929, but Jews continued to arrive, especially after Hitler's rise to power in 1933. In 1931 Palestine's 174,000 Jews constituted 17% of the total population; by 1941, there were 474,000 Jews, 30% of the total.

Growing Palestinian Arab opposition to Zionism and the policies of the British Mandate, especially regarding Jewish immigration, led to the Arab Revolt (1936–39), in which about 400 Jewish civilians and 200 British soldiers were killed. The Mandatory government suppressed the uprising with considerable violence, killing some 5000 Palestinian Arabs. Palestinian Jews took advantage of the Arab economic boycott to increase their economic autonomy – for instance, by establishing an independent port in Tel Aviv. However, the Arab Revolt succeeded in convincing the British – who, in case of war with Germany, would surely need Arab oil and political goodwill – to severely limit Jewish immigration to Palestine. Just as the Jews of Europe were becoming increasingly desperate to flee Hitler (the Nazis allowed Jews to leave Germany until late 1941 provided they could find a country to take them), the doors of Palestine slammed shut. Even after WWII, the British prevented Holocaust survivors from reaching Palestine, outraging Jewish public opinion in Palestine and the United States; refugees who tried to run the blockade were imprisoned on Cyprus.

Baptist lay preacher Thomas Cook led a party of middle-class English tourists to Jerusalem in 1869. They camped outside the walls for tea. Criminals, at that time, were still being publicly decapitated by sword at Jaffa Gate.

Zionism struck a heroic chord in Hollywood. Paul Newman starred in *Exodus* (1960), based on Leon Uris's bestseller about a boat carrying illegal Jewish immigrants; and Kirk Douglas played an American war hero who joined the war for Israel's independence in *Cast a Giant Shadow* (1966).

1291	16th century	1799	1837
The Mamluks take Akko, the Crusaders' last stronghold, ending Christian rule in Palestine until the arrival of the British in 1917.	Tsfat (Safed) becomes a centre of Jewish scholarship and Kabbalah (Jewish mysticism) with the arrival of Jerusalem-born Isaac Luria (the Ari) and Sephardic rabbis fleeing the Spanish Inquisition.	Napoleon captures Gaza, Jaffa (where he massacres thousands of POWs) and Haifa but fails to take Akko and doesn't get anywhere near Jerusalem. Abruptly leaves his army and returns to France.	Massive earthquake hits the Galilee, flattening much of Tsfat, where over 2000 people are killed, and claiming 600 lives in Tiberias.

ZIONISM

The Jewish Virtual Library (www.jewishvirtuallibrary.org) defines Zionism as 'the national movement for the return of the Jewish people to their homeland and the resumption of Jewish sovereignty in the Land of Israel'. The biblical word 'Zion' (Tziyon) refers both to Jerusalem, towards which Jews have prayed since the time of the Temple, and to the Land of Israel.

According to the historian Binyamin Neuberger, 'political Zionism, the national liberation movement of the Jewish people, emerged in the 19th century within the context of the liberal nationalism then sweeping through Europe. Central to Zionist thought is the concept of the Land of Israel as the historical birthplace of the Jewish people, and the belief that Jewish life elsewhere is a life of exile'.

This theme also appears in Israel's Declaration of Independence (1948), which states: *'The Land of Israel was the birthplace of the Jewish people. Here their spiritual, religious and political identity was shaped. Here they first attained to statehood, created cultural values of national and universal significance and gave to the world the eternal Book of Books. After being forcibly exiled from their land, the people kept faith with it throughout their dispersion and never ceased to pray and hope for their return to it and for the restoration in it of their political freedom.'*

Among Zionism's practical goals: to provide the Jewish people – seen by Zionists as no less a nation than the Czechs, the Hungarians or the French – with national self-determination in a world made up of nation-states; and to offer individual Jews a place of refuge from anti-Semitic discrimination and persecution.

By 1947 the British government, exhausted by WWII and tired of both Arab and Jewish violence in Palestine, turned the problem over to the two-year-old UN. In a moment of rare agreement between the United States and the Soviet Union in 1947, the UN General Assembly voted in favour of partitioning Palestine into two independent states, one Jewish, the other Arab, with Jerusalem under a 'special international regime'. Palestinian Jews accepted the plan in principle, but Palestinian Arabs, and nearby Arab countries, rejected it. Arab bands immediately began attacking Jewish targets. The protection of Palestinian Jewish communities, economic interests and transport was led by the Haganah, an underground military organisation that would soon become the Israel Defence Forces (IDF).

As soon as the British left, at midnight on 14 May 1948, the Jews proclaimed the establishment of an independent Jewish state and the armies of Egypt, Syria, Jordan, Lebanon and Iraq invaded Palestine. British Field Marshall Bernard Montgomery, who won fame for his North African desert campaigns during WWII, commented that Israel would survive no longer than three weeks. But to the Arab states' – and the world's – surprise the 650,000 Palestinian Jews were not defeated but rather took

The history of Palestine during the British Mandate comes alive through individual stories in the excellent *One Palestine, Complete* (2001) by Israel's leading popular historian, Tom Segev.

1882–1903	1909	1910	1916
Pogroms in Russia spark the First Aliya, the first organised Zionist immigration to Palestine. Agricultural settlements such as Metula, Rosh Pina, Zichron Ya'akov and Rishon LeZion are established.	Led by Meir Dizengoff, 66 families found Tel Aviv on sand dunes north of Jaffa. The 5 hectares purchased by the group are parcelled out by lottery.	The first kibbutz, Degania, is established by socialist 'pioneers' from Russia at the southern end of the Sea of Galilee, on land purchased in 1904.	The secret Sykes-Picot Agreement divvies up the Ottoman Empire into spheres of influence. Palestine, Transjordan and southern Iraq are earmarked for Britain; France gets Lebanon and Syria.

IMMIGRATION

control of 77% of Mandatory Palestine (the Partition Plan offered them 56%), though this did not include Jerusalem's Old City. Jordan occupied (and annexed) the West Bank and East Jerusalem, expelling the residents of the Old City's Jewish quarter; Egypt took control of an area that came to be known as the Gaza Strip.

Independence & Catastrophe

The 1948 Arab–Israeli War brought independence for Israel, a place of refuge for Holocaust survivors and Jewish refugees from the Arab countries, and a guarantee that Jews fleeing persecution would always have country that would take them in. But for the Palestinian Arabs the 1948 war is remembered as Al-Naqba, the Catastrophe.

At the start of the conflict, at least 800,000 Arabs lived in what was to become Israel. By the end of the war, 160,000 Arabs remained in areas under Israeli control. Though Israeli Prime Minister David Ben-Gurion frequently said that 'Israel did not expel a single Arab', it's clear that while many Palestinian Arabs fled their homes to escape fighting, others were forced out of their towns and villages by Israeli military units. Other factors that contributed to the Arab exodus were the early flight of the economic elite to neighbouring countries, and a lack of both national solidarity (partly the result of internecine violence in the 1930s) and nationalist consciousness among the largely illiterate rural population.

After Israel became independent, impoverished Jewish refugees began flooding in – from British internment camps on Cyprus (set up by the British to hold Jews intercepted on the way to Palestine), from 'displaced persons' camps in postwar Europe (including hundreds of thousands of Holocaust survivors), from countries soon to be locked tight behind the Iron Curtain (eg Bulgaria), and from Arab countries whose ancient Jewish communities became targets of anti-Jewish violence (eg Iraq, Yemen and Syria). Within three years, Israel's Jewish population more than doubled.

War & Terrorism

In the spring of 1967 Arab capitals – especially Cairo – were seething with calls to liberate all of historic Palestine from what they saw as an illegitimate occupation by Jewish Israelis, in the name of pan-Arab nationalism. Egyptian President Gamal Abdel Nasser closed the Straits of Tiran to Israeli shipping (including oil shipments from Iran, at the time an ally of Israel), ordered UN peacekeeping forces to withdraw from Sinai, and made rousing speeches listened to with rapt attention by tens of millions across the Arab world. Jordan and Syria massed troops on their borders with Israel. Terrified Israelis took Nasser at his word – on 3 May

Israelis call immigration to Israel *aliyah*, from a Hebrew root meaning 'to ascend'. Moving from Israel to another country is sometimes derisively called *yeridah* ('going down'). The Israeli government has special programmes to encourage emigrants to return.

1917	1918	1925	1929
In the Balfour Declaration, the British government expresses support for a 'Jewish national home' in Palestine. British forces under General Allenby capture Jerusalem from the Ottomans.	British forces take northern Palestine from the Ottomans. In one of the world's last cavalry charges, an Indian cavalry brigade captures Haifa.	The Hebrew University of Jerusalem is founded atop Mt Scopus. Members of the first Board of Governors include Albert Einstein, Sigmund Freud and Martin Buber.	Arab–Jewish riots erupt due to a disagreement over Jewish access to the Western Wall. Many of Hebron's Jews are sheltered by Muslim neighbours but 67 are killed by mobs.

he declared, 'our basic objective will be the destruction of Israel' – and wondered if their fate would be similar to that of the Jews of Europe.

On 6 June, Israel launched a pre-emptive attack on its Arab neighbours, devastating their air forces and then, in a three-front land war, the armies of Syria, Egypt and Jordan. In less than a week – that's why the conflict came to be known as Six Day War (www.sixdaywar.co.uk) – Israel captured Sinai and Gaza from Egypt, the West Bank and East Jerusalem from Jordan, and the Golan from Syria.

Israelis reacted to the victory with nothing less than euphoria, and many could find no other explanation than divine intervention. Some saw the triumph as proof that the messianic process was well and truly underway and sought to settle the newly captured lands (see p258). At the time, few Israelis were able to see the political, moral and demographic difficulties Israeli control of the Palestinian Territories would entail.

In 1973 Egypt and Syria launched a surprise, two-front attack on Yom Kippur, the holiest day of the Jewish calendar. Unprepared because of intelligence failures born of post-1967 hubris, Israel was initially forced to withdraw but soon rallied and, with enormous casualties on both sides, pushed the Arab armies back. However, initial Egyptian battlefield successes made it possible for Egyptian President Anwar Sadat to portray the Yom Kippur War as a victory. And although in tactical and strategic terms it was Israel that had won on the battlefield, Israelis never saw the war as a victory.

Thoroughly discredited by both the failures of the Yom Kippur War and the Labor Party's perceived corruption and lassitude, Prime Minister Golda Meir ended her political career in 1974. Three years later, the Labor Party itself, at the head of every government since 1948, was voted out of office, in part by Mizrahi (Asian and North African) Jews angry at their economic and political marginalisation. Menahem Begin, a right-wing former underground fighter (some would say terrorist because of his organisation's attacks on Arab civilians), became prime minister. But when Egyptian President Anwar Sadat stunned the world by travelling to Jerusalem (1977) and offered to make peace with Israel in return for an Israeli withdrawal from Sinai and promises (never fulfilled) of progress towards a Palestinian state, Begin accepted. With a beaming US President Jimmy Carter looking on, Begin and Sadat signed the Camp David Accords in 1978.

Israel completed its evacuation of Sinai, including 7000 settlers, in spring 1982, just six weeks before simmering tensions between Lebanon-based PLO forces and Israel, and the attempted assassination of the Israeli ambassador to the UK by an anti-PLO Palestinian faction, were used by Israel's general-turned-defence minister Ariel Sharon to justify launching a full-scale invasion of Lebanon, intended to drive the PLO out of Lebanon and install a pro-Israel Christian regime. The war divided

REFUGEE CAMPS

There are 20 refugee camps administered by the UN Relief and Works Agency (UNRWA) in the West Bank. The Gaza Strip has eight, and there's one in East Jerusalem. Over 50% of Palestinians are listed by the UN as refugees.

1939–45

Six million European Jews are murdered by the Nazis and their local collaborators. Many Palestinian Jews volunteer for service in the British Army. Zionists smuggle Jewish refugees into Palestine.

1946

Etzel (Irgun) underground paramilitary fighters under Menahem Begin blow up the south wing of Jerusalem's King David Hotel, a British military command centre, killing 91.

» Ruins of King David Hotel

1947

The UN General Assembly votes to partition Palestine into Jewish and Arab states, a plan accepted in principle by the Zionists but rejected by the Arabs. Fighting engulfs Palestine.

Israelis to an unprecedented degree, especially as it dragged on for years, until 1985 (Israeli forces occupied a 'security zone' on Lebanese territory until May 2000). Many Israelis believed that the war was launched without proper government approval, and even more felt that their country was tainted when IDF soldiers failed to stop their Christian Lebanese allies from massacring Palestinians in the Beirut refugee camps of Sabra and Shatila in September 1982. A mass demonstration against the war and the massacre attracted 400,000 people in Tel Aviv, the largest civil demonstration in Israel's history. (Israel's ongoing trauma from the First Lebanon War was the subject of the 2008 Oscar-nominated animated film *Waltz with Bashir*.)

Meanwhile, Palestinians waited in Israeli occupied areas, in refugee camps in neighbouring countries, and across the Arab world and beyond for a solution to their plight. In 1964 the Arab League, made up of representatives of 22 Arabic-speaking nations, set up the Palestine Liberation Organisation (PLO). But it wasn't until after the Arab defeat in the 1967 Six-Day War that a Palestinian leader willing to defy the Arab League won control of the PLO.

Born in Cairo in 1929, Yasser Arafat was in Kuwait working as an engineer in the late 1950s when he founded Fatah, a reverse Arabic acronym for 'Palestine Liberation Movement' and also the word for 'victory'. It was through the Fatah faction that he took over the PLO in 1969. From exile in Jordan and later Lebanon and Tunisia, he launched a campaign of hijackings, bombings and attacks against civilian targets designed to weaken Israel (instead, Israel responded with a determined campaign that included cross-border commando operations and assassinations) and keep the Palestinian problem in the international headlines (in this he certainly succeeded).

In 1987 a popular uprising against Israeli rule broke out in the West Bank and Gaza. Known as the First Intifada (Arabic for 'shaking off'), it was a spontaneous eruption of strikes, stones and Molotov cocktails by frustrated youths. Arafat, based in Tunis, was at first out of touch with grass-roots events in the Palestinian Territories, but he soon took control, garnering worldwide sympathy for the Palestinian cause.

In 1988 Arafat publicly renounced terrorism and effectively recognised Israel. Five years later, Israel (under Yitzhak Rabin) and the PLO signed the Oslo Accords, so named because secret negotiations in the Norwegian capital laid the basis for an agreement under which Israel would hand over control of territory to the Palestinians in stages, beginning with the major towns of the West Bank and Gaza. The toughest issues – the future of Jerusalem and Palestinian refugees' 'Right of Return' – were to be negotiated at the end of a five-year interim period. The Oslo formula was,

The most famous Palestinian poet, Mahmoud Darwish, wrote many works of nostalgia for the lost homeland, its tastes and smells and place names. In one of his best-known poems he wrote: 'We have a country of words.' He died in 2008.

Arafat made the chequered *keffiyeh* (traditional Arab men's head-gear) famous around the world. His was black and white, the colours favoured by Fatah, and he arranged the folds to form an elongated triangular shaped like Palestine. Red-and-white *keffiyehs* are often worn by Jordanian Bedouin, leftist Palestinian groups and Hamas.

1948	1948–70s	1951	1956
British leave Palestine, Zionist forces hold five Arab armies and local militias at bay, 700,000 Palestinian Arabs become refugees, State of Israel is declared.	Some 600,000 Jews leave, flee or are expelled from Arab countries such as Syria, Iraq, Egypt, Libya and Morocco and find refuge in Israel; many endure years in transit camps.	Jordan's King Abdullah I is assassinated on Al-Haram al-Sharif/ Temple Mount in Jerusalem by a Palestinian nationalist. His grandson becomes King Hussein and rules until 1999.	After Egypt closes off the Red Sea to Israeli shipping, Israel captures Sinai. Britain and France try to use the conflict as a pretext to retake the Suez Canal.

essentially, 'land for peace' based on the 'two-state solution' proposed by the UN in 1947.

The Oslo Era

Yasser Arafat arrived in Gaza to head the new Palestinian Authority (PA) in July 1994. Israel handed over the remaining towns, both in the Gaza Strip and the West Bank, over the next few years. But the Oslo Accords didn't bring real peace. Rather, they drove those on both sides who opposed the compromises necessary for peace to greater acts of violence. Hamas and Islamic Jihad took their terrorism to new heights with suicide bombings against Israeli civilians. Israel hit back by assassinating Hamas and Islamic Jihad leaders, using tactics that often resulted in civilian casualties. Military incursions and settler violence against local Palestinians increased.

Perhaps the biggest blow to the peace process came in November 1995, when a right-wing Orthodox Israeli gunned down Prime Minister Yitzhak Rabin after a Tel Aviv peace rally. The assassination was the culmination of several years of incitement from nationalist Israelis (especially Jewish settlers) bitterly opposed to Rabin's agreement to give up part of the 'Land of Israel'. Many Orthodox Jews (though not the ultra-Orthodox, who are non- or anti-Zionist) believe that the biblical lands they call Judea and Samaria (ie the West Bank) – and, at the time, Gaza – came to be under Israeli control as part of a divinely ordained process heralding the beginning of the messianic era. Relinquishing control of land they see as Israel's God-given birthright would do no less than put an end to the messianic process. For messianists there can be no greater crime.

For most Israelis Rabin's killing was nothing less than a national nightmare, and it accomplished much of what the assassin had hoped by robbing the peace process of an advocate whose military background – as a brigade commander in 1948 and later as chief of staff in the 1967 war – inspired Israelis to trust him on security issues.

Rabin's death was followed by a string of Hamas suicide bombings that helped bring a right-wing coalition led by Binyamin Netanyahu to power. But in 1999 a centre-left coalition government led by former chief of staff Ehud Barak took office. Barak said he wanted 'separation' from the Palestinians and was willing to give up almost all of the West Bank, Gaza and East Jerusalem. Barak persuaded US president Bill Clinton to hold a summit at Camp David in summer 2000 wanting to strike a final peace deal, despite the fact that US diplomats told him Arafat wasn't ready to move that fast. When the talks failed, widespread violence broke out. Most media at the time blamed Israel's Likud Party leader Ariel Sharon because of his visit to Jerusalem's Temple Mount, which Palestinians called 'a provocation'.

ARAB CITIZENS

Israel's Arab citizens – Palestinian Arabs who remained in their homes in 1948 and their descendants – lived under military law until 1966. They now number some 1.6 million; most live in the Galilee. Arabs living in East Jerusalem have blue Israeli ID cards but most aren't Israeli citizens.

1967

In six days, Israel defeats Egypt, Jordan and Syria, more than tripling its territory. Israelis can pray at the Western Wall for the first time since 1948.

1972

Palestinian terrorists belonging to Yasser Arafat's Fatah kill 11 Israeli athletes and coaches at the Munich Olympics. Golda Meir gives the order to hunt down the killers and assassinate them.

ALEXANDRA BOULAT/VII/CORBIS ©

» Graves of murdered Israeli athletes, Kiryat Shaul cemetery

At first Arafat saw unleashing violence as a way to pressure Israel into making concessions, but he quickly lost control to young, local Fatah leaders who felt he hadn't given them enough power since his return from exile – they accused him of giving all the top military and political jobs to corrupt old party hacks who'd been with him in Beirut and Tunis. The young Fatah leaders quickly allied with Hamas and Islamic Jihad, eventually launching a wave of suicide bombings.

Israeli public opinion hardened and in 2001 Ariel Sharon, a tough-talking former general who spoke privately of the Intifada as an 'existential danger' to Israel, and who had opposed Barak's efforts to reach a deal with Arafat, was elected prime minister. Sharon sent tanks to occupy West Bank towns previously ceded to Arafat, made frequent, bloody incursions into Gaza, and carried out 'targeted assassinations' of presumed terrorist leaders. He refused to guarantee that if Arafat left the West Bank he would be allowed to return, so the Palestinian leader found himself confined to his Ramallah compound. Depressed and sick, Arafat's command of events and – according to some aides – reality weakened until his death in November 2004. Over the course of the Second Intifada (2000–05), over 1000 Israelis, 70% of them civilians, were killed by Palestinians and some 4700 Palestinians, many of them civilians, were killed by Israelis, according to the Israeli human rights group B'Tselem (www.btselem.org).

With his old enemy out of the way, Sharon – contradicting his reputation as an incorrigible hardliner – forged ahead with a radical plan to 'disengage' from the Palestinians, building the Separation Fence (see p268) around (most of) the West Bank – despite furious opposition from Jewish settlers – and pulling out of isolated settlements. In August 2005 he completed the hugely controversial evacuation of all 8600 Israeli settlers from the Gaza Strip and four settlements in the northern West Bank. In January 2006 Sharon suffered a massive stroke; Jewish settlers saw it as divine punishment for his betrayal of the Land of Israel. In early 2012 Sharon was still in a coma.

Recent History

Sharon's deputy, Ehud Olmert, won election as prime minister in March 2006 on a platform that – although he, too, had a long record as a hawk – promised a further pull-back from much of the West Bank. But in 2006 Hamas swept Palestinian parliamentary elections. In response to this, the European Union and the USA cut off aid, demanding that Hamas recognise Israel, renounce terrorism and accept peace deals signed by previous Palestinian governments (the money began to flow once more a few months later, but donors still insisted on bypassing Hamas-run ministries and giving the money direct to institutions on the ground).

ARAB NAMES

Arab men are often referred to as Abu (meaning 'father of') followed by the name of their eldest son. Arafat was known popularly as Abu Ammar. But that wasn't because he had a son – he had a daughter, Zahwa, born in 1995. He chose the name of a follower of the Prophet Mohammed as his *nom de guerre*.

1973	**1978**	**1987–93**	**1991**
Egypt and Syria launch a surprise attack on Yom Kippur, the holiest Jewish holiday.	Israel and Egypt sign the Camp David Accords. Israel opens an embassy in Cairo, Egypt establishes one in Tel Aviv, and Sinai is returned to Egypt.	Palestinian frustration with occupation explodes in the First Intifada. The IDF, trained to fight standing armies, responds ineffectively; Palestinian casualties generate international condemnation.	Arafat supports Saddam Hussein's invasion and annexation of Kuwait. In response, Kuwait and other Gulf nations cut off PLO funding and expel Palestinians.

WHAT IS HAMAS?

In 1987 Islamist leaders in Gaza set up the Palestinian wing of Egypt's Muslim Brotherhood, calling it Harakat al-Muqawama al-Islamiya (Islamic Resistance Movement). Better known by its acronym, Hamas, the organisation seeks to establish a Palestinian Islamic state in all of what is now Israel, the West Bank and Gaza. Because it has refused to renounce violence against Israeli civilians (eg suicide bombing and rocket attacks against Israeli towns and cities), Hamas is classified as a 'terrorist group' by the United States, Canada, the European Union, the UK, Japan and Israel.

By the early 1990s, Hamas – funded by Gulf countries and, later, Iran – was gaining status among Palestinians, not only for its uncompromising opposition to Israel but also for running youth clubs, medical clinics and schools in poor neighbourhoods. Whereas Arafat's Fatah Party was seen as corrupt to the core, Hamas was considered both pious and honest.

In 2005 the group agreed with Arafat's successor, Mahmoud Abbas, to accept a role in parliamentary politics. In the PA elections of January 2006, Hamas won a surprise majority in the Palestinian Legislative Council (the PA parliament), in large part because voters were sick of Fatah's corruption.

The new Hamas government refused to recognise Israel, renounce violence or recognise peace agreements signed by the PA – as demanded by Western countries – and found itself shunned. It also faced internal opposition from Fatah gunmen loath to give up their power. Later, in a bloody coup, it forced Fatah out of Gaza and embarked on a campaign of missile attacks against Israeli towns and villages that culminated in Israel's devastating assault on the Gaza Strip around New Year 2009. Since then, Hamas and Israel have had a tenuous ceasefire. Many of the recent missile and infiltration attacks against Israel have been carried out by Gaza's smaller, even more radical Islamist groups.

In the wake of the Arab Spring uprisings of 2011, Hamas eased up on trying to impose strict Islamic law in Gaza, signalled its intention to move its headquarters out of an increasingly unstable Damascus, and indicated that it may turn away from 'armed struggle' in favour of mobilising the masses, a strategy that has worked well for Islamist movements across North Africa.

In summer 2006 Hezbollah guerrillas kidnapped two Israeli soldiers patrolling on the Israeli side of the Israel–Lebanon border. Israel entered a brief war with the Iranian-backed Lebanese militia, in which the Shiite group launched thousands of rockets at Israeli cities, towns and villages, bringing northern Israel to a terrified halt. The scale of Israel's bombing attacks on Lebanese towns was widely condemned and the war was a diplomatic disaster for Israel, but six years later a tenuous ceasefire was still holding.

1993	1994	1995	2000–05
Israeli Prime Minister Yitzhak Rabin and PLO Chairman Yasser Arafat, sworn enemies for decades, sign the Oslo Accords at the White House with an uneasy handshake.	Israel and Jordan sign a peace treaty, delimiting their long border and guaranteeing Jordan a share of Jordan River water. Embassies are opened in Amman and Ramat Gan.	After a peace rally in Tel Aviv, Israeli Prime Minister Yitzhak Rabin is assassinated by a right-wing Jewish extremist. The killing contributes to the breakdown of the Oslo peace process.	The Second Intifada brings scores of suicide bombings to Israeli cities and towns, leading to deadly IDF incursions into Palestinian towns and deepening bitterness on both sides.

SECOND INTIFADA

In spring 2007, Hamas gunmen ran their Fatah counterparts out of the Gaza Strip after several days of fighting. Fatah officials who didn't make it out were tortured, and some killed. A few were thrown to their deaths from tall buildings. Fatah responded with the arrest of Hamas men – some were tortured, too – in the West Bank, which remained under their control. Since then, the US and the EU have continued to send significant aid to the Fatah-led Palestinian Authority in the West Bank, while Iran has smuggled money and weapons to Hamas in Gaza. Israel's unilateral withdrawal from Gaza came to be seen by some Israelis as a serious strategic blunder.

In 2001 Hamas and Islamic Jihad began launching missiles from Gaza into the northern Negev. After Israel's 2006 withdrawal from Gaza these attacks escalated, and over time homemade Qassam rockets were replaced by Iranian-supplied 122mm Grads capable of hitting Be'er Sheva and Rishon LeZion and perhaps Tel Aviv, though Sderot bore the brunt of the attacks and Tel Aviv was never actually hit. In very late 2008, Gazan militants opened up a weekend barrage of dozens of rockets. Casualties in southern Israeli towns such as Sderot were negligible, but the terror brought to local residents was significant. A ceasefire between Israel and Hamas was brokered by Egypt but it never held, and the rockets continued. Israel launched a major offensive, dubbed Operation Cast Lead, aimed at halting the missile attacks. The battles raged for three weeks and, in the end, much of Gaza's infrastructure was destroyed, thousands were homeless, and there were shortages of fuel and the materials needed to rebuild. According to the Israeli human rights organisation B'Tselem, during the operation 1397 Palestinians were killed by Israelis (Israel claims a large majority were militants) and five Israeli soldiers were killed by Palestinians. But Hamas remained in control and dug new smuggling tunnels to circumvent Israel's much-criticised blockade of Gaza, significantly eased for civilian goods in June 2010, and Egypt's sealing of the Rafah border crossing, ended right after the 2011 fall of the Mubarak regime.

Despite everything, a tenuous ceasefire between Hamas and Israel was still holding, more or less, in early 2012.

Few Palestinian fighters had long careers during the Second Intifada. At one point in 2003, 11 successive leaders of Islamic Jihad in the West Bank town of Jenin were either arrested or killed by Israeli troops within a week of taking their position – sometimes on the very day they were made leader.

2004	2005	2006	2011
Yasser Arafat dies at age 75, of unexplained causes, in a Paris hospital and is buried in Ramallah. Conspiracy theories abound; some claim he was poisoned.	Israel unilaterally withdraws from the Gaza Strip, evacuating 21 settlements. Jewish settlers are outraged and radicalised; Palestinians condemn Israel's continued control of land, sea and air access.	Attacks on the Galilee by Iranian-backed Hezbollah lead to Israel's Second Lebanon War. The hard-line Islamist movement Hamas defeats pro-two-state Fatah in Palestinian parliamentary elections.	Radical Jewish settlers carry out 'Price Tag' attacks on Palestinian property and IDF soldiers in an effort to deter the Israeli government from carrying out court-ordered demolitions of illegal West Bank outposts.

People of Israel & the Palestinian Territories

Although it's the world's only Jewish state, Israel is far from homogenous, and a short visit will reveal faces of every colour. By contrast, the Palestinian Territories (not including Jewish settlements) are almost wholly Arab, with only small pockets of minorities such as Samaritans and Bedouins. The pull of the land binds those living in Israel and the Palestinian Territories – Jewish, Muslim or Christian – perhaps sometimes too close for comfort.

As well as about 5.5 million Jews, Israel is home to Arab Muslims, Arab Christians, Druze, Bedouin and various other smaller groups, including the Circassians and Samaritans. Most Palestinians are Sunni Muslim; the West Bank's population is also around 8% Christian.

Among Jews, too, there's just no generalising: much of Israel's Jewish population has come from countries throughout the world, and there are significant cultural differences – particularly among the older generations – between those with European, North African, Ethiopian and Arab heritage. Add in varying levels of religiosity, from atheist all the way up the stairway to heaven to ultra-Orthodox, and a complex cultural picture emerges.

Jews

Jews have inhabited the land of Israel for a few millennia – although their populations have waxed and waned – but the immigration of large numbers of Diaspora Jews was mainly a 20th-century phenomenon. Economic opportunities and spiritual commitments – and, for many, a desire to live and raise children without facing anti-Semitism – have seen the entrance of Russians, Eastern Europeans, South Americans, Moroccans, Yemenites, Syrians, Ethiopians, Indians, Iraqis and British, French and American Jews, to name but a few.

No matter what their origin, most Israelis are united by the belief that the state exists to be a haven for historically persecuted Jews. But Zionism has not come cheap, and three generations have grown in a state of war, insecurity and instability. This reality has done much to shape the national character: a native-born Jew is known as a *sabra* (a prickly pear, or cactus fruit), although in fairness you'll find as many easy-going Israelis as hot-tempered ones.

Behind their tough, warrior image, many Israelis identify closely with European culture, fashion and trends. They are global travellers (it's almost a rite of passage to travel the world after a stint in the army), leaders in the high-tech world (with medical and technical innovations in

Relative to its population, Israel is the largest immigrant-absorbing country on earth. During the 1990s around 900,000 Russians emigrated to the country, boosting the Jewish population by 20%.

RELIGIOUS PRACTICES

incredible supply), proficient in the English language and surprisingly obsessed with the annual Eurovision Song Contest, in which they're active and enthusiastic participants.

Sephardim

Sepharad is the old Hebrew name for Spain, and these Jews are descendants of those expelled from Spain and Portugal at the end of the 15th century. Most of the Jews in Palestine until the 19th century were Sephardim; other Sephardim lived in Constantinople, Amsterdam, Greece, the Balkans, South America and northern Morocco, among other places, where many became prominent academics, physicians and philosophers, contributing to the rich and influential cultural legacy of the Sephardim. Some, too, stayed on in the Iberian region; a 2008 study published in the *American Journal of Genetics* suggests that as much as 17.5% of the current population of Spain and Portugal has some form of Sephardic Jewish ancestry. Around 725,000 Israeli Jews are Sephardim, with Sephardi Jews making up around 15% to 20% of the world's total Jewish population.

The traditional language of the Sephardim is known as Ladino, a Romance language combining old Spanish, old Portuguese and Hebrew and – depending on where exiles from Spain settled – elements of Turkish, Greek, Arabic and French. Though many regional dialects originally existed, it's the eastern (Balkan) form of the language that's today being kept alive in Israel, by its use in media from specialist radio stations to community newspapers.

Ashkenazim

Today's Ashkenazi Jews originate from Germany (in classic Hebrew, *Ashkenaz* refers to Germany), along with Central and Eastern Europe. Some are also descendants of Ashkenazim who emigrated to North and South America, South Africa and Australia between the 16th and 20th centuries.

Some cultural, linguistic and genetic evidence suggests that many Ashkenazim originally emigrated to Europe from the Middle East around CE 800. One theory suggests these 'wandering Jews' were traders who married from local populations and converted their brides to Judaism, which would account for their European physical features.

> Subtle differences exist between Ashkenazi and Sephardi religious practices. Holidays such as Passover are celebrated slightly differently, with varying prohibitions on foods; prayers, too, are performed with variations between the two groups.

THE LAW OF RETURN

Theodor Herzl, the Hungarian Jew who founded political Zionism, dreamt of creating a place where all Jews could live without persecution. His goals were eventually made a reality with the Law of Return, legislation passed by the Knesset in 1950 that guaranteed Israeli citizenship to any Jew who wanted it.

The process is simple: a prospective *oleh* (immigrant) first applies through the Department of Immigration and Absorption or through Israeli consulates abroad; proof of Judaism, Jewish ancestry or conversion to Judaism must be presented, often in the form of parents' *ketubah* (wedding certificate) or a letter from a rabbi back home; the *oleh* then makes *aliyah* (ascent), becoming an Israeli citizen and being provided with the accompanying benefits, including Hebrew language lessons and a financial assistance package, and duties, including army service.

The 1990s saw Israel and its settlements in the Territories absorb hundreds of thousands of *olim* (immigrants), many from Russia and Ethiopia. The masses of immigrants have also played a key political function by keeping the Jewish voting block well ahead of that of Israeli Arabs, most of whom tend to have large families. *Olim* numbers have fallen off in recent years, with around 18,000 arriving each year.

The classic language of the Ashkenazim is Yiddish, a mixture of medieval German and Hebrew, written in Hebrew characters. Though its use has waned considerably, you might still hear the older generations – and some ultra-Orthodox Jews – conversing in Yiddish.

In 1931 the population of Ashkenazi Jews in Europe was around 8.8 million. After the Holocaust, only about a third of that population survived. Despite this, Ashkenazi Jews still comprise around 80% of the world's Jewish population, though in Israel the Ashkenazim constitute a minority among Jews.

Mizrahim

The word *Mizrahi* means Easterner, and the term loosely defines those Jews who originated in North African, Middle Eastern and Central Asian countries such as Yemen, Iraq, Persia (modern-day Iran), Afghanistan, Georgia and Uzbekistan, as well as India and Pakistan. The term *Mizrahi* can also describe those Jews who never left Israel.

Mizrahi Jews began emigrating to Palestine in the 1880s from Yemen. Their numbers swelled after 1948, largely after Arab populations rejected them and in some cases forced their emigration; in 1956, for example, 25,000 Jews were expelled from Egypt by government order. In the same way as Ashkenazi Jews had Yiddish and Sephardim conversed in Ladino, Mizrahi Jews traditionally spoke Maghrebi, a type of Judeo-Arabic dialect (and many brought regional dialects from their former countries).

In the early years of the Israeli state, the Mizrahim suffered discrimination at the hands of the Ashkenazi, and many were forcibly settled in the Negev or remote (in Israeli terms, at least) border areas, though recent years have brought them into the mainstream. Intermarriage between Ashkenazi and Mizrahi has become common, and pop culture equally includes both groups.

Beta Israel

You may know the Beta Israel better as Ethiopian Jews; also sometimes known by the slightly derogatory term Falasha, or 'exiles'. These Jews, who now number around 121,000 in Israel, were largely airlifted to Israel from Ethiopia (together with some from Sudan) in 1984, 1985 and 1991. New immigrants still continue to trickle in today.

No one is quite sure how Jews got to Ethiopia in the first place, although it's possible they were converted by Yemenite-Jewish traders. Another theory suggests they are descendants of the House of King Solomon, who, during his reign, had an intimate relationship with the Queen of Sheba. Others suggest they are descended from a group of Jews that separated from Moses and went south during the biblical Exodus.

The transition to their new home proved difficult for many of the Beta Israel and they are still among the poorest people in the country. Social and cultural differences have kept most Beta Israel communities separated from mainstream society, though the gap has narrowed in recent years as the younger generation takes a more integrated place in Israeli society. The best known among them is Ethiopian-Israeli actress model Esti Mamo, best known for modelling in *Elle* and *Vogue* magazines.

Muslims

Sunni Muslims make up the overwhelming majority of the Palestinian population, and around 70% of the Israeli Arab population. Israel's Central Bureau of Statistics reports that by 2025 the Muslim population of Israel will reach 2 million and make up 22% of the population.

Around 39% of Muslims live in northern population centres, including Nazareth and Haifa, although the highest concentration is in

In Israel Mizrahi Jews are sometimes also referred to under the umbrella term Sephardi, since some Mizrahi religious practices are similar to Sephardi religious rites.

PEOPLE OF ISRAEL & THE PALESTINIAN TERRITORIES

ASHKENAZI JEWS

Ashkenazi Jews make up just 0.25% of the world population, yet they have won 28% of Nobel prizes for economics, physics, chemistry and medicine. Ashkenazi Jews also make up half of the world's chess champions.

AFRICAN HEBREW ISRAELITES

The African Hebrew Israelites, better known as the Black Hebrews, are African-Americans who claim descent from the Ten Lost Tribes of Israel. This concept developed in the late 19th century when several congregations (such as the Church of God and Saints of Christ, founded in 1896, and the Church of the Living God, the Pillar Ground of Truth for All Nations, founded in 1886) emerged from former Christian groups in the USA, and started adhering to traditional Jewish practices, including the observance of Sabbath and the other biblical holidays. In 1966 Chicago-born Ben Carter, also known as Ben Ammi Ben Israel, had visions that he, too, was a direct descendant of the Israelites and began preaching of a return to the Holy Land. The first members of his flock reached Israel, via Liberia, in 1969 and the group has since been based in Dimona (where they follow a strict regime of exercise and vegan cuisine). Today they number around 3000 people and have had permanent residency status since 2003, making them subject to mandatory service in the army.

Jerusalem, home to about 200,000 Muslims (21% of the Muslim population). Although Israeli Muslims are in the political minority, Muslims do maintain control of their holy sites, including the Dome of the Rock and Al-Aqsa Mosque in Jerusalem and the Ibrahimi Mosque in Hebron. Unlike the Arab residents of Haifa, who have Israeli citizenship (and passports), Arab residents of East Jerusalem have only ID cards. These cards permit travel within Israel and the West Bank but, as they are not passports, special permission (and plenty of red tape) is required for East Jerusalem residents to leave the country.

Traditionally, Palestinian Muslims have been moderate in their beliefs and practices; the rise of Palestinian Muslim fundamentalism over the course of the last 30 years has been attributed to a number of factors including the 1979 Islamic Revolution in Iran, which emphasised a return to religious Muslim governance over secular rule, and to the rise of the first Palestinian intifada, which spawned a Jihadist mentality among some extremists. Gaza, in particular, has become a fundamentalist Islamic enclave in recent years, with Hamas forcibly taking the helm and seeking to impose strict religious laws on its population.

The Palestinian people have made significant strides in developing their land for the better and have set down the foundations of what they hope will one day be an independent Palestine. Ramallah in particular is an example of what can be achieved in times of peace as the city is brimming with commerce, restaurants, new hotels and even a stock exchange. Palestinian culture is also alive and well, and a number of Palestinians have achieved international success, notably the award-winning poet Mahmoud Darwish.

Israeli Muslims have long faced a conflict of interests as they struggle to carve out a place within Israeli society but also remain sympathetic to Palestinians in their fight for an independent state. Although it is more common to observe Al-Naqba (the Catastrophe) – the anniversary of Palestinian refugees' displacement on 15 May 1948 – in the Palestinian Territories, some Israeli Muslims do use the day to protest the state of Israel.

> Simplified, the split between Sunni and Shiite Muslims stems from the death of the Prophet Mohammed. Those who believed his successor should be chosen from among his followers became Sunni Muslims; those who thought leadership should be kept in the family (thus going to Mohammed's cousin and brother-in-law, Ali) became Shiites.

Christians

Before the establishment of Israel, Arab Christians made up around 10% of the population of Palestine. Traditionally affluent and educated, they had the means to escape in 1948 (and since), and did so. Today Arab Christians total around 175,000 in Israel and the Palestinian Territories combined, about 2% of the total population. Most of Israel's Christians are clustered in Jerusalem and Nazareth; in the Palestinian Territories, they are grouped around Bethlehem and Ramallah.

As well as Arab Christians, Israel and the Palestinian Territories are also home to Armenian, Russian and Egyptian Christians, foreign clergymen, monks, nuns and others working for Christian organisations. Most Christian holy sites are administered by overseas churches such as the Greek Orthodox Church. Armenians, Copts, Assyrians, Roman Catholics and Protestants also lay claim to various holy sites, and disputes arise frequently over how to share their stewardship. Sometimes the only solution has been to give the keys to Muslim family caretakers, in the hope of stopping centuries-old feuds.

Druze

The Druze are a social and religious group who speak Arabic and practise a secretive religion that is an offshoot of Islam. Like Muslims, the Druze believe in Allah and his prophets, but they believe that Mohammed was succeeded in the 11th century by the divinely appointed ruler, Fatimid Caliph al-Hakim bi-Amr Allah. Also contrary to Islamic belief, the Druze believe in reincarnation; for this reason, headstones on their graves carry no name.

Within Druze society there is a select inner core made up of men and women who have passed a series of difficult tests and are considered to have led exemplary lifestyles of honesty and modesty. The men are identifiable by their white turbans, and only these *uqqal* (the wise) are permitted to read the Druze holy books and take part in the Thursday-night religious ceremonies. The rest of the community, *juhhal* (the ignorant), are not permitted to study the scriptures.

Most Druze communities actually live in the bordering countries of Lebanon and Syria; in Israel they inhabit a few villages in the Galilee, on Mt Carmel and in the Golan. One of their most important religious sites is the tomb of Jethro, located near Tiberias. Jethro was the non-Jewish father-in-law of Moses who assisted the Jews through the desert and accepted monotheism.

Bedouin

The term 'Bedouin' is Arabic for 'desert dweller' and refers to the nomad-pastoralist groups that traditionally live in the desert regions from Egypt to the Arabian Desert. Some 150,000 Bedouin (who consider themselves Arab) live in the Negev Desert while 60,000 live in the Galilee area. The Bedouin, who practise Sunni Islam and speak Arabic, are today sometimes referred to as 'Negev Arabs'.

Land disputes with Israel have pushed the Bedouin onto ever-decreasing plots of land and only around 10% are able to maintain a traditional pastoral lifestyle. Some settlements have been established; however, these are often illegal – there are currently some 45 unrecognised Bedouin villages in the Negev.

Israel has long attempted to move the Bedouin to established towns so the land can be used for military, agricultural and industrial purposes. The Bedouin living in remote desert outposts assert that their forefathers have tended this land (mostly desert, and not of much use for development) for centuries, that they remain rooted to it and that they have nowhere else to go. Israel has offered to rent tracts of land to the Bedouin, who have so far declined.

The land disputes have created increasing tension between the Israeli government and the Bedouin – in some areas home have been demolished and rebuilt several times over. But the disputes are more ideological than political, and many young Bedouin still show their support for Israel by joining the army (although they are not required to do so).

PEOPLE OF ISRAEL & THE PALESTINIAN TERRITORIES

DRUZE

The symbol of the Druze is a five-coloured star, with each colour symbolising one of their principles: green (the universal mind), yellow (the universal soul), red (the truth/word), blue (the antagonist/cause) and white (the protagonist/effect).

To find out more about the Bedouin, get hold of a copy of *Citizen Nawi*, a documentary that describes the fate of the South Hebron Hills Bedouin, and the courageous work of Israeli human rights activist Ezra Nawi.

Circassians

A Caucasian people of Muslim faith, the Circassians number around 4000. They originated in the Caucasian Mountains of Russia and emigrated to Palestine in the 1890s. The community is concentrated in the Galilee villages of Kfar Kama and Reyhaniye. Like the Druze, male Circassians are must perform three years military service in the Israel Defence Forces (IDF); female Circassians are exempt.

Samaritans

Samaritans are one of the world's smallest religious communities, numbering around 700 people, though in Roman times it's thought their numbers ran to around one million. They claim to be both Palestinians and Israelites – they speak Arabic but pray in ancient Hebrew.

The small population, coupled with their refusal to accept converts, has caused a history of genetic disease. To counter this, male Samaritans have been allowed to seek a non-Samaritan Jewish wife, a difficult task since few non-Samaritan women are willing to accept their strict rules of segregation. Nowadays, all marriages must first be given approval by a geneticist.

More challenges faced the Samaritans in Nablus during the First Intifada, during which they were targeted for their close ties with Israel, and tensions with local Muslims forced them to abandon the city and take refuge on Mt Gerizim (see p280); they have been there ever since.

Since 2007 an estimated 30,000 migrants from Africa have entered Israel, usually by paying thousands of dollars to Sinai Bedouins to smuggle them over the border. Most claim to be political asylum seekers from Eritrea or Sudan and find themselves in limbo while their cases are reviewed.

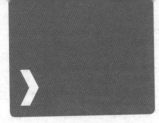

Hummus & Olives: Regional Food

In the beginning there was food, and lots of it. Yes, a quick flick through the Torah, New Testament or Quran will tell you that food has always played a significant role in the Middle East. The Scriptures are stuffed with banquets and feasts, and to this day meals mean far more than scheduled daily breaks from work or play. Food is identity, family and tradition. Here, food is home.

A relatively small area of land, Israel and the Palestinian Territories encompass a veritable universe of cuisine. Within Israel, you can generally divide home cooking into two camps: Ashkenazi (Jews of Eastern European heritage) and Sephardi/Mizrahi (Jews of Iberian, Balkan, North African or Middle Eastern origin). But like its people and music, Israeli food is increasingly becoming a fusion of cultures. The myriad of influences include Iraqi, Moroccan, Polish, Hungarian, Russian, French, Yemenite and many more.

The dish that unites both Jews and Arabs alike is undoubtedly hummus. Served warm with fresh pita bread, it can be eaten with fuul (fava bean paste), tahina (sesame seed paste) or the classic fried felafel. But there's much more beyond the chickpea...

Olives are found all over the region and complement dishes such as *labneh (labaneh)*, a yoghurt-type cheese that's smothered in olive oil and sprinkled with *zaatar* (a blend of spices that includes hyssop, sumac and

Heavenly Hummus

» Ali Caravan, Jaffa (p150)

» Hummus Said, Akko (p186)

» Abu Shukhri, Abu Ghosh (p105)

» Abu Shukri, Jerusalem (p92)

» Nadima, Wadi Nisnas (p170)

A VEGETARIAN BONANZA

There are few places in the world so satisfying to travel in for vegetarians as Israel and the Palestinian Territories.

Local fast food, in particular, is a vegetarian's delight, while salads are frequently served in supersized bowls with bread. In Middle Eastern–style fish or meat restaurants, the tableful of mezze-style plates you'll receive are likely to include beetroot, aubergine in tomato sauce, hummus and olives. Even in top-end, meat-heavy restaurants, you're sure to find a good vegetarian selection. In most major cities there are a growing number of health restaurants, such as the chain Fresh Kitchen, that offer a wide choice of veggie sandwiches, pastas and casseroles, and many dairy kosher cafes have strictly nonmeat menus.

Going veggie is usually more cost-effective, too. Fast food such as hummus, felafel, *sabich* and *bourekas* are all cheap, and sometimes just as filling as a meat option.

This book uses the 🌱 icon to let you know that a restaurant is exclusively vegetarian, while if a restaurant is also vegan this will be indicated in the text.

SPICY SAUCES

sesame). Seasonal fruits such as grapes, apricots, peaches, oranges, lemons, plums, pears, watermelons, strawberries, pomegranates and dates are all grown locally.

For a taste of Iraq, try *kuba* (delicious dough balls stuffed with meat) or *sabich* (grilled aubergine, boiled potato and egg in a pita). The Yemenite *jachnun* is an oddly addictive, highly calorific, rolled length of dough served with a hard-boiled egg, strained tomatoes and schug relish (a spicy sauce made from red or green peppers). *Shakshuka* is a spicy Moroccan egg and tomato stew, generally served at breakfast. *Bourekas* (stuffed cheese pastries made with flaky dough) and shwarma (sliced grilled meat from a spit) are thought to have come from Turkey. Immigrants from Eastern Europe brought blintzes (crêpes), schnitzel, bagels and a heavy, slow-cooked stew, traditionally eaten at midday on Shabbat, called *cholent* or *chunt*.

Israelis, Palestinians, Bedouins and Druze all love a good barbecue and on sunny weekends you're likely to see families gathering in parks to chargrill some red meat, served, of course, with bread and hummus.

When to Eat

If asked if you would like any *hareef* (hot sauce such as Yemenite schug) or *amba* (Iraqi-style mango chutney) with your felafel, *sabich* or hummus, think carefully. These spicy sauces often leave more than a slight tang on the tongue.

The real question in this part of the world is, 'when not to eat?' At any time of the day or night (especially in Tel Aviv and its surrounding suburbs), Israelis can be seen eating out. Although, in general, most Israelis eat their main meal at lunchtime, city-dwellers think nothing of going out to grab a heavy hamburger, felafel or shwarma at 10pm or later. Weekend breakfasts are long, lavish and leisurely, consisting of eggs, salads, fresh juice, bread, cheeses, olives and coffee. Thursday night is the busiest night out for drinking, while Friday nights are frequently reserved for family dinners, with younger generations heading off to bars and nightclubs after having their fill of mum's cooking.

In Arab or Palestinian towns you'll find many businesses shut up shop at midday – even in cosmopolitan Ramallah and Bethlehem – and their proprietors head home for a long family lunch. It may sound strange to Westerners, but most Arabs swear that the best time to eat hummus is early in the morning, served fresh from the pot.

Habits & Customs

Arabs, Bedouin and Druze often cook their breads in a *taboun* (clay oven), which in Israel is also used for pizzas and *bourekas* (stuffed pastries).

Israel and the Palestinian Territories' religious Jews and Muslims observe specific sets of dietary laws, the former known as kosher and the latter as halal. Though they have a number of elements in common (for example the prohibition of pork and the same basic methods of slaughter), there are marked differences between the two, and a number of subtle grades of both practices.

Generally speaking, keeping kosher means not mixing meat and dairy products, and refraining from the consumption of pork, shellfish or wild fowl; as in Muslim slaughter houses, animals for consumption must be killed while fully conscious, their throats slit with a non-serrated blade. In largely secular Israel, keeping kosher in restaurants is a matter of choice, with kosher restaurants generally divided between 'dairy' (basically vegetarian) and 'meat' restaurants. In Tel Aviv, however, you'll find kosher restaurants the exception rather than the rule, and pork and shrimp are in no short supply. Alcohol isn't prohibited within Judaism; on the contrary, most Jewish festivals involve reciting the *kiddush* (blessing over wine) and you'll find some excellent kosher – and nonkosher – wines in Israel.

Because the Palestinian Territories are predominantly Muslim, food is handled according to halal standards. Again, you'll find few bacon sandwiches here, but there are no issues with eating sea creatures such as lobster, oysters and squid under Islamic law. Alcohol, on the other hand, is not permitted within Islam and you'll find it's mostly (though not entirely) Christians patronising Palestinian bars.

Festivals & Special Occasions

Israel

Food has always been crucial to all Jewish festivals and special occasions, either notable for its prevalence (as at weddings, bar/bat mitzvahs or Passover) or its absence (as at Yom Kippur, the Day of Atonement, when a 25-hour fast is kept).

Many Israeli families, whether religious or not, keep to the tradition of the Shabbat (Sabbath) dinner: a meal held together on a Friday evening, which commences, in some homes, with the lighting of Shabbat candles and the sipping of wine. In religious families, all work is forbidden on Shabbat, from 18 minutes before sundown on Friday to one hour after sundown on Saturday, and thus slow-cooked dishes make up Saturday's lunchtime fare.

At Israeli weddings and bar/bat mitzvahs, food is especially important. For these events, families typically invite a few hundred people to enjoy a huge hot buffet of meat, fish, cooked vegetables and rice, before the night descends into a party.

Food also has a part to play at funerals: when Jews mourn a member of their immediate family, Judaism requires that they sit *shiva*, ie stay at home in mourning for seven days after the funeral. Some continue the

A question you're likely to hear at breakfast time in Israel: would you like *betzei ayin* (sunny-side-up), *beitzim mekushkashot* (scrambled), a *chavita* (omelette) or just a *beitza kasha* (hard-boiled egg)?

HUMMUS & OLIVES: REGIONAL FOOD FESTIVALS & SPECIAL OCCASIONS

YALLA, LET'S EAT!

For every Jewish holiday, there's an accompanying set of foods, which appear in the shops a few weeks beforehand. Here are a few of the key ingredients in the Jewish calendar.

» **Passover (Pesach)** Bitter herbs, salt water, a lamb shank bone, *haroset* (a sweet paste of grated apple, nuts, sweet wine and perhaps dates) and a boiled egg each symbolise aspects of the Exodus story. A typical Ashkenazi feast includes chicken soup, gefilte fish (poached cod or carp balls) and plenty of wine. Bread, however, is off the menu (even selling it is forbidden by law in Jewish areas) and is replaced by matzah, those unleavened crackers, made of just flour and water, that you either love or hate.

» **Shavuot** Celebrating the revelation at Sinai, Shavuot is a time when anything goes, so long as it's dairy; cheese-based dishes make a big appearance on Israeli menus.

» **Rosh HaShanah** Jewish New Year comes in for a sweet start with honey-dipped apples, sweet round *challah* bread and honey cake.

» **Yom Kippur** Nothing at all; many Israelis (religious and secular) fast for 25 hours, then break it with a feast.

» **Sukkot** Known by Christians as the Feast of the Tabernacles, Sukkot commemorates the wandering of the Israelites in the desert. Observant Jews eat supper in a *sukkah* (rectangular hut with a flat roof made of branches), which is usually decorated with fruits of the autumn harvest.

» **Hanukkah** Stuff yourself with *sufganiot* (jam doughnuts) – an Israeli contribution to the holiday – and fried potato latkes (pancakes) to commemorate the Jewish Festival of Light and the rededication of the Temple in Jerusalem.

» **Tu B'Shevat** An assortment of dried fruits and nuts are devoured on the New Year for Trees, a time when kids and adults alike plant trees.

» **Purim** *Oznei Haman* ('Ears of Haman'): triangular pastries with poppy-seed, prune or date filling, commemorating the defeat of the arch-villain, Hamam, in the Purim story.

The Mediterranean Menu

If the Bible were to be rewritten today, the Holy Land probably wouldn't be called the 'land of milk and honey' but rather the 'land of meatballs and hummus'. Just like the people, food here is a Mediterranean mix of European and Middle Eastern flavours, with more than a pinch of spice. Here's a taste of the local food and drink...

Saint Pita

1 Baking and breaking bread is another tradition that unites all peoples in the region. What is hummus without pita, shwarma without *laffa* or Shabbat without *challah*?

Olives to Die For

2 Olives often come as a simple side dish with meals or glasses of beer but they do have an almost religious significance in Israel. Mentioned in the Bible numerous times, the olive tree is a symbol of abundance, blessing and peace.

A Culture of Coffee

3 Coffee is part of the constitution. Israelis seem to plan their day around their next *kafeh hafuch* (a cappuccino) or *kafeh shachor* (Turkish black coffee). In Tel Aviv, making coffee is an art form – look out for flowery patterns in your froth.

Felafel Phenomena

4 The undisputed king of Israeli fast food is the felafel, a fried ball of ground chickpeas served with hummus, tahina and salad. Be warned: this vegetarian snack is very, very addictive.

The Heart of Hummus

5 You won't travel far in Israel and the Palestinian Territories without seeing a plate of warm hummus. Made from chickpeas, garlic, olive oil and additional spices, it's usually served with pita bread – perfect for brunch, lunch, dinner or all of the above.

Clockwise from top left
1. Pita breads 2. An array of olives 3. Coffee 4. Felafel

tradition of eating a symbolic meal of bread, to signify sustenance, and boiled eggs and lentils, whose circular shape represents continuation of life. Others find their fridges and freezers overflowing, as every guest paying a condolence call brings along a pie, cake or casserole.

The role of food in Israeli Arab households is similar to the customs followed in the Palestinian Territories; read on for more details.

Palestinian Territories

Ramadan is the Muslim period of fasting, when the observant abstain from eating (along with drinks, cigarettes and sex) during a whole month's daylight hours. Many awaken before sunrise to eat, since they won't eat again until the *iftar*, the daily breaking-of-the-fast feast at dusk. The best-known treat of this season is *qatayif*, a pancake folded over a cluster of crushed nuts or small mound of cheese and drizzled with sugar syrup. For savoury significance, lamb is served during the feast of sacrifice, Eid al-Adha.

During periods of mourning, bitter Arab coffee replaces the sugared variety. When a baby is born, relatives might prepare *mughly*, a spice-laden rice pudding said to aid lactation.

For the big holidays and celebrations, certain things are givens: grainy cookies made of buttery semolina and stuffed with dates or nuts, called *maamool*, and a host of honeyed pastries and sweets including baklava, are carried into host homes in wrapped bakery trays by invited guests.

Where to Eat & Drink

There is no topping Tel Aviv when it comes to quality and variety. In recent years, Tel Aviv and its neighbour Jaffa have become international-calibre dining destinations, with food options for every budget, and an especially bumper crop of high-end individual brasseries and 'chef restaurants'. Jerusalem, too, has plenty of dining choices, though many of them, unlike Tel Aviv, are kosher. However, unique dining experiences can be found all over the country, ranging from seafood institutions in Akko to Bedouin blowouts in the Negev, and from locally raised steaks on the Golan to vegetarian feasts in Amirim in the Upper Galilee.

Although Be'er Sheva and Jerusalem both have lively student scenes, the best bars are found in Tel Aviv. Aside from sports pubs and dance bars, the city is home to a new crop of boutique breweries serving inter-

The 'big cheeses' in Israel are *Bulgarit* (Bulgarian cheese, similar to feta), *emek* (a yellow cheese), *Tsfatit* (a soft, set cheese, originally from Tsfat) and – a huge national favourite – cottage cheese.

The three 'M's – *mjadarah* (rice and lentils topped with fried onions), *mensef* (bread covered in broiled lamb and rice) and *maklubi* ('upside-down' layers of chicken or lamb in rice) – are Bedouin and Palestinian specialities.

FRUIT OF THE VINE

Israel's love affair with wine goes back a long way. The ancient Israelites, Greeks, Romans and Nabataeans all cultivated wine in the region due to its fertile land and excellent grape-growing climate. The modern Israeli wine industry was founded by Baron Edmond de Rothschild who, in 1892, helped establish the **Carmel Winery** (www.carmelwines.co.il/en) in Rishon LeZion (south of Jaffa) and Zichron Ya'acov (south of Haifa); both vineyards still operate today.

The country's current wine revolution, however, began in the early '80s, when the Upper Galilee and Golan regions were planted out with grapes to create cabernets, merlots, chardonnays, sauvignon blancs and other popular varieties. Now you can even find new Israeli wineries in the Judean Hills and the arid Negev Highlands (see p237). Israeli wines, from the old established names to the exclusive tiny boutique ventures, are generally akin to Australian and Californian wines in taste and liveliness.

Notable wineries include **Tishbi** (www.tishbi.com) in Binyamina, the **Golan Heights Winery** (www.golanwines.co.il) on the Golan and **Yatir** (www.yatir.net) in Arad. In the West Bank, you might also occasionally spot a wine ('*nabid*' in Arabic) produced by the monks of the Cremisan monastery, in Beit Jala, near Bethlehem.

national and Israeli beers. For high-quality wineries, head to the Golan Heights, Carmel Mountains or Negev Highlands.

In the Palestinian Territories, Ramallah and Bethlehem both sport the best top-end dining options, though the very best food is generally cheap and cheerful: the felafel, grilled meats and even the *ka'ek* (elongated sesame bagels). Nablus, meanwhile, is justifiably famous for its sweets. Come here for hot *kunafeh,* a flat cheese cake, served hot, made with melted white Nabulsi cheese topped with orange-coloured vermicelli-like pastry and soaked in rosewater syrup. While in Hebron, look out for *kedra* (a rice and lamb dish, infused with saffron and steamed inside a ceramic jar).

Local Brews

» Goldstar, dark lager

» Maccabee, pale lager

» Alexander, boutique ale

» Taybeh, Palestinian beer

HUMMUS & OLIVES: REGIONAL FOOD WHERE TO EAT & DRINK

Daily Life

Israelis

Values & Lifestyle

Israel's Western-style democracy and global economic reach provide the framework for a modern, progressive state, but the country's incredible patchwork of ethnic groups, belief systems, languages and family stories make for a wide array of worldviews, personal and family priorities, and lifestyles.

In Tel Aviv, secular and modern Orthodox families eat, shop, work and play with an intensity and panache that have more in common with Silicon Valley, Wall Street, Berlin's arts scene, gay pride parades and East Asian globalisation than with the city's poor suburbs or Jerusalem. Meanwhile, the residents of the country's 74 remaining 'communal' kibbutzim still live lives of 1950s-style socialist equality. And in Haredi (ultra-Orthodox) neighbourhoods such as Jerusalem's Mea She'arim, residents strive to preserve (or recreate) the lifestyle of 18th-century Eastern Europe.

Israel society was founded on socialist principles, exemplified by the shared community life of the kibbutz. But the vast majority of contemporary Israelis have shifted to a decidedly bourgeois, consumer-driven existence. Increased wealth and a love of the outdoors have made them an active lot: hiking, cycling, windsurfing, backpacking, camping and other leisure activities are hugely popular. Hebrew culture and the arts are immensely important so reading literature and going out to concerts, the theatre and films is woven into the fabric of Israeli-Jewish life.

In the Muslim Arab, Christian Arab, Bedouin, Druze and Circassian villages of the Galilee and the Negev, the pace of life is heavily influenced by religion (generally moderate and Western-oriented among Christians and Circassians, quite traditional among Muslims and Druze), economic realities (including discrimination) and the latest news from the Palestinian Territories and the Knesset. Young people often live at home until they get married.

However, certain aspects of life are made a high priority by almost all Israelis. First and foremost among all ethnic groups is devotion to family. Young Jews may leave the nest at a relatively early age to serve in the army, backpack through Southeast Asia, study, and live with a boyfriend or girlfriend, but the weekly ritual of Shabbat keeps families close, drawing children – even after they're married – back to their parents' home to light candles according to time-honoured tradition.

Military Service

Israel's military has been part of daily life since the country's birth, and for most young Israeli Jews (except the ultra-Orthodox) entering the army is a rite of passage. Israel Defence Forces (IDF) service is compulsory for Jewish, Druze and Circassian men (three years) and for non-

---

Among Israeli Jews, 42% define themselves as 'secular', 38% as 'traditional' to one degree or another, 12% as modern Orthodox and 8% as ultra-Orthodox (Haredi). Source: a 2009 survey by Israel's Central Bureau of Statistics.

Israel is home to 400,000 users of 'kosher' mobile phones. The phones block access to content that is deemed inappropriate and they also lack text messaging (to prevent illicit flirting). Some of the latest models come with a Yiddish interface and Hassidic ringtones.

Orthodox Jewish women (two years); some Bedouin and Christian men volunteer to serve. Reservists can be called up (though most aren't) for training every year or two, generally until age 40 for men and until age 24 (or until the birth of their first child) for women. Soldiers are everywhere (especially, it seems, on buses and trains), and while it remains a jarring sight for first-time visitors, Israelis are unfazed by the proliferation of automatic weapons. If asked, some may answer that while being armed to the teeth is hardly ideal, it sure beats cowering from anti-Jewish mobs as their grandparents had to do in Germany, Poland, Russia, Iraq or Morocco.

The shadow of the Holocaust is always hovering in the background – in the way Israelis perceive their vulnerability to the prospect of Iranian nuclear weapons, in the way they respond to suicide bombings and missiles fired from Gaza, and in the way they relate to reports of the anti-Semitism faced by some Diaspora Jews.

Women

Israeli women have freedom, status and opportunities on a par with their European counterparts and have played significant roles in the economy, politics and even the military (Israel is the only country to have a military draft for women). However, as in Ottoman times, marriage and divorce remain in the hands of the ultra-Orthodox–dominated Chief Rabbinate, which tends to favour male prerogatives over women's rights.

In addition, Israel's ultra-Orthodox communities have become noticeably more extremist in recent years, laying down strict rules that are aimed at separating men and women. The restrictions include segregated buses and footpaths, as well as the banning of women from advertisements and interviews on radio stations. Mainstream Israeli society largely disapproves of the rules and Israeli president Shimon Peres has called for the extremists to stand down.

SACRED BREAD

DAILY LIFE ISRAELIS

According to the Bible, the withholding of bread (Job 22:7) from the poor is a sin, which is why in Israel you will see bags of bread left hanging on the outside of garbage cans. Bread is considered sacred and a prayer must be said before it's eaten.

JEWS & RELIGION

Judaism – as a religion, a nationality and a civilisation – has a significant impact on the daily lives of all Israeli Jews. For the Orthodox and especially the ultra-Orthodox (Haredim), virtually every action and decision is somehow connected to Halacha (Jewish law), as interpreted by over 2000 years of legal precedent. Secular Jews pay little attention to the daily discipline of Jewish observance, but their lives are still defined by the weekly rhythm of Shabbat and the annual cycle of Jewish holidays. Many Jewish Israelis define themselves not as 'secular' (ie ideologically secularist) but as traditional (*masorti*) – that is, they observe some traditions but not all of them. For instance, young people may have Shabbat (Friday night) dinner with their parents before heading out to a discotheque.

In recent years Israeli Jews have been showing increasing religiosity. Secular Jews are keeping more Shabbat rituals, traditional Jews are becoming a bit more traditional, and the modern and ultra-Orthodox are choosing to follow ever-stricter interpretations of Halacha.

The exponential growth of the Haredi community is creating all sorts of frictions – for example, in formerly secular neighbourhoods in which new Haredi residents demand that roads be closed on the Sabbath and buses segregated.

Most schools run by the ultra-Orthodox teach only religious subjects, providing virtually no education in science, maths, history, literature or English and producing generations of young people with few job skills. A significant majority of ultra-Orthodox men never work; instead they are supported by government subsidies while studying in *yeshivot* (religious seminaries). Haredi women, who are not bound by the Halachic command to spend every waking moment on religious study, are entering the workforce in increasing numbers.

FAMILY BUDGETS

Palestinians

Values & Lifestyle

The ebb and flow of Palestinian daily life depends largely on the security situation in the Palestinian Territories. Gaza is in particularly dire straits as the Israeli blockade imposed after the Hamas takeover of 2007, though loosened in recent years, has constricted the local economy, leaving huge numbers of people out of work and dependent on international aid. The situation in the West Bank has improved greatly since the end of the Second Intifada (circa 2005), and the removal of most internal checkpoints has made it easier for Palestinians to travel between home and work or school.

The Palestinians are determined to make the best of their tenuous situation. Family bonds are unbreakable and are often made stronger by intra-family business partnerships. Family income is typically sunk into a large home so everyone can live under one roof, with separate units for each nuclear family.

Palestinian men often spend their leisure time in the local coffeehouse, where old-timers play backgammon and snack on sticky baklava. Meals are usually taken at home, and the dinner table often resembles a banquet hall with an endless array of salads, soups and main courses. Palestinians are also intimately attached to their land, especially their olive groves, and often return to home villages to help with the harvest in October and November.

Gaza is largely controlled by Muslim fundamentalists but much of the West Bank retains a moderate outlook, and Ramallah in particular exhibits the trappings of modern, Western living, including fast cars, health clubs and late-night bars. Football and basketball are both popular sports, played by young Palestinians on makeshift fields and courts across the Territories. And while images of the Palestinian youths hurling rocks at Israeli soldiers have become ingrained on the world's consciousness, surveys show that only 8% of young Palestinians believe that violence is a useful political tool.

> Palestinian men are the breadwinners in most families, but in a typical household the wife handles the accounts. After budgeting her husband's earnings she hands him back some walking-around cash, called 'cigarette money'.

Employment & Income

Palestinians earn far less than the average Israeli (the annual per-capita income in the West Bank is just US$2900, compared with Israel's US$29,800), a factor that has done much to keep Palestinians frustrated with their lot. With a high unemployment rate and a spectacular birth rate (an average of seven children per woman), the average Palestinian home is both overcrowded and poor.

Women

Though Palestinian women, like many women worldwide, have traditionally assumed the role of home-based caregiver, recent years have seen more women encouraged to enter higher education and to work outside the home. Over the last several decades, women have slowly made their mark on Palestinian politics – Ramallah currently boasts its first female mayor, Janet Michael.

> Gays and lesbians live an open lifestyle in Tel Aviv and other cities, but their lifestyle in Jerusalem is more cautious and conservative. This conservatism can lead some Haredim to stray from their marriages in order to engage in secret, same-sex relationships.

Government & Politics

Israeli Government

Israel is a parliamentary democracy headed by a prime minister. Government decisions are made by the cabinet, presided over by the prime minister; its members (ministers) have executive responsibility for government ministries. The 120-member unicameral legislature, the Knesset, is elected by national proportional representation every four years (although elections are almost always called early). Israel also has a president, whose role is largely ceremonial, except that he or she must consent to the dissolution of parliament and, after elections, decide which party leader will be given the first shot at forming a coalition. The parliament elects the president for a term of seven years.

There is no separation of religion and state in Israel. Marriage and divorce are controlled by Jewish, Muslim and Christian religious courts, which do not perform intermarriages. As there is no civil marriage, couples of mixed religious background wishing to wed can do so only outside Israel (eg in Cyprus).

One unusual feature of the Israeli Knesset is that the winning party in elections doesn't necessarily end up as the party in charge. Any winning party must form a coalition comprising at least 61 seats of the Knesset; if the winning party fails to secure majority support within an amount of time allotted by the president, the next party in line will attempt to do so. This is precisely what happened in the 2009 elections.

Until 2009 Israel's leading party for several years was Kadima (Forward), founded in 2005 by Ariel Sharon following his sudden departure from the right-wing Likud Party. Kadima, which won 29 seats in the 2006 parliamentary elections, billed itself as a centrist party, promoting a secular civil agenda. Its platform was based on partial disengagement from the Palestinian Territories, a reduction in the influence of Orthodox Jewish religious groups and a free-market economy with adequate welfare support. Sharon's sudden stroke in January 2006, however, brought his deputy Ehud Olmert to the head of the party and the government.

Olmert soon found himself embroiled in foreign and domestic strife as Israel engaged in armed conflict in both Gaza and Lebanon. Popular support for Kadima waned until elections were finally held in February 2009. Olmert's personal popularity also took a nosedive because of accusations of bribery and corruption (he was indicted in early 2012). Kadima still won by a fraction (taking 28 Knesset seats, against the Likud party's 27 seats), but, despite the attention surrounding Tzippi Livni as Olmert's successor and the first female prime minister since Golda Meir, Kadima was unable to form the requisite coalition.

Golda Meir was the world's third female prime minister and known as the 'Iron Lady' long before the nickname was bequeathed to Margaret Thatcher.

Iranian-born Moshe Katsav, president of Israel from 2000 to 2007, resigned after being accused of serious sexual misconduct towards a former female subordinate and was eventually convicted of two counts of rape. In December 2011, still proclaiming his innocence, he began serving a seven-year term at Ma'asiyahu Prison in Ramla.

Binyamin Netanyahu, leader of the right-wing Likud party, succeeded where Kadima failed, bringing some far-right extremist elements (some of whom advocate the establishment of Jewish religious law, or that Israel should encompass the whole of historic Palestine, including the current West Bank and Gaza Strip) into the coalition. He assumed the office of prime minister in April 2009.

Following President Barack Obama's 'New Beginning' speech in Cairo in June 2009, Netanyahu endorsed the idea of a Palestinian state alongside Israel in his 'Bar-Ilan' speech, although any further effort to hold talks with the Palestinians ended in an impasse. In 2011 relations between the two leaders cooled after Netanyahu lectured Obama in the Oval Office, warning him not to chase 'illusions' of Middle East peace and stating that a return to the 1967 borders would be impossible.

Meanwhile, the left-leaning Labor Party fared poorly in the 2009 elections, slipping from 19 to 13 seats (down from 56 in 1969). Its founding ideology was a mix of Zionism and socialism (this was the party of David Ben-Gurion, Shimon Peres and Yitzhak Rabin), but has recently been criticised for its wavering, having been compared to the 'Third Way' of British Labour under Tony Blair. In January 2011 Labour leader and Defence Minister Ehud Barak resigned from the party, taking other Knesset members with him to form Si'at Ha'Atzma'ut (the Independence Party).

More than 20 other parties also battled for seats in 2009, with, in total, 65 seats falling to right-wing parties. General elections are next scheduled for November 2013 but observers say a vote is likely earlier than that.

Palestinian Authority

The Palestinian Authority (Palestinian National Authority; PA or PNA) was established in 1994 as an interim body to rule for five years while a bona fide Palestinian government was established. According to the Oslo Accords (see p380), the PA was to assume control over urban areas and villages in the Palestinian Territories (rural areas and roads would still be under Israeli control). Ongoing failures in the negotiations prevented the establishment of an independent state and the PA remains the governing body.

The PA is headed by a president, elected once every four years. In January 2005 Mahmoud Abbas (also known as Abu Mazen) won the presidency with 62% of the vote. In January 2009, however, when Abbas' tenure ran out, he extended his term by another year. The one-year extension ran out and Abbas remains in power with no indication of a power change.

Abbas has enjoyed only tepid support over the years but he got a big boost from the Palestinian public in September 2011 when he submitted an application to the UN General Assembly as that body's 194th member state.

The Palestinian legislative council (parliament) is a unicameral body with 132 members, who are elected from 16 districts in the West Bank and Gaza. The leading party in the council selects a prime minister and a government. In January 2006, the Islamist Hamas party triumphed in elections held throughout the Palestinian Territories, and on 29 March 2006, Ismail Haniyeh was sworn in as prime minister. Immediately, the USA, European Union, Canada and Israel froze all Palestinian Authority funding, since they consider Hamas a terrorist organisation.

Though Fatah, under President Abbas, and Hamas, under Prime Minister Haniyeh, briefly came together with a coalition government, Hamas' bloody takeover of Gaza in June 2007 prompted Abbas to dismiss the government, along with Haniyeh, and appoint an ex-World Bank official, Salam Fayyad, as the PA's technocrat prime minister. Hamas,

The Palestinian-run Jerusalem Media & Information Centre (www.jmcc.org) provides news on the conflict and polling and other services to journalists and documentarians.

The respected, non-profit, non-partisan Middle East Media Research Institute (www.memri.org) provides translations of articles and TV clips in Arabic, whose message is often very different from that of official English-language statements and sound bites.

WHO'S WHO IN PALESTINIAN POLITICS

» **Palestine Liberation Organisation (PLO)** Founded in 1964, this political and paramilitary group is considered by the UN to be the 'sole legitimate representative of the Palestinian people'. Since the Palestinian Territories aren't recognised by the UN as an independent state, there is no recognition within the UN (except in Unesco) of the PA or the PLC. But in order for Palestinians to have some sort of presence in the UN, the PLO, an organisation distinct from the government, holds a permanent observer role at the UN General Assembly, though it can't vote. In 1991, the USA ceased to consider the PLO a terrorist organisation.

» **Palestinian National Council (PNC)** The legislative body of the PLO, with some 669 members representing West Bank, Gazan and Diaspora Palestinians. It is responsible for electing the PLO's decision-making 18-member Executive Body.

» **Palestinian Authority (PA)** The current democratically elected Palestinian government (designed as an interim body), with its president elected separately every four years.

» **Palestinian Legislative Council (PLC)** The Palestinian parliament, comprising 132 members.

» **Fatah** The oldest political party in the Palestinian Territories, Fatah (Conquest), was founded by Yasser Arafat and a handful of refugees in the late 1950s. Fatah is a secular, nationalist party that sits left of centre. For most of its early existence, Fatah was a terrorist organisation that carried out attacks against Israeli targets in the Middle East and Europe in the 1970s. Attempts to reconcile with Israel brought it swiftly into the mainstream (for example, it outwardly renounced terror) and it dominated Palestinian politics and the Palestinian Authority until about 2006, when its main rival, the Islamist group Hamas, won victories in local, and later national, elections.

» **Hamas** The charter of Hamas, written in 1988, calls for the destruction of the State of Israel through 'armed struggle' (including terrorism) and the establishment of a Palestinian Islamic state in what is now the territory of Israel, the Gaza Strip and the West Bank. See What is Hamas?, p385, for more.

however, retained control of Gaza and continues to assert that it is a democratically, and thus legitimately, elected leadership.

The West Bank and Gaza are now governed by two separate governments. The internationally recognised, Fatah-backed PA government sits in the West Bank, with Abbas as its president and Fayyad its prime minister. Gaza, meanwhile, is ruled by a marginalised, isolated Hamas government, ruling with an iron fist, with Haniyeh its prime minister and Aziz Duwaik, originally a professor of urban geography, as Speaker of the Palestinian Legislative Council. With Abbas now in power beyond his elected term, Hamas now recognises Duwaik as the Palestinian acting president. However, in January 2012 Duwaik was arrested by the Israeli army and sentenced to six months' detention without charges.

In July 2009 Hamas appeared to soften its stance against Israel when Khaled Mashal, a Damascus-based official, announced it would consider a peace plan that saw a Palestinian state based on 1967 borders. Haniyeh made similar comments in 2010 but, despite the change in tone, Hamas has not changed its charter, which calls for the destruction of Israel and the creation of an Islamic state on the land that is currently Israel, the West Bank and the Gaza Strip.

Hamas, by Matthew Levitt, is essential reading material for anyone interested in Palestinian politics. The well-researched exposé details the rise of Hamas from terror network to an efficient, disciplined political force.

Judaism, Christianity & Islam

Israel and the Palestinian Territories are the birthplace of two of the three great monotheistic faiths, Judaism and Christianity; the youngest of the trio, Islam, considers Jerusalem to be its third-holiest city. And another world religion, the Baha'i faith, has its holiest sites in Haifa and Akko (see p161).

Judaism

One of the oldest religions still practised, Judaism is based on a covenantal relationship between the Jewish people and God. The most succinct summary of Jewish theology and Judaism's strict monotheism is to be found in the Shema prayer, which reads, 'Hear O Israel, the Lord is your God, the Lord is One'.

According to the Torah (the first five books of the Hebrew Bible), the covenant between God and the Jewish people began with the first monotheist, Abraham (19th century BCE), forefather of both Jews and Muslims. It was later confirmed and elaborated at Mt Sinai (13th century BCE), where the Israelites – in addition to receiving the Ten Commandments – were transformed from a tribal grouping into a people. The Jewish people is eternally bound by this covenant – this is the meaning of being 'chosen' – and is required not only to obey God's *mitzvot* (commandments) but also to demonstrate, through exemplary conduct, the truth of God's oneness to all the nations of the world.

Judaism holds that God is present in history and in the actions of human beings. Evil occurs when human beings wilfully and deliberately ignore God's will, good when they follow the rules He has laid down. Humans have both free will and moral agency: they can choose to follow either their evil impulses or their better natures.

Jewish history can be divided into two periods: before and after the destruction of the Second Temple in Jerusalem in 70 CE. Before that momentous year, Jewish ritual and service to God were focused on animal sacrifices carried out in the Temple in Jerusalem by the *kohanim* (members of the priestly class, from whom Jews with the family name of Cohen are descended). After the destruction of Jerusalem, sacrifices ceased and Judaism turned to prayer, meditation and study as the main media of communication with the Divine. Over the next few centuries, Judaism's Oral Law was put into writing in the Mishna and further elaborated in the Talmud; much of the latter, written in Aramaic, reads like a shorthand protocol of legal deliberations.

Before the Holocaust, there were about 18 million Jews worldwide. Today, there are estimated to be about 13 million Jews, including about 6 million each in Israel and the United States.

Over the next 1500 years, generation after generation of sages – issuing legal rulings and teaching in places such as Babylonia (Iraq), Egypt, Spain, Tsfat (in the Galilee) and Lithuania – debated and refined both Jewish theology and the 613 commandments of Halacha (Jewish law). Orthodox Judaism (the most conservative of the religion's streams) holds that the Oral Law, in its entirely, was given at Mt Sinai, while the Reform, Conservative and Reconstructionist Movements believe that Judaism has always been dynamic and proactive, changing and developing over the generations as it had to deal with new ideas and new circumstances.

Today, ultra-Orthodox (Haredi) rabbis – many of whom are non-Zionist (ie are at best ambivalent about the role of the State of Israel in Jewish history) – have exclusive control of state-supported Jewish religious practice in Israel through the Chief Rabbinate, despite the fact that their followers constitute only a small minority of the country's Jewish population. In the Diaspora, the vast majority of Jews belong to the liberal (progressive) movements or are not affiliated with any movement.

Although most Jews have lived in the Diaspora for most of Jewish history – in theological terms, they were exiled from the Land of Israel as punishment for disobeying God's commandments – Jerusalem, Zion and Israel have played a central role in Judaism ever since God repeatedly promised the Land of Israel to the Children of Israel in the Torah. When praying, Jews face Jerusalem, and virtually all synagogues are built with the Torah ark facing the Holy City.

Christianity

Christianity is based on the life and teachings of Jesus of Nazareth, a Jew who lived in Judea and Galilee during the 1st century CE; on his crucifixion by the Romans; and on his resurrection three days later, as related in the New Testament.

Christianity started out as a movement within Judaism, and most of Jesus's followers, known as the Apostles, were Jews. Like many Jews of his time, Jesus was critical of the decadence and materialism of Jerusalem's ruling class and contemptuous of Roman authority. But after his death, the insistence of Jesus's followers that he was the Messiah caused Christianity to become increasingly distinct from Judaism. The anti-Jewish polemics of some early Christians, written at a time when Christianity was a beleaguered sect persecuted by the Romans, would have serious implications in later centuries, when Christianity became all-powerful in Europe.

JUDAISM, CHRISTIANITY & ISLAM ARAB RELIGION CHRISTIANITY

In 1920, one in 10 Palestinian Arabs was Christian; today, just one in 75 residents of the Palestinian Territories is. Bethlehem, which in 1948 was 85% Christian, is now more than three-quarters Muslim.

JEWISH HEADCOVERINGS

If you see a man wearing a small, round, convex skullcap, chances are he is a religious Jew.

There is no commandment specifying that Jewish men cover their heads. Rather, wearing a *kippa* (*yarmulke* in Yiddish, skullcap in English) is merely a tradition, albeit one that is well entrenched. All male visitors to Jewish holy sites are asked to cover their heads – a *kippa* is fine, of course, but so is any kind of hat.

It is often possible to infer a Jew's background, religious orientation and even political beliefs by the type of *kippa* he – or her husband – wears. Zionist Orthodox Jews, including West Bank settlers, usually go for crocheted *kippot* with designs around the edges, while ultra-Orthodox (Haredi) men, of both the Hasidic and Litvak streams, generally wear black velvet or cloth *kippot* of medium size. The Bukharian Jews of Central Asia wear pillbox caps decorated with embroidery. An extra-large crocheted *kippa* is a sign that the wearer is probably either a follower of the Braslav Hassidic movement or a messianic Jewish West Bank settler. (Don't confuse such *kippot* with the white, crocheted skullcaps worn by Hajjis, ie Muslims who have made the pilgrimage to Mecca.)

According to the New Testament, the Angel Gabriel – in an event known as the Annunciation – appeared to Mary in Nazareth and informed her that she would conceive and give birth to the Son of God. Jesus was born in Bethlehem (in Christian terminology and art, his birth is known as the Nativity) but grew up back in Nazareth, where later on he preached. Much of his ministry – and many of his best-known miracles – took place around the Sea of Galilee, in places such as Capernaum, Korazim, Bethsaida and Kursi. The Sermon on the Mount was delivered just up the hill from Capernaum on the Mount of the Beatitudes, while the Transfiguration took place on Mt Tabor. Places believed to correspond to all these venues can be visited.

At the age of 33 or so Jesus, whose growing influence had caused alarm among Jewish and Roman authorities alike, was accused of sedition and condemned to death by the Roman prefect of Judaea, Pontius Pilate. Christians believe that his suffering was foretold in the Hebrew Bible. According to the New Testament, after the Last Supper Jesus was arrested in Gethsemane; put on trial before the Sanhedrin (Jewish supreme court), Pontius Pilate and even Herod the Great (the Roman-appointed king of Judaea) himself; condemned to death; and mocked by Roman soldiers as he was led to Golgotha (Calvary), where he was crucified. Three days after his burial (Entombment), his tomb was found to be empty, evidence of his Resurrection.

The followers of Jesus came to be known as Christians (Christ is a Greek-derived title meaning 'Anointed One'), believing him to be the son of God and the Messiah (the English word 'messiah' comes from the Hebrew *mashiach,* which means 'anointed one'). Jews did not (and do not) accept Jesus as the Messiah or as the Son of God – this difference is the defining theological disagreement between the two faiths. Muslims consider Jesus to be a messenger of God and a prophet but do not believe that he was crucified or that he atoned for humankind's sins.

In about 325 CE, Helena (Constantine the Great's mother) identified what she believed to be the location of Jesus's crucifixion and burial, marking the site with a predecessor of today's Church of the Holy Sepulchre. The First Crusade (1095–99) was launched in part to ensure Christian access to this site.

The ownership of holy sites in Israel and the Palestinian Territories has long been a subject of contention among the country's various Christian denominations. At a number of sites in Jerusalem and Bethlehem, relations are still governed by a 'status quo' agreement drawn up in Ottoman times. The Holy Land's largest denomination, the Greek Orthodox Church – almost all of whose local members are Arabic-speaking Palestinians – has jurisdiction over more than half of Jerusalem's Church of the Holy Sepulchre and a large portion of Bethlehem's Church of the Nativity.

Islam

Founded by the Prophet Mohammed (570–632 CE), who lived in what is now Saudi Arabia, Islam is based on belief in the absolute oneness of God (Allah) and in the revelations of His final prophet, Mohammed. The Arabic word *islam* means 'absolute submission' to God and His word.

Mohammed began preaching to the people of Mecca in about 610 CE, calling on them to renounce idolatry, believe in one God and prepare themselves for the Day of Judgment, when all humans would be held accountable for their actions.

Islam's sacred scripture is the Quran (Koran), which was revealed to Mohammed over the course of two decades. Believed by Muslims to be God's infallible word, it consists of 114 *suras* (chapters) written in highly

Only about 1400 Christians still live in Gaza. Since the Hamas takeover, Islamist hard-liners have killed the owner of a Gaza City Christian bookshop for alleged proselytising (2007), bombed the Gaza City YMCA (2008) and attacked several churches.

In 1993 the late King Hussein of Jordan – out-manoeuvring the Saudis – donated funds to refurbish the golden dome of Jerusalem's Dome of the Rock. The exterior is now covered by 80 kg of 24-carat gold leaf.

THE FIVE PILLARS OF ISLAM

» **Shahadah** Islam's confession of faith, the Shahadah sums up the Islamic belief in the absolute oneness of God and the finality of Mohammed's prophecy: 'There is no God but Allah, and Mohammed is the messenger of Allah'. Anyone who recites the Shahadah – which appears on the flag of Saudi Arabia – three times, in front of witnesses, becomes a Muslim.

» **Salat** The obligation to pray to God, without an intermediary, five times a day (dawn, midday, late afternoon, sunset and night). Prayers are performed facing Mecca and can be undertaken anywhere, except on Friday at noon, when men must attend congregational prayers in a mosque.

» **Zakat** Muslims are required to give alms to the poor worth one-fortieth of their income. The West Bank and Gaza have around 80 *zakat* committees that oversee the distribution of charitable donations.

» **Sawm** During Ramadan, the ninth month of the Islamic calendar, nothing must pass through the lips (food, cigarettes or drinks), and sex is prohibited, from dawn until dusk.

» **Hajj** The pilgrimage to Mecca, which every Muslim who is able should make at least once in their lifetime.

complex – and often poetic – classical Arabic. The Quran presents God as the omnipresent creator and sustainer of the world, infinite in His wisdom and power. Sayings and acts attributed to the Prophet, believed to illustrate correct Islamic behaviour and beliefs, are known as *hadith*.

Islam and Judaism share common roots, and Muslims consider Adam, Noah, Abraham, Isaac, Jacob, Joseph and Moses to be prophets. As a result, Jews and Muslims share a number of holy sites, including Al-Haram ash-Sharif/Temple Mount in Jerusalem and the Ibrahimi Mosque/Cave of Machpelah (Tomb of the Patriarchs) in Hebron. Because of their close scriptural links, Muslims consider both Jews and Christians to be an *ahl al-Kitab*, a 'people of the Book'. Judaism has always seen Islam as a fellow monotheistic faith (because of the Trinity, Jewish sages weren't always so sure about Christianity).

Muslims believe that Mohammed visited Jerusalem on his 'Night Journey', during which his steed Buraq took him from Mecca to Jerusalem in a single night. He then ascended to heaven from the stone around which the Dome of the Rock was later built, returning with revelations for the faithful. For a brief period, Mohammed instructed Muslims to pray towards Jerusalem.

Almost all Palestinian Muslims belong to Sunni Islam, by far the religion's largest branch; so do the vast majority of Egyptians, Jordanians and Syrians. The Lebanese Hezbollah movement, like its patrons in Iran, is Shiite (Shi'a). Syria's ruling elite belongs to a heterodox offshoot of Shi'ite Islam known as Alawite (Alawi).

Excellent primers on the Muslim faith include *Inside Islam* (2002), edited by John Miller and Aaron Kenedi, and *Islam: A Short History* (2000) by Karen Armstrong. For wide-ranging historical analyses, try *Islam and the West* (1994) or *The Crisis of Islam* (2004) by Bernard Lewis.

Arts

Literature

Israeli Literature

Israelis are enormously proud of the revival of the Hebrew language and the creation of modern Hebrew literature, seeing them as the crowning cultural achievements of the Zionist movement.

Some classic names to keep an eye out for (their major works are available in English translation):

» **Yosef Hayim Brenner** (1881–1921) His novels and poems of show both his passion for, and his critique of, the Zionist movement's efforts to create a tough, new 'Hebrew' civilisation in Palestine.

» **Shmuel Yosef Agnon** (1888–1970) Israel's only Nobel winner was concerned with the dichotomy between traditional Jewish and modern life.

» **Rachel Bluwstein** (1890–1931) Known in Israel simply as Rachel, she has long been the nation's most-beloved poet.

» **Yehuda Amichai** (1924–2000) He captured the public's imagination with his gently ironic explorations of daily life.

» **Ephraim Kishon** (1924–2005) The works of the brilliant Hungarian-born satirist skewer Israeli society and universal human foibles.

» **Aharon Appelfeld** (b 1932) In novels such as *Badenheim 1939* (1978), the Holocaust hovers just off-stage.

» **AB Yehoshua** (b 1936) Described by Harold Bloom as an 'Israeli Faulkner', he particularly shines in *The Lover* (1977), set against the backdrop of the 1973 Yom Kippur War.

» **Amos Oz** (b 1939) His works paint bleak but compelling pictures of an Israel few visitors encounter.

» **David Grossman** (b 1954) The novelist established his reputation with *The Yellow Wind* (1987), a critical look at Israel's occupation of the Palestinian Territories.

Palestinian Literature

Until recent years, poetry remained the most common form of literary expression in Palestinian circles, and the politically oriented poet Mahmoud Darwish (1941–2008) remains its leading light. Two of his last collections, *Why Did You Leave the Horse Alone?* (1995) and *Unfortunately, It Was Paradise* (2003), are typically lyrical and nostalgic.

It wasn't until the 1960s that narrative fiction appeared on the Palestinian literary scene. Emile Habibi (1922–96) and Tawfiq Zayad (1929–94), Israeli Arabs who long served as members of the Knesset, both wrote highly regarded works of fiction. Habibi's *Secret Life of Saeed the Pesoptimist* (1974) is a brilliant, tragicomic tale dealing with the difficulties facing Palestinians who became Israeli citizens after 1948. The stunning

---

Attended by 600 publishers from 30 countries, the huge Jerusalem International Book Fair has been held in odd-numbered years since 1963. It's here that the prestigious Jerusalem Prize for Literature is awarded.

A hugely popular book carnival called the Hebrew Book Week (www.sfarim.org. il, in Hebrew) brings scores of publishers' book stalls – and steep discounts – to public squares in about a dozen Israeli cities every June.

debut work of Ghassan Kanafani (1936–72), *Men in the Sun* (1963), includes a novella and a collection of short stories delving into the lives, hopes and shattered dreams of its Palestinian characters. In *The Inheritance* (2005), Sahar Khalifeh (b 1942) provides frequently chilling insights into the lives of Palestinian women, both in the Palestinian Territories and abroad.

Music

Israeli Music

Israeli music is a rich tapestry of modes, scales and vocal styles that cross back and forth between East and West. The country was producing 'world music' before the category ever existed.

Israelis of all ages listen to songs from decades past without necessarily thinking of them as 'retro'. Among the still-popular greats of the mid-20th century is Yemenite singer Shoshana Damari (1923–2006), famous for her incredibly guttural pronunciation of the letter *'ayn*. Naomi Shemer (1930–2004) composed much of the soundtrack of Israel's 1960s, 1970s and 1980s, including the iconic – though rarely heard (except in Diaspora Jewish communities) – 'Jerusalem of Gold' (1967).

Despite the 1965 banning of a Beatles tour by Israel's cultural commissars, rock quickly made itself a long-term fixture on the local music scene thanks to groups such as Poogy (Kaveret), Mashina, Teapacks (named after Tipp-Ex, the correction fluid) and Benzin. Rock has waxed and waned alongside the anthems of classic Israeli pop – names to listen for include Shlomo Artzi, Arik Einstein, Matti Caspi, Shalom Hanoch, Yehudit Ravitz, Assaf Amdursky and, more recently, Aviv Geffen. Idan Raichel introduced Ethiopian melodies to a mainstream audience.

Among the Israeli hip-hop artists and groups you may come across are Shabak Samech, HaDag Nachash, Subliminal, the Shadow and the Israeli-Palestinian group DAM. One of the most exuberant performers of dance music as been **Dana International** (www.danainternational.co.il), a half-Yemenite transsexual who won the Eurovision Song Contest in 1998.

Mizrahi (Oriental or Eastern) music, with its Middle Eastern and Mediterranean scales and rhythms, has its roots in the melodies of North Africa (especially Umm Kulthum–era Egypt and mid-century Morocco), Iraq and Yemen. For decades it was banned from the radio – the Ashkenazi cultural elite feared 'Levantinisation' – so to find the work of artists such as Zohar Argov (1955–87) and Haim Moshe (b 1956), you had to head to the grunge of Tel Aviv's central bus station.

These days, though, Mizrahi music may just be Israel's most popular genre. Old-timers **Shlomo Bar** (www.shlomobar.com) and **Yair Dalal** (www.yairdalal.com), inspired by the traditional Jewish music of Morocco and Iraq respectively, are still performing alongside superstars **Sarit Hadad** (www.sarit-hadad.com), who has been described as Israel's Britney Spears, and **Amir Benayoun**, whose genre-defying concerts mix love songs and medieval Jewish liturgical poems. Moshe Peretz also enjoys crossing the line from Mizrahi to mainstream and back again.

Another popular trend is using Jewish religious vocabulary and soundscapes to access ethnicity. Over the last few years, performers such as Etti Ankri, Ehud Banai, David D'Or, Kobi Oz, Berry Sakharof and Gilad Segev have turned towards traditional – mainly Sephardic and Mizrahi – liturgical poetry and melodies, producing works with massive mainstream popularity.

Mizrahi music has fared much better than its traditional Ashkenazi counterpart, Klezmer. Born in the shtetls of Eastern Europe, Jewish 'soul' can take you swiftly from ecstasy to the depths of despair – but it has

MUSIC
FESTIVALS

Israel's best musical festivities include the twice-a-year Abu Gosh Vocal Music Festival (www.agfestival.co.il), Eilat's Red Sea Jazz Festival (www.redseajazz eilat.com) and, for dance music, Tel Aviv's annual Love Parade.

remained a niche taste. You can check it out at the Tsfat Klezmer Festival (p233).

Israel also has a strong Western classical tradition thanks to Jewish refugees from Nazism and post-Soviet immigrants from Russia. The **Israel Philharmonic Orchestra** (www.ipo.co.il) – whose first concert, in 1936, was conducted by Arturo Toscanini – is world renowned.

Palestinian Music

To listen to some genuine Palestinian folk music, go to www.barghouti.com/folklore/voice. Many of the songs were recorded live at Palestinian weddings, where the art form is practised at its best.

In addition to catchy Arabic pop from Beirut and Cairo, visitors to the West Bank might also come across traditional folk music, dominated by the sounds of the *oud* (a stringed instrument whose resonator is shaped like a pear), the *daf* (tambourine) and the *ney* (flute).

A phenomenon currently sweeping the Palestinian Territories is locally produced rap music. From Gaza's first hip-hop group, PR (Palestinian Rappers), to the genre's main exponents, **Dam Rap** (www.damrap.com), the music frequently deals with the themes of occupation, the difficulties of daily life and resistance. Dam Rap is actually a group of Israeli Arabs from the impoverished city of Lod, not far from Ben-Gurion airport. Identifying both with Palestinians and Israelis, they rap in a heady mixture of Hebrew, Arabic and English.

Theatre & Dance

Israeli Theatre

Per capita, Israelis attend the theatre more frequently than almost any other people. Most performances are in Hebrew, with a few in Arabic, Russian and Yiddish. Some troupes offer English supertitle translations once a week or more; attending is a great way to immerse yourself in the local culture.

Tel Aviv and Jaffa have a profusion of companies and venues, and in Jerusalem there are frequent festivals, both large and small. **Festival Akko** (www.accofestival.co.il) brings fringe productions to Akko each fall.

Israel's biggest festival of the performing arts, the Israel Festival (www.israel-festival.org.il), is held every year in May and June in Jerusalem.

Many contemporary Israeli plays tackle the hot political topics and social issues of the day. In recent years, the Holocaust, *refuseniks*, the West Bank occupation, suicide and homosexuality within Orthodox Judaism have all been explored onstage. Playwrights to keep an eye out for include Hanoch Levin (1942–99), provocative enough to have had several of his plays censored in the 1970s, Nissim Aloni (1926–98), Yehoshua Sobol (b 1939), Hillel Mittelpunkt (b 1952) and Shmuel Hasfari (b 1954).

Attending a musical performed by the Yiddish troupe **Yiddishpiel** (www.yiddishpiel.co.il) is like a quick trip to pre-Holocaust Eastern Europe, though performances are heavy on nostalgia and the subtitles are in Hebrew and Russian.

For something very unusual and poignant, head to Jaffa's **Nalaga'at Centre** (www.nalagaat.org.il), home to the world's only deaf-blind theatre company.

Palestinian Theatre

Palestinian theatre, long an important expression of Palestinian national aspirations, has been censored by the British, suppressed and harassed by the Israelis, battered by conflict and closures and, most recently, targeted by Islamists. Nevertheless, Palestinian actors and directors carry on. Two of the main centres of Palestinian theatre are the **Palestinian National Theatre** (www.pnt-pal.org) in East Jerusalem, founded in 1984 by the El-Hakawati Theatre Company, and **Al-Kasaba Theatre & Cinematheque** (www.alkasaba.org) in Ramallah.

In 2011 Palestinian theatre suffered two heavy blows. Juliano Mer-Khamis (1958–2011), the Palestinian-Israeli founder of Jenin's **Freedom**

ISRAEL FESTIVAL

Theatre (www.thefreedomtheatre.org), was murdered by unknown masked gunmen in Jenin; and François Abu Salem (1951–2011), founder of the Palestinian National Theatre, was found dead, a possible suicide, at his home in Ramallah.

Israeli Dance

Israel has a several world-renowned professional dance companies. The acclaimed **Bat Sheva Dance Company** (www.batsheva.co.il), founded by Martha Graham in 1964, is based at Tel Aviv's **Susanne Dellal Centre** (www.suzannedellal.org.il); it is now led by celebrated choreographer Ohad Naharin (b 1952). The **Kibbutz Contemporary Dance Company** (www.kcdc.co.il) performs around the country.

For something completely different, catch a noisy, raucous, energetic performance by Jaffa-based **Mayumana** (www.mayumana.com), Israel's answer to Stomp.

In the realm of folk dancing, Israel is famous for the hora, brought from Romania by 19th-century immigrants. The best place to see folk dancing is at the **Carmiel Dance Festival** (www.karmielfestival.co.il), held over three days in early July in Carmiel, in the central Galilee.

Palestinian Dance

The most popular Palestinian folk dance is a line dance called the dabke. One of the best Palestinian dance groups is **El-Funoun** (www.el-funoun.org), based in Al-Bireh in the West Bank.

Visual Arts

Israeli Visual Arts

Jerusalem's **Bezalel Academy of Arts & Design** (www.bezalel.ac.il), established in 1906 to provide training for European-educated artists and Yemenite artisans, developed a distinctive style combining biblical themes with the sinuous, curvaceous lines of art nouveau (Judendstil). Today, the academy remains one of the most exciting forces on Israel's art scene.

During the 1930s, German-Jewish artists fleeing Nazism brought with them the bold forms of German expressionism. The New Horizons group, which strove to create visual art in line with European movements, emerged after 1948 and remained dominant until the 1960s. Romanian-born Marcel Janco, one of the founders of the Dada cultural

THEATRE FESTIVAL

The fantastic Israeli Fringe Theatre Festival (www.accofestival.co.il) in Akko hosts Israeli plays and street theatre every year during the Sukkoth holiday.

THE WRITING ON THE WALL

Most images of Israel's contentious Separation Fence show blank grey stretches of dismal concrete panelling. But like the Berlin Wall of the 1980s, its surfaces – especially those on the Palestinian side – have been appropriated as a blank canvas for artistic outpourings.

Some of the myriad messages painted on its smooth surface speak of hope; others are angry; still more are defiant or ironic; while some enterprising locals have added their restaurant menus to the mix. There are graffiti projects by international professionals, simple painted murals created by schoolchildren, and visitors' spray-canned protests in a spectrum of languages. Some Palestinians think the 'writing on the wall' is an important form of communication with the outside world; others feel that painting on it legitimises its existence and shouldn't be done at all. The most heavily decorated section of wall is to the right of the Bethlehem checkpoint as you enter from Israel, and further on, towards Aida Refugee Camp. British graffiti artist Banksy is one of the best known to add his mark, along with Pink Floyd's Roger Waters, who appropriately added his lyrics from 'The Wall' to the real thing.

JUDAICA

movement, immigrated to Palestine in 1941 and later established the artists' village of Ein Hod, where there's a museum of his work.

In Israel's cities, keep an eye out for modern sculpture – works range from provocative to whimsical.

Israel's leading art museums are Jerusalem's **Israel Museum** (www.english.imjnet.org.il) and the **Tel Aviv Museum of Art** (www.tamuseum.com), whose new wing, designed by Preston Scott Cohen, opened in 2011. Both have superb permanent collections and put on often-outstanding shows featuring Israeli artists. For details on the country's many museums, try surfing http://ilmuseums.com.

Palestinian Visual Arts

Contemporary Palestinian art became distinct from traditional craft-based art during the 1960s. In the West Bank, the best places to see visual art are Ramallah's **Khalil Sakakini Centre** (www.sakakini.org), the **International Centre of Bethlehem** (Dar Annadwa; www.annadwa.org) and the Bethlehem Peace Center.

Arab and Palestinian art is featured at the **Umm el-Fahem Art Gallery** (http://umelfahemgallery.org), in the Israeli-Arab town of Umm al-Fahm. Jerusalem's **Museum on the Seam** (www.mots.org.il) makes a special effort to exhibit works by Arab and Muslim artists.

Cinema

Israeli Film

Israeli cinema has come a long way since the silent footage of the late Ottoman era, the heroic documentaries of the 1930s and 1940s, and the comic *borekas* movies (named after a flaky Balkan pastry) that dominated big screens during the 1970s. In recent years, Israeli films – many of which take a highly critical look at Israeli society and policies – have been garnering prizes at major film festivals, including Cannes, Berlin, Toronto and Sundance.

The country's first cinema, the Eden, opened in 1914 Tel Aviv, on the edge of Neve Tzedek. Today, there are thriving cinematheques in **Haifa** (www.haifacin.co.il, in Hebrew), **Jerusalem** (www.jer-cin.org.il) and **Tel Aviv** (www.cinema.co.il, in Hebrew), which opened a flash new wing in 2011.

Israeli celebrations of the Seventh Art include:

» **Docaviv International Documentary Film Festival** (www.docaviv.co.il) in Tel Aviv

» **Haifa International Film Festival** (www.haifaff.co.il)

» **International Student Film Festival** (www.taufilmfest.com) in Tel Aviv

The best places in Israel to find creative, joyous Judaica (Jewish ritual objects) are Jerusalem (eg Yoel Moshe Salomon St), Tsfat (the Synagogue Quarter and the Artists' Quarter) and Tel Aviv's Nahalat Binyamin crafts market (Tuesday and Friday).

CONFLICT FLICKS

The Israeli-Palestinian conflict provides the backdrop for a host of powerful, award-winning documentaries by Palestinians and Israelis (or both working together), including Juliano Mer-Khamis' *Arna's Children* (2003), about a children's theatre group in Jenin; the hard-hitting *Death in Gaza* (2004), whose director, James Miller, was killed during production (the IDF claims he was caught in crossfire); Yoav Shamir's *5 Days* (2005), which looks at the Israeli pullout from Gaza; Shlomi Eldar's *Precious Life* (2010), about the relationships formed during a Gaza baby's medical treatment in Israel; Ra'anan Alexandrowicz's *Law in These Parts* (2011), about Israel's military legal system in the West Bank; and *5 Broken Cameras* (2011) by Emad Burnat on the anti–Separation Fence protests at Bil'in.

To take the edge off these tension-filled flicks, check out Ari Sandel's zany **West Bank Story** (2005; www.westbankstory.com), a spoof on the musical West Side Story.

» **Jerusalem Film Festival** (www.jff.org.il)

» **Other Israel Film Festival** (www.otherisrael.org) focusing on Israel's minorities, including its Arab citizens

» **Tel Aviv International LGBT Film Festival** (www.tlvfest.com)

For a complete database of made-in-Israel movies, see the website of the Manhattan-based **Israel Film Center** (www.israelfilmcenter.org).

Palestinian Film

Cinema in the Palestinian Territories is hampered by a dearth of resources and film schools and by threats from Islamists. Nevertheless, the **Palestinian Social Cinema Arts Association** (http://pscaa.wordpress.com) is working to develop the Seventh Art in the Palestinian Territories.

Most feature-length Palestinian movies are international productions shot, but not completely produced, in the region. The first Palestinian film nominated for an Oscar was the controversial *Paradise Now* (2005), directed by Nazareth-born, Netherlands-based Hany Abu-Assad, which puts a human face on Palestinian suicide bombers.

The West Bank has two movie venues, the **Al-Kasaba Theatre & Cinematheque** (www.alkasaba.org) in Ramallah and the internationally supported **Cinema Jenin** (www.cinemajenin.org). Cinema has done less well in Gaza, where all films must be approved by Hamas censors; a brief shot of a woman's uncovered hair is enough to get a movie banned. In 2010 Hamas released *The Great Liberation*, which depicts of the destruction of Israel in computer-generated graphic detail.

ARTS CINEMA

Shashat (www.shashat.org), a Palestinian NGO focusing on women in cinema, holds a Palestinian women's film festival each fall.

Environment

Professor Alon Tal & Daniel Robinson

Flora & Fauna

The ecology and environment of Israel and the Palestinian Territories are as extraordinary as the country's history. As described in the Bible, the Land of Israel is teeming with life, and even the casual reader of Scripture will notice that nature served as a central inspiration and motif for the psalmists and prophets.

The land's strategic location at the meeting point of three continents has made it attractive to empires for millennia, but this very same geography has also created a unique ecological mix. African tropical mammals such as the hyrax live alongside Asian mammals such as the Indian porcupine and the relatively rare European marten. In the arid Negev, for instance, travellers can feel an African influence in the isolated acacia stands, with the nimble antelopes and the towering horns of the ibex. In the Galilee, Mediterranean forests, with their gnarled oaks, almonds and sycamores, can be found in the Carmel and Meron regions, offering what may be the most authentic extant examples of the wooded vistas that provided the backdrop for biblical tales such as the slaying of Absalom in Gilead, or for the imagery of Isaiah's prophecies.

The introduction of firearms during the 19th century soon led to the devastation of the country's large mammals and birds. Cheetahs, bears, ostriches and crocodiles were just a few of the animals hunted to extinction. A determined policy of conservation during much of modern Israel's history has stemmed this tragic tide.

Much of the natural (and naturally malarial) wetlands that once characterised the central and northern parts of Israel and the Palestinian Territories were drained long ago, erasing much of their unique flora and fauna. But small sanctuaries such as Ein Afek and the Hula Nature Reserve have retained the feel of the original local swamps and are home to a rich assortment of birds and even lumbering water buffalo.

Plants have also benefited from Israel's conservation policies. From about January through to March (later at higher elevations), hillsides are literally carpeted with yellow, orange, red, pink, purple and white wildflowers. The anemones and cyclamens of the Be'eri Forest in the northern Negev and the Beit Keshet forest near Nazareth are particularly astonishing. Irises can be found on Mt Gilboa, and native orchids in the Jerusalem Hills. During the 1960s, Israel's first environmental campaign succeeded in persuading Israelis to refrain from picking wildflowers.

Israel's 128 surviving indigenous mammal species are, for the most part, holding their own, due to restrictions on hunting and a system of nature reserves, which now cover some 25% of Israel's land. However, nature reserves are no panacea for biodiversity loss. Many are minuscule in size and isolated, providing only limited protection for local species. Moreover, many of the reserves in the south are also used as military fzones. Sometimes this

Professor Alon Tal founded the Israel Union for Environmental Defence and the Arava Institute for Environmental Studies, and has served as chair of Life and Environment, Israel's umbrella group for green organisations.

A dozen species of bat, two of them critically endangered, have found cool, secluded warm-season shelter in abandoned Israel Defence Forces (IDF) bunkers along the Jordan River, unused since the 1994 Israel-Jordan peace treaty.

OPERATION HAI-BAR

Over the past 45 years, an initiative known as Hai-Bar (literally 'wildlife') took on the challenge of reintroducing animal species that appear in the Bible but later became extinct in Israel. This was accomplished by bringing together a small number of animals from other parts of the region and patiently breeding them until they could be gradually reintroduced to their natural habitats. In a parallel initiative, birds of prey, whose populations were ravaged by profligate pesticide usage during the 1950s, were also gradually returned to the wild.

While some zoologists question the authenticity of a few of the selected mammal species, the Hai-Bar program has largely been a success. Starting with the wild ass, which appears in Isaiah's prophesies, various animals were quietly reintroduced to the country's open spaces. A small group of Persian fallow deer was secretly airlifted from Iran in 1978 on the last El Al flight to leave before Khomeini's revolution. These shy animals have taken hold in the Galilee reserve of Akhziv and in the hills west of Jerusalem. The Arabian oryx, whose straight parallel horns, viewed from the side, gave Crusaders the impression that they were unicorns, are also back. The two Hai-Bar centres – one at Yotvata and the other on Mt Carmel – are being downsized, having completed most of their planned reintroductions, but are still well worth a visit for animal or Bible fans.

overlap works to nature's advantage, as civilian visitors are allowed in only at weekends and on holidays. But the soldiers, tanks and jet bombers cause serious disruption, especially for four-legged inhabitants of these areas.

Deforestation & Reafforestation

Centuries of tree-cutting for firewood and charcoal caused Palestine to lose much of its vegetation. The final (axe) blow came during WWI, when the Ottoman military felled the country's last remaining forests to supply fuel for the railways. Aerial photographs from the period confirm that the destruction of local oak forests was almost complete. (A tiny patch of primary oak forest can still be seen at Alonei Yitzhak Nature Reserve, 10km east of Caesarea.)

Israel's modern landscape reflects an impressive afforestation effort began over a century ago. Early Zionist settlers were avid planters of trees, and since Israel's founding over 260 million trees have been planted, mainly by the Jewish National Fund (JNF; www.kkl.org.il). The new forests (eg along the main road up to Jerusalem) have been criticised by ecologists, who dislike conifer monocultures, and have stirred the resentment by Israel's Arab citizens, who see them as symbols of Jewish domination. But in recent years, the JNF has grown more sensitive and has diversified its plantings, reafforesting largely with local species and preserving native vegetation. A statutory master plan has zoned some 10% of the Israeli countryside as forests intended to serve a variety of recreational and ecological functions.

For generations of Jews around the world, planting trees has become an expression of solidarity with Zionism and the State of Israel. Most of the JNF forests lack the authenticity of old-growth woods, but the massive tree plantings nonetheless constitute a significant achievement in landscape restoration, most notably in the arid south, where pine stands thrive in areas with as little as 100mm of precipitation, and around the Sea of Galilee, which – as can be seen in old photographs – was almost denuded of trees by the end of Ottoman rule.

ECOLOGY BOOK

In *The Natural History of the Bible* (2007), Daniel Hillel, a world-renowned soil physicist and water management expert, examines local ecology's influence on the people and world of the Scriptures.

Oil's Important but Water's Essential

Access to water is absolutely crucial in this arid region – without it humans, animals and plants quite simply cannot survive. That's why King Hezekiah put so much effort into building a tunnel to ensure Jerusalem's

Ongoing tensions have made it difficult for Palestinian environmentalists to address the Palestinian Territories' enormous environmental challenges. Some Palestinians, struggling to feed their families, see issues such as nature conservation and air pollution as luxuries best left for later.

PARK ACCESS

The Israel Nature & Parks Authority (www.parks.org.il) administers most of Israel's national parks. Save money by buying a six-park 'Green Card' for 105NIS or an all-park card for 145NIS, both valid for two weeks.

water supply in time of siege, and why similar technology was used at Tel Hatzor. And that's why in Palestinian–Israeli peace negotiations, three of the most difficult issues are being left for last: Jerusalem, the fate of Palestinian refugees and water.

As soon as Israel declared independence, it began to plan the transport of water from the relatively wet Galilee to the dryer south. By the 1960s, thanks to the reservoirs and tunnels of the 130km National Water Carrier – and despite clashes with Syria over water rights – prodigious quantities of water were being piped to the Negev Desert, where farming settlements there flourished. But water was still in short supply, precipitating Israelis' invention of modern drip-irrigation, now used around the world (including by countries hostile to Israel), and the extensive recycling of sewage water for use in agriculture.

But technological intervention has not been without its price, and the over-pumping of groundwater has salinised aquifers all along the coast. Today, the most critical situation is in Gaza. Nitrate levels and salinity in Gaza's aquifers were already excessive during the period of Egyptian control before 1967, but dozens of unlicensed wells, dug after Israel evacuated the region, have exacerbated the massive seawater intrusion.

During the 1950s, the Hula wetlands in the northern Galilee were drained to create farmland, obliterating important bird habitats and a key nutrient sink for the Sea of Galilee. The diversion of spring water and winter run-off for agriculture, industry and home use has destroyed the aquatic habitats of many of Israel's streams, a situation made worse by sewerage run-off from the Palestinian cities of the West Bank.

There are, however, some bright spots. Over the past 18 years, the Alexander River (www.restorationplanning.com), 13km south of Caesarea, has been cleaned up and rehabilitated. In 2003 it won the prestigious Riverprize awarded by the Australia-based International River Foundation (www.riverfoundation.org.au).

The most conspicuous victim of Israel's water management prowess has been the Dead Sea. These days, the amount of water flowing annually into the world's lowest lake is one billion cubic metres *less* than would be naturally. As a result, the sea is rapidly shrinking, with the water level dropping at 1.2m per year. Sinkholes have begun to form around the shoreline, posing a safety hazard and undermining agriculture and the tourist trade. There have long been proposals to refill the Dead Sea with seawater either from the Mediterranean, through a 'Med–Dead Canal', or from the Red Sea, via a 'Red–Dead Canal' (and to use the difference in altitude to generate hydroelectricity). But while the latter is still on the table and is supported by Jordan, it lacks funding and environmentalists are ambivalent about possible impacts.

Israeli scientists have also been trying to find less interventionist ways to maximise water use. The ancients – especially the Nabataeans – developed sophisticated techniques to channel rare desert cloudbursts in order to make agriculture possible even in the arid central Negev. Modern scientists are trying to rediscover ancient techniques at an experimental farm near the Nabataean ruins of Avdat (p314).

At the other end of the technology spectrum, reverse-osmosis desalination technology is playing an ever more important role in Israel's water management strategy and will soon supply 20% of the country's water (and 60% of household water). Thanks to a breakthrough in the efficiency of the membranes through which sea water is filtered, it now costs a mere US$0.52 to produce 1 cu m (1000L) of drinkable water. The Ashkelon Sea Water Reverse Osmosis (SWRO) Plant on the Mediterranean coast is one of the largest such facilities in the world.

HALF A BILLION BIRDS

It's a common misconception that birds migrate because they can't take the cold. In fact, their feathers keep them warm enough to survive even brutally cold winters. Rather, Northern Hemisphere birds 'fly south' to find food. Each autumn, before cooling weather starts to limit insect supplies and vegetation, they leave chilly Europe and tropical Asia for Africa. But it is unwise to stay in these southern climes beyond the winter because the competition for food is simply too stiff, especially given all the extra calories needed for breeding. So the birds head back to the north, where they can feast on the once-again abundant insects.

This long-distance commute means that twice a year, half a billion birds from an unbelievable 283 species fly over the Jordan Valley (part of the Great Rift Valley, aka the Syrian-African Rift Valley), making it the largest avian fly-way in the world. Compressed into a narrow corridor along the eastern edge of Israel and the Palestinian Territories, the area's topography creates astonishing opportunities for birdwatchers.

A number of sites offer rewarding experiences even for those who are not inclined to rise before the sun, binoculars in hand, to identify arcane avian species. These websites have some great information and useful links.

» **Agamon HaHula** (www.agamon-hula.co.il) These reconstituted wetlands in the Upper Galilee are a favourite stopover of migrating cranes.

» **International Center for the Study of Bird Migration in Latrun** (www.birds.org.il) A Russian-made radar station tracks birds for ornithologists – and for the safety of civil and military aviation.

» **Kibbutz Lotan** (www.birdingisrael.com) Runs ecological education programs, including introductions to birding.

» **International Birding & Research Center** (www.eilat-birds.org) An old garbage dump near Eilat has been turned into a salt marsh where exhausted birds can refuel.

The energy demands of SWRO facilities are prodigious, and their discharged brine, which contains chemicals and metals, may have consequences when returned to the sea. But generally, there is optimism that innovation will resolve Israel's chronic water scarcity and sustain the country's agriculture – in addition to reducing the danger of regional conflicts over water, a natural resource that's even more critical than oil.

Development Perils & Successes

The population of Israel and the Palestinian Territories has grown by over a million people a decade since 1948, making today's population roughly seven times larger than it was back then. Simultaneously, Israel, initially a poor developing nation, has developed a moderately prosperous Western economy. The country's industrialisation, building construction and enthusiasm for highways have generated pollution and sprawl comparable to those the West. However, because of Israel's small size, these are often felt more acutely. If Israel has been innovative in water management, it has fallen far behind in other areas.

For example, air pollution in many Israeli and Palestinian cities is worse than almost anywhere in Europe, and periodically reaches dangerous levels. On the solar energy front, little has improved since a 1970s building code required that all homes install solar panels to heat water, though the Ben-Gurion National Solar Energy Center at the university's Sde Boker campus offers a fascinating technological tour (reservations can be made by calling Shoshana Dann ☎08-659 6934). Local waste management is surprisingly underdeveloped, with recycling rates well below those in Western Europe. Burial of rubbish at inexpensive and municipal landfills is the default option, despite the dwindling reserves of available real estate. (Maybe policymakers just want to be generous to future archaeologists.)

SOLAR POWER

Israel's first solar power station, the Solar Flower (www.aora-solar.com), consists of a 30m tower and tracking mirrors (heliostats) that follow the sun's rays. Situated at Kibbutz Samar near Eilat, it can generate enough electricity for 50 households.

ONLINE ENVIRONMENTAL RESOURCES

For details on the state of the environment – and what's being done about it – in Israel and the Palestinian Territories, see the websites of the following environmental organisations:

» **Adam Teva v'Din** (Israel Union for Environmental Defence; www.adamteva.org.il) Israel's premier advocacy organisation plays hardball in the courts, suing polluters and lethargic government agencies.

» **Applied Research Institute of Jerusalem** (www.arij.org) An independent Palestinian research and advocacy organisation.

» **Arava Institute for Environmental Studies** (www.arava.org) A teaching and research centre that brings Israelis, Palestinians and Jordanians to Kibbutz Ketura near Eilat.

» **Blaustein Institutes for Desert Research** (http://cmsprod.bgu.ac.il/Eng/Units/bidr) Researches desertification and sustainable living in arid lands.

» **Friends of the Earth Middle East** (www.foeme.org) Promotes cooperation between Israeli, Palestinian and Jordanian environmentalists.

» **Galilee Society** (www.gal-soc.org) Israel's leading Arab environmental activist group.

» **Heschel Center for Environmental Learning & Leadership** (www.heschel.org.il) Studies sustainability issues in Israel and has innovative environmental education programs.

» **House of Water & Environment** (www.hwe.org.ps) Ramallah-based NGO with expertise in water resources.

» **Israel Nature & National Parks Protection Authority** (www.parks.org.il) Manages Israel's nature reserves and archaeological sites.

» **Israeli Ministry of Environmental Protection** (www.sviva.gov.il) An increasingly powerful government ministry responsible for environmental regulation and enforcement. Their website is a treasure trove of date.

» **Jewish National Fund** (www.kkl.org.il in Israel, www.jnf.org in USA) Serves as Israel's forest service, and has a long history of planting trees.

» **Life & Environment** (www.sviva.net) Umbrella organisation for over 100 Israeli environmental organisations.

» **Palestine Wildlife Society** (www.wildlife-pal.org) An educational and research NGO with a particular expertise in birds.

» **Palestinian Ministry of Environmental Affairs** (www.mena.gov.ps) Charged with environmental regulation and education.

» **Society for the Protection of Nature in Israel** (SPNI; www.teva.org.il in Hebrew, www.aspni.org in English) Israel's oldest and largest environmental organisation.

Sprawl has also emerged as a serious problem, as more affluence has generated inefficient land-use patterns. In the past, most Israelis lived in apartment buildings, but their aspirations to move 'up and out' into 'villas' (single-family homes) have led to a proliferation of low-density communities based on a two-cars-per-family lifestyle. Open spaces have given way to roads and suburbs. Environmentalists have fought hard to stop this trend, but with only isolated success. However, during the late 1990s, a major campaign to curb construction near beaches produced dramatic results. Laws now protect the coastline, banning most construction within 300m of the water line and guaranteeing public access to the beaches.

Israel's environmental movement has grown more powerful in recent years. At the local government level, 'green' parties have begun to find a constituency. As the country begins to adopt European standards and many industries become more environmentally conscientious, real inroads into ingrained habits and ways of thinking are being made. However, the ever-increasing populations of Israel and the Palestinian Territories continue to make sustainable development ever more important – and more challenging.

Survival Guide

Safe Travel

Is it safe?! This is the question you'll hear endlessly from friends and family back home when you announce your intentions to travel to Israel and/or the Palestinian Territories. But despite the headlines and the inherent risk in any travel these days, your chances of getting caught up in an act of violence are extremely low. (Despite all the wars and terrorism, Israeli men have the 5th-longest life expectancy in the world.) Still, it's always a good idea to play it safe, plan ahead and heed advice from locals.

The following government websites offer travel advisories and information on current hot spots. Israelis and Palestinians often agree that if they err it's on the side of caution.

US State Department (http://travel.state.gov)

Australian Department of Foreign Affairs (www. smartraveller.gov.au)

British Foreign Office (www.fco.gov.uk)

Canadian Department of Foreign Affairs www.dfait -maeci.gc.ca

AIRPORT & BORDER SECURITY

Israeli airport security unabashedly uses profiling – but not necessarily in the way you might think. In 1986, a pregnant Irish woman, Anne Mary Murphy, almost boarded an El Al 747 in London with Semtex explosive hidden in the lining of her luggage – it had been placed there without her knowledge by her Jordanian boyfriend, Nezar Hindawi, who's still in prison in the UK. Ever since then, Israeli security officials have been on the lookout for anyone who might unwittingly serve as a suicide bomber, with young, unmarried Western females near the top of the profiling list.

In general, Israel allows in bona fide tourists. But if officials suspect that you're coming to take part in pro-Palestinian political activities, or even visit the West Bank for reasons other than Christian pilgrimage, they may ask a lot of questions. Having a Muslim name and passport stamps from places like Syria, Lebanon or Iran may also result in some pointed questions. The one sure way to get grilled is to sound evasive or to contradict yourself – the security screeners are trained to try to trip you up.

New arrivals at Ben-Gurion airport should be prepared for lengthy questioning and bag searches – though they should also be prepared to be pleasantly surprised. If you end up being grilled, your best bet is to smile and be as polite as you can possibly manage after that long, late-night flight. When exiting the country, you may find that security is often stricter than when coming in – after all, you're about to board an aircraft.

At the Allenby Bridge Crossing between the West Bank and Jordan, inspections and questioning are often particularly thorough. Sometimes, Israeli authorities give visitors an entry stamp that is valid for the Palestinian Authority but not Israel.

SECURITY MEASURES IN ISRAEL

For obvious reasons Israel has some of the most stringent security policies in the world. Streets, highways, markets and public facilities are cordoned off on the basis

TRAFFIC ACCIDENTS

Since 1948, more Israelis have died in traffic accidents (about 31,000) than as a result of wars and military action (22,867 as of mid-2011) and terrorism (2443). Fortunately, traffic fatalities are going down: in 2011 there were 'only' 399 traffic deaths, compared with an average of 621 in the 1990s. By comparison, 21 people were killed in terrorist and rocket attacks in 2011.

of intelligence (eg regarding a possible suicide bombing) that isn't usually made public, and abandoned shopping bags, backpacks and parcels are picked up by bomb squad robots and blown up. In recent years the number of annual terrorist attacks inside Israel has dropped to the single digits (by comparison, in March 2002 alone over 130 Israelis were killed in Palestinian attacks), but it pays to remain vigilant about suspicious people (or packages), especially when travelling by public bus. Keep an eye on the news and heed local travel advice while on the road.

When entering bus or rail terminals, shopping malls, many supermarkets and all sorts of other public venues (though many fewer than a few years back), your bags are likely to be searched – and in some cases X-rayed. You will also be checked with a metal detector wand or a body search and probably asked, '*Yesh lecha neshek?*' ('Do you have a gun?') It's amazing how quickly you'll get used to this – and may expect to have your handbag searched at your local shopping mall long after you've returned home.

SAFE TRAVEL IN THE WEST BANK

In recent years, travel in Palestinian Authority–controlled areas of the West Bank has generally been safe for non-Israelis.

Road passage between many Palestinian West Bank towns and Israel is regulated by Israeli army roadblocks, which can range from a row of tyre-piercing stakes laid on the asphalt to a toll booth–type drive-through structure to the constructions resembling maximum security prisons near Bethlehem and at Qalandia, near Ramallah. Here you'll need to show a foreign passport (Israel forbids its citizens to enter Palestinian-controlled areas) and answer some questions.

GAS MASKS

Because of the possibility of attack by chemical weapons (Syria is among the countries believed to possess mustard gas and nerve agents), Israel's **Home Front Command** (www.oref.org.il) has issued fitted gas masks to Israeli adults and special super-pressure hoods for infants and young children. If the Israeli government determines that a real and present danger of a chemical attack exists, masks will also be distributed to tourists, as they were in 1991 and 2003. In 2012 the masks were said to be in short supply, which is why the government is trying to figure out a tactful way to collect unused masks from the family members of people who have died.

Be very careful wherever there is friction between Jewish settlers and local Palestinians, eg Hebron and some of the radical settlements and outposts around Nablus and the Hebron Hills. Visitors could also find themselves caught in a confrontation between 'Hilltop Youth' (see p258) and the IDF or police. Non-Israeli Jews shouldn't have problems in the West Bank but don't wear outward signs of Judaism or you might be mistaken for a settler.

Israeli soldiers use night-vision goggles so if you are walking near a checkpoint or the Separation Fence at night you are likely to be spotted and, possibly, deemed a potential threat by a 19-year-old Israeli draftee.

A few tips for safe travel in the West Bank:

» Always carry your passport.
» If it's your first visit to the West Bank, especially to places like Hebron, Nablus or Jenin, its best to go with a guide or on a tour – not necessarily because it's dangerous but because these areas are geographically and politically complex and bringing a good guide will help to make sense of it all.
» Don't wander into the refugee camps on your own. Bring a local guide.
» Travel during daylight hours. The West Bank is disorienting enough (with poor road signage, roadblocks and checkpoints) in the daytime;

travelling after dark will only add to the confusion.
» Dress modestly. Cover up those bare shoulders and legs – you'll blend in with the crowd a bit better and won't cause inadvertent offence. This applies to both men and women (but especially women).
» Couples should resist the urge to show public displays of affection.
» Avoid political demonstrations, which often get out of hand and can turn into violent confrontations between Palestinians and Israeli soldiers.
» Use caution when approaching road blocks and checkpoints – Israeli soldiers are on high alert at all times, and causing unnecessary anxiety could lead to all sorts of problems and confrontations. Remember: they have no idea that you're just a curious visitor.

THE SITUATION IN GAZA

In recent years Gaza has become lawless and extremely dangerous. The territory is ruled by the Palestinian Islamist movement Hamas, whose gunmen have used violence (including extrajudicial killings) against supporters of Fatah (see p370), people suspected of collaborating with Israel, locals accused of 'immoral' behaviour and Christians suspected of

WHAT TO DO IN A ROCKET ATTACK

Say you're visiting friends in Be'er Sheva or hanging out on the beach in Ashkelon when the air raid sirens go off – what do you do? This scenario is not very likely, but missiles fired from Gaza hit as far north as Rishon LeZion, just 15km from the centre of Tel Aviv, in 2011.

According to the **Home Front Command** (www.oref.org.il), if you're indoors you should immediately head to the nearest Mamad (reinforced concrete room) and close the heavy steel door and window, or to a conventional bomb shelter if there's time. Depending on how far from the launch site you are and whether the projectile is a locally made Qassam or an Iranian-supplied 122mm Grad, you may have just a few tens of seconds to get ready for impact.

If you're in a building without a Mamad (only buildings constructed after the First Gulf War have them), head to a regular room situated 'farthest from the direction of the threat, with the smallest possible number of outside walls, windows and openings'; another option is to take shelter in an interior staircase or a corridor. If you're on the top floor of a building, descend two floors – but not all the way to ground floor.

If you are outdoors or in a vehicle, enter the nearest building and follow the above instructions. If you're in an exposed area, 'lie on the ground face-down and cover your head with your hands'.

If there are no additional instructions (eg on the radio), you can come out of hiding after 10 minutes.

proselytising. In addition, the members of radical Islamist factions, some allied with the 'global jihad' movement, have been involved in armed clashes with Hamas and have carried out kidnappings, including of foreign volunteers who came to Gaza to support the Palestinian cause. And then there's always the possibility of being hit by Israel Defence Forces (IDF) fire – sometimes from helicopter gunships – aimed at squads launching rockets into southern Israel.

POLITICAL PROTESTS

Israel is a democracy so political protests are a legally protected right – but the West Bank is not part of Israel. Rather, it is 'administered' by the Israeli army (ie is under military rule), which means that while the law (or military orders) are rarely enforced when it comes to settlers, harsh measures – including truncheons, tear gas, stun grenades and rubber bullets – are often used against Palestinian protesters (and the left-wing Israelis who sometimes join

them), eg at the weekly anti-Separation Fence demos in Bil'in. If you show up at a protest rally, even just to watch, you stop being an innocent outsider and become a participant in the conflict, with all that implies.

Even if you steer well clear of the IDF and Jewish settlers during a visit to the West Bank, make sure you don't inadvertently get caught between rival Palestinian factions.

Even within Israel demonstrations can get out of hand, as often happens when ultra-Orthodox Jews confront the police in Mea She'arim or Beit Shemesh (see p43).

In short, activism can be a dangerous business in Israel and the Palestinian Territories, especially if you don't know what you're doing.

MINEFIELDS

Some parts of Israel and the Palestinian Territories – particularly along the Jordanian border and around the periphery of the Golan Heights – are still sown with anti-personnel mines. Fortunately, known mined areas

are indicated in pink on topographical maps (see p431) and are fenced with barbed wire sporting dangling red (or rust) triangles and/or yellow and red 'Danger Mines!' signs.

Since some marked hiking trails pass through mined areas and army firing zones, where there's a small chance you'll come across unexploded ordnance (UXO), the best way to avoid becoming a statistic is to stick closely to marked trails. Especially on the Golan, never climb over or through a barbed-wire fence. In the Jordan Valley and the Arava, flash floods sometimes wash away old mines, depositing them outside known minefields. Wherever you are, never, ever touch anything that looks like it might be an old artillery shell, grenade or mine!

If you find yourself in a mined area, retrace your steps only if you can clearly see your footprints. If not, stay where you are and call for help. If someone is injured in a minefield, do not rush in to assist even if they are crying out for help – find someone who knows how to enter a mined area safely.

Directory A–Z

Accommodation

Both Israel and the Palestinian Territories offer accommodation options for every budget. In Israel, expect prices – though not always standards – on a par with Western Europe. The West Bank and Gaza are quite a bit cheaper, with many of the best options clustered in Ramallah and Bethlehem.

Accommodation prices in Israel vary spectacularly with the day of the week and the season. In general, 'weekday' rates run from Saturday to Wednesday or Thursday and 'weekend' rates apply on Friday and sometimes Thursday (many Israelis don't work on Friday). Some establishments, including B&Bs, apply two-night minimums at weekends.

In most parts of the country, prices rise to 'weekend' levels during July and August. The exceptions: extremely hot areas such as the Dead Sea and on the shores of the Sea of Galilee. Some urban hotels (eg in Tel Aviv) have the chutzpah to impose a seven-night minimum stay during the summer.

Jewish holidays such as the week-long Passover and Sukkot festivals, Shavuot and Rosh HaShanah bring 'high-high season' prices, especially in popular getaways such as the Galilee, the Golan Heights and Eilat. At these times, book well in advance. (On Yom Kippur most Jewish Israelis stay home.)

Room prices in the Palestinian Territories remain fairly constant year-round, the exception being in Bethlehem, where rates rise around Christmas and Easter. Book well ahead if you're planning on travel at these times.

Prices given in shekels include VAT (16%), which foreign tourists don't have to pay. As a result, some establishments give tourists a discount on their regular shekel rates.

B&Bs (Tzimmerim)

The most common form of accommodation in the Upper Galilee and Golan is the *tzimmer* (or *zimmer*). No one really knows how this particular German word came to symbolise, for Israelis, all that's idyllic about a cabin in the country, though some suggest it was originally an attempt to copy the 'Zimmer Frei' signs of Germany's alpine guesthouses. Prices are generally upper-midrange.

A *tzimmer* is often a glorified wooden cabin with rustic, varnished-pine decor, satellite TV and a kitchen corner complete with table-top stove and small fridge. *Tzimmers'* most oft-touted and highly prized feature is the jacuzzi – normally in the bedroom. Some places offer a great breakfast, just like a proper B&B, but others assume you'll cook your own, ask the day before if you want to special-order (for 100NIS per couple) or offer vouchers so you can go out to breakfast.

To find a *tzimmer* (this book only mentions a tiny fraction of what's available), keep an eye out for signs on the street or check the following websites:

» www.zimmeril.com
» www.israel-tours-hotel.com

SLEEPING PRICE CATEGORIES

Prices in our listings are for double rooms with breakfast in the high (but not 'high-high', holiday) season.

	ISRAEL	PALESTINIAN TERRITORIES
Budget ($)	under 350NIS	under 260NIS
Midrange ($$)	350NIS to 600NIS	260NIS-400NIS
Top End ($$$)	above 600NIS	above 400NIS

BOOK YOUR STAY ONLINE

For more reviews by Lonely Planet authors, check out http://hotels.lonelyplanet.com. You'll find independent reviews, as well as recommendations on the best places to stay. Best of all, you can book online.

» www.weekend.co.il (in Hebrew)
» www.zimmer.co.il (in Hebrew)

In the Palestinian Territories, guesthouses are plentiful and make a good-value alternative hotels or hostels. Bethlehem, in particular, has some attractive, atmospheric options. Another option is a homestay – the **Hospitality Club** (www.hospitalityclub.org) has a number of Palestinian members offering travellers a bed for the night.

Beach Huts

Down Sinai way, backpackers will delight in the sometimes ramshackle but always cheap bungalows and beach huts scattered along the Red Sea sands. They are incredibly basic – a palm-frond shelter with a floor of carpets and cushions can cost as little as E£20 per person.

Camping

The cheapest way to stay overnight is in a tent (or at least a sleeping bag). Particularly mellow are some of the sites around the northeastern shore of the Sea of Galilee, many of which charge per car (they're free if you arrive on foot). Paying a fee for admission or parking gets you security, a decent shower block and toilet facilities.

Camping is forbidden inside nature reserves. Fortunately, various public and private bodies run inexpensive **camping sites** (www.campingil.org.il) at about 100 places around the country, including 22 operated by the **Nature and Parks Authority** (☎3639, 1222-3639; www.parks.org.il, search for 'over-

night campgrounds'). Some are equipped with shade roofs (so you don't need a tent), lighting, toilets, showers and barbecue pits. In Hebrew, ask for a *chenyon laila* or an *orchan laila*.

In the Palestinian Territories, camping should be avoided due to general security concerns.

Hostels & Field Schools

Almost three dozen independent hostels and guesthouses in all parts of the country, including some of the country's best accommodation deals (dorm beds for 100NIS), are members of **Israel Hostels** (ILH; www.hostels-israel.com). If you're interested in meeting other travellers, these places are usually your best bet.

Israel's 19 official Hostelling International (HI) hostels and guesthouses – significantly upgraded since the days of no-frills dorms and timer-activated communal showers – offer clean, well-appointed rooms and copious breakfasts. When school's out, they're especially popular with families. For details, check out the website of the **Israel Youth Hostels Association** (☎1-599-510 511; www.iyha.org.il/eng).

The **Society for the Protection of Nature in Israel** (☎03-638 8688, 057-200 3030; www.teva.org.il/english) runs nine field schools (*bet sefer sadeh*) in areas of high ecological value. Often used by school groups, they offer basic but serviceable accommodation to independent travellers. During holiday periods, they're hugely popular with Israeli families.

In Jerusalem, pilgrims' hostels run by religious organisations serve mainly, but not exclusively, religious travellers. As you would expect, they lack the party atmosphere of some independent hostels but are a secure and solid-value way to stay in the Old City. Accommodation for pilgrims can also be found around the Sea of Galilee.

In the Palestinian Territories, Bethlehem has a wide range of pilgrims' hostels.

Hotels

Israel's hotels and guesthouses range from grim to gorgeous. Generally speaking, hotel prices are highest in Tel Aviv, Eilat and Jerusalem.

In order to attract observant Jewish guests, most hotels serve only kosher food and modify their routines on Shabbat and Jewish holidays.

In the Palestinian Territories, most decent hotels, as well as some guesthouses, are in Ramallah and Bethlehem, though a few new hotels have recently been built elsewhere on the West Bank. **Palestine Hotels** (www.palestinehotels.com) is an excellent hotel booking website.

Kibbutz Guesthouses

Capitalising on their beautiful, usually rural locations,

quite a few kibbutzim offer midrange guesthouse accommodation. Often constructed in the socialist era but significantly upgraded since, these establishments allow access to kibbutz facilities, including the swimming pool, and serve delicious kibbutz-style breakfasts. For details and reservations, check out the **Kibbutz Hotels Chain** (☎03-560 8118; www.kibbutz.co.il).

Activities

Archaeological Digs

For details on archaeological digs that welcome paying volunteers, check out these websites:

Biblical Archaeology Society (http://digs.bib-arch.org/digs)

Hebrew University of Jerusalem (http://archaeology.huji.ac.il/news/excavations.asp)

Israeli Foreign Ministry (www.mfa.gov.il; search for 'Archaeological Excavations')

Birdwatching

Some 500 million birds pass through Israel twice a year, once on their way south to Africa for the winter and again on their way north to Europe and northern Asia for the summer. It's no surprise, then, that the country – especially along the Mediterranean coast, in the Hula Valley (p226) and around Eilat – is one of the world's foremost venues for birding. For details, see the website of the **Israel Ornithological Center** (IOC; www.teva.org.il/english/ioc) and p419. Gatherings of twitchers (birdwatchers) include the **Hula Valley Bird Festival** (www.hulabirdfestival.org).

Cycling

Mountain biking has become hugely popular in Israel in recent years, especially among hi-tech yuppies with SUVs (a stereotype but not an untrue one). Many cycling trails go through forests managed by the **Jewish National Fund** (www.kkl.org.il); for details, click 'Cycling Routes' on its website. **Shvil Net** (www.shvil.net) publishes Hebrew-language cycling guides that include detailed topographical maps.

This guide lists places that rent bikes.

Races are regularly held in locales such as the Dead Sea; many are sponsored by the **Israel Cycling Federation** (http://ofanaim.org.il). There is also a variety of annual long-distance rides, such as the **Arava Institute & Hazon Israel Ride** (www.hazon.org/programs/israel-ride) and the **ALYN Hospital International Charity Bike Ride** (www.alynride.org). Cycling organisations that run group rides include **Israel Spokes** (www.israelspokes.com). Popular Hebrew-only cycling forums, great for finding local clubs, group rides and equipment, include **Shvoong** (www.harim.co.il), **Groopy** (http://groopy.co.il) and **Harim** (www.harim.co.il).

Companies and cycling groups offering organised two-wheeled tours of Israel:

Cyclenix (www.cyclenix.com)

EcoBike Cycling Vacations (www.ecobike.co.il)

Genesis Cycling (http://genesiscycling.com)

Israel Cycling Tours (www.israelcycling.com)

Israel Pedals (www.israelpedals.co.il)

SK Bike Tours (www.skbike.co.il)

Urban cycling is highly developed in Tel Aviv thanks to over 100km of dedicated by paths and lanes (see p109). For details on getting around the country by bicycle, see p437.

Some airlines allow you to bring along your bicycle for a reasonable fee while others charge a small fortune.

Hiking

With its unbelievably diverse terrain – ranging from the alpine slopes of Mt Hermon to the parched wadis of the Negev – and almost 10,000km of marked trails, Israel offers some truly superb hiking. The country gets little or no precipitation for at least half the year so Israelis can plan outings without having to worry about getting rained on – and, because water is so precious, love nothing more than to spend a summer's day sloshing through a spring-fed stream shaded by lush vegetation. Whenever you hit the trails, don't forget to bring a hat and plenty of water, and plan your day so you can make it back before dark.

At national parks and nature reserves (www.parks.org.il), walking maps with English text are usually handed out when you pay your admission fee. In other areas, the best maps to have – in part because they indicate minefields and live-fire zones used for Israel Defence Forces (IDF) training – are the 1:50,000-scale topographical maps produced by the Society for the Protection of Nature in Israel (SPNI; see p431).

The website **Tiuli** (www.tiuli.com), run by Lametayel, Israel's largest camping equipment store, has details in English on the hiking options available around the country. The SPNI's **Mokedteva** (www.mokedteva.co.il, in Hebrew) has up-to-date information on weather, hiking routes, trail difficulty, trail closures and special events.

Popular long-distance trails (from north to south):

Israel National Trail (Shvil Yisra'el; www.israelnationaltrail.com, www.teva.org.il/english/israelnationaltrail) Rambles for 940km through Israel's least-populated and most-scenic areas, from Kibbutz Dan in the north to Taba on the Red Sea. Trail blazes are orange, blue and white.

Golan Trail (Shvil Hagolan; www.golantrail.com) Runs for 125km along the eastern edge of the Golan Heights (see p253).

Sea-to-Sea Hike (Masa MiYam l'Yam) A 70km route from the Mediterranean (Achziv Beach) to the Sea of Galilee (near Ginnosar) via Mt Meron and Amud Stream. Takes three to five days.

Jesus Trail (www.jesustrail.com) A 65km route from Nazareth's Church of the Annunciation to Capernaum on the Sea of Galilee (see p190). Passes through Christian, Jewish, Muslim, Bedouin and Druze communities.

Gospel Trail Runs from Nazareth's Mt Precipice to Capernaum, avoiding built-up areas. Inaugurated in late 2011 by Israel's Ministry of Tourism.

Sea of Galilee Circuit (Shvil Sovev Kineret, Kinneret Trail) Circumnavigates the Sea of Galilee. Of the planned 60km, 35km have already been built (see p213).

Nativity Trail Stretches 160km from Nazareth to Bethlehem, mostly through the beautiful landscapes of the northern West Bank. Must be done with a guide – for details, contact Hijazi Travel (http://hijazih.wordpress.com).

Jerusalem Trail (www.jerusalemtrail.com) A 42km circuit that connects the Israel National Trail with Jerusalem, looping through the Jerusalem Hills and around the Old City.

On the West Bank, it's generally not a good idea to wander around the countryside unaccompanied. Consult local organisations for up-to-date information on areas considered safe; Jericho and environs are usually a good bet. You might want to pick up a copy of *Walking in Palestine* by Tony Howard and Di Taylor.

Scuba Diving

The Red Sea has some of the world's most spectacular and species-rich coral reefs. Good value scuba courses – and dive packages – are available in Eilat, but the underwater life is a lot more dazzling across the border in Sinai. The waters of the Mediterranean aren't nearly as colourful but at places like Caesarea you can explore Atlantis-like ancient ruins.

Windsurfing

Israel's only Olympic gold medal was won by windsurfer Gal Fridman at the 2004 Athens games, so it comes as no surprise that the country offers world-class sailing conditions. Popular venues include the Mediterranean coast, the Red Sea and even the Sea of Galilee.

Business Hours

Opening hours in Israel:

ATMs Generally operate 24 hours a day, seven days a week.

Banks Most are open from 8.30am to sometime between 12.30pm and 2pm Monday to Thursday, and in addition a couple of afternoons a week from 3pm or 4pm until as late as 6.30pm. Many branches are open on Sunday, and some also open on Friday morning.

Bars & Pubs Hours are highly variable, but many – especially in Tel Aviv – are open until the wee hours.

SHABBAT

The Jewish Sabbath, known in Hebrew as Shabbat, begins 18 minutes (36 minutes in Jerusalem) before sundown on Friday and lasts until an hour after sundown on Saturday (technically, until three stars can be seen in the heavens, according to Jewish law). In mostly Orthodox neighbourhoods (eg much of Jerusalem), the arrival of Shabbat is marked with a siren.

'Status-quo' agreements in many cities, including Jerusalem and Tel Aviv, allow restaurants, places of entertainment (theatres, cinemas, discos, bars etc), museums and small groceries – but not retail shops – to stay open on Shabbat. In Tel Aviv and on land owned by kibbutzim, some stores keep their doors open on Shabbat, using non-Jewish staff to avoid fines from the Ministry of Labor and Social Affairs, which – to avoid employing Jews on the Sabbath – sends out only non-Jewish (usually Druze) inspectors!

In predominantly Muslim areas (East Jerusalem, Akko's Old City, parts of Jaffa, the West Bank and Gaza) many businesses are closed all day Friday but remain open on Saturday. Christian-owned businesses (concentrated in Nazareth, Bethlehem and the Armenian and Christian quarters of Jerusalem's Old City) are often closed on Sunday.

National parks, nature reserves and most museums are open seven days a week but close earlier (2pm or 3pm) on Friday afternoon. Christian sites may be closed on Sunday morning, while mosques are usually closed to visitors on Friday.

Thursday and Friday are the biggest nights out.

Clubs & Discos The trendiest boogie joints don't open their doors until after midnight, closing around dawn. In Tel Aviv and Eilat most operate seven days a week, while in Haifa and Jerusalem they only open on weekends (ie Thursday and Friday nights).

Post Offices Generally open from 8am to 12.30pm or 1pm Sunday to Thursday, with many reopening from 3.30pm to 6pm on certain days. Some big city branches dispense with the siesta. Friday hours are 8am to noon.

Restaurants Hours are highly variable, with some establishments (eg hummus shops) winding down mid-afternoon and others serving hot dishes until well after midnight. A few upmarket establishments close between lunch and dinner. Most kosher restaurants are closed on Shabbat (Friday night and Saturday).

Shopping Malls Generally open from 9.30am or 10am to 9.30am or 10pm Sunday to Thursday and until 2pm or 3pm on Friday and the eves of Jewish holidays.

Shops Usually open from 9am to 6pm or later Sunday to Thursday and until 2pm or 3pm on Friday and the eves of Jewish holidays.

Customs Regulations

Israel allows travellers 18 and over to import duty-free up to 1L of spirits and 2L of wine, 250mL of perfume, 250g of tobacco products, and gifts worth no more than US$200. Live animals can be brought into Israel but require lots of advance paperwork. Fresh meat, pornography and 900MHz cordless phones are prohibited.

Dangers & Annoyances

For information on dealing with security-related problems, see p422. For tips on safe hiking, see p247 and p290. The peculiarities of swimming in the Dead Sea are covered on p288.

Theft

Theft is as much a problem in Israel and the Palestinian Territories as it is in any other country, so take the usual precautions: don't leave valuables in your room or vehicle, and use a money belt. In hostels, it's wise to check your most valuable belongings and documents into the front-desk safe. On intercity buses, it's fine to stow large bags in the luggage hold, but keep valuables with you inside. Crowded tourist spots and crowded markets are obvious haunts for pickpockets, so stay aware of what's happening around you. Bike theft is rampant so use a massive chain lock and never leave an expensive bike on the street overnight.

Discount Cards

A Hostelling International (HI) card is useful for discounts at official HI hostels. An International Student Identity Card (ISIC) doesn't get anywhere near as many discounts as it once did (none, for instance, are available on public transport).

Some museums and sights offer discounts to senior citizens, though to qualify you may not only need to be 'senior' but also a 'citizen'.

If you're visiting lots of the national parks and historical sites run by the **Israel Nature & Parks Authority** (INPA; www.parks.org.il), you can save by purchasing a 14-day Green Card, which gets you into all 65 INPA sites for just 145NIS (a six-park version costs 105NIS).

Electricity

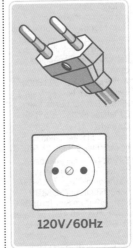

120V/60Hz

120V/60Hz

Embassies & Consulates

Jerusalem may be Israel's capital, but the vagaries of international politics have led most diplomatic missions to locate in or near Tel Aviv. A few countries maintain consulates in Jerusalem, Haifa and/or Eilat.

Most diplomatic missions are open in the morning from Monday to Thursday or Friday, and some for longer hours. The following are in Tel Aviv unless specified otherwise:

Australia (☏03-693 5000; www.israel.embassy.gov.au; 28th fl, Discount Bank Tower, 23 Yehuda HaLevi St, 65136)

Canada (☏03-636 3300; www.canadainternational. gc.ca/israel; 3 Nirim St, 67060)

Egypt (www.egyptembassy. net for Egyptian embassy in Washington) Eilat (☏08-637 6882; 68 Afrouni St, 88119 Eilat; ◷9-11am Sun-Thu); Tel Aviv (☏03-546 4151; 54 Basel St, 64239; ◷9-11am Sun-Tue) In Eilat, deliver your passport, application and one passport-sized photo in the morning and pick up the visa around 2pm the same day. In Tel Aviv the process may take a few days.

France Jerusalem (☏02-625 9481; www.consulfrance-jeru salem.org; 5 Paul Émile Botta St, 91076); Tel Aviv (☏03-520 8500; www.ambafrance-il.org; 112 Herbert Samuel Esplanade, 63572)

Germany (☏03-693 1313; www.tel-aviv.diplo.de, in German & Hebrew; 19th fl, 3 Daniel Frisch St, 64731)

Ireland (☏03-696 4166; www. embassyofireland.co.il; 17th fl, 3 Daniel Frisch St, 64731)

Jordan (☏03-751 7722; www. jordanembassytelaviv.gov. jo; 10th fl, 14 Abba Hillel St, Ramat Gan) You can apply in the morning and pick your visa up around 2pm the same day; bring one passport-sized photo. Linked to adjacent Tel Aviv by Dan bus 66.

Netherlands (☏03-754 0777; http://israel.nlambas sade.org; 14 Abba Hillel St, Ramat Gan, 52506)

New Zealand (☏03-695 1869; www.mfat.govt.nz; 3 Daniel Frisch St, 64731)

Turkey (☏03-524 1101; 202 HaYarkon St, 63405)

UK Jerusalem (☏02-541 4100; www.ukinjerusalem. fco.gov.uk; 19 Nashashibi St, Sheikh Jarrah, 97200); Tel Aviv Consular Section (☏03-725 1222; www.ukinisrael.fco.gov. uk; 6th fl, Migdalor Bldg, 1 Ben Yehuda St, 63801)

USA Haifa (☏04-853 1470; 26 Ben-Gurion Ave, 35023); Jerusalem (☏02-622 7230; http://jerusalem.usconsulate. gov; 18 Agron Rd, 94190); Tel Aviv (☏03-519 7475; http:// israel.usembassy.gov; 71 HaYarkon St, 63903)

Food

For details on Israeli and Palestinian cuisine, see p393.

Two useful websites listing thousands of restaurants, cafes and bars all over Israel:
» www.restaurants-in-israel. co.il
» www.restaurants.co.il

EATING PRICE CATEGORIES

The price of a restaurant's average main dish determines which price category it's in.

	ISRAEL	PALESTINIAN TERRITORIES
Budget ($)	under 30NIS	under 35NIS
Midrange ($$)	30NIS to 70NIS	35NIS-55NIS
Top End ($$$)	above 70NIS	above 55NIS

Gay & Lesbian Travellers

Israel is home to an open and lively gay scene. Tel Aviv, named 'Best City of 2011' in a worldwide poll of the readers of **GayCities** (www.gaycities. com, http://telaviv.gaycities. com), has a number of gay hang-outs and plenty of rainbow-coloured flags fluttering over the streets. The resort town of Eilat is gay friendly, although the scene is mostly Israeli tourists. Haifa and Jerusalem have smaller gay communities. Orthodox Judaism, Islam and most of the Holy Land's Christian churches are opposed to homosexuality, so it's appropriate to be circumspect in religious neighbourhoods. There are no laws in Israel against homosexuality.

Local organisations, offering support, information, contacts and events, are based in Tel Aviv (see p139) and Jerusalem (see p97).

Gay culture is extremely hidden in the Palestinian Territories, and hundreds of gay Palestinians have fled to Israel for their own safety (although this has become increasingly difficult with tight border controls). To better understand the difficult plight of gay and lesbian Palestinians, check out:
» www.globalgayz.com/ middle-east/palestine
» www.aswatgroup.org.

Insurance

It's a good idea to take out a travel insurance policy before leaving for Israel. In addition to the usual coverage for sickness (hospital visits can be expensive in Israel) or theft, tailor your insurance to your specific needs (eg make sure the policy includes scuba diving and skiing if you plan to partake).

Worldwide travellers' coverage is available online at www.lonelyplanet.com/ bookings/insurance.do.

If you'll be staying in Israel for at least three to six months, even on a tourist visa, it's possible to get pretty complete medical coverage at reasonable rates through one of the country's HMOs. For details, drop by one of the offices of:

» **Me'uchedet** (☑03-520 2323; www.meuhedet.co.il)

» **Maccabi Healthcare Services** (☑3555; www.maccabi4u.co.il)

» **Clalit** (☑2700, 1222-2700; www.clalit-global.co.il)

Internet Access

There are wi-fi hots spots all over Israel (eg in all McDonald's branches) and in quite a few places in the Palestinian Territories. Wi-fi is also available on some intra-city buses (though it's rather slow). HI youth hostels and many fancy hotels charge for wi-fi and the use of internet computers; at other hostels and in midrange hotels wi-fi is often free. Internet cafes are becoming scarce but, where available, appear in city listings under Information.

Throughout this book we use @ to indicate places that have internet computers; a 🛜 symbol denotes wi-fi (not necessarily free). For useful web resources, see p17.

Legal Matters

Smoking is banned in all enclosed public spaces; violators – or the owners of the place where scofflaws light up – can face on-the-spot fines. It is illegal to drive any sort of motorised vehicle on any beach.

Visitors to Israel – unlike Israeli citizens – are not allowed to proselytise. Religion is a sensitive matter here so sharing your faith's 'good news' too enthusiastically can lead to angry locals and complications with the police.

If you're arrested, there's little your embassy can do

for you while the legal process plays itself out, other than sending a low-ranking diplomat to visit you.

Palestinian police are not permitted to arrest tourists, but can detain a tourist until Israeli military forces arrive on the scene.

Maps

Tourist office maps, when available, tend to be rudimentary. Excellent road maps of Israel and the Palestinian Territories are published by a Tel Aviv–based company called **Mapa** (www.mapa.co.il, in Hebrew) and sold at all bookshops; its website has a detailed Hebrew-language map of the whole country. The databases used by **Google Maps** (www.maps.google.com) and GPS-based navigational devices are as developed as in most Western countries.

For hikers, the **Society for the Protection of Nature in Israel** (SPNI; www.teva.org.il), known in Hebrew as *HaChevra l'Haganat HaTeva*, publishes a series of 20 1:50,000-scale topographical trail maps (*mapot simun shvilim*), available only in Hebrew. Not only do they indicate nature reserves (shown in green with the name in purple) and all marked hiking trails, but they also show areas used by the IDF for live-fire military exercises (*shitchei esh;* indicated in pink) and the location of old minefields (*sdot mokshim;* in pink with a border of red triangles). The maps (82NIS if purchased directly from the SPNI) are sold at bookshops; waterproof versions may cost a bit more.

Money

ATMs

ATMs are widespread, and Visa, MasterCard and, increasingly, American Express

and Diners cards are accepted almost everywhere. Most – but not all – ATMs do Visa and MasterCard cash advances.

Cash

The official currency is the Israeli New Shekel (NIS or ILS), known simply as the shekel (shekelim in the plural). Rates at the time of printing are found on p16.

The shekel is divided into 100 agorot. Coins come in denominations of 10 and 50 agorot (marked ½ shekel) and one, two and five NIS; notes come in denominations of 10, 20, 50, 100 and 200NIS.

Prices in this book are quoted in shekels except where the establishment quotes prices in dollars or euros. Because tourists are not subject to Israel's Value Added Tax (VAT) of 16%, most top-end hotels, HI hostels, car-hire companies and airlines have shekel rates for locals and US dollar rates for foreigners.

Tourists who pay in local currency are entitled to a VAT refund on many items purchased in Israeli shops (check with the cashier before you buy). Purchases must be wrapped in sealed, partially transparent plastic, and the original invoice must be legible without opening the parcel. Claim your refund from the counter in the departures lounge of Ben-Gurion airport.

The Palestinian Territories do not have their own currency. Rather, they use Israeli shekels and, to a lesser degree, Jordanian dinars and US dollars.

Moneychangers

Exchange rates vary little from place to place, but banks may charge a hefty commission. The best deals are usually available at larger post office branches and independent exchange bureaux, which don't charge commissions.

Tipping

Until recently, tipping wasn't an issue in Israel, but these days restaurant bills arrive with a 10% to 12% addition for service, or a notice informing you that service is not included. Waiters in the Palestinian Territories will usually be very grateful for any gratuity. Taxi drivers on both sides of the Green Line do not expect tips.

Travellers Cheques & Wire Transfers

Travellers cheques can be changed at most banks but charges can be as high as 20NIS per cheque; instead use a no-commission exchange bureau or the post office.

Post offices offer Western Union international money-transfer services.

Post

Sent with **Israel Post** (www.israelpost.co.il), letters and postcards to North America and Australasia take seven to 10 days to arrive; to Europe it's a bit less. Incoming mail takes three or four days from Europe and around a week from other places. A domestic letter weighing up to 50gm costs 1.70NIS. Internationally, postcards and airmail letters cost 4NIS to Europe and 5.80NIS to North America or Australia.

For express service, options include **DHL** (www.dhl.co.il) and **UPS** (www.ups.com); Israel Post's EMS (Express Mail Service) is cheaper but slower and not as reliable.

Telephone

Costs

Domestic land-line-to-land-line calls are cheap, but calling a mobile phone from a land line or another mobile can cost 0.60NIS a minute or more. Be careful when you use the phone in your hotel room – hotels often charge exorbitant rates.

Mobile Phones

Nothing matches the convenience of having your own mobile phone, but although overseas mobile phones work in Israel (so long as your gadget can handle 900/1800 MHz), roaming charges can be ruinous. Fortunately, Israel's three main mobile phone companies, **Orange** (Big Talk; www.orange.co.il, in Hebrew), **Pelefon** (Talk & Go; www.pelephone.co.il, in Hebrew) and **Cellcom** (www.cellcom.co.il, in Hebrew) all offer pay-as-you-go SIM cards at their many outlets. A variety of online companies also sell Israeli SIMs internationally.

Throughout this guide, numbers starting with 05 plus a third digit are for mobiles. To call a local land line from a mobile phone, always dial the area code.

If you are near Israel's borders (especially with Jordan), you may discover that your mobile phone has switched to a Jordanian network. Manually switch your gadget back to your Israeli network or you may clock up pricey roaming charges.

Phone Codes

Israel's country code is ✆972; the Palestinian Territories use both ✆972 and ✆970. To call from abroad, dial your international access code followed by the country code, the local area code (minus the zero) and the subscriber number. In this book, all phone numbers include area codes.

To call abroad from Israel, available international access codes include ✆012 (012 Smile), ✆013 (013 Netvision) and ✆014 (Bezeq) and ✆018 (018). All offer remarkably cheap rates to most countries, though it pays to find out what their latest offers are.

Phonecards

Prepaid local and international calls can be made using a variety of phonecards, sold at post offices, lottery kiosks and newsstands

Time

Except for a few days at the beginning of daylight savings time (summer time) and several weeks at the end of daylight savings time, Israel is two hours ahead of GMT/UTC, seven hours ahead of New York, 10 hours ahead of San Francisco and eight or nine hours behind Melbourne.

Israel goes on daylight savings time at 2am on the last Friday before 2 April, more or less like Europe and North America. But because of demands by ultra-Orthodox political parties, it returns to winter time at 2am on the Sunday between Rosh HaShana and Yom Kippur, ie four to seven weeks before Europe and North America. The rationale is that without daylight savings time the Yom Kippur fast ends a whole hour earlier – but it also begins an hour earlier...

Tourist Information

Nearly every major Israeli city has a tourist office. Staff will send you off with maps and more brochures than you can carry. Some also organise city walking tours. The only tourist office in the Palestinian Territories is in Bethlehem.

Useful websites include:

» www.goisrael.com – website of Israel's Ministry of Tourism

» www.thisweekinpalestine.com – details on what's happening in the Palestinian Territories

» www.parks.org.il – Israel Nature & Parks Authority

» www.travelujah.com – useful information for Christian travellers

» www.igoogledisrael.com – tips on travelling and living in Israel from a veteran British expat

Travellers with Disabilities

In Israel, access for people in wheelchairs and with other disabilities has improved significantly in recent years. Hotels, hostels and other accommodation are required to have at least one room available for wheelchair users, and many tourist sites such as museums and historic sites can accommodate people with disabilities. Many nature reserves have trails that are wheelchair accessible (see www.parks.org.il). Restaurants are a mixed bag, with few claiming to be fully accessible (ie including bathrooms).

The Palestinian Territories are less well equipped and getting around is made more difficult by road checkpoints, which are usually crossed on foot; lines for these can be long and crowded and sometimes require moving over and around barriers.

Access in Israel & the Palestinian Authority (www.accessinisrael.org) by Gordon Couch provides the low-down for travellers with mobility restrictions. Published in 2000, it's old but still relevant. Some information is also available from **Access Israel** (www.aisrael.org).

The **Yad Sarah Organisation** (02-644 4444; www.yadsarah.org; 124 Herzl Blvd, Jerusalem) lends wheelchairs, crutches and other mobility aids free of charge (deposit required).

Visas

Israel

In general, Western visitors to Israel and the Palestinian Territories are issued free tourist (B-2) visas. You need a passport that's valid for at least six months from the date of entry. (For specifics on who qualifies, visit www.mfa.gov.il and click on 'About the Ministry' and then 'Consular Service'.)

Most visas issued at an entry point are valid for 90 days. But travellers, eg those entering by land from Egypt or Jordan, may be given just 30 days or even two weeks – it's up to the discretion of the border control official.

We've heard reports of Israeli authorities at Allenby–King Hussein Bridge and Ben Gurion airport issuing entry stamps (eg to people of Palestinian or Arab ancestry) reading 'Palestinian Authority Only', making it difficult or impossible to get past the IDF roadblocks that regulate traffic from the West Bank into Israel. (If you receive such a stamp at the airport, it's not clear how you're supposed to get to the West Bank without violating its provisions.) Conversely, authorities at the airport have been known to require that travellers sign a form declaring that they will not enter the Palestinian Authority without permission from Israeli authorities.

Kibbutz volunteers must secure a volunteer's visa (see p434).

If there is any indication that you are coming to participate in pro-Palestinian protests or are seeking illegal employment, you may find yourself on the next flight home.

For information on the implications of an Israeli stamp in your passport, see p30.

VISA EXTENSIONS

To extend a tourist (B-2) visa beyond the time given you upon entry, you can either:

» Apply to extend your visa (170NIS).

» Do a 'visa run' to Egypt (Sinai) or Jordan. This might get you an additional three months – or just one. Ask other travellers for the latest low-down.

Visas are extended by the **Population Immigration & Border Authority** (1-700-551 111; www.piba.gov.il, in Hebrew; generally 8am-noon Sun-Tue & Thu), part of the **Ministry of the Interior** (for information 3450 or 1222-3450), whose offices include **Jerusalem** (1 Shlomzion HaMalka St), **Tel Aviv** (Kiryat HaMamshala, 125 Menachem Begin Rd) and **Eilat** (2nd fl, HaKenyon HaAdom, HaTemarim Blvd).

Bring a passport valid for at least six months beyond the requested extension period, a recent photo, a letter explaining why you want/need an extension (plus documentation), and evidence of sufficient funds for the extended stay. Offices in smaller towns are often easier and faster to deal with.

If you would qualify for an *oleh* (immigrant) visa under Israel's Law of Return, ie have at least one Jewish grandparent or have converted to Judaism and have documentation demonstrating this, it's very easy to extend your tourist visa for as long as you'd like, or even become an Israeli citizen.

You can be fined if you overstay your visa, though travellers who overstay by just a few days report no hassles or fines.

Egypt

In general, Western visitors arriving in Egypt overland have to arrange an Egyptian visa in advance (if you fly to Egypt, you can usually get a visa upon arrival). But for travel to Sinai's Red Sea coast, officials at the Eilat–Taba border issue free Sinai-only visas that are valid for 14 days of travel along the coast between Taba and Sharm el-Sheikh, and to Mt Sinai and St Katherine's Monastery. These visas are not valid for diving at Ras Mohammed National Park near Sharm el-Sheikh.

OVERSEAS PALESTINIANS

According to the US State Department, 'Israeli authorities might consider as Palestinian anyone who has a Palestinian identification number, was born in the West Bank or Gaza, or was born in the United States but has parents or grandparents who were born or lived in the West Bank or Gaza'. Even if they hold US citizenship, the Israeli government may require that a person so designated travel to Israel and/or the West Bank using a Palestinian Authority passport.

If you're planning to continue overland to other parts of Egypt, you'll almost certainly need to arrange an Egyptian visa (single entry US$15 to US$20, multiple entry US$15 to US$25) in advance. For Egypt's consular offices in Israel, see p430.

Jordan

Nearly all nationalities require a visa to enter Jordan. Conveniently, single-entry, extendable, two-week visas are issued with a minimum of fuss at:

» The Jordan River–Sheikh Hussein crossing (visa costs JD20), 30km south of the Sea of Galilee.

» The Yitzhak Rabin–Wadi Araba crossing (visa is free), a few kilometres north of Eilat and Aqaba.

» The ferry from Nuweiba in Sinai (visa is free).

Note: visas are *not* available at the Allenby–King Hussein Bridge crossing.

Contact a Jordanian embassy or consulate for a visa (single/multiple entry JD20/60 or 88/168NIS; see p429) if:

» you want to enter Jordan via Allenby–King Hussein Bridge.

» you need a multiple-entry visa (valid for six months).

» at-the-border visas are not available to people of your nationality.

Note: if you crossed into the West Bank and/or Israel through Allenby–King Hussein Bridge *and* re-enter Jordan the same way, you do not need to apply for a new Jordanian visa, provided you return within the validity of your Jordanian visa or its extension. Remember to keep the stamped exit slip and present it on returning.

Volunteering

Israel and the Palestinian Territories abound with volunteer opportunities. In Israel these are mainly of the kibbutz variety (for archaeological digs, see p427), while in the Palestinian Territories they're mostly helping the various NGOs that endeavour to improve everyday life for Palestinian children, women and others.

For a list of Israeli organisations interested in foreign volunteers, go to the websites of **Ruach Tova** (www.ruachtova.org) or the **National Council on Volunteering** (www.ivolunteer. org.il); for the latter, click on 'Volunteer Opportunities' and then 'Visitors'.

Israel

KIBBUTZIM

Since Israel's founding, hundreds of thousands of young people (especially Europeans) have spent time as kibbutz volunteers. For many, the months spent mucking cow sheds, washing up in the communal dining room or picking vegetables was a highlight of their youth.

These days, the kibbutz movement is well past its heyday, with all but 70 of the country's 270 kibbutzim (the plural of 'kibbutz') having decided to transform themselves into non-communal villages. However, it is still possible to volunteer on a couple of dozen kibbutzim.

The work is manual (often in the dining hall, laundry or tourist services), the work weeks are long (seven or eight hours a day, six days a week) and the monetary compensation mere pocket money (400NIS a month), but you get housing (in a room for two to four people), food, laundry service, health insurance, the chance to meet other young people and learn some Hebrew, and an unparalleled opportunity to immerse yourself in kibbutz life. Volunteers have access to sports facilities, the pool, cultural events (eg movies in the evening) and the pub. Tours and activities are often available on days off (three a month). For one Brit's inside perspective, see www.kibbutzvolunteer.com.

Kibbutz volunteers must be between the ages of 19 (or perhaps 18) and 35 and be willing to commit for between two and six months. You must apply in your home country at least a month before you planned arrival; a medical form is required. You're unlikely to know in advance which kibbutz has space. You have to pay for your own air travel, pitch in for health insurance (three/six months 340/440NIS) and cover the cost of a volunteer's visa (three/six months 110/200NIS).

For citizens of the US and Canada:

Kibbutz Program Centre (☑001-212 462 2764, fax 001-212-462-2765; www.kibbutzprogramcenter.org; Ste 1004, 114 W 26th St, New York, NY 10001)

For candidates from everywhere else:

Kibbutz Program Centre (☎03-524 6154/6, fax 03-5239966; www.kibbutz.org.il/volunteers; 6 Frishman St, Tel Aviv; ⊗8.30am-2.30pm Sun-Thu)

Palestinian Territories

There are manifold volunteer opportunities across the West Bank. Groups that welcome volunteers include:

» **Al-Rowwad Centre** (p275)
» **Freedom Theatre** (www.thefreedomtheatre.org)
» **Hope Flowers School** (☎02-274 0693; www.hopeflowersschool.org)
» **Palestinian Circus School** (www.palcircus.ps)
» **Tent of Nations** (☎02-274 3071; www.tentofnations.org)
» **Ibdaa Cultural Centre** (p275)

Weights & Measures

Israel, the West Bank and Gaza all follow the international metric system of weights and measures.

Women Travellers

Female travellers generally feel as free and comfortable in Israel as they would in any Western country, though it's important to follow sensible travel advice, such as not hitchhiking alone, and other precautions one generally adheres to back home. During daylight hours, exercise caution in labyrinthine old cities (eg Akko and Bethlehem) and in lonely parts of tourist areas (eg beaches near Tel Aviv and Eilat); avoid these areas at night. On some beaches on both sides of the Green Line, foreign women may attract unwanted attention. Palestinian men are generally very respectful towards women and travelling in the West Bank is almost always hassle-free.

Keep in mind local dress codes. While tight-fitting, revealing clothing is common in many parts of Israel and on evenings out in Ramallah or Bethlehem, it may make locals uncomfortable in the more religiously conservative parts of Jerusalem and the West Bank, and is likely to be met with overt hostility in ultra-Orthodox Jewish neighbourhoods. When visiting such areas (as well as when visiting religious sites), the best bet for women travellers is to wear a long skirt and a shirt with long sleeves (long trousers are OK in Muslim and Christian areas). For Muslim sites, also bring a scarf to cover your hair.

Work

Travellers used to be able to turn up in Tel Aviv and find plenty of casual work in bars and restaurants, but authorities have been cracking down on businesses hiring illegal workers and opportunities are now slim. Your best chances for gainful employment are through Tel Aviv guesthouses and restaurants near the beach. Guesthouses may be able to help find you a job, but only if you are staying there. Nevertheless, it doesn't hurt to scour the classified ads in *Jerusalem Post* and *Ha'aretz* for employment.

Working legally requires a permit from the Ministry of the Interior and, as in North America or Western Europe, these aren't easy to get – with one exception. If you would qualify for an *oleh* (immigrant) visa – ie if you have at least one Jewish parent or grandparent – you can get a working visa with relative ease.

If you do find work and discover that you have been cheated by your employer, you can get free advice from **Kav l'Oved Workers' Hotline** (☎03-688 3766; www.kavlaoved.org.il; 4th fl, 75 Nachalat Binyamin St, Tel Aviv); see the website for the times English-speaking staff are on hand.

Transport

GETTING THERE & AWAY

Israel has land borders and peace treaties with Egypt and Jordan, so it's easy to combine a visit to Israel and the Palestinian Territories with a trip to Petra and/or to the Red Sea coast of Sinai. For information on entering and exiting Israel and the Palestinian Territories by land, see p27.

For details on visas to Israel, Jordan and Egypt, see p433.

For implications on the possible implications of having an Israeli entry stamp in your passport, see p30.

Flights and tours can be booked online at www.lonelyplanet.com/bookings.

Air

Airports

Israel's main gateway is **Ben-Gurion International Airport** (IATA code: TLV; ☑arrivals & departures 03-972 3333; www.iaa.gov.il), situated 50km northwest of Jerusalem and 18km southeast of central Tel Aviv. Its ultramodern international terminal, finished in 2004 at a cost of US$1 billion, handles about 11 million passengers a year. For details on arrivals and departures, go to the website and click 'Ben Gurion Airport', then 'Passenger Services' and finally 'On Line Flights'.

Airport security is tight, so international travellers should check in at least three hours prior to their flight – when flying both to and from Israel.

A handful of European charter flights touch down at **Ovda airport** (IATA code: VDA; ☑1-700-705 022; www.iaa.gov.il), 60km north of Eilat.

Airlines

Israel's privatised flag carrier, **El Al** (LY; ☑03-977 1111; www.elal.co.il) has direct flights to several dozen cities in Europe and the Former Soviet Union, as well as long-haul non-stop services to New York, Newark, Toronto, Los Angeles, Mumbai, Bangkok, Seoul, Hong Kong and Beijing; some flights to Asian destinations are codeshares. Known for having the tightest security in the business, the company was privatised in 2005, leading to a significant improvement in service. El Al is not a member of any of the three global airline alliances (Star Alliance, OneWorld and Skyteam). **Sundor** (www.sundor.co.il) is El Al's charter subsidiary.

Some of the cheapest flights from North America to Tel Aviv are offered by **Air Canada** (www.aircanada.com) via Toronto, or **US Airways** (www.usairways.com) via Philadelphia. A variety of European carriers offer trans-Atlantic services with a stopover in their hub city, making it easy to combine travel to Israel with a visit to London, Paris, Frankfurt, Amsterdam or Rome.

Almost all the major European airlines have flights to

CLIMATE CHANGE & TRAVEL

Every form of transport that relies on carbon-based fuel generates CO_2, the main cause of human-induced climate change. Modern travel is dependent on aeroplanes, which might use less fuel per kilometre per person than most cars but travel much greater distances. The altitude at which aircraft emit gases (including CO_2) and particles also contributes to their climate change impact. Many websites offer 'carbon calculators' that allow people to estimate the carbon emissions generated by their journey and, for those who wish to do so, to offset the impact of the greenhouse gases emitted with contributions to portfolios of climate-friendly initiatives throughout the world. Lonely Planet offsets the carbon footprint of all staff and author travel.

Tel Aviv. Budget and charter airlines that link Tel Aviv with Europe but may not pop up on air-ticket search engines (eg www.orbitz.com, www.expedia.com, www.kayak.com and www.travelocity.com) include:

» **Air Baltic** (www.airbaltic.com)

» **Air Berlin** (www.airberlin.com)

» **Air Méditerranée** (www.air-mediterranee.fr)

» **Arkia** (www.arkia.com)

» **Brussels Airlines** (www.brusselsairlines.com)

» **Cimber Sterling** (www.cimber.com)

» **easyJet** (www.easyjet.com)

» **Enter** (www.enterair.pl)

» **German Wings** (www.germanwings.com)

» **Israir** (www.israirairlines.com)

» **Jet2** (www.easyjet.com)

» **Jetairfly** (www.jetairfly.com)

» **Meridiana** (www.meridiana.it)

» **Niki** (www.flyniki.com)

» **Norwegian** (www.norwegian.com)

» **Smartwings** (www.smartwings.net)

» **TUI** (www.tuifly.com)

» **Vueling** (www.vueling.com)

The only Middle Eastern cities with direct services to Tel Aviv are Istanbul, served by **Turkish Airlines** (www.turkishairlines.com); Cairo, served by Air Sinai (a subsidiary of Egyptair); and Amman, served by **Royal Jordanian** (www.rj.com).

El Al has non-stop flights – some of them codeshare (eg with Thai) – to/from eastern Asia, as does **Korean Air** (www.koreanair.com), but the cheapest way to get to/from South, Southeast and East Asia is often via Istanbul on Turkish Airways, via Addis Ababa on **Ethiopian Airlines** (www.flyethiopian.com), or via Amman on carriers such as Royal Jordanian, Qatar Airways (with a stop over in Doha), Emirates (via

Dubai) and Etihad (via Abu Dhabi).

Israel is rarely an allowable stop on round-the-world (RTW) itineraries, but Cairo is usually possible.

Tickets

In Israel and some European countries, good deals are sometimes available from the Israeli student travel agency **ISSTA** (☏03-777 7777; www.issta.com; 109 Ben Yehuda St, Tel Aviv), which has branches around the country.

Daka 90 (☏03-636 6883; www.daka90.co.il, in Hebrew & Russian), whose name means 'at the last minute', sometimes advertises inexpensive flights, including one-ways.

Many Israeli backpackers on their way to South, Southeast or East Asia, or Australia book through **FLYeast** (☏09-970 0400; www.flyeast.co.il, in Hebrew), which specialises in inexpensive one-way and round-trip flights via Amman and then Doha, Dubai or Abu Dhabi (yes, Israelis are allowed to transit through those hubs). You can either fly the Tel Aviv–Amman leg or – to save a bit of money – take the bus.

Land

For details on land travel between Israel and the Palestinian Territories, Jordan and Egypt, see p27.

Sea

Passenger ferry services from Haifa to Limassol, Cyprus have been suspended. For details on the ferry from Aqaba (Jordan) to Nuqeiba (Sinai, Egypt), see p29.

GETTING AROUND

Israel has an efficient and inexpensive public transport system, with buses going everywhere and trains connecting the main cities.

The West Bank is served by local buses that travel between cities and East Jerusalem, and by a plethora of shared and private taxis. There are no connections whatsoever between Gaza and the West Bank.

Air

Flights to Eilat from Tel Aviv's Sde Dov airport, Ben-Gurion airport's domestic terminal and Haifa are handled by:
Arkia (www.arkia.com)
El Al (www.elal.co.il)
Israir (www.israirairlines.com)

Deals are often available on-line, with one-ways going for as little as 79NIS from Ben-Gurion (the price of a bus ticket).

Bicycle

Cycling is a great way to get around Israel. Highways have wide shoulders (though drivers can be politely described as erratic, and cycling is forbidden on some major intercity routes) and there is a growing number of off-road bike trails and scenic byways. The distances between tourist attractions, cities and villages are relatively short. Biking is also a great way to meet people and experience the country at ground level. And best of all, it's free and environmentally friendly.

The main drawback to cycling in Israel, other than the risk of being run over, is the heat. Always set off as early as possible and carry plenty of water. Choose your route carefully; while the coastal plain is flat enough, the Upper Galilee, the Golan and the Dead Sea region have lots of steep hills, and the Negev Desert and the Jordan Valley can be mercilessly hot. One of the best bike trips is around the Sea of Galilee (bikes can be hired in Tiberias). Bicycles can be taken on buses but you may need to pay an extra luggage charge. Bikes (except folding bikes with cloth covers) aren't allowed on trains.

Some bike shops in Israel will rent out bikes by the week; others will buy a bike back from you at a fair price if you purchase it in their shop. You'll find plenty of bike shops in Jerusalem, Haifa, Tel Aviv (eg along HaHashmona'im St) and other cities; two of the largest are **Rosen & Meentz** (www.rosen-meents.co.il) and **Matzman & Merutz** (www. matzman-merutz.co.il). Bike hire isn't really an option in the Palestinian Territories, but if you have a bike there shouldn't be a problem bringing it through the checkpoints.

If you choose to fly with your own bicycle, contact your airline ahead of time to ask about baggage restrictions and associated costs. Bike shops can give you a bike box.

For information on cycling tours and competitions, see p427. For information on cycling in Tel Aviv and the city's bike path network, see p109.

Bus

Israel

Almost every town and village has bus service at least a few times a day, though from mid-afternoon on Friday until Saturday after dark, most intercity buses don't run at all (the lines to Eilat and Majdal Shams are exceptions). In this book, information on bus travel appears at the end of each listing, under Getting There & Away.

Sample one-way fares include:

» Jerusalem to Tel Aviv – 18NIS

» Tel Aviv to Kiryat Shmona – 47NIS

» Tel Aviv to Eilat – 75NIS
Return tickets – also good for two one-ways or for two passengers travelling together – cost 15% less

than two single tickets. On some lines, a *kartisiya* (kar-tees-ee-*yah*), a punch card valid for six or eight trips, can also save you money. Students no longer qualify for discounts.

Israel no longer has two bus monopolies but rather about 20 private companies that compete for routes in Ministry of Transport tenders. The **Public Transportation Info Center** (☎1-900-72-1111; www.bus.co.il), easy to use once you figure it out, provides details in English on all bus companies' routes, times and prices. To get information on bus schedules by SMS (text message), send a question (in Hebrew only) to ☎4949.

Bus companies you're likely to run across include:

» **Dan** (☎03-639 4444; www. dan.co.il)

» **Egged** (☎2800, 03-694 8888; www.egged.co.il)

» **Kavim** (☎03-606 6055; www.kavim-t.co.il, in Hebrew)

» **Metropoline** (☎5900, 1222-5900; www.metropoline. com, in Hebrew)

» **Nateev Express** (☎04-6463921/3/7; www.nateevex press.com, in Hebrew)

» **Nazareth Tourism & Transport** (NTT; ☎1-599-559 559; www.ntt-buses.com, in Hebrew)

» **Rama** (☎8787, 3254; www. golanbus.co.il)

» **Veolia** (☎6686; www.con nex.co.il)

The only bus tickets that need to be (or can be) ordered in advance are Egged tickets to/from Eilat, reserve by website or phone. Note: at research time, the system only accepted Israeli credit cards.

West Bank

In East Jerusalem and the West Bank, a number of small, Arab-run bus companies provide public transport. Unlike their counterparts in Israel, they operate right through the weekend.

Car & Motorcycle

To drive a vehicle in Israel and the Palestinian Territories, all you need is your regular driving licence (an international driving licence is not required).

Israel's automobile association is known as **Memsi** (☎02-625 9711; www.memsi. co.il, in Hebrew; 31 Ben Yehuda St, Jerusalem).

Hire

Having your own wheels lets you travel at your own pace, get lost along back roads and – if necessary – cover a lot of ground in a short amount of time. It doesn't make much sense to have a car in Jerusalem or Tel Aviv – parking can be a huge hassle – but it's a great idea in the Galilee, Golan and Negev, where many towns and villages are served by just a handful of buses a day.

Israel's biggest concentration of rental agencies is along Tel Aviv's HaYarkon St (one block in from the beach), but most companies have offices around the country (see city listings for details). These include:

» **Avis** (www.avis.co.il)

» **Budget** (www.budget.co.il)

» **Cal Auto** (www.calauto.co.il) One of the cheapest, with prices from 99NIS a day.

» **Eldan** (www.eldan.co.il) The only company with an office in Kiryat Shmona.

» **Hertz** (www.hertz.co.il) The only company with a Dead Sea office.

Car hire with insurance and unlimited kilometres costs as little as US$200 per week or US$600 per month. Israelis have to pay VAT (16%) on car rental but tourists do not. Discounts are available on-line; there's a surcharge for airport pick-up.

Read the fine print on your insurance contract carefully, especially regarding the excess (deductible). If you do not take the insurance option, you may be liable for any damages to the vehicle whether you caused them or not, and for damage to another car or property. You may already be covered by your personal travel insurance, so be sure to check with your insurer before setting off.

Note that most Israeli rental agencies forbid you to take their cars into the Palestinian Territories; Green Peace is a notable exception (see p103).

Road Conditions

The condition of most Israeli roads is quite good, but a visible minority of Israeli drivers can be extremely unpredictable and drive, in general, far more aggressively than in the USA, the UK or Australia. Drive carefully – and defensively – at all times.

North–south highways are designated using even numbers, while east–west routes have odd numbers; in general, numbers rise as you go south-to-north and west-to-east. Thus, Rte 2 runs along the Mediterranean coast while Rte 90 hugs the country's eastern border with Jordan; Israel's northernmost road – in Upper Galilee – is Rte 99. Rte 1, an exception to this sequencing, links Tel Aviv with Jerusalem and the Dead Sea.

Israel has three toll roads:
» Rte 6 (Kvish Shesh; www.kvish6.co.il, in Hebrew, Arabic and Russian), which runs up the centre of the country for 138km. Bills for tolls – up to 32NIS – are sent to car owners on the basis of a national database of licence plate numbers.
» Carmel Tunnels (www.carmeltunnels.co.il, in Hebrew; one/two sections 6/12NIS) The two segments run under Mt Carmel south of Haifa.
» Fast Lane (Nativ Mahir; www.fastlane.co.il, in Hebrew) A 13km quick lane from Ben-Gurion Airport to Tel Aviv. Tariffs vary based on traffic conditions.

In the West Bank (except on roads reserved for Jewish settlers), the traffic is far less fast-moving, and can be held up by checkpoints, road blocks or donkey carts. For more information on driving on the West Bank, see p271.

Road Rules

Vehicles drive on the right-hand side of the road in Israel and the Palestinian Territories; seatbelts are required at all times. Unless you have a hands-free set, using a mobile phone while driving is illegal and subject to a fine of 1000NIS.

Road signs are marked in English, Hebrew and (usually) Arabic. The best road maps are produced by **Mapa** (www.mapa.co.il, in Hebrew) and are available at all bookshops.

Car headlights must always be on whenever you're driving on an intercity road, except when daylight savings time is in force.

Israeli police cars always have their blue (sometimes red-and-blue) lights flashing, so seeing police lights in your rear-view mirror doesn't mean you're in trouble (if you are, they'll make that clear with a loud hailer).

Hitching

Although hitching was once a common way of getting around Israel, increasing reports of violent crime make this a risky business and we do not recommend it. Women should not hitch without male companions and all travellers should be circumspect about the cars they get into. The local method of soliciting a lift is simply to point an index finger at the road. Hitching is still most common in the Upper Galilee and Golan regions.

Local Transport

Bicycle

Bike paths have been going up in cities all over Israel, but the most developed network is in Tel Aviv – see p109 and p145 for details. Details on bike rental appear in local listings.

Bus

Buses are used widely within larger cities. If you don't read Hebrew, or you are new to a city, it can be a little difficult to figure out the bus routes – just ask locals where your stop is and which bus to take. You can also ask advice from any bus driver passing by. See Getting Around under city listings for local details.

Taxi

'Special' (ie nonshared, or 'private') taxis can be very convenient but a few unscrupulous drivers overcharge tourists. The best way to avoid getting ripped off is to confidently give a street address, a cross street and directions. It's almost always to your advantage to use the meter (by law the driver has to put it on if you ask). A trip across town in Jerusalem or Tel Aviv shouldn't cost more than 30NIS to 35NIS.

Metre fall is 11.10NIS (9.50NIS in Eilat). Tariff 2 (25% more expensive than Tariff 1) applies between 9pm and 5.30am and on Shabbat and Jewish holidays. Wait time costs 86NIS per hour. Legitimate surcharges include:
» Pick-up at Ben-Gurion airport – 5NIS
» Piece of luggage (not including hand luggage) – 4NIS
» Third and fourth passengers– 4NIS each
» Phone order – 4.70NIS.

Taxi drivers do not expect tips, but in the absence of a rip-off attempt, it's fine to refuse a shekel or two in change.

Sherut (Shared Taxi)

To Israelis it's a sherut (sheh-root) while the Palestinians call it a service (pronounced ser-vees) taxi, but whatever name you use, shared taxis are a useful way to get around. These vehicles, often 13-seat minivans, operate on a fixed route for a fixed price, like a bus except that they don't have fixed stops. If you don't know the fare, ask your fellow passengers.

Sheruts are generally quicker than buses. They begin their run from a recognised taxi rank, but leave only when they're full so you may have to hang around for a while, although rarely more than 20 minutes. You can get out anywhere you like but you'll still pay the full fare. Many sheruts operate 24/7 and are the only means of public transport in Israel during Shabbat, when prices rise slightly. Throughout this book, we've quoted weekday prices, unless otherwise stated.

On the West Bank, shared taxis are plentiful and can take the form of chugging old Mercedes cars as well as minibuses. They can often be found near main town squares, eg in Ramallah.

For details on the daily sherut from Nazareth to Jenin, see p200.

Tours

Numerous companies offer day trips and tours in and around Israel, with a growing number of companies operating on the West Bank, too. Tours are great if you're short on time, or if you've a special interest; those run by the Society for the Protection of Nature in Israel (SPNI), for example, are terrific for nature enthusiasts. See p427 for information on cycling tours. Also see individual destination chapters for more tour options, including walking tours.

On the West Bank, a tour can be a good way of getting oriented, particularly if you're hesitant about going alone.

Israel

Society for the Protection of Nature in Israel (SPNI; ☑03-638 8688; www. teva.org.il) Runs highly regarded nature hikes (eg to see spring wildflowers) suitable for the whole family; mainly for Israelis so tour guides speak Hebrew – but SPNI outings are a good way to meet locals.

Abraham Hostel (☑02-650 2200; www.abraham-hostel-jerusalem.com) Runs excellent day tours of Jerusalem, the Dead Sea, Masada, Bethlehem and other sites. Also goes to Petra.

Bein Harim Tours (☑03-542 2000; www.beinharim.co.il) Custom tours around Israel and trips to Petra and Sinai.

Mike's Centre Tours & Transport (☑02-630 2000; www.mikescentre.com; tours per person US$50) Runs popular day trips from Jerusalem.

Touring Israel (☑077-450 3900; www.touringisrael.com) Tailor-made, top-end trips around Israel.

United Tours (☑03-617 3333; www.unitedtours.co.il) Large operator with one- and two-day trips all over the country.

Palestinian Territories

For more information on West Bank tours, see p258 and p266.

Green Olive Tours (☑03-721 9540, 054-693 4433; www.greenolivetours.com) Offers a wide variety of insightful day trips and multiday tours in both Israel and the West Bank.

Hijazi Travel (☑059-952 3844; http://hijazih.wordpress. com) Owner Hijazi Eid specialises in West Bank hiking and trekking, as well as city tours.

Alternative Tourism Group (☑02-277 2151; www.atg.ps) Culture, religion and politics, as well as walks along the Nazareth-to-Bethlehem Nativity Trail.

Abu Hassan Alternative Tours (☑052-286 4205; www. alternativetours.ps) Offers 'touristic' and 'political' day tours.

Train

Israel Railways (☑5770 or 03-611 7000; www.rail.co.il) runs a comfortable and generally convenient network of passenger rail services; details on services are also available from the **Public Transportation Info Center** (☑1-900-721 111; www.bus. co.il). Return tickets are 10% cheaper than two one-ways; children under 10 get a 20% discount. Trains do not run from mid-afternoon Friday until Saturday night. Unlike the buses, the train system is wheelchair accessible.

The system's scenic but slow original line, inaugurated in 1892, links three Tel Aviv stations with Beit Shemesh and Jerusalem (22.50NIS, 1¾ hours), while the heavily used main line runs along the coast linking Tel Aviv with Herzliyya (9NIS), Netanya (15.50NIS), Atlit (30.50NIS), Haifa (30.50NIS), Akko (39NIS) and Nahariya (44.50NIS) – and affording fine views of the Mediterranean. From Tel Aviv there are spurs to (clockwise from the north) Kfar Saba; Ben-Gurion airport (15NIS, runs pretty much 24 hours) and Modi'in; Kiryat Gat, Be'er Sheva (30NIS) and Dimona; Rehovot and Ashkelon; Rishon Letzion; and Bat Yam and Yavne-West.

Construction is underway on a US$2 billion high-speed rail link between Tel Aviv and Jerusalem (28 minutes), with a stop on the way at Ben-Gurion airport. The planned completion date is 2017. There has been a plan to run a rail line down to Eilat for decades.

Health

While it's never nice to be injured or become sick while you're travelling, you can at least take some comfort in the knowledge that Israel has world-class medical facilities. The medical facilities available in the Palestinian Territories are of a lower standard, but you can rest assured that a hospital in Israel is never too far away.

While standards of health are high in Israel, there are several location-specific conditions for travellers to be aware of, particularly dehydration, heat exhaustion and sunburn.

IN ISRAEL & THE PALESTINIAN TERRITORIES

Availability & Cost of Health Care

Israel has first-rate state-funded hospitals across the country, plus a number of private hospitals and clinics. For a list of hospitals, see www.science.co.il/hospitals.asp. Large cities in the Palestinian Territories have reasonable hospital facilities, but these can be crowded or short on supplies.

Pharmacies *(beit merka-chat)* in Israel are common on city streets, and pharmacists will speak English and can give advice about what medicine to take if you describe your problem. In cities, at least one pharmacy is always on call *(beit merkachat toran)* – phone ☑106 (the local municipal hotline) for details, or check out the links at www.onlineisrael.info/search-internet/health/city (in Hebrew). Some branches of Super Pharm are open 24 hours. In the Palestinian Territories, medicine may be expired so check the date.

If you require any prescribed medication, take enough from home to get you through your trip and bring a copy of the prescription in case you need a refill. Note: Israeli pharmacies can accept only prescriptions issued by Israeli doctors.

Private dental clinics are found anywhere from suburban streets to shopping malls. Standards of dental care are high, but keep in mind that your travel insurance will not usually cover you for anything other than emergency dental treatment.

Infectious Diseases

Leishmaniasis

Spread through the bite of an infected sandfly, leishmaniasis can cause a slowly

---

TRAVEL HEALTH WEBSITES

It's usually a good idea to consult a government travel health website before departure.

» **Australia** (www.smartraveller.gov.au) Lets you download the brochure *Travelling Well*.

» **Canada** (www.hc-sc.gc.ca/hl-vs/travel-voyage/index-eng.php).

» **UK** (www.doh.gov.uk) Search for the booklet *Health Information for Overseas Travel* (the 'Yellow Book').

» **USA** (http://wwwnc.cdc.gov/travel).

» **World Health Organization** (www.who.int/ith/en) You can download the book *International Travel & Health*.

» **MD Travel Health** (www.mdtravelhealth.com) Provides country-by-country travel health recommendations.

growing skin lump or ulcer. It may develop into a serious life-threatening fever, usually accompanied by anaemia and weight loss. Infected dogs are also carriers of the infection. Sandfly bites should be avoided whenever possible.

Rabies

Rabies is rare but present in Israel and the Palestinian Territories so avoid contact with stray dogs and wild animals such as foxes.

Spread through bites or licks on broken skin from an infected animal, rabies is fatal. Animal handlers should be vaccinated, as should those travelling to remote areas where a reliable source of post-bite vaccine is not available within 24 hours. Three injections are needed over a month. If you have not been vaccinated, you will need a course of five injections starting within 24 hours or as soon as possible after the injury. Vaccination does not provide you with immunity; it merely buys you more time to seek appropriate medical help.

Traveller's Diarrhoea

Traveller's diarrhoea can occur with a simple change of diet, so even though Israeli food and water are generally healthy you may get an upset stomach simply because your body is not accustomed to the new foods – it may take a few days to adjust. Keep in mind that in summer outdoor food spoils quickly, so this is a good time to avoid hole-in-the-wall shwarma and felafel joints because hummus goes bad quickly. (Eating hummus in an indoor restaurant is likely to be safer.) Be even more careful in the Palestinian Territories.

If you develop diarrhoea, be sure to drink plenty of fluids, preferably an oral re-hydration solution containing salt and sugar. A few loose stools don't require treatment, but if you start having more than four or five stools a day you should start taking an antibiotic (usually a quinolone drug) and an antidiarrhoeal agent (such as loperamide). If diarrhoea is bloody, persists for more than 72 hours, or is accompanied by fever, shaking chills or severe abdominal pain, you should seek medical attention.

Environmental Hazards

Heat Illness

Heat exhaustion is one of the most common ailments among travellers in Israel and the Palestinian Territories. This occurs following heavy sweating and excessive fluid loss with inadequate replacement of fluids and salt. It is particularly common in hot climates when taking unaccustomed exercise before full acclimatisation. Symptoms include headache, dizziness and tiredness. Dehydration is already happening by the time you feel thirsty – aim to drink enough water that you produce pale, diluted urine. The treatment of heat exhaustion consists of replacing fluid with water or fruit juice or both, and cooling by cold water and fans. The treatment of the salt loss component consists of salty fluids as in soup or broth, and adding a little more table salt to foods than usual.

Heat stroke is much more serious. This occurs when the body's heat-regulating mechanism breaks down. An excessive rise in body temperature leads to sweating ceasing, irrational and hyperactive behaviour and eventually loss of consciousness and death. Rapid cooling by spraying the body with water and fanning is an ideal treatment. Emergency fluid and electrolyte replacement by intravenous drip is usually also required.

Insect Bites & Stings

Mosquitoes may not carry malaria but can cause irritation and infected bites. Using DEET-based insect repellents will prevent bites. Mosquitoes also spread dengue fever.

Bees and wasps cause real problems only to those with a severe allergy (anaphylaxis). If you have a severe allergy to bee or wasp stings you should carry an adrenaline injection or similar.

Sandflies are located around the Mediterranean beaches. They usually cause only a nasty itchy bite, but can carry a rare skin disorder called cutaneous leishmaniasis. Bites may be prevented by using DEET-based repellents.

The number of jellyfish has been increasing over the years, thanks to overfishing in the Mediterranean (fish eat jellyfish, and in the absence of predators the jellyfish have boomed). The jellyfish sting is irritating, but in most cases it wears off in about 10 or 15 minutes. A

IF YOU REQUIRE MEDICAL CARE

For emergency first aid or evacuation by ambulance to a hospital in Israel, call the country's national emergency medical service, **Magen David Adom** (☎101), on any phone. Magen David Adom stations also provide after-hours first aid.

In the West Bank and Gaza, Palestinian hospitals can take care of most health problems but for anything serious, you're better off transferring to an Israeli hospital such as one of the two Hadassah Hospital campuses in Jerusalem.

For less urgent matters, you can:

» ask at your hotel for a nearby physician's office

» check the list of doctors on the website of the **US Embassy** (http://israel.usembassy.gov/consular/acs/doctors.html)

» in the Jerusalem area, contact **Terem Emergency Medical Centers** (☎1-599-520 520; www.terem.com) or the **Jerusalem Medical Center** (☎02-561 0297)

» in Tel Aviv, contact **Tel Aviv Doctor** (☎054-941 4243; www.telaviv-doctor.com).

If you become seriously ill, you may want to contact your embassy or consulate.

---

particularly strong sting (or a sting to the face or genitals) requires an evaluation by a physician.

Scorpions are frequently found in arid or dry climates. They can cause a painful bite, which is rarely life threatening.

Bedbugs are occasionally found in hostels and cheap hotels. They lead to very itchy, lumpy bites. Spraying the mattress with an appropriate insect killer will do a good job of getting rid of them.

Scabies are also sometimes found in cheap accommodation. These tiny mites live in the skin, particularly between the fingers. They cause an intensely itchy rash. Scabies are easily treated with lotion available from pharmacies; people who you come into contact with also need treating to avoid spreading scabies between asymptomatic carriers.

Snake Bites

The vast majority of the snakes that live in Israel and the Palestinian Territories are not poisonous – but some, such as the Palestine viper (*tzefa*; *Vipera palaestinae*), are. Do not walk barefoot or stick your hand into holes or cracks.

If bitten by a snake, do not panic. Half of those bitten by venomous snakes are not actually injected with poison (envenomed). Immobilise the bitten limb with a splint (eg a stick) and apply a bandage over the site with firm pressure, similar to a bandage over a sprain. Do not apply a tourniquet, or cut or suck the bite. Get the victim to medical help as soon as possible so that antivenene can be given if necessary.

Water

Tap water is safe to drink in Israel, but often has an unpleasant taste (in some areas it is slightly saline) so many Israelis use filters or spring water dispensers at home. Bottled water is available everywhere. Do not drink water from rivers or lakes as it may contain bacteria or viruses that can cause diarrhoea or vomiting.

Language

HEBREW

Hebrew is the national language of Israel, with seven to eight million speakers worldwide. It's written from right to left in its own alphabet.

Read our coloured pronunciation guides as if they were English and you'll be understood. Most sounds have equivalents in English. Note that a is pronounced as 'ah', ai as in 'aisle', e as in 'bet', i as the 'ea' in 'heat', o as 'oh' and u as the 'oo' in 'boot'. Both kh (like the 'ch' in the Scottish *loch*) and r (similar to the French 'r') are guttural sounds, pronounced at the back of the throat. The apostrophe (') indicates the glottal stop (like the pause in the middle of 'uh-oh'). The stressed syllables are indicated with italics.

Basics

Hello.	שלום.	sha·*lom*
Goodbye.	להתראות.	le·hit·ra·*ot*
Yes.	כן.	ken
No.	לא.	lo
Please.	בבקשה.	be·va·ka·*sha*
Thank you.	תודה.	to·*da*
Excuse me./Sorry.	סליחה.	sli·*kha*

How are you?

מה נשמע?	ma nish·*ma*

Fine. And you?

טוב, תודה.	tov to·*da*
ואתה/ואת?	ve·a·*ta*/ve·*at* (m/f)

What's your name?

איך קוראים לך?	ekh kor·*im* le·*kha*/lakh (m/f)

My name is ...

שמי ...	shmi ...

Do you speak English?

אתה מדבר אנגלית?	a·*ta* me·da·*ber* ang·*lit* (m)
את מדברת אנגלית?	at me·da·*be*·ret ang·*lit* (f)

I don't understand.

אני לא מבין/מבינה.	a·*ni* lo me·*vin*/me·vi·*na* (m/f)

Accommodation

Where's a ...?	איפה ...?	*e*·fo ...
campsite	אתר הקמפינג	a·*tar* ha·*kemp*·ing
guesthouse	בית ההארחה	bet ha·'a·ra·*kha*
hotel	בית המלון	bet ma·*lon*
youth hostel	אכסניית הנוער	akh·sa·ni·*yat* *no*·ar

Signs – Hebrew

Entrance	כניסה
Exit	יציאה
Open	פתוח
Closed	סגור
Information	מודיעין
Prohibited	אסור
Toilets	שירותים
Men	גברים
Women	נשים

Do you have a ... room?	יש לך ?... חדר	yesh le·kha/lakh khe·der ... (m/f)
single	ליחיד	le·ya·khid
double	זוגי	zu·gi

How much is it per ...?	כמה זה עולה ל ...?	ka·ma ze o·le le ...
night	לילה	lai·la
person	אדם	a·dam

Eating & Drinking

Can you recommend a ...?	אתה יכול להמליץ על ...? את יכולה להמליץ על ...?	a·ta ya·khol le·ham·lits al ... (m) at ye·cho·la le·ham·lits al ... (f)
cafe	בית קפה	bet ka·fe
restaurant	מסעדה	mis·a·da

What would you recommend?
מה אתה ממליץ? — ma a·ta mam·lits (m)
מה את ממליצה? — ma at mam·li·tsa (f)

What's the local speciality?
מה המאכל המקומי? — ma ha·ma·'a·khal ha·me·ko·mi

Do you have vegetarian food?
יש לכם אוכל — yesh la·khem o·khel
צמחוני? — tsim·kho·ni

I'd like the ..., please.	אני צריך/ צריכה את ... , בבקשה.	a·ni tsa·rikh/ tsri·kha et ... be·va·ka·sha (m/f)
bill	החשבון	ha·khesh·bon
menu	התפריט	ha·taf·rit

Numbers – Hebrew

1	אחת	a·khat
2	שתיים	shta·yim
3	שלוש	sha·losh
4	ארבע	ar·ba
5	חמש	kha·mesh
6	שש	shesh
7	שבע	she·va
8	שמונה	shmo·ne
9	תשע	te·sha
10	עשר	e·ser
100	מאה	me·a
1000	אלף	e·lef

Note that English numerals are used in modern Hebrew text.

Emergencies

Help!	הצילו!	ha·tsi·lu
Go away!	לך מפה!	lekh mi·po

Call ...!	תקשר ל ...!	tit·ka·sher le ...
a doctor	רופא	ro·fe/ro·fa (m/f)
the police	משטרה	mish·ta·ra

I'm lost.
אני אבוד. — a·ni a·vud (m)
אני אבודה. — a·ni a·vu·da (f)

Where are the toilets?
איפה השירותים? — e·fo ha·she·ru·tim

I'm sick.
אני חולה. — a·ni kho·le/kho·la (m/f)

Shopping & Services

I'm looking for ...
אני מחפש ... — a·ni me·kha·pes ... (m)
אני מחפשת ... — a·ni me·kha·pe·set ... (f)

Can I look at it?
אפשר להסתכל — ef·shar le·his·ta·kel
על זה? — al ze

Do you have any others?
יש לך אחרים? — yesh le·kha/lakh a·khe·rim (m/f)

How much is it?
כמה זה עולה? — ka·ma ze o·le

That's too expensive.
זה יקר מדי. — ze ya·kar mi·dai

There's a mistake in the bill.
יש טעות בחשבון. — yesh ta·ut ha·khesh·bon

Where's an ATM?
איפה יש כספומט? — e·fo yesh kas·po·mat

Transport & Directions

Is this the ... to (Haifa)?	האם זה/ זאת ה ... ל(חיפה)?	ha·im ze/ zot ha ... le·(khai·fa) (m/f)
boat	אוניה	o·ni·ya (f)
bus	אוטובוס	o·to·bus (m)
plane	מטוס	ma·tos (m)
train	רכבת	ra·ke·vet (f)

What time's the ... bus?	באיזה שעה האוטובוס ה ...?	be·e·ze sha·a ha·o·to·bus ha ...
first	ראשון	ri·shon
last	אחרון	a·kha·ron

One ... ticket, please.	כרטיס אחד ... בבקשה.	kar·tis e·khad ... be·va·ka·sha
one-way	לכיוון אחד	le·ki·vun e·khad
return	הלוך ושוב	ha·lokh va·shov

How much is it to ...?
כמה זה ל ...? — ka·ma ze le ...

Please take me to (this address).
תיקח/תיקחי אותי (לכתובת הזאת) בבקשה. — ti·kakh/tik·khi o·ti (lak·to·vet ha·zot) be·va·ka·sha (m/f)

Where's the (market)?
איפה ה (שוק)? — e·fo ha (shuk)

Can you show me (on the map)?
אתה/את יכול להראות (לי על המפה)? — a·ta/at ya·khol/ye·kho·la le·har·ot (li al ha·ma·pa) (m/f)

What's the address?
מה הכתובת? — ma hak·to·vet

ARABIC

The Arabic variety spoken in the Palestinian Territories (and provided in this section) is known as Levantine Arabic. Note that there are significant differences between this colloquial language and the MSA (Modern Standard Arabic), which is the official written language in the Arab world, used in schools, administration and the media. Arabic is written from right to left in Arabic script.

In our pronunciation guides a is pronounced as in 'act', aa as the 'a' in 'father', ae as the 'ai' in 'air', aw as in 'law', ay as in 'say', e as in 'bet', ee as in 'see', i as in 'hit', oo as in 'zoo', u as in 'put', gh is a guttural sound (like the Parisian French 'r'), r is trilled, dh is pronounced as the 'th' in 'that', th as in 'thin' and kh as the 'ch' in the Scottish loch. The apostrophe (') indicates the glottal stop (like the pause in the middle of 'uh-oh').

Basics

Hello.	مرحبا.	mar·ha·ba
Goodbye.	خاطرك.	khaa·trak (m)
	خاطرك.	khaa·trik (f)
Yes.	ايه.	'eeh
No.	لا.	laa
Please.	اذا بتريد.	'i·za bit·reed (m)
	اذا بتريدي.	'i·za bit·ree·dee (f)
Thank you.	شكراً.	shuk·ran
Excuse me.	عفواً.	'af·wan
Sorry.	أسف.	'aa·sif (m)
	أسفة.	'aas·fe (f)

Numbers – Arabic

1	١	واحد	waa·hed
2	٢	اثنين	'it·nayn
3	٣	ثلاثة	ta·laa·te
4	٤	اربع	'ar·ba'
5	٥	خمسة	kham·se
6	٦	ستة	sit·te
7	٧	سبعة	sab·'a
8	٨	ثمانية	ta·maa·ne
9	٩	تسعة	tis·'a
10	١٠	عشرة	'ash·ra
100	١٠٠	مية	mi·e
1000	١٠٠٠	الف	'elf

Note that Arabic numerals, unlike letters, are written from left to right.

How are you?
كيف؟/كيفك؟ — ki·fak/ki·fik (m/f)

Fine, thanks. And you?
منيح./منيحة. — mneeh/mnee·ha (m/f)
وأنت/أنتي؟ — oo 'ent/'en·tee (m/f)

What's your name?
شو اسمك؟ — shoo 'es·mak (m)
شو اسمك؟ — shoo 'es·mik (f)

My name is ...
اسمي ... — 'es·mee ...

Do you speak English?
بتحكي إنكليزي؟ — btah·kee ing·lee·zee

I don't understand.
ما فهمت. — maa fa·he·met

Accommodation

Where's a ...?	وين ...؟	wen ...
campsite	مخيّم	mu·khay·yam
guesthouse	بيت الضيوف	bayt id·du·yoof
hotel	فندق	fun·du'
youth hostel	فندق شباب	fun·du' sha·baab

Do you have a ... room?	في عندكن غرفة ...؟	fee 'ind·kun ghur·fe ...
single	بتخت منفرد	bi·takht mun·fa·rid
double	بتخت مزدوّج	bi·takht muz·daw·wej

How much is it per ...?	قديش لـ...؟	'ad·deesh li·...
night	ليلة	lay·le
person	شخص	shakhs

Eating & Drinking

Can you recommend a ...?	بتوصي بـ...؟	bit·waa·see bi·...
cafe	مقهى	ma'·ha
restaurant	مطعم	mat·am

What would you recommend?
بشو بتوصي؟ bi·shoo btoo·see

What's the local speciality?
شو الوجبة الخاصة؟ shoo il·waj·be il·khaa·se

Do you have vegetarian food?
في عندكن طعام نباتي؟ fee 'ind·kun ta·'aam na·baa·tee

I'd like the ..., please.	بدي .... لو سمحت.	bid·dee ... law sa·maht
bill	الحساب	il·hi·saab
menu	قائمة الطعام	'ae·'i·met it·ta·'aam

Emergencies

Help!	ساعد! ساعدي!	saa·'id (m) saa·'i·dee (f)
Go away! (to a man/woman)	روح!/ روحي!	rooh/ roo·hee

Call ...!	اتصل بـ...!	'it·ta·sil bi·...
a doctor	دكتور	duk·toor
the police	الشرطة	ish·shur·ta

I'm lost.
أنا ضائع. 'a·na daa·'i' (m)
أنا ضائعة. 'a·na daa·'i·'e (f)

Where are the toilets?
وين الحمامات؟ wen il·ham·maa·maat

I'm sick.
أنا مريض. 'a·na ma·reed (m)
أنا مريضة. 'a·na ma·ree·de (f)

Shopping & Services

I'm looking for ...
بدور عن ... bi·daw·wer 'an ...

Can I look at it?
ورجني ياه؟ war·ji·nee yaah (m)
ورجيني ياه؟ war·jee·nee yaah (f)

Do you have any others?
في عندكن غيره؟ fee 'ind·kun ghay·ru

How much is it?
قديش هقه؟ 'ad·deesh ha·'·u

That's too expensive.
هيدا غالي اكتير. ha·da ghaa·lee 'ik·teer

There's a mistake in the bill.
في خطأ بالحساب. fee kha·ta' bil·hi·saab

Where's an ATM?
وين جهاز الصرافة؟ wen je·haez is·sa·raa·fe

Transport & Directions

Is this the ... to (Petra)?	هدا الـ ... لـ(بيترا)؟	ha·da il· ... la·(bee·tra)
boat	سفينة	sfee·ne
bus	باص	baas
plane	طائرة	taa·'i·re
train	قطار	'i·taar

What time's the ... bus?	أمتى الباص الـ...؟	'em·ta il·baas il·...
first	اول	'aw·wel
last	اخر	'aa·khir

One ... ticket, please.	تذكرة ... اذا بتريد.	taz·ki·re ... 'i·za bit·reed
one-way	ذهاب	za·haab
return	ذهاب واياب	za·haab oo 'ee·yaab

How much is it to ...?
قديش الاجرة لـ...؟ 'ad·deesh il·'uj·re la ...

Please take me to (this address).
اوصلني عند (هيدا العنوان). 'oo·sal·nee 'ind (ha·da il·'un·waan)

Where's the (market)?
وين الـ(سوق)؟ wen il·(soo')

Can you show me (on the map)?
بتورجني (عالخريطة)؟ btwar·ji·nee ('al·kha·ree·te)

What's the address?
شو العنوان؟ shoo il·'un·waan

GLOSSARY

The language origin of non-English terms is noted in brackets: Hebrew (H) and Arabic (A). Singular and plural is noted as (s) and (pl) while masculine and feminine terms are noted as (mas) and (fem).

ablaq (A) – in architecture, alternating bands of light and dark stone

abu (A) – father (of), often used as part of a name; see also *umm*

agorot (H) – smallest unit of the shekel; 1 shekel = 100 agorot

ain (A) – water spring or source; also *ein*

al (A) – the definite article, 'the'; also spelled 'el-' or with the L replaced by the letter that follows it, eg ash-sharif

aliya (H) – immigration to Israel (literally 'going up')

b'seder (H) – OK

bab (A) – door, gate

bakashot *(H)* – a cycle of petitionary prayers sung in synagogues that follow some Sephardic rites (eg those from Aleppo, Syria) in the early hours of Shabbat during the winter months

be'er (H) – well

beit knesset (H) – synagogue

beit merkachat (H) – pharmacy

beit/beth (H) – house

bimah (H) – central platform in a synagogue

bir (A) – well

birkat habayit (H) – blessing for the home

burj (A) – fortress or tower

caravanserai (A) – see *khan*

daf (A) – tambourine

derekh (H) – street or road

ein (H) – spring

Eretz Yisra'el (H) – the Land of Israel

Eretz Yisra'el HaShlema (H) – the Greater Land of Israel, a term once used by the Jewish settler movement to refer to the territory that they believe God promised the People of Israel (includes the West Bank and the Golan Heights and, for some, still Gaza)

gadol (H) – big

gan (H) – garden or park

Haganah (H) – literally 'defence'; the Jewish underground army during the British Mandate; the forerunner of the modern-day Israel Defence Forces (IDF)

hajj (A) – annual Muslim pilgrimage to Mecca

Hamas (A) – Harakat al-Muqaama al-Islamiya; militant Islamic organisation that aims to create an Islamic state in the pre-1948 territory of Palestine

hammam (A) – public bathhouse

har (H) – mountain

haraam (A) – literally 'forbidden'; holy sanctuary

Hared/Harediya/ Haredim/Harediyot (H, mas s/fem s/mas pl/fem pl) – an ultra-Orthodox Jew, a member of either a Hasidic group or one of the groups opposed to Hasidism, known as Litvaks ('Lithuanians') or 'Misnagdim' ('opponents')

Hasid/Hasidim (H, mas s/ mas pl) – member of an ultra-Orthodox groups with mystical tendencies founded in Poland in the 18th century by the Ba'al Shem Tov

hazzanut (H) – Jewish liturgical singing

Hebrew Bible – the Old Testament

Hezbollah (A) – Iranian-backed Shiite political party and militia active in Lebanon

hof (H) – beach

hurva (H) – ruin

IDF – Israel Defence Forces; the national army

iftar (A) – the daily, dusk breaking-of-the-fast feast during Ramadan

intifada (A) – literally 'shaking off'; term Palestinians use to describe an uprising against Israel. The First Intifada lasted from 1987 to 1990. The Second Intifada lasted from 2001 to 2005

Islam (A) – literally 'voluntary surrender to the will of God (Allah)'; the religion of the vast majority of Palestinian people

israa' (A) – the 'Night Journey' of the Prophet Mohammed from Mecca to Jerusalem

juhhal (A) – literally 'the ignorant'; members of the Druze community who are not *uqqal*

kafr (A) – village

kashrut (H) – religious dietary laws, ie the rules of keeping *kosher*

katan *(H)* – small

keffiyeh (A) – the black-and-white chequered Palestinian Arab headscarf

ketuba (H) – Jewish wedding contract

kfar – village

khan (A) – also called a *caravanserai*, a travellers' inn usually constructed on main trade routes, with accommodation on the 1st floor and stables and storage on the ground floor around a central courtyard

khirbet (A) – ruins (of)

kibbutz/kibbutzim (H, s/ pl) – a communal settlement run cooperatively by its members; kibbutzim, once based solely on farming, are now involved in a wide range of industries; see also *moshav*

kibbutznik (H) – member of a *kibbutz*

kikar (H) – square; roundabout

kippa/kippot (H, s/pl) – skullcap worn by observant Jewish men (and among reform and conservative Jews, sometimes by women); known in Yiddish as a *yarmulke*

Klezmer (H) – traditional music of Eastern European Jews, often described as traditional Jewish soul music

Knesset (H) – Israeli Parliament

Koran (A) – see *Quran*

kosher (H) – food prepared according to Jewish dietary law; see also *kashrut*

ma'ayan (H) – spring, pool

madrassa (A) – theological school, especially one associated with a mosque

majdal (A) – tower

makhtesh (H) – erosion cirque

matkot *(H)* – Israeli beach ping pong

menorah (H) – a seven-branched candelabrum that adorned the ancient Temple in Jerusalem and has been a Jewish symbol ever since; it is now the official symbol of the State of Israel

mi'raj (A) – the Prophet Mohammed's ascent from Jerusalem to Heaven

midrahov (H) – pedestrian mall

mihrab (A) – prayer niche in a mosque, indicating the direction of Mecca

mikveh (H) – Jewish ritual immersion bath

minaret (A) – the tower of a mosque; from which the call to prayer is traditionally sung

minbar (A) – pulpit used for mosque sermons

mishkan (H) – portable house of worship

mitnachel (H) – Jewish West Bank settler; sometimes considered pejorative

mitzvah (H) – a commandment or obligation; a good deed

Mizrahi/Mizrahim (H, s/pl) – a Jew from one of the Middle East Jewish communities, eg from one of the Islamic countries such as Morocco, Yemen or Iraq; this term is often used interchangeably with Sephardi, though technically only the descendants of Jews expelled from Spain are Sephardim

moshav/moshavim (H, s/pl) – cooperative settlement, with a mix of private and collective housing and economic activity; see also kibbutz

moshavnik (H) – a member of a moshav

muqarna (A) – corbel; architectural decorative devices resembling stalactites

nahal (H) – river

Naqba (A) – literally the 'Catastrophe'; this is what the Palestinians call the 1948 Arab–Israeli War

nargileh (A) – water pipe; see also *sheesha*

ney (A) – flute

oleh/olah/olim/olot (H, s mas/s fem/pl mas/pl fem) – immigrant

PA – Palestinian Authority

PFLP – Popular Front for the Liberation of Palestine

PLO – Palestine Liberation Organisation

PNC – Palestinian National Council, ruling body of the PLO

Quran (A) – the sacred book of the Muslims

ras (A) – headland

refusenik (H) – originally a Jew in the Soviet Union who was denied permission to emigrate to Israel; sometimes used today to refer to Israelis who refuse to serve in the IDF in the West Bank

rehov (H) – street

ribat (A, H) – pilgrim hostel or hospice

sabil (A) – public drinking fountain

sabra (H) – literally 'prickly pear'; native-born Israeli

servees (A) – term used for small bus or service taxi in the Palestinian Territories, see also *sherut*

settler – a term for Israelis who have created new communities on territory captured from Jordan, Egypt and Syria during the 1967 Six Day War; the Hebrew word for settler is *mitnachel*

sha'ar (H) – gate

shabab (A) – literally, 'youths'; young Palestinians who formed the backbone of the intifadas by confronting the IDF and throwing stones

Shabbat (H) – the Jewish Sabbath observed from sundown on Friday evening to an hour after sundown on Saturday

shalom (H) – peace; hello; goodbye

Shari'a (A) – Muslim law

Shechina (H) – divine presence

sheesha (A) – water pipe, term used in Egypt; see also *nargileh*

sheikh – (A) learned or old man

shekel/sh'kalim (H, s/pl) – Israeli monetary unit

Shema (H) – Judaism's central statement of belief in the oneness of God

sherut (H) – shared taxi, service taxi; Israeli minivans that operate on fixed routes, in or between cities; see also servees

shiva (H) – ritual week-long period of mourning for first-degree relatives

shofar (H) – ram's horn traditionally blown on Rosh HaShana and Yom Kippur

shtetl (H) – small, traditional Eastern European Jewish village

sukkah/sukkot (H, s/pl) – small dwellings built during the feast of Sukkot

taboun (H) – a clay oven

tel (H) – a hill; in archaeology, a mound built up as

successive cities were built and destroyed on the same site

Torah (H) – the Five Books of Moses, ie the first five books of the Hebrew Bible (the Old Testament); also called the Pentateuch

tsadik/tsadika (H, s mas/s fem) – a righteous person

Tzahal (H) – Hebrew acronym for the Israel Defence Forces (IDF)

tzimmer (H) – literally 'room' in German; B&B or holiday-cabin accommodation; also spelled 'zimmer'

tzitzit (H) – white tassels worn by orthodox Jewish men, attached to the four corners of a square undergarment; also the knotted fringes on the prayer shawl

ulpan/ulpanim (H, s/pl) – language school

umm (A) – mother (of); feminine equivalent of *abu*

UNRWA – UN Relief & Works Agency for Palestine Refugees

uqqal (A) – the wise; the select inner core of the Druze community; see also *juhhal*

wadi (A) – river that's dry except during downpours

WZO – World Zionist Organisation

ya'ar (H) – forest

yad (H) – hand; memorial

yeshiva/yeshivot (H, s/pl) – Jewish religious seminary or school

zimmer (H) – see *tzimmer*

behind the scenes

SEND US YOUR FEEDBACK

We love to hear from travellers – your comments keep us on our toes and help make our books better. Our well-travelled team reads every word on what you loved or loathed about this book. Although we cannot reply individually to postal submissions, we always guarantee that your feedback goes straight to the appropriate authors, in time for the next edition. Each person who sends us information is thanked in the next edition – the most useful submissions are rewarded with a selection of digital PDF chapters.

Visit **lonelyplanet.com/contact** to submit your updates and suggestions or to ask for help. Our award-winning website also features inspirational travel stories, news and discussions.

Note: We may edit, reproduce and incorporate your comments in Lonely Planet products such as guidebooks, websites and digital products, so let us know if you don't want your comments reproduced or your name acknowledged. For a copy of our privacy policy visit lonelyplanet.com/privacy.

OUR READERS

Many thanks to the travellers who used the last edition and wrote to us with helpful hints, useful advice and interesting anecdotes:

Dan Arenson, Cecilia Arias, Garry Aslanyan, Mohammed Barakat, Josh Berk, Catherine Black, Jan R Blok, Carolin Bruecker, Yaron Burgin, David Campbell, Victor Clarke, Eli Direktor, Yaniv Divekar, David Drake, Bettina Dunkel, Andreas Eskerod, Rainer Feichter, Cyril Galland, Aline Gaub, John Grech, Massimiliano Gugole, Sofie Hviid, Lars Jensen, Peter Kargaard, Sharon Keld, Lisanne Kerstens, Jennifer Killen, Hanna Lomeland & Ofer Hadad, Nigel Mackenzie, Don Madge, Aaron Magid, David Marchesi, Lena Moser, Rachel Nassif, Carl O'Connor, Marcus Pailing, Thomas Paschold, Maarten Pullen, Clive Roper, Alex Rosen, Dov Ruckenstein, David Silverstone, Kristel Sjouw, James Smith, Camilla Standhart, Ward Van Alphen & Jolanda Maas, Christine Van Der Veer, Roman Varinsky, George Vick, Márcia Vinha, Carmen Werner Davidson, Grit Wesser, Jeff White, Heidi Wikström, Heleen Witte, Qian Xiaoyan, Ziv Zafir

AUTHOR THANKS

Daniel Robinson

Special thanks to (from north to south) Ofer Bashan, Yafa Na'ar, Dudu Pilas, Hanoch Tal, Joel Friedman, Inbar Rubin, Amichai and Tehila Yisraeli, Hezi Segev, Tal Ben David, Aviva Minoff, Avraham Loewenthal, Baruch Adler, Daniel Flatauer, David Friedman, Eyal Riess, Hava Lustig, Moshe Tov Kreps, Yair Moore, Naomi (Korazim NP), Katerina Halperin, Amir Zouabi, Amir Zubij, Daher Zeidani, the Fauzi Azar staff (especially Sami), Guy Côte, Joseph Marotta, Maoz Yinon, Martina Shama, Ramzi Haj, Sister Noriko, Tony Kanaza, Sarah Yefet, Yafa Kfir and Amiram, Meir Doron, Nissim Bados, Yair Huri, Yaron Burgin, David Berger, Gabi Zentner, Alon Reuven, Jacky Almakayyes, Raz Zabar and Gil Shkedi. The extraordinary backstopping and forebearance of my wife, Rachel Safman, made this project possible. I dedicate my parts of this volume my first-born son, Yair Lev Robinson.

Michael Kohn

A mighty thank you to editor Kate Morgan and fellow author Daniel Robinson for pulling this project together. In Israel, I received much help and camaraderie from Gal Mor and Yaron Burgin (Abraham Hostels), Katy and Ze'ev (Port Inn) Fred Schlomka (Green Olive Tours), Danny Flax (Allenby B&B), Imad

Muna (Educational Bookshop), Mike (Mike's Center) and my West Bank taxi drivers Waleed, Zafer and Bashir. A special shalom to Einav, Gal and the twins, Omri in Tel Aviv and Danny Golan in Jerusalem. Lastly, to Baigal and Molly who braved many long plane, train and automobile rides to make the journey with me, you made this the best trip yet.

Dan Savery Raz

Thanks to Erez Naim for being my human GPS in the Negev, Daniel Robinson for his Tel Aviv tips (kurtosh anyone?), Jason Levy for his balanced knowledge of Gaza and the ecofriendly volunteers of Kibbutz Lotan. Once again, I am indebted to all my family, especially Mum, Revi and Yossi, Orit (for the car) and Evelyn (for the kuba). Big shout to Dad for being a rock star and Shiri Miller Raz for sharing the journey.

Jessica Lee

On the road a big thanks to Claire Craig, Salma Nassar, Eric Monkaba, Muhammad Ali, Gordon Wilkinson, Zoltan Matrahazi, and especially Salama Abd Rabbo. Back in Cairo huge cheers to Sameh Tawfik, Mark Walgemoet, Sarah Bruford, Paula Maiorano and Julian 'Whijul' White. While at Lonely Planet many thanks to Michael Benanav and Zora O'Neill for awesome advice and to Kate Morgan for putting up with my endless questions.

Jenny Walker

Returning to Petra is always the greatest of pleasures, not just on account of the spectacular ancient city, but also because the kind folk of Wadi Musa continue to go out of their way to be hospitable. While their assistance in researching this chapter is very much appreciated, I reserve greatest thanks for my beloved husband, Sam Owen, who accompanied me during research and assisted immeasurably in resourcing further background information during write-up.

ACKNOWLEDGMENTS

Climate map data adapted from Peel MC, Finlayson BL & McMahon TA (2007) 'Updated World Map of the Köppen-Geiger Climate Classification', Hydrology and Earth System Sciences, 11, 163344.

Illustrations p50–1, p346–7 by Michael Weldon.

Cover photograph: Roman ruins, Tel Beit She'an, Beit She'an National Park, Michael DeFreitas/Getty Images

Many of the images in this guide are available for licensing from Lonely Planet Images: www.lonelyplanetimages.com.

THIS BOOK

This 7th edition of Lonely Planet's Israel & the Palestinian Territories guidebook was researched and written by Daniel Robinson (coordinating author), Michael Kohn, Dan Savery Raz, Jessica Lee and Jenny Walker. The previous edition was written by Amelia Thomas (coordinating author), Michael Kohn, Miriam Raphael and Dan Savery Raz. This guidebook was commissioned in Lonely Planet's Melbourne office, and produced by the following:

Commissioning Editors Suzannah Shwer, Kate Morgan, Kathleen Munnelly, Glenn van der Knijff

Coordinating Editor Kate Whitfield

Coordinating Cartographers Julie Dodkins, Marc Milinkovic

Coordinating Layout Designer Kerrianne Southway

Managing Editors Brigitte Ellemor, Anna Metcalfe, Martine Power

Managing Cartographers Shahara Ahmed, Alison Lyall, Adrian Persoglia

Managing Layout Designer Chris Girdler

Assisting Editors Andrew Bain, Jackey Coyle, Cathryn Game, Carly Hall, Kim Hutchins, Ross Taylor, Helen Yeates

Assisting Cartographers Karusha Ganga, James Leversha

Cover Research Naomi Parker

Internal Image Research Aude Vauconsant

Language Content Annelies Mertens

Thanks to Elin Berglund, Ryan Evans, Larissa Frost, Dan Goldberg, Martin Heng, Andi Jones, Karyn Noble, Marg Toohey, Gerard Walker

index

how to use this book

These symbols will help you find the listings you want:

🚗 Driving   🧍 Hiking   🚲 Biking

These symbols give you the vital information for each listing:

☎	Telephone Numbers	🛜	Wi-Fi Access	🚌	Bus
☺	Opening Hours	🏊	Swimming Pool	⛴	Ferry
P	Parking	🥗	Vegetarian Selection	Ⓜ	Metro
⊖	Nonsmoking	🍴	English-Language Menu	S	Subway
❄	Air-Conditioning	👪	Family-Friendly	🚋	Tram
@	Internet Access	🐾	Pet-Friendly	🚆	Train

Reviews are organised by author preference

Look out for these icons:

TOP CHOICE   Our author's recommendation

FREE   No payment required

🍃   A green or sustainable option

Our authors have nominated these places as demonstrating a strong commitment to sustainability – for example by supporting local communities and producers, operating in an environmentally friendly way, or supporting conservation projects.

Map Legend

Sights
- 🏖 Beach
- 🏛 Buddhist
- 🏰 Castle
- ✝ Christian
- 🕉 Hindu
- ☪ Islamic
- ✡ Jewish
- 🗿 Monument
- 🏛 Museum/Gallery
- 🏚 Ruin
- 🍷 Winery/Vineyard
- 🦁 Zoo
- ⊙ Other Sight

Activities, Courses & Tours
- 🤿 Diving/Snorkelling
- 🛶 Canoeing/Kayaking
- 🎿 Skiing
- 🏄 Surfing
- 🏊 Swimming/Pool
- 🚶 Walking
- 🌊 Windsurfing
- ⊕ Other Activity/Course/Tour

Sleeping
- 🛏 Sleeping
- ⛺ Camping

Eating
- 🍴 Eating

Drinking
- ☕ Drinking
- ☕ Cafe

Entertainment
- 🎭 Entertainment

Shopping
- 🛍 Shopping

Information
- 💲 Bank
- 🏛 Embassy/Consulate
- ➕ Hospital/Medical
- @ Internet
- 👮 Police
- ✉ Post Office
- ☎ Telephone
- 🚻 Toilet
- ❶ Tourist Information
- • Other Information

Transport
- ✈ Airport
- ⊗ Border Crossing
- 🚌 Bus
- ⊕ Cable Car/Funicular
- 🚴 Cycling
- ⊖ Ferry
- Ⓜ Metro
- 🚝 Monorail
- P Parking
- ⛽ Petrol Station
- 🚕 Taxi
- 🚆 Train/Railway
- 🚋 Tram
- • Other Transport

Routes
Tollway
Freeway
Primary
Secondary
Tertiary
Lane
Unsealed Road
Plaza/Mall
Steps
Tunnel
Pedestrian Overpass
Walking Tour
Walking Tour Detour
Path

Geographic
- 🏠 Hut/Shelter
- 🚨 Lighthouse
- 👁 Lookout
- ▲ Mountain/Volcano
- 🌴 Oasis
- 🌳 Park
-)(Pass
- 🧺 Picnic Area
- 💧 Waterfall

Population
- ★ Capital (National)
- ◉ Capital (State/Province)
- ● City/Large Town
- ● Town/Village

Boundaries
- ––– International
- –––– State/Province
- – – Disputed
- Regional/Suburb
- Marine Park
- Cliff
- Wall

Hydrography
- River/Creek
- Intermittent River
- Swamp/Mangrove
- Reef
- Canal
- Water
- Dry/Salt/Intermittent Lake
- Glacier

Areas
- Beach/Desert
- Cemetery (Christian)
- Cemetery (Other)
- Park/Forest
- Sportsground
- Sight (Building)
- Top Sight (Building)

Jessica Lee

Sinai Jessica escaped small-town New Zealand and high-tailed it for the road at the age of 18, spending much of her twenties traipsing extensively through Asia, Africa and Latin America. She washed up in Egypt in 2004 where she fell in love with the Arabic language and the incredible hospitality of the people. Since 2007 she has lived in the Middle East full-time, mostly based in Cairo, and has authored several guidebooks to the region. She tweets about things Middle Eastern @jessofarabia.

Read more about Jess at:
lonelyplanet.com/members/jessicalee1

Contributing Author

Professor Alon Tal co-wrote the Environment chapter. He founded the Israel Union for Environmental Defense and the Arava Institute for Environmental Studies, and has served as chair of Life and Environment, Israel's umbrella group for green organisations. He is a professor of the Desert Ecology Department at Ben-Gurion University, and heads the Jewish National Fund's sustainable development committee.

OUR STORY

A beat-up old car, a few dollars in the pocket and a sense of adventure. In 1972 that's all Tony and Maureen Wheeler needed for the trip of a lifetime – across Europe and Asia overland to Australia. It took several months, and at the end – broke but inspired – they sat at their kitchen table writing and stapling together their first travel guide, *Across Asia on the Cheap*. Within a week they'd sold 1500 copies. Lonely Planet was born. Today, Lonely Planet has offices in Melbourne, London and Oakland, with more than 600 staff and writers. We share Tony's belief that 'a great guidebook should do three things: inform, educate and amuse'.

OUR WRITERS

Daniel Robinson

Coordinating Author, Lower Galilee & Sea of Galilee, Upper Galilee & Golan, The Dead Sea Brought up near San Francisco and Chicago, Daniel spent part of his childhood in Jerusalem, a bit of his youth at Kibbutz Lotan and many years in Tel Aviv, where he worked on a PhD in late Ottoman history, covered suicide bombings for the AP, and helped lead the local Critical Mass campaign for bike paths. A Lonely Planet author since 1989, he holds a BA in Near Eastern Studies from Princeton and an MA in Jewish History from Tel Aviv University. His favourite activities include cycling Tel Aviv's historic avenues, hiking around Ein Gedi, and birdwatching in the Hula and Arava Valleys.

Read more about Daniel at:
lonelyplanet.com/members/daniel_robinson

Michael Kohn

Jerusalem, Haifa & the North Coast, West Bank After studying journalism at the University of California, Michael hopped an overseas flight and launched a career as a foreign correspondent, reporting for media outlets including the BBC World Service and Reuters. His first trip to Israel was in 1987 when at age 15 he embarked on a six-week student tour. He returned years later to update Lonely Planet's *Middle East* guide and a reconnection with Israel commenced. He has since worked on three editions of *Israel & the Palestinian Territories*. When not travelling for LP he lives northern California.

Dan Savery Raz

Tel Aviv, The Negev, The Gaza Strip Dan travelled around Europe and North America for Channel 4's *A Place in the Sun* magazine before moving from leafy London to sandy Tel Aviv with his wife in 2008. Now a real 'Tel Avivi', he can often be found walking his dog, Boots, or dipping into a plate of hummus. A contributor to Lonely Planet's *Best in Travel, Happy* and *Street Food*, he has also written articles for *Haaretz*. Dan occasionally dabbles in fiction and published *The Last Stanza* – a poetry anthology that fundraised for African refugees in Tel Aviv; for details see www.danscribe.com.

Read more about Dan at:
lonelyplanet.com/members/Dansaveryraz

Jenny Walker

Petra Jenny Walker's first involvement with Arabia was as a student, collecting butterflies for her father's book on entomology. Convinced she and her mum were the first Western women to brew tea in the desolate interior, she returned to university to see if that were true. Her studies resulted in a dissertation on Doughty and Lawrence (BA Hons) and a thesis on the Arabic Orient (MPhil, University of Oxford). Jenny has travelled in more than 100 countries from Panama to Mongolia. She is Associate Dean (Professional Development) at Caledonian University College of Engineering, Oman.

OVER PAGE | MORE WRITERS

Published by Lonely Planet Publications Pty Ltd
ABN 36 005 607 983
7th edition – July 2012
ISBN 978 1 74179 936 1
© Lonely Planet 2012   Photographs © as indicated 2012
10 9 8 7 6 5 4 3 2 1
Printed in China

Although the authors and Lonely Planet have taken all reasonable care in preparing this book, we make no warranty about the accuracy or completeness of its content and, to the maximum extent permitted, disclaim all liability arising from its use.